COOK'S

ILLUSTRATED

~ 2011 ~

$35.00

Published by
America's Test Kitchen
17 Station Street
Brookline, MA 02445

ISBN-13: 978-1-936493-01-2
ISBN-10: 1-936493-01-2
ISSN: 1933-639X

To get home delivery of *Cook's Illustrated* magazine, call 800-526-8442 inside the U.S., or 515-247-7571 if calling from outside the U.S., or subscribe online at www.cooksillustrated.com.

In addition to *Cook's Illustrated* Hardbound Annual Editions available from each year of publication (1993–2011), America's Test Kitchen offers the following cookbooks and DVD sets:

THE BEST RECIPE SERIES
Soups, Stews & Chilis
More Best Recipes
The Best Skillet Recipes
The Best Slow & Easy Recipes
The Best Chicken Recipes
The Best International Recipe
The Best Make-Ahead Recipe
The Best 30-Minute Recipe
The Best Light Recipe
The Cook's Illustrated Guide to Grilling and Barbecue
Best American Side Dishes
The Best Cover & Bake Recipes
The New Best Recipe
Steaks, Chops, Roasts, and Ribs
Baking Illustrated
Perfect Vegetables
Italian Classics
The Best American Classics
The Best One-Dish Suppers
The America's Test Kitchen Menu Cookbook

AMERICA'S TEST KITCHEN ANNUALS
The Best of America's Test Kitchen (2007–2012 Editions)
Cooking for Two (2009–2011 Editions))
Light & Healthy (2010 and 2011 Editions)

THE AMERICA'S TEST KITCHEN SERIES DVD SETS
(featuring each season's episodes from our hit public television series)
The *America's Test Kitchen* 4-DVD Set (2002–2011 Seasons)
The *America's Test Kitchen* 2-DVD Set (2001 Season)

THE AMERICA'S TEST KITCHEN SERIES COMPANION COOKBOOKS
America's Test Kitchen: The TV Companion Cookbook (2012)
America's Test Kitchen: The TV Companion Cookbook (2011)
The Complete America's Test Kitchen TV Show Cookbook (2010)
America's Test Kitchen: The TV Companion Cookbook (2009)
Behind the Scenes with America's Test Kitchen (2008)
Test Kitchen Favorites (2007)
Cooking at Home with America's Test Kitchen (2006)
America's Test Kitchen Live! (2005)
Inside America's Test Kitchen (2004)
Here in America's Test Kitchen (2003)
The America's Test Kitchen Cookbook (2002)

THE COOK'S COUNTRY SERIES
America's Best Lost Recipes
The Cook's Country Cookbook
Best Grilling Recipes
Best Lost Suppers
Best Potluck Recipes
Blue Ribbon Desserts
From Our Grandmothers' Kitchens

ADDITIONAL BOOKS FROM AMERICA'S TEST KITCHEN
The America's Test Kitchen Family Cookbook
The America's Test Kitchen Family Baking Book
The America's Test Kitchen Healthy Family Cookbook
The Best Simple Recipes
Slow Cooker Revolution
Cook's Country Annual Hardbound (2005–2011 Editions)
1993–2011 Cook's Illustrated Master Index

Visit our online bookstore at www.cooksillustrated.com to order any of our cookbooks and DVDs listed above. You can also order subscriptions, gift subscriptions, and any of our cookbooks and DVDs by calling 800-611-0759 inside the U.S., or at 515-246-6911 if calling from outside the U.S.

BC = Back Cover

COOK'S
ILLUSTRATED

Our Favorite Chili
We Tried Every Trick in the Book

Thin-Crust Pizza
Finally, a Foolproof Crust

Better Glazed Salmon

Spaghetti al Limone
Creamy, Zesty, Quick

Keys to Perfect Cookies

Old-Fashioned Gingerbread Cake

Do You Need a Paring Knife?
In a Word—Yes!

Rating Red Wine Vinegar
Split Pea and Ham Soup
Classic Caesar Salad
Nut-Crusted Chicken Cutlets
Weeknight Spanakopita
Easy Couscous Side Dishes

www.CooksIllustrated.com
$5.95 U.S./$6.95 CANADA

0 74470 62805 7

0 2>

CONTENTS
January & February 2011

COOK'S ILLUSTRATED

Founder and Editor   Christopher Kimball
Editorial Director   Jack Bishop
Executive Editor, Magazines   John Willoughby
Executive Editor   Amanda Agee
Test Kitchen Director   Erin McMurrer
Managing Editor   Rebecca Hays
Senior Editors   Keith Dresser
  Lisa McManus
Associate Features Editor   Elizabeth Bomze
Copy Editors   Nell Beram
  Amy Graves
Associate Editor   Bryan Roof
Test Cooks   Andrea Geary
  Andrew Janjigian
  Yvonne Ruperti
Assistant Editor   Taizeth Sierra
Executive Assistant   Christine Gordon
Editorial Assistant   Shannon Hatch
Test Kitchen Manager   Gina Nistico
Senior Kitchen Assistant   Leah Rovner
Kitchen Assistants   Maria Elena Delgado
  Ena Gudiel
  Edward Tundidor
Executive Producer   Melissa Baldino
Associate Producer   Stephanie Stender
Contributing Editors   Matthew Card
  Dawn Yanagihara
Consulting Editor   Scott Brueggeman
Science Editor   Guy Crosby, Ph.D.

Managing Editor, Special Issues   Todd Meier
Assistant Editor, Special Issues   Chris Dudley
Assistant Test Cook, Special Issues   Danielle DeSiato-Hallman
Editorial Assistant, Special Issues   Brittany Allen

Online Managing Editor   David Tytell
Online Editor   Kate Mason
Online Media Producer   Peter Tannenbaum
Online Assistant Editor   Mari Levine
Online Editorial Assistant   Eric Grzymkowski

Design Director   Amy Klee
Art Director   Julie Bozzo
Designer   Lindsey Timko
Deputy Art Director, Marketing/Web   Christine Vo
Staff Photographer   Daniel J. van Ackere

Vice President, Marketing   David Mack
Circulation Director   Doug Wicinski
Circulation & Fulfillment Manager   Carrie Horan
Partnership Marketing Manager   Pamela Putprush
Marketing Assistant   Lauren Perkins
Database & Direct Mail Director   Adam Perry
Senior Database Analyst   Marina Sakharova
Product Operations Director   Steven Browall
Product Promotions Director   Tom Conway
E-Commerce Marketing Director   Hugh Buchan
E-Commerce Marketing Manager   Laurel Zeidman
E-Commerce Marketing Coordinator   Sandra Greenberg
Marketing Copywriter   David Goldberg
Customer Service Manager   Jacqueline Valerio
Customer Service Representatives   Jillian Nannicelli
  Kate Sokol

Sponsorship Sales Director   Marcy McCreary
Retail Sales & Marketing Manager   Emily Logan
Sponsorship & Marketing Coordinator   Bailey Vatalaro

Production Director   Guy Rochford
Senior Project Manager   Alice Carpenter
Production & Traffic Coordinator   Kate Hux
Senior Production Manager   Jessica L. Quirk
Asset & Workflow Manager   Andrew Mannone
Production & Imaging Specialists   Judy Blomquist
  Heather Dube
  Lauren Pettapiece

Technology Director   Rocco Lombardo
Lead Developer   Scott Thompson
Web Developers   Christopher Candelora
  James Madden
  Robert Martinez
Senior Web Production Coordinator   Evan Davis
Web Production Assistant   Jennifer Millett
Systems Administrator   Marcus Walser

VP, New Media Product Development   Barry Kelly
Lead Developer   Bharat Ruparel
Senior Information Architect   Melissa MacQuarrie
Social Media Manager   Steph Yiu
Web Developer   Anand Kumar

Chief Financial Officer   Sharyn Chabot
Human Resources Director   Adele Shapiro
Controller   Mandy Shito
Financial Director   Wayne Saville
Senior Accountant   Aaron Goranson
Staff Accountant   Connie Forbes
Accounts Payable Specialist   Steven Kasha
Office Manager   Michael Pickett
Receptionist   Henrietta Murray
Publicity   Deborah Broide

PRINTED IN THE USA

GOAT CHEESES

GOAT CHEESES Spanish Ibores is similar to Parmesan, but for its paprika-rubbed rind and slightly bitter bite. Majorero, indigenous to the Canary Islands, has a subtle acidic aftertaste. Holland's goat Gouda is nutty, with a salty crunch. Norwegian Ekte Gjetost has a brownish hue achieved as the whey's sugars caramelize. Elegant Mothais-sur-feuille ripens in a chestnut leaf. Departing from wheel and log forms are herbaceous Fleur Verte (flower-shaped), grassy Clochette (cellar-aged in bell form), and lemony Valençay (with an ashen exterior and pyramid shape). While Bucheron and Sainte-Maure de Touraine come in logs, the former's buttery interior features concentric rings (the inner chalky, the outer creamy), and the latter's blue rind hides its trademark long straw, used to facilitate handling.

COVER (Bananas): Robert Papp; BACK COVER (Goat Cheeses): John Burgoyne

America's TEST KITCHEN

A CHILD'S WINTER IN VERMONT

Whether the snowflakes were larger because I was small or because nature was more outspoken in those years, more impetuous and likelier to shower the hills behind our cabin with helter-skelter curtains of deep snowfall, I am not resolved, but childhood's winter was ruled by the elements, our young eyes open to the possibilities of a winter storm, as if our small village was at the whim of something that lived deep in the woods, rarely seen but feared. People were smaller then in a world that was ruled by forces that were carried on a distant wind, to alight on our roofs and back roads, the frozen powder having been made elsewhere and transported from wild peaks, a place just beyond our country store, down the dirt road, and on out into the world.

It was a winter when we still used a party line, ringing up Mrs. Lomberg to place a call, the black earpiece held tightly to the head, speaking too loudly into the cone-shaped receiver and knowing that conversations were overheard and sipped, like the first pull of hot maple syrup. It was a winter followed by a summer when we hand-cranked our own peach ice cream, the wooden paddle snow-kissed, almost-frozen sweet cream dripping onto the chin, wiped casually with a sticky finger. It was a winter when the Franklin stove was ripping hot, popping the creosote in the metal flue, and a fall when the crows perched royally on the dead, bare branches of a giant oak that had stood forever on the perimeter of our upper hay field, and I would take a dozen lazy shots with a 22, the birds unfluttered and remote.

Winter came that year without a cursory handshake, a freezing October rain weighing down branches still festooned with burnt umber leaves, the weight of the ice cracking limbs in half, felling whole trees, sinking power lines. And then it snowed hard and often, feathery fins of powdered fluff running atop the split rails, icicles hanging down from frozen gutters and snapped off in a ragged line with the handle of a broom. On one chilly Sunday, our father, desperate to escape his cabin fever, braved the iced toboggan run that was our road and crashed the army jeep into a snowbank just below Charlie Bentley's place. He walked home, unbowed, and tried a second breakout, this time in our blue Scout, burying its nose a hay wagon short of his first attempt. He remained a prisoner that day, unaware that it was a day of liberation.

Then December came, and it was a season of woolly mittens and Bean boots, of gut-strung snowshoes, of Flexible Flyers and Flying Saucers, of green-checked wool pants bedecked with baubles of ice that were plucked off like burrs in fall, hitching a ride as we strode past unawares. Out the back door, our father would place a jug of hard cider, the water freezing beneath a skim of high alcohol, just the thing before dinner, feet stretched toward the reddening black stove, his cheeks and spirits aglow.

And then Christmas descended, the giant tree dragged stump first through the porch door on Christmas Eve. The lights were untangled in quiet succession and tested, ornaments checked and rewired with new hangers, and then the last touch, the draping of icicles, at which point my sister and I broke free, turning Christmas Eve into a chaos of slapdash silvery confetti, the tree appearing to have caught a frontal wind of flotsam and jetsam, all sense of Christian order abandoned to pagan enthusiasms. And then day arrived, and the stockings were opened before breakfast: a bazaar of tiny balsa planes, red plastic ball-in-a-cup magic tricks, hand buzzers, red hots, finger puppets, tiny picture books, metal puzzle rings, flowers that blossomed in water and then, digging deeply into the heel and toe, a plastic compass, a small Davy Crockett pocketknife, and a black tin police car with a red rooftop light. Pancakes and our own sausage patties for breakfast, and then off to bigger things: a camera, a telescope, a rubber band

Christopher Kimball

airplane, and a slingshot. And then a mad rush into the deep snow, sledding down the side hill past the burn barrel and brush piles, across the dirt driveway, down off into the lower meadow toward the line of maples by the road, secretly hoping for a collision, a cartwheel of limbs and cold snow down the neck, to lie in a heap at the very bottom of the ride, at the very top of winter's frozen possibilities, staring empty and happy up into the thick pewter sky.

And then the day ebbed, the thermometer dropped toward zero, and it was the smack of backgammon pieces on the board my father had bought in Cairo during the war, mother-of-pearl inlays and the smell of exotic wood as my pieces shuttled back home and then off. Or a late afternoon of cribbage and eggnog in enormous clear plastic glasses with brightly colored dry flies inset as if in amber. Or a quiet hour upstairs, with the original edition of *The Wizard of Oz*, not the friendly Hollywood version, but a place of threatening Hammerheads and Glinda's palace in Quadling Country. And then Christmas dinner, the pot roast, the mashed potatoes, the green beans, the baking powder biscuits with tilted top hats, and then the molasses-black, brandy-soaked Christmas pudding, served and eaten with a backdrop of falling snow. After dinner, we cracked open the back door and turned on the outside light to check if our footprints had yet to be filled in, to see if the snow would pile up against the door, making us prisoners for a day or a week, holed up at the center of our small log cabin universe.

I have always remembered that year as the truest winter and the best of Christmases but am still hopeful that a storm will travel across unknown peaks to bury our small town once again and rekindle our faith in childhood and the fear of something lurking deep in the woods, just this side of dangerous and on the other side of imagination.

FOR INQUIRIES, ORDERS, OR MORE INFORMATION

www.CooksIllustrated.com
At www.CooksIllustrated.com, you can order books and subscriptions, sign up for our free e-newsletter, or renew your magazine subscription. Join the website and gain access to 18 years of *Cook's Illustrated* recipes, equipment tests, and ingredient tastings, as well as companion videos for every recipe in this issue.

COOKBOOKS
We sell more than 50 cookbooks by the editors of *Cook's Illustrated*.
To order, visit our bookstore at www.CooksIllustrated.com.

COOK'S ILLUSTRATED MAGAZINE
Cook's Illustrated magazine (ISSN 1068-2821), number 108, is published bimonthly by Boston Common Press Limited Partnership, 17 Station St., Brookline, MA 02445. Copyright 2011 Boston Common Press Limited Partnership. Periodicals postage paid at Boston, Mass., and additional mailing offices USPS #012487. Publications Mail Agreement No. 40020778. Return undeliverable Canadian addresses to P.O. Box 875, Station A, Windsor, ON N9A 6P2. POSTMASTER: Send address changes to Cook's Illustrated, P.O. Box 6018, Harlan, IA 51593-1518. For subscription and gift subscription orders, subscription inquiries, or change-of-address notices, visit us at www.AmericasTestKitchen.com/customerservice or write us at Cook's Illustrated, P.O. Box 6018, Harlan, IA 51593-1518.

FOR LIST RENTAL INFORMATION, CONTACT Specialists Marketing Services, Inc., 777 Terrace Ave., 4th Floor, Hasbrouck Heights, NJ 07604; 201-865-5800.
EDITORIAL OFFICE 17 Station St., Brookline, MA 02445; 617-232-1000; fax 617-232-1572. Subscription inquiries, visit www.AmericasTestKitchen.com/customerservice or call 800-526-8442.
POSTMASTER Send all new orders, subscription inquiries, and change-of-address notices to Cook's Illustrated, P.O. Box 6018, Harlan, IA 51593-1518.

ILLUSTRATION: RANDY GLASS

Pine Mouth

Can you explain this crazy thing that happened to me? Recently I ate pesto made with pine nuts, and for several days afterward, everything I ate or drank left a bitter metallic taste in my mouth. What was going on?

ELIZABETH WALKER
TAOS, N.M.

➤The reaction you describe is indeed bizarre—but not entirely uncommon. In fact, the condition has a Facebook page, and numerous blogs are devoted to the subject. Called "pine mouth," the phenomenon was first reported by a Belgian anesthesiologist in 2001. Those affected report that eating pine nuts temporarily alters their sense of taste, making most food and drink (including water) taste bitter or metallic. The nuts themselves taste fine; the condition emerges hours or even days after ingestion and lingers for as long as two weeks.

While the syndrome can clearly be linked to the consumption of pine nuts, its underlying explanation remains a mystery. One theory is that the reaction stems from rancid nuts. The most recent hypothesis, from research conducted at the Nestlé Research Center in Lausanne, Switzerland, suggests that new types of pine nuts introduced to the marketplace from China (now one of the largest—and cheapest—suppliers of the foodstuff) may be to blame. According to newspaper reports, the Swiss researchers found at least two Chinese species for sale that had never previously been used for human consumption.

The good news? While the symptoms of pine mouth are downright uncomfortable, the condition is temporary and does not seem to present any long-lasting health concerns. But until the true source of pine mouth is understood, we recommend purchasing Middle-Eastern or European-grown (and more expensive) pine nuts and refrigerating or freezing them in a well-sealed container to stave off rancidity.

SAFER BET
To minimize the chance of "pine mouth," seek out nuts grown in the Middle East or Europe.

Microwaving with Plastic

I've heard that plastic wrap can release harmful chemicals into food during microwaving. Is this true?

KLEA MCKENNA
SAN FRANCISCO, CALIF.

➤The chemicals contained in some plastic wraps (and in some plastic containers) are potentially harmful if the plastic is heated to the point that it melts or burns (at lower temperatures, plastic is essentially inert). To avoid exposure to these chemicals, the U.S. Food and Drug Administration recommends using only wrap and containers that are marked "microwave-safe"—many manufacturers have recently reformulated their products, which now carry this label—and leaving several inches of room between the food and the plastic wrap during cooking. This advice is particularly important if the food is high in fat or oil, since most of the suspect chemicals in plastic are fat (rather than water) soluble. Our advice: Use ceramic or glass cookware for microwaving, and instead of plastic wrap, cover food with an overturned microwave-safe bowl or plate. In the test kitchen, we have found that this retains moisture just as well as plastic wrap, with zero risk.

ZERO RISK
To prevent the leaching of harmful chemicals, cover food with a plate instead of plastic wrap in the microwave.

Salt Substitutes

What does the test kitchen think about salt substitutes? Are some brands better than others?

DIANE BOERI
WORCESTER, MASS.

➤Salt substitutes typically replace some or all of the sodium chloride (table salt) with potassium chloride, a salty-tasting mineral. We tasted four brands (Biosalt, Morton Lite Salt, LoSalt, and French's NoSalt) against the real stuff in three applications: cooked into rice, sprinkled on popcorn, and simply dissolved in water.

Three of the substitutes were deemed acceptable, if slightly off tasting, while the fourth, NoSalt, stood out as extremely bitter. Why the difference? As it turns out, potassium chloride is naturally bitter, and the likable salt substitutes buffered this bitterness with varying amounts of real table salt. NoSalt, on the other hand, contains no sodium chloride.

If you want to use a salt substitute, you'll find that those containing at least some sodium chloride will taste a whole lot better than those that have none at all.

Bakewell Cream

Our family recently moved to Maine, and I've seen an unusual product for sale in the grocery store called Bakewell Cream. What is it?

COURTNEY NALIBOFF
NORTH HAVEN, MAINE

➤Bakewell Cream was invented during World War II, when cream of tartar and baking powder were in short supply. The product contains no dairy: The "cream" in its name refers to its use in traditional Maine cream biscuits. It's actually a mixture of sodium pyrophosphate, a mineral acid, and cornstarch, added to prevent moisture absorption. It can be substituted for cream of tartar or combined in a 2:1 ratio with baking soda as a replacement for baking powder.

We mixed Bakewell Cream with baking soda and used it in our cream biscuit and sugar cookie recipes, finding that it performed just fine as a leavener. As a substitute for cream of tartar, however, it failed to impress: Our cream of tartar meringues were perfectly crisp and bright white, while those containing Bakewell Cream browned before they were fully cooked, leaving their centers gummy. The explanation? It all comes down to pH levels. Browning reactions occur more readily in alkaline environments—such as egg whites. Acidic cream of tartar works rapidly to reduce the pH of egg whites, thereby warding off browning. Sodium pyrophosphate, on the other hand, becomes acidic only when heated in the presence of water. The Bakewell Cream meringues, then, didn't turn acidic until they were fully heated in the oven, by which time it was too late to prevent them from browning.

In the Thick of It

I often use tapioca to thicken fruit pies. Can pearl tapioca, Minute tapioca, and tapioca flour be used interchangeably?

MARGARET COOKE
OAKLAND, CALIF.

➤In the test kitchen, we usually turn to Minute tapioca to thicken our fruit pies. Coarsely ground and precooked, it dissolves easily during baking, especially after it has been pulverized in a spice grinder. To see how other types of tapioca stack up, we weighed tapioca flour and ground pearl tapioca to match the 19-gram weight of 2 tablespoons of Minute tapioca and used them in our Sweet Cherry Pie. Both products produced great results, the only minor difference being that the pearl tapioca left minuscule gelatinous spheres in the filling.

The bottom line: While we still prefer to use finely ground Minute tapioca because it's easy to find, other tapioca products can be substituted.

How to Read a Steakhouse Menu

What do the terms "Kobe beef," "Wagyu beef," and "American Wagyu" mean exactly?

ADAM GRAVES
AUSTIN, TEXAS

➤Wagyu is a breed of cattle originally raised in Kobe, the capital city of Japan's Hyogo prefecture. Wagyu have been bred for centuries for their rich intramuscular fat, the source of the buttery-tasting, supremely tender meat. Wagyu cattle boast extra fat since they spend an average of one year longer in the feedlot than regular cattle, and end up weighing between 200 and 400 pounds more at slaughter. What's more, the fat in Wagyu beef is genetically predisposed to be about 70 percent desirable unsaturated fat and about 30 percent saturated fat, while the reverse is true for conventional American cattle.

In order to earn the designation "Kobe beef," the Wagyu must come from Kobe and meet strict production standards that govern that appellation. Since all beef exports from Japan are currently prohibited because of an outbreak of foot-and-mouth disease, any Wagyu consumed stateside are domestically raised. The "American Wagyu" or "American-Style Kobe Beef" that appears on some menus is usually a cross between Wagyu and Angus, but the U.S. Department of Agriculture requires that the animal be at least 50 percent Wagyu and remain in the feedlot for at least 350 days to receive these designations.

Snake River Farms, located in Idaho, has one of the largest herds of American Wagyu. When we tasted its beef ($18 to $50 per pound, depending on the cut) against regular prime beef ($13 to $30/pound), the Wagyu proved itself a delicacy worthy of an occasional splurge: It was strikingly rich, juicy, and tender. The prime beef was also very good, but its texture and taste weren't quite as luxuriant.

AMERICAN WAGYU **PRIME BEEF**
The extensive marbling in American Wagyu beef sets it apart from regular beef.

Sweetening Out-of-Season Corn

I've read that cooking out-of-season corn on the cob in water along with a little whole milk and sugar improves its taste. Does this trick work?

JACKI BECKER
BRIDGEPORT, CONN.

➤Just-picked corn contains a great deal of sugar and very little starch, which is why ultra-fresh corn on the cob is such a treat. However, problems arise very soon after harvest, when natural sugars start to convert into bland starch, and the process only continues during transport or storage.

Any tactic for offsetting flavor deterioration seems worth a try, so we boiled out-of-season corn four ways: in 1 gallon of plain water, in the same amount of water mixed with 1 cup of milk, in water mixed with 1 cup of milk and 4 teaspoons of sugar, and in water sweetened with 4 teaspoons of sugar (our go-to test kitchen technique). The corn cooked in plain water was virtually tasteless, as was the sample pulled from the water-milk bath.

So although adding milk proved unnecessary, a little sugar did the trick—4 teaspoons per gallon of plain water brought out the bright flavor of the kernels. Why? Corn contains proteins called prolamines, whose bitterness becomes more pronounced as the sugar concentration declines. When sugar is added to the cooking water, it's absorbed by the kernels, helping restore their sweetness and mask bitterness.

Emulsifying with Egg Beaters

I enjoy making homemade mayonnaise but am concerned about consuming raw egg yolks. Can a pasteurized egg product be used instead?

TOM BASS
BILOXI, MISS.

➤Egg Beaters is one of the only pasteurized egg options available to most consumers, but we had our doubts about its ability to serve as a good substitute for real eggs in something creamy like mayonnaise. Real egg yolks contain the emulsifying agent lecithin, which helps thicken mayonnaise, whereas Egg Beaters is made from egg whites and therefore contains no lecithin. That said, we gave it a whirl in our Garlic Mayonnaise, replacing the two egg yolks with ¼ cup of Egg Beaters. The result? An incredibly thick emulsion, albeit slightly less rich-tasting than the real thing.

Encouraged, we went on to make Egg Beaters–based hollandaise sauce and Caesar dressing, both with great success. For a final cooked application, we prepared our Classic Crème Brûlée, swapping in the Egg Beaters for the prescribed 12 large yolks. The resulting custard was remarkably creamy but unacceptably dull, its flavor eliciting comparison to "insipid vanilla pudding."

How does this product work? The secret is vegetable gums. Unlike lecithin, which forms a barrier around water droplets, making it difficult for them to separate, gums simply add viscosity, helping mixtures coalesce into a suspension. The lesson: If you're concerned about consuming raw egg yolks, Egg Beaters could be your answer. Just don't swap it for large quantities of yolks, as in custard desserts.

Erratum

In a review of remote thermometers (Sept./Oct. 2010), we incorrectly stated that the CDN Wireless Probe Thermometer and Timer (model WT1) could not be set for temperatures lower than 170 degrees. While it is possible to override the preset temperatures, we found the process difficult and time-consuming, and still do not recommend this device.

SEND US YOUR QUESTIONS We will provide a complimentary one-year subscription for each letter we print. Send your inquiry, name, address, and daytime telephone number to Notes from Readers, Cook's Illustrated, P.O. Box 470589, Brookline, MA 02447, or to notesfromreaders@AmericasTestKitchen.com.

Quick Tips

⋟ COMPILED BY SHANNON FRIEDMANN HATCH ⋞

Clump-Free Sugar

Gregory Sarafin of Center Moriches, N.Y., tried everything to stop his sugar from turning into a solid white brick. Airtight glass containers helped, but the sweet stuff ultimately still caked. Now he has a new weapon: his potato masher. With a few strokes, the sugar breaks up into granules.

Temperature Cheat Sheet

Eileen Baione of Jensen Beach, Fla., can never remember the target doneness temperatures for various cuts of meat and poultry, desserts, and bread. Her solution? She attaches to the thermometer's protective case a laminated index card featuring the desired internal temperatures for the foods she makes most.

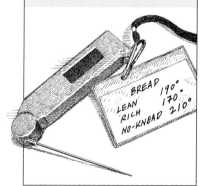

Spreading Cold Butter

Cecelia Rooney of Point Pleasant, N.J., often runs into this common problem: She wants butter for her toast but forgot to leave it out to soften. Crisis averted: She has discovered that a vegetable peeler will cut a thin ribbon that's easy to spread.

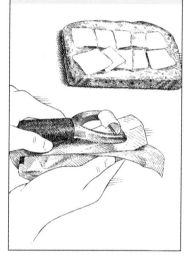

Great Plate Warmer

Earl Schenberg of St. Louis, Mo., has figured out a way to prevent his room-temperature plates from cooling down his hot breakfast. While his bread is toasting, he places the plates on top of the toaster oven. The radiating heat warms them right up and delivers eggs, pancakes, and other breakfast items to the table still hot.

Plastic-Bag Hideaway

Looking for a way to corral her unwieldy (and ever-growing) pile of plastic bags, Dimple Dudley of Newbern, Tenn., discovered that an empty paper towel roll makes a great hideaway. She can stuff up to 20 bags inside.

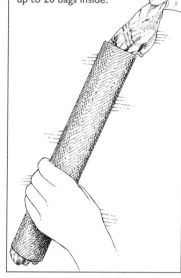

Just a Splash of Oil

Tired of fumbling with the cap to the olive oil when cooking, Karen Koster of Austin, Texas, devised a one-handed plan. She pours the oil into an old ketchup bottle. Now whenever she needs a splash of oil, she just flips the top and squirts it into the pan.

Grease, Lightning Fast

Sheila Censorio of Block Island, R.I., has found a smart way to grease cake pans:

1. Save empty butter wrappers in a zipper-lock bag in the freezer.
2. Whenever a recipe calls for a greased pan, pull out one wrapper and wipe it on the pan's surface. Each wrapper usually has just enough butter clinging to it to grease a pan.

SEND US YOUR TIP We will provide a complimentary one-year subscription for each tip we print. Send your tip, name, and address to Quick Tips, Cook's Illustrated, P.O. Box 470589, Brookline, MA 02447, or to quicktips@AmericasTestKitchen.com.

ILLUSTRATION: JOHN BURGOYNE

Better Flour Duster

When rolling out biscuits, pie pastry, or pizza dough, Latrice Gainey of Timmonsville, S.C., was covering her work surface with drifts of wasted flour until she figured out a better method. She now keeps a clean, dry cheese shaker (like the kind at a pizza parlor) filled with flour and sprinkles just what she needs.

Hash Browns, Simplified

Preparing hash browns can occupy a lot of kitchen real estate: countertop for grating, sink for rinsing, clean surface for laying out paper towels for drying—and that's all before the potatoes make it to the frying pan. Rob Razzano of El Cajon, Calif., has trimmed the method by placing the grated potatoes directly in the basket of his salad spinner. From here, he can rinse them and then spin away the moisture.

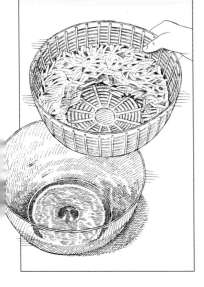

Stay-Put Parchment Paper

Rolling out cookie dough between two sheets of parchment paper (which prevents the dough from sticking) is a breeze with this method from Sarah Mahler of Cumberland, R.I.

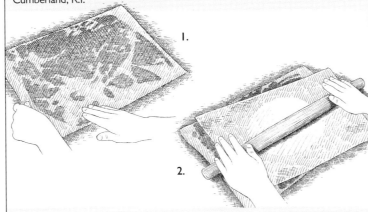

1. Sprinkle water on a clean surface and lay a sheet of waxed or parchment paper on top. The water will cling to the paper and hold it in place, creating a stick-free surface for the dough.
2. Place the dough on the paper and place another sheet on top. Roll out the dough and cut cookies; toss the paper for quick cleanup.

Keeping Leftover Pie Intact

Storing uneaten pie can be tricky. Toppings such as fresh fruit, meringue, and whipped cream can get crushed against a container. Nike Lewis of Cary, N.C., has found an unconventional use for a large, round storage container. When turned upside down, the lid acts as the plate for the leftover pie, while the container's bowl acts as a dome that preserves any topping's integrity.

Perfect Panini

Paul Villien of New Orleans, La., has found a way to mimic the popular griddle sandwiches without investing in a panini press.

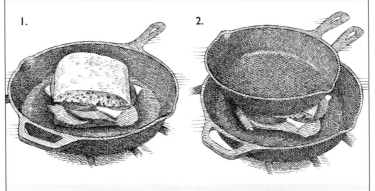

1. Set a large, seasoned, oiled cast-iron skillet over medium-high heat; place assembled sandwich inside.
2. Place a smaller cast-iron skillet (or other heavy pot) on top of the sandwich to press. Cook until the bottom of the sandwich is golden brown, then flip and repeat the process on the other side.

Keeping Hand Towels at Hand

Hand towels draped over oven-door handles often fall to the floor. Emily Lewis of Eustis, Fla., has devised a way to keep hers in place.

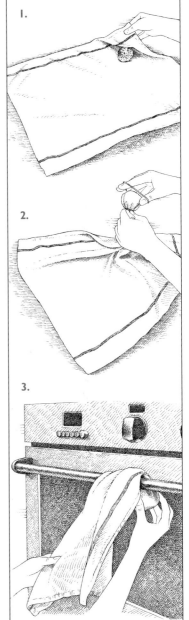

1. Lay a towel flat on the counter and place a crumpled ball of aluminum foil, about 1½ inches in diameter, at one corner.
2. Fold that corner over the ball and secure it with a rubber band.
3. Feed the loose end of the towel up and over the oven-door handle and pull the fabric down in front, leaving the foil ball hanging behind like a pulley weight.

Foolproof Thin-Crust Pizza

With ovens that reach only 500 degrees and dough that's impossible to stretch thin, even the savviest home cooks struggle to produce parlor-quality pies. We set out to change that.

⇒ BY ANDREW JANJIGIAN ⇐

Pizza was the first food I learned to make as a kid, and I've been determined to perfect it ever since. Over the years, my dogged pursuit of the ideal crust—thin, crisp, and spottily charred on the exterior; tender yet chewy within—has led me into exhaustive research and experiments, and even compelled me to extremes. I've been known to override the lock on my oven during its white-hot cleaning cycle. I've even built a wood-fired oven in my backyard.

But despite those efforts, I had yet to produce a recipe that was both reliable and reasonable for someone baking in a conventional oven. After the 10 to 12 minutes necessary to crisp the crust, the interior inevitably turns dry and tough. Plus, the raw dough itself is a devil to work with: Too wet and it becomes sticky; too dry and it's a stiff, dense wad. And forget stretching it into a neat circle; most of the time it either rips or springs back like a rubber band. If I were really going to bring home the kind of pizza I've come to crave when dining out, I'd have to take each element back to the drawing board.

Testing the Water

Like other lean doughs, pizza tends to have a short ingredient list (often just flour, water, salt, and yeast), so each element counts for a lot. Flour was the obvious first consideration, and I opted for high-protein (about 13 percent by weight) bread flour. It's a typical choice when a chewy, nicely tanned crust is the goal, since the proteins both encourage gluten development and brown easily.

The other major factor is the hydration level of the dough—in other words, the weight of the water in relation to the weight of the flour. From my recent work on focaccia (Sept./Oct. 2010), I knew that low-hydration doughs (55 to 70 percent water) generally result in the type of tight, even crumb you might find in sandwich bread, whereas a higher hydration (70 percent and up) produces the looser, airier, more bubbly crumb typical of rustic

The puffy edge of our pizza provides a good handle before tapering down to a thin layer in the center.

artisan-style breads. Figuring my goal was somewhere in the middle, I started my testing by mixing together five moderately wet doughs (from 58 to 67 percent hydration), kneading all the ingredients with our preferred food-processor method. (A more conventional stand-mixer method might take 15 to 20 minutes before the dough turns into a shiny, elastic mass, but we've recently found that a food processor turns out comparably kneaded results in less than two minutes.) I let the dough proof at room temperature for a few hours, shaped and topped the pies with our quick no-cook pizza sauce (a placeholder at this stage) and a generous handful of shredded mozzarella, and shuttled them onto blazing hot (500-degree) baking stones to cook. I pulled them out roughly 10 minutes later, once the crusts had puffed up a bit and blistered in spots and the cheese was melted and spotty brown.

Just as I'd expected, the lower-hydration doughs were not only stiff and difficult to shape into even rounds when raw, but also tough to chew once baked. But really wet doughs weren't ideal either; though they emerged significantly more tender from the oven, all that water had made the raw dough so

sticky and soft that it tended to tear when stretched. The best of the bunch fell at about 61 percent—enough to stretch easily without ripping or sticking to my fingers and retain moisture as it baked. With further experimentation, I found that I could raise the hydration level to 63 percent and still be able to handle this stickier dough by adding a little extra flour to the exterior as I shaped and stretched the pie. Such a judicious use of "bench flour" allowed me to increase the hydration of the dough while still maintaining the ability to shape it easily.

Cold Storage

With this dough I had a good jumping-off point, but pizza perfection was still a long way away. First off, instead of being thin and just a bit floppy, like a good parlor pie, my crust was bready and overinflated—more like focaccia than pizza—even when stretched as thinly as possible. Even more troubling, the dough was lacking in flavor, save for a strong yeastiness.

Simply dialing back on the yeast seemed like an obvious test—and did help deflate the too-puffy crust just a bit. But it also wiped out what little flavor the dough started with. Since keeping the yeast to a minimum was a given, I clearly needed an altogether different approach to fermentation.

First, a little background on the relationship between fermentation and dough's texture and flavor. When dough is first mixed, tiny "seed" bubbles form that expand with carbon dioxide at two different junctures: once when the bread is proofed and again when a last burst of carbon dioxide is produced during the first few minutes of baking. The larger the bubbles in the dough prior to baking, the more open and puffy the final dough will be. One way to minimize the size of the bubbles is to chill the dough as it proofs. Aside from producing finer, tighter air bubbles, cold fermentation has the added benefit of creating more flavorful dough. Why? Because at lower temperatures, yeast produces less carbon dioxide and more of the initial side products of fermentation: flavorful sugars, alcohol, and acids (see "Keeping Inflation Down").

With that in mind, I mixed up a new batch of dough and immediately placed it in the refrigerator to proof. The next day, I pulled it out, divided and shaped it into rounds, and let it warm to room temperature while I preheated my baking stone. I was skeptical at first; unlike the room temperature–proofed batch, this dough looked pretty unremarkable, showing none of the telltale signs of active

Dough that shrinks back when you roll it out is one of the pesky factors that keep a crust from ever baking up truly thin.

1. ADD JUST ENOUGH WATER Create a relatively wet—but not too wet—dough, which stretches without tearing and stays tender once baked.

2. PROOF IN FRIDGE Chill the dough in the refrigerator for at least 24 hours. This leads to less rise, a more flexible dough that holds its shape, and a thinner (and more flavorful) final crust.

3. DIVIDE Halve dough and shape into balls. Place on lightly oiled baking sheet and cover with oiled plastic wrap. Let rest 1 hour to allow dough to return to room temperature.

4. FLATTEN On well-floured surface and using fingertips, gently flatten dough into 8-inch disk, leaving outer edge slightly thicker than center to create a fatter "handle."

5. STRETCH With hands, stretch dough into 12-inch round, working along edges and giving dough quarter turns. Transfer to well-floured peel and stretch to 13-inch round.

---

fermentation such as an airy, bubbly structure. But one sniff of its heady, slightly boozy aroma clearly indicated that plenty had been happening beneath the surface. Furthermore, this tighter, smoother mass of dough proved much easier to work with, pulling effortlessly into a circle that gradually tapered in thickness from edge to center. I shouldn't have been surprised by this latter development. Besides slowing carbon dioxide production, chilling dough slows down gluten development so that dough literally stays looser, making it easier to stretch and hold its shape without snapping back. And the pizza it produced? Vastly better than previous attempts: Though not perfect, the dough was more complexly flavored and crisp than any other pie I'd made, with an interior that boasted decent tenderness and chew. Even the rim offered just the right degree of puffiness and functioned as an ample handle.

I had to wonder: If 24 hours of cold fermentation had such a dramatic effect on the dough, what would happen if I left it in the fridge even longer? Three days later, I had my answer. I'd mixed together and chilled a batch of dough each day over a 72-hour period, and the pizza bake-off proved that its flavor improved as time went by. (Push the fermentation beyond three days, however, and the yeast finally starts to produce a surplus of carbon dioxide, rendering the dough puffy.) True, cold fermented dough wasn't exactly quick, but the recipe was a snap to make. Plus, the long rest wasn't altogether inconvenient; with a little planning, this dough had great make-ahead potential.

Hot Stone

But the crust's crispness—or lack thereof—continued to nag me. Adding a tablespoon of oil to the dough helped a bit, but not enough. I had one other idea about how to encourage more crunch and color: sugar. We often sprinkle a spoonful over poultry skin to help it darken and crisp up in the oven, and I saw no reason the same trick couldn't be used here. I worked 2 teaspoons into the dough and, sure enough, the next pizza I pulled from the oven was tinged a slightly deeper shade of brown. But it still wasn't enough.

The real problem was the same one I'd been trying to address with all of my radical pizza-baking experiments over the years: The fact that home ovens simply don't get hot enough to produce a deeply browned crust before the interior crumb dries out and toughens. The best solution has always been the hottest setting on the oven dial and a pizza stone, which soaks up the radiating heat like a sponge. Following that logic, most recipes call for the stone to be placed as low in the oven as possible, where it gets maximum exposure to the main heating element. But when I thought about it, that technique didn't really make sense—and I even had an industry clue to prove it: commercial pizza ovens. These wide, shallow chambers quickly reflect heat from the floor back onto the top of the pie as it cooks, preventing the crust from drying out before the toppings have browned. Obviously I couldn't alter the shape of my oven—but I could move the stone up closer to the top to narrow the gap between the

stone and the ceiling. After a series of tests with thermocouples and an infrared thermometer, I found the best position for the stone is really as close to the top of the oven as possible—about 4 inches or so from the ceiling, which left just enough headroom to comfortably house the pie. (See "Shrink Your Headroom," page 8.) When I pulled this latest attempt from my newfangled setup, the results were a revelation: Everything had baked in sync, producing a pizza that was thoroughly crisp, well-browned on both top and bottom, and slightly chewy, just like a good parlor slice.

To Top It Off

I had my perfect foundation; all I had left to do was tweak the toppings. The no-cook sauce I'd been using—canned whole tomatoes, garlic, olive oil, and spices pureed in the food processor—needed just a quick jolt of flavor, so I added a splash of red wine vinegar to enhance the tomatoes' bright acidity. As

---

SCIENCE EXPERIMENT Keeping Inflation Down

The biggest factor contributing to a crust that turns out thick versus thin is the size of the air bubbles in the dough before it goes into the oven. The more the bubbles expand with carbon dioxide as the dough ferments (or "proofs"), the thicker the final crust. Could a longer rise in the refrigerator fix the problem?

EXPERIMENT
We made two batches of dough, leaving one to rise at room temperature for four hours and placing the other in the refrigerator for 24 hours, then baked them both according to our recipe.

RESULTS
The dough left to rise at room temperature produced a crust that puffed up like focaccia, while the dough that rose in the fridge baked up with smaller bubbles and boasted far more flavor.

EXPLANATION
Fermentation is a two-phase process: First, the carbohydrates in the dough are converted by the yeast to sugars, alcohol, and acids. Next, these convert to carbon dioxide, expanding the bubbles created in the dough when it was first mixed. At room temperature, the process moves rapidly to the production of carbon dioxide. But in the fridge, the process is slowed way down. With enough time, the complex-tasting sugars, alcohol, and acids form, but very little carbon dioxide gets converted, so the bubbles in the dough stay small and the crust bakes up both thin and more flavorful.

PUFFY AND BLAND   **THIN AND FLAVORFUL**

for the cheese, I supplemented the creamy, stretchy mozzarella with a fistful of sharp, salty, finely grated Parmesan. And that's where I stopped. Of course, additional toppings are fine (provided one doesn't use too heavy a hand); but for me, this simple-to-make, simply dressed pie bakes up perfect as-is.

THIN-CRUST PIZZA
MAKES TWO 13-INCH PIZZAS

NOTE: Our preferred brand of whole-milk mozzarella is Dragone. You can shape the second dough ball while the first pizza bakes, but don't top the pizza until right before you bake it. If you don't have a baking stone, bake the pizzas on an overturned and preheated rimmed baking sheet. It is important to use ice water in the dough to prevent overheating the dough while in the food processor. Semolina flour is ideal for dusting the peel; use it in place of bread flour if you have it. The sauce will yield more than needed in the recipe; extra sauce can be refrigerated for up to a week or frozen for up to a month. For our free recipe for Thin-Crust White Pizza, go to www.CooksIllustrated.com/feb11.

Dough
- 3 cups (16½ ounces) bread flour, plus more for work surface (see note)
- 2 teaspoons sugar
- ½ teaspoon instant or rapid-rise yeast
- 1⅓ cups (about 10½ ounces) ice water (see note)
- 1 tablespoon vegetable oil, plus more for work surface
- 1½ teaspoons table salt

Sauce
- 1 (28-ounce) can whole peeled tomatoes, drained and liquid discarded
- 1 tablespoon extra-virgin olive oil
- 1 teaspoon red wine vinegar
- 2 medium garlic cloves, minced or pressed through garlic press (about 2 teaspoons)
- 1 teaspoon table salt
- 1 teaspoon dried oregano
- ¼ teaspoon ground black pepper

Cheese
- 1 ounce finely grated Parmesan cheese (about ½ cup)
- 8 ounces shredded whole-milk mozzarella (about 2 cups) (see note)

1. FOR THE DOUGH: In food processor fitted with metal blade, process flour, sugar, and yeast until combined, about 2 seconds. With machine running, slowly add water through feed tube; process until dough is just combined and no dry flour remains, about 10 seconds. Let dough stand 10 minutes.

2. Add oil and salt to dough and process until dough forms satiny, sticky ball that clears sides of workbowl, 30 to 60 seconds. Remove dough from bowl, knead briefly on lightly oiled countertop until smooth, about

1 minute. Shape dough into tight ball and place in large, lightly oiled bowl. Cover tightly with plastic wrap and refrigerate for at least 24 hours and up to 3 days.

3. FOR THE SAUCE: Process all ingredients in food processor until smooth, about 30 seconds. Transfer to medium bowl or container and refrigerate until ready to use.

4. TO BAKE THE PIZZA: One hour before baking pizza, adjust oven rack to second highest position (rack should be about 4 to 5 inches below broiler), set pizza stone on rack, and heat oven to 500 degrees. Remove dough from refrigerator and divide in half. Shape each half into smooth, tight ball. Place on lightly oiled baking sheet, spacing them at least 3 inches apart; cover loosely with plastic wrap coated with nonstick cooking spray; let stand for 1 hour.

5. Coat 1 ball of dough generously with flour and place on well-floured countertop. Using fingertips, gently flatten into 8-inch disk, leaving 1 inch of outer edge slightly thicker than center. Using hands, gently stretch disk into 12-inch round, working along edges and giving disk quarter turns as you stretch. Transfer dough to well-floured peel and stretch into 13-inch round. Using back of spoon or ladle, spread ½ cup tomato sauce in thin layer over surface of dough, leaving ¼-inch border around edge. Sprinkle ¼ cup Parmesan evenly over sauce, followed by 1 cup mozzarella. Slide pizza carefully onto stone and bake until crust is well browned and cheese is bubbly and beginning to brown, 10 to 12 minutes, rotating pizza halfway through. Remove pizza and place on wire rack for 5 minutes before slicing and serving. Repeat step 5 to shape, top, and bake second pizza.

Topping Tips

We like our Thin-Crust Pizza simply dressed with tomato sauce and handfuls of shredded mozzarella and Parmesan, but additional toppings are always an option—provided they're prepared correctly and added judiciously. (An overloaded pie will bake up soggy.) Here are a few guidelines for how to handle different types of toppings:

HEARTY VEGETABLES
Aim for a maximum of 6 ounces per pie, spread out in a single layer. Vegetables such as onions, peppers, and mushrooms should be thinly sliced and lightly sautéed (or microwaved for a minute or two along with a little olive oil) before using.

DELICATE VEGETABLES AND HERBS
Leafy greens and herbs like spinach and basil are best placed beneath the cheese to protect them or added raw to the fully cooked pizza.

MEATS
Proteins (no more than 4 ounces per pie) should be precooked and drained to remove excess fat. We like to poach meats like sausage (broken up into ½-inch chunks), pepperoni, or ground beef for 4 to 5 minutes in a wide skillet along with ¼ cup of water, which helps to render the fat while keeping the meat moist.

Nut-Crusted Chicken Cutlets

How do you get chicken cutlets with a rich, nutty crust? As it turns out, by holding back on the nuts.

> BY ANDREW JANJIGIAN <

Incorporating chopped nuts into the coating of a boneless, skinless chicken breast not only adds a new, more robust flavor element, but also boosts the crust's crunch factor. But in my experience this technique comes with some problems: The crust becomes dense and leaden, and the rich flavor of the nuts rarely comes through. Plus it's all too easy to dry out a lean boneless breast.

Ensuring juicy, flavorful meat was a simple fix: I salted the cutlets (poking them with a fork first helps the salt penetrate) and rested them briefly before dredging and frying. For the crust, I wondered if a simple "breading" of nuts would help, but when I dredged the cutlets in flour, dipped them in beaten eggs, and dragged them through chopped almonds, the crushed pieces barely adhered to the meat. Using bread crumbs in the final dredge, which would absorb liquid from the eggs to help act as glue, was definitely going to be necessary. A mixture of half nuts and half Japanese panko—coarser and crunchier than conventional bread crumbs—gave me just the light, crisp texture I wanted. To improve flavor, I added Dijon mustard to the egg wash, and lemon zest, fresh thyme, and a dash of cayenne to the nut-crumb mixture.

But the crust still wasn't particularly nutty—and batch frying the cutlets was a hassle. Reviewing my research recipes, I noticed a few that baked the breaded cutlets. No question: "Oven frying" would be easier. And maybe the circulating oven heat would also toast the nuts and deepen their flavor. I breaded the next batch, arranged the cutlets on a wire rack set in a sheet pan, and baked them until they were cooked through. About 20 minutes later, the chicken emerged juicy and shrouded in an even, golden crust but—infuriatingly—no more nutty-tasting than before.

Adding more almonds only robbed the crust of the panko's crispness. Pretoasting them helped, but not enough to warrant the extra step. What I really needed was a way to add more nuttiness without adding more nuts. Then it hit me. We've achieved exactly this result in other recipes by calling on a powerhouse ingredient: browned butter. Gently heating butter until its milk solids take on a rich, deeply bronzed color brings out its inherent nuttiness. I gave it a shot, swirling a large butter knob in a skillet for about five minutes and then cooking the panko, ground nuts, and a minced shallot in the browned butter until fragrant and russet-colored. My tasters reached for second helpings of this latest batch. The technique worked equally well with pecans, pistachios, hazelnuts, and peanuts, making this an easy weeknight dish I could turn to again and again.

NUT-CRUSTED CHICKEN CUTLETS WITH LEMON AND THYME
SERVES 4

NOTE: This recipe is best with almonds, but works well with any type of nut. If your chicken breasts have the tenderloin attached, remove it and save it for another use. For our free recipes for Nut-Crusted Chicken Cutlets with Bacon and Nut-Crusted Chicken Cutlets with Lime and Chipotle, go to www.CooksIllustrated.com/feb11.

- 4 boneless, skinless chicken breasts (6 to 8 ounces each), trimmed of excess fat (see note) Kosher salt
- 1 cup roughly chopped almonds (see note)
- 4 tablespoons (½ stick) unsalted butter, cut into 4 pieces
- 1 medium shallot, minced (about 3 tablespoons)
- 1 cup panko (Japanese-style bread crumbs)
- 2 teaspoons finely grated zest from 1 lemon, zested lemon cut into 4 wedges
- 1 teaspoon minced fresh thyme leaves
- ⅛ teaspoon cayenne pepper
- 3 large eggs
- 2 teaspoons Dijon mustard
- ¼ teaspoon ground black pepper
- 1 cup unbleached all-purpose flour

1. Adjust oven rack to lower-middle position and heat oven to 350 degrees. Using fork, poke thickest half of each breast 5 to 6 times. Place on wire rack set in rimmed baking sheet and evenly sprinkle each breast with ½ teaspoon kosher salt (or ¼ teaspoon table salt). Refrigerate, uncovered, while preparing coating.

2. Process nuts in food processor until they resemble coarse meal, about 20 one-second pulses. Heat butter in 12-inch skillet over medium heat; cook, swirling pan constantly, until butter turns golden brown and has nutty aroma, 4 to 5 minutes. Add shallot and ½ teaspoon kosher salt (or ¼ teaspoon table salt); cook, stirring constantly, until just beginning to brown, about 2 minutes. Reduce heat to medium-low, add panko and ground nuts; cook, stirring frequently, until golden brown, 10 to 12 minutes. Transfer panko mixture to shallow dish or pie plate and stir in lemon zest, thyme, and cayenne.

Browning the nuts and panko in butter deepens the coating's color—and flavor.

3. Lightly beat eggs, mustard, and black pepper together in second shallow dish or pie plate. Place flour in third shallow dish or pie plate. Pat chicken dry with paper towels. Working with 1 piece at a time, dredge chicken breast in flour, shaking off excess, then coat with egg mixture, allowing excess to drip off. Coat all sides of chicken with panko mixture, pressing gently so that crumbs adhere. Transfer breaded chicken to clean wire rack set in rimmed baking sheet and repeat with remaining chicken.

4. Bake until instant-read thermometer inserted into thickest part of chicken registers 160 degrees, 20 to 25 minutes. Let rest 5 minutes before serving with lemon wedges.

NUT-CRUSTED CHICKEN CUTLETS WITH ORANGE AND OREGANO

NOTE: This version works particularly well with pistachios or hazelnuts.

Follow recipe for Nut-Crusted Chicken Cutlets with Lemon and Thyme, substituting 1 teaspoon orange zest for lemon zest (reserving orange wedges for garnish) and oregano for thyme.

Better Glazed Salmon

Glazed salmon usually falls victim to the harsh heat of the broiler. We turned down the heat to bump up the flavor.

⇒ BY BRYAN ROOF ⇐

There are few better ways to highlight the rich, silky flesh of salmon than by offsetting it with a sweet-tart glaze. Most recipes brush the fish with a sticky mixture and then place it a few inches from the broiler element, basting it every minute or so to ensure a substantial coating. Of course, I didn't relish the idea of repeatedly reaching into a hot oven, but the method seemed viable enough. When I tried it, however, the sugary glaze charred, and as can happen with thick cuts of meat, a band of leathery overcooked flesh developed on the outside, with only the very center of the salmon exhibiting the translucent, buttery texture I was looking for.

Bye-Bye, Broiler

The problem was the broiler. It was simply too hard to pinpoint the proper doneness using such extreme heat, and repeatedly opening and closing the oven door to apply the glaze only complicated matters. But I had another idea: So-called slow-cooked salmon is a popular restaurant dish these days, and the approach reverses the tactic I'd been trying. The fish bakes in a low-temperature oven, rendering its flesh terrifically moist and tender. The likely trade-off would be a well-lacquered exterior, but I thought it was worth a shot. I switched the oven to "bake," moved the rack to the middle position, and gently cooked the fish plain (I'd address the glaze later). After 10 minutes at 300 degrees, the salmon was cooked perfectly.

Now that my salmon was succulent and pink throughout, I had only one problem: Tasters missed the slightly crusty, flavorful browned exterior of the broiled fish. Cranking the heat back up was out of the question. Instead, I briefly seared each side of the fish in a hot skillet before transferring it to the low oven. But while the crust was nicely browned, one bite revealed that I had virtually negated the benefits of my slow-cooked technique. The outer layer of the fish was tough and dry—reminiscent of the broiled recipes I'd tried.

For the most evenly cooked results, portion a whole center-cut fillet into four equal pieces.

What I needed to do was more rapidly caramelize the fillets before their exteriors had a chance to turn tough and leathery—and that's when I remembered a favorite test kitchen technique: To expedite browning on everything from pork tenderloin to tuna, we lightly sprinkle the flesh with sugar. Here, I tried brown sugar (for its subtle molasses flavor), and it took only a minute for a delicate, flavorful crust to form. I then seared the skin side of the fish for

another minute to promote even cooking and transferred the skillet to the oven. Seven minutes later, I had just what I wanted: a golden brown exterior and a pink, wonderfully moist interior.

Sticking To It

That just left me with the glaze. I combined more brown sugar with vinegar, then added mirin, soy sauce, and mustard to create a teriyaki-inspired varnish that would serve as a perfect foil to the rich, fatty salmon. I brought the mixture to a boil in a saucepan; reduced it for five minutes, when it was thick enough to coat the back of a spoon; then brushed it over the seared salmon fillets. But even before I got the fish into the oven, much of the glaze slid off and pooled in the bottom of the pan. Basting the salmon every couple of minutes would certainly help, but I hated to go that tedious route.

Another obvious remedy would be to further thicken the glaze, so I tried adding a small amount of cornstarch to the mixture. The result? Better, but too much of the sauce still dribbled down the sides of the fish. Adding more cornstarch was not an option; any more than a teaspoon rendered the mixture gummy and gloppy. I was running out of ideas when an altogether different approach occurred to me: What if instead of trying to create a tackier glaze, I worked on getting the salmon itself to have more "stickability"? I had a hunch that rubbing cornstarch on the surface of the fish would add texture, essentially creating tiny nooks and crannies to trap the glaze.

Fingers crossed, I combined ¼ teaspoon of cornstarch with the brown sugar I was already rubbing on the fish, plus ½ teaspoon of kosher salt for seasoning, and then seared the fillets. As I'd hoped, the surface

---

SCIENCE White, Out

What's the white stuff that sometimes mysteriously forms on salmon and sometimes doesn't? This film is a protein called albumin. When the muscle fibers in the fish are heated, they contract, pushing the moisture-filled albumin to the surface of the flesh. Once this protein reaches temperatures between 140 and 150 degrees, its moisture is squeezed out, and it congeals and turns white. Not only does the white albumin detract from the salmon's appearance, but its formation indicates a loss of moisture in the fish.

Cooking salmon at a low temperature can mitigate albumin coagulation. Gentle cooking results in less intense muscle contractions, so that less of the albumin moves to the surface of the fish and more of it stays trapped in the flesh. The fish not only stays more moist, but it looks better, too. –B.R.

HIGH HEAT = MORE WHITE STUFF

LOW HEAT = LESS WHITE STUFF

was now quite coarse, mottled all over with tiny peaks and valleys. I proceeded with the recipe, spooning the glossy glaze over the salmon and then transferring it to the low oven. This time the mixture stuck, resulting in a glistening, well-lacquered exterior.

With my glaze holding fast to the fillets, I whipped up three more variations: a fruity pomegranate version spiked with balsamic vinegar, an Asian barbecue mixture drawing sweetness from hoisin sauce and tartness from rice vinegar, and a salty, citrusy orange-miso version.

Not only was this adapted restaurant technique easier and more foolproof than the frequent basting method in other recipes, but I had dinner on the table in about 20 minutes.

GLAZED SALMON
SERVES 4

NOTE: Use center-cut salmon fillets of similar thickness so that they cook at the same rate. The best way to ensure uniformity is to buy a 1½- to 2-pound whole center-cut fillet and cut it into 4 pieces. Prepare the glaze before you cook the salmon. If your nonstick skillet isn't ovensafe, sear the salmon as directed in step 2, then transfer it to a rimmed baking sheet, glaze it, and bake it as directed in step 3.

- 1 teaspoon light brown sugar
- ½ teaspoon kosher salt
- ¼ teaspoon cornstarch
- 4 center-cut skin-on salmon fillets, 6 to 8 ounces each (see note)
  Ground black pepper
- 1 teaspoon vegetable oil
- 1 recipe glaze (recipes follow)

1. Adjust oven rack to middle position and heat oven to 300 degrees. Combine brown sugar, salt, and cornstarch in small bowl. Pat salmon dry with paper towels and season with pepper. Sprinkle brown sugar mixture evenly over top of flesh side of salmon, rubbing to distribute.

2. Heat oil in 12-inch ovensafe nonstick skillet over medium-high heat until just smoking. Place salmon, flesh side down, in skillet and cook until well browned, about 1 minute. Using tongs, carefully flip salmon and cook on skin side for 1 minute.

3. Remove skillet from heat and spoon glaze evenly over salmon fillets. Transfer skillet to oven and cook until center of thickest part of fillets registers 125 degrees on instant-read thermometer and is still translucent when cut into with paring knife, 7 to 10 minutes. Transfer fillets to platter or individual plates and serve.

SOY-MUSTARD GLAZE
MAKES ABOUT ½ CUP

NOTE: Mirin, a sweet Japanese rice wine, can be found in Asian markets and the international section of most supermarkets.

- 3 tablespoons light brown sugar
- 2 tablespoons soy sauce
- 2 tablespoons mirin (see note)
- 1 tablespoon sherry vinegar
- 1 tablespoon whole grain mustard
- 1 tablespoon water
- 1 teaspoon cornstarch
- ⅛ teaspoon red pepper flakes

Whisk ingredients together in small saucepan. Bring to boil over medium-high heat; simmer until thickened, about 1 minute. Remove from heat and cover to keep warm.

POMEGRANATE-BALSAMIC GLAZE
MAKES ABOUT ½ CUP

- 3 tablespoons light brown sugar
- 3 tablespoons pomegranate juice
- 2 tablespoons balsamic vinegar
- 1 tablespoon whole grain mustard
- 1 teaspoon cornstarch
  Pinch cayenne pepper

Whisk ingredients together in small saucepan. Bring to boil over medium-high heat; simmer until thickened, about 1 minute. Remove from heat and cover to keep warm.

ASIAN BARBECUE GLAZE
MAKES ABOUT ½ CUP

- 2 tablespoons ketchup
- 2 tablespoons hoisin sauce
- 2 tablespoons rice vinegar
- 2 tablespoons light brown sugar
- 1 tablespoon soy sauce
- 1 tablespoon toasted sesame oil
- 2 teaspoons Asian chili-garlic sauce
- 1 teaspoon grated fresh ginger

Whisk ingredients together in small saucepan. Bring to boil over medium-high heat; simmer until thickened, about 3 minutes. Remove from heat and cover to keep warm.

ORANGE-MISO GLAZE
MAKES ABOUT ½ CUP

- ¼ cup juice plus 1 teaspoon finely grated zest from 2 oranges
- 2 tablespoons white miso
- 1 tablespoon light brown sugar
- 1 tablespoon rice vinegar
- 1 tablespoon whole grain mustard
- ¾ teaspoon cornstarch
  Pinch cayenne pepper

Whisk ingredients together in small saucepan. Bring to boil over medium-high heat; simmer until thickened, about 1 minute. Remove from heat and cover to keep warm.

A Better Way to Cook Couscous

Back-of-the-package instructions may be simple, but too often they yield a tasteless, soggy mess. To cook couscous properly, we had to think outside the box.

≳ BY MARCUS WALSER ≲

Although couscous traditionally functions as a sauce absorber beneath North African stews and braises, it works equally well as a lighter, quicker alternative to everyday side dishes like rice pilaf and mashed potatoes. The tiny grains of pasta, made by rubbing together moistened semolina granules, readily adapt to any number of flavorful add-ins—from grassy fresh herbs like cilantro and parsley to heady spices like cumin and coriander and sweeter elements like raisins and dates. Best of all, the whole operation, from box to bowl, takes about five minutes.

At least that's what the back-of-the-box instructions say. I quickly realized that such convenience comes at a cost. No matter how precisely I followed the directions—measure and boil water, stir in couscous, cover and let stand off heat for five minutes, fluff with fork—the results were discouragingly similar to wet sand: bland, blown-out pebbles that stuck together in clumps. And it wasn't just one brand's poor instruction. Every box I bought spelled out the same steps.

I'm no expert on North African cuisine, but I'd read enough about couscous to know that it has far more potential than my efforts were suggesting. Then, as I was researching how the grains are made, I realized my problem: the box—both its contents and its cooking instructions. According to traditional couscous-making practices, the uncooked grains are steamed twice in a double boiler–shaped vessel called a *couscoussière*, from which the grains emerge fluffy and separate. The commercial staple we find on grocery store shelves, however, is far more processed: The grains are flash-steamed and dried before packaging. When exposed to the rigors of further cooking, this parcooked couscous—more or less a convenience product—turns to mush. That's why the box instructions are so simple: A quick reconstitution in boiling water is all the grains can stand.

To bring some much-needed flavor to the dish, I tried dry-toasting the grains in the pan and then stirring in boiling water—but that got me nowhere: The pasta grains burned before they had a chance to develop any real flavor. Then I recalled a popular trick used on another grain that, without some

finesse, can also cook up woefully bland: rice. The "pilaf method," according to widely accepted rice and grain cookery, calls for briefly sautéing the grains in hot fat before liquid is introduced. So for my next batch of couscous, I melted a small amount of butter, which, as I'd hoped, coated the grains nicely, allowing them to brown gently and uniformly and helping them cook up fluffy and separate. (Plus, with butter in the pan, I could briefly sauté all sorts of add-ins, like spices, garlic, shallots, and even grated carrot.) To bump up the flavor even further, I replaced half of the water called for in the box instructions with chicken broth. Now I was getting somewhere: After absorbing the hot stock-based liquid, the couscous grains were flavorful enough to stand on the plate without a sauce. With my technique established, I developed simple flavor variations by adding dried fruit, nuts, and zest to the couscous.

Satisfied with my recipe, I figured my work was just about done—until I spied the two dirty pans in the sink. Given that the dish took all of five minutes to cook, I was determined to do better when it came to cleanup. Then it dawned on me: Since my saucepan was already hot from toasting the grains, why not simply add room-temperature liquid to it instead of going to the trouble to heat the liquid in a separate pan? Sure enough, that did it. The residual heat from the pan boiled the liquid almost instantly—it was like deglazing a skillet after searing. On went the lid, and after a brief rest and a quick fluff with a fork, my couscous was done—with much better flavor (and just minutes' more effort) than I got from the box method.

BASIC COUSCOUS
SERVES 4 TO 6

- 2 tablespoons unsalted butter
- 2 cups couscous
- 1 cup water
- 1 cup low-sodium chicken broth
- 1 teaspoon table salt
  Ground black pepper

Heat butter in medium saucepan over medium-high heat. When foaming subsides, add couscous and cook, stirring frequently, until grains are just beginning to brown, about 5 minutes. Add water, broth, and salt; stir briefly to combine, cover, and remove pan from heat. Let stand until grains are tender, about 7 minutes. Uncover and fluff grains with fork. Season with pepper to taste and serve.

COUSCOUS WITH DATES AND PISTACHIOS

Follow recipe for Basic Couscous, increasing butter to 3 tablespoons and adding 1 tablespoon finely grated fresh ginger, ½ teaspoon ground cardamom, and ½ cup chopped dates to saucepan with couscous. Increase amount of water to 1¼ cups. Stir ¾ cup coarsely chopped toasted pistachios, 3 tablespoons minced fresh cilantro leaves, and 2 teaspoons lemon juice into couscous before serving.

COUSCOUS WITH DRIED CHERRIES AND PECANS

Follow recipe for Basic Couscous, increasing butter to 3 tablespoons and adding 2 minced garlic cloves, ¾ teaspoon garam masala, ⅛ teaspoon cayenne pepper, and ½ cup coarsely chopped dried cherries to saucepan with couscous. Increase amount of water to 1¼ cups. Stir ¾ cup coarsely chopped toasted pecans, 2 thinly sliced scallions, and 2 teaspoons lemon juice into couscous before serving.

COUSCOUS WITH CARROTS, RAISINS, AND PINE NUTS

Follow recipe for Basic Couscous, increasing butter to 3 tablespoons. Once foaming subsides, add 2 grated medium carrots and ½ teaspoon ground cinnamon; cook, stirring frequently, until carrot softens, about 2 minutes. Continue with recipe, adding ½ cup raisins to saucepan with couscous and increasing water to 1¼ cups. Stir ¾ cup toasted pine nuts, 3 tablespoons minced fresh cilantro leaves, ½ teaspoon finely grated orange zest, and 1 tablespoon orange juice into couscous before serving.

COUSCOUS WITH SHALLOTS, GARLIC, AND ALMONDS

Follow recipe for Basic Couscous, increasing butter to 3 tablespoons. Once foaming subsides, add 3 thinly sliced shallots and cook, stirring frequently, until softened and lightly browned, about 5 minutes. Add 1 minced garlic clove and cook until fragrant, about 30 seconds. Continue with recipe, stirring ¾ cup toasted sliced almonds, ¼ cup minced fresh parsley leaves, 2 teaspoons lemon juice, and ½ teaspoon finely grated lemon zest into couscous before serving.

See Us Create Flavorful Couscous
Video available FREE for 4 months at
www.CooksIllustrated.com/feb11

Our Favorite Chili

We built the best basic chili from the ground up, and then entered the strange world of secret ingredients to determine what's legit and what's just laughable.

≥ BY ANDREA GEARY ≤

C hili devotees (or "chiliheads," as they are known) are an opinionated, even cheerily belligerent bunch. Each cook will swear that the only chili worth eating is his or her own: rich with slow-cooked meat and redolent with chile peppers and spices, all bound in an unctuous sauce. But chili is basically just meat cooked with ground chiles; how could one be so much better than another? The key, any chilihead will tell you, lies in the all-powerful "secret ingredients."

I lost count of the references unearthed in my research to the intriguing additions that could magically improve a humble pot of chili, but the specifics were hard to nail down. (Chiliheads are as secretive as they are argumentative.) It took a lot of digging to compile a list. The Internet yielded fascinating new leads, like prunes floated atop the simmering chili (removed before serving), and obscure cookbooks revealed a couple of others (chocolate, beer). Chiliheads were reluctant to reveal the key to their own success; luckily, they could occasionally be coaxed to divulge the details of other cooks' recipes, including one chili that was thickened with "just a touch of peanut butter."

Inspired by these inventive (some might say wacky) cooks, I was determined to make my own ultimate chili. Before I began developing my recipe, I looked one more place for ideas: chili cook-offs. Who, I reasoned, would know more about producing the ultimate chili than these die-hard cooks who labor 40 weekends per year to defend their bragging rights? It turns out that the chili cook-off circuit is a fascinating world unto itself, but my sleuthing yielded little in the way of practical instruction (see "The Truth About Championship Chili," page 15).

What's Your Beef?

Enticing as my ever-increasing list of secret ingredients was, it was getting me nowhere until I developed a basic recipe that these strange additions could embellish. Adopting the opinionated swagger of a veteran chili cook, I brashly laid down my own ground rules: To live up to my high expectations, my chili would have to be all beef (diced, not ground), and it would have pinto beans, tomatoes, onions, and garlic. These last four ingredients are actually highly

We build spicy complexity by toasting and grinding whole chiles and then stirring in a few surprise ingredients.

controversial in some parts of the United States, but: my recipe, my rules. It's the chilihead way.

I began by testing five different cuts of beef: flap meat, brisket, chuck-eye roast, skirt steak, and short ribs, all in ¾-inch dice, and all browned before going into the pot with sautéed onions, jalapeños, and garlic; diced tomatoes; beef broth; and quick-brined pinto beans. For the sake of simplicity, I seasoned each pot with ⅓ cup of chili powder.

Though the short ribs were extremely tender, some tasters felt that they tasted too much like pot roast. (Not to mention that it took $40 worth of them to make just one pot of chili.) The brisket was wonderfully beefy but lean and a bit tough. The clear winner was chuck-eye roast, favored for its tenderness and rich flavor. The beans were praised for their soft, creamy texture (attributed to the hour-long brine), and tasters embraced the addition of the tomatoes and aromatics. But I was far from home free: My tasters also complained that the chili powder gave the dish a gritty, dusty texture, and the flavor was "less than vibrant."

Getting Down to the Nitty-Gritty

Making my own chili powder seemed the best way to solve both of those problems, so I decided to give it a try. Of all the dried chiles that are available in most supermarkets, I chose anchos for their earthiness and árbols for their smooth heat. I removed the stems and seeds from six dried ancho chiles and four dried árbol chiles, then toasted the anchos in a dry skillet until they were fragrant (the very thin árbols burned when I tried to toast them). After cooling the anchos, I ground them in a spice grinder along with the árbols and 2 teaspoons each of cumin and oregano, both common seasonings in commercial chili powder blends. The sauce in chili made with my own blend was not only much more deeply flavored but also remarkably smooth. Why was the batch made with the supermarket chili powder so gritty in comparison?

Research revealed that at many processing plants dried chiles are ground whole—stems, seeds, and all. The stems and seeds never break down completely, and that's what gives some commercial powders that sandy texture. Making chili powder is undeniably a time-consuming step, but for my ultimate chili it was worth it.

Nevertheless, before venturing into the world of secret ingredients, I wondered if I could streamline my recipe a bit. Finding I was spending far too much time trimming the chuck-eye roast of fat and sinew, I switched to blade steak, which also comes from the chuck and was simpler to break down into ¾-inch chunks; it took half the time and my tasters were none the wiser. Rather than grind the chiles in successive batches in a tiny spice grinder, I pulverized them all at once in the food processor, adding a bit of stock to encourage the chile pieces to engage with the blade rather than simply fly around the larger bowl. The puree still wasn't quite as fine as I wanted it to be, but I'd address that later. I also used the food processor to chop the onions and jalapeños. Since stovetop cooking required occasional

Andrea Makes Her Chili
Video available FREE for 4 months at
www.CooksIllustrated.com/feb11

stirring to prevent scorching, I moved the bulk of the cooking to the gentler heat of the oven, where it could simmer unattended for 90 minutes.

Secret Weapons

Happy with my basic recipe, I was ready to spring a series of unlikely ingredients on my colleagues. My research had indicated that chili cooks' secret weapons tended to fall into five categories: cooking liquids, complexity builders, sweeteners, meat enhancers, and thickeners. In a series of blind tastings, I set out to separate the wonderful from the simply weird.

At this point, the only liquid in my recipe was the predictable beef broth. In my next four pots of chili I added Guinness, red wine, coffee, and lager to the mix. The stout gave the chili a bitter edge and flattened out the bright notes of the jalapeños and tomatoes, and the wine was too tangy. Tasted just 30 minutes into the cooking time, the coffee seemed promising, but it did not end well, becoming as bitter and acidic as the dregs in the office urn. The lightly hoppy flavor of the lager, however, complemented the tomatoes, onions, and jalapeños beautifully—not so surprising, perhaps, since chili and beer pair well by tradition. Lager was in.

Next up: the complexity builders, ingredients that add depth without being readily discernible. Cloves and cinnamon were deemed too identifiable and sweet, but members of the chocolate family— unsweetened chocolate, unsweetened cocoa, and bittersweet chocolate—performed well, with tasters appreciating the complexity that each provided. Since I would be sweetening the pot in the next test, I named the unsweetened cocoa the winner in this round and added it to my recipe.

Getting the Fundamentals Right

No secret ingredient can make up for a dish that takes too many shortcuts. Here's how we laid the groundwork for a top-notch bowl of chili.

TYPICAL STARTING POINTS		UPPING THE ANTE
GROUND BEEF  Ground chuck can't help but turn dry and nubbly after hours of cooking in the chili pot.		**WHOLE BLADE STEAK**  Starting with whole steak allows us to cut the meat into beefy chunks that stay moist and tender.
BOTTLED CHILI POWDER  Commercial chili powders lack depth, and the ground seeds and stems they often contain will turn the stew gritty.		**THREE KINDS OF CHILES**  For complex chile flavor, we grind dried ancho and árbol chiles into a paste. Fresh jalapeños bring grassy heat.
CANNED BEANS  They're certainly convenient, but canned beans can also be bland and mushy.		**BRINED DRIED BEANS** Soaking dried beans in brine before cooking seasons them throughout and contributes to creamier texture.

The aim of adding a sweet ingredient to chili is to smooth out any sharp or acidic flavors without making the dish noticeably sweet. I had high hopes for the two prunes left to float on the top of the simmering chili, but that technique was too subtle for my tasters. Four ounces of Coca-Cola added to the pot had the surprising effect of enhancing the tomato flavor too much, and brown sugar was "OK but kind of boring." The winner in this round? Molasses, which lent the chili an "earthy, smoky depth" that tasters loved.

The next category, meat enhancers, yielded the most surprising results. Many cooks swear by the practice of augmenting their chili with "umami bombs" in the form of anchovies, soy sauce, mushrooms, or even Marmite (and competitive cooks tend to go straight for the MSG in the form of stock cubes or Sazón Goya). I found that adding such ingredients dramatically increased the meaty flavor of the chili, but in doing so they threw the balance of chiles, aromatics, and spices out of whack. It was just too meaty, or as one taster observed, "like chewing on a bouillon cube." Tasters even persuaded me to switch from beef broth to chicken broth, citing better balance. Good-quality meat was meaty enough, thanks.

On to the most eagerly anticipated test of them all: peanut butter. Intended to thicken the chili, it's not as bizarre as you might think. Mexican cooks often add ground seeds and nuts to mole to give it richness, texture, and depth, so why not add peanut butter to chili? I tested more prosaic thickeners as well: flour and the traditional masa (dough made with limed corn, then dried and ground).

The flour subtly thickened the chili, but it didn't offer anything in terms of flavor. The peanut butter, on the other hand, lent a "big roasted flavor" to the chili, but it also left a strange aftertaste that

STEP BY STEP | OUR BEST-EVER CHILI

1. QUICK-BRINE beans by bringing to boil in salt solution and letting stand 1 hour.

2. TOAST ancho chiles in skillet to enhance flavor.

3. MAKE PASTE by grinding toasted anchos, dried árbols, spices, cornmeal, and broth.

4. SAUTÉ onions, jalapeños, and garlic in Dutch oven.

5. ADD chili paste, tomatoes, molasses, broth, and beans to Dutch oven. Stir to combine.

6. SEAR beef in batches in skillet until well-browned; transfer to Dutch oven.

7. DEGLAZE skillet with lager between batches and scrape up fond; add to Dutch oven.

8. TRANSFER chili to oven and cook until meat and beans are fully tender, 1½ to 2 hours.

had tasters simply saying "yuck." The masa was well received for its thickening properties and the subtle corn flavor it contributed, but even for ultimate chili I balked at buying a 4-pound bag of masa just to use 3 tablespoons. This is where I introduced my own quirky ingredient to the pantheon of secret ingredients. I found that when I added 3 tablespoons of cornmeal to my food processor chili paste, its bulk helped me achieve a finer grind, and it accomplished the thickening goal admirably.

Other cooks might accuse me of being full of beans, but this chili, with its tender beef and complex sauce, plus its own secret ingredients, is one I will defend with the vigor of the most seasoned chilihead.

OUR FAVORITE CHILI
SERVES 6 TO 8

NOTE: A 4-pound chuck-eye roast, well trimmed of fat, can be substituted for the steak. Because much of the chili flavor is held in the fat of this dish, refrain from skimming fat from the surface. Wear gloves when working with both dried and fresh chiles. Dried New Mexican or guajillo chiles make a good substitute for the anchos; each dried árbol may be substituted with ⅛ teaspoon cayenne. If you prefer not to work with any whole dried chiles, the anchos and árbols can be replaced with ½ cup commercial chili powder and ¼ to ½ teaspoon cayenne pepper, though the texture of the chili will be slightly compromised. Good choices for condiments include diced avocado, chopped red onion, chopped cilantro leaves, lime wedges, sour cream, and shredded Monterey Jack or cheddar cheese. The chili can be made up to 3 days in advance.

    Table salt
½ pound dried pinto beans (about 1 cup), rinsed and picked over
6 dried ancho chiles (about 1¾ ounces), stems and seeds removed, and flesh torn into 1-inch pieces (see note)
2–4 dried árbol chiles, stems removed, pods split, seeds removed (see note)
3 tablespoons cornmeal
2 teaspoons dried oregano
2 teaspoons ground cumin
2 teaspoons cocoa powder
2½ cups low-sodium chicken broth
2 medium onions, cut into ¾-inch pieces (about 2 cups)
3 small jalapeño chiles, stems and seeds removed and discarded, flesh cut into ½-inch pieces
3 tablespoons vegetable oil
4 medium garlic cloves, minced or pressed through garlic press (about 4 teaspoons)
1 (14.5-ounce) can diced tomatoes
2 teaspoons light molasses
3½ pounds blade steak, ¾ inch thick, trimmed of gristle and fat and cut into ¾-inch pieces (see note)
1 (12-ounce) bottle mild lager, such as Budweiser

1. Combine 3 tablespoons salt, 4 quarts water, and beans in large Dutch oven and bring to boil over high heat. Remove pot from heat, cover, and let stand 1 hour. Drain and rinse well.

2. Adjust oven rack to lower-middle position and heat oven to 300 degrees. Place ancho chiles in 12-inch skillet set over medium-high heat; toast, stirring frequently, until flesh is fragrant, 4 to 6 minutes, reducing heat if chiles begin to smoke. Transfer to bowl of food processor and cool. Do not wash out skillet.

3. Add árbol chiles, cornmeal, oregano, cumin, cocoa, and ½ teaspoon salt to food processor with toasted ancho chiles; process until finely ground, about 2 minutes. With processor running, very slowly add ½ cup broth until smooth paste forms, about 45 seconds, scraping down sides of bowl as necessary. Transfer paste to small bowl. Place onions in now-empty processor bowl and pulse until roughly chopped, about four 1-second pulses. Add jalapeños and pulse until consistency of chunky salsa, about four 1-second pulses, scraping down bowl as necessary.

4. Heat 1 tablespoon oil in large Dutch oven over medium-high heat. Add onion mixture and cook, stirring occasionally, until moisture has evaporated and vegetables are softened, 7 to 9 minutes. Add garlic and cook until fragrant, about 1 minute. Add chili paste, tomatoes, and molasses; stir until chili paste is thoroughly combined. Add remaining 2 cups broth and drained beans; bring to boil, then reduce heat to simmer.

5. Meanwhile, heat 1 tablespoon oil in 12-inch skillet over medium-high heat until shimmering. Pat beef dry with paper towels and sprinkle with 1 teaspoon salt. Add half of beef and cook until browned on all sides, about 10 minutes. Transfer meat to Dutch oven. Add ½ bottle lager to skillet, scraping bottom of pan to loosen any browned bits, and bring to simmer. Transfer lager to Dutch oven. Repeat with remaining tablespoon oil, steak, and lager. Once last addition of lager has been added to Dutch oven, stir to combine and return mixture to simmer.

6. Cover pot and transfer to oven. Cook until meat and beans are fully tender, 1½ to 2 hours. Let chili stand, uncovered, 10 minutes. Stir well and season to taste with salt before serving.

The Truth About Championship Chili
The Terlingua International Chili Championship is, according to 2006 champion Dana Plocheck, "the Masters of chili," so I was delighted when my research turned up the winning recipes from the past 20 years. That delight turned to disbelief, however, as I pored over each recipe: Not one champ from this West Texas competition included so much as a diced onion or bell pepper to flavor the pot, and the chile flavor was supplied not by fresh or dried chiles, but exclusively by supermarket (or mail-order) chili powder. Nor did any of the recipes boast any novel yet promising "secret" ingredients that might be fun to try in my own chili. (Who could get inspired by dried chicken granules or packets of Sazón Goya?) In fact, all of the winning recipes looked astonishingly similar.

Turns out that cook-off chili can be disqualified for having any distinguishing features—including obvious bits of chopped tomatoes or onions. Therefore, cooks strive to make their chili look just like their competitors'. In fact, the only way to make a chili taste distinctive is to apply layer after layer of seasoning and spice. And that is precisely what participants do, adding successive "dumps" (the word competitors use for their custom-mixed spice packets) to the chili pot over the course of the cooking time. Secrets like these might just be better off remaining secret.–A.G.

Secret Weapons ... or Weird Extras?

When chili cook-offs proved a bust, we combed the Internet for claims of "secret" ingredients to see if any would actually improve our recipe. Most were better left on the shelf.

YOU'RE IN!
Cornmeal brought great body to the sauce, while beer, molasses, and unsweetened cocoa added depth and complexity.

DIDN'T CUT IT
We'll pass on ingredients like peanut butter, red wine, cola, prunes, and coffee. "Umami bombs" such as anchovies and shiitake mushrooms are also off our list.

Secrets to Perfect Cookies

Cookies couldn't be simpler to make. So why do they so often turn out irregularly shaped, unevenly baked, and lacking the desired texture? Here's everything you need to know to bake the perfect batch. BY KEITH DRESSER

MAKING THE DOUGH

Measure Accurately

In tests, we've found that the most common way of measuring dry ingredients—spooning them into the measuring cup—is also the least accurate. Since even the slightest variation in an amount can have a direct effect on your cookie (a tiny bit too much flour, for example, and the cookie will be dry; too little and the cookie will bake up flat), it's important to measure precisely.

PREFERRED METHOD
For the greatest accuracy, weigh sugar and flour.

SECOND BEST
Dip a measuring cup into flour or sugar and scoop away excess with a straight edge.

Use Butter at Optimal Temperature

Whether softened or melted, proper butter temperature is as critical in a simple sugar cookie as it is in the fanciest cake.

➤ Properly softened butter (65 to 67 degrees, or roughly room temperature) allows air to be pumped into the butter for tender texture in the final cookie. Two good cues: The butter should give slightly when pressed but still hold its shape, and it should bend without cracking or breaking.

➤ When a recipe calls for melted butter, make sure it's lukewarm (85 to 90 degrees) before adding it to the dough. Butter that's too warm can cook the dough (or the eggs in it) and cause clumps.

Speedy Way to Soften Butter

Avoid microwaving to soften cold butter—it's easy to soften it too much or even melt it. Instead, cut the butter into small pieces. By the time you've preheated the oven and measured the remaining ingredients, the pieces should be near 65 degrees.

PORTIONING THE DOUGH

Drop and Roll

With drop cookies, we usually go beyond merely depositing tablespoons of dough on the cookie sheet. Instead, we prefer to roll the dough between our hands to create uniformly shaped balls that bake evenly.

A Better Way to Roll

With roll-and-cut cookies, there's always a danger of working too much flour into the dough during rolling and producing dry cookies. We like to roll out the dough between two large sheets of parchment paper instead of on a floured counter. Chill the rolled-out dough in the fridge for 10 minutes to make cutting easier.

BAKING

Don't Forget to Preheat

To keep cookies from spreading too much, it is important to expose them to an immediate blast of heat. It takes at least 15 minutes for a standard oven to reach the desired temperature.

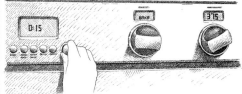

PREPARING THE PAN

Use a Parchment Liner

Don't grease your sheets—the extra fat can cause cookies to bake unevenly. Instead, line the baking sheet with parchment. Its slick surface allows cookies to easily release. (Waxed paper isn't a good substitute—high temperature can make the wax coating melt.) To keep parchment flat on the pan, put a small dab of dough on each corner of the baking sheet.

Make a Sling

With their gooey centers, it's nearly impossible to remove some bar cookies from the pan without tearing or crumbling. Here's our easy solution:

1. Place two sheets of foil or parchment paper perpendicular to each other in the baking pan, pushing into the corners and up the sides. Spray with nonstick cooking spray.

2. After the bar cookies have baked and cooled, use the overhang to lift the whole thing from the pan. Cut into portions.

Use an Oven Thermometer

Oven temperatures can be off by as much as 50 degrees. Always use an oven thermometer to tell you what's really going on inside. (Our new favorite is profiled on page 11.)

TROUBLESHOOTING

PROBLEM: The last cookies always seem short on chips
SOLUTION: Reserve some morsels to add later
➤ When chocolate chips, nuts, or raisins are in the mix, the last few cookies from a batch never seem to have as many of these goodies as the first few. To get around this, reserve some of the mix-ins and stir them into the dough after about half of it has been scooped out.

PROBLEM: Cookies don't add up to the correct yield
SOLUTION: Use a portion scoop
➤ When cookies are portioned out larger or smaller than the recipe directs, they may not produce the intended texture. To ensure consistent size and the proper yield, we use a portion scoop. (We keep many different sizes on hand for just this purpose. A typical cookie requires a #30 scoop.)

PROBLEM: Cookies keep burning on bottom
SOLUTION: Use a light-colored baking sheet and line with parchment paper
➤ We typically don't like light-colored bakeware since it doesn't absorb heat as well as darker finishes, leading to spotty browning. But the cookie sheet is the exception. All of the dark nonstick cookie sheets we've tested consistently overbrown the bottoms of cookies. Light-colored sheets, on the other hand, prevent overbrowning but are prone to sticking. We get around this by baking cookies on parchment paper.

PROBLEM: Chewy cookies that aren't chewy
SOLUTION: Underbake
➤ To ensure a chewy texture, take cookies out of the oven when they are still slightly underdone, which often means they will droop over the end of a spatula. Crevices should appear moist and edges on smooth cookies should be lightly browned.

PROBLEM: Cookies run together
SOLUTION: Bake in staggered rows
➤ When scoops of dough are placed too close together on the sheet, the cookies can fuse together. To ensure enough space between cookies, alternate the rows. For example, place three cookies in the first row, two in the second, three in the third, and so on.

PROBLEM: Unevenly baked batches
SOLUTION: Rotate during baking
➤ The temperature in most ovens varies from front to back, top to bottom—even side to side. To prevent uneven baking, rotate the cookie sheet partway through baking so that the back side faces front.

PROBLEM: It's hard to tell when dark chocolate cookies are done
SOLUTION: Press the middle
➤ Most cookies, irrespective of texture, are done when pressing them lightly with your finger leaves just a slight indentation.

PROBLEM: Cookies left in oven too long
SOLUTION: Cool immediately on rack
➤ If you become distracted and leave your cookies in the oven a minute or two too long, all is not lost. Remove the baking sheet from the oven and, instead of allowing the cookies to set on the sheet, immediately transfer them to a wire rack, where they will cool more quickly.

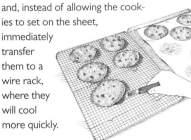

PROBLEM: Overly crisp edges
SOLUTION: Briefly chill dough and don't use a hot sheet
➤ If your kitchen is particularly hot, the butter in the dough can start to melt, softening the dough and leading to overcooked edges. If the dough seems too soft, chill it for 10 to 15 minutes before portioning.
➤ Putting raw dough on cookie sheets still warm from the oven can cause them to begin spreading, leading to burnt edges. Always allow baking sheets to cool completely before adding more batches. To expedite cooling, rinse warm—but not hot—sheet under cold tap water.

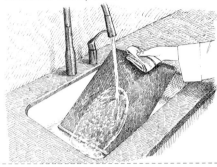

PROBLEM: Chewy cookies dry out too quickly
SOLUTION: Store with bread
➤ To keep chewy cookies from turning dry and brittle, store them in a zipper-lock bag at room temperature with a small piece of bread (no more than half of a slice) placed inside.

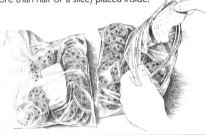

Freeze 'n' Bake Cookies

Almost all cookie dough can be successfully frozen. But instead of freezing it in a solid block, try portioning the dough first. This allows you to bake as many cookies as you like—even just three or four—when the craving strikes. Simply portion the dough on a parchment-lined baking sheet and freeze until hard. Transfer the unbaked cookies to a zipper-lock bag and return them to the freezer. There's no need to thaw the dough before baking; just increase the baking time by 1 or 2 minutes.

Classic Caesar Salad

Hold the chicken and other dubious updates. Great Caesar salad is all about making tweaks to the original's pungent, garlicky dressing and crispy croutons. But what tweaks?

⋟ BY MATTHEW CARD ⋞

Caesar salad, as invented 90-odd years ago by restaurateur Caesar Cardini (or his brother, depending on which myth you believe), is an endangered species. These days, the original version has been all but eclipsed by ersatz variations that throw in chicken or fish, bind the salad in pita wraps, or squeeze it into BLTs. If it's global cuisine you want, there's Thai-style Caesar spiked with fish sauce and cilantro, or chile-flavored Mexican Caesar topped with tortilla chips. I'm all for ad-libbing, but not when it means transforming a great and simple concept into something unrecognizable.

I wanted to strip away the superfluous trappings that plague modern recipes and return to the basics that made this salad a culinary sensation in the first place: crisp-tender romaine lettuce napped in a creamy, garlicky dressing boasting a pleasing salty undertone, with crunchy, savory croutons strewn throughout.

Well Dressed

The only problem with getting back to the original? With numerous claims made on authorship, there's no one dressing formula to use as a benchmark. I was left to concoct my own version from ingredients that most sources, at least, agreed were classic: extra-virgin olive oil, lemon juice, eggs, garlic, Worcestershire sauce, Parmesan cheese, and anchovies. I immediately discovered that there was work to be done here. For starters, my tasters agreed that extra-virgin olive oil was too fruity and bitter, its robust flavor clearly at odds with the other assertive elements in the dressing. The solution: Cut it with a 3:1 ratio of neutral-tasting canola oil.

I moved on to consider the eggs, which in Caesar dressing have a dual purpose: They temper the strong ingredients without making the dressing greasy, and they effectively "glue" the dressing to the lettuce. I found that the waterlogged whites in whole eggs were washing out the flavor, so I went with two yolks instead. But as to how the yolks should be treated, the recipes I consulted were divided. Some—including Cardini's—suggest coddling. In theory, this process—briefly simmering the eggs, shells on, in water—thickens their texture and, in turn, thickens the dressing. But when we compared dressings made with coddled and raw yolks, the difference was negligible; plus, coddling was a fussy step that I would just as soon avoid. (That said, some sources suggest coddling as a prophylactic measure against possible bacteria. If this is a concern, a pasteurized egg substitute such as Egg Beaters works just fine.)

It was on to the garlic. Well aware that the dressing's flavor depends on how the stuff is prepared, I worked my way through a series of tests—everything from finely chopping the cloves with salt to rubbing whole cloves around the interior of the serving bowl. Ultimately, my tasters favored garlic transformed

To be sure there's deep flavor in every part of this salad, we toss our crisp-chewy croutons with minced garlic and grated Parmesan.

into pulp on a rasp-style grater. The fine paste virtually disappeared into the dressing, suffusing it with a robust (though far from aggressive) flavor, especially when I followed the advice of an old French wives' tale and allowed it to steep in the lemon juice for a few minutes before introducing the rest of the dressing ingredients (see "Tempering Garlic's Bite").

But when it came to the anchovies, I found that I wanted more than most recipes call for. In fact, there's no record that Cardini included the minnows in his version, so I started with a judicious two fillets and worked my way up to six. When thoroughly minced, the fish were reduced to roughly a tablespoon, and their richly savory—not fishy—flavor was evenly dispersed throughout the dressing. Per tradition, a shot of Worcestershire sauce and a fistful of wispy grated Parmesan added even more complexity.

My one lingering complaint? The dressing, which I'd been simply whisking together in the serving bowl, tended to break, leaving some romaine leaves greasy with oil and others merely saturated with garlicky lemon juice. I got far better results when I tried beating the egg yolks, anchovies, and Worcestershire sauce into the lemon juice and garlic, and then slowly whisking in the oil and half of the cheese to build a sturdy emulsion.

Make Your Own Anchovy Paste

START WHOLE
The deep flavor of good-quality oil-packed fillets is a must in this recipe. The fishier, flatter taste of commercial anchovy paste won't do.

MASH UP
Even small bits of anchovy can be distracting in Caesar salad. Finely slice the fillets and mash with a fork to create a paste that contributes savory—not fishy—flavor.

Crispy, Crunchy, Chewy

But my work wasn't done. As the only other major component of Caesar salad, the croutons had to be perfect—nothing like the hard, desiccated specimens in most restaurant versions. I wanted more flavor, but also some contrast between the crust and interior crumb. That eliminated squishy supermarket sandwich loaves, as well as their textural opposite, super-crusty French baguettes. In the end, the bubbly, chewy center and crisp exterior of ciabatta worked best.

To get my croutons golden brown, I toasted, broiled, and fried ¾-inch cubes, eventually discovering that crisping the bread in a hot pan slicked with extra-virgin olive oil produced the most flavorful results—albeit unevenly browned and a bit parched in the center. Brainstorming for ways to keep the middle moist (and just a little chewy), I thought of panzanella (Italian bread salad), in which stale pieces of bread are reconstituted in water and squeezed of excess moisture before being added to the salad. On the one hand, introducing water seemed silly, since part of my goal was a crisp crust. But what if just enough water could preserve the crouton's moistness while the exterior browned in the skillet?

I sprinkled the bite-size cubes with a little water and salt, transferred them to an oiled nonstick skillet, and proceeded with my recipe. The result? Croutons that were perfectly tender at the center, and browned and crunchy as could be around the edges. Our science editor explained the results: Water gelatinizes the starch in the bread, simultaneously breaking some of it down to glucose. As it cooks, the gelatinized starch turns crispy on the exterior but remains tender within. And the glucose? Like all sugars, it hastens browning—a good thing when it comes to croutons.

For a flavor boost, I tossed the still-hot cubes with a paste of raw garlic and extra-virgin olive oil and dusted them with grated Parmesan. So good were these little beauties that I had to hide them from pilfering fingers while I prepared the rest of the salad.

Once the crisp romaine was dressed, there were just two last-minute tweaks: a table-side squeeze of fresh lemon juice for brightness and a shower of extra Parmesan. Finally, I'd brought Caesar back from the brink of extinction, staying true to the classic and managing to coax the best out of each component.

CAESAR SALAD
SERVES 4 TO 6

NOTE: If you can't find ciabatta, a similar crusty, rustic loaf of bread can be substituted. A quarter cup of Egg Beaters may be substituted for the egg yolks. Since anchovy fillets vary in size, more than 6 fillets may be necessary to yield 1 tablespoon of minced anchovies. The easiest way to turn garlic cloves into a paste is to grate them on a rasp-style grater.

Croutons

5	tablespoons extra-virgin olive oil
½	teaspoon garlic paste from 1 medium clove (see note)
½ – ¾	loaf ciabatta, cut into ¾-inch cubes (about 5 cups) (see note)
¼	cup water
¼	teaspoon table salt
2	tablespoons finely grated Parmesan

Salad

¾	teaspoon garlic paste from 1 large clove (see note)
2–3	tablespoons juice from 1 to 2 lemons
½	teaspoon Worcestershire sauce
6	anchovy fillets, patted dry with paper towels, minced fine, and mashed to paste with fork (1 tablespoon) (see note)
2	large egg yolks (see note)
5	tablespoons canola oil
5	teaspoons extra-virgin olive oil
1½	ounces finely grated Parmesan (about ¾ cup) Ground black pepper
2–3	romaine hearts, cut crosswise into ¾-inch-thick slices, rinsed, and dried very well (8 to 9 lightly pressed cups)

1. FOR THE CROUTONS: Combine 1 tablespoon oil and garlic paste in small bowl; set aside. Place bread cubes in large bowl. Sprinkle with water and salt. Toss, squeezing gently so bread absorbs water. Place remaining 4 tablespoons oil and soaked bread cubes in 12-inch nonstick skillet. Cook over medium-high heat, stirring frequently, until browned and crisp, 7 to 10 minutes.

2. Remove skillet from heat, push croutons to sides of skillet to clear center; add garlic/oil mixture to clearing and cook with residual heat of pan, 10 seconds. Sprinkle with Parmesan; toss until garlic and Parmesan are evenly distributed. Transfer croutons to bowl; set aside.

---

3. FOR THE SALAD: Whisk garlic paste and 2 tablespoons lemon juice together in large bowl. Let stand 10 minutes.

4. Whisk Worcestershire sauce, anchovies, and egg yolks into garlic/lemon juice mixture. While whisking constantly, drizzle canola oil and extra-virgin olive oil into bowl in slow, steady stream until fully emulsified. Add ½ cup Parmesan and pepper to taste; whisk until incorporated.

5. Add romaine to dressing and toss to coat. Add croutons and mix gently until evenly distributed. Taste and season with up to additional 1 tablespoon lemon juice. Serve immediately, passing remaining ¼ cup Parmesan separately.

TECHNIQUE | A BETTER KIND OF CROUTON

Most modern-day croutons used in Caesar salad are crunchy through and through. We designed ours to be crispy on the outside but chewy in the middle, a far better complement to the crisp-tender romaine leaves.

1. MOISTEN Sprinkling bread cubes with water and then squeezing them moistens their interior.

2. CRISP UP Frying the dampened cubes in oil crisps their exteriors while the moist interior retains some chew.

Rethinking Split Pea Soup

Simmering a leftover ham shank used to be a frugal way to stretch a meal. But what if you have to make do without the backbone of this soup?

⇒ BY KEITH DRESSER ⇐

Split pea soup used to be the thing to make after serving a roast ham for Sunday supper. Once you were done frying ham and eggs for breakfast and shaving off meaty slabs for ham sandwiches at lunch, you would drop the bone (with hunks of meat still clinging to it) into a big soup pot with a bag of split peas and cover it with water. After hours of simmering, the meat would fall off the bone, the fat would melt into the broth, and the peas would disintegrate and thicken the rib-sticking potage.

That was the idea, anyway. But in my experience, this thrifty dish has never amounted to anything greater than the sum of its parts. Too often it turns into an overly thick—dare I say sludgy—green mash with one-note flavor. Plus, these days, I rarely serve roast ham, so procuring a leftover bone is not as simple as reaching into my refrigerator. But the thought of what this dish is meant to be—a spoon-coating, richly flavorful broth studded with tender shreds of sweet-smoky meat—was enough to send me back to the kitchen.

Without a ham bone, I had to find an equally flavorful replacement. Most of the recipes I found swapped in ham hocks, but these fatty, sinewy knuckle pieces (I tried both fresh and smoked) only rendered my soup greasy. Plus, unless you find a particularly substantial specimen, hocks tend to be skimpy on meat, making a supplemental form of pork necessary.

My tasters wanted plenty of ham strewn throughout the pot, so I made a point of shopping for meatier alternatives and returned to the test kitchen with Canadian bacon and ham steak. The former was disappointing. Unlike regular strip American bacon made from fat-streaked (read: flavorful) pork belly, the Canadian version comes from the lean loin region of the pig, and its meek flavor barely broke through the thick fog of peas. Ham steak, however, was a welcome addition to the pot; after quartering the slab and letting it simmer in the broth (a classic base of water fortified with sautéed onion and garlic, carrots and celery added midway through cooking to preserve their texture, bay leaves, and a pair of thyme sprigs) for about 45 minutes, the liquid had taken on significantly fuller pork flavor, and the ham itself was tender enough to pull into meaty shreds with a pair of forks.

But as my tasters rightly pointed out, the ham steak was hardly an equal substitute for bone. We all agreed that the soup was still lacking richness and could use more smokiness—a perfect job for

American bacon, I figured. (Apparently, two forms of pork were going to be necessary after all.) But the quick fix I was hoping for proved elusive. I crisped a few strips and added them to the pot only to find that they overwhelmed the ham and peas. Instead, I slid raw bacon into the soup along with the ham steak, which offered subtler flavor, and the slices could be fished out right before serving.

As for the peas, I knew from experience that the presoaking step in many recipes was not only unnecessary, but also unfavorable. Unsoaked peas break down just as readily as soaked peas, and the resulting soup is actually more flavorful, since they absorb the pork-enriched broth.

All that was left to do was work up a few garnishes. A handful of fresh peas seemed appropriate; their sweetness popped against the hearty, smoky broth. Fresh chopped mint leaves and a drizzle of good balsamic vinegar added freshness and sweetness, respectively, and punched up the flavors even more. Finally, I floated gently fried croutons on the surface. As my tasters ladled out second (and even third) helpings, I knew that I'd reworked this stodgy supper into an updated classic.

SPLIT PEA AND HAM SOUP
SERVES 6 TO 8

NOTE: Four ounces of regular sliced bacon can be used, but the thinner slices are a little harder to remove from the soup. Depending on the age and brand of split peas, the consistency of the soup may vary slightly. If the soup is too thin at the end of step 3, increase the heat and simmer, uncovered, until the desired consistency is reached. If it is too thick, thin it with a little water. Serve the soup sprinkled with Buttery Croutons, fresh peas, and chopped mint and drizzled with aged balsamic vinegar. The soup can be made up to 3 days in advance. If necessary, thin it with water when reheating.

- 2 tablespoons unsalted butter
- 1 large onion, chopped fine (about 1½ cups)
  Table salt
- 2 medium garlic cloves, minced or pressed through garlic press (about 2 teaspoons)
- 7 cups water
- 1 ham steak (about 1 pound), skin removed, cut into quarters
- 3 slices (about 4 ounces) thick-cut bacon (see note)

- 1 pound green split peas (about 2 cups), picked through and rinsed
- 2 sprigs fresh thyme
- 2 bay leaves
- 2 medium carrots, peeled and cut into ½-inch pieces (about 1 cup)
- 1 medium celery rib, cut into ½-inch pieces (about ½ cup)
  Ground black pepper

1. Heat butter in large Dutch oven over medium-high heat. When foaming subsides, add onion and ½ teaspoon salt; cook, stirring frequently, until softened, about 3 to 4 minutes. Add garlic and cook until fragrant, about 30 seconds. Add water, ham steak, bacon, peas, thyme, and bay leaves. Increase heat to high and bring to simmer, stirring frequently to keep peas from sticking to bottom. Reduce heat to low, cover, and simmer until peas are tender but not falling apart, about 45 minutes.

2. Remove ham steak, cover with foil or plastic wrap to prevent drying out, and set aside. Stir in carrots and celery; continue to simmer, covered, until vegetables are tender and peas have almost completely broken down, about 30 minutes longer.

3. When cool enough to handle, shred ham into small bite-size pieces with two forks. Remove and discard thyme sprigs, bay leaves, and bacon slices. Stir ham back into soup and return to simmer. Season to taste with salt and pepper; serve.

BUTTERY CROUTONS
MAKES ABOUT 2 CUPS

- 3 tablespoons unsalted butter
- 1 tablespoon olive oil
- 3 large slices high-quality sandwich bread, cut into ½-inch cubes (about 2 cups)
  Table salt

Heat butter and oil in 12-inch skillet over medium heat. When foaming subsides, add bread cubes and cook, stirring frequently, until golden brown, about 10 minutes. Transfer croutons to paper towel–lined plate and season with salt to taste.

Spaghetti al Limone

Unaccustomed to the spotlight, lemon can turn temperamental in this quick-hit Italian classic—unless you provide it with the perfect costars.

⇒ BY RACHEL TOOMEY KELSEY ⇐

I had one of the best bites of pasta in my life while sitting on a veranda framed by lemon trees on the island of Capri, just a few miles off Italy's Amalfi coast. Called spaghetti al limone, the al dente noodles barely seemed sauced at all. Yet every forkful burst with bright, bracing lemon flavor, moistened with just enough fruity olive oil to coat each delicate strand.

Back home, I wondered if the balmy sunlight (mixed with crisp pinot grigio) had blurred my recollection of that pasta. Under the sobering lights of the test kitchen, my attempts to re-create the dish were exercises in frustration. The sauce came out greasy—or worse, slid right off the pasta. And the lemon was unreliable: bright and tangy one batch, harshly acidic the next.

I wanted a clingy sauce with loads of lemon flavor, not mouth-puckering sourness. A survey of the literature revealed that spaghetti al limone recipes run the gamut from dairy-laden Alfredo variants to complicated reductions of citrus and wine. But the style I was after was more like a warm pasta salad: a basic vinaigrette of lemon juice and olive oil tossed with hot pasta.

Lemon was the star of this show, so I started there. I found that anything less than ¼ cup of juice per pound of pasta and the flavor faded into the background. But the threshold was ruthlessly small: Even a bit beyond that had tasters puckering. To boost the lemon's power without extra acidity, I stirred in a generous dose of grated zest, which added fragrant floral notes.

Unfortunately, to balance out the acidity of even this modest amount of lemon juice, I needed a whopping 1½ cups of olive oil—excessive for a dish meant for the weeknight-dinner rotation. Rolling back the oil, I tried tempering the sourness instead with garlic, shallot, even sugar. While the sweet, pungent complexity of the shallot was a keeper, the sauce remained too tart.

So far I'd been steadfast in my purist approach, keeping the lemon and olive oil at center stage. But I was hitting a wall. I was looking for spaghetti al limone, not spaghetti al olio, I reasoned. Would tasters prefer all that heady lemon flavor in one of the dairy-based sauces I'd dismissed?

I made two versions of my working recipe—one with olive oil, the other substituting cream—and had tasters sample them side by side. The cream really did a number on the lemon flavor, mitigating the sourness. On the other hand, tasters missed the fruity olive oil flavor. Even the leftovers (an unofficial

Tempering the tart lemon juice in this dish with both oil and cream makes for a bright, glossy sauce.

gauge of taster enthusiasm) offered no clues: Exactly half a batch of each remained.

Defeated, I dumped all the leftovers into a single container, toting it home for my husband's dinner. To my surprise, he loved it; he had nothing but compliments for this two-batch hybrid. Curious, I took a bite. It was excellent: The sourness was gone, the flavor of the olive oil came through, and the spaghetti wasn't greasy. And remarkably, the lemon flavor also seemed more pronounced than in any version thus far. On further research, I learned that dairy fat does double duty with lemon flavor. First, it dampens the sourness by neutralizing some of the acids in the juice. But it also augments the part of a lemon's flavor profile (the oils) responsible for the fruity, floral notes by working in tandem with the olive oil to emulsify those flavors into a form that really coats the tastebuds. By combining the dairy fat with the olive oil fat, at least in theory, I could solve all my problems.

To find out, I whipped up a batch using both oil and cream. As tasters sang my praises, I knew I was on the right track. Fiddling with the proportions of oil to cream, I found that 1:1 was the ideal ratio. To keep the fat reasonably low while still yielding enough sauce to coat the spaghetti, I incorporated some of the starchy pasta water, an age-old Italian trick.

One last problem: The sauce wasn't clinging to the pasta well. Tinkering with the cooking method, I let the sauced pasta sit, covered, for two minutes to absorb the flavors and let the sauce thicken. I finished the dish with nutty Parmesan cheese (a common addition), chopped fresh basil, and a drizzle of olive oil. Bright, floral, and balanced, with a fruity olive oil bite, my final dish tasted as pure and simple as the one I enjoyed in Capri—and I'm the only one who knows it isn't.

SPAGHETTI WITH LEMON AND OLIVE OIL (AL LIMONE)
SERVES 4 TO 6

NOTE: Let the dish rest briefly before serving so the flavors develop and the sauce thickens.

Table salt
1 pound spaghetti
¼ cup extra-virgin olive oil, plus more for serving
1 medium shallot, minced (about 3 tablespoons)
¼ cup heavy cream
2 teaspoons finely grated zest and ¼ cup juice from 3 lemons
1 ounce finely grated Parmesan cheese (about ½ cup), plus more for serving
Ground black pepper
2 tablespoons shredded fresh basil leaves

1. Bring 4 quarts water to boil in large Dutch oven over high heat. Add 1 tablespoon salt and pasta to boiling water; cook, stirring frequently, until al dente. Reserve 1¾ cups cooking water, drain pasta into colander, and set aside.

2. Heat 1 tablespoon oil in now-empty Dutch oven over medium heat until shimmering. Add shallot and ½ teaspoon salt; cook until shallot is softened, about 2 minutes. Whisk 1½ cups of reserved pasta cooking water and cream into pot; bring to simmer and cook for 2 minutes. Remove pot from heat, return pasta, and stir until coated. Stir in remaining 3 tablespoons oil, lemon zest, lemon juice, cheese, and ½ teaspoon pepper.

3. Cover and let pasta stand 2 minutes, tossing frequently and adjusting consistency with remaining ¼ cup reserved pasta water if necessary. Stir in basil and season with salt and pepper to taste. Serve, drizzling individual portions with oil and sprinkling with cheese.

Greek Spinach Pie Done Right

Ideally, spanakopita is a hot and flavorful one-dish meal encased in a crispy, buttery crust.
Yet most versions fall flat—a Greek tragedy in need of a happy ending.

≥ BY BRYAN ROOF ≤

Spanakopita's roots run deep in Greek culture, and it's not hard to understand the enduring appeal. This savory spinach "pie" trades on a flaky phyllo crust—wafer-thin sheets of oven-crisped dough—that gives way to a delectably moist filling of tender greens and salty feta, kicked up with lemon, garlic, herbs, and spices. What's not to love?

Plenty, at least stateside. The lackluster versions served at unambitious Greek-American diners bear more resemblance to lukewarm lawn clippings encased in a wet paper bag than the crispy-pillowy pride of Hellenic home cooking. A step up from there, the tidy spinach-and-phyllo turnovers found in supermarket freezers at least get the crispiness right. Yet the paltry ratio of filling to buttery crust places these tasty bites squarely in hors d'oeuvre territory.

My goal was to bring back the features that made spanakopita such a mealtime favorite in the first place—a casserole-style pie with a perfect balance of zesty spinach filling to shatteringly crisp phyllo crust—and I didn't want it to require an all-day stint in the kitchen. To that end, I decided to go with frozen phyllo sheets rather than homemade pastry: I wanted a weeknight meal, not a weeklong project.

Turning Over a New Leaf

Most recipes for spanakopita follow the same basic series of steps: Transparently thin sheets of phyllo—unleavened dough made from flour, water, and lemon juice or vinegar—are layered to form a bottom crust, usually in a 13 by 9-inch baking pan. Each layer receives a brush of melted butter to contribute rich flavor and boost browning. On top of that goes the cheesy spinach filling, followed by another layering of delicate phyllo sheets, which forms the top crust. Baked at a high temperature (to ensure a golden-brown top), the piping-hot pie is cooled and sliced into serving portions.

Fresh spinach is a must in the filling, which we brighten with scallions, grated lemon zest, and fresh mint and dill.

To get my bearings, I baked off several versions that I came across in various Greek cookbooks (as well as a few family recipes kindly offered up from colleagues), confirming that store-bought frozen phyllo dough (thawed and handled properly; see "Tips for Taming Phyllo," page 31) was plenty reliable, save for some niggling texture issues involving the bottom crust. (I would deal with those later.) But the filling, by contrast, needed some serious work.

I decided to start with the main ingredient—the spinach—and come up with the perfect filling from there. To my surprise, many of the recipes I came across in my research called for canned spinach—but knowing the sad, lifeless state of most canned fruits and vegetables, I refused to go there. Instead, I narrowed my options to frozen spinach, fresh baby leaves, and fresh adult greens. After loading up my cart, I headed back to the test kitchen for a daylong spinach-tasting extravaganza.

Using a bare-bones filling of spinach, feta, and egg (for binding), I needed but one test to rule out frozen. The weak flavor and woody, stringy texture were nonstarters. In the end, tasters favored the bolder flavor of the mature fresh spinach. Happily, all the methods I tried for precooking it (sautéing, boiling, microwaving, steaming) worked well for these hearty leaves, so I went with the push-button convenience of the microwave. Follow-up tests revealed that coarsely chopping the spinach and thoroughly squeezing out its excess moisture yielded superior texture and maximum flavor.

With the green stuff in good shape, I moved on to the other major component: the dairy. Feta rides shotgun to spinach in spanakopita, and the right amount can make or break the dish. I found that simply crumbling the rich, pungent cheese (in the end, 12 ounces) into fine pieces helped it spread evenly through the sea of green, ensuring a salty tang in every bite. To buffer the assertiveness of the feta and add textural contrast, many recipes incorporate soft dairy into the mix as well. I tried everything. Cream cheese gave the spanakopita the consistency of spinach dip; ricotta and cottage cheese cooked up into rubbery curds. Sour cream and yogurt fared better, but thicker Greek yogurt—go figure!—turned out the best batch to date.

Some of the recipes I tested even included a third dairy component in the filling: a hard sheep's milk cheese called kefalograviera, which builds complexity. I wanted depth of flavor, but not the hassle of scouring specialty markets for such an obscure item. In the end, another, far more readily available hard sheep's milk cheese, Pecorino Romano, made a stand-up substitute.

A few final flavor tweaks: Grassy scallions trumped onions, leeks, and shallots; the more-robust flavor of raw minced garlic beat out sautéed; a generous scattering of dill and mint provided a burst of freshness. A little nutmeg, cayenne, and a dose of lemon (juice plus grated zest) added fragrant warmth and brightness, respectively.

Getting to the Bottom of It

With a filling worthy of Mount Olympus, I was ready to move on to that one maddening texture issue: the crust. The top crust was flaky and golden-brown. But no matter how I sliced it, the bottom crust ended up soggy. I tried adjusting the oven temperature, to no avail. Had I missed a clue during my initial survey of spanakopita recipes, too distracted by the lousy fillings to pick up on some clever trick? No—reviewing my notes, I realized every recipe I had tested was plagued by the same problem.

In fact, the store-bought frozen turnovers were the only versions to achieve crispy bottom crusts. Though I was reluctant to take on the labor-intensive task of turning spanakopita into bite-size triangles for the purposes of weeknight dinner (the triangles didn't really add up to a meal anyway), I decided to bake off a batch just to see what made them work so well. Aside from their cunning shape, the big difference here was the ratio of phyllo to filling in each bite. While not nearly enough filling for my purposes, it was hard to argue with the crispiness of the triangles.

But could adjusting the ratio of phyllo to filling be the key to success in a casserole version as well? Studying my current recipe, I measured the height of the spinach layer: just shy of 2 inches. I supposed dialing it back was worth a shot. But when I tried this, I didn't start seeing increased crispiness on the bottom of the crust until the filling was reduced to almost half its original volume—and at that point, I was cutting into the number of servings. Plus the bottom, while improved, was still nowhere close to where I wanted it to be.

Then it occurred to me that no matter how much I reduced the filling, the thick, high walls of the baking dish would still trap any moisture coming off it, in effect helping to "steam" the crust instead of crisping it. So, what if I moved the pie to the flat surface of a baking sheet, which would allow excess liquid to evaporate far more readily? Sure enough, this proved to be an excellent move.

For starters, the assembly was easier. In the baking dish, the phyllo sheets, which were bigger than the vessel, would bunch up on the sides and corners. (And trimming them to fit was far too fussy.) A typical 18 by 13-inch baking sheet, on the other hand, was plenty big enough to accommodate the full size of the 14 by 9-inch dough sheets. I layered 10 pieces of phyllo for the bottom crust, carefully painting each sheet with butter, then spread my spinach filling over top, which was now about ¾ inch thick—more than the paltry smear in those spanakopita triangles but less than half as much as the filling in the casserole dish. I covered the spinach with eight more buttered layers of phyllo. As a last-minute brainstorm, I also took the grated Pecorino Romano I was using in the filling and sprinkled it between the first six layers instead, which helped glue them together and fixed the annoying, recurrent problem of having this tissue-thin pastry slide off when sliced. I scored the top few layers of phyllo with the tip of my knife to make it easier to cut once cooked, and transferred the baking sheet to a 425-degree oven.

Twenty-five minutes later, what emerged from the oven was a beautiful spanakopita with crispiness on the top and—sure enough—on the bottom.

In the end, all this classic needed was a modern twist to make it great. What started as a Greek tragedy was now a real showstopper.

The average square of spinach pie served up in a Greek diner is so flawed, we're surprised anyone ever orders it.

PROBLEM: Top sheets of phyllo fall off when pie is sliced, leaving filling virtually exposed •
SOLUTION: A sprinkling of grated Pecorino Romano (substituting for a Greek sheep's milk cheese) between some of the top layers of phyllo glues them together more firmly than the usual butter alone, so the top crust stays put.

PROBLEM: Dull-tasting, woody filling made with • frozen spinach
SOLUTION: We use chopped fresh mature spinach (not baby leaves, which contribute only weak taste) pre-cooked in the microwave, squeezed of excess moisture, and brightened with fresh herbs, lemon juice, and zest.

PROBLEM: Soggy bottom crust •
SOLUTION: A thinner layer of filling cuts down on moisture, and baking the pie on a baking sheet, not in a baking dish, allows excess liquid to evaporate so the crust can crisp up.

GREEK SPINACH AND FETA PIE (SPANAKOPITA)

SERVES 6 TO 8 AS A MAIN DISH OR
10 TO 12 AS AN APPETIZER

NOTE: Full-fat sour cream can be substituted for whole-milk Greek yogurt. Phyllo dough is also available in larger 14 by 18-inch sheets; if using, cut them in half to make 14 by 9-inch sheets. Don't thaw the phyllo in the microwave—let it sit in the refrigerator overnight or on the countertop for four to five hours. For more tips on working with phyllo, see page 31. To make ahead, freeze the spanakopita on the baking sheet, wrapped well in plastic wrap, or cut the spanakopita in half crosswise and freeze smaller sections on a plate. Bake the spanakopita frozen, increasing the baking time by 5 to 10 minutes.

Filling

- 2 (10-ounce) bags curly leaf spinach, rinsed
- ¼ cup water
- 12 ounces feta cheese, rinsed, patted dry, and crumbled into fine pieces (about 3 cups)
- ¾ cup whole-milk Greek yogurt (see note)
- 4 medium scallions, sliced thin (about ½ cup)
- 2 large eggs, beaten
- ¼ cup minced fresh mint leaves
- 2 tablespoons minced fresh dill leaves
- 3 medium garlic cloves, minced or pressed through garlic press (about 1 tablespoon)
- 1 teaspoon grated zest plus 1 tablespoon juice from 1 lemon
- 1 teaspoon ground nutmeg
- ½ teaspoon ground black pepper
- ¼ teaspoon table salt
- ⅛ teaspoon cayenne pepper

Phyllo Layers

- 7 tablespoons unsalted butter, melted
- ½ pound (14 by 9-inch) phyllo, thawed (see note)
- 1½ ounces Pecorino Romano cheese, grated fine (about ¾ cup)
- 2 teaspoons sesame seeds (optional)

1. FOR THE FILLING: Place spinach and water in large microwave-safe bowl. Cover bowl with large dinner plate. Microwave on high power until spinach is wilted and decreased in volume by half, about 5 minutes. Using potholders, remove bowl from microwave and keep covered, 1 minute. Carefully remove plate and transfer spinach to colander set in sink. Using back of rubber spatula, gently press spinach against colander to release excess liquid. Transfer spinach to cutting board and roughly chop. Transfer spinach to clean kitchen towel and squeeze to remove excess water. Place drained spinach in large bowl. Add remaining filling ingredients and mix until thoroughly combined. (Filling can be made up to 24 hours in advance and stored in the refrigerator.)

2. FOR THE PHYLLO LAYERS: Adjust oven rack to lower-middle position and heat oven to 425 degrees. Line rimmed baking sheet with parchment paper. Using pastry brush, lightly brush 14 by 9-inch rectangle in center of parchment with melted butter to cover area same size as phyllo. Lay 1 phyllo sheet on buttered parchment, and brush thoroughly with melted butter. Repeat with 9 more phyllo sheets, brushing each with butter (you should have total of 10 layers of phyllo).

3. Spread spinach mixture evenly over phyllo, leaving ¼-inch border on all sides. Cover spinach with 6 more phyllo sheets, brushing each with butter and sprinkling each with about 2 tablespoons Pecorino cheese. Lay 2 more phyllo sheets on top, brushing each with butter (these layers should not be sprinkled with Pecorino).

4. Working from center outward, use palms of your hands to compress layers and press out any air pockets. Using sharp knife, score pie through the top 3 layers of phyllo into 24 equal pieces. Sprinkle with sesame seeds (if using). Bake until phyllo is golden and crisp, 20 to 25 minutes. Cool on baking sheet 10 minutes or up to 2 hours. Slide spanakopita, still on parchment, to cutting board. Cut into squares and serve.

Overhauling Gingerbread Cake

This snack cake's moist, tender crumb typically comes at a price: a gummy, sunken center.
And we wanted the glut of extraneous spices gone, too.

> BY YVONNE RUPERTI

As I stepped through the faux-vintage gates of the "living museum" at Plimoth Plantation, I was hoping for salvation. Or at least insight into a cake that dates back to the Colonial era. After a week of baking countless batches of uninspired gingerbread cake, I still lacked a workable baseline recipe. The cake I had in mind was moist through and through and utterly simple—a snack cake that would bake in a square pan. But almost without exception, every recipe I tried that had the moistness I wanted also suffered from a dense, sunken center. Equally disappointing, flavors ran the gamut from barely gingery to addled with enough spices to make a curry fan cry for mercy. So much for simple: This cake had me flummoxed.

So, at the urging of well-intentioned colleagues, I had come to spend a day at this circa-1627 Pilgrim village in Plymouth, Mass., hoping to glean some Colonial wisdom that might help my cake bake up both moist and even. When the museum's culinarian showed up bearing a stack of weathered cookbooks, I was sure I'd come to the right place. But as we prepared these vintage recipes, my optimism faded. Apparently, early Americans liked their gingerbread dry and dense as bricks—an effect exacerbated in a few recipes by a curious kneading step. (Kneading helps develop the glutens in flour, providing structure to bread but rendering cakes and cookies tough.) In cakes so dry, the issue of wet, sunken centers never came up.

Dejected, I bid my hosts a polite "good-morrow" and headed back to the test kitchen to regroup.

Spice Exploration

Cobbling together a basic working recipe from the best of the flawed versions I'd come across, I decided to put the structural problems on hold and focus on fixing flavor first.

This plain-looking cake boasts plenty of flavor—and dresses up nicely with lightly sweetened whipped cream.

Using a simple dump-and-stir method, I mixed the wet ingredients (molasses, water, melted butter, a couple of eggs) in one bowl and the dry ingredients (flour, baking soda, baking powder, brown sugar, salt) in another. For now, I opted for a purist's approach to the spice rack, expunging all options but a single tablespoon of ground ginger. Gently folding the wets into the dries, I poured the batter into an 8-inch square cake pan and baked it at 350 degrees for 40 minutes.

As expected, the cake's center collapsed. But with the extraneous spices out of the way, I was able to focus on the ginger. Bumping the ground ginger up to 2 tablespoons yielded an assertive bite, though it lacked complexity. I tried folding in grated fresh ginger with the dried. Sure enough, the pungent notes of the fresh root made the flavor sing.

What about the other spices, which I'd left in temporary exile? Options like cardamom, nutmeg, and cloves weren't terrible but shifted the gingerbread too far into spice-cake territory. In the end, only two "guest" spices made the cut: cinnamon and, in an unexpected twist, fresh-ground black pepper, which worked in tandem with all that potent ginger to produce a warm, complex, lingering heat.

Eyeing the liquid components, I suspected that using water was a missed opportunity. Buttermilk added tanginess but dulled the ginger. Ginger ale, ginger beer, and hard apple cider all seemed likely contenders, but baking rendered them undetectable. Dark stout, on the other hand, had a bittersweet flavor that brought out the caramel undertones of the molasses. To minimize its booziness, I tried gently heating the stout to cook off some of the alcohol—a somewhat fussy step that side-by-side tests nonetheless proved worthwhile.

Finally, I found that swapping out the butter for cleaner-tasting vegetable oil and replacing a quarter of the brown sugar with granulated cleared the way to let all those spice flavors come through.

Sturdy As She Goes

Now that the flavor was coming along nicely, I was more determined than ever to solve the sinking problem. Baking the cake in a Bundt pan might have alleviated the collapse, but not without the fussy steps of greasing and flouring the conical center and turning out the finished cake for serving. Not to mention the fact that not everybody has this type of pan. But I had another idea: Bucking the usual protocol for cakes, a few of the recipes I tested incorporated

RECIPE TESTING
Not So Gingerly with Gingerbread

Most cake batters require a gentle touch to avoid developing glutens in the flour and, thus, a tough crumb. But vigorous stirring actually gave our super-wet gingerbread batter the structure necessary to keep the center from collapsing.

**GENTLY STIRRED BATTER =
SUNKEN CAKE CENTER**

the baking soda with the wet ingredients instead of the other dry ones (including the baking powder). The reason? Too much acid in a batter lessens the baking powder's ability to leaven the cake. Baking powder contains just the right amounts of both acid and alkalai, which react to produce carbon dioxide for leavening. But if too much acid is present from other sources, it will neutralize some of the acid in the baking powder, reducing its effectiveness. Thus baking soda, an alkali, is used to neutralize acidic ingredients before they get incorporated into the batter. With gingerbread, the typical culprits are molasses and brown sugar, but my recipe also included stout—a triple threat of acidity that might well be thwarting the rise. I made the recipe again, this time stirring the half-teaspoon of baking soda right into the warm stout, followed by the molasses and brown sugar. It was a modest success. While the center still fell, it wasn't nearly as drastic—more of a buckle than a crater.

My batter was quite loose, so I wondered if the flour-to-liquid ratio was off. Would a drier gingerbread be a sturdier gingerbread? I tried decreasing the stout and oil. No dice: Though the cake's center stayed mostly propped up, it wasn't worth the marked decrease in moistness. An extra egg made the texture sturdier—but rubbery. Adjusting the amount of leaveners up and down produced cakes that ranged from dense and squat to light and pillowy, but they all shared one trait: that blasted sunken center.

Oof. My kingdom for better structure. I was getting close to calling it quits—or at least calling for some blemish-masking sleight of hand involving powdered sugar—when I reached a breakthrough. It was a casual conversation with a colleague about that fruitless trip (weeks earlier) to Plimoth Plantation that got me thinking about the gingerbread I'd made there. Structure, I mused, was about the only thing those tough little bricks had going for them. Which is when I remembered the unusual kneading step.

Kneading—as well as energetic beating—contributes strength and structure by developing the glutens in flour. But gluten development is the enemy of tenderness, which is why cake recipes generally incorporate the flour gently at the end of mixing, after the heavy-duty butter creaming is done. Tenderness I had in spades; structure, I could use. Could roughing up the batter a bit strengthen the crumb?

Departing from my current method of delicately folding the wet ingredients into the dry, I added only about a third of the wets, then mixed vigorously to form a smooth paste. I incorporated the remaining wet ingredients in two more installments, mixing until smooth after each addition. I put the cake in the oven, crossed my fingers, and waited. Sure enough, this cake was a real looker—nary a crater in sight. Fragrant, moist, bold-flavored, and beautiful, this was the gingerbread cake I'd been dreaming of.

Silently, I made a mental note to respect my elders. Sometimes, it turns out, history bears repeating.

Keys to Richer, Zingier Flavor

BITTERSWEET BEER
Dark stout contributes deep, caramelized notes.

FLAVOR-FREE FAT
Clean, neutral-tasting oil brings key flavors into clear relief.

A ROOTY BOOST
Fresh ginger kicks up the fiery, pungent notes of dried ginger.

BACKSEAT SPICES
Black pepper and cinnamon complement—without overwhelming—the ginger.

CLASSIC GINGERBREAD CAKE
MAKES ONE 8-INCH SQUARE CAKE, SERVING 8 TO 10

NOTE: This cake packs potent yet well-balanced, fragrant, spicy heat. If you are particularly sensitive to spice, you can decrease the amount of dried ginger to 1 tablespoon. Guinness is the test kitchen's favorite brand of stout. Avoid opening the oven door until the minimum baking time has elapsed. If your cake pan has thin walls, you might want to wrap it with premade cake strips or make your own from cheesecloth and foil (see page 30). This extra insulation will help ensure that the edges of the cake don't overbake. Serve the gingerbread plain or with lightly sweetened whipped cream. Leftovers can be wrapped in plastic wrap and stored at room temperature for 2 days.

- ¾ cup stout (see note)
- ½ teaspoon baking soda
- ⅔ cup mild molasses
- ¾ cup (5¼ ounces) packed light brown sugar
- ¼ cup (1¾ ounces) granulated sugar
- 1½ cups (7½ ounces) unbleached all-purpose flour, plus extra for dusting pan
- 2 tablespoons ground ginger (see note)
- ½ teaspoon baking powder
- ½ teaspoon table salt
- ¼ teaspoon ground cinnamon
- ¼ teaspoon finely ground black pepper
- 2 large eggs
- ⅓ cup vegetable oil
- 1 tablespoon finely grated fresh ginger

1. Adjust oven rack to middle position and heat oven to 350 degrees. Grease and flour 8-inch square baking pan.

2. Bring stout to boil in medium saucepan over medium heat, stirring occasionally. Remove from heat and stir in baking soda (mixture will foam vigorously). When foaming subsides, stir in molasses, brown sugar, and granulated sugar until dissolved; set mixture aside. Whisk flour, ground ginger, baking powder, salt, cinnamon, and pepper together in large bowl; set aside.

3. Transfer stout mixture to large bowl. Whisk in eggs, oil, and grated ginger until combined. Whisk wet mixture into flour mixture in thirds, stirring vigorously until completely smooth after each addition.

4. Transfer batter to prepared pan and gently tap pan against counter 3 or 4 times to dislodge any large air bubbles. Bake until top of cake is just firm to touch and toothpick inserted into center comes out clean, 35 to 45 minutes. Cool cake in pan on wire rack, about 1½ hours. Cut into squares and serve warm or at room temperature.

EQUIPMENT TESTING Cake Strips

Cake strips are designed to correct uneven baking by insulating the outside of a cake pan; the more-even heat prevents doming and cracking and keeps the edges of the cake from overbaking. We wrapped four strips, made from silicone or damp aluminized fabric, around 8-inch square, 9-inch round, and 13 by 9-inch pans filled with cake batter, and compared them with homemade strips (see page 30).

Its ability to be custom-cut to any size pan gave our homemade version an edge. But for greater convenience, our pick is Rose's Heavenly Cake Strip ($9.99). This silicone band snapped around 9-inch round and 8- and (with some preheating) 9-inch square pans and turned out cakes that were level and consistently moist from edge to center. The only downfall? It won't fit a larger pan. For complete testing results, go to: www.CooksIllustrated.com/feb11. –Amy Graves

OH, SNAP
ROSE LEVY BAKEWARE
Rose's Heavenly Cake Strip
Price: $9.99
Comments: This silicone band slips around a cake pan, with no presoaking or jiggering into place. Yellow cakes emerged level and moist; gingerbread showed no cracks or doming. Too bad it doesn't fit all pan sizes.

The Best Paring Knife

Is it worth shelling out the bucks for forged German steel, or can a $5 blade make the cut?

⇒ BY LISA McMANUS ⇐

Nothing can compare with a chef's knife when it comes to sawing through large cuts of meat, chopping chunky vegetables, or transforming herbs into mince. But for detail work—hulling strawberries, coring fruit, scraping out vanilla beans, or trimming away a tough patch of silver skin on a roast—smaller, more maneuverable paring knives are far better tools. Their blades can be as stumpy as 2¾ inches or as long as 5 inches, and they come in a range of shapes. We've long preferred the versatility of the classic style, with its slightly curved blade and pointed tip resembling a mini chef's knife. (See "Paring Knife Menagerie" for a rundown of more specialized shapes.)

Since our last review, in 2006, two German makers have introduced changes to the geometry of their knives, and some of the cooks in the test kitchen have raised concerns about the flimsiness of our previous favorite, from Victorinox. So we decided to take another look at these blades.

We armed ourselves with 10 of the latest models, most boasting our ideal blade length of 3 to 3½ inches, in a wide variety of prices—from our current favorite and bargain buy from Victorinox ($4.95) to a gleaming forged blade from Shun that cost 14 times as much. We then subjected the knives to a range of tasks to determine their maneuverability, comfort, and precision.

Core Issues

Since the foremost function of a paring knife (as opposed to a chef's knife) is to offer greater control for in-hand detail work, we started our assessments at the very tip of the blade. We slipped each knife into fresh strawberries, evaluating how easily we could glide the point around the hull to remove the stem and the whitish core without losing much fruit. Ultra-fine tips allowed us to effortlessly make deft cuts, while blunter tips clumsily jutted into the berries and left raggedy holes in the fruit.

The strawberry test confirmed that a blade much longer than 3½ inches compromises precision and agility. The longest blade in our lineup—the 4-inch

Paring Knife Menagerie

The world of paring knives includes specialty blades like the "bird's beak" and "sheep's foot" styles, both of which are named for their resemblance to animal appendages. The former's narrow, deeply curved blade is a chef favorite for carving vegetables into intricate shapes. The latter has a rounded tip and a straight blade, like a miniature santoku knife. We pitted one such blade, the Wüsthof Classic 3" Hollow-Ground Sheep's Foot Paring Knife ($54.95), against our all-purpose winner (also from Wüsthof), and found that the sheep's foot configuration worked well for precise slicing jobs done on a cutting board, like julienning small fruits and vegetables. But skinning curvy apples and digging the cores out of delicate strawberries was another matter. Here, the broad, asymmetrical tip of the sheep's foot was a handicap compared to the slim, more-flexible spear-point tip of the all-purpose model. The Wüsthof Classic 2½" Bird's Beak Paring Knife ($49.95) has the opposite problem: designed only for hand-held carving, its hooked blade is no good for slicing on a cutting board.

The bottom line: These specialty knives have their uses, but neither is a replacement for our favorite all-purpose blade. –L.M.

BIRD'S BEAK
Best for decorative carving in the hand.

SHEEP'S FOOT
Best for straight cuts on a cutting board.

ALL-PURPOSE
Best for cutting and peeling, in the hand or on a cutting board.

sibling to our favorite 3¼-inch Victorinox knife—had trouble navigating the inside of a berry. That said, its extra length was a plus for bisecting a bulbous apple and slicing a block of cheddar. But as soon as we switched back to the more intricate work of trimming apple cores, this longer blade just got in the way.

We also found that we preferred knives that had a more even balance between blade and handle, which made them feel almost like an extension of our hands. The handles on some models, like the $70 Shun, were so weighty that they actually seemed to be pulling the blade away from the food as we sliced. Heavier handles also made hand-held tasks like hulling strawberries or coring apples more awkward.

Sharp Differences

Another crucial component to any good knife is the actual sharpness of the blade. Take sectioning oranges: The goal is to remove perfect juice-filled segments intact and uncrushed, and only a very sharp blade can slip into each section and right up against the membrane that divides the flesh. Some knives left us with oozing orange scraps; others turned out a neat heap of orange wedges, crisply cut and full of juice. Same deal with mincing shallots and slicing fibrous ginger root. While the top performers reduced the aromatics with ease, other models struggled to make clean, sweeping cuts through the foods.

But were the more successful knives performing better simply because their factory edges were

sharper? Curious, we took a closer look at the blades on our front-runners. As it turned out, the two top-scoring knives, the Wüsthof Classic with PEtec 3½-Inch Paring Knife ($39.95) and its close runner-up, the Four Star 3-Inch Paring Knife by Henckels ($24.99), both recently underwent "East-West" makeovers, their cutting edges changed to a typical Japanese 14- or 15-degree bevel angle per side, as opposed to a traditional Western angle of 19 to 22 degrees. (The Victorinox, our 2006 favorite, uses a similar angle: 17 degrees.) Did changing the angle improve the performance? Maybe. But when we later ran the German knives through a sharpener that brought the angle closer to that of a more traditional Western edge, our testers couldn't detect much difference in the cutting ability of the knives.

So, while those new edge angles seem to be a plus, they are only one of several factors that make these German paring knives so successful: well-shaped blades with sharply pointed tips; compact overall length; good handle-to-blade balance, weight, and proportion; and comfortable grips that feel secure and don't slip, no matter if you're cutting in the hand or on a board.

Don't get us wrong. We still like our old favorite (and current Best Buy), the 3¼-inch Victorinox, a light knife with a slim, sharp blade. And you can't beat its low price. But for those who appreciate working with the more secure feel of a solidly built paring knife, the Wüsthof is a near-perfect tool.

TESTING PARING KNIVES

We tested 10 paring knives, using testers with differing knife skills and hand sizes to determine which functioned best for most cooks. All knives were purchased online. Sources for the winner and Best Buy are listed on page 32.

PRECISION: We hulled strawberries, cored apples, sectioned oranges, and minced shallots, giving highest marks to knives that were maneuverable and felt very sharp but safe in our hands. Since precision is the principal advantage of paring knives, we gave extra weight to these results.

PEELING: We peeled apples and oranges and trimmed fresh ginger root, looking for a knife with good maneuverability around curves and the ability to peel thinly and precisely with little waste.

CUTTING: We sliced apples, fibrous ginger roots, and cheddar cheese blocks, looking for blade strength, sharpness, and appropriate length.

USER-FRIENDLINESS: We rated each knife on features that made using it easier, more comfortable, and secure.

EDGE RETENTION: We sliced sheets of paper before and after testing, preferring knives that arrived sharp and kept their edge.

Keeping the Edge

To maintain their narrow Asian-style factory edges, we prefer to sharpen our top two paring knives—one by Wüsthof, the other by Henckels—on our favorite manual Asian sharpener, the Chef's Choice 463 ($40). But you can also hone these blades on a Western sharpener. It will widen the cutting angle by 5 degrees—not enough to detract significantly from the knife's overall performance. In fact, in a side-by-side blind comparison of knives sharpened with the Asian-style Chef's Choice and our favorite manual sharpener for Western knives from AccuSharp ($11), only a few testers could detect a difference as they sliced tomatoes with the Western edge.

**CHEF'S CHOICE
ASIAN-STYLE SHARPENER**

HIGHLY RECOMMENDED | **PERFORMANCE** | **TESTERS' COMMENTS**

WÜSTHOF Classic with PEtec, 3½-inch
Model: 4066
Price: $39.95
Weight: 2⅛ ounces

Precision: ★★★
Peeling: ★★★
Cutting: ★★★
User-friendliness: ★★★
Edge Retention: ★★½

This razor-sharp knife with "Precision Edge Technology—PEtec" was comfortable and well proportioned. A recent redesign gave it a narrower blade angle of 14 degrees (previously 19 degrees) on each side and a new plastic handle that feels like hard, smooth wood.

HENCKELS Four Star Paring Knife, 3-inch
Model: 31070-080 (Note: -083 is same knife, packaged in box)
Price: $24.99
Weight: 1⅝ ounces

Precision: ★★★
Peeling: ★★★
Cutting: ★★½
User-friendliness: ★★½
Edge Retention: ★★★

This knife with a super-sharp edge and 15-degree blade angle would have tied with the winning Wüsthof but for its slightly too short 3-inch blade. That said, most testers preferred its "grippier" handle, and our final paper-slicing test showed that it retained its edge a bit better than the Wüsthof.

VICTORINOX Fibrox Paring Knife, 3¼-inch
BEST BUY
Model: 40600
Price: $4.95
Weight: ¾ ounce

Precision: ★★★
Peeling: ★★★
Cutting: ★★★
User-friendliness: ★★
Edge Retention: ★★½

At a fraction of the price of the top two knives, this sharp, precise blade is a real bargain—and feels more secure in the hand than its 4-inch sibling. Our only gripe? It's a featherweight compared with other models and feels a bit flimsy and plasticky.

RECOMMENDED | **PERFORMANCE** | **TESTERS' COMMENTS**

KUHN RIKON Paring Knife Colori 1 Nonstick, 3½-inch
Model: 2808
Price: $10
Weight: 1⅛ ounce (without sheath)

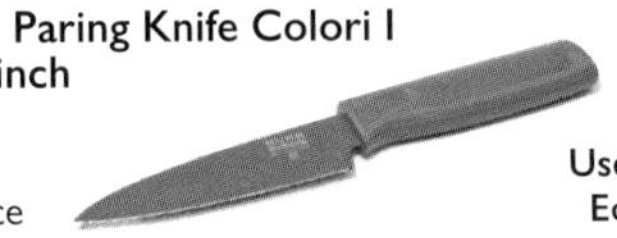

Precision: ★★
Peeling: ★★½
Cutting: ★★★
User-friendliness: ★★½
Edge Retention: ★★½

This inexpensive, lightweight knife was comfortable to hold and came with a snug sheath. Its stiff, non-stick-coated blade felt a bit unwieldy for intricate tasks—and the coating itself was generally superfluous—but the cutting edge was razor-sharp and slid through shallots with ease.

DEXTER-RUSSELL V-Lo Paring Knife, 3½-inch
Model: V105-CP
Price: $7.30
Weight: ¾ ounce

Precision: ★★
Peeling: ★★
Cutting: ★★
User-friendliness: ★★½
Edge Retention: ★★

While we appreciated this knife's sharp blade, the ribbed, slim-waisted plastic handle and extreme lightweight design divided testers' votes: Those with small hands deemed it "a pleasure to hold," while those with large hands felt that it was "too insubstantial" and "like a toy."

VICTORINOX Fibrox Paring Knife, 4-inch
Model: 40501
Price: $4.95
Weight: ¾ ounce

Precision: ★
Peeling: ★★½
Cutting: ★★½
User-friendliness: ★★
Edge Retention: ★★½

"Nice, sharp" blade. But while the extra ¾ inch on this larger Victorinox twin came in handy for slicing fruit and cheese, it was too much metal for most testers, who complained that the elongated blade felt unwieldy during intricate tasks like hulling berries.

RECOMMENDED WITH RESERVATIONS | **PERFORMANCE** | **TESTERS' COMMENTS**

SHUN Classic Paring Knife, 3½-inch
Model: DM0700
Price: $70
Weight: 2⅛ ounces

Precision: ★½
Peeling: ★★½
Cutting: ★★★
User-friendliness: ★
Edge Retention: ★★½

Though wonderfully sharp, this knife was handle-heavy and slick, making it awkward for hand-held cutting tasks like berry hulling. And at nearly twice the cost of our winner—and 14 times the cost of our Best Buy—we just couldn't bring ourselves to shell out for it.

KYOCERA Ceramic Blade Revolution Series Paring Knife, 3-inch
Model: FK-075
Price: $26.95
Weight: 1½ ounces

Precision: ★
Peeling: ★★
Cutting: ★★★
User-friendliness: ★★
Edge Retention: ★★

While the sharp ceramic blade slices beautifully, this knife came with an annoying list of "don'ts": Don't drop, flex, or knock it; don't turn the blade sideways to crush garlic; don't run it through the dishwasher; etc. Plus, it can't be honed on a traditional sharpener, and its fat, rounded tip got in the way of precision work.

CHICAGO CUTLERY Walnut Tradition Slant Tip Paring Knife, 3-inch
Model: 102-SP
Price: $13.11
Weight: 1¼ ounces

Precision: ★★
Peeling: ★★★
Cutting: ★
User-friendliness: ★
Edge Retention: ★★

This knife's diminutive blade (which measures just 2¾ inches) fell short in many cutting tasks, and its square wooden handle felt disproportionately huge. That said, its narrow tip is well designed for detail work, nimbly hulling berries and working its way around the contours of an apple core.

NEW WEST KNIFEWORKS Paring Knife, 3-inch
Model: Fusionwood
Price: $49
Weight: 2⅛ ounces

Precision: ½
Peeling: ★★
Cutting: ★★
User-friendliness: ★
Edge Retention: ★★★

This knife was lovely to look at and retained its edge very well. But we struggled with its heavy handle and upturned tip, which made almost every task—from hulling berries to mincing shallots and working our way around apple seeds and cores—a bit of a hassle.

Revisiting Red Wine Vinegar

Does aging make a difference in vinegar, or does it all boil down to the grapes you start with?

⇛ BY DIANA BURRELL ⇚

Lately, choosing red wine vinegar at the supermarket gives me the same nervous feeling as trying to pick the right wine for dinner guests. As with balsamic vinegars, the number of red wine vinegars in the condiment aisle has exploded in the past decade. I can choose between brand name vinegars my mother has used for years and newer ones that boast impressive European pedigrees. Is French better than American? Does aged red wine vinegar provide more depth of flavor? Will a pan deglazed with vinegar that began life as a Zinfandel or Pinot Noir create a sauce that's more piquant than one flavored with vinegar simply labeled "red"? Considering that some vinegars cost less than 20 cents per ounce, are the ones that cost four or five times as much actually worth the money?

We last tasted red wine vinegars in 2003. Given the proliferation of options since, we decided that it was time to take a fresh look.

Pure Pucker

Food scientist Harold McGee aptly calls vinegar "the natural sequel to an alcoholic fermentation." For centuries, humankind supplied the wine, and nature provided it with bacteria (Acetobacter aceti), which, with the help of oxygen, metabolizes wine's ethyl alcohol and converts it into the acetic acid that gives vinegar its distinctive sharp scent and mouth-puckering flavor. Today, most commercial red wine vinegars are produced via two distinct methods. The first, the Orléans method, was developed in the 14th century. To start fermentation, oak barrels of wine are inoculated with a "mother of vinegar"—a cellulose glob loaded with acetic acid bacteria from an established vinegar. Periodically, vinegar is drawn off and fresh wine added, and the process continues until all the alcohol is converted into acetic acid. Some argue that this method makes for a more flavorful wine vinegar because it gives the flavor compounds time to develop and mature. But it's also expensive, since it takes months before the vinegar is ready for the market.

In the second, more modern method, wine and bacteria are put in an acetator, a stainless-steel machine that rapidly circulates oxygen through red wine to feed the bacteria. This method converts alcohol into acetic acid in about a day, although some of these rapidly produced vinegars are then put in barrels for additional aging and, presumably, improved flavor.

Domestic varieties of red wine vinegar are typically just 5 to 6 percent acetic acid, while imports are usually in the 7-percent range; the strength is determined by a dilution with water. But the unique flavor profile of a vinegar is not only influenced by acetic acid but also by naturally occurring flavor compounds from the base wine, as well as by new compounds created during the production process. The question was, which of these factors would actually make a difference to our tasters?

Straight Up

We asked 21 staff members to taste and rate 10 red wine vinegars, selected from a list of top-selling national supermarket brands. Our lineup included our previous winner, Spectrum Naturals Organic Red Wine Vinegar, along with Pompeian, another top-ranked vinegar from that tasting, as well as Star, Heinz, Holland House, Colavita, and Regina. We also pulled in some international newcomers: Laurent du Clos, a French import, and Lucini and Monari Federzoni, both from Italy.

Most cooks don't do shots of vinegar unless they're masochists, but I was curious to learn if we'd get some early preferences right out of the bottle. I assumed that tasters would be partial to the vinegars that were sweet and less harsh, since they'd be tasting these potent substances straight. In fact, the favorite in this round fell right in the middle of the rankings for sweetness and harshness. Tasters, it seemed, liked full flavor and a little sharpness.

While I wasn't confident that we had a front-runner yet, the plain tasting did reveal that some of the vinegars had unpleasant off-flavors and aromas, the most common being the smell of nail polish remover, or acetone. This was not surprising, since any traces of alcohol left in vinegar will bond chemically with acetic acid to create ethyl acetate, a compound that has the same distinctive scent as the acetone found in nail polish remover. "A little bit is OK," said Mary Ellen Camire, a professor of food science and nutrition at the University of Maine, explaining that acetate can give vinegar a pleasing fruitiness. "But too much can indicate a production failure."

Sweet and Sour

Next we tasted the vinegars as they would actually be used—in a simple vinaigrette served with butter lettuce and in pickled onions. Surprisingly, some of the harsher vinegars, such as Monari Federzoni and Lucini, which had made tasters choke in the plain tasting, were experienced as relatively sweet in the vinaigrette. How could this be?

I recalled that the mayonnaise we had used to help

emulsify the vinaigrette contained a small amount of sugar. Our science editor confirmed that the strong, highly acidic vinegars were acting synergistically with this sugar to heighten its sweet taste. Less acidic vinegars, on the other hand, were being pushed into the background, allowing the strong flavor compounds in the extra-virgin olive oil and the mustard to mask sweetness. This told me that a good vinegar needs some muscle in the form of acidity to tease out all the flavors from the bunch.

But in the end, these highly acidic vinegars lost the battle with our tasters. The most expensive of the supermarket brands—Lucini Pinot Noir Italian Wine Vinegar, running $9.99 for 8.5 ounces—ended up tied for last place with the other most acidic entry, Monari Federzoni. The majority of tasters simply found them too harsh, especially when sampled plain or in pickled onions. However, since they scored well in our vinaigrette tasting, they might be worth buying if you like a strong, bracing vinegar to dress your salads.

At the top of the heap, French import Laurent du Clos knocked our former favorite, Spectrum Naturals, down a couple of notches with its crisp red wine flavor balanced by stronger than average acidity and subtle sweetness. While this vinegar gets its start in an acetator and then is aged in wooden barrels for two months before bottling, we weren't convinced that aging was the reason that our tasters gravitated toward this brand. Several of our lowest-

TASTING RED WINE VINEGARS

In three blind tastings, 21 *Cook's Illustrated* staff members tasted 10 red wine vinegars, from a list of top-selling national brands compiled by the Chicago-based market research firm SymphonyIRI Group. We sent the vinegars to an independent laboratory to test for sugar levels, acetic acid as a percentage of volume, and the type of grapes present in the vinegar. We sampled the vinegars in a plain tasting, then in two cooking applications—vinaigrette and pickled onions—and rated the vinegars on harshness, sweetness, and presence of red wine flavor. Results were averaged, and red wine vinegars appear below in order of preference. All vinegars were purchased at Boston-area supermarkets.

RECOMMENDED

LAURENT DU CLOS Red Wine Vinegar
Price: $5.99 for 16.9 fl. oz. (35 cents per oz.)
Acidity: 6.12%
Sugar: None detected
Type of Grape: Vinifera, red and white
Comments: "Good red wine flavor" won the day for this French import. Tasters liked the "nicely rich," "well-balanced," and "fruity" flavor that came through in the pickled onions, and they praised the "clean, light, pleasant taste" and "subtle zing" it added to the vinaigrette.

POMPEIAN Gourmet Red Wine Vinegar
Price: $3.99 for 16 fl. oz. (25 cents per oz.)
Acidity: 5.14%
Sugar: 0.5%
Type of Grape: Concord
Comments: Tasters were enthusiastic about this "very mild, sweet, pleasant" red wine vinegar with "tang" that was in "harmonious balance." It was "not harsh at all," but had a "bright, potent taste" with "really pleasing red wine flavor."

RECOMMENDED WITH RESERVATIONS

SPECTRUM NATURALS Organic Red Wine Vinegar
Price: $5.99 for 16.9 fl. oz. (35 cents per oz.)
Acidity: 6.06%
Sugar: None detected
Type of Grape: Concord/Vinifera-type grapes
Comments: Tasters praised our former favorite supermarket brand's "winy" and "fruity" taste with "buttery" and "briny" undertones, but it stumbled in the pickled onions, inspiring remarks about its "watery," "thin," and "wimpy" flavor.

HEINZ Gourmet Red Wine Vinegar
Price: $3.99 for 12 fl. oz. (33 cents per oz.)
Acidity: 5.32%
Sugar: None detected
Type of Grape: Concord
Comments: Tasted on its own, this domestic red wine vinegar was deemed "bright and sweet with good red wine flavor." Once cooked, however, a few tasters noticed a "sour, almost fermented taste" that was "too harsh" to let the wine flavor through.

HOLLAND HOUSE Red Wine Vinegar
Price: $2.89 for 12 fl. oz. (24 cents per oz.)
Acidity: 5.2%
Sugar: 0.3%
Type of Grape: Concord
Comments: Some tasters liked its "tart," "fruity," and "cherry/nectarine" notes, but this vinegar also received the most complaints about its "acetone" or "nail polish remover" smell and taste.

RECOMMENDED WITH RESERVATIONS (CONTINUED)

REGINA Red Wine Vinegar
Price: $2.49 for 12 fl. oz. (21 cents per oz.)
Acidity: 5.2%
Sugar: None detected
Type of Grape: Vinifera
Comments: Distinguishing itself with its perceived sweetness, this vinegar with "berry" and "floral" notes didn't offend, nor did it wow tasters, whose comments included "middle-of-the-road quality" and "no zip or zing."

COLAVITA Red Wine Vinegar
Price: $2.99 for 17 fl. oz. (18 cents per oz.)
Acidity: 6.3%
Sugar: 0.9%
Type of Grape: Vinifera
Comments: Some tasters appreciated this vinegar's "winy and sweet" flavor and "nice balance" with "just the right tang." Others, however, found it "harsh," "sour," and "sharp" with a "saccharine aftertaste."

STAR Red Wine Vinegar
Price: $2.39 for 12 fl. oz. (20 cents per oz.)
Acidity: 5.08%
Sugar: None detected
Type of Grape: Vinifera
Comments: This vinegar had a "bright and zippy" presence in vinaigrette and a "refreshing bite" in the pickled onions, but its lack of "real red wine taste" allowed the acidity to prevail, making it harsh for some.

LUCINI Pinot Noir Italian Wine Vinegar
Price: $9.99 for 8.5 oz. ($1.18 per oz.)
Acidity: 7.28%
Sugar: None detected
Type of Grape: Vinifera
Comments: "Pucker city!" wrote one taster about this "strong" and "punchy" Tuscan import, the most acidic vinegar we tasted. But one taster in the vinaigrette round claimed, "It's the first time … I've picked out red wine flavor."

MONARI FEDERZONI Red Wine Vinegar
Price: $3.99 for 16.9 fl. oz. (24 cents per oz.)
Acidity: 7.16%
Sugar: None detected
Type of Grape: Vinifera
Comments: This "strong, pungent, and jarring" Italian vinegar garnered little praise from our tasters because of its overwhelming acidity. One wrote, "I'd like the sample better if it wasn't so harsh. It has nice sweetness and flavor." A few tasters liked its "robust, aged flavor" and thought it was "tangier than the others" in a vinaigrette.

---

ranking vinegars were also aged.

There is one characteristic shared by all three top vinegars: They're blends. Laurent du Clos is made from a mix of red and white vinifera grapes, Pompeian adds an aged vinegar sourced from Spain to its domestically produced vinegar, and Spectrum is created from a combination of sweet Concord grapes and winy vinifera-type grapes. (It's worth noting that our favorite high-end vinegar, O Zinfandel, adds Bing cherry juice to heighten the flavor of its base vinegar.) Multiple varieties of grapes create vinegar with a complex and pleasing taste—aging is not necessarily required.

For everyday red wine vinegar, Laurent du Clos is hard to beat. At 35 cents per ounce, it's not the least expensive brand we tasted, but that's a reasonable price for a vinegar that doesn't compromise on flavor.

DID YOU KNOW? All products reviewed by America's Test Kitchen, home of *Cook's Illustrated* and *Cook's Country* magazines, are independently chosen, researched, and reviewed by our editors. We buy products for testing at retail locations and do not accept unsolicited samples for testing. We do not accept or receive payment or consideration from product manufacturers or retailers. Manufacturers and retailers are not told in advance of publication which products we have recommended. We list suggested sources for recommended products as a convenience to our readers but do not endorse specific retailers.

The Ultimate Way to Season Cast Iron

For years we've seasoned cast-iron cookware in the test kitchen by placing it over medium heat and wiping out the pan with coats of vegetable oil until its surface turns dark and shiny. When a pan starts to look patchy, we simply repeat the process. But when we heard about a new method that creates a slick surface so indestructible that touch-ups are almost never necessary, we were intrigued. Developed by blogger Sheryl Canter, the approach calls for treating the pan with multiple coats of flaxseed oil between hour-long stints in the oven.

We carried out Canter's approach on new, unseasoned cast-iron skillets and compared them with pans treated with vegetable oil—and the results amazed us. The flaxseed oil so effectively bonded to the skillets, forming a sheer, stick-resistant veneer, that even a run through our commercial dishwasher with a squirt of degreaser left them totally unscathed. But the vegetable oil–treated skillets showed rusty spots and patchiness when they emerged from the dishwasher, requiring reseasoning before use.

Why did the new treatment work so well? Flaxseed oil is the food-grade equivalent of linseed oil, used by artists to give their paintings a hard, polished finish, and it boasts six times the amount of omega-3 fatty acids as vegetable oil. Over prolonged exposure to high heat, these fatty acids combine to form a strong, solid matrix that polymerizes to the pan's surface.

Although lengthy, seasoning with flaxseed oil is a mainly hands-off undertaking. We highly recommend the treatment:

1. Warm an unseasoned pan (either new or stripped of seasoning*) for 15 minutes in a 200-degree oven to open its pores.
2. Remove the pan from the oven. Place 1 tablespoon flaxseed oil in the pan and, using tongs, rub the oil into the surface with paper towels. With fresh paper towels, thoroughly wipe out the pan to remove excess oil.
3. Place the oiled pan upside down in a cold oven, then set the oven to its maximum baking temperature. Once the oven reaches its maximum temperature, heat the pan for one hour. Turn off the oven; cool the pan in the oven for at least two hours.
4. Repeat the process five more times, or until the pan develops a dark, semi-matte surface.

*To strip a cast-iron pan of seasoning, spray it with oven cleaner, wait 30 minutes, wash with soapy water, and thoroughly wipe with paper towels.

FLAXSEED OIL   VEGETABLE OIL

Even after a run in the dishwasher, the pan seasoned with flaxseed oil held on to its perfect seasoning. The pan seasoned with vegetable oil did not.

A Better Dust for Your Peel: Semolina

One of the keys to success in making any pizza, including our Thin-Crust Pizza (page 8), is ensuring that your perfectly formed pie easily slides off the peel and onto the stone, without any rips or tears to the bottom of the crust. To prevent the dough from sticking, many recipes advise using cornmeal or bread crumbs. While both coatings work, they also leave a gritty or crunchy residue on the bottom of the pizza. We typically call for a generous dusting of flour, but even this isn't the perfect solution, as too much flour on the peel can lend a dusty, raw-flour taste to the crust, while too little will allow the dough to stick. The best approach is to spring for a bag of semolina flour. This coarsely ground wheat doesn't char as easily as all-purpose flour, so you can make two pies in succession without brushing off the stone. And almost any amount of semolina will allow pizza to release easily without leaving too gritty a residue.

Mellowing Out EVOO

Fruity, peppery extra-virgin olive oil is our go-to for dressing salads, dipping bread, or drizzling over grilled vegetables. But sometimes recipes call for regular olive oil (usually labeled "pure" on the bottle) because its milder taste allows the other flavors of the dish to come to the fore. To avoid having to keep bottles of both on hand, we wondered if we could make our own by mixing EVOO with a neutral-flavored oil like canola. We concocted blends of the two oils in various ratios, tasting them plain and emulsified into aïoli and mayonnaise. We found that 1 part EVOO and 3 parts canola oil produced a flavor virtually identical to regular olive oil.

Wizened Ginger, Faded Flavor

We rarely use up an entire knob of fresh ginger in one go, and we routinely store the remainder in the fridge. But after a few weeks, the root tends to shrivel and dry out. Is this an indication that it's no longer suitable for cooking?

Two batches of stir-fried broccoli later, we had our answer. Though tasters found both dishes acceptable, the sample made with fresh, plump ginger packed spicy heat and "zing," while the broccoli made with a more wizened specimen turned out "mild" and "flat." Why? As ginger ages, it loses its signature pungency from the compound gingerol. During storage—and even as it's heated—gingerol converts into a more mild-flavored compound called zingerone, which, despite its sharp-sounding name, is far less assertive than its precursor. Lesson learned: If possible, buy small pieces of ginger and use it while it's fresh. And if you're polishing off an older piece, be prepared to use more than the recipe calls for and add it as close as possible to the end of cooking.

STEP BY STEP | INSULATING CAKE STRIP: HOME EDITION

Cake strips promote more even baking, preventing doming and cracking as well as keeping the edges of a cake from overbaking. This extra insulation is particularly important if the walls of your pan are thin.

1. SOAK STRIP Soak 2 by 32-inch piece of cheesecloth or folded newspaper with water. Gently wring out excess water.

2. FOLD IN FOIL Place damp strip at bottom of 36-inch length of foil. Repeatedly fold foil over dampened strip to cover to make 2 by 36-inch strip.

3. WRAP AROUND PAN Mold insulating strip around pan and pinch ends together to seal.

4. SECURE To ensure insulating strip stays in place around pan, secure with twine.

Grate Expectations

When we run a recipe calling for a grated hard cheese such as Parmesan or Pecorino Romano, we always include not only the weight but also the grate size desired. As the chart below amply demonstrates, this is because volume can vary significantly depending on size: The same 1 ounce of cheese can equal ½ cup of grated cheese—or half of that amount. So always follow the directions for grate size: It can dramatically impact the outcome of your recipe.

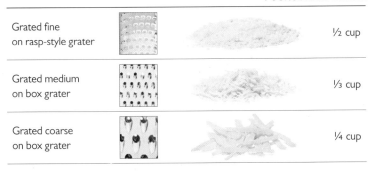

			I OUNCE HARD CHEESE
Grated fine on rasp-style grater			½ cup
Grated medium on box grater			⅓ cup
Grated coarse on box grater			¼ cup

Storing Fresh Loose Carrots

In tests, we've found carrots with green tops still attached have better flavor than those sold already trimmed. But what's the best way to store them? Since the vegetable will continue to feed the leafy tops in storage, should you remove the tops when you get home from the market? We purchased several bunches of carrots, left the tops intact on half, and removed the tops from the other half. We then stored the carrots in our refrigerator's crisper drawer for two weeks. When we examined the samples, those stored with their tops attached were extremely limp, indicating moisture loss. But to our surprise, the trimmed carrots fared only slightly better.

Clearly, we needed to reevaluate our storage method. We repeated the test, this time placing both trimmed and untrimmed batches in open zipper-lock bags—a setup that trapped most of their moisture but allowed some to escape. After two weeks, the carrots with their tops on had still softened significantly, while the trimmed ones were just as firm and sweet-tasting as they had been two weeks prior.

IN THE BAG
Store carrots trimmed of leafy tops in an open zipper-lock bag.

Precise Water Temperature for the Perfect Loaf

A full-flavored, properly risen loaf of bread depends on more than just the right mix of ingredients. The temperature of the dough as it begins proofing, or rising, affects the rate of fermentation and, in turn, the flavor and texture of the finished product. The optimal temperature for most bread doughs is 75 degrees. To arrive at this temperature, you usually can't manipulate variables such as the temperature of the room, flour, or starter (if using). Instead, professional bakers use a simple mathematical formula to calculate the temperature of the one variable they can control: the water. This formula also takes into account the amount of heat generated by the specific mixing method. Hand-kneaded doughs have a so-called friction factor of 5 degrees, while the friction factor of stand mixers is 20 degrees, and the very vigorous action of a food processor is 25 degrees.

To calculate the ideal water temperature, multiply the optimal dough temperature of 75 by 3 (multiply by 4 if the recipe includes a starter). Then subtract the temperatures of the room, flour, and starter (if applicable) and the friction factor from this figure.

For example, for dough kneaded in a stand mixer (friction factor of 20) when the room, flour, and starter temperatures are all 71 degrees, you would need a water temperature of 67 degrees: $(75 \times 4) - 71 - 71 - 71 - 20 = 67$.

This trustworthy formula will help ensure the perfect loaf.

Sharpening Serrated Knives

Our favorite manual and electric knife sharpeners restore hair-splitting sharpness to dull blades with just a few strokes, but until recently we'd never tested either manufacturer's claim that the tools work equally well with serrated blades. Generally speaking, serrated edges don't need to be honed and sharpened nearly as often as smooth blades; because their pointed teeth do most of the work and the finer scallop-shaped serrations follow the points through the food, the edges endure less friction and degrade more slowly. And as for serrated-specific sharpeners, we've previously found them disappointing and recommended that serrated knives be sharpened by a professional. But we were curious about how these knives would fare in a traditional sharpener, so we gathered half a dozen pointed-, scalloped-, and saw toothed–edge knives that were too dull to slice through a loaf of crusty bread or a ripe tomato and ran them through a series of sharpening tests.

Alas, our Rolls-Royce of electric sharpeners—the Chef'sChoice 130 Professional Sharpening Station ($149.95)—didn't cut it; after the manufacturer-prescribed 10 strokes, the edge improved only marginally. But our favorite manual sharpener, the AccuSharp Knife and Tool Sharpener ($9.49), restored an edge that sliced through crusty bread and cleaved juicy tomatoes with ease. Why the sharp difference? It came down to mechanics. With the electric sharpener, two spinning wheels sharpen merely the edges and tips of the serrated knives, not the valleys between these tips. The manual tool, by contrast, allows the V-shaped tungsten carbide to ride up and down the different serrations (pointed, scalloped, and saw toothed), sharpening not only the edges and tips, but the deep valleys too. That being the case, we'll skip the pricey professional job and grab the AccuSharp from the tool drawer.

ACCUSHARP KNIFE SHARPENER

TECHNIQUE | TIPS FOR TAMING PHYLLO

Frozen packaged phyllo dough functions as light, flaky pastry in traditional Greek dishes such as baklava and spanakopita and as a ready-made tart crust or wrapper for both sweet and savory fillings. But the tendency of these paper-thin sheets to tear, dry out quickly, or stick together can be maddening. Here are some tips for mastering this delicate dough.

1. COVER WITH PLASTIC AND A DAMP TOWEL To help prevent cracking, phyllo must be kept moist until you're ready to work with it. The usual approach is to cover the stack with a damp towel. But it's all too easy to overmoisten the towel and turn the dough sticky. We prefer to cover the stack with plastic wrap and then a damp towel. The weight of the towel will keep the plastic wrap flush against the phyllo.

2. STAGGER THE CRACKS Because phyllo is so fragile, some sheets crack and even tear while still in the box. Don't worry about rips, just make sure to adjust the orientation of the sheets as you stack them so that cracks in different sheets don't line up.

3. TRIM STUCK EDGES When phyllo sheets emerge from the box fused at their edges, don't try to separate the sheets. Instead, trim the fused portion and discard.

⇒ BY TAIZETH SIERRA & AMY GRAVES ⇐

NEW PRODUCT **Ultimate Chicken Roaster**

Perfection in one pan? That's what All-Clad promises with its new Stainless Steel Ultimate Chicken Roaster ($179.95), designed to produce flawlessly roasted chicken and vegetables in the same dish. A detachable 9-inch metal arm suspends the chicken over a small, solidly made tri-ply roasting pan, which holds the vegetables; there are high, easy-to-grasp handles at either end.

But while every test produced a chicken with moist, tender meat, getting crispy skin was a crapshoot. Birds bigger than 4 pounds, trussed or not, drooped onto the vegetables, interfering with air circulation and even browning of both elements and drowning the vegetables in drippings. Only birds of 4 pounds or less came out with perfect, golden skin, but some of the vegetables stayed pale, and the smaller chickens didn't weigh enough to keep the inadequately anchored arm firmly in place (at one point it even fell off, dropping the chicken into the pan).

The bottom line: This pan is suitable only for small birds, but even then you won't get perfection. It's easier than using a traditional roasting rack and flipping the chicken, but when we compared it with our favorite (and cheaper) vertical roaster, Norpro's Vertical Roaster with Infuser ($27.95), set into a roasting pan and surrounded by vegetables, we saw no real advantages to the new gadget.

ARMED ROBBERY
The high-priced Ultimate Chicken Roaster offers no advantage over our favorite (and far less expensive) vertical roaster from Norpro.

NEW PRODUCT **Silicone Salt Storer**

The Prepara Pop Savor ($19.95) takes the design of a traditional "salt pig"—a hooded ceramic vessel that cooks fill with salt for seasoning—and fashions the cover from soft silicone to make a closeable lid that keeps out dirt and moisture. To test its usefulness, we successively filled the container with salt, sugar, and ice cream sprinkles, using the salt to season food during cooking. We also left the container next to the stove while frying bacon. As promised, the durable "pop" top flipped open and kept its contents shielded from splattered grease when closed. The attached half-teaspoon measuring spoon was accurate, though superfluous for those of us who prefer to grab a pinch with our fingers. Our only gripe? The 3½-inch opening was a little cramped for a few testers with large hands.

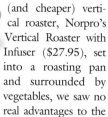

STOVESIDE STORAGE
The soft, silicone flip-top lid on the Prepara Pop Savor shelters salt and opens with the flick of a finger.

NEW PRODUCT **Thermapen Protector**

We're big fans of ThermoWorks' Splash-Proof Super-Fast Thermapen thermometer ($96), but this water-resistant update to the original model is not heat-resistant and will suffer some melting and cracking if left too close to a hot grill or stove for an extended period of time. As a protective measure, ThermoWorks now offers a silicone boot ($6) that fits snugly over the thermometer. To see how much heat it can take, we placed two Thermapens—one fitted with the boot and one left bare—next to the stove, half an inch from a pan radiating 550-degree heat. Ten minutes later, the surface of the unprotected Thermapen reached 175 degrees and showed signs of damage (melting, blistering, and discoloration), while the boot-clad Thermapen withstood the heat for more than 20 minutes as the temperature from the stove increased exponentially. Although the damage

BOOT UP
Covering our favorite Thermapen thermometer with a tailor-made silicone boot protects it from radiant heat.

was merely cosmetic (both Thermapens continued to work perfectly), we think this small investment is worthwhile to protect our favorite instant-read thermometer.

EQUIPMENT TESTING **Universal Pan Lid**

Many skillets—including our favorite stainless fry pans from All-Clad—come without lids, and shelling out for matching covers to each individual pan ($33.95 to $49.95 each) seems wasteful. Wondering if an inexpensive universal lid would do just as well—most models sport grooved rings ranging from 8 to 12 inches in diameter and claim to fit a variety of standard-size pans—we boiled water and prepared French omelets, rice pilaf, and braised vegetables (all of which require a tight-fitting lid) in our favorite All-Clad 8-, 10-, and 12-inch skillets and 4-quart saucepan, covering each vessel with four different universal lids and its All-Clad counterpart. Unfortunately, none of the lids was a one-size-fits-all solution—their roughly 12-inch diameters loosely covered the 8-inch skillet and saucepan—though most fit snugly on larger skillets. Our favorite, the Progressive Stainless-Steel Universal Fry Pan Lid ($14.99), featured an adjustable vent that prevented steam pressure from building up, helping it stay put on both the 10- and 12-inch skillets. In fact, it even kept more liquid from evaporating than the All-Clad lids themselves—and at a fraction of the price.

SNUG AND CHEAP
The inexpensive Progressive Stainless-Steel Universal Fry Pan Lid can replace name-brand lids for 10- and 12-inch skillets.

Sources

The following are mail-order sources for items recommended in this issue. Prices were current at press time and do not include shipping. Contact companies to confirm or visit www.CooksIllustrated.com for updates.

PAGE 11: OVEN THERMOMETER
- Cooper-Atkins 24HP Oven Thermometer: $5.95, item #COO-24HP-01-1, Northwestern Cutlery (888-248-4449, **www.nwcutlery.com**).

PAGE 25: CAKE STRIP
- Rose's Heavenly Cake Strip: $9.99, item #12420, Fante's Kitchen Wares Shop (800-443-2683, **www.fantes.com**).

PAGE 27: PARING KNIVES
- Wüsthof Classic 3½-inch Paring Knife with PEtec: $39.95, item #2600393, Williams-Sonoma (877-812-6235, **www.williams-sonoma.com**).
- Victorinox 3¼-inch Paring Knife: $4.95, item #242240, Cooking.com (800-663-8810, **www.cooking.com**).

PAGE 32: SILICONE SALT STORER
- Pop Savor: $19.95, item #PP02-PSR100, Prepara (888-878-8665, **www.prepara.com**).

PAGE 32: THERMAPEN PROTECTOR
- Silicone Boot for Thermapen: $6, item #THS-830-260, ThermoWorks (800-393-6434, **www.thermoworks.com**).

PAGE 32: UNIVERSAL PAN LID
- Progressive Stainless-Steel Universal Fry Pan Lid SS-31: $14.99, item #6141, Kitchen Kapers (800-455-5567, **www.kitchenkapers.com**).

U.S. POSTAL SERVICE STATEMENT OF OWNERSHIP, MANAGEMENT AND CIRCULATION

1. Publication Title: Cook's Illustrated; 2. Publication No. 1068-2821; 3. Filing Date: 9/28/10; 4. Issue Frequency: Jan/Feb, Mar/Apr, May/Jun, Jul/Aug, Sep/Oct, Nov/Dec; 5. No. of Issues Published Annually: 6; 6. Annual Subscription Price: $35.70; 7. Complete Mailing Address of Known Office of Publication: 17 Station Street, Brookline, MA 02445; 8. Complete Mailing Address of Headquarters or General Business Office of Publisher: 17 Station Street, Brookline, MA 02445; 9. Full Names and Complete Mailing Address of Publisher, Editor and Managing Editor: Publisher: Christopher Kimball, 17 Station Street, Brookline, MA 02445; Editor: Jack Bishop, 17 Station Street, Brookline, MA 02445; Managing Editor: Rebecca Hays, 17 Station Street, Brookline, MA 02445; 10. Owner: Boston Common Press Limited Partnership, Christopher Kimball, 17 Station Street, Brookline, MA 02445; 11. Known Bondholders, Mortgagees, and Other Securities: None; 12. Tax Status: Has Not Changed During Preceding 12 Months; 13. Publication Title: Cook's Illustrated; 14. Issue Date for Circulation Data Below: September/October 2010; 15a. Total Number of Copies: 1,053,420 (Sep/Oct 2010: 1,037,748); b. Paid Circulation: (1) Mailed Outside-County Paid Subscriptions Stated on PS Form 3541: 800,694 (Sep/Oct 2010: 798,138); (2) Mailed In-County Paid Subscriptions Stated on PS Form 3541: 0 (Sep/Oct 2010: 0); (3) Paid Distribution Outside the Mail Including Sales Through Dealers and Carriers, Street Vendors, Counter Sales, and Other Paid Distribution Outside the USPS: 88,225 (Sep/Oct 2010: 85,811); (4) Paid Distribution by Other Classes of Mail through the USPS: 0 (Sep/Oct 2010: 0); c. Total Paid Distribution: 888,919 (Sep/Oct 2010: 883,949); d. Free or Nominal Rate Distribution: (1) Free or Nominal Rate Outside-County Copies Included on PS Form 3541: 4,753 (Sep/Oct 2010: 4,461); (2) Free or Nominal Rate In-County Copies Included on Form PS 3541: 0 (Sep/Oct 2010: 0); (3) Free or Nominal Rate Copies Mailed at Other Classes Through the USPS: 0 (Sep/Oct 2010: 0); (4) Free or Nominal Rate Distribution Outside the Mail: 50 (Sep/Oct 2010: 50); e. Total Free or Nominal Rate Distribution: 4,803 (Sep/Oct 2010: 4,511); f. Total Distribution: 893,721 (Sep/Oct 2010: 888,460); g. Copies Not Distributed: 159,698 (Sep/Oct 2010: 149,288); h. Total: 1,053,420 (Sep/Oct 2010: 1,037,748); i. Percent Paid: 99.46% (Sep/Oct 2010: 99.49%).

INDEX
January & February 2011

NEW RECIPES ON THE WEB
Available free for 4 months at
www.CooksIllustrated.com/feb11

Nut-Crusted Chicken Cutlets with Bacon
Nut-Crusted Chicken Cutlets with Lime and
  Chipotle
Thin-Crust White Pizza

COOK'S VIDEOS
Available for members at
www.CooksIllustrated.com

BASIC COUSCOUS
How to create flavorful couscous

CAESAR SALAD
Crouton secrets

CLASSIC GINGERBREAD CAKE
See how we add ginger flavor

GLAZED SALMON
Steps to great glazed salmon

GREEK SPINACH AND FETA PIE
Bryan builds the layers

NUT-CRUSTED CHICKEN CUTLETS
Look: Nut crust perfected

OUR FAVORITE CHILI
Andrea makes her favorite chili

SPAGHETTI WITH OLIVE OIL AND LEMON
It's simple: See for yourself

SPLIT PEA AND HAM SOUP
Building soup from the ground up

TESTING PARING KNIVES
Get in on the actual tests

THIN-CRUST PIZZA
Look: The crust stays stretched

AMERICA'S TEST KITCHEN
Public television's most popular cooking show

Join the millions of home cooks who watch our show, *America's Test Kitchen*, on public television every week. For more information, including recipes and program times, visit www.AmericasTestKitchenTV.com.

DOWNLOAD OUR FREE Cook's Illustrated iPhone App

Inside you'll find a collection of our top recipes, along with videos that explain how to make them. You can also access many of our most popular taste test results, useful kitchen timers, and an interactive shopping list that helps you plan ahead. Are you a member of CooksIllustrated.com? If so, you'll have access to every recipe, video, and taste test on the website. Go to CooksIllustrated.com/iPhone.

Classic Gingerbread Cake, 25

Nut-Crusted Chicken Cutlets, 9

Caesar Salad, 19

Our Favorite Chili, 15

Basic Couscous, 12

Thin-Crust Pizza, 8

Glazed Salmon, 11

Spaghetti with Lemon and Olive Oil, 21

Split Pea and Ham Soup, 20

Greek Spinach and Feta Pie, 23

PHOTOGRAPHY: CARL TREMBLAY; STYLING: MARIE PIRAINO

Fleur Verte

Ekte Gjetost

Valençay

Mothais-sur-feuille

Clochette

Majorero

Goat Gouda

Ibores

Bucheron

Sainte-Maure de Touraine

GOAT CHEESES

NUMBER 109

MARCH & APRIL 2011

COOK'S
ILLUSTRATED

Dressing Up Steaks
Shortcut to 4-Star Pan Sauce

Peruvian Roast Chicken
Crisp Skin, Real Latin Flavor

Quick Mushroom Ragu

Broccoli-Cheese Soup
Throw Out the Rule Book

Rating Peanut Butters
"Natural" Gets Creamed

Secrets to Perfect Whole-Wheat Bread

Should You Buy a $250 Toaster Oven?

Herb-Crusted Fish Fillets
Real Boston Cream Pie
Crispy Potato Galette
All About Butter
Cuban Black Beans and Rice

www.CooksIllustrated.com
$5.95 U.S./$6.95 CANADA

0 74470 62805 7

0 4>

CONTENTS
March & April 2011

COOK'S ILLUSTRATED

Founder and Editor — Christopher Kimball
Editorial Director — Jack Bishop
Executive Editor, Magazines — John Willoughby
Executive Editor — Amanda Agee
Test Kitchen Director — Erin McMurrer
Managing Editor — Rebecca Hays
Senior Editors — Keith Dresser
Lisa McManus
Associate Features Editor — Elizabeth Bomze
Senior Copy Editor — Catherine Tumber
Copy Editor — Nell Beram
Associate Editors — Amy Graves
Bryan Roof
Test Cooks — Andrea Geary
Andrew Janjigian
Yvonne Ruperti
Dan Souza
Assistant Editor — Taizeth Sierra
Executive Assistant — Christine Gordon
Editorial Assistant — Shannon Friedmann Hatch
Assistant Test Kitchen Director — Gina Nistico
Senior Kitchen Assistant — Leah Rovner
Kitchen Assistants — Maria Elena Delgado
Ena Gudiel
Edward Tundidor
Executive Producer — Melissa Baldino
Associate Producer — Stephanie Stender
Contributing Editors — Matthew Card
Dawn Yanagihara
Consulting Editor — Scott Brueggeman
Science Editor — Guy Crosby, Ph.D.

Managing Editor, Special Issues — Todd Meier
Assistant Editor, Special Issues — Chris Dudley
Assistant Test Kitchen, Special Issues — Danielle DeSiato-Hallman
Editorial Assistant, Special Issues — Brittany Allen

Online Managing Editor — David Tytell
Online Editor — Kate Mason
Online Assistant Editor — Mari Levine
Online Editorial Assistant — Eric Grzymkowski
Online Media Producer — Peter Tannenbaum
Media Producer — Alexandra Pournaras
Associate Editor/Camera Operator — Nick Dakoulas
Assistant Editor/Camera Operator — Jesse Prent

Design Director — Amy Klee
Art Director — Julie Bozzo
Designer — Lindsey Timko
Deputy Art Director, Marketing/Web — Christine Vo
Staff Photographer — Daniel J. van Ackere

Vice President, Marketing — David Mack
Circulation Director — Doug Wicinski
Circulation & Fulfillment Manager — Carrie Horan
Partnership Marketing Manager — Pamela Putprush
Marketing Assistant — Lauren Perkins
Database & Direct Mail Director — Adam Perry
Senior Database Analyst — Marina Sakharova
Product Operations Director — Steven Browall
Product Promotions Director — Tom Conway
E-Commerce Marketing Director — Hugh Buchan
E-Commerce Marketing Manager — Laurel Zeidman
E-Commerce Marketing Coordinator — Sandra Greenberg
Marketing Copywriter — David Goldberg
Customer Service Manager — Jacqueline Valerio
Customer Service Representatives — Jillian Nannicelli
Kate Sokol

Sponsorship Sales Director — Marcy McCreary
Retail Sales & Marketing Manager — Emily Logan
Sponsorship & Marketing Coordinator — Bailey Vatalaro

Production Director — Guy Rochford
Senior Project Manager — Alice Carpenter
Production & Traffic Coordinator — Kate Hux
Senior Production Manager — Jessica L. Quirk
Asset & Workflow Manager — Andrew Mannone
Production & Imaging Specialists — Judy Blomquist
Heather Dube
Lauren Pettapiece

Technology Director — Rocco Lombardo
Lead Developer — Scott Thompson
Web Developers — Bach Bui
Christopher Candelora
James Madden
Robert Martinez
Tikky Shiwala
Senior Web Production Coordinator — Evan Davis
Web Production Assistants — Debbie Chiang
Jennifer Millett
Systems Administrator — Marcus Walser

VP, New Media Product Development — Barry Kelly
Lead Developer — Bharat Ruparel
Senior Information Architect — Melissa MacQuarrie
Social Media Manager — Steph Yiu
Graphic Designer — Eggert Ragnarsson
Web Developer — Anand Kumar

Chief Financial Officer — Sharyn Chabot
Human Resources Director — Adele Shapiro
Controller — Mandy Shito
Financial Director — Wayne Saville
Senior Accountant — Aaron Goranson
Staff Accountant — Connie Forbes
Accounts Payable Specialist — Steven Kasha
Office Manager — Michael Pickett
Receptionist — Henrietta Murray
Publicity — Deborah Broide

PRINTED IN THE USA

TAPROOTS Many plants anchor themselves to the earth with a taproot—a vertical transport for nutrients and water. Carrots, perhaps the most iconic taproot, are culinary chameleons, boasting a sweet taste that works in everything from stir-fries to cream cheese–frosted layer cakes. Once roasted or pureed into soup, creamy parsnips develop a sweet nuttiness. Crisp, spicy radishes and apple-like jícama are typically served raw. Rutabagas are larger than turnips and have a similar sweet, peppery taste. Beneath the gnarled, homely surface of celeriac, or celery root, waits flesh with the combined flavor of celery and parsley. Rough-skinned burdock adds earthy sweetness to Japanese dishes. Some say salsify tastes of oysters; others say artichoke hearts. Jewel-toned beets are the beauties of the taproot world; their rich, sweet flesh can be served raw, roasted, steamed, or pickled.

COVER (Asparagus): Robert Papp; BACK COVER (Taproots): John Burgoyne

America's TEST KITCHEN

America's Test Kitchen is a very real 2,500-square-foot kitchen located just outside of Boston. It is the home of *Cook's Illustrated* and *Cook's Country* magazines and is the workday destination of more than three dozen test cooks, editors, and cookware specialists. Our mission is to test recipes over and over again until we understand how and why they work and until we arrive at the best version. We also test kitchen equipment and supermarket ingredients in search of brands that offer the best value and performance. You can watch us work by tuning in to America's Test Kitchen (www.AmericasTestKitchenTV.com) on public television.

PICKUP TRUCK RULES

Two years ago, I saw a bumper sticker plastered on the back window of a Ford 250. It said, POSSUM: THE OTHER WHITE MEAT. Amusing, to be sure, but this quip also represents the self-reliance and sense of humor of pickup truck culture. Here is a quick rundown of the other maxims that define this way of life.

Rule Number 1: Do It; Don't Talk About It. Experts are the folks who never give advice. If you are always telling someone how to do something, you probably don't know how to do it yourself.

Rule Number 2: Never Ask If You Can Help; Just Help. A friend was unloading lumber off of a pickup truck when a neighbor stopped by to borrow something. He asked if he could help, was told that no assistance was necessary, and then watched for 20 minutes as my friend unloaded his truck. You never need permission to help.

Rule Number 3: Some Dogs Are Pickup Truck Dogs and Some Aren't. Rabbit dogs (beagles) stay outside all winter, but Labs, good for bird hunting, are kept inside and ride in the pickup next to the driver. It's not fair, but it's a fact of life: Some dogs are pickup truck dogs and some aren't.

Rule Number 4: Saturday Is a Workday (Sundays Are Half Days). The only thing worse than working is not working. If you are not out of the house and on the road by 7 a.m., well, you aren't working hard enough. And be careful about stopping for lunch—it slows you down.

Rule Number 5: The Garage Is a Family Room. The garage is full of expensive toys (tools), and it has a kerosene heater for cold days and a small refrigerator for the coffee creamer and Labatts. It's a good place to rehash hunting stories and catch up with neighbors. The first place to look for a neighbor on a Saturday is in the garage, not in the house.

Rule Number 6: There Are Ford People and Chevy People. If you drive a Ford pickup, you don't have much to say to those who drive Chevys, even if it costs you $3,000 to replace a $60 part due to poor engineering. Only flatlanders buy Nissans.

Rule Number 7: The Past Is Present, the Future Is Tomorrow. Everyone and everything that has gone before still exists, like the long-departed bachelor farmers who used to attend covered dish suppers at the corner house, or the time Baldwin Brook overflowed its banks and changed course. The future is always a day away.

Rule Number 8: You're from Where? The universe stops at the town line. If you're from the next town, you are a friend, not a neighbor. If you're from two towns away, you are from "out of town." If you're from three towns away, you need a passport.

Rule Number 9: Real Men Carry Pocket Knives. Your pickup has a towing strap, a portable battery charger, a come-along, and a toolbox just behind the cab. You can pull a tractor out of a ditch, loosen a frozen bolt, hang a door, fix a lawn mower, sharpen a chain saw, and start a fire with green wood. The only thing that can't be fixed is your teenage daughter—the one who just got three new tattoos.

Rule Number 10: Weather Means Business. Weather only matters when it affects your livelihood: snowplowing, sugaring (cold nights, warm days), haying, and planting. The rest of the time, weather is just conversation.

Christopher Kimball

Rule Number 11: Your Cheatin' Heart. Go ahead and fall in love with Reba McEntire or any other country music singer, since Nashville is more than two towns away. The waitress at the Bog, the local watering hole, is definitely *not* cute—that is, if you wish to continue speaking in a deep voice.

Rule Number 12: Hunting Is Not a Sport; It's a Religion. Hunting is a form of pagan worship that is only allowed for two weeks in November. The rest of the time, you talk about it. That's why conversations with people who don't hunt are so short: There isn't much else to talk about.

Rule Number 13: NASCAR Is Not a Sport Either (see Rule Number 12). When NASCAR is on, the remote, the armchair, and the living room are yours. If you can't get to a TV, you turn on the radio. That's why they make big construction-site radios that are battery-powered: In an emergency, you can listen to NASCAR in the woods.

Rule Number 14: Real Men Entertain in the Basement. That's where you keep your hunting gear, your pellet stove, and the old dog-haired sofa that's not good enough for upstairs. The living room is for women, the Christmas tree, framed graduation photos of the kids, and the bird dog (and, of course, NASCAR Sundays).

Rule Number 15: The Country Store Is the Internet. The local store is a repository of every piece of gossip or news about heartbreak, illness, feuds, and coming events. To go "on line" in the country, just go down to the country store. To "log in," just speak to the person behind the counter.

FOR INQUIRIES, ORDERS, OR MORE INFORMATION

www.CooksIllustrated.com
At www.CooksIllustrated.com, you can order books and subscriptions, sign up for our free e-newsletter, or renew your magazine subscription. Join the website and gain access to 18 years of *Cook's Illustrated* recipes, equipment tests, and ingredient tastings, as well as companion videos for every recipe in this issue.

COOKBOOKS
We sell more than 50 cookbooks by the editors of *Cook's Illustrated*. To order, visit our bookstore at www.CooksIllustrated.com.

COOK'S ILLUSTRATED MAGAZINE
Cook's Illustrated magazine (ISSN 1068-2821), number 109, is published bimonthly by Boston Common Press Limited Partnership, 17 Station St., Brookline, MA 02445. Copyright 2011 Boston Common Press Limited Partnership. Periodicals postage paid at Boston, Mass., and additional mailing offices USPS #012487. Publications Mail Agreement No. 40020778. Return undeliverable Canadian addresses to P.O. Box 875, Station A, Windsor, ON N9A 6P2. POSTMASTER: Send address changes to Cook's Illustrated, P.O. Box 6018, Harlan, IA 51593-1518. For subscription and gift subscription orders, subscription inquiries, or change-of-address notices, visit us at www.AmericasTestKitchen.com/customerservice or write us at Cook's Illustrated, P.O. Box 6018, Harlan, IA 51593-1518.

FOR LIST RENTAL INFORMATION, CONTACT Specialists Marketing Services, Inc., 777 Terrace Ave., 4th Floor, Hasbrouck Heights, NJ 07604; 201-865-5800.

EDITORIAL OFFICE 17 Station St., Brookline, MA 02445; 617-232-1000; fax 617-232-1572. Subscription inquiries, visit www.AmericasTestKitchen.com/customerservice or call 800-526-8442.

POSTMASTER Send all new orders, subscription inquiries, and change-of-address notices to Cook's Illustrated, P.O. Box 6018, Harlan, IA 51593-1518.

⇒ ANDREA GEARY & ANDREW JANJIGIAN ⇐

Cake Miracle Worker?

Have you ever used a product from King Arthur called Cake Enhancer? Would you recommend it?

PAM MEADOWS
SAN DIEGO, CALIF.

➤The King Arthur Flour Company describes its Cake Enhancer as a "miracle ingredient." When added to cake batter at the creaming stage, it supposedly renders the crumb soft and moist and increases shelf life. The mysterious product contains rice starch, polyglycerol esters, and mono- and diglycerides—the same additives found in many boxed cake mixes and commercial baked goods.

Intrigued, we ordered the product, used it to "enhance" our favorite fluffy yellow cake, and compared the results with the same cake baked as usual. On the first day, the cakes tasted identical and shared the same soft, tender, and moist crumb. On the third day, tasters found the enhanced cake slightly more moist and tender than the unenhanced cake, and they rated it more favorably.

Here's how Cake Enhancer works: Over time, the starches in any baked good will begin to retrograde, bonding together more tightly and becoming harder and firmer. As this happens, the starches absorb any available water in the crumb, turning it drier and tougher. The additives in Cake Enhancer significantly slow starch retrogradation, so the cake tastes better longer.

Our conclusion: King Arthur Cake Enhancer will help keep a three-day-old homemade cake tasting fresher, but in our experience, cakes are usually eaten long before they get that old. In most instances, there will be no reason to stir in this packet of additives.

CAKE ENHANCER
This "miracle" product from King Arthur prolongs the shelf life of cakes.

Evaporated Milk in a Pinch?

If I don't have regular whole milk on hand, can I substitute evaporated milk in baked goods and desserts?

JIM McCORMICK
VALDOSTA, GA.

➤Evaporated milk is made by slowly heating milk to remove about half of its water—a process that develops a light golden color and mildly sweet flavor. Nestlé states that Carnation evaporated milk can be substituted in a 1:1 ratio for regular whole milk. To test this claim, we opened a few cans to make sponge cake, vanilla pudding, and Parker House rolls, and compared the results with the same recipes made with regular whole milk. The results were imperfect across the board: The evaporated-milk cake exhibited a firmer structure than the cake made with regular milk. And although the consistency of the evaporated-milk pudding was acceptable, its delicate vanilla flavor was marred by caramel undertones. The Parker House rolls made with evaporated milk emerged from the oven more stunted and much darker than rolls made with regular milk.

The bottom line: Evaporated milk is a poor substitute for regular milk. The reason? It contains about 6.6 percent fat and 10 percent caramelized lactose (milk sugar), versus the 3.3 percent fat and 4.5 percent lactose in regular milk—differences significant enough to interfere with proper structure in baked goods.

Better Than Butter?

I've seen a new Land O'Lakes product in the supermarket called Fresh Buttery Taste Spread. How does it stack up to real butter?

ELIZABETH HERTEL
PROVIDENCE, R.I.

➤Fresh Buttery Taste Spread is a soybean oil–based product with a label touting "70 percent less saturated fat than butter, 0 grams of trans fat per serving, and no cholesterol." We compared the spread to regular unsalted Land O'Lakes butter smeared on bread and baked into pound cake, chocolate chip cookies, and pie crust. On their toast, tasters unanimously preferred the real butter, complaining about an "artificial" taste and a "plasticky" texture in the spread. This soybean-oil product's performance in baked goods was also less than perfect, yielding cake, cookies, and pie crust that were unusually dense. Why would this be so? It is likely that the spread contains a higher percentage of water than unsalted butter—and we've found that even small amounts of extra water added to baked goods can lead to increased gluten development and a tougher, denser crumb.

About the only thing that Land O'Lakes Fresh Buttery Taste Spread did well was spread easily—but it wasn't worth the trade-off in flavor.

STICK WITH BUTTER
Land O'Lakes Fresh Buttery Taste Spread can't compete with real butter.

Getting (R)amped Up

I have been seeing a lot of ramps at farmers' markets. What are they, and how should I use them?

PEGGY EVANS
SANTA MONICA, CALIF.

➤The ramp (also known as wild leek, wild garlic, or ramson) is a member of the onion family that sprouts up in early spring in woodlands as far-flung as Canada, North Carolina, Missouri, and Minnesota. The bulb of the vegetable looks a little like scallion, but the leaves are flatter and broader, closely resembling those of the lily of the valley. Both bulb and leaves can be used raw or cooked in applications that call for onions, leeks, or scallions. To prepare ramps, trim off the roots and remove any loose or discolored skin that clings to the bulbs, then rinse well.

We sampled ramps sautéed in butter and tossed with pasta, as well as pickled in a simple vinegar mixture. Tasters described the flavor as slightly more pungent than the more familiar alliums, with hints of garlic and chive. We also tasted the raw leaves, finding them slightly grassy, reminiscent of a mild jalapeño.

LEEKS GONE WILD
Wild leeks, or ramps, have an onion-like pungency and a slightly peppery bite.

Shades of Rhubarb

Is it important to seek out rhubarb that's red versus green? Is the red color an indication of greater ripeness and better flavor?

CHARLES NATHAN
GREENVILLE, S.C.

➤We simmered chunks of red and green rhubarb in separate batches with orange juice and sugar (to soften the plant's tartness) and asked tasters to compare them. All tasters found the red rhubarb to be far more appealing to look at, but they judged the green rhubarb just as vibrant in terms of taste. It turns out that a red color in rhubarb, a product of anthocyanin pigments, varies according to variety and is not necessarily an indication of ripeness. These pigments are nearly tasteless—in fact, they are used in natural food colorings because their flavor is virtually undetectable even in high concentrations. Red or green, rhubarb's sour flavor is mainly due to the presence of oxalic and citric acids. So, for a better-looking dish, seek out the scarlet stalks, but the green ones will taste just as delicious.

Brighter, Greener Pesto

I've heard that you can prevent pesto from darkening by blanching the basil before putting it in the food processor. Does this trick really work?

STEPHEN THOMSON
DEDHAM, MASS.

➤ To find out, we made two batches of pesto: one with fresh basil and one with blanched leaves. The pesto made with fresh basil started to darken as soon as we scooped it out of the food processor, but the blanched batch stayed bright green even after sitting for a few hours on the counter. When we sampled the sauces, tasters found them virtually identical in flavor. The good news continued: After an entire week in the refrigerator, the blanched-basil pesto was still a brilliant green, as was a sample that we froze for three weeks and then thawed. The sample that had been frozen tasted great, too.

Here's why blanching works: Cutting, processing, or bruising activates enzymes within the basil leaf that promote rapid oxidation, darkening its bright green color. Blanching (dunking the leaves in boiling water for 20 to 30 seconds, then plunging them into ice water) inactivates those enzymes, so the color holds fast.

If you're making a limited quantity of pesto to use right away, blanching is hardly worth the trouble. But if you're transforming a bumper crop into a year's worth of pesto, the process will ensure vivid color that lasts.

BLANCHED = BRIGHT   **UNBLANCHED = DULL**

To set the brilliant green color of basil, blanch it.

Parchment That Won't Get Parched

Is it okay to heat parchment paper higher than the temperature range listed on the packaging? Your recipes sometimes call for this.

RANDY NEWMANN
ENFIELD, CONN.

➤ Most parchment paper is rated for use at temperatures no higher than 420 to 450 degrees. But it's true—we occasionally recommend using this liner for bread and pizza baked as high as 500 degrees. Phone calls to several manufacturers, including Regency and Reynolds, put any safety worries to rest: Using parchment at higher-than-recommended temperatures does not release noxious chemicals, and the paper will not burn. But there's no question that it can darken and turn brittle. For pizza and other flatbreads that bake in 20 minutes or less, the parchment doesn't turn brittle quickly enough for it to be an issue. For dishes that are in the oven at high temperatures for more than 30 minutes, such as our Almost No-Knead Bread, parchment can break down enough to fall apart—a particular issue in this recipe, in which we use the parchment as "handles" to remove the bread from the hot pan. In this case, we'd recommend seeking out paper rated for use at the highest temperature available (Regency brand, rated for up to 450 degrees, is the one we recommend for prolonged high-heat applications) and placing a strip of folded aluminum foil (4 or 5 inches wide) beneath the parchment when baking. The foil had no detrimental effect on the color or texture of the bread we baked, and it made for easy removal of the loaves, even after the parchment itself had become brittle.

The Thick and Thin of Asparagus

Sometimes the asparagus stalks at my local market are as thin as pencils; other times they're fat and meaty. Is thickness an indication of maturity? And does size affect taste?

JANET POTTER
NEWARK, N.J.

➤ Asparagus spears are the plant shoots of an underground crown that can produce for up to 20 years. The thickness of a spear has nothing to do with its age—that is, a thin spear will not mature into a thicker spear. Rather, diameter is determined by two factors: the age of the entire plant (younger crowns produce more slender stalks) and its variety.

So, which size is preferable? We snapped off the woody bottoms of fat and skinny spears and tasted them side by side, both steamed and tossed with olive oil and salt. While both types tasted equally sweet, nutty, and grassy, we expected the delicate-looking thin spears to be more tender. To our surprise, the thicker spears actually had the better texture (if only by a hair). The reason? The vegetable's fiber is slightly more concentrated in thinner spears.

Since thick and thin spears are both good bets, choose the size that best suits your cooking method. Thicker stalks are better for broiling and roasting because they will stand up to the intense dry heat that would quickly shrivel skinnier spears. We also like thicker spears for grilling since they are easier to manipulate. Quick-cooking thinner spears are good candidates for steaming and stir-frying.

DID YOU KNOW? All products reviewed by America's Test Kitchen, home of *Cook's Illustrated* and *Cook's Country* magazines, are independently chosen, researched, and reviewed by our editors. We buy products for testing at retail locations and do not accept unsolicited samples for testing. We do not accept or receive payment or consideration from product manufacturers or retailers. Manufacturers and retailers are not told in advance of publication which products we have recommended. We list suggested sources for recommended products as a convenience to our readers but do not endorse specific retailers.

SEND US YOUR QUESTIONS We will provide a complimentary one-year subscription for each letter we print. Send your inquiry, name, address, and daytime telephone number to Notes from Readers, *Cook's Illustrated*, P.O. Box 470589, Brookline, MA 02447, or to NotesFromReaders@AmericasTestKitchen.com.

WHAT IS IT?

Can you tell me what this device is? It's been in my mother's utensil drawer for as long as we can remember, but we've never known how to use it.

SUZANNE McCRAIG
WAYLAND, MASS.

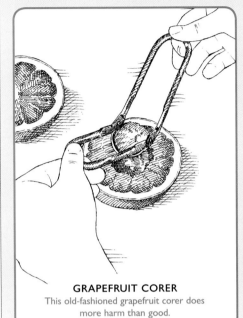

GRAPEFRUIT CORER
This old-fashioned grapefruit corer does more harm than good.

Your item is a grapefruit corer, manufactured by the Turner & Seymour Manufacturing Company of Torrington, Connecticut. The tool was first patented in 1923 and then refined at least three more times in the decade that followed. The device, which measures about 4½ inches high, is made from stainless steel. As its name indicates, the apparatus was designed to remove the middle portion of a grapefruit halved along the equator so that the fruit is easier to eat. The operator forces the circular blade through the fruit and then pulls the handles apart to loosen the core. However, when we put this corer to the test, the cutter struggled to make its way through the flesh, nearly demolishing the grapefruit. And when we finally succeeded in freeing the core, it was no easier to spoon bites from the fruit than had we left the core intact. We'll pass on this antique tool, preferring to use a simple grapefruit spoon to get the job done.

Quick Tips

≥ COMPILED BY SHANNON FRIEDMANN HATCH ≤

Put a Cork on It

Drew Sartin of Birmingham, Ala., has kitchen cabinets that always slam shut after someone reaches for dishes, spices, or other culinary sundries. In lieu of buying adhesive-backed felt to soften the blow, he sliced a wine cork into thin disks and glued them onto the inside corners of the cabinets.

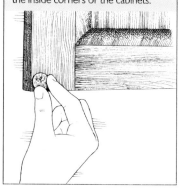

Slicing to the End

Slicing to the very end of oblong foods like zucchini, cucumber, and salami can be dicey work, which is why Cori Ander of St. Anthony, Minn., came up with this technique. She spears one end of the food with a corn holder just deep enough for the prongs to get a good grip. She then grasps the corn holder, leaving her fingers out of harm's way as she slices all the way to the end.

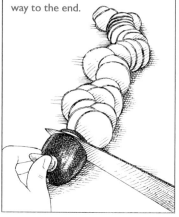

Seeding Peppers

Jeffrey Dunn of Philadelphia, Pa., uses a grapefruit spoon to scrape the seeds and veins out of fiery chiles and mild bell peppers. The spoon's serrated edge pulls the veins from the inner core and walls, and its rounded sides glide around the chile or bell pepper more easily than a knife.

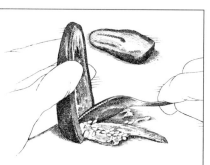

When the Pit Sticks to the Knife

In the test kitchen, we remove the pit from a halved avocado by inserting a knife into the pit and twisting the base of the fruit to release it. But what's the best way to remove the speared pit from the knife? Two readers chime in:

A. Allison White of Huntington, W.Va., places her thumb and forefinger on either side of the blade where the top of the pit meets the blade, as if giving the blade a pinch. With a little downward pressure from her fingers, the pit falls right off.
B. A firm tap of the pit against the cutting board works for Kerry Jones of Sag Harbor, N.Y.—the pit splits right in two. Problem solved.

Cutting Kernels

Paula Osorio of Loveland, Ohio, uses her mandoline to quickly take corn off the cob. After setting the mandoline to ¼-inch thickness and placing a pie plate underneath to catch the kernels, she grips the corn with a kitchen towel for safety, then strips each ear in four quick sweeps down the blade.

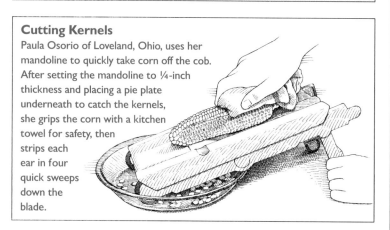

Making a Decorative Ice Ring

When Lori Melucci of Lincoln, R.I., isn't baking cakes with her Bundt pan, she uses it to mold a decorative ice ring for punch.

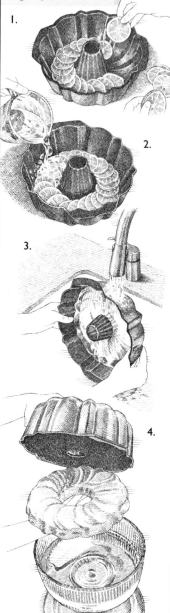

1. Arrange a layer of thinly sliced citrus rings over the bottom of a Bundt pan. Pour enough cold water over the fruit to barely cover. Freeze until firm, about 1 hour.
2. Add enough ice water to cover the fruit by 1½ inches (about 2 cups). Freeze until firm, about 3 hours.
3. When you're ready to use the ice ring, run the bottom of the mold under warm water until the ice ring releases.
4. Place the ring in your punch bowl.

Cracking Pistachios with Ease

With their partially open shells, pistachios are great for snacking—but inevitably there's a handful of nuts in the mix with the shells sealed tight. Jennifer Cain of Brooklyn, N.Y., has discovered that her garlic press offers an easy way to open them up.

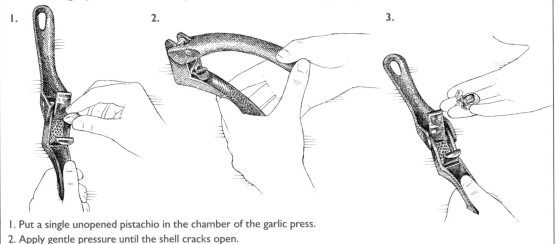

1. Put a single unopened pistachio in the chamber of the garlic press.
2. Apply gentle pressure until the shell cracks open.
3. Remove the pistachio and discard the broken shell.

Quick Pour

Carl Foreman of Middlefield, Conn., literally cuts corners when pouring out an entire box of broth—and eliminates the usual glug.

1. Open the container's plastic tab and peel off its seal.
2. Lift the opposite end's glued cardboard corner. Snip it off with a sharp pair of kitchen shears. Squeeze the box to open the slit, then pour from that end.

Really Fast Fries

By using his apple slicer, DL Smith of Dexter, Mich., gets his spuds cut and ready for the fryer in no time.

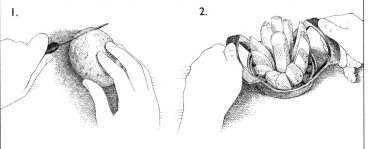

1. Slice one end of the potato to create a stable base. Set the potato cut side down on the cutting board.
2. Push the apple slicer down over the potato, sectioning it into steak fry–size wedges. Cut the center cylinder in half lengthwise before cooking.

Lazy Cook's Lattice

Jane Ikemura of Los Angeles, Calif., has found an easy way to make straight lattice strips to top her pies.

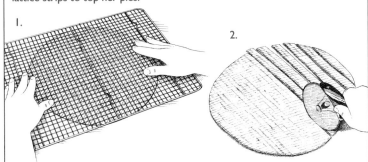

1. Roll out the dough according to the recipe, then lightly press the top of a cooling rack into the dough.
2. Using the rack's indentations as your guide cut the dough into 1¼-inch strips (every fourth line works with our winning model from CIA Bakeware) with a pizza wheel.

Keeping the Chill in Chilled Pastry

Sharon Edgar of Santa Rosa, Calif., has a trick for keeping pastry dough—and the butter it contains—as cold as possible as she rolls it out, helping to ensure the flakiest biscuits and pie crusts.

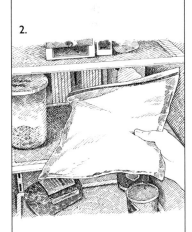

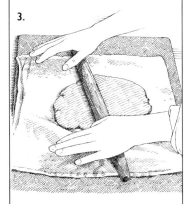

1. Cut a sheet of cotton canvas (available at fabric stores) into a 16-inch square; launder and dry.
2. Fold the canvas, place it in a zipper-lock bag, and freeze.
3. When you're ready to use it, unfold the canvas and lay it on the countertop, sprinkle it with flour, and place the dough on top to roll.

The Ultimate Steak Sauce

Could we bring the ultra-rich flavor and glossy consistency of a classic French demi-glace to steak sauce without spending all day roasting bones and reducing stock?

§ BY ANDREW JANJIGIAN €

It's easy enough to finish a seared steak with a quick pan sauce or a knob of flavored butter, but anyone who's dined in a fine French restaurant knows that nothing compares to a sauce made with the ultra-savory, full-bodied reduction known as demi-glace. The preparation has been a hallmark of haute cuisine since the days of the 19th-century French chef Auguste Escoffier, and chefs trained in classic French technique tend to keep a supply on hand not only to dress up steak, but as a meaty flavor foundation for soups, sauces, and sautés.

But making demi-glace is another matter. The time-consuming process is really only feasible in a restaurant kitchen. The process in a nutshell: Veal bones are roasted for a couple of hours with aromatics; the roasting pan is deglazed, releasing all the flavorful browned bits that will help enrich the stock; the whole works are transferred to a stock pot with wine and several quarts of water where it all gurgles gently for at least six hours. The stock is then strained and reduced to an ultra-concentrated, glossy, silky essence.

I wasn't about to delve into such fussy work in my own kitchen. But this rich, velvety sauce is too good to be left only to restaurant chefs. Surely with some experimenting I could find a shortcut.

Cutting Corners

The test kitchen already has a good technique for pan-searing steaks (our preferred cuts are strip and rib-eyes), so I immediately got to work on the demi-glace. I started by browning carrot, onion, and garlic chunks in a Dutch oven before deglazing with a little red wine and beef broth. Once the mixture had boiled down and thickened a bit, I took a taste. The result wasn't terrible, but its flavor was thin and it had no real body to speak of—hardly something that could stand as the backbone to a sauce.

I had one quick idea for amping up the flavor: In a traditional demi-glace, the vegetables are usually cut into large chunks, which break down and release

Our quick demi-glace makes a rich, silky base for countless pan sauces.

Watch This Sauce Take Shape
Video available FREE for 4 months at www.CooksIllustrated.com/apr11

flavor over the course of roasting and simmering. But since I needed big flavor fast, I pulsed the aromatics in the food processor until they were roughly chopped, figuring their increased surface area would offer more opportunity for flavorful browning. I also added mushrooms and tomato paste (another component common in traditional demi-glace), knowing that both ingredients' meat-mimicking glutamates would increase the savory flavor. Sure enough, this batch—which I further enhanced with thyme, bay leaves, and peppercorns; then deglazed with red wine and a quart of beef broth; and reduced for about 25 minutes—showed definite flavor improvement. But it still didn't win over my tasters. Even after I'd worked this latest version into a classic herb pan sauce, they unenthusiastically pushed pieces of steak around in the still-thin reduction. My faux base still wasn't fooling anybody.

Building a Semi-Demi

There was no doubt what was missing: Without the meatiness and unctuous gelatin given up by roasted veal bones, my attempt would never be as savory or silky-textured as the real deal. I was at a loss for my next move, when a colleague reminded me of a similar conundrum when we tried to make full-bodied chicken soup without the time-consuming step of slow-simmering a chicken carcass. Our secret there? Ground chicken. The choice actually makes a lot of sense, as the goal with any stock is to extract as much flavor from the meat as possible—and the finer the bits, the quicker the flavor is extracted. Figuring the same principle would apply here, I grabbed a half pound of ground beef and browned it along with tomato paste for about 10 minutes before adding the vegetables. This was the breakthrough I'd been looking for: Though still not as full-bodied as I'd like, this base more than hinted at the flavor of roasted bones.

The consistency issue was a little trickier. Calves' bones are particularly rich in collagen, which prolonged roasting and simmering breaks down into rich gelatin. Even when I reduced my base to a near-syrupy consistency, the effect wasn't at all the same. But I did have something in my kitchen cupboard that might help: powdered gelatin. I stirred two packages into the final reduction (after straining the solids) and boiled it down to half a cup. As I'd hoped, this was all it took to turn my quick demi-glace silky and viscous.

This time, when I worked the base into my final steak sauces—fresh herbs, brandy with green peppercorns, and port wine were our favorites—my tasters mopped up every last drop. Admittedly, classically trained French chefs might be able to tell the difference between my "semi demi" and the true approach—but I'd bet they'd still want the recipe.

SAUCE BASE
MAKES ½ CUP

NOTE: The sauce base recipe yields more than called for in the steak recipe; leftovers can be refrigerated for up to 3 days or frozen for up to one month. Our preferred brands of beef broth are Rachael Ray Stock-in-a-Box and College Inn Bold Stock.

- 1 small onion, peeled and cut into rough ½-inch pieces
- 1 small carrot, peeled and cut into rough ½-inch pieces
- 8 ounces cremini mushrooms, stems trimmed and caps wiped clean and halved
- 2 medium garlic cloves, peeled
- 1 tablespoon vegetable oil
- 8 ounces 85 percent lean ground beef
- 1 tablespoon tomato paste
- 2 cups dry red wine
- 4 cups low-sodium beef broth (see note)
- 4 sprigs fresh thyme
- 2 bay leaves
- 2 teaspoons whole black peppercorns
- 2 packages (5 teaspoons) unflavored powdered gelatin

1. Process onion, carrot, mushrooms, and garlic in food processor into ⅛-inch pieces, 10 to 12 one-second pulses, scraping down sides of bowl as needed.

2. Heat oil in Dutch oven over medium-high heat until shimmering; add beef and tomato paste and cook, stirring frequently, until beef is well browned, 8 to 10 minutes. Add vegetable mixture and cook, stirring occasionally, until any exuded moisture has evaporated, about 8 minutes. Add wine and bring to simmer, scraping bottom of pan with wooden spoon to loosen browned bits. Add beef broth, thyme, bay leaves, and peppercorns; bring to boil. Reduce heat and gently boil, occasionally scraping bottom and sides of pot and skimming fat from surface, until reduced to 2 cups, 20 to 25 minutes.

3. Strain mixture through fine-mesh strainer set over small saucepan, pressing on solids with rubber spatula to extract as much liquid as possible (you should have about 1 cup stock). Sprinkle gelatin over stock and stir to dissolve. Place saucepan over medium-high heat and bring stock to boil. Gently boil, stirring occasionally, until reduced to ½ cup, 5 to 7 minutes. Remove from heat and cover to keep warm.

Two Routes to Super-Rich Sauce

Traditional French demi-glace relies on veal bones for its flavor and takes a full day to prepare. Our modern approach substitutes ground beef and gelatin and dramatically shortcuts the process.

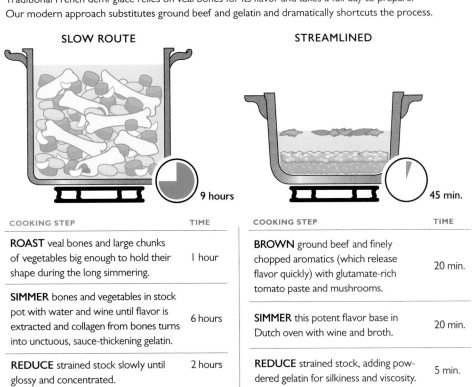

SLOW ROUTE		STREAMLINED	
	9 hours		45 min.
COOKING STEP	**TIME**	**COOKING STEP**	**TIME**
ROAST veal bones and large chunks of vegetables big enough to hold their shape during the long simmering.	1 hour	**BROWN** ground beef and finely chopped aromatics (which release flavor quickly) with glutamate-rich tomato paste and mushrooms.	20 min.
SIMMER bones and vegetables in stock pot with water and wine until flavor is extracted and collagen from bones turns into unctuous, sauce-thickening gelatin.	6 hours	**SIMMER** this potent flavor base in Dutch oven with wine and broth.	20 min.
REDUCE strained stock slowly until glossy and concentrated.	2 hours	**REDUCE** strained stock, adding powdered gelatin for silkiness and viscosity.	5 min.

PAN-SEARED STEAKS WITH HERB SAUCE
SERVES 4

NOTE: We like this sauce with strip or rib-eye steaks, but it will work with any type of pan-seared steak.

Steaks

- 1 tablespoon vegetable oil
- 4 boneless strip or rib-eye steaks, 1 to 1¼ inches thick (about 8 ounces each) (see note)
   Table salt and ground black pepper

Herb Sauce

- 1 small shallot, minced (about 2 tablespoons)
- ½ cup white wine
- ¼ cup Sauce Base (½ recipe)
- ¼ teaspoon white wine vinegar
- 1½ teaspoons minced fresh chives
- 1½ teaspoons minced fresh parsley leaves
- 1 teaspoon minced fresh tarragon leaves
- 1 tablespoon unsalted butter
   Table salt and ground black pepper

1. **FOR THE STEAKS:** Heat oil in 12-inch heavy-bottomed skillet over medium-high heat until smoking. Meanwhile, pat steaks dry with paper towels and season both sides with salt and pepper. Lay steaks in pan, leaving ¼ inch between them. Cook, not moving steaks, until well browned, about 4 minutes. Using tongs, flip steaks and continue to cook until instant-read thermometer inserted in center registers 120 degrees for rare to medium-rare, 3 to 7 minutes. Remove steaks to platter and tent loosely with foil while preparing herb sauce.

2. **FOR THE HERB SAUCE:** Return now-empty skillet to medium-low heat; add shallot and cook, stirring constantly, until lightly browned, about 2 minutes. Add wine and bring to simmer, scraping bottom of pan with wooden spoon to loosen browned bits. Add ¼ cup Sauce Base, vinegar, and any accumulated juices from steak; return to simmer and cook until slightly reduced, about 1 minute. Off heat, whisk in chives, parsley, tarragon, and butter; season with salt and pepper to taste. Spoon sauce over steaks and serve immediately.

PAN-SEARED STEAKS WITH BRANDY AND GREEN-PEPPERCORN SAUCE

Follow recipe for Pan-Seared Steaks with Herb Sauce, substituting brandy for white wine and red wine vinegar for white wine vinegar. Omit chives, parsley, tarragon, and butter. In step 2, add ¼ cup heavy cream, 2 tablespoons rinsed green peppercorns, and ¼ teaspoon chopped fresh thyme to skillet along with Sauce Base and vinegar.

PAN-SEARED STEAKS WITH PORT WINE SAUCE

Follow recipe for Pan-Seared Steaks with Herb Sauce, substituting ruby port for white wine and balsamic vinegar for white wine vinegar. Substitute ¼ teaspoon chopped fresh thyme for chives, parsley, and tarragon.

Simplifying Potato Galette

This crisp, earthy-tasting potato cake would be the perfect side dish—if it weren't for all the fussy layering. And does the cake have to fall apart when you slice it?

⇒ BY MATTHEW CARD ⇐

About once a year, I feel compelled to make *pommes Anna*, the classic French potato cake in which thin-sliced potatoes are tossed with clarified butter, tightly shingled in a skillet, and cooked slowly on the stovetop. The results can be glorious: a crisp, deeply bronzed crust encasing a creamy center that tastes of earthy, well-seasoned potatoes and sweet butter. It's about as good as non-deep-fried potatoes can get.

But despite my fondness for it, the galette is strictly special-occasion fare in my house. It's not the ingredient list—that part's brief. But thinly slicing and then diligently layering all those potato disks takes more time and attention to detail than I usually want to spend.

That said, plenty of existing recipes promise to make the dish "easy," "simple," and "foolproof," but I have yet to find one that really delivers on all counts. Only one that I've tried produced anything resembling the classic potato galette, and it differed from the others in two ways: First, it was roasted in a very hot (450-degree) oven, where the steady, ambient heat cooked the three-odd pounds of potatoes evenly (no chalky bits of raw tuber) and colored them nicely brown. Second, only the first layer of ⅛-inch-thick potato slices was neatly arranged; the rest were casually packed into the pan, eliminating most of the usual tedious layering work. Then, following tradition, the cooked galette was inverted out of the skillet, its crisp, golden exterior hiding the haphazard arrangement within.

But the recipe got me only halfway to my goal. The whole operation was still fussier than I wanted, and while the exterior of this improvised galette more or less looked the part, the tightly fused, striated layers that are the hallmark of classic pommes Anna were gone. And as soon as the knife hit the crust, the underlying slices slid apart.

To help ensure the potato cake slices cleanly, cut the raw potatoes no more than ⅛ inch thick.

Easing the Way

So, there was obvious potential in roasting, and I had a simple (if not totally foolproof) assembly method for the cake—but everything else in the recipe was up for consideration. For starters, there was the pan. Pommes Anna is traditionally cooked in a cast-iron skillet, which absorbs heat beautifully and turns out a galette with a substantial, deeply browned crust. But considering that this new iteration was cooked in the oven—and that inverting the already heavy vessel when it's full and searing hot can be intimidating—wasn't a baking pan worth a try? But as I tested my way through square, round, ovoid, rectangular, and springform pans, every one either warped in the hot oven or failed to generate much of a crust. A skillet really was the best tool for the job, though for convenience's sake—and to avoid a risk of the cake sticking to the pan bottom—I opted to forgo cast iron in favor of an oven-safe nonstick model.

Of course I'd need to compensate for the lighter, thinner pan's browning inadequacies, so I started fiddling with the placement of the oven rack on which the potatoes were cooking. Not surprisingly, the farther I lowered the rack toward the main heating element, the deeper the spuds browned. On the advice of several colleagues, I tried to eke out even more color and flavor by placing a pizza stone under the skillet. Sure enough, the thick slab (which absorbs heat in much the same way as a cast-iron skillet) guaranteed even browning—but it also required preheating for an hour and more heavy lifting than I wanted. Ultimately, I devised a much simpler two-pronged approach that worked equally well: First I got the galette cooking on the stovetop (where the direct flame jump-started the browning process), then I slid the pan onto the bottom rack of the hot oven. That gave me great browning with no stone.

Then there was the laborious clarifying step required by most recipes. This traditional technique involves barely simmering the butter until its water has just cooked off, then removing its milk solids. The idea is that milk solids in whole butter can cause the potatoes to stick to the bottom of the pan. But when I whipped up batches of my working recipe with clarified and whole butter, I couldn't tell the difference between the two. One more complication out of the way.

Starch Swap

I was pleased with my progress—the galette was deeply bronzed—but one lingering problem remained: How to keep the potatoes from sliding away from each other into a messy heap when I sliced it? One contributing factor, I realized, was my informal assembly method. Simply dumping most of the potatoes into the skillet may have been easy, but the bond between the piled-on slices was fairly haphazard. Still, the lack of adhesiveness often seemed exacerbated by the potatoes themselves. Sometimes they seemed to have more starchy glue, other times they cooked up overly dry. Up to this point I'd been using russet potatoes, which virtually every pommes Anna recipe, classic or otherwise, calls for. Switching to Yukon Golds didn't help. Though tasters preferred their buttery, sweet flavor, their texture was just as unreliable as the russets, and they weren't any better at keeping the layers together.

After giving it some thought, I realized that the variable "stick-ability" of the potatoes—whether Yukons or russets—had a simple explanation: The starch in any potato is always going to be a wild card, since it changes considerably depending how long the potato has been out of the ground. To eliminate this as a variable, one of my colleagues had a suggestion: Wash away the potato starch and find another means of gluing the slices together. Though counterintuitive, the idea was not entirely unfamiliar. A few years back we developed a recipe for potato *roesti* (pommes Anna's Swiss cousin, made with shredded spuds) in which we first rinsed the potatoes of their surface starch, then tossed them with a smidge of cornstarch to ensure cohesion.

Hopeful that the technique might transfer to my sliced potatoes—I decided to stick with the more flavorful Yukons—I proceeded with my working recipe, swirling the slices in a bowl of cold water to wash away their starch, then thoroughly patting them dry. (Excess moisture also impedes bonding.) Then I added a tablespoon of cornstarch to the melted butter, tossed the two components together, and proceeded with assembly. The result? Big improvement. Though the galette still wasn't quite as dense and compact as a meticulously layered pommes Anna is, at least the slices adhered to one another more reliably.

So what could I do about that loose layering of potatoes? Some recipes suggest occasionally tamping down on the galette as it cooks to compress the slices, but I wondered if more constant contact might be better. I placed a foil-wrapped brick on top of the cake for the first part of the cooking, and the layers did indeed stick together somewhat better, but unevenly—the outer rim was still loose. Rummaging around for something broader and rounder, I spied the cake pan I'd discarded earlier in my testing and thought of a novel deployment. I filled the center with pie weights, placed it on the cake, pressed down firmly, and left it on during the first 20 minutes of baking (with a sheet of nonstick-sprayed aluminum foil in between to prevent the pan bottom from sticking). After removing the cake pan halfway through cooking to allow the top layer of potatoes to take on a little color, I was delighted to find the cake not only uniformly browned, but nicely compacted as well.

The exhaustive testing paid off. Once flipped out of the pan, my crispy potato cake revealed itself to be perfectly browned and, better yet, perfectly whole. A few cuts with a serrated knife and it was ready

HOW WE MADE GALETTE EASIER

1. REMOVE RANDOM STARCH Rinsing the sliced potatoes and patting them dry removes their surface starch— which can vary considerably, depending on the potatoes' age.

2. ADD SPECIFIC STARCH Tossing the potatoes in a mixture of cornstarch and melted butter adds back a fixed amount of starch for sticking power.

3. FREE-FORM IT Dumping—instead of meticulously layering—most of the potatoes onto a single neatly arranged layer cuts out much of the usual fuss.

4. PRESS IT DOWN Pressing down on the galette with a pan full of pie weights compresses the slices so they stick to each other. Leave the pan on during baking for further compression.

to serve—completely looking the part of a classic pommes Anna. I, however, knew the truth: It took an easy few minutes to assemble, cooked largely unattended, and, best yet, was foolproof.

POTATO GALETTE
SERVES 6 TO 8

NOTE: In order for the potato cake to hold together, it is important to slice the potatoes no more than ⅛ inch (3 mm) thick and to make sure the slices are thoroughly dried before assembling the cake. Use a mandoline slicer or the slicing attachment of a food processor to slice the potatoes uniformly thin. A pound of dried beans, rice, or coins can be substituted for the pie weights. For an alternate method for unmolding the galette, see page 31.

2½   pounds (5 to 6 large) Yukon Gold potatoes, scrubbed and sliced ⅛ inch thick (see note)
5   tablespoons unsalted butter, melted
1   tablespoon cornstarch
1   teaspoon table salt
½   teaspoon ground black pepper
1½   teaspoons chopped fresh rosemary leaves (optional)

1. Adjust oven rack to lowest position and heat oven to 450 degrees. Place potatoes in large bowl and fill with cold water. Using hands, swirl to remove excess starch, then drain in colander. Spread potatoes onto kitchen towels and thoroughly dry.

2. Whisk 4 tablespoons butter, cornstarch, salt, pepper, and rosemary (if using) together in large bowl. Add dried potatoes and toss until thoroughly coated. Place remaining tablespoon butter in heavy bottomed 10-inch ovenproof nonstick skillet and swirl to coat. Place 1 potato slice in center of skillet then overlap slices in circle around center slice, followed by outer circle of overlapping slices. Gently place remaining sliced potatoes on top of first layer, arranging so they form even thickness.

3. Place skillet over medium-high heat and cook

until sizzling and potatoes around edge of skillet start to turn translucent, about 5 minutes. Spray 12-inch square of foil with nonstick cooking spray. Place foil, sprayed side down, on top of potatoes. Place 9-inch cake pan on top of foil and fill with 2 cups pie weights. Firmly press down on cake pan to compress potatoes. Transfer skillet to oven and bake 20 minutes.

4. Remove cake pan and foil from skillet. Continue to cook until potatoes are tender when paring knife is inserted in center, 20 to 25 minutes. Return skillet to medium heat on stovetop and cook, gently shaking pan (use potholder—handle will be hot), until galette releases from sides of pan, 2 to 3 minutes.

5. Off heat, place cutting board over skillet. With hands protected by oven mitts or potholders, using 1 hand to hold cutting board in place and 1 hand on skillet handle, carefully invert skillet and cutting board together. Lift skillet off galette. Using serrated knife, gently cut into wedges and serve immediately.

Peruvian Garlic-Lime Chicken

Authentic versions of this spit-roasted bird boast an evenly bronzed exterior, moist meat, and robust seasoning. We hoped that an oven—and supermarket staples—could do the job.

⇒ BY BRYAN ROOF ⇐

Peruvian chicken joints have recently developed something of a cult following in the United States, and for good reason. The rotisserie bird that they serve, known as *pollo a la brasa* in the mother country, is deeply bronzed from its slow rotation in a wood-fired oven and impressively seasoned with garlic, spices, lime juice, chiles, and a paste made with *huacatay*, or black mint. Off the spit, the chicken is carved and served with a garlicky, faintly spicy, mayonnaise-like sauce.

I didn't want my lack of a rotisserie to stop me from re-creating this phenomenal dish at home. But when I started researching recipes, I realized that trying to achieve the smokiness and evenly browned skin of the authentic version wasn't going to be as simple as throwing a well-seasoned bird into the oven. I would also have to replicate the flavors of hard-to-find black mint paste, along with the Peruvian *aji* peppers that give both the chicken and the dipping sauce their signature subtle heat.

First (Marin)ade

Nary a piece of chicken passes through the test kitchen without being rubbed with salt or soaked in a brine. Since salting is our preferred technique when bronzed, well-rendered skin is the goal, I started there. (Both techniques render the bird flavorful and juicy. But while salting helps lock in the bird's existing juices, brining introduces extra moisture to the meat and yields comparatively flabby skin.) After letting the salt seep in for about an hour, I took cues from a few recipes I'd found and coated the exterior of the bird with a simple paste of garlic, extra-virgin olive oil, lime juice, and cumin that I had pureed in the blender. (I'd worry about the mint and smoke flavors later.) I then set the chicken on a V-rack in a roasting pan and cranked the oven to a blazing 450 degrees in hopes of replicating the rotisserie flame. About 45 minutes later the chicken

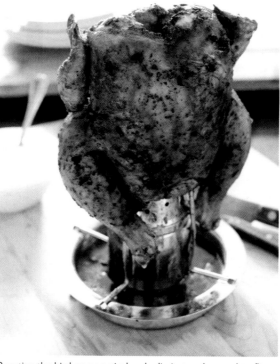

Roasting the bird on a vertical rack eliminates the need to flip the chicken during cooking.

was brown, all right—but only on one side. What's more, despite the salting treatment, the white meat was parched from all that high-heat exposure, and the punchy flavors from the paste were literally skin-deep at best.

Actually, the lack of flavor made sense. While developing our recipe for marinated beef kebabs, a test kitchen colleague learned that none of the flavors in a marinade (including garlic, spices, and acids) penetrate much beyond the exterior of the meat, no matter how long you leave it to soak—with one exception. Only

salt and other compounds of sodium travel farther into the meat the longer it sits. The flavors of my wet paste would never be more than superficial, no matter how long I let the bird marinate, so two things—salt and plenty of time—would be key to heightening those heady flavors and seasoning the meat.

Since both the salt and the paste were being rubbed onto the chicken, I combined the two flavor components into one step, this time mixing a generous 2 tablespoons of kosher salt into the paste. Instead of merely rubbing it over the skin, I also spread the paste under the skin directly against the meat for maximum penetration; I then let the bird rest for six hours before roasting. The result? Much improved taste. Though my marinade was still missing a few of the trademark elements, the salt in the paste had worked its magic and ramped up the chicken's flavor from skin to bone. (Further testing revealed that it was fine to marinate the bird for up to 24 hours.)

My next test took me back to the supermarket, where I shopped for a replacement for the herbaceous, slightly earthy black mint paste. Fresh ordinary mint was the best option, so I worked a handful of the leaves into my next batch of paste, along with some dried oregano, grated lime zest (to satisfy those who'd requested more citrus flavor but didn't want too much acidity), black pepper, sugar, and just a teaspoon of finely minced habanero chile (a little of this fiery pepper goes a long way). Now the tangy spice flavors of my chicken were popping.

Vertical Horizon

Back to my other major hurdle: replacing the rotisserie. While my goal wasn't necessarily crisp skin—the skin on the chicken I'd eaten in restaurants was well rendered but not crackly—I did want it evenly browned, and the V-rack just wasn't working. One option was to flip the chicken several times during cooking, but with a hefty amount of wet paste

Approximating the Flavors of Peru

MINT AND OREGANO
The combination of fresh mint and dried oregano replicates the clean, faintly woodsy flavor of Peruvian black mint (huacatay) paste.

TWO TYPES OF CHILE
Spicy aji peppers are integral to the marinade and dipping sauce. We replaced the aji with a fiery habanero in the marinade and pickled jalapeno in the sauce.

SMOKED PAPRIKA
The smoked version of this brick-red powder imitates the wood-fired flavors of a rotisserie.

Distributing the flavorful paste both over and under the skin ensures the best taste, and storing the chicken in a zipper-lock bag helps contain the mess. Be sure to wear gloves when working with chiles.

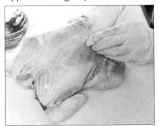

1. SLIP IT UNDER Loosen skin from over thighs and breast and rub half of paste directly over meat.

2. RUB IT OVER Spread remaining paste over skin of entire chicken.

3. CHILL THE BIRD Place chicken in gallon zipper-lock bag and refrigerate for 6 to 24 hours.

slathered on the bird, this turned out to be a messy proposition—not to mention an outright pain. My other idea was a vertical roaster, which cooks the chicken standing upright and allows the heat to circulate freely around the bird for evenly cooked results. I proceeded with my recipe, placing the marinated bird over the roaster's tall cone and setting the whole package on a baking sheet to cook. I knew I was on to something this time: There was no awkward flipping, and the fat dripped freely out of the bird, allowing the skin to render and brown. But it wasn't a perfect solution: The rotisserie's subtle smokiness was predictably absent, and without the roasting-pan walls to shield it from the blasting heat, the white meat was still dry.

There was only one way to keep the chicken from dehydrating: lowering the oven temperature. Indeed, when I roasted the next bird at a relatively gentle 325 degrees, the meat was tender and juicy—but the skin was only lightly tanned. Stuck between these two opposing ideals, I opted for a two-pronged approach that we've used before in the test kitchen. Once the low-roasted chicken was almost cooked through, I let it rest briefly at room temperature, cranked the oven to 500 degrees, added a little water to the roasting pan (to prevent the rendered fat from smoking), and returned the chicken to the much-hotter oven to brown thoroughly. At last: perfectly cooked meat and skin. That left just the missing smoke flavor to resolve.

Nothing about my roasting technique was going to infuse smokiness—but I did have something in my spice cabinet that might help. Smoked paprika, which has recently become widely available, isn't a traditional part of the Peruvian marinade, but 2 teaspoons mixed into the paste turned out to be a pretty close approximation of the real thing.

Finally, there was the sauce. The ideal texture is thinner than traditional mayonnaise but still viscous enough to coat the chicken when dunked. With that in mind, I whipped a whole egg (instead of just a yolk, as in traditional mayonnaise) and vegetable oil in the food processor with a little water, onion, lime juice, cilantro, yellow mustard, and garlic. The consistency was right—but it lacked the punch of those elusive aji peppers. The next best thing? A pickled jalapeño, which kicked up the acidity a notch, too.

Looking over my recipe, I was surprised at how easily I'd been able to replicate the authentic flavors with a few supermarket staples and a vertical roaster. But I wasn't surprised that among my fellow test cooks, this Peruvian mainstay had developed a cult following of its own.

PERUVIAN ROAST CHICKEN WITH GARLIC AND LIME
SERVES 4

NOTE: This recipe calls for a vertical poultry roaster. If you don't have one, substitute a 12-ounce can of beer. Open the beer and pour out (or drink) about half of the liquid. Spray the can lightly with nonstick cooking spray and proceed with the recipe. If the top of the chicken is becoming too dark during roasting in step 3, place a 7-inch-square piece of foil over the neck and wingtips. If habanero chiles are unavailable, 1 tablespoon of minced serrano chile can be substituted. Wear gloves when working with hot chiles.

- 3 tablespoons extra-virgin olive oil
- ¼ cup lightly packed fresh mint leaves
- 2 tablespoons kosher salt
- 6 medium garlic cloves, peeled and roughly chopped
- 1 tablespoon ground black pepper
- 1 tablespoon ground cumin
- 1 tablespoon sugar
- 2 teaspoons smoked paprika
- 2 teaspoons dried oregano
- 2 teaspoons finely grated zest and ¼ cup juice from 2 limes
- 1 teaspoon minced habanero chile (see note)
- 1 (3½- to 4-pound) whole chicken

1. Process all ingredients except chicken in blender until smooth paste forms, 10 to 20 seconds. Using fingers or handle of wooden spoon, carefully loosen skin over thighs and breast and remove any excess fat. Rub half of paste beneath skin of chicken. Spread entire exterior surface of chicken with remaining paste. Tuck wingtips underneath chicken. Place chicken in gallon-size zipper-lock bag

and refrigerate at least 6 hours and up to 24 hours.

2. Adjust oven rack to lowest position and heat oven to 325 degrees. Place vertical roaster on rimmed baking sheet. Slide chicken onto vertical roaster so chicken stands upright and breast is perpendicular to bottom of pan. Roast until skin just begins to turn golden and instant-read thermometer inserted into thickest part of breast registers 140 degrees, 45 to 55 minutes. Carefully remove chicken and pan from oven and increase oven temperature to 500 degrees.

3. When oven is heated to 500 degrees, place 1 cup water in bottom of pan and return pan to oven. Roast until entire skin is browned and crisp and instant-read thermometer registers 160 degrees inserted in thickest part of breast and 175 degrees in thickest part of thigh, about 20 minutes (replenish water as necessary to keep pan from smoking), rotating bird 180 degrees halfway through cooking.

4. Carefully remove chicken from oven and let rest, still on vertical roaster, 20 minutes. Using kitchen towel, carefully lift chicken off vertical roaster and onto platter or cutting board. Carve chicken and serve, passing Spicy Mayonnaise separately.

SPICY MAYONNAISE
MAKES ABOUT 1 CUP

NOTE: If you have concerns about consuming raw eggs, ¼ cup of an egg substitute can be used in place of the egg.

- 1 large egg (see note)
- 2 tablespoons water
- 1 tablespoon minced onion
- 1 tablespoon juice from 1 lime
- 1 tablespoon minced fresh cilantro
- 1 tablespoon canned pickled jalapeño, minced
- 1 medium garlic clove, minced or pressed through garlic press (about 1 teaspoon)
- 1 teaspoon yellow mustard
- ½ teaspoon kosher salt
- 1 cup vegetable oil

Process all ingredients except oil in food processor until finely chopped, about 5 seconds. With machine running, slowly drizzle in oil in steady stream until mayonnaise-like consistency is reached, scraping down bowl as necessary.

Standing Upright

In lieu of a rotisserie, we cook the chicken on our favorite vertical roaster from Norpro ($27.95). While it doesn't spin the bird over an open flame, it does allow the oven's heat to sweep evenly over the bird for a well-browned exterior, and it catches the rendered drippings in the reservoir at its base.

NORPRO VERTICAL ROASTER

Rethinking Broccoli-Cheese Soup

When simply adding more broccoli didn't generate enough vegetable flavor in our soup, we did some further research—and then threw out the rule book on vegetable cookery.

> BY ANDREA GEARY ⋲

If truth-in-advertising rules applied to recipe titles, broccoli-cheese soup would be called "Cheesy Cream of Cheese Soup Garnished with Broccoli." Giving the broccoli top billing might lure you into thinking the dish will be full of this nutrient-rich vegetable, but most times you can barely detect its presence. I was determined to create a soup in which the cheese enhanced rather than camouflaged my favorite vegetable.

In most cases, the amount of broccoli called for doesn't stand a chance—usually a mere pound hidden beneath two to three cups of sharp cheddar and a glut of cream. The most obvious first step to try, then, was to reverse the proportions of broccoli and cheese. Following the typical approach but upping the broccoli to a full 2 pounds, I blanched the broccoli while sweating onions and other aromatics in another pot. I combined these ingredients with chicken broth and some of the broccoli cooking water, pureed them, returned the liquid to the pot, and stirred in a cup of shredded cheese and ¼ cup of cream. But to my chagrin, tasters frowned as they took their first bites. Despite the soup's lovely bright green color, its vegetable flavor hadn't much improved.

Roasting the broccoli until browned before combining it with the other ingredients would be a surefire way to bump up its flavor—but it would also muddy the soup's color. Plus, I was reluctant to take the trouble. So it was back to the books. Eventually I came across something completely different and almost comically counterintuitive: Cook the everliving daylights out of the broccoli. I'd always thought overcooking intensified broccoli's off-putting sulfur flavors, so I probably would have dismissed this method had it not been for the source: Alice Waters. The renowned California chef is famous for getting the best out of fresh produce. Following her technique, I briefly sautéed the chopped florets and stems in a little butter, added about a cup of water, covered the pot, and let it simmer for a full hour. The results looked like olive-drab mush (so much for not muddying the appearance), but the flavor was remarkably improved—complex, with no trace of sulfur.

Curious, I queried our science editor for an explanation. It turns out that when moist heat breaks

See Us Break Broccoli Rules

Video available FREE for 4 months at www.CooksIllustrated.com/apr11

Cooking the daylights out of the broccoli is the key to this soup's sweet, nutty vegetable flavor. Who knew?

down the vegetable's cell walls, it triggers the formation of sulfur-containing compounds called isothiocyanates. The longer the broccoli is cooked, the more these compounds are produced and the more pungent the broccoli's taste—but only up to a point. With really prolonged heating, the isothiocyanates break down into less pungent compounds, the most volatile of which eventually evaporate, leaving only nutty, sweet flavors behind.

This was unquestionably a breakthrough. When I incorporated the super-overcooked broccoli into my soup, its flavor stood up nicely against the rich, sharp cheddar. But all wasn't perfect: The soup now had an unappealing gray cast, and I wasn't keen on minding the pot for an hour. Our science editor had a suggestion: Add baking soda to the cooking water. He predicted just a pinch would accelerate the breakdown of the broccoli's cell walls and more quickly transform the sulfurous compounds into more pleasant ones. When I tried his suggestion, the results were striking. After 20 minutes of braising, the broccoli was fully softened—and just as sweet and nutty as the long-cooked batch. Only one problem remained: the soup's drab color.

This time the inspiration for my solution came not from Alice Waters but from Popeye. Just two ounces of fresh baby spinach added right before I pureed the soup ensured a bright color and also enhanced the vegetable flavor.

As for the cheese, I found that incorporating just

3 ounces of cheddar, along with half that amount of Parmesan, gave the soup enough cheesy flavor without making it heavy. And the cream? Everyone agreed that the soup was plenty rich without it. Once I floated a few crisp croutons on top of each portion, I knew my broccoli soup makeover was complete.

BROCCOLI-CHEESE SOUP
SERVES 6 TO 8

NOTE: To make a vegetarian version of this soup, substitute vegetable broth for the chicken broth. For our free recipe for Buttery Croutons, go to www.CooksIllustrated.com/apr11.

- 2 tablespoons unsalted butter
- 2 pounds broccoli, florets roughly chopped into 1-inch pieces, stems trimmed, peeled, and cut into ¼-inch-thick slices
- 1 medium onion, roughly chopped (about 1 cup)
- 2 medium garlic cloves, minced or pressed through garlic press (about 2 teaspoons)
- 1½ teaspoons dry mustard powder
- Pinch cayenne pepper
- Table salt
- 3–4 cups water
- ¼ teaspoon baking soda
- 2 cups low-sodium chicken broth (see note)
- 2 ounces baby spinach (2 loosely packed cups)
- 3 ounces sharp cheddar cheese, shredded (¾ cup)
- 1½ ounces Parmesan cheese, grated fine (about ¾ cup), plus extra for serving
- Ground black pepper

1. Heat butter in large Dutch oven over medium-high heat. When foaming subsides, add broccoli, onion, garlic, dry mustard, cayenne, and 1 teaspoon salt. Cook, stirring frequently, until fragrant, about 6 minutes. Add 1 cup water and baking soda. Bring to simmer, cover, and cook until broccoli is very soft, about 20 minutes, stirring once during cooking.

2. Add broth and 2 cups water and increase heat to medium-high. When mixture begins to simmer, stir in spinach and cook until wilted, about 1 minute. Transfer half of soup to blender, add cheddar and Parmesan, and process until smooth, about 1 minute. Transfer soup to medium bowl and repeat with remaining soup. Return soup to Dutch oven, place over medium heat and bring to simmer. Adjust consistency of soup with up to 1 cup water. Season to taste with salt and pepper. Serve, passing extra Parmesan separately.

Quick Mushroom Ragu

Making a true, long-simmered Italian meat sauce means tending the pot for hours. Is it possible to achieve deep, satisfying flavor in just 30 minutes?

≥ BY BRYAN ROOF ≤

You'd never find a respectable Tuscan trattoria saucing a bowl of pasta with an overly sweet, dried herb–infused red sauce and calling it a "ragu"—but that's exactly the profile that most Americans recognize from the jarred versions that line supermarket shelves. In Italy, a true ragu combines tomatoes, meat, and hours of slow simmering to produce a rib-sticking, ultra-savory sauce that clings tightly to the pasta. A proper Italian ragu, in other words, is a labor of love.

But there are plenty of occasions when all that love and simmering is simply not possible. The jarred stuff is one option. Another, which embodies real depth of flavor and meaty richness and can be on the table in about 30 minutes, is mushroom ragu. Based on a Tuscan dish known as *spaghetti alla boscaiola*, or "woodsman's pasta," this ragu combines the naturally hearty texture of fresh mushrooms with the concentrated meaty flavor of dried ones.

My working recipe started with a carry-over: Pancetta is one ingredient of a traditional meat ragu that also finds its way into mushroom ragu, helping to make up for the lean nature of the mushrooms. Chopped bits of the salt-cured pork are first rendered, then the fat is used to sauté the remaining ingredients. Pancetta's meaty flavor, though subtle in the grand scheme of things, adds backbone to the sauce while still relinquishing the leading role to the mushrooms.

Since fresh mushrooms give the sauce bulk, I decided to go with one of the meatiest kinds: portobellos. I started with just one, removing the mushroom's gills—the dark, feathery grooves on the cap's underside—prior to cooking to keep the sauce from turning muddy. I then chopped the portobello into bite-size pieces that would blend into the sauce yet maintain a noticeable presence.

If fresh mushrooms offer meaty texture, then dried mushrooms offer ultra-concentrated flavor. Smoky porcini are among the most savory of the dehydrated varieties, and they seemed the natural choice in this Tuscan-inspired dish. I began by soaking half an ounce in boiling water for 10 minutes, then mincing the damp, shriveled pieces and adding them to the skillet along with the rendered pancetta, a little olive oil, the chopped portobello, and sliced garlic. After about five minutes, the fresh mushrooms had started to brown. In went chopped fresh tomatoes, and after about 20 minutes of simmering, the sauce had thickened nicely. When I tasted it, however, I was disappointed to find that it had nothing close to the earthy richness I wanted.

I tried adding another portobello cap—and liked the bulk it provided—but it barely made an impact on flavor. A far more potent solution was to increase the dried porcini to a full ounce. This so greatly deepened the flavor that I decided to keep going. I strained the soaking liquid left over from rehydrating the mushrooms, which I knew would have picked up a lot of porcini flavor, and added it to the sauce. Replacing the water in the recipe with chicken broth fortified the ragu even more. The mushroom flavor was finally in a good place; now I could return to the tomatoes.

Canned tomatoes are far more reliable than fresh at this time of year, and I tried several types. Crushed tomatoes proved too thick, and diced tomatoes, which are treated with calcium chloride, stayed unpleasantly firm. Tasters preferred the softer yet hearty texture of whole tomatoes that I had crushed by hand. A tablespoon of tomato paste rounded out the sauce.

With the last-minute addition of fresh rosemary and red pepper flakes, the sauce took on brightness and heat. Even without an abundance of meat and hours of simmering, this was a ragu worthy of the name.

A double dose of mushrooms—fresh portobellos and dried porcini—makes a hearty, flavorful sauce.

SPAGHETTI WITH MUSHROOM AND TOMATO SAUCE
SERVES 4

NOTE: Use a spoon to scrape the dark brown gills from the portobellos.

- 1 ounce dried porcini mushrooms, rinsed well
- 1 cup low-sodium chicken broth
- 4 ounces pancetta, cut into ½-inch pieces
- ½ pound (2 large) portobello mushrooms, stems and gills removed and discarded, caps cut into ½-inch pieces (about 1½ cups) (see note)
- 3 tablespoons extra-virgin olive oil
- 4 medium garlic cloves, peeled and sliced thin
- 1 tablespoon tomato paste
- 2 teaspoons minced fresh rosemary leaves
- 1 (14.5-ounce) can whole tomatoes, roughly crushed by hand
  Table salt and ground black pepper
- 1 pound spaghetti
  Grated Pecorino Romano cheese, for serving

1. Place porcini and broth in small microwave-safe bowl; cover with plastic wrap and cut several steam vents in plastic with paring knife. Microwave on high power 1 minute, until broth is steaming. Let stand until mushrooms soften, about 10 minutes. Lift mushrooms from broth with fork and finely chop. Strain broth through fine-mesh strainer lined with large coffee filter into medium bowl. Set aside mushrooms and broth.

2. Heat pancetta in 12-inch skillet over medium heat; cook, stirring occasionally, until rendered and crisp, 7 to 10 minutes. Add portobellos, chopped porcini, olive oil, garlic, tomato paste, and rosemary; cook, stirring occasionally, until all liquid has evaporated and tomato paste starts to brown, 5 to 7 minutes. Add reserved chicken broth, crushed tomatoes, and their juices; increase heat to high and bring to simmer. Reduce heat to medium-low and simmer until thickened, 15 to 20 minutes. Season with salt and pepper to taste.

3. While sauce simmers, bring 4 quarts water to boil in large Dutch oven. Add 1 tablespoon salt and pasta; cook until al dente. Drain pasta, reserving ½ cup cooking water, and return to pot. Add sauce to pasta and toss to combine. Adjust consistency with reserved pasta water and season with salt and pepper to taste. Serve, passing Pecorino separately.

Wicked Good Boston Cream Pie

This triple-component dessert would deserve a revival—if only we could make the filling foolproof and keep the glaze from cracking off.

⇒ BY ANDREA GEARY ⇐

Legend has it that Boston cream pie was invented in the 1850s at Boston's landmark Parker House Hotel. A creative baker produced what was to become a wildly popular dessert by simply pouring chocolate glaze onto a cream-filled cake. So why is this dessert called a "pie"? Food historians theorize that home cooks transferred the concept to the most common form of bakeware in the mid-19th-century kitchen: a pie plate.

But today Boston cream pie is rarely made at home, through no fault of its taste: It's hard to beat the trifecta of tender sponge cake layered with vanilla-scented pastry cream and covered in a rich chocolate glaze. The reason home cooks avoid making it is that there are so many opportunities for failure. Sponge cakes are scary: Separating eggs, whipping, folding—this is no easy feat for the uninitiated, and the resulting crumb can be dry and tasteless. And pastry cream? It could curdle—or worse, never thicken. As for the glaze, well, chocolate is famously capricious, at times seizing up unexpectedly, at others looking deceptively glossy going on the cake, only to set up dull and gritty.

But when Boston cream pie hits all the marks, there really is no better dessert. As a native Bostonian, I wanted to pay homage to my roots by leading the dessert's revival with a fail-safe recipe.

The Cake

Boston cream pie is traditionally made from a genoise-like sponge cake: lean, practically weightless layers leavened only by the air whipped into the eggs in the batter. When I baked the genoise from the Parker House Hotel's own recipe, I identified three problems with this style of cake. First, it's fussy and unreliable. The whipped eggs must be gently folded with the flour so as not to deflate the egg mixture, leading to a cake that's dense instead of airy. Second, with a high concentration of egg and little fat, the crumb can be too lean and tough for modern tastes. Finally, low-fat

The key to a shiny glaze? Corn syrup added to chocolate ganache.

cakes require quite a bit of sugar for structure (think angel food cake), and with so little butter to balance it, genoise often ends up tasting overly sweet. While a traditional genoise may have satisfied diners in the 1850s, today we crave a soft, moist, and tender crumb.

With all that in mind, I baked a traditional American yellow cake containing just over two sticks of butter. I wasn't surprised when tasters heartily approved—the cake was incredibly moist. But there was more work to be done: A truly great Boston cream pie boasts contrasting flavors and textures. With an overly rich cake, the lush pastry cream would be lost, not showcased.

Looking for middle ground, I came across another cake that was actually trendy during Boston cream pie's heyday: the hot-milk sponge cake. This cake contains more butter than a genoise, yielding a tender crumb, but it still has considerably less fat than a traditional yellow cake. The mixing method involves whipping eggs with sugar, then simply stirring in the remaining ingredients (including warm milk)—no finicky folding or separating of eggs required. And because the batter is bolstered with a fair amount of baking powder, it doesn't rely solely on the whipped eggs for lift.

After I baked up a batch and offered slices to tasters, I knew that I'd nailed it. Not only had the cake been supremely easy to prepare, but its light texture

and subtle flavor were shaping up to be the perfect platform for a creamy filling. Baking the batter in two pans eliminated the need to slice a single cake horizontally before adding the filling.

The Cream

Next up: pastry cream. This filling is typically made by bringing dairy (we prefer half-and-half) to a simmer and then using it to temper—or slowly raise the temperature of—a mixture of egg yolks, sugar, and cornstarch or flour. The mixture is then returned to the heat and whisked until it has thickened and the eggs are lightly cooked. But if insufficiently heated or overwhisked, the pastry cream will not reach the proper consistency, which presents a particular problem in Boston cream pie: If its texture is too loose, the cream will squish out when the cake is sliced.

I'd always been under the impression that cornstarch and flour are equally good options in pastry cream. But when I experimented with both, I found flour to be far more reliable (see "Thickener Face-Off: Flour vs. Cornstarch"). To achieve a slightly sturdier texture that would be good for slicing, I also tried adding gelatin. My tasters quickly nixed that idea: Even a small amount led to a rubbery texture.

After some reflection, I thought of another ingredient that might provide body: butter. I mixed 4 tablespoons (along with a spoonful of vanilla) into the cooked mixture of yolks, sugar, half-and-half, and flour, and then dipped in my spoon for a taste. The butter reinforced the richness of the pastry cream, enhancing its luxurious flavor. And once the butter-enriched cream was spread on the cake and refrigerated, it sliced cleanly and held fast between the layers while still maintaining a silky smoothness.

The Glaze

With a moist, tender cake and perfect pastry cream ready to go, it was time to address the glaze. The key was to create a smooth mixture that would cling to the top of the cake and drip artistically down its sides, retaining softness and shine after refrigeration. The Parker House Hotel recipe calls for melted chocolate thickened with a fondant (water and sugar cooked to the "soft ball" stage). The glaze went on easily but formed a firm shell when chilled. Other glazes made with just chocolate and heavy cream (called ganache) looked beautifully shiny as they were poured on the cake, only to dry to a dull matte brown. And both types of glaze failed to bond with the cake beneath, forming a skin that separated from the cake when it was sliced.

My glaze needed shine and flexibility. Corn syrup held promise, and sure enough, adding a couple of spoonfuls to a mixture of heavy cream and melted chocolate gave the ganache luster with staying power. The glaze also clung nicely to the cake, holding on to the crumb during slicing. It turns out that the sugar molecules in corn syrup form a perfectly smooth surface, reflecting light waves in the same direction, creating shine. Corn syrup also acts as a plasticizer, making the glaze flexible rather than brittle so that it adheres to the cake instead of peeling off.

As I assembled the last in a long series of Boston cream pies, I knew that I'd finally developed a fear-free recipe to make this Bostonian proud. Sure, there are three components, but I'd figured out ways to guarantee success with each.

BOSTON CREAM PIE
SERVES 8 TO 10

NOTE: Chill the assembled cake for at least 3 hours to make it easy to cut and serve.

Pastry Cream

2	cups half-and-half
6	large egg yolks
½	cup (3½ ounces) sugar
	Pinch table salt
¼	cup unbleached all-purpose flour
4	tablespoons cold unsalted butter, cut into four pieces
1½	teaspoons vanilla extract

Cake

1½	cups (7½ ounces) unbleached all-purpose flour
1½	teaspoons baking powder
¾	teaspoon table salt
¾	cup whole milk
6	tablespoons (¾ stick) unsalted butter
1½	teaspoons vanilla extract
3	large eggs
1½	cups (10½ ounces) sugar

Glaze

½	cup heavy cream
2	tablespoons light corn syrup
4	ounces bittersweet chocolate, chopped fine

1. FOR THE PASTRY CREAM: Heat half-and-half in medium saucepan over medium heat until just simmering. Meanwhile, whisk yolks, sugar, and salt in medium bowl until smooth. Add flour to yolk mixture and whisk until incorporated. Remove half-and-half from heat and, whisking constantly, slowly add ½ cup to yolk mixture to temper. Whisking constantly, return tempered yolk mixture to half-and-half in saucepan.

2. Return saucepan to medium heat and cook, whisking constantly, until mixture thickens slightly, about 1 minute. Reduce heat to medium-low and continue to simmer, whisking constantly, 8 minutes.

3. Increase heat to medium and cook, whisking vigorously, until bubbles burst on surface, 1 to 2 minutes. Remove saucepan from heat; whisk in butter and vanilla until butter is melted and incorporated. Strain pastry cream through fine-mesh strainer set over medium bowl. Press lightly greased parchment paper directly on surface and refrigerate until set, at least 2 hours and up to 24 hours.

4. FOR THE CAKE: Adjust oven rack to middle position and heat oven to 325 degrees. Lightly grease two 9-inch round cake pans with nonstick cooking spray and line with parchment. Whisk flour, baking powder, and salt together in medium bowl. Heat milk and butter in small saucepan over low heat until butter is melted. Remove from heat, add vanilla, and cover to keep warm.

5. In stand mixer fitted with whisk attachment, whip eggs and sugar at high speed until light and airy, about 5 minutes. Remove mixer bowl from stand. Add hot milk mixture and whisk by hand until incorporated. Add dry ingredients and whisk until incorporated.

6. Working quickly, divide batter evenly between prepared pans. Bake until tops are light brown and toothpick inserted in center of cakes comes out clean, 20 to 22 minutes.

7. Transfer cakes to wire rack and cool completely in pan, about 2 hours. Run small plastic knife around edge of pans, then invert cakes onto wire rack. Carefully remove parchment, then reinvert cakes.

8. TO ASSEMBLE: Place one cake round on large plate. Whisk pastry cream briefly, then spoon onto center of cake. Using offset spatula, spread evenly to cake edge. Place second layer on pastry cream, bottom side up, making sure layers line up properly. Press lightly on top of cake to level. Refrigerate cake while preparing glaze.

9. FOR THE GLAZE: Bring cream and corn syrup to simmer in small saucepan over medium heat. Remove from heat and add chocolate. Whisk gently until smooth, 30 seconds. Let stand, whisking occasionally, until thickened slightly, about 5 minutes.

10. Pour glaze onto center of cake. Use offset spatula to spread glaze to edge of cake, letting excess drip decoratively down sides. Chill finished cake 3 hours before slicing. Cake may be made up to 24 hours before serving.

For the Best Pie, Ditch Tradition

We deconstructed the recipe for Boston Cream Pie invented by the Parker House hotel—and found it needed a complete overhaul.

DULL, HARD GLAZE

The original glaze dries to a hard, dull-looking shell that won't bond with the cake. And who really wants brittle piped frosting on top?

OVERLY LEAN, SWEET CAKE

The traditional sponge cake is too lean and sweet for modern tastes. And if you don't know what you're doing, it will bake up flat instead of airy.

RUNNY FILLING

It's all too easy to create a pastry cream that's too thin, leading to a filling that dribbles down the cake.

Butter 101

We don't just slather it on toast or whip it into cakes. In the test kitchen, butter is what makes for juicier chicken breasts, more tender omelets, and creamier mashed potatoes. BY KEITH DRESSER

BUYING AND STORING BASICS

Shopping

SALTED OR UNSALTED? In the test kitchen, we use unsalted butter almost exclusively and add our own salt to recipes. Why? First, the amount of salt in salted butter varies from brand to brand—on average ⅓ teaspoon a stick—which makes offering a universal conversion impossible. Second, salted butter almost always contains more water, which can interfere with gluten development—particularly important in baking. (Biscuits made with salted butter were noticeably mushy.) Third, salt masks butter's naturally sweet, delicate flavors; in butter-specific recipes like beurre blanc and buttercream frosting, we found that extra salt to be overwhelming.

PLAIN OR PREMIUM? While you hear a lot about the higher fat content in premium butters, they actually contain only about a gram more per tablespoon than regular butter, and even our tasters had trouble telling the difference. The real distinction is culturing—the process of fermenting the cream before churning it that builds tangy, complex flavors. That said, these nuances are subtle in most cooked applications, so we save the expensive cultured stuff for spreading on toast.

**FAVORITE
EVERYDAY BUTTER**
Land O'Lakes Unsalted Butter

**FAVORITE
PREMIUM BUTTER**
Lurpak Unsalted Butter

Whipped Butter: A Stand-In for Stick?

Whipped butter, made by beating air into butter, makes a creamy spread but isn't always a good alternative to stick butter for cooking. While testers couldn't tell the difference in baked goods, they found the aerated butter "foamy" and "plastic-like" in uncooked applications such as frosting. If you want to use whipped butter, base your substitution on weight, not volume. (Adding air increases the volume, not the weight.) A standard tub of whipped butter weighs 8 ounces, equal to two sticks of butter.

Tooling Around

Butter Keeper

Chilling butter keeps it from spoiling, but also makes it too stiff to spread on toast. That's where a butter keeper comes in: Shaped like a mini crock, the top of this two-part vessel is filled with softened butter while the base holds water (which is changed every few days). When the lid is put in place, the water forms a seal around the butter, protecting it from light and air. We found that butter kept this way stayed fresh for a month.
➤**Test Kitchen Favorite:** Norpro Butter Keeper ($8.95)

Butter Measuring Knife

Improperly wrapped sticks of butter—or unmarked blocks—make measuring a guessing game. We like this reversible ruler-like paddle knife that accurately measures and neatly cuts both stick butter and the fatter, block-style kind (though it's too narrow for pound-block butter).
➤**Test Kitchen Favorite:** KitchenArt Pro Measuring Butter Knife ($10.96)

Storing

Placed in the back of the fridge where it's coldest (not in the small door compartment), butter will keep for 2½ weeks. In tests we've found that any longer and it can turn rancid as its fatty acids oxidize. For longer storage (up to four months), move it to the freezer. Also, since butter quickly picks up odors and flavors, we like to slip the sticks into a zipper-lock bag.

GAUGING BUTTER TEMPERATURE

Butter temperature can dramatically affect the texture of baked goods. For the most accurate results, we check the temperature with an instant-read thermometer. The following tactile clues will also provide a good gauge.

CHILLED
(about 35 degrees)
➤**Method:** Cut butter into small pieces; freeze until very firm, 10 to 15 minutes.
➤**How to Test It:** Press with a finger—it should be cold and unyielding.
➤**Why It Matters:** Cold butter melts during baking, leaving behind small pockets of air that create flaky layers in recipes like pie dough and croissants.

SOFTENED
(65 to 67 degrees)
➤**Method:** Let refrigerated butter sit at room temperature for about 30 minutes.
➤**How to Test It:** The stick will easily bend without breaking and give slightly when pressed.
➤**Why It Matters:** Softened butter is flexible enough to be whipped but firm enough to retain the incorporated air—vital to making cakes with a tender crumb.

MELTED AND COOLED
(85 to 90 degrees)
➤**Method:** Melt butter in a small saucepan or microwave-safe bowl; cool about 5 minutes.
➤**How to Test It:** The butter should be fluid and slightly warm.
➤**Why It Matters:** Butter is roughly 16 percent water; when it's melted, the water breaks from the emulsion and helps create gluten for chewier cookies.

COOKING TIPS AND TECHNIQUES

WAIT FOR BUTTER TO STOP FOAMING BEFORE SAUTÉING

➤ **Why Do It:** Sautéing is best done in hot fat. When foaming subsides, it's an easy visual cue that the melted butter is hot enough for cooking. More specifically, it indicates that all the water in the butter (about 16 percent by weight) has evaporated, and the temperature can rise above water's boiling point of 212 degrees. As foaming subsides, butter continues heating and finally smokes at 250 to 300 degrees. (To sauté in butter at higher temperatures, use clarified butter.)

USE COLD—NOT SOFTENED— BUTTER FOR PASTRY

➤ **Why Do It:** Good, light pastry and biscuits depend on distinct pieces of cold, solid butter distributed throughout the dough that melt during baking and leave behind pockets of air. To keep the butter cold during mixing, we use a food processor, but you can also grate frozen butter into the dry ingredients using the large holes of a box grater.

ADD COLD BUTTER TO PAN SAUCES

➤ **Why Do It:** Swirling a tablespoon or two of cold butter into a pan sauce right before serving adds both richness and body. (Cold, firm butter resists separation, while the water in softened butter separates more easily and can lead to a broken emulsion.) Cut the butter into tablespoon-size chunks so that it melts quickly.

SLIP BUTTER UNDER THE SKIN OF CHICKEN BREASTS

➤ **Why Do It:** Notoriously dry and chalky, roast chicken breasts can be transformed with softened butter. Two tablespoons of unsalted butter mixed with ½ teaspoon salt and spread underneath the skin of a whole breast before roasting will baste the white meat, keeping it juicy while adding flavor.

ADD BUTTER BEFORE DAIRY IN MASHED POTATOES

➤ **Why Do It:** If the dairy is stirred into the hot cooked potatoes before the butter, the water in the dairy will combine with the potatoes' starch, making them gummy. When melted butter is added first, the fat coats the starch molecules and prevents them from reacting with the water in the dairy. The result? Smoother, more velvety mashed potatoes.

ADD BUTTER BITS TO UNCOOKED EGGS FOR OMELETS

➤ **Why Do It:** Whisking a tablespoon of cold, diced butter into the eggs before cooking is the secret to a soft, creamy omelet. Without butter, the proteins in egg whites form tight, cross-linked bonds, yielding a dense, rubbery version of the French classic. But with our method, the eggs cook as the butter melts and disperses, coating the proteins and stopping them from linking.

CLARIFYING CLARIFIED BUTTER AND GHEE

Clarified Butter
Butter is mostly made up of fat, but it also contains small amounts of proteins, carbohydrates, minerals (the milk solids), and water, all of which are distributed throughout the fat in an emulsion. When butter is heated, this emulsion is broken, causing the different components to separate according to density and chemical predisposition. The pure fat left standing is called clarified butter.

Since clarified butter has a higher smoke point than whole butter (clarified ranges from 350–375 degrees, whole butter from 250–300 degrees), food can be seared in it without the danger of milk solids burning and becoming bitter. The second, and more specific, application is working with phyllo dough. We've found that clarified butter's pure fat produces particularly flaky, crispy layers.

Ghee
Ghee, a butter product used throughout Indian cooking, takes clarification a step further by simmering the butter until all the moisture is evaporated and the milk solids begin to brown, giving the fat a slightly nutty flavor and aroma. You can find ghee in unrefrigerated jars (100 percent fat is shelf stable) at Indian and Middle Eastern markets, as well as in natural foods stores. The two products can be used interchangeably, but ghee will lend foods cooked in it a slightly richer, more buttery flavor.

Simple Butter Recipes

GARLIC COMPOUND BUTTER
MAKES 4 TABLESPOONS

Using fork, beat 4 tablespoons softened unsalted butter, ½ teaspoon finely grated lemon zest, 1 tablespoon minced fresh parsley, 1 minced garlic clove, ½ teaspoon salt, and ground black pepper to taste in small bowl until combined. Serve as a topping on steak, pork chops, or fish.

FOOLPROOF HOLLANDAISE SAUCE
MAKES ABOUT 2 CUPS

Whisk 12 tablespoons softened unsalted butter and 6 large egg yolks in large heat-resistant bowl set over medium saucepan filled with ½ inch of barely simmering water (don't let bowl touch water) until mixture is smooth and homogeneous. Slowly add ½ cup boiling water and cook, whisking constantly, until thickened and sauce registers 160 degrees on instant-read thermometer, 7 to 10 minutes. Off heat, stir in 2 teaspoons lemon juice and ⅛ teaspoon cayenne. Season with salt to taste. Serve immediately over prepared asparagus or eggs Benedict.

BROWN BUTTER SAUCE
MAKES ABOUT ¼ CUP

Melt 4 tablespoons unsalted butter, cut into 4 pieces, in small, heavy-bottomed, traditional (not nonstick) skillet over medium-low heat. Continue to cook, swirling constantly, until butter is dark golden brown and has nutty aroma, 1 to 3 minutes. Remove pan from heat and let stand 1½ minutes. Add 1 tablespoon lemon juice, 1 tablespoon chopped parsley, and salt and pepper to taste; swirl pan to combine. Let milk solids settle to bottom of pan, about 10 seconds. Drizzle liquid over gnocchi, mushrooms, steak, or fish, leaving as many solids behind as possible.

WHITE BUTTER SAUCE
MAKES ABOUT ⅔ CUP

Bring 3 tablespoons dry white wine, 2 tablespoons white wine vinegar, 1 tablespoon minced shallots, and pinch salt to boil in small, heavy-bottomed saucepan over medium-high heat. Reduce heat to medium-low and simmer until reduced by two-thirds, about 5 minutes. Whisk in 1 tablespoon heavy cream. Increase heat to high and add 8 tablespoons cold unsalted butter, cut into 4 pieces. Whisk vigorously until butter is incorporated and forms thick, pale yellow sauce, 30 to 60 seconds. Remove pan from heat and serve sauce immediately with fish or vegetables.

Cuban Black Beans and Rice

Cooking beans and rice in a single vessel sounds like a straightforward one-pot meal—
that is, until both elements cook up mushy and bland.

⇒ BY YVONNE RUPERTI ⇐

Rice and beans has always been a sustenance dish to me—satisfying, surely, but a bit mundane. So I was intrigued when a friend returned from a trip to Miami and raved about a Cuban version in which black beans and rice are cooked together with aromatic vegetables, spices, and pork to create either a hearty main course or a flavorful side dish. Traditionally called *Moros y Cristianos*, this dish is unique in that the rice is cooked in the inky concentrated liquid left over from cooking the beans, which renders the grains just as flavorful. This was definitely a dish I wanted to cook at home.

Most of the recipes that I found followed the same method: Sauté pork (usually salt pork or bacon) in a Dutch oven until crisp; lightly brown aromatic vegetables and spices in the rendered fat; then stir in uncooked rice, followed by the already cooked black beans and their cooking liquid. Cover and gently simmer until the liquid has been absorbed and the rice is tender.

Sounded easy enough. But after cooking up a few pots, my problems became clear: Sometimes I had bland rice studded with insipid beans—hardly worth the effort. Other times I ended up with poorly cooked rice: either a moist, gluey mash or grains scorched on the bottom but still undercooked on the top (the liquid having boiled away). My goal: a dish that was not just richly flavorful, but foolproof.

Flavor Makers

To get the flavor right, I knew I needed to perfect the *sofrito*. This mixture of aromatic vegetables, spices, and herbs is a cornerstone of Latin cooking and the starting point for this dish. The specific elements in the mix differ from one Latin cuisine to another, but a Cuban sofrito usually consists of a "holy trinity" of onion, green pepper, and garlic, typically flavored with cumin and oregano.

I quickly found that pureeing the vegetables for the sofrito before combining them with the beans

A last-minute squeeze of lime juice punches up this dish's rich, earthy flavors.

and rice was not the way to go here; the resulting paste muddied the texture of the dish and eliminated the possibility of browning the sofrito in a skillet first. Chopping the vegetables (or pulsing them in a food processor) into quarter-inch dice was a better option. After crisping 6 ounces of diced salt pork (bacon made an acceptable substitute), I added the onion, pepper, cumin, and oregano, and sautéed the sofrito for 15 minutes in the rendered fat and a splash of extra-virgin olive oil until the mixture was golden brown and flavorful. Then I added some garlic to the mix.

The only problem? There just wasn't enough of that rich flavor. I needed this sofrito to be the backbone to a big pot of beans and rice, not just give it a mild overtone. Increasing the spices helped, but only to a point; overdoing it made the dish dusty and harsh. I thought that doubling the amount of sofrito would do the trick—and flavorwise, it did—but the sheer volume of moist vegetables weighed down the rice and beans in a kind of sofrito sludge. Did all of the veggies have to go directly into the sofrito? Since I had been pre-cooking the soaked beans in plain water, I wondered if I could use the extra veggies to infuse the beans and thereby increase the overall flavor of the dish. With that in mind, I put half an onion, half a green pepper, half a

garlic head, and bay leaves in with the beans to simmer. When the beans were just cooked, I sampled them. It turned out to be a good idea—both the beans and their cooking liquid were full-flavored and would lend that quality to the rice as well. The results were even better when I swapped half of the water for chicken broth.

Rescuing the Rice

With the flavor of the dish where I wanted it, I turned to the rice. I had hoped to forgo the traditional extra step of rinsing the rice before cooking, but a side-by-side comparison clearly showed that washing off the excess starch from the grains helps prevent them from turning sticky and clumping together. Plus, I was already using the starchy black bean cooking liquid to cook the rice, so removing the extra surface starch from the rice grains was particularly important.

Fixing the scorched-yet-undercooked rice was a little trickier. It's a fine line between gummy rice and undercooked rice because the beans, sofrito, and pork all add moisture to the pot. I tinkered around a bit with extra liquid; after a few sodden pots of beans and rice, I found that 2½ cups was the correct amount of bean liquid to get 1½ cups of rice cooked through in about 30 minutes. But even at the lowest heat setting, I found that the mixture at the bottom of the pot was still scorching while the rice grains at the top remained almost crunchy. The problem made sense: With the stove's flame hitting only the underside of the pot, the bottom layer of rice burned while the grains at the top barely cooked at all. That's when I recalled our oven-baked rice technique, in which the all-around, indirect heat cooks the pot's contents gently and evenly. I brought the rice, beans, and liquid (including a splash of red wine vinegar for brightness) to a simmer, gave the mixture a stir, covered the vessel, and slid it into a 350-degree oven. After about the same time as it took to cook on the stove, I removed the pot, fluffed

What's a Sofrito?

A sofrito serves as the fundamental flavor base for many Cuban dishes, including this one. The combination of onion, green pepper, and garlic (and often cumin and oregano) is a close relative of the French *mirepoix*, which features onion, carrot, and celery. **CUBAN FLAVOR BASE**

1. ENRICH BEANS
Simmering the beans in water and chicken broth bolstered with salt, garlic, bell pepper, onion, and garlic adds extra flavor.

2. RINSE RICE Washing excess starch off the rice with plenty of cool running water helps the grains cook up fluffy, not sticky.

3. DEEPEN SOFRITO FLAVOR Lightly browning the sofrito vegetables and spices with the rendered salt pork adds complex, meaty flavor.

4. ADD BEAN COOKING LIQUID Cooking the rice and beans in the reserved bean cooking liquid plus red wine vinegar imbues the dish with flavor.

5. BAKE IN OVEN Baking the beans and rice eliminates the crusty bottom that can form when the dish is cooked on the stove.

the contents with a fork, and let it sit for five minutes. Finally, perfectly cooked rice from top to bottom.

As a final touch, a sprinkling of thinly sliced scallions and a squeeze of lime brought the dish to life. And for a meatless version, a tablespoon of tomato paste cooked with the sofrito laced the dish with *umami* presence. Forget about packing your bags—this was a taste of Cuba that you could make in any kitchen.

CUBAN-STYLE BLACK BEANS AND RICE (MOROS Y CRISTIANOS)
SERVES 6 TO 8 AS AN ENTREE AND 8 TO 10 AS A SIDE DISH

NOTE: Serve this recipe as a side dish or as a main course with a simple green salad. It is important to use lean—not fatty—salt pork. If you can't find it, substitute six slices of bacon. If using bacon, decrease the cooking time in step 4 to eight minutes. For a vegetarian version of this recipe, use water instead of chicken broth, omit the salt pork, add 1 tablespoon of tomato paste with the vegetables in step 4, and increase the amount of salt in step 5 to 1½ teaspoons.

	Table salt
1	cup dried black beans, rinsed and picked over
2	cups low-sodium chicken broth (see note)
2	cups water
2	large green bell peppers, halved and seeded
1	large onion, halved at equator and peeled, root end left intact
1	head garlic, 5 medium cloves removed and minced or pressed through garlic press (about 5 teaspoons), remaining head halved at equator with skin left intact
2	bay leaves
1½	cups long grain white rice
2	tablespoons olive oil
6	ounces lean salt pork, cut into ¼-inch dice (see note)
1	tablespoon minced fresh oregano leaves
4	teaspoons ground cumin
2	tablespoons red wine vinegar
2	medium scallions, sliced thin
1	lime, cut into 8 wedges

1. Dissolve 1½ tablespoons salt in 2 quarts cold water in large bowl or container. Add beans and soak at room temperature for at least 8 hours and up to 24 hours. Drain and rinse well.

2. In large Dutch oven with tight-fitting lid, stir together drained beans, broth, water, 1 pepper half, 1 onion half (with root end), halved garlic head, bay leaves, and 1 teaspoon salt. Bring to simmer over medium-high heat, cover, and reduce heat to low. Cook until beans are just soft, 30 to 40 minutes. Using tongs, remove and discard pepper, onion, garlic, and bay leaves. Drain beans in colander set over large bowl, reserving 2½ cups bean cooking liquid. (If you don't have enough bean cooking liquid, add water to equal 2½ cups.) Do not wash out Dutch oven.

3. Adjust oven rack to middle position and heat oven to 350 degrees. Place rice in large fine-mesh strainer and rinse under cold running water until water runs clear, about 1½ minutes. Shake strainer vigorously to remove all excess water; set rice aside. Cut remaining peppers and onion into 2-inch pieces and process in food processor until broken into rough ¼-inch pieces, about eight 1-second pulses, scraping down sides of bowl as necessary; set vegetables aside.

4. In now-empty Dutch oven, heat 1 tablespoon oil and salt pork over medium-low heat; cook, stirring frequently, until lightly browned and rendered, 15 to 20 minutes. Add remaining tablespoon oil, chopped peppers and onion, oregano, and cumin. Increase heat to medium and continue to cook, stirring frequently, until vegetables are softened and beginning to brown, 10 to 15 minutes longer. Add minced garlic and cook, stirring constantly, until fragrant, about 1 minute. Add rice and stir to coat, about 30 seconds.

5. Stir in beans, reserved bean cooking liquid, vinegar, and ½ teaspoon salt. Increase heat to medium-high and bring to simmer. Cover and transfer to oven. Bake until liquid is absorbed and rice is tender, about 30 minutes. Fluff with fork and let rest, uncovered, 5 minutes. Serve, passing scallion and lime wedges separately.

TASTING Dried Black Beans

Canned beans may be convenient, but their flavor and texture never measure up to dried. We tested three brands of dried black beans by sampling them cooked plain and in Cuban-Style Black Beans and Rice. Surprisingly, the mail-order heirloom variety became blown out and mushy, while the beans from the two national supermarket brands emerged from the pot perfectly intact and creamy. Our favorite was Goya Dried Black Beans, which offered "nutty," "buttery" bean flavor and a reliably uniform texture. For complete tasting results, go to www.CooksIllustrated.com/apr11.
—Taizeth Sierra

DREAM BEANS
GOYA Dried Black Beans
Price: $1.69 per pound
Comments: Our favorite beans had "nice meaty flavor" and "just enough chew."

HO-HUM
EDEN Organic Dry Black Turtle Beans
Price: $3.20 per pound
Comments: Tasters considered these runners-up "average all around."

TASTY BUT TESTY
RANCHO GORDO Midnight Black Beans
Price: $4.95 per pound, plus shipping (mail-order)
Comments: Because these beans never behaved consistently when cooked, an "almost perfect" flavor still couldn't keep them out of last place.

Better Baked Sole Fillets

Delicate sole demands precise timing and a gentle touch. Was there a way to roll those requirements into a more fail-safe approach?

⇒ BY DAWN YANAGIHARA ⇐

I love the subtle flavor and fine texture of sole, but it's nearly impossible to translate this fish into a simple, foolproof weeknight meal. For starters, every cooking method has its drawbacks. Both sautéing and pan-frying yield nice golden color, but a hot skillet can overcook the thin fillets in a flash. Plus, sole's footprint is wide, meaning the fillets must be cooked in batches. Poaching, meanwhile, is gentler—but also downright bland without a flavorful poaching liquid and sauce for serving.

Baking, however, struck me as both forgiving and convenient, though the technique was not without fault. Of the recipes I turned up, most were uninspired (coated with plain bread crumbs), overwrought (wrapped artfully around blanched asparagus), or both (en papillote with zucchini), so I selected a few of the more sensible options and gave them a go.

Simply laying the fillets flat on a baking sheet seemed promising—until they broke into pieces when I transferred them to dinner plates. Rolling them into compact bundles eased the transport from baking dish to plate, but the trade-off was a thicker piece of fish that cooked unevenly.

But the technique itself—baking rolled fillets—showed promise, so I experimented with oven temperatures (300 to 450 degrees) to even out the cooking. After 30 minutes at 325 degrees, the fillets were nicely done from edge to center. Covering the baking dish with foil offered the delicate fish further protection from the drying heat of the oven.

With the cooking method settled, I set out to ramp up the still-flat flavor: I sprinkled the fillets with salt and pepper and minced fresh herbs and lemon zest, drizzled them with melted butter, rolled them, drizzled more butter, and put them in the oven. The flavor? Better, but still mild. Once I worked a clove of minced garlic into the butter and a slather of Dijon mustard over each fillet, the flavor popped.

All I had left to address? The baked fillets' one-dimensional texture and unappetizing pallor. A topping of panko (Japanese-style bread crumbs) toasted in butter along with garlic offered a possible solution to both problems, but adding a measure of herbs to the crumbs once they were cooled made it even better. As for when to add the crumbs, they absorbed moisture and lost their lovely crispness when added at the outset, but lacked cohesion with the fish when sprinkled on after cooking. I compromised with a hybrid technique, removing the foil with 5 to 10 minutes remaining, basting the fillets with pan juices, topping them with most of the toasted crumbs, and then returning them to the oven uncovered. Just before serving, I sprinkled on the remaining crumbs. This way, most of the crumbs fused to the fish and the final showering offered delicate crispness.

Fuss-free and foolproof, these crumb-topped, herb-filled fillets were exactly what I had hoped to create: fish suitable for a weeknight dinner, yet impressive and elegant enough to serve to company.

BAKED SOLE FILLETS WITH HERBS AND BREAD CRUMBS
SERVES 6

NOTE: Try to purchase fillets of similar size. If using smaller fillets (about 3 ounces each), serve 2 fillets per person and reduce the baking time in step 3 to 20 minutes. We strongly advise against using frozen fish in this recipe. Freezing can undermine the texture of the fish, making it hard to roll. Fresh basil or dill can be used in place of the tarragon.

- 3 tablespoons minced fresh parsley leaves
- 3 tablespoons minced fresh chives
- 1 tablespoon minced fresh tarragon leaves (see note)
- 1 teaspoon finely grated zest from 1 lemon
- 5 tablespoons unsalted butter, cut into pieces
- 2 medium garlic cloves, minced or pressed through garlic press (about 2 teaspoons)
- 6 boneless, skinless sole or flounder fillets (about 6 ounces each) (see note)
  Kosher salt and ground black pepper
- 1 tablespoon Dijon mustard
- ⅔ cup panko (Japanese-style bread crumbs)
  Lemon wedges for serving

1. Adjust oven rack to middle position and heat oven to 325 degrees. Combine parsley, chives, and tarragon in small bowl. Measure out 1 tablespoon herb mixture and set aside for bread crumbs, then stir lemon zest into remaining herbs.

2. Heat 4 tablespoons butter in 8-inch skillet over medium heat until just melted. Add 1 teaspoon minced garlic and cook, stirring frequently, until fragrant, 1 to 2 minutes. Set skillet aside.

Coated inside and out with butter and rolled into tight cylinders, these fillets cook up moist—and intact.

3. Pat fillets dry with paper towels and season both sides with salt and pepper. Turn fillets skinned side up with tail end pointing away from you. Spread ½ teaspoon mustard on each fillet, sprinkle each evenly with about 1 tablespoon herb–lemon zest mixture, and drizzle each with about 1½ teaspoons garlic butter. Tightly roll fillets from thick end to form cylinders. Set fillets seam side down in 13 by 9-inch baking dish. Drizzle remaining garlic butter over fillets, cover baking dish with aluminum foil, and bake 25 minutes. Wipe out skillet but do not wash.

4. While fillets are baking, add remaining tablespoon butter to now-empty skillet and melt over medium heat. Add panko and cook, stirring frequently, until crumbs are deep golden brown, 5 to 8 minutes. Reduce heat to low, add remaining teaspoon minced garlic, and cook, stirring constantly, until garlic is fragrant and evenly distributed in crumbs, about 1 minute. Transfer to small bowl and stir in ¼ teaspoon salt and pepper to taste. Let cool, then stir in reserved tablespoon herb mixture.

5. After fillets have baked 25 minutes, remove baking dish from oven. Baste fillets with melted garlic butter from baking dish, sprinkle with all but 3 tablespoons bread crumbs, and continue to bake, uncovered, until internal temperature registers about 135 degrees on instant-read thermometer, 6 to 10 minutes longer. Using thin metal spatula, transfer fillets to individual plates, sprinkle with remaining bread crumbs, and serve with lemon wedges.

Rescuing Snow Peas

Typically used as filler in stir-fries, snow peas can stand on their own—as long as they don't wither away in the heat.

≥ BY RACHEL TOOMEY KELSEY ≤

The typical destination for snow peas is a stir-fry, where the pods almost always serve as filler—never as the focal point. But if the average stir-fry served up in Chinese restaurants is anything to go by, you wouldn't want the vegetable to be any more prominent. The pods are often greasy and limp, with all their delicate flavor cooked out of them.

But why should this have to be the case? If executed properly, the fast-paced, high-heat method of stir-frying would seem like the ideal approach for cooking the pods and bringing out their sweet, grassy flavor while preserving their crisp bite.

It took just one test to demonstrate that things weren't quite that simple. I heated a couple of tablespoons of vegetable oil in a large skillet over a high flame and tossed in a few handfuls of snow peas. But after several minutes of frantic stirring, I found that I had produced the oily pods I recognized from Chinese takeout. And while some of the pods retained a bit of crisp texture, too many had turned floppy. And their subtly sweet flavor? Far too subtle.

I never intended for the snow peas to stand entirely on their own—they'd need a few supporting ingredients to bolster their understated taste. But before I added anything else to the dish, I wanted to try an obvious method for bumping up the pods' natural flavor: browning. When vegetables are cooked over intense heat, their natural sugars caramelize, causing them to take on nutty, concentrated flavors. But the food has to be relatively stationary to let browning happen—the constant motion of stir-frying would only thwart the process. I decided to treat the peas as we do when searing meat to create a well-browned crust: I didn't move them until the high heat had done its work. Sure enough, this approach put me on a better track. With 12 ounces of peas (enough for four people) in the pan, most of the pods were in contact with the hot surface.

After one minute of almost undisturbed cooking—I gave them a single stir after 30 seconds—the peas emerged bright green, crisp, and freckled with a few spots indicative of good browning. I then reverted to constant stirring for another minute or two, until the pods were fully cooked through.

My new sauté method helped considerably, and I cut down the oil to just 1 tablespoon to fix the greasiness problem. But the peas still needed more depth. When I tried to increase browning by leaving them untouched in the pan for a few extra minutes, I was back to a skillet full of limp, overcooked pods. I had another idea—a trick that the test kitchen often uses to promote better browning: sugar. Just ⅛ teaspoon sprinkled over the peas as they went into the hot pan, along with salt and pepper, kicked up the color in the few minutes the vegetables needed to cook through.

Now it was time for those complementary flavors. Shallot seemed like a good place to start, but when I sautéed the minced aromatic before adding the snow peas to the skillet, it ended up burning and turning bitter by the time my peas had finished cooking. Instead, I treated the shallot like garlic, which also has a tendency to burn quickly. I made a clearing in the center of the skillet after the peas were well browned and then cooked the shallot with a splash of oil until just fragrant. Much better.

For a final flavor punch, I added some acidity in the form of lemon juice (lime juice or vinegar works too) and a hit of fresh herbs that drew out those shy grassy flavors. I had turned these once-second-fiddle pods into a real standout side dish of their own.

SAUTÉED SNOW PEAS WITH LEMON AND PARSLEY
SERVES 4

NOTE: Chives or tarragon can be used in place of the parsley.

- 1 tablespoon vegetable oil
- 1 small shallot, minced (about 2 tablespoons)
- 1 teaspoon finely grated lemon zest plus 1 teaspoon juice from 1 lemon
  Table salt and ground black pepper
- ⅛ teaspoon sugar
- ¾ pound snow peas, tips pulled off and strings removed
- 1 tablespoon minced fresh parsley leaves (see note)

1. Combine 1 teaspoon oil, shallot, and lemon zest in small bowl. Combine ¼ teaspoon salt, ⅛ teaspoon pepper, and sugar in second small bowl.

2. Heat remaining 2 teaspoons oil in 12-inch nonstick skillet over high heat until just smoking. Add snow peas, sprinkle with salt mixture, and cook, without stirring, 30 seconds. Stir and continue to cook, without stirring, 30 seconds longer. Continue to cook, stirring constantly, until peas are crisp-tender, 1 to 2 minutes longer.

3. Push peas to sides of skillet; add shallot mixture to clearing and cook, mashing with spatula, until fragrant, about 30 seconds. Toss to combine shallot mixture with vegetables. Transfer peas to bowl and stir in lemon juice and parsley. Season with salt and pepper, and serve.

SAUTÉED SNOW PEAS WITH GINGER, GARLIC, AND SCALLION

Follow recipe for Sautéed Snow Peas with Lemon and Parsley, substituting 2 minced garlic cloves, 2 teaspoons grated fresh ginger, and 2 minced scallion whites for shallot and lemon zest, and red pepper flakes for black pepper. In step 3, substitute rice vinegar for lemon juice and 2 sliced scallion greens for parsley.

SAUTÉED SNOW PEAS WITH GARLIC, CUMIN, AND CILANTRO

Follow recipe for Sautéed Snow Peas with Lemon and Parsley, substituting 2 minced garlic cloves and ½ teaspoon toasted and lightly crushed cumin seed for shallot, and ½ teaspoon lime zest for lemon zest. In step 3, substitute lime juice for lemon juice and cilantro for parsley.

SAUTÉED SNOW PEAS WITH SHALLOT, LEMON GRASS, AND BASIL

Follow recipe for Sautéed Snow Peas with Lemon and Parsley, substituting 2 teaspoons minced fresh lemon grass for lemon zest. In step 3, substitute lime juice for lemon juice and basil for parsley.

Watch Us Sauté Them
Video available FREE for 4 months at
www.CooksIllustrated.com/apr11

TECHNIQUE | NO MORE STRINGS

Along the seam of each pod is a fine, wiry "string" that should be removed before cooking. To pull it off, simply grasp one of the ends and pull gently along the length of the pod.

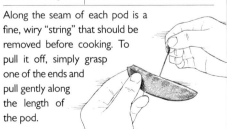

Whole-Wheat Sandwich Bread

Most whole-wheat breads are either squat bricks or white bread in drag. We wanted a hearty yet light-textured sandwich loaf that really tasted like wheat.

⇉ BY ANDREW JANJIGIAN ⇇

Most recipes for whole-wheat sandwich bread lead to one of two pitfalls. They either pay lip service to being "whole wheat," yielding loaves containing so little of the whole-grain stuff that they resemble the fluffy, squishy bread you find at the supermarket, or they call for so much whole wheat that the loaves bake up coarse and dense, crumbling as soon as you slice into them. These squat breads may boast strong wheat flavor, but it's often accompanied by a bitter, musty edge. I wanted to create sandwich bread with a full-blown nutty—but not bitter—taste and a hearty yet soft crumb that sliced neatly.

The Whole (Grain) Problem

The cornerstone of any good bread is gluten—the network of proteins that forms when the flour is kneaded with water and provides structure for the loaf. The challenge when making whole-wheat bread is that the very thing that gives it character and distinguishes it from white bread—the presence of bran, the outer layer of the cereal grain that's stripped away in refined flour—is also an impediment to gluten development. The fiber in bran has sharp edges that tend to cut the gluten strands, weakening their bonds and making the dough less able to contain gases during proofing and baking. When there's too much whole wheat in the mix, the upshot is a heavy, crumbly loaf. Bran is also what makes whole wheat bitter.

Since baking with whole-wheat flour leads to a minefield of issues, I decided to start with a known quantity—a good white-flour recipe—and then work my way backward to "unrefine" it. I consulted my friend Richard Miscovich, a baking instructor at Johnson & Wales University, in Providence, R.I., who gave me his trusted recipe for a white-flour *pain de mie*, the French equivalent of our sandwich bread.

Our bread packs twice as much whole wheat as most other sandwich loaves but still bakes up tender and faintly sweet.

To see firsthand the effects of swapping in whole-wheat flour, I made a series of loaves, replacing a portion of the 3 cups of all-purpose white flour in Miscovich's recipe with whole wheat in amounts from 25 to 100 percent. Because whole-wheat flour absorbs more liquid than its refined counterpart, I incrementally increased the amount of water as well to keep the dough pliant and workable. Per Miscovich's method, I mixed the dough, turned it midway through the first rise to remove large gas bubbles and promote even fermentation, and shaped it into loaves. Before putting the bread in the oven, I poured boiling water into an empty loaf pan that I'd positioned on the bottom rack. The water would supply steam—a common bread baker's technique that prevents the crust from drying out before the loaves have fully expanded. I then placed the loaves in the oven on a preheated

baking stone (its heat would help ensure a maximum amount of rise before the crumb set, locking in volume).

Once the breads' crusts turned a burnished mahogany color, I pulled them from the oven and let them cool. I'm not exaggerating when I say that these loaves were a motley crew—they ranged from tall, airy beauties to compact bricks. In fact, the results followed my expectations exactly: The higher the percentage of whole-wheat flour, the squatter the loaf and the denser the crumb.

After sampling slices from each loaf, my tasters and I concluded that 40 percent whole-wheat flour was as high as I could go before the texture began to take a turn for the worse. But I was facing a catch-22: The flavor contributed by this amount of whole wheat—while decent—was still far from the full-fledged wheat taste I was after, but if I added any more whole-wheat flour, the lack of gluten would interfere with the bread's structure.

There was one immediate thing I could try to get the proportion of whole wheat up a notch without impacting the height of the bread or its texture: Substitute bread flour for all-purpose flour. Thanks to the boost in gluten development from its extra protein, I was able to bump up the amount of whole-wheat flour to 50 percent. But if I wanted to up the count even further, I'd need another approach.

Super Soaker

Delving into more bread research, I uncovered a crucial piece of information: Many whole-grain bread recipes require soaking the grains in some of the water or other liquid from the recipe before incorporating them into the dough. A prolonged soak—most sources recommended overnight—

Whole-Wheat Extremes

Whole-wheat sandwich breads typically fall into one of two categories: squishy, Wonder Bread–like loaves or rock-solid specimens that are dense enough to support a brick.

LIGHTWEIGHT

HEAVYWEIGHT

accomplishes three things: First and foremost, it softens the grain's fiber, thereby preventing the sharp edges from puncturing and deflating the dough. Second, the hydrating effect also prevents the grains from robbing moisture from the dough, which would toughen the crumb. Third, steeping the grains activates the wheat's enzymes, converting some starches into sugars and, in turn, reducing bitterness and coaxing out a sweet flavor (see "Soaking Wheat for Better Bread").

A soaker dough might be just the thing that would allow me to ramp up the percentage of whole-wheat flour without any negative impact. I made another series of breads, incrementally increasing the whole wheat as far as I dared beyond 40 percent. This time I mixed the wheat flour in each batch with the milk I was already using until it formed a rough dough. I kneaded it briefly, then covered the bowl and let it rest on the counter overnight. The next morning, I broke each soaker dough into small pieces that would be easier to knead with the remaining ingredients (white flour, water, yeast, sugar, butter, and salt) and baked off the loaves. The results were even better than I had hoped: I was able to bring the total proportion of wheat flour up to 60 percent—a full 10 percent more than in my last attempt—with no decrease in loaf volume. Even better, the flavor of this bread was considerably more wheaty than any loaf I'd baked so far and boasted just the right hint of bitterness.

To add even more wheat flavor to the bread, I made another batch, mixing a small amount of wheat germ into the soaker. The germ, which is removed along with the bran during the milling process, is a significant source of not only the whole grain's nutrition but also its sweet flavor. Just as I'd hoped, it strengthened the bread's wheat taste even further, and everyone agreed that I'd taken that flavor as far as it could go. But my work was not yet done. I wanted this loaf to be the best it could be.

Getting a Head(y) Start

I'd baked enough bread over the years to know that the difference between a good-tasting loaf and one that offers the most robust, well-developed flavor can boil down to the use of a *biga* (also known as a starter or preferment). When left to sit overnight, this mixture of flour, water, and yeast develops a full range of unique flavors that give bread even more character.

My recipe was already an overnight process, so just before making the soaker I mixed the bread flour and water with a small amount of yeast and left the two bowls to sit at room temperature. But then I thought of something: The biga had used up all the remaining liquid in my dough.

Usually when I make bread, I use cold water to help keep the dough cool during the kneading process—the friction causes the dough's temperature to rise and can lead to an overproofed product whose flavor and texture both suffer. But all the liquid in my recipe was now incorporated into either the biga or the soaker—and after their overnight rest, both would be at room temperature.

There was nothing to do about the biga—it needed to rest at around 75 degrees to properly ferment. But I wondered if I could get away with refrigerating the soaker as it sat overnight and then using it to keep the final dough's temperature cool.

Fortunately, the refrigerator did not inhibit the soaking process one bit, and when I kneaded the chilled soaker with the room-temperature biga the next morning, the finished dough came out of the mixer at an ideal 75 degrees. I then proofed, shaped, and baked the dough as before. The result? A unanimous thumbs-up from my tasters, all of whom appreciated the bread's newfound complexity.

Finishing Touches

Now that I had my basic recipe figured out, there were just two minor tests to sort through. White sugar had been working fine, but when I experimented with brown sugar, molasses, and honey, my tasters voted for the honey, citing superior flavor and complexity. And then there was the fat. Butter was making the bread just a tad too tender and rich. No problem: Cutting back on the fat by more than half was a good start, and then swapping out even more of the butter for vegetable oil was an easy fix.

That was the last batch I pulled out of the oven—a hearty yet soft-textured loaf that sliced cleanly and offered up an earthy, faintly sweet flavor with just a hint of bitterness. And just to be sure it functioned well in all applications, I made toast, grilled cheese sandwiches, and tuna melts, all with great success. Admittedly, making this bread was not a speedy process, but the results were worth the wait.

1. MAKE BIGA Combine bread flour, water, and yeast and let mixture rest overnight to create bubbly, aromatic starter dough.

2. MAKE SOAKER Steep whole-wheat flour and wheat germ in milk to hydrate bran and help reduce its bitterness.

3. KNEAD SOAKER Briefly knead soaker, then chill overnight to ensure that final dough reaches proper temperature.

4. COMBINE BIGA AND SOAKER Tear soaker into 1-inch pieces and mix with biga (and remaining ingredients). Knead, then let rise 45 minutes.

5. FOLD AND TURN Deflate center of dough, then fold it in on itself. Turn bowl 90 degrees; fold again. Repeat for total of 8 folds. Let rise 45 minutes.

6. DIVIDE AND PRESS Halve dough and pat each portion into 8 by 17-inch rectangle, with short side facing you.

7. ROLL Roll each sheet toward you into tight cylinder. Keep roll taut by tucking it under itself as you go. Pinch seams to seal.

8. PLACE AND RISE Place each loaf seam side down in prepared loaf pans. Let dough rise until almost doubled in size, 60 to 90 minutes.

9. ADD STEAM Place empty loaf pan on lower oven rack and fill with boiling water. Steam prevents crust from drying out before loaves expand.

10. SLASH TOPS Using knife blade, make shallow slash down center of each loaf to stop bread from tearing randomly when it rises. Bake 40 to 50 minutes.

WHOLE-WHEAT SANDWICH BREAD
MAKES TWO 9 BY 5-INCH LOAVES

NOTE: You can hand-knead the dough, but we've found that it's easy to add too much flour during the kneading stage, resulting in a slightly tougher loaf. Wheat germ is usually found either in the baking aisle near the flours or with hot cereals such as oatmeal. Leftover bread can be wrapped in a double layer of plastic wrap and stored at room temperature for 3 days. To freeze the bread for up to 1 month, wrap it with an additional layer of aluminum foil.

Biga
- 2 cups (11 ounces) bread flour
- 1 cup (8 ounces) warm water (100–110 degrees)
- ½ teaspoon instant or rapid-rise yeast

Soaker
- 3 cups (16½ ounces) whole-wheat flour, plus extra for kneading
- ½ cup wheat germ (see note)
- 2 cups (16 ounces) whole milk

Dough
- ¼ cup honey
- 4 teaspoons table salt
- 2 tablespoons instant or rapid-rise yeast
- 6 tablespoons unsalted butter, softened
- 2 tablespoons vegetable oil
   Bread flour for work surface

1. FOR THE BIGA: Combine bread flour, water, and yeast in large bowl and stir with wooden spoon until uniform mass forms and no dry flour remains, about 1 minute. Cover bowl tightly with plastic wrap and let stand at room temperature (70 degrees) overnight (at least 8 hours and up to 24 hours).

2. FOR THE SOAKER: Combine whole-wheat flour, wheat germ, and milk in large bowl and stir with wooden spoon until shaggy mass forms, about 1 minute. Turn out dough onto lightly floured work surface and knead until smooth, 2 to 3 minutes. Return soaker to bowl, cover tightly with plastic wrap, and refrigerate overnight (at least 8 hours and up to 24 hours).

3. FOR THE DOUGH: Tear soaker apart into 1-inch pieces and place in bowl of stand mixer fitted with dough hook. Add biga, honey, salt, yeast, butter, and oil. Mix on low speed until cohesive mass starts to form, about 2 minutes. Increase speed to medium and knead until dough is smooth and elastic, 8 to 10 minutes. Turn out dough onto lightly floured counter and knead 1 minute. Shape dough into ball and place in lightly greased container. Cover tightly with plastic wrap and allow to rise at room temperature 45 minutes.

4. Gently press down on center of dough to deflate. Holding edge of dough with fingertips, fold partially risen dough over itself by gently lifting and folding edge of dough toward middle. Turn bowl 90 degrees; fold again. Turn bowl and fold dough 6 more times (total of 8 folds). Cover and allow to rise at room temperature until doubled in volume, about 45 minutes.

5. Adjust oven racks to middle and lowest positions, place baking stone on middle rack, and heat oven to 400 degrees. Spray two 8½ by 4½-inch loaf pans with nonstick cooking spray. Transfer dough to well-floured counter and divide into 2 pieces. Working with 1 ball of dough at a time, pat each into 8 by 17-inch rectangle. With short side facing you, roll dough toward you into firm cylinder, keeping roll taut by tucking it under itself as you go. Turn loaf seam side up and pinch it closed. Place loaf seam side down in prepared loaf pan, pressing gently into corners. Repeat with second ball of dough. Cover loaves loosely with plastic wrap and allow to rise at room temperature until almost doubled in size, 60 to 90 minutes (top of loaves should rise about 1 inch over lip of pan).

6. Place empty loaf pan or other heatproof pan on bottom oven rack and bring 2 cups water to boil on stovetop. Using sharp serrated knife or single-edge razor blade, make one ¼-inch-deep slash lengthwise down center of each loaf. Pour boiling water into empty loaf pan in oven and set loaves on baking stone. Reduce oven temperature to 350 degrees. Bake until crust is dark brown and internal temperature registers 200 degrees on instant-read thermometer, 40 to 50 minutes, rotating loaves 180 degrees and side to side halfway through baking.

7. Transfer pans to wire rack and let cool 5 minutes. Remove loaves from pans, return to rack, and cool to room temperature, about 2 hours.

The Reinvention of Peanut Butter

"Natural" peanut butter used to mean an oil slick on top and a texture so stiff you could stand a stick in it. Is the new breed of butters any better? And what exactly makes them "natural"?

≥ BY DIANA BURRELL ≤

Selecting a jar of peanut butter never used to be complicated. Once you aligned yourself with either the creamy or the crunchy camp, you had two basic choices: conventional peanut butters made with hydrogenated oil and other additives, or the barely processed versions containing just nuts and maybe a pinch of salt. In the past, we've been firm believers in the conventional kind. As much as we might like the idea of a healthier spread made only with ground-up nuts, we've found that these generally offer the texture of Spackle and a taste sorely in need of added salt and sweeteners—and yes, hydrogenated fat.(Let's be clear: Hydrogenated fat is not the same as partially hydrogenated fat, a trans fat that we all want to avoid.)

But these days it seems as though manufacturers have literally gone nuts, cramming supermarket shelves with not only the familiar options, but also everything else they can think of to increase market share. You'll find organic varieties; reduced-fat specimens; sea-salt, no-salt, and low-salt versions; and omega 3–enriched spreads—not to mention "no-stir," "honey-roasted," and "whipped" styles. From our vantage point, the most intriguing development has been the proliferation of peanut butters now declaring themselves "natural." Would these spreads offer a taste and texture good enough to lure us away from the "unnatural" conventional butters made with hydrogenated oil?

To answer that question, I went to the supermarket and came home with a staggering number of peanut butters—15 creamy spreads and 13 crunchy ones. I separated out the crunchy butters for their own tasting (see "While We Were at It: Tasting Crunchy P. B.," page 26), then proceeded to whittle the creamy ones down to a more manageable number in a series of preliminary tasting rounds. The final lineup boasted four representatives from the conventional category, five brands with "natural" in their names, and one organic style.

The Fine Print

Before dipping in our spoons, we spun the jars around to examine their contents. We were immediately disabused of any notion that "natural" on the label meant bare-bones peanuts. Only one jar—Smucker's Natural—contained just peanuts (and less than 1 percent salt). The other four included some of the same additives found in conventional butters, including sweeteners and salt, as well as molasses and even flax seed oil. But instead of hydrogenated fat, they contained palm oil.

The prevalence of palm oil in the so-called natural butters (the organic brand contained it, too) made me curious, so I did a little research. It turns out that because the U.S. Food and Drug Administration (FDA) doesn't regulate the term "natural," manufacturers can literally put almost anything in the jar and still use that label. It also turns out that in terms of saturated fat, palm oil is as much of a culprit as hydrogenated oil. Palm oil, in fact, is made up of about 55 percent saturated fat. When I examined their nutrition labels again, I found that most of the "natural" peanut butters made with this oil contained at least 3 grams of saturated fat per serving—the same amount as conventional spreads made with hydrogenated oil. Bottom line: If a "natural" peanut butter has palm oil in it, it probably doesn't belong in the health food aisle any more than a conventional peanut butter does. (It's worth noting that a pure peanut butter may not be all that deserving of a spot there either. The closest thing to an additive-free spread in our lineup, Smucker's Natural, contains 2.5 grams of saturated fat per serving.)

Sticking Points

But the real question before us was how these palm-oil products would taste—and spread—compared with other brands. So I rallied my colleagues to sample the peanut butters straight up in a blind tasting; peanut butter cookies and spicy satay sauce would follow later.

After everyone put down their spoons, I had one key finding: While some tasters were staunchly in favor of a particular flavor profile—some preferred a sweeter peanut butter, others liked a good hit of salt, and many voted in favor of products that struck a good balance between the two—the bottom line was all about texture. As they had in the past, the creamiest, most spreadable peanut butters—even those with less-than-robust peanut flavor—jumped to the top of the chart. To our surprise, these included not only the conventional butters but a couple of the "natural" styles as well.

At the same time, samples that were gritty and sludgy (Smucker's Natural, Smart Balance All Natural Rich Roast), dribbly and goopy (MaraNatha Organic No Stir), or too sticky (Peanut Butter & Co. No-Stir Natural Smooth Operator) were panned,

Keeping Peanut Butter Creamy, Artificially and "Naturally"

The earliest mass-produced peanut butters didn't contain any added fat. But just like the single-ingredient peanut butters manufactured today (and the ones you can grind yourself at the supermarket), their texture was so stiff from the inevitable separation of oil from the ground-up nuts that grocers received the spreads in tubs with instructions to stir frequently with a wooden paddle. The separated oil had another problem: It was prone to rancidity. A chemist named Joseph L. Rosefield solved both problems in 1922 by removing some of the natural peanut oil, which is liquid at room temperature, and replacing it with hydrogenated oil, an animal or vegetable fat chemically altered to include more saturated fatty acids to make it solid at room temperature. The result: a shelf-stable, semisolid spread.

These days, an increasing number of peanut butter manufacturers are replacing hydrogenated fat with palm oil, a naturally highly saturated fat that works much the same way. But though such a product may call itself "natural," the exact melting point of the palm oil can be subject to as much manipulation as that of hydrogenated fat. Despite this, we found palm oil to be less effective in keeping a peanut butter smooth and creamy. And "natural" or not, it contributes a comparable amount of saturated fat to the mix as hydrogenated oil.

—D.B.

SUPER CREAMY
The hydrogenated fat in our winner, Skippy Peanut Butter, means that no oil separates out, for a supremely creamy texture.

LESS CREAMY
The palm oil in this "natural" peanut butter from Peanut Butter & Co. wasn't fully effective in keeping the spread emulsified.

OIL SLICK
Smucker's Natural is made from nothing but ground peanuts and a little salt—and it's got a thick film of oil on top to prove it.

MARCH & APRIL 2011

25

no matter how nutty or well rounded they tasted.

How much would creaminess and peanut flavor matter once the samples were baked into cookies and mixed into satay sauce? Turns out texture was again the number-one factor: Dry, gritty peanut butters like Smucker's and Smart Balance made for predictably dry, gritty cookies. And the sauces they made? Unpalatably "stiff" and "pasty." Meanwhile, creamier samples, particularly the two top-ranking "natural" brands from the plain tasting, turned out cookies with "nice softness" and "satisfying chew," along with sauces with such good consistency that tasters were happy to "eat them by the spoonful."

That said, MaraNatha, whose "runny," "mouth-coating" texture stranded it near the bottom rungs in the plain tasting, actually took bronze in the cookie round, where its more fluid composition lent moisture to the dough and turned out "sturdy" yet "pleasantly soft" cookies. Furthermore, the satay sauce brought out a flaw in the winner of our plain tasting—namely that its somewhat "muted" peanut flavor became even more faded in the presence of spicy ingredients and tart lime juice.

Tried and (Still) True

When we tallied our final results, nobody was especially surprised by the overall champ. As it had when we evaluated peanut butters in both 2001 and 2006, regular old hydrogenated oil–based Skippy took top honors for a supremely "smooth," "creamy" texture that even made up for what a few tasters deemed a "slightly weak" nutty flavor. Nor were we particularly stunned when the only truly additive-free peanut butter in the bunch (not counting its tiny bit of salt)—Smucker's Natural—fell to the bottom of the rankings due to a texture that tasters deemed "inedible" and, when baked into cookies, as intractable as a "hockey puck."

What did surprise us, however, was the very close runner-up: Jif Natural, one of two palm oil–based peanut butters to make the "recommended" list. Like Skippy, it garnered praise for a "wonderfully" smooth texture. Tasters also praised its "dark roast-y" flavor, which we attribute in part to the inclusion of molasses, an ingredient common to three out of our five favorite peanut butters (and absent in four of the five lower-ranking contenders).

Like the other favored palm-oil brand (Skippy Natural), Jif Natural is not actually a peanut butter but a "spread." By FDA regulations, if a product has less than 90 percent peanuts and more than 55 percent fat, it must be labeled a "spread." Nomenclature aside, the extra fat in Jif Natural may have contributed to a creaminess on a par with regular Skippy, even in the absence of hydrogenated fat.

Maybe someday manufacturers will figure out a way to make an übercreamy, full-flavored peanut butter with just the nuts. In the meantime, we'll be making our PB&Js with our longtime favorite, regular Skippy Peanut Butter.

While We Were at It: Tasting Crunchy Peanut Butter

Though we don't use it as much as the creamy stuff for cooking purposes, crunchy peanut butter occupies a prime spot in many home kitchen pantries.

We selected 13 brands, eliminating six in an initial pretasting: Arrowhead Mills Crunchy Valencia Peanut Butter; Arrowhead Mills Organic Crunchy Valencia Peanut Butter; MaraNatha Natural with Salt, Crunchy & Roasted Peanut Butter; MaraNatha Natural No Stir Crunchy & Sweet Peanut Butter; Jif Regular Peanut Butter, Extra Crunchy; Skippy Super Chunk Peanut Butter. We then sampled the remaining seven crunchy spreads to figure out which ones had the best peanut flavor, texture, and balance of sweetness and saltiness.

Not surprisingly, our favorites—and least favorites—tracked almost identically with the results from the creamy tasting. Smucker's Organic Chunky, Smart Balance All Natural Rich Roast Chunky, and MaraNatha Organic No Stir Crunchy all suffered from texture flaws, with tasters condemning them for "grainy," "gritty" consistencies and, particularly in the case of MaraNatha, for being so "soupy" and "viscous" that it was "hard to eat." In some instances, their flavors were no help either; the hints of "fishiness" that we picked up on in the creamy Smart Balance were just as present in this chunkier batch.

Likewise, tasters gravitated toward the crunchy versions of Jif and Skippy Natural, our two favorite palm oil–based peanut butters from the creamy tasting. In fact, both of these spreads beat out their conventional equivalents (eliminated after the pretasting), with tasters praising their sweet-salty balance, "strong roasted flavor," and "really good crunch." –D.B.

Improving on Nature?

We wondered if we could convert our bottom-ranked peanut butter, Smucker's Natural, into an approximation of top-ranked Skippy's by making it less natural. So we gooped it up: We opened a new jar, poured off the oil on top, then dumped it into a food processor and processed it until creamy with a big gob of solid Crisco and generous amounts of salt and sugar. Our tasters' verdict? The doctored Smucker's Natural was far creamier and tastier than the original, but still couldn't compare to Skippy's. In this case, we'll leave the chemistry to the corporate experts.

RECOMMENDED

JIF Natural Crunchy Peanut Butter Spread
Price: $2.79 for 18 oz. (15 cents per oz.)
Comments: With "nice roasted-peanut flavor," "well-balanced" sweetness that reminded tasters of "honey," and "good crunch," this sibling to our creamy runner-up was "a joy to eat" and our favorite of the bunch.

SKIPPY Natural Super Chunk Peanut Butter Spread
Price: $2.39 for 18 oz. (13 cents per oz.)
Comments: Tasters most enjoyed that this peanut butter offered a "good amount of crunch" but was still "rich, thick, and smooth around the chunks." Though some people found it a tad "salty," most noted that its flavor was "balanced" and "not too sweet."

PEANUT BUTTER & CO. Crunch Time No-Stir Natural Peanut Butter
Price: $4.49 for 16 oz. (28 cents per oz.)
Comments: Though multiple tasters found this sample "very sugary," others felt that sweetness helped balance out its "roasty—almost bitter" edge. Meanwhile, it won fans for a good "crunchy to smooth ratio."

RECOMMENDED, CONTINUED

PETER PAN Crunchy Peanut Butter
Price: $2.89 for 16.3 oz. (18 cents per oz.)
Comments: Tasters found this sample "faux chunky" with "not many bits." That said, others noted that the creamy portion around the chunks was "smooth" and "melts nicely in your mouth."

NOT RECOMMENDED

SMUCKER'S Organic Chunky Peanut Butter
Price: $4.89 for 16 oz. (31 cents per oz.)
Comments: As one taster pointed out, this sample tasted like "real peanuts"—though that wasn't a compliment. The majority of tasters found this all-natural specimen "bland," "greasy," and undersalted with a texture that was "tacky" and "gritty."

SMART BALANCE All Natural Rich Roast Chunky Peanut Butter
Price: $3.19 for 16 oz. (20 cents per oz.)
Comments: The crunchy version of this peanut butter racked up complaints about its "fishy," "earthy, dirt-like" off-flavors—likely caused by the addition of flax seed oil, which spoils easily. Even worse, tasters found the salt so overwhelming that it "masked the peanut flavor."

TASTING CREAMY PEANUT BUTTER

Twenty-one *Cook's Illustrated* staff members tasted 10 creamy peanut butters in four blind tastings; the peanut butters were culled from a list of top-selling national brands compiled by the Chicago-based market research firm SymphonyIRI Group. We eliminated the following brands in a series of pretastings: Simply Jif, MaraNatha Natural Peanut Butter with Salt, MaraNatha Natural No-Stir Peanut Butter, MaraNatha Organic Peanut Butter with Salt, Arrowhead Mills Creamy Valencia Peanut Butter, Arrowhead Mills Organic Creamy Valencia Peanut Butter, and Smucker's Organic Peanut Butter. We judged our final panel of peanut butters in two plain tastings, then tasted them in peanut butter cookies and in a spicy satay sauce. We asked our tasters to rate the peanut butters for peanut flavor, sweetness, saltiness, and texture. Results were averaged, and peanut butters are listed below in order of preference. The peanut butters were also sent to an independent laboratory to be tested for sugar and salt levels. All peanut butters were purchased at Boston-area supermarkets or ordered online.

RECOMMENDED

SKIPPY Peanut Butter
Price: $2.39 for 16.3-oz. jar (15 cents per oz.)
Total Sugar: 10.7%
Salt: 1.25%
Ingredients: Roasted peanuts, sugar, hydrogenated vegetable oils (cottonseed, soybean, and rapeseed) to prevent separation, salt
Comments: In a contest that hinged on texture, tasters thought this "smooth," "creamy" sample was "swell" and gave it top honors, both plain and baked into cookies. Its rave reviews even compensated for a slightly "weak" nut flavor that didn't come through as well as that of other brands in the pungent satay sauce.

JIF Natural Peanut Butter Spread
Price: $2.29 for 18-oz. jar (13 cents per oz.)
Total Sugar: 11.5%
Salt: 0.61%
Ingredients: Peanuts, sugar, palm oil, contains 2% or less of salt, molasses
Comments: The big favorite in satay sauce, this peanut butter's "dark, roasted flavor"—helped by the addition of molasses—stood out particularly well against the other heady ingredients, and it made cookies with "nice sweet-salty balance." Plus, as the top-rated palm oil–based sample, it was "creamy," "thick," and better emulsified than other "natural" contenders.

REESE'S Peanut Butter
Price: $2.59 for 18-oz. jar (14 cents per oz.)
Total Sugar: 9.9%
Salt: 1.11%
Ingredients: Roasted peanuts, sugar, peanut oil, hydrogenated vegetable oil (contains rapeseed, cottonseed, and soybean oils), salt, molasses, monoglycerides, and cornstarch
Comments: "This is what peanut butter should be like," declared one happy taster, noting specifically this product's "good," "thick" texture and "powerful peanut flavor." In satay sauce, however, some tasters felt that heavier body made for a "pasty" end result.

JIF Peanut Butter
Price: $2.29 for 18-oz. jar (13 cents per oz.)
Total Sugar: 10.7%
Salt: 1.26%
Ingredients: Roasted peanuts, sugar, contains 2% or less of molasses, fully hydrogenated vegetable oils (rapeseed and soybean), mono- and diglycerides, salt
Comments: This classic peanut butter lived up to its "creamy, rich" reputation and turned out a "nice, chewy" batch of cookies. But some tasters felt that the chiles and other ingredients in satay sauce overpowered its "sweet, mellow" flavor.

SKIPPY Natural Peanut Butter Spread
Price: $2.39 for 15-oz. jar (16 cents per oz.)
Total Sugar: 8.8%
Salt: 1.26%
Ingredients: Roasted peanuts, sugar, palm oil, salt
Comments: The only other palm oil–based peanut butter to make the "recommended" cut, this contender had a "looser" texture than its winning sibling but still won fans for being "super-smooth." Tasters thought it made an especially "well-balanced," "complex" peanut sauce.

RECOMMENDED WITH RESERVATIONS

PEANUT BUTTER & CO. No-Stir Natural Smooth Operator
Price: $4.49 for 18-oz. jar (25 cents per oz.)
Total Sugar: 8.7%
Salt: 0.85%
Ingredients: Peanuts, evaporated cane juice, palm fruit oil, salt
Comments: Though it says "no-stir" on the label, this "stiff" palm oil–enriched peanut butter was "weeping oil" and came across as "greasy" to some tasters. However, it turned out a respectable batch of cookies—"chewy in the center, crisp and short at the edge"—and made "perfectly good" satay sauce.

MARANATHA Organic No Stir Peanut Butter
Price: $5.69 for 16-oz. jar (36 cents per oz.)
Total Sugar: 9.3%
Salt: 0.51%
Ingredients: Organic dry roasted peanuts, organic palm oil, organic unrefined cane sugar, salt
Comments: On the one hand, this organic peanut butter produced cookies that were "soft and sturdy" yet "moist," with "knockout peanut flavor." On the other hand, eating it straight from the jar was nearly impossible; its "loose," "liquid-y," and "dribbly" consistency had one taster wonder if it was "peanut soup."

PETER PAN Peanut Butter
Price: $2.49 for 18-oz. jar (14 cents per oz.)
Total Sugar: 10.8%
Salt: 1.11%
Ingredients: Roasted peanuts, sugar, less than 2% of hydrogenated vegetable oils (cottonseed and rapeseed), salt, partially hydrogenated cottonseed oil
Comments: Though this peanut butter offered an ideally "cushiony, smooth" texture, it also left an "off-putting," "waxy," "stale" aftertaste that, according to some tasters, also plagued the cookies.

NOT RECOMMENDED

SMART BALANCE All Natural Rich Roast Peanut Butter
Price: $3.59 for 16-oz. jar (22 cents per oz.)
Total Sugar: 8.2%
Salt: 1.19%
Ingredients: Peanuts, evaporated cane juice, natural oil blend (palm fruit and flax seed oils), salt, molasses
Comments: Besides being unpalatably "tacky" and "sludgy," this "natural" peanut butter suffered from an awful "fishy" flavor with a "weird acidic aftertaste" that tasters noted in all three applications. Our best guess as to the culprit? The inclusion of flax seed oil, an unsaturated fat that's highly susceptible to rancidity.

SMUCKER'S Natural Peanut Butter
Price: $2.69 for 16-oz. jar (17 cents per oz.)
Total Sugar: 3.9%
Salt: 0.50%
Ingredients: Peanuts, contains 1 percent or less of salt
Comments: With its only additive a negligible amount of salt, the only truly natural peanut butter in the lineup elicited comments ranging from mild dissatisfaction ("needs enhancement with salt and sugar") to outright disgust ("slithery," "chalky," "inedible"). Cookies were "dry and crumbly" with a "hockey puck" texture, and the satay sauce was "stiff," "gritty," and "gloppy."

The Best Toaster Oven

Do you really need to spend $250 to get a good piece of toast?

⇒ BY LISA McMANUS ⇐

First, the good news: Toaster ovens have improved—a little. In 2007, we were hard-pressed to find one that could eke out a decent piece of toast. Today, testing 10 new models, including a makeover of our former winner from Krups, a slice of golden-brown toast is no longer quite so hard to get. The bad news? They're not cheap. The least expensive model we tested was $60; a good half of them were $150 or more. Manufacturers justify these prices by offering a slew of different features, including some we never imagined desirable in a toaster oven: a food dehydrator, a chicken rotisserie, a bun warmer, even a built-in meat probe. Assumptions about what a toaster oven should do have changed, too: More are called countertop ovens, leaving "toast" right out of the equation.

Daily Bread

As cooks, we appreciate the merits of a small second oven, handy for preparing single portions and side dishes, melting cheese on sandwiches, and keeping the kitchen cool in hot weather. A toaster oven takes half the time of a full-size oven to preheat, and is more energy-efficient for small tasks. Toasting is still important, though: If these ovens can't toast a simple slice of bread, what are the chances they can handle cookies, chicken, or pizza?

We began our tests simply by making toast, buying dozens of loaves of our favorite white bread and toasting slice after slice on each oven's "medium" toast setting. Five of the 10 models easily surpassed the performance of their 2007 counterparts. Two were a total disappointment, doing little more than heating up the slices: After several minutes, their "toast" was almost as white as it was before going in.

A good toaster oven should radiate intense heat for broiling and browning. To test for this ability we made dark toast. A few brands failed miserably: One model's darkest setting (out of nine choices) produced black smoke and a chunk of inedible charcoal. Another's dial ticked away as it burned the bread to a crisp. Only two ended up capable of producing both deeply browned toast and good medium toast.

Toasting six slices of bread at a time gave us an excellent snapshot of heating patterns. The best performers—including the two models that excelled in our other toasting tests—browned evenly across both sides of the six slices, while lesser ovens had hot and cold spots, yielding mottled results.

Roast and Bake

If we're paying top dollar for a toaster oven claiming it can perform a wide range of functions, it better be able to carry them out. So we set up these ovens with a range of bigger cooking challenges, from melting cheese on tuna sandwiches and thin-crust pizzas to heating dense casseroles of frozen macaroni and cheese. We tried baking crisp lemon cookies and roasting 4-pound chickens. Those ovens that failed to toast evenly, we found, also did poor work melting cheese uniformly across sandwiches and pizza, leaving some areas still solid and others overly browned. Instead of becoming shapely disks with light golden edges, cookies baked in these models emerged as blobs with randomly browned surfaces. Macaroni and cheese was still cool in the center after over an hour of baking, with the edges drying out. And a few ovens always seemed to take longer to get the job done—we actually gave up on one after it failed to melt cheese on pizza in a reasonable amount of time, or fully cook a chicken after two hours. (A backup copy of this oven performed just as poorly.)

Interior space was also an issue. Squeezing a whole chicken into the narrow confines of a few of the ovens was nearly impossible. The most cramped was horizontally divided, with a bun-warming chamber on top that left little room in the oven beneath. Unsurprisingly, perhaps, the ovens tall enough to easily accommodate a whole chicken—including one with a rotisserie—failed to cook anything else especially well, because foods less voluminous than chicken sat too far away from their heating elements.

After compiling the results of each test, it was clear that the ovens that aced our toasting tests were also best at general cooking. But why were they so successful? We did one last trial, setting all the ovens to 350 degrees and hooking up each one to a thermocouple to gauge accuracy. True to form, the wimpy ovens barely reached 315 degrees; others varied wildly, hitting far above and below the mark; and the best climbed closest to the 350-degree target and stayed there.

Top Choice

Two ovens distinguished themselves with consistently good performance, but only one was truly exemplary: The Smart Oven by Breville ($249.95) achieved a perfect score. Toast browned evenly on every setting, whether we wanted one slice or six. Cookies, a tuna melt, pizza, mac and cheese, and chicken were

Bad for Toast, Bad for Baking

We found that if an oven couldn't produce nice, evenly browned toast, this was a pretty good indicator that it couldn't perform any of its other functions well, including basic baking. The toast and sugar cookies below were made in the Cuisinart Convection Toaster Oven ($179), which we don't recommend.

UNEVENLY BROWNED   **UNEVENLY BAKED**

thoroughly and uniformly cooked. This oven was big enough for chicken but sufficiently compact for browning toast and baking smaller foods. Its five heating elements (most models had four)—three rods on top, two below—cycle on and off keyed to preset programs for different foods, directing heat where needed (though we found the presets easy to customize, and the oven "remembers" your adjustments). Its heating elements are quartz, which heats and cools faster than the nickel and chromium heating apparatus found in most toaster ovens. It is thus more responsive, provides steadier heat, and eliminates the usual toaster oven pitfall: the hot spots that form directly under the elements.

Interestingly, the Breville Smart Oven has an unusual mechanism for maintaining its rock-steady heating. Most toaster ovens operate with an "on/off" switch—they get hotter until they literally switch off, and then cool gradually until they switch back on, maintaining an average temperature close to what you want. By contrast, the Breville operates with a sort of "dimmer" switch, staying on but varying the intensity to sustain the desired temperature.

If $250 is too much, the Hamilton Beach Set & Forget Toaster Oven with Convection Cooking ($99.99) is our Best Buy. At less than half the price of the Breville, it is similarly proportioned, striking the balance between adequate interior space and concentrated heating. Its elements are not as sophisticated, but it was one of the most accurate ovens and produced consistently acceptable food. Both ovens were also remarkably simple to use, unlike others with thick manuals and confusing buttons. Our winners required no learning curve.

Watch the Testing in Progress
Video available FREE for 4 months at
www.CooksIllustrated.com/apr11

TESTING TOASTER OVENS

We tested 10 toaster ovens, all claiming to hold a 12-inch pizza or six slices of toast; most also offered convection settings. Prices listed were paid at online retailers. Ovens appear in order of preference. See page 32 for sources for the winners.

TOASTING:

We made single slices of toast (using white bread) on medium and dark settings, preferring models that produced evenly golden-brown medium toast, with crisp exteriors and moist interiors; and dark toast that was a deep, appealing brown, not burned. We also toasted multiple batches of six slices to evaluate the heating patterns in the ovens, rating highly those that produced uniformly browned batches. Scores on these tasks were averaged.

COOKING:

We baked lemon cookies, melted cheese on tuna sandwiches, heated frozen pizzas and macaroni and cheese casseroles, and roasted whole chickens, averaging the scores from each test.

USER-FRIENDLINESS:

We looked for solid construction, easy cleanup, and straightforward controls that didn't constantly send us back to the manual.

ACCURACY:

Using a thermocouple to gauge accuracy, we tested how well empty ovens held the standard temperature of 350 degrees.

	PERFORMANCE	TESTERS' COMMENTS

HIGHLY RECOMMENDED

The Smart Oven by BREVILLE
Model: BOV800 XL
Price: $249.95

Toasting: ★★★
Cooking: ★★★
User-friendliness: ★★★
Accuracy: ★★★

While the price makes us wince, this well-designed oven aced every test and was simple to use. Food browned and cooked uniformly, whether we were roasting chicken, toasting bread, or melting cheese. Five quartz elements consistently cooled and reheated, producing steady, controlled heat.

RECOMMENDED

BEST BUY

HAMILTON BEACH Set & Forget Toaster Oven with Convection Cooking
Model: 31230
Price: $99.99

Toasting: ★★★
Cooking: ★★
User-friendliness: ★★★
Accuracy: ★★

Clearly designed control buttons, a helpful electronic display, and an easy-to-understand manual made using this oven a snap. Not quite as accurate as our winner, it still produced golden-brown toast and crisp-skinned roast chicken. Pizza and cookies baked a tiny bit unevenly. We liked its meat probe.

RECOMMENDED WITH RESERVATIONS

BLACK & DECKER Digital Convection Oven
Model: CTO6305
Price: $89.99

Toasting: ★★★
Cooking: ★★
User-friendliness: ★★★
Accuracy: ★

This oven's performance was acceptable but a little uneven. Its elements cycled far lower when we set it for 350 degrees. Cookies and chicken browned unevenly, though mac and cheese and pizza were fine; toast was terrific with one slice but a little patchy in multiple batches.

KRUPS 6-Slice Convection Toaster Oven
Model: FBC2
Price: $149.99

Toasting: ★
Cooking: ★★
User-friendliness: ★★★
Accuracy: ★★

A more pared-down version of our previous winner from Krups, which was discontinued, this oven just doesn't measure up to new competition. Ironically, the earlier Krups made decent toast. This time, single slices of toast were its biggest downfall, coloring too much or barely at all.

DUALIT Professional Mini Oven
Model: 89100
Price: $249.95

Toasting: ★★
Cooking: ★★★
User-friendliness: ★★
Accuracy: ★

Solidly built and simple to set, this pricey oven was well lit with a large window—a good thing, since testing confirmed that it ran so hot (cycling as high as 428 degrees when we wanted 350) that we usually had to stand by, ready to yank out the food early, before it overcooked. Still, it cooked evenly and well.

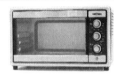

OSTER 6081 Channel 6-Slice Toaster Oven
Model: 6801
Price: $58.01

Toasting: ★★★
Cooking: ★★
User-friendliness: ★
Accuracy: ★★

This was the cheapest model in the lineup, and its slightly tinny feel and badly designed controls made that clear: Knobs are labeled underneath and hard to set without stooping; settings are printed in low-contrast color. But its heat was relatively accurate and the cooking, including toast, was surprisingly above par.

NOT RECOMMENDED

CUISINART Convection Toaster Oven
Model: TOB-195
Price: $179

Toasting: ★★
Cooking: ★★
User-friendliness: ★★
Accuracy: ★

Toast turned out light when we wanted it medium or dark, plus it always colored unevenly. Cookies, pizza, and tuna melts also came out with darker patches where they'd been under the elements. Chicken cooked well but made a smoky, greasy mess. Its controls (with 16 buttons!) required multiple steps.

DE'LONGHI ESCLUSIVO Convection Toaster Oven
Model: DO1289
Price: $149.95

Toasting: ★
Cooking: ★★★
User-friendliness: ★
Accuracy: ★★

Though it was relatively accurate, baked perfect cookies, and heated a casserole thoroughly, this oven took forever to cook. Toast was perfect on top, but pale on bottom. Its ridiculously confusing controls gave us a headache. We didn't even bother trying its food-dehydrator setting.

T-FAL Avante Elite Toaster Oven
Model: OT8085002
Price: $89.99

Toasting: ★★
Cooking: ★
User-friendliness: ★
Accuracy: ★★

This oven (and a backup copy) started out strong but failed halfway through cooking. Roast chicken was still only half-cooked after nearly two hours. When pizza cheese failed to bubble long after the recommended cooking time, we gave up. We hated the design.

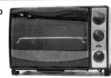

WEST BEND Countertop Oven with Rotisserie
Model: 74706
Price: $97.37

Toasting: ★
Cooking: ★★
User-friendliness: ★
Accuracy: ★

The only thing we liked about this cheaply made, poorly designed oven was its rotisserie, which helped produce a juicy golden bird despite its temperature being way off the mark, dipping as low as 226 degrees when set to 350 in our accuracy test. Toast stayed white on the bottom; pizza cheese never fully melted.

⇒ BY ANDREW JANJIGIAN & DAN SOUZA ⇐

Getting the Best Zest

Which tool is best for harvesting zest from lemons and other citrus fruits: a plain old vegetable peeler, a "channel" zester that pushes thin strings of zest through a row of tiny holes as you drag it across the fruit, or a rasp-style grater (originally a wood-working tool) that turns out sawdust-like bits of zest? Zest produced by the first two tools generally requires mincing before it can be added to recipes, and some cooks worry that this leaves too much of the essential oils on the cutting board, with less for the dish. We used all three methods to zest lemons, mincing the larger zest from the peeler and channel zester with a knife, and adding them all to lemon pound cake and our recipe for Spaghetti with Lemon and Olive Oil (January/February 2011). The result? Tasters found all the samples equally lemony. If no one way of zesting is best for flavor, we'll stick with the convenience of a rasp grater.

Caramel in the Microwave

Many cooks shy away from making caramel. The process involves nothing more than melting sugar on the stovetop, but it can be tricky nonetheless. The sugar must be heated slowly and carefully to avoid overcooking—an all-too-easy occurrence even when you're using a thermometer. And there's always the risk of getting splattered by the molten syrup as you stir. We recently learned of an easier, virtually hands-off approach: Use the microwave. Stir 1 cup of sugar, 2 tablespoons of corn syrup (added to help keep the caramel from recrystallizing), 2 tablespoons of water, and ⅛ teaspoon of lemon juice together in a 2-cup microwave-safe measuring cup or glass bowl. Microwave on full power until the mixture is just beginning to brown, 5 to 8 minutes (depending on the strength of your microwave). Remove the caramel from the microwave and let it sit on a dry surface for 5 minutes or until it darkens to a rich honey

brown. To make cara-
mel sauce, add ½ cup
of hot heavy cream a
few tablespoons at a
time (so the caramel
won't seize up), fol-
lowed by 1 tablespoon
of butter. Caramel
doesn't get any easier
than this.

STARTING TO BROWN   **IT'S DONE!**

TECHNIQUE | A BETTER WAY TO COAT YOUR LOAVES

The standard method for coating loaf bread with seeds, grains, or bran calls for misting or brushing the outside of the loaf with water before sprinkling seeds on the dough. When we tried this approach on our Whole-Wheat Sandwich Bread (page 24), we had a devil of a time sprinkling the seeds evenly over the loaf and noticed that far too many of the seeds fell off despite our efforts. We like the following method, which does a better job of moistening the dough without overwetting it (and causing seeds to slide off) while guaranteeing a thorough, even coating.

1. Place the shaped dough on a moist-ened, lightly wrung-out clean kitchen towel spread on a work surface; roll back and forth to moisten.

2. Spread about a ¼-inch layer of seeds on a second baking sheet. Roll the moistened loaf back and forth, pressing the dough gently against the seeds to ensure that they stick.

TEST KITCHEN TIP Yes, You Can Freeze Garlic

We occasionally find ourselves with too much fresh garlic on hand. Rather than let-ting the excess sprout before we can use it, we wanted a way to keep it in suspended animation. Here's our recommendation: Peel the cloves, mince or press them through a garlic press, and place the mince in a bowl. Add enough neutral-flavored oil (not extra-virgin olive oil, in case the dish you need it for calls for something else) to coat (about ½ teaspoon per clove), then spoon heaping teaspoons of the mixture onto a baking sheet. Place the baking sheet in the freezer until the garlic is firm, then transfer the frozen portions to a freezer-safe bag or container. The frozen garlic will keep for up to a month with no loss in flavor. Tasters were unable to distinguish the frozen garlic from freshly minced when we used both in pasta with garlic and oil.

TECHNIQUE | FOR EVENLY SHAPED PIZZA, DRAPE YOUR DOUGH

Stretching pizza dough into a symmetrical round of even thickness is easier said than done. It can stretch unevenly or even tear, leading to a misshapen finished pizza. That's why we were intrigued to learn about a new method—one that relies on the steady, evenly distributed pull of gravity to get the job done.

1. For a typical 12-inch pizza, press the dough into an 8-inch round on a well-floured countertop.

2. Drape half of the dough over the counter. Lift the top half of the dough off the counter, with your hands at approximately 10 and 2 o'clock.

3. Rotate the dough clockwise, using your left hand to feed the dough to your right hand, meeting at 12 o'clock. Continue until gravity has pulled it to a 12-inch diameter.

4. Return the fully stretched dough to the countertop or transfer it to a pizza peel for topping.

Much like a frittata or roesti, our Potato Galette (page 9) must be inverted out of the hot, heavy pan for serving—a step that can literally make or break the presentation. Here's our foolproof method for getting this (and other similar items that are cooked in a skillet) from pan to platter without having to flip the unwieldy pan.

 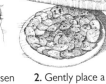 

1. With a spatula, loosen the galette or other cake and slide it out of the skillet onto a large plate.

2. Gently place a cutting board over the galette. Do not use an overly heavy board, which may crush the cake.

3. Flip the plate over so the board is on the bottom. Remove the plate, and the galette is ready to be sliced and served.

Taking the Pulse of Your Food Processor

Recipes using a food processor to chop or grind ingredients often call for "one-second pulses." But what exactly does this mean? Should you hold down the button for a full second and then release it? Or just press it for a microsecond, release it, and wait a full second before pressing down again? The answer depends on your machine. We tried different brands and observed what happened when we depressed their pulse buttons. Some, like our favorite, KitchenAid KFP750, instantly spun and continued to rotate a second after we lifted our finger off the button. Others, like the Viking Food Processor and Cuisinart Custom 14-Cup, came to a halt as soon as we lifted up, requiring us to keep the button depressed to complete a "pulse." To ensure that you get the right results when a recipe calls for a certain number of pulses, check your processor and find out what exactly happens to the blade—so you'll know whether to release the pulse button right away or keep it depressed to get a full one-second spin.

Minimizing Moisture Loss in Meat

For large cuts of meat or poultry, we often advocate a low-and-slow cooking method (with a short hit of intense heat at the very end to brown the exterior) rather than the more traditional high-temperature roasting all the way through. We find that this approach allows the center to come up to the desired internal temperature with less risk of overcooking the outer layers. But we recently conducted an experiment that proves that even cooking isn't the only benefit of slow-roasting: It also helps minimize the loss of flavorful juices (and fat).

We took two identical 6-pound rib roasts (trimmed of fat) and roasted one at 450 degrees and the other at 250 degrees until each was medium-rare, or 125 degrees, at the center. We then weighed the cooked roasts. The slow-cooked roast had lost about 9.25 percent of its starting weight, while the high-temperature roast had lost nearly 25 percent of its original weight. Why the difference? It's simple: Proteins shrink less and express less moisture and fat when cooked at moderate temperatures than at high heat.

So the next time you're tempted to turn up the heat on your roast, think twice.

250° OVEN   **450° OVEN**
High heat caused one 6-pound roast to lose significantly more moisture and fat than the same size roast cooked at a lower temperature.

Hold the Salt, Season with Vinegar

Every cook seasons with salt, which works its magic as an enhancer of flavors mainly by suppressing our perception of bitterness. As off-putting flavors recede, underlying flavors come to the fore. But many great chefs have another flavor enhancer in their arsenal: vinegar. Like salt, acids such as vinegar or lemon juice compete with bitter flavor compounds, lessening our perception of these tastes as they "brighten" remaining ones. We use vinegar to enliven the flavor of everything from soups and stews to sauces. Instead of just reaching for the salt shaker to boost the final flavor of a dish, consider a touch of vinegar as well. Use a plain white wine vinegar (ideally of at least 6 percent acidity, so a little goes a long way) or one matched to the other flavors of the dish (such as red wine vinegar in a sauce containing red wine). With just a dash, or about ⅛ teaspoon, you may find you need that much less salt.

Toning Down Raw Onion's Bite

We've often heard the claim that soaking sliced or chopped raw onions in liquid can mellow their harsh taste by drawing out the pungent sulfur compounds known as thiosulfinates that are produced when the onion is cut. But what kind of liquid and how long of a soak? We tested three of the most commonly recommended liquids—water, milk, and vinegar—by soaking the cut onions in each for 5 and 15 minutes. We found that 15 minutes was necessary for any of the treatments to be effective. The vinegar soak did rid the onions of much of their burn, but it was replaced by an equally strong sour taste, even after thorough rinsing. Milk was also very effective at removing the sulfur compounds, but it left the onions tasting washed-out. The best method—better than even plain water—was our own: a baking-soda solution (1 tablespoon per cup of water). Unlike the other methods, which merely do their best to leach away the offending sulfur compounds, the alkaline baking soda neutralizes sulfenic acid, the immediate precursor to the harsh-tasting thiosulfinates, and prevents them from forming in the first place. Just be sure to rinse the onions thoroughly before using to remove any soapy baking-soda taste.

NEUTRALIZE IT
A 15-minute soak in a solution of baking soda and water tames the pungent taste of sliced or chopped raw onions.

Low-Temp Pasta?

Most instructions for cooking dried pasta are invariably the same: Drop the noodles into a pot of boiling water, bring it back to a boil, and keep it bubbling vigorously until the pasta is done. We already broke with this conventional wisdom by showing that you can cook pasta in a lot less water than is typically called for, as long as you don't mind stirring it frequently.

Now we've learned that you don't need to hold your pasta water at a rolling boil either. In fact, you don't even need to keep the pot on the heat. The pasta will cook just fine if you take the pot off the burner as soon as you add the pasta, cover it immediately, stir once or twice during the first minute, cover again, and leave it to sit for the recommended cooking time. We tested this method with spaghetti, shells, farfalle, and ziti, using the full 4 quarts of water recommended per pound, and we found that the texture was identical to that of pasta we boiled the conventional way.

Here's why the approach works: Starches absorb water at approximately 180 degrees. As long as the water is at a rolling boil (212 degrees) when you add the pasta and your kitchen is at normal room temperature, the water will remain well above 180 degrees off the heat for longer than the typical 8 to 10 minutes it takes for the pasta to cook through. In our tests, the water temperature had only cooled to about 195 degrees by the time the pasta was al dente. (In a cooler-than-normal kitchen, the pasta might take a minute or two longer to reach the proper texture, and the water temperature might drop a little more.)

Does this mean we're going to stop boiling our pasta? Maybe not. But it's nice to know we have the option.

≥ BY AMY GRAVES & TAIZETH SIERRA ≤

EQUIPMENT UPDATE **Kitchen Rulers**

We often specify exact measurements in our recipes, and traditionally we've used an ordinary steel ruler to guide us. But do rulers specifically designed for the kitchen have anything special to offer? We picked up two regular 18-inch steel rulers and compared them with two specialty rulers: the wooden Fox Run Magnetic Kitchen Ruler ($1.49), which doubles as an oven rack push-puller, and the Mercer Stainless Cut Ruler and Chef Tool ($11.45). We sliced cookie dough and chopped vegetables, using the rulers to achieve uniform-size pieces that ensure even cooking.

A good ruler must be accurate and have a straight edge; the Fox Run ruler failed on both counts. The markings on two different rulers didn't line up, and both copies were warped. While we were impressed by the Mercer culinary measuring tool, which is printed with a wealth of information, from common conversions to food storage temperatures, its 5-inch width was too bulky for everyday use. In the end, a basic office-supply-store ruler, the Empire 18-inch Stainless Steel Ruler ($8.49), which has large, easy-to-read markings, was the best tool by any measure.

JUST THE BASICS
The Empire 18-inch Stainless Steel Ruler, designed for office use, also fits the bill in the kitchen.

NEW PRODUCT **Clever Coffee Dripper**

The most flavorful coffee is brewed with water between 195 and 205 degrees and steeped for six minutes. Many people prefer a Melitta cone since it offers control over these variables. The Clever Coffee Dripper ($12.50) is a plastic cone similar to the Melitta, with a couple of improving twists: It has a lid to keep water hotter than the open cone, as well as a shutoff valve that holds back the dripping coffee so it can steep more fully, as in a French press. And because it uses a regular coffee filter, this device gives you full-bodied coffee without the French press's sediment. The coffee releases only when you place the cone on a cup, and it stops flowing when you lift it off. One quibble: The manufacturer claims that the tool can make 10, 15, or 30 ounces of coffee. We brewed 10 ounces with good results; 15 ounces was trickier, as the amount of fluid lifted the grounds dangerously close to the rim. For 30 ounces you must fill the cone twice with water, making the first batch of coffee too strong and the second too weak. But for smaller batches, the Clever Coffee Dripper is a success.

A SMART DRIP
The Clever Coffee Dripper offers improvements over the traditional drip cone.

EQUIPMENT TESTING **Pullman Loaf Pans**

A Pullman loaf pan is a bread pan with a slide-on lid; it produces a squared-off loaf with a compact crumb that's perfect for sandwiches. In this country, the pans are commonly associated with the cramped kitchens of 19th-century Pullman railcars, where the flat-topped breads that the pans produced were easier to stack than domed loaves. We purchased three models and baked off a round of sandwich breads to see how each pan performed.

We can't recommend two of the pans: the Matfer Bourgeat Bread Pan with Cover ($71.95) and the Paderno World Cuisine Blue Steel Bread Pan with Cover ($48.88). Each is made from uncoated steel, and both reacted with the canola-based cooking spray we used, discoloring and giving off a fishy odor. Neither pan came with care instructions, but we later learned that uncoated steel pans like these should be continuously seasoned and kept dry—like cast iron—or they may stick, discolor, and/or rust. When we want a squared-off loaf, we'll go with the fuss-free nonstick aluminized steel surface of the USA Pan 13 by 4-inch Pullman Loaf Pan & Cover ($33.95).

ALL SQUARED AWAY
The Pullman Loaf Pan & Cover from USA Pan baked perfect, flat-topped, crisp-cornered loaves.

NEW PRODUCT **Silicone Microwave Lid**

The Japanese-made Piggy Steamer ($18), a 7-inch circle of thin silicone with a thicker, raised center shaped like the face of a pig, turns out to be not only whimsical but also functional. As a microwave plate cover or bowl cover, it's unbreakable and stays cool, with protruding ears that serve as convenient handles. (The nostrils vent steam—and are used in Japan for lifting the lid with chopsticks.) In Japan, the lid is typically placed directly on food. For microwave reheating, we rested it directly on rice on a plate and across the tops of bowls of soup and pasta sauce. The rice became steamy without drying out; the soup and pasta sauce emerged piping hot, and the lid kept the microwave splatter-free. We love this funny, floppy lid, which easily washes clean and is also effective for opening jar lids.

THAT'LL DO, PIG
This whimsical lid makes a stay-cool bowl cover for the microwave and doubles as a jar opener.

NEW PRODUCT **Kitchen Calculator**

Converting recipes with metric measures can be daunting, as can scaling recipes for different numbers of servings. The KitchenCalc Handheld Kitchen Calculator and Timer ($24.95) is designed to simplify both tasks. We pulled out an old French recipe for eight people written in grams and converted it into five servings and American measures. Though the buttons looked intimidating, with individual keys for units of measure, the manual gave us clear instructions, and in no time we'd converted the recipe. It also saved us from making the mistake of converting fluid ounces into weight. We could have used any calculator, but the culinary-specific KitchenCalc, which comes with a clear plastic cover to protect it from kitchen messes, saved us time and effort.

CALCULATING FRIEND
The KitchenCalc solves kitchen math problems.

Sources

The following are mail-order sources for items recommended in this issue. Prices were current at press time and do not include shipping. Contact companies to confirm information or visit www.CooksIllustrated.com for updates.

PAGE 6: WINE OPENER
• Oggi Nautilus Corkscrew: $24.99, item #W7305, Wine Stuff (800-946-3788, www.winestuff.com).

PAGE 29: TOASTER OVENS
• The Smart Oven by Breville, $249.95, item #BOV800XL, Cutlery and More (800-650-9866, cutleryandmore.com).
• Hamilton Beach Set & Forget Toaster Oven with Convection Cooking, $99.99, item #31230, Hamilton Beach (800-851-8900, www.hamiltonbeach.com).

PAGE 32: RULER
• Empire 18-inch Stainless Steel Ruler: $8.49, item #27318, Home Depot (800-466-3337, www.homedepot.com).

PAGE 32: CLEVER COFFEE DRIPPER
• Clever Coffee Dripper: $12.50, Elemental Coffee Roasters (405-633-1703, www.elementalcoffeeroasters.com).

PAGE 32: PULLMAN LOAF PAN
• USA Pan 13 by 4-inch Pullman Loaf Pan & Cover: $33.95, item #02-2613, ChefTools.com (206-933-0700, www.cheftools.com).

PAGE 32: PIGGY STEAMER
• Piggy Steamer: $18, item #72606, MoMA Store (800-851-4509, www.momastore.org).

PAGE 32: KITCHEN CALCULATOR
• KitchenCalc Handheld Kitchen Calculator and Timer: $24.95, item #8300-BXB, Calculated Industries (800-854-8075, www.calculated.com).

INDEX
March & April 2011

NEW RECIPE ON THE WEB
Available free for 4 months at
www.CooksIllustrated.com/apr11

Buttery Croutons

  **COOK'S LIVE VIDEOS**
Available for members at
www.CooksIllustrated.com

BAKED SOLE FILLETS WITH HERBS AND BREAD CRUMBS
See How We Roll

BOSTON CREAM PIE
Assembling a Classic

BROCCOLI-CHEESE SOUP
Watch Us Break Broccoli Rules

CUBAN-STYLE BLACK BEANS AND RICE (*MOROS Y CRISTIANOS*)
Opposites Come Together

PERUVIAN ROAST CHICKEN
How the Vertical Roaster Works

POTATO GALETTE
Look—It Holds Together

SAUCE BASE
An Elegant Sauce Takes Shape

SAUTÉED SNOW PEAS
The Way to Cook Them

SPAGHETTI WITH MUSHROOM AND TOMATO SAUCE
Bryan Builds His Ragu

TESTING: TOASTER OVENS
Putting Them to the Test

WHOLE-WHEAT SANDWICH BREAD
Andrew Guides You, from Flour to Loaf

AMERICA'S TEST KITCHEN TV
Public television's most popular cooking show

Join the millions of home cooks who watch our show, *America's Test Kitchen*, on public television every week. For more information, including recipes and program times, visit www.AmericasTestKitchenTV.com.

AMERICA'S TEST KITCHEN RADIO
Tune in to our new radio program featuring answers to listener call-in questions, ingredient taste test and equipment review segments, and in-depth reporting on a variety of topics. To listen to episodes, visit www.AmericasTestKitchen.com/Radio.

DOWNLOAD OUR FREE *Cook's Illustrated* **iPhone App**

Inside you'll find a collection of our top recipes, along with videos that explain how to make them. You can also access many of our most popular taste test results, useful kitchen timers, and an interactive shopping list that helps you plan ahead. Are you a member of CooksIllustrated.com? If so, you'll have access to every recipe, video, and taste test on the website. Go to CooksIllustrated.com/iPhone.

Follow us on Twitter: twitter.com/TestKitchen
Find us on Facebook: facebook.com/CooksIllustrated

Peruvian Roast Chicken with Garlic and Lime, 11

Sautéed Snow Peas with Lemon and Parsley, 21

Broccoli-Cheese Soup, 12

Boston Cream Pie, 15

Pan-Seared Steak with Herb Sauce, 7

Potato Galette, 9

Spaghetti with Mushroom and Tomato Sauce, 13

Cuban-Style Black Beans and Rice, 19

Baked Sole Fillets with Herbs and Bread Crumbs, 20

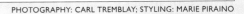
Whole-Wheat Sandwich Bread, 24

PHOTOGRAPHY: CARL TREMBLAY; STYLING: MARIE PIRAINO

Celery Root

Carrot

Parsnip

Jícama

Beet

Rutabaga

Radish

Burdock

Salsify

Turnip

TAPROOTS

NUMBER 110

MAY & JUNE 2011

COOK'S
ILLUSTRATED

Easy Grilled Pork Roast
Secrets of Bone-In Grilling

Real Pub-Style Burgers
Sear First, Roast Later

Barbecued Chicken Kebabs
Bacon to the Rescue

Fresh Strawberry Pie
Whole Berries, Pure Flavor

Real Pasta Primavera

Rating Greek Yogurts
Be Smart, Buy Greek

Liquid Measuring Cups
Classic Model Beats Upstarts

Sweet and Tangy Coleslaw
New Grilling Sauces
Best Grilled Scallops
A Guide to Cooking Greens
Perfect Crêpes at Home
Indonesian–Style Fried Rice

www.CooksIllustrated.com
$5.95 U.S./$6.95 CANADA

0 74470 62805 7

0 6>

CONTENTS
May & June 2011

COOK'S ILLUSTRATED

Founder and Editor	Christopher Kimball
Editorial Director	Jack Bishop
Executive Editor, Magazines	John Willoughby
Executive Editor	Amanda Agee
Test Kitchen Director	Erin McMurrer
Managing Editor	Rebecca Hays
Senior Editors	Keith Dresser
	Lisa McManus
	Bryan Roof
Associate Features Editor	Elizabeth Bomze
Senior Copy Editor	Catherine Tumber
Copy Editor	Nell Beram
Associate Editors	Andrea Geary
	Amy Graves
	Andrew Janjigian
	Yvonne Ruperti
	Dan Souza
Assistant Editors	Hannah Crowley
	Taizeth Sierra
Executive Assistant	Christine Gordon
Editorial Assistant	Shannon Friedmann Hatch
Assistant Test Kitchen Director	Gina Nistico
Senior Kitchen Assistant	Leah Rovner
Kitchen Assistants	Maria Elena Delgado
	Ena Gudiel
Executive Producer	Melissa Baldino
Associate Producer	Stephanie Stender
Contributing Editors	Matthew Card
	Dawn Yanagihara
Consulting Editor	Scott Brueggeman
Science Editor	Guy Crosby, Ph.D.
Managing Editor, Special Issues	Todd Meier
Assistant Editor, Special Issues	Chris Dudley
Assistant Test Cook, Special Issues	Danielle DeSiato-Hallman
Editorial Assistant, Special Issues	Brittany Allen
Online Managing Editor	David Tytell
Online Editor	Kate Mason
Online Assistant Editors	Eric Grzymkowski
	Mari Levine
Video Operations Manager	Peter Tannenbaum
Media Producer	Alexandra Pournaras
Associate Editor/Camera Operator	Nick Dakoulas
Assistant Editor/Camera Operator	Jesse Prent
Design Director	Amy Klee
Art Director, Magazines	Julie Bozzo
Designer	Lindsey Timko
Art Director, Marketing/Web	Christine Vo
Associate Art Directors, Marketing/Web	Erica Lee
	Jody Lee
Designers, Marketing/Web	Elaina Natario
	Mariah Tarvainen
Staff Photographer	Daniel J. van Ackere
Vice President, Marketing	David Mack
Circulation Director	Doug Wicinski
Circulation & Fulfillment Manager	Carrie Horan
Partnership Marketing Manager	Pamela Putprush
Marketing Assistant	Lauren Perkins
Database & Direct Mail Director	Adam Perry
Senior Database Analyst	Marina Sakharova
Product Operations Director	Steven Browall
Product Promotions Director	Tom Conway
E-Commerce Marketing Director	Hugh Buchan
E-Commerce Marketing Manager	Laurel Zeidman
E-Commerce Marketing Coordinator	Sandra Greenberg
Marketing Copywriter	David Goldberg
Customer Service Manager	Jacqueline Valerio
Customer Service Representatives	Jillian Nannicelli
	Kate Sokol
Sponsorship Sales Director	Marcy McCreary
Retail Sales & Marketing Manager	Emily Logan
Client Service Manager, Sponsorship	Bailey Snyder
Production Director	Guy Rochford
Senior Project Manager	Alice Carpenter
Production & Traffic Coordinator	Kate Hux
Senior Production Manager	Jessica L. Quirk
Asset & Workflow Manager	Andrew Mannone
Production & Imaging Specialists	Judy Blomquist
	Heather Dube
	Lauren Pettapiece
Technology Director	Rocco Lombardo
Systems Administrator	Marcus Walser
Lead Developer	Scott Thompson
Software Architect	Robert Martinez
Web Developer II	Christopher Candelora
Web Developers	Bach Bui
	James Madden
	Alphonse Shiwala
Business Analyst	Wendy Tsang
Quality Assurance Specialist	Micquella Bradford
IT Support Specialist	Geoffrey Clark
Senior Web Production Coordinator	Evan Davis
Web Production Assistant	Debbie Chiang
VP New Media Product Development	Barry Kelly
Lead Developer	Bharat Ruparel
Senior Information Architect	Melissa MacQuarrie
Social Media Manager	Steph Yiu
Graphic Designer	Eggert Ragnarsson
Web Developer	Brian Runk
Instructional Designer	Miriam Manglani
Chief Financial Officer	Sharyn Chabot
Human Resources Director	Adele Shapiro
Controller	Mandy Shito
Financial Director	Wayne Saville
Senior Accountant	Aaron Goranson
Staff Accountant	Connie Forbes
Accounts Payable Specialist	Steven Kasha
Office Manager	Michael Pickett
Receptionist	Henrietta Murray
Publicity	Deborah Broide

PRINTED IN THE USA

CHERRIES

CHERRIES are often high in acidity, and the glossy, burgundy Bing and crimson Van are no exceptions. Both promise tartness at first bite, followed by a flood of sweetness. The late-season Skeena—a plum-colored variety—is juicy, meaty, and sweet, while crisp, heart-shaped Sweethearts hide a muted tang beneath their garnet exterior. Golden Rainiers, with their variegated yellow-orange color, have tender, sweet flesh. Sour cherries can be unrelentingly tart and are best used for baking. Montmorency (also known as pie cherries), North Star, and Early Richmond (one of the first sour cherries to debut each season) typically fill cobblers and pies. Vibrant Balatons, with their pleasant bite reminiscent of green grapes, are ideal for juicing or making jam.

COVER (Blueberries): Robert Papp; BACK COVER (Cherries): John Burgoyne

America's TEST KITCHEN

America's Test Kitchen is a 2,500-square-foot kitchen located just outside of Boston. It is the home of Cook's Illustrated and Cook's Country magazines and is the workday destination of more than three dozen test cooks, editors, and cookware specialists. Our mission is to test recipes over and over again until we understand how and why they work and until we arrive at the best version. We also test kitchen equipment and supermarket ingredients in search of brands that offer the best value and performance. You can watch us work by tuning in to America's Test Kitchen (www.AmericasTestKitchenTV.com) on public television.

ON THE SUNNY SIDE

There was too much snow this winter for rabbit hunting, and my pickup got stuck just below Orval's cabin on a thick sheet of ice. Large snowbanks were still piled around on Easter. So, in an effort to cheer myself up, I offer a few of my favorite Vermont stories, told by folks who are experts at finding humor in the worst possible situations with a cocktail of sardonic wit, self-deprecation, and an appreciation of the random absurdity of life.

A Texan was visiting Vermont and stopped to talk to a farmer on the side of the road.

"Glad to meet you," said the Texan. "Nice place you got here. How much land you got?"

"Pretty good-size farm for around here—'bout two hundred acres."

"Where I come from that's an awful small place," remarked the Texan. "Down in Texas, I drive for most of the morning before I get to the corner of my ranch."

"Ayuh," the old-timer commiserated, "I had a truck like that once, but I got rid of it."

A New Yorker with a Great Dane on a leash tried to board a bus in Bennington, Vermont. The driver opened the bus door and, looking out at the pair, said, "You can't get on this bus."

"Why not?" snapped the New Yorker.

"No dogs allowed," countered the driver.

The New Yorker, throwing aside all sense of common decency, shouted, "OK, you know what you can do with your bloody bus!"

Equal to the occasion, the driver replied, "If you do the same with your dog, you can get on!"

A substitute minister went to a small rural church and found that there was only one man in the congregation. The preacher asked him if he wanted him to perform the service anyway.

The man thought a bit and then said, "Well, Reverend, if I put some hay in the wagon and go down to the pasture to feed the cows and only one shows up, I feed her."

So the minister went through most of the service, including a full-length sermon. Afterward, he asked the lone member of the congregation what he thought of it.

"Well, Reverend, I'll tell you. If I put some hay in the wagon and go down to the pasture to feed the cows and only one cow shows up, I don't give her the whole damn load."

One particularly wet spring, Arlo Benson missed seeing his neighbor, Seth Perkins, for several days and got worried. Arlo drove around to Seth's place and found him sitting in his pickup in the yard, mud up to his hubcaps.

"Howdy, Seth," said Arlo. "You all right?"

"Ayuh," said Seth.

There was a pause and then Arlo said, "You stuck?"

"I would be," replied Seth, "if I tried to move."

Many years ago, land values in Vermont started to rise. So a sharp real estate speculator came up from the city and drove way back into the country to pick up some cheap land that he would soon turn around and sell at a big profit.

He drove around until he came upon a hill farm, miles from civilization, and saw a farmer by the side of the road. After some conversation, the flatlander said, "I'd like to buy about five hundred dollars' worth of land from you."

Christopher Kimball

"Good," said the farmer, "that's very good. Go fetch your wheelbarrow and I'll fill it up for you!"

A man from Quechee, Vermont, was taking the train from North Station in Boston to White River Junction. The train was crowded and a well-dressed city man sat down beside him. After getting acquainted, the Bostonian said:

"You say you are just a Vermont farmer, but I am impressed with your intelligence and common sense. To pass the time, I suggest that we play a game."

"Well, what's your game?"

"I suggest that we each ask the other a question and if we can't answer the other fellow's question, we give him a dollar."

"Well now, that might be a good game but I don't think that the terms are quite fair."

"What's wrong with the terms?"

"Well, you're a city man, probably well educated and traveled. I'm just a poor Vermont farmer—only went through grammar school and spent all the rest of my life on the farm. So, I suggest that if you can't answer my question you give me a dollar, but if I can't answer your question I give you fifty cents."

"That seems fair enough; let's play. You ask the first question."

"Well, I'd like to know what it is that has three legs and flies."

After some thought the city man said, "Damned if I know. Here's your dollar."

"OK," said the Vermonter, "what's your question?"

"I'd like to know what it is that has three legs and flies."

"Damned if I know. Here's your fifty cents."

FOR INQUIRIES, ORDERS, OR MORE INFORMATION

www.CooksIllustrated.com
At www.CooksIllustrated.com, you can order books and subscriptions, sign up for our free e-newsletter, or renew your magazine subscription. Join the website and gain access to 18 years of *Cook's Illustrated* recipes, equipment tests, and ingredient tastings, as well as companion videos for every recipe in this issue.

COOKBOOKS
We sell more than 50 cookbooks by the editors of *Cook's Illustrated*. To order, visit our bookstore at www.CooksIllustrated.com.

COOK'S ILLUSTRATED MAGAZINE
Cook's Illustrated magazine (ISSN 1068-2821), number 110, is published bimonthly by Boston Common Press Limited Partnership, 17 Station St., Brookline, MA 02445. Copyright 2011 Boston Common Press Limited Partnership. Periodicals postage paid at Boston, Mass., and additional mailing offices USPS #012487. Publications Mail Agreement No. 40020778. Return undeliverable Canadian addresses to P.O. Box 875, Station A, Windsor, ON N9A 6P2. POSTMASTER: Send address changes to Cook's Illustrated, P.O. Box 6018, Harlan, IA 51593-1518. For subscription and gift subscription orders, subscription inquiries, or change-of-address notices, visit us at www.AmericasTestKitchen.com/customerservice or write us at Cook's Illustrated, P.O. Box 6018, Harlan, IA 51593-1518.

FOR LIST RENTAL INFORMATION Specialists Marketing Services, Inc., 777 Terrace Ave., 4th Floor, Hasbrouck Heights, NJ 07604; 201-865-5800.
EDITORIAL OFFICE 17 Station St., Brookline, MA 02445; 617-232-1000; fax 617-232-1572. Subscription inquiries: Visit www.AmericasTestKitchen.com/customerservice or call 800-526-8442.
POSTMASTER Send all new orders, subscription inquiries, and change-of-address notices to Cook's Illustrated, P.O. Box 6018, Harlan, IA 51593-1518.

Shrimp vs. Prawn

I have a Malaysian cookbook that calls for prawns, but my grocery store sells only shrimp. Is there really any difference?

ANDREW DRAPER
HOLLAND, MICH.

➤Biologically speaking, there is a difference between shrimp and prawns, and it's mainly about gill structure—a distinguishing feature that is hard for the consumer to spot and is typically lost during processing and cooking. This simple fact may be why the terms are often used interchangeably or can vary depending on factors as random as custom and geography. "Prawn" is a term often used in the southern U.S., for example, while northerners might refer to the same specimen as "shrimp." In Britain and in many Asian countries, it's all about size: Small crustaceans are called shrimp; larger ones, prawns. Size is actually not a good indication of a true shrimp or a true prawn, as each comes in a wide range of sizes, depending on the species. Taste won't provide a clue either: As we found in our shrimp and prawn boil here in the test kitchen, each type can sometimes taste more or less sweet, again depending on the species.

The bottom line: We found no problem substituting one for the other in any recipe. The most important thing is to make sure that the count per pound (which indicates the size) is correct so that the same cooking times will apply.

SHRIMP
In shrimp, the thorax (the section just behind the head) extends over both the head and the abdomen like a band.

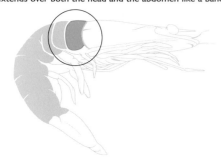

PRAWN
In prawns, the head overlaps the thorax, which overlaps the abdomen, much like the shingles on a roof.

Making Bananas Last

Is there any way to slow the ripening of bananas? I can never eat an entire bunch before they become overripe.

JAMES NEAL
CINCINNATI, OHIO

➤Most people store bananas on the countertop, and we wondered if chilling the fruit could slow ripening. To find out, we left 12 pounds of bananas at room temperature for three days until they were perfectly ripe (signified by a firm but yielding texture). We then moved half of the bananas into the refrigerator, leaving the remainder at room temperature.

For the next few days, the bananas were nearly indistinguishable. After four days, however, the room-temperature fruit became markedly soft and mushy, while the refrigerated fruit remained firm, despite blackened skins. We continued to taste the refrigerated bananas after the room-temperature samples had been discarded and were delighted to discover that they lasted an additional five days (so, almost two weeks after purchase) before the flesh became overripe.

The explanation is simple: As a banana ripens, it emits a gas called ethylene and develops acids that aid in ripening. Cool temperatures slow down the production of ethylene and acids, thereby decelerating ripening. However, refrigeration also causes the cell walls of the peel to break down, releasing enzymes that cause the formation of black-brown pigments.

Appealing Carrots

Is it really necessary to peel carrots?

EVELYN HAMALAINEN
CHELMSFORD, MASS.

➤To test whether peeling carrots has a noticeable effect on their flavor or texture, we compared batches of scrubbed unpeeled carrots with peeled carrots. We tasted the samples raw, cut into coins and glazed, and roasted in a 425-degree oven.

Although a few tasters found the unpeeled raw carrots to be earthier tasting than their stripped siblings, most were distracted by their "dusty exterior" and "bitter finish." The results were even more clear-cut when the carrots were cooked. Tasters unanimously preferred the peel-free carrots in the glazed and roasted samples. In both cases, the skins on the unpeeled carrots became wrinkled, tough, and gritty. Their flavor was "again earthier, but not in a good way" and they weren't particularly appealing looking. On the other hand, the peeled versions remained bright orange, tender, and sweet.

In sum: It takes only an extra minute or two to peel carrots. We think it's time well spent.

Red Wine Substitute

Several years ago, you wrote that white vermouth could be substituted for white wine in a recipe that calls for just a small amount. Can I also substitute red vermouth for red wine?

JOHN LEWIS
NEW BRUNSWICK, N.J.

➤Red vermouth is sweeter than white vermouth (and considerably sweeter than red wine), so we were unsure that it would make a suitable substitute. To find out, we prepared two dishes—pot roast braised in ½ cup of red wine and pan-seared steak with a red wine pan sauce—first following the recipe as written and then subbing red vermouth for the red wine. We were happy to find that in both cases the vermouth made a sweeter yet still acceptable dish—a boon for cooks who don't want to open a whole bottle of wine only to use a relatively small amount, since vermouth keeps for several weeks once opened. If the extra sweetness bothers you, try toning it down with a few drops of lemon juice or red wine vinegar.

RED WINE STAND-IN
Keep long-lasting red vermouth on hand to use in recipes that call for a small amount of red wine.

To Seed or Not to Seed

Is it true that tomato seeds will turn fresh tomato sauce bitter?

HANNAH CROSS
ATLANTA, GA.

➤Many recipes for tomato sauce call for first seeding the tomatoes, a process that can be a chore for large batches. To see if skipping this step would leave us with a bitter sauce, we compared a batch of tomato sauce in which we had seeded beefsteak tomatoes with one in which we hadn't. In the past, we've found that the gel surrounding the seeds is rich in savory glutamates (more glutamates, even, than the flesh of the tomato), so we pushed the guts from the seeded tomatoes through a fine-mesh strainer, ensuring that only the seeds were left behind and preserving the gel. Out of curiosity, we sampled the raw seeds straight up and found them to be completely benign.

Forty minutes of simmering in the sauce didn't change a thing; our tasters still detected no bitterness in the tomatoes and in fact found the sauces identical in flavor. Since the seeds don't harm the flavor and removing them is a hassle, we'll be leaving them in. If you choose to remove the seeds for aesthetic reasons, be sure to strain off and use the flavorful gel that surrounds them.

Lighten Your Loaf

What is vital wheat gluten? Should I be adding it to my homemade breads?

THOMAS MARTIN
OMAHA, NEB.

➤Vital wheat gluten (also known simply as "gluten") is the protein component of wheat flour. To isolate the gluten, manufacturers combine flour with water to make dough and knead it to develop the gluten network. The dough is subsequently rinsed in water until all of the starch is removed and only the rubbery gluten remains, which is then dried and ground before packaging.

Professional bakers add vital wheat gluten to strengthen dough so it retains more gas, which results in greater volume and a lighter crumb. Extra gluten is beneficial in "gluten-challenged" dough containing lower gluten flours (like whole wheat or rye) or sharp or bulky components (nuts, seeds, or bran) that can sever gluten strands. It can also enhance the chewiness of breads like bagels.

When we tried the product in a hearty whole-wheat bread, adding 1½ teaspoons per cup of whole-wheat flour according to the manufacturer's guidelines, we found that it rose ½ inch higher than the bread made without it. Added to a bagel recipe, it generated a crisp exterior and chewy interior, despite the fact that we used ordinary all-purpose flour instead of the specialized high-gluten flour the recipe called for.

VITAL WHEAT GLUTEN

Our conclusion: If you want to lighten up a dense loaf or ensure chewiness in breads like bagels without having to resort to special mail-order flour, vital wheat gluten (available in supermarkets) is worth trying.

Spinach on Your Teeth

I always wash my spinach thoroughly before I cook it, but it still leaves a chalky residue on my teeth. Why?

FRANK HARLEY
AMARILLO, TEXAS

➤Spinach contains oxalic acid, which is released when the cell walls are ruptured, first by cooking and later by chewing. The oxalic acid combines with the calcium in saliva (and in the spinach itself) to form tiny calcium oxalate crystals that cling to the teeth, leaving behind a dry, dusty sensation. Not surprisingly, we found that the effect is exaggerated when the spinach is combined with dairy, since milk and cheese products contain far more calcium than saliva does to combine with the oxalic acid. If you are especially sensitive to this phenomenon, you could try eating your spinach raw, since without the rupturing of cells that occurs during cooking, there will be less oxalate available to form the oxalate crystals.

WHAT IS IT?

My sister used to love buying the showcased kitchen gadgets at the New York State Fair in the 1940s. She handed down this tool to me, but she was never sure what it was used for. Do you know?

DONNA C. DESIATO
LIVERPOOL, N.Y.

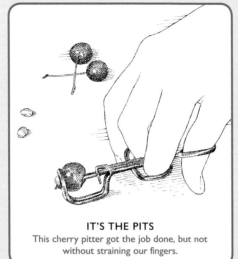

IT'S THE PITS
This cherry pitter got the job done, but not without straining our fingers.

Your item is an antique fruit pitter, invented by John Clark Brown in 1935. Created especially for cherries, the tool was designed to be operated single-handedly, leaving one hand free to load and unload the fruit. A plunger operated by the user's thumb pushes against the cherry resting in a small hopper, forcing the pit through a hole in the hopper. The device's stiff wire construction measures 4½ inches tall, and the unit we got our hands on still appeared to be in great working order. However, after pitting several pounds of cherries and a few olives, we had some seriously sore fingers. While it may have been a model of innovation in its day, cherry pitters have come a long way since the 1930s. (For information on our favorite modern cherry pitter, see page 32.)

You Say . . . Kumato?

My grocery store recently started stocking strange-looking dark brown tomatoes called Kumatoes. Are they any good?

KAREN CORBETT
ROCHESTER, N.Y.

➤The Kumato, a tomato variety with a startling brownish green color, was introduced to the U.S. market two years ago and is available year-round, imported from Europe. Its unusual appearance has created speculation that the Kumato is a genetically modified fruit, but it is actually the product of natural crossbreeding among several varieties, including some wild Mediterranean specimens.

We compared Kumatoes with standard supermarket vine-ripened tomatoes, sampling them plain and in cooked tomato sauce and raw salsa. In all cases, tasters found the Kumatoes sweeter than the ordinary tomatoes, which made sense: The Kumato was bred to have a higher fructose content than traditional vine-ripened tomatoes. Tasters also preferred the Kumato for its dense, meaty texture; the vine-ripened tomato was described as comparatively mealy and watery.

The bottom line: The Kumato may not be a match for a locally grown, late-summer farm stand beauty, but if you're buying fresh tomatoes out of season, it's a far better bet than the ordinary supermarket offerings.

KUMATOES
Purchased out of season, brownish green Kumatoes offer a sweeter flavor and meatier texture than ordinary vine-ripened supermarket tomatoes.

BPA in Beer Can Chicken?

Since the interior of beer cans is coated with an epoxy that contains Bisphenol A (BPA), is the popular method of cooking a chicken perched on an open can really a good idea?

ROBIN O'LEARY
BIRMINGHAM, ALA.

➤Some studies have linked BPA to cancer and other harmful health effects. To evaluate the ramifications of cooking chicken on a beer can, we roasted two whole birds, one set on an open beer can containing 6 ounces of beer and the other on a stainless-steel vertical roaster with the same amount of beer poured into the reservoir. After roasting the chickens, we collected their drippings and stripped each carcass, grinding the meat and skin to create homogeneous samples. We sent the samples to a lab to be evaluated for BPA content.

In each chicken, the BPA measured less than 20 micrograms per kilogram, leading us to believe that the beer can cooking method is safe. (The Food and Drug Administration's current standard for exposure is 50 micrograms per kilogram of body weight for adults, or 3,400 micrograms per day for a 150-pound person.) For those who have any remaining concerns, there is always the vertical roaster (our favorite is the Norpro Vertical Roaster with Infuser, $27.95), which works just as well as a low-tech option.

SEND US YOUR QUESTIONS We will provide a complimentary one-year subscription for each letter we print. Send your inquiry, name, address, and daytime telephone number to Notes from Readers, *Cook's Illustrated*, P.O. Box 470589, Brookline, MA 02447, or to NotesFromReaders@ AmericasTestKitchen.com.

Quick Tips

⇒ COMPILED BY SHANNON FRIEDMANN HATCH ⇐

Picture-Perfect Recipes

Keeping recipes splatter-free is no longer an issue for Maureen Broomall of Pepperell, Mass. She prints them out on water-resistant photo paper so she can wipe away any spills. Plus, its heavy weight makes it more durable than a regular recipe card, and the 4x6 size fits perfectly in her recipe box.

Quicker Cherry Pitting

Alyssa Gilberti of Brighton, Mass., has worked out an efficient way to pit cherries using a takeout utensil and a glass bottle. Place a cherry over the mouth of a clean, empty glass bottle (choose one with a small mouth, such as a wine or soda bottle). Using the blunt end of a chopstick, pierce through the center of the cherry, pushing the pit through the flesh and skin and into the bottle.

Deviled Eggs On the Go

The deviled egg is all about presentation—bright yellow filling piped into the hollow of a cooked egg white—so packing a dozen for a picnic or a party can be daunting. Errin Chapin of Medfield, Mass., prevents overturned eggs by placing each one in a paper cupcake liner and then arranging them in a single layer in a plastic storage container.

Frothy Milk Without a Steamer

Gloria Lynch of Colorado Springs, Colo., loves adding foamy steamed milk to her coffee to make café au lait. But instead of investing in a steamer, she uses her microwave and French press to create hot, frothy milk.

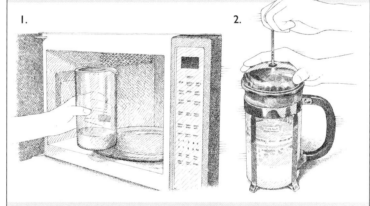

1. Remove the glass container from a French press and pour in at least enough cold milk to reach the bottom edge of the plunger when it's put in place.
2. Microwave the milk in the glass container for 10 to 20 seconds. Reassemble the press and pump the plunger up and down until foam develops.

Patching Cracked Shells

Rather than throw away pie pastry trimmings, Melissa Borrell of Annville, Pa., saves the scraps for patchwork. If there are any cracks or holes after prebaking a pie shell, she spackles them with the leftover dough, pressing it into place, and then finishes baking according to the recipe.

DIY Airtight Seal

Exposure to air can make bread quickly go from fresh to stale, and twist ties and rubber bands hardly guarantee an airtight seal. Glenn Baker of Decatur, Ill., uses this technique to keep his loaves as fresh as possible.

1. Cut off the neck of an empty plastic bottle; reserve the neck and lid.
2. Pull the top edge of the plastic bread bag through the bottle's neck.
3. Press the air out of the bag, fold the top of the bag down, and then screw on the bottle's lid to seal.

ILLUSTRATION: JOHN BURGOYNE

No More "Mystery Meat"

Gene Koury of Chico, Calif., often freezes raw meat for later use and offers this simple labeling trick. After wrapping the meat in plastic wrap and placing it in a zipper-lock freezer bag, he cuts off the grocery label and puts it inside, facing out. At a glance he knows the exact cut, weight, and—most important—date of purchase, allowing him to gauge how long the meat has been lingering in the freezer.

Get a (Better) Grip

Rubber wristbands and bracelets can do more than promote a favorite team, charity, or cause. Ellen McEwen of Monterey, Calif., uses them to open stubborn jar lids. Wrapping the wristband around the lid helps her gain traction as she twists.

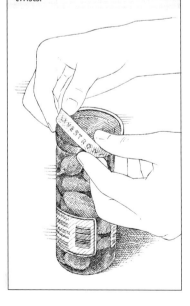

Ice Water Shake-Up

When recipes like pie dough call for ice water, it can be a challenge to pour just the water, not the cubes as well. Andreas Weiger of Burlington, Wis., uses a tool from his wet bar to ensure a controlled pour.

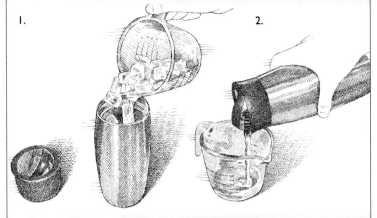

1. Fill a cocktail shaker with the desired amount of water. Add ice and affix the lid.
2. Shake vigorously, then pour the water through the strainer, leaving the ice in the base.

Grinding Solution

Hope Hilton of Harpswell, Maine, has a clever way to grind whole spices without a spice grinder. She purchases peppercorns in glass jars with removable grinding mechanisms, which she finds in the spice section of her supermarket.

1. After reserving their contents for later use, she fills the now-empty jars with cumin, coriander, fennel seed, and more.
2. The spices can now be ground as needed.

Quick Trivet Substitute

In the midst of a cooking marathon, Kevin Holland of Palm Coast, Fla., found himself with two hot baking sheets and only one trivet. Here's how he improvised: He flipped over four large spoons and laid them on the countertop a few inches apart. Then he set the hot baking sheet on top of the spoons to cool.

Recycled Picnic Plates

Styrofoam is not recycled in Augusta, Ga., where Rebecca Burke lives. To give the narrow Styrofoam trays that often accompany prepackaged fresh produce a second life, she washes them and stashes them in her cooler to use as plates for picnics.

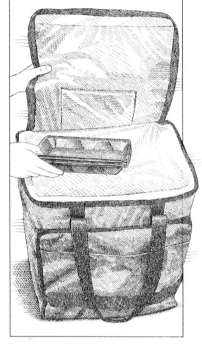

Level Measuring

Carolyn Baker of McCormick, S.C., stores a clean Popsicle stick in her dry-ingredient containers. Instead of having to grab for a butter knife or other straight edge to sweep away the excess when measuring flour or sugar, she already has her leveling tool at hand.

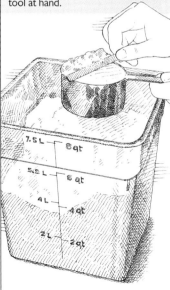

Rescuing Barbecued Chicken Kebabs

Stripped of protective fatty skin, barbecued chicken kebabs don't stand a chance on a fiery grill. But what if the chicken gets a little help from a pig?

⇒ BY MATTHEW CARD ⇐

In theory, barbecued chicken kebabs sound pretty great: char-streaked chunks of juicy meat lacquered with sweet-sharp barbecue sauce. Using skewers sounds easy, too—a fast-and-loose sort of way to capture the charms of barbecued chicken without the time and patience needed to cook a whole bird or the focus essential to tending a host of mixed parts. Ah, but if only the kebabs lived up to that promise. The quandary is that without an insulating layer of skin, even the fattiest thigh meat can dry out and toughen when exposed to the blazing heat of the grill. And forget about ultra-lean, skinless breast meat: It's a lost cause. Simply slathering barbecue sauce onto skewered chicken chunks—the approach embraced by most recipes—does little to address this fundamental problem. In fact, it's often one of the ruining factors: If applied too early or in too great a volume, the sauce drips off the meat, burns, and fixes the chicken fast to the grill.

Rubbed the Right Way

My goal was simple: juicy, tender chicken with plenty of sticky-sweet, smoke-tinged flavor. I wanted an everyday sort of recipe, one that would work equally well with white or dark meat (skewered separately since they cook at different rates) and brushed with a no-nonsense homemade barbecue sauce. But before I got to the sauce (I would use a simple ketchup-based placeholder for now), I had to ensure that the meat was as moist and tender as possible. Brining was the natural next step.

When meat soaks in salty water, the salt helps pull the liquid into the meat, plumping the chicken and thoroughly seasoning it. The salt also denatures the meat proteins, creating gaps that trap water and guard against drying out. But brining isn't a cure-all: When I made kebabs with chicken breasts and thighs that I brined after cutting them into pieces (1-inch chunks cooked through relatively quickly yet required enough time on the grill to pick up smoky flavor), the brine made the meat so slick and wet that any barbecue sauce I brushed on toward the end of cooking dribbled off.

Would a dry method work better? Sure enough, a heavily salted dry spice mixture (I let the rubbed chicken sit for 30 minutes before grilling) was just

To ensure that our homemade barbecue sauce caramelizes—but doesn't burn—we brush it on toward the end of cooking.

the ticket. As the mixture sat, the salt drew the juices to the surface of the chicken pieces, where they mixed with the seasonings and then flowed back into the chicken. The rub also crisped up on the chicken's exterior as it cooked, forming a craggy surface that the sauce could really cling to. To avoid overpowering the chicken, I steered clear of outspoken spices, settling on both sweet and smoked paprika, the former contributing depth and the latter helping to boost the overall smokiness of the dish. A few teaspoons of sugar added to the rub aided in browning, pleasantly complicating flavor.

When Chicken Meets Pig

With its ruddy exterior, my chicken now looked the part, but the meat was still not quite moist enough and, despite the improvements made by the spices, lacked sufficient depth of flavor. In a hunt for a solution, I read up on Middle Eastern kebab cookery. I learned that Turkish chefs skewer slices of pure lamb fat between lamb chunks before grilling. The fat melts during cooking, continually basting the lean meat.

Using musky lamb fat in a chicken recipe seemed

too weird, but what about another fatty yet more complementary meat: smoky bacon? I cut several strips into 1-inch pieces and spliced the chicken pieces with the fatty squares before putting the kebabs on the grill. Unfortunately, by the time the chicken was cooked through, the bacon—tightly wedged as it was between the chicken chunks—had failed to crisp. For my next attempt, I tried wrapping strips of bacon around the kebabs in a spiral-like helix. This time, the bacon turned crunchy, but its flavor overwhelmed the chicken's more delicate taste.

If strips didn't work, how about rendered bacon fat? I liberally coated the prepared kebabs with drippings from freshly cooked bacon and set them on the grill grate. Within minutes, the fat trickled into the coals and prompted flare-ups, blackening most of the chicken. What wasn't burnt, however, was moist and tasted addictively smoky.

If raw strips were too much of a good thing and rendered fat dripped off too quickly, was there an in-between solution? This time around, I finely diced a few slices of bacon and mixed them with the chicken chunks, salt, and spices. After giving the kebabs a 30-minute rest in the refrigerator, I grilled them over a modified two-level, moderately hot fire. (I had piled all of the coals on one side of the grill and left the other half empty to create a cooler "safety zone" on which to momentarily set the kebabs in the event of a flare-up.) Once the chicken was browned on one side (this took about two minutes), I flipped it a quarter turn, giving me nearly done meat in about eight minutes. At this point, I brushed barbecue sauce onto the kebabs, leaving them on the grill for just a minute or two longer to give the sauce a chance to caramelize. (Adding the sauce any earlier is a surefire route to scorched chicken.) The bacon bits clung tenaciously to the chicken, producing the best results yet.

But I wasn't finished. The bacon hadn't cooked evenly: Some bits were overly crisp and others still a little limp. I had an idea that would take care of the problem: grinding the bacon into a spreadable paste. Admittedly, the concept was a bit wacky, but I'd come this far with bacon, so why not? I tossed a couple of strips of raw bacon into a food processor and ground them down to a paste, which I then mixed with the chicken chunks and dry rub. As before, I rested the coated chicken in the refrigerator for half an hour before putting it on the grill. The chicken looked beautiful when it came off the fire: deeply browned and covered in a thick, shiny glaze,

Making Bacon Play Nice

In an effort to give lean chicken a little protective fat and smokier flavor, we played around with bacon until we hit upon an approach that worked.

TOO FLABBY
Bacon pieces wedged between the chicken chunks never fully cooked.

TOO BACON-Y
Whole strips of bacon wrapped around the chicken overpowered the chicken flavor.

TORCHED
Basting the chicken with bacon drippings led to flare-ups.

WINNING SOLUTION
Coating the chicken in a paste made of finely processed bacon did the trick.

---

with no burnt bacon bits in sight. But to my great disappointment, not to mention puzzlement, the chicken was now dry and had lost flavor. I repeated the test to make sure this batch wasn't a fluke and got the same results.

What could be going on? The only thing I was doing differently was coating the chicken in paste rather than simply mixing it with small pieces of the smoked meat combined with the salt, sugar, and spices. Then it occurred to me: Maybe the fatty ground-up bacon was adhering so well to the chicken that it was acting as a barrier to the salt, which now couldn't penetrate the meat. What if I first salted the meat for 30 minutes, then tossed it with the sugar, spices, and bacon paste right before I put it on the grill? This simple change was the answer: The chicken was juicy, tender, and full-flavored, with a smoky depth that complemented the barbecue sauce.

Now about that sauce . . . To enliven my classic ketchup, mustard, and cider vinegar mixture, I stirred in some grated onion and Worcestershire sauce. A spoonful of brown sugar and a little molasses added just enough bittersweet flavor to counter the sauce's tanginess. Simmered for a few minutes, the mixture tasted bright and balanced and boasted a thick, smooth texture that clung well to the chicken. As I watched this final batch of supremely moist, smoky, perfectly cooked kebabs disappear as fast as I could pull them off the grill, I knew that this recipe had realized its full potential.

CHARCOAL-GRILLED BARBECUED CHICKEN KEBABS
SERVES 6

NOTE: We prefer flavorful thigh meat for these kebabs, but you can use white meat. Whichever you choose, don't mix white and dark meat on the same skewer since they cook at different rates. If you have thin pieces of chicken, cut them larger than 1 inch and roll or fold them into approximately 1-inch cubes. Use the large holes on a box grater to grate the onion.

Sauce
- ½ cup ketchup
- ¼ cup light or mild molasses
- 2 tablespoons grated onion (see note)
- 2 tablespoons Worcestershire sauce
- 2 tablespoons Dijon mustard
- 2 tablespoons cider vinegar
- 1 tablespoon light brown sugar

Kebabs
- 2 pounds boneless, skinless chicken thighs or breasts, trimmed of excess fat and cut into 1-inch cubes (see note)
- 2 teaspoons kosher salt
- 2 tablespoons sweet paprika
- 4 teaspoons sugar
- 2 teaspoons smoked paprika
- 2 slices bacon, cut into ½-inch pieces
- 4 12-inch metal skewers

1. FOR THE SAUCE: Bring all ingredients to simmer in small saucepan over medium heat; cook, stirring occasionally, until sauce reaches ketchup-like consistency and is reduced to about 1 cup, 5 to 7 minutes. Transfer ½ cup sauce to small bowl and set aside remaining sauce to serve with cooked chicken.

2. FOR THE KEBABS: Toss chicken and salt in large bowl; cover with plastic wrap and refrigerate for at least 30 minutes and up to 1 hour.

3. Light large chimney starter three-quarters filled with charcoal (4½ quarts, about 75 briquettes) and allow to burn until coals are fully ignited and partially covered with thin layer of ash, about 20 minutes. Arrange all coals in even layer over half of grill bottom, leaving other half empty. Position cooking grate over coals, cover grill, and heat grate until hot, about 5 minutes. Scrape grate clean with grill brush.

4. While grill heats, pat chicken dry with paper towels. Combine sweet paprika, sugar, and smoked paprika in small bowl. Process bacon in food processor until smooth paste forms, 30 to 45 seconds, scraping down bowl twice during processing. Add bacon paste and spice mixture to chicken; mix with hands or rubber spatula until ingredients are thoroughly blended and chicken is completely coated. Thread meat onto skewers, rolling or folding meat as necessary to maintain 1-inch cubes.

5. Place kebabs over coals and grill, turning one-quarter turn every 2 to 2½ minutes until well browned and slightly charred, 8 minutes for breasts or 10 minutes for thighs. (If flare-ups occur, slide kebabs to cool side of grill until fire dies down.) Brush top surface of kebabs with ¼ cup sauce; flip and cook until sauce is brown in spots, about 1 minute. Brush second side with remaining ¼ cup sauce; flip and continue to cook until brown in spots and instant-read thermometer inserted in center of meat registers 160 degrees for breasts and 175 degrees for thighs, about 1 minute longer. Remove kebabs from grill and let rest for 5 minutes. Serve, passing reserved barbecue sauce separately.

GAS-GRILLED BARBECUED CHICKEN KEBABS

Follow recipe for Charcoal-Grilled Barbecued Chicken Kebabs through step 2. Turn all burners to high, close lid, and heat grill until hot, about 15 minutes. Scrape cooking grate clean with grill brush. Leave primary burner on high and turn off other burner(s). Continue with recipe from step 4, placing kebabs over primary burner and grilling with lid down.

The Secrets of Bone-In Pork Roast

A boneless pork roast sure is convenient. But is something important lost when those bones are cut away? We went out to the grill (and into the lab) to find out.

> BY ADAM RIED <

Most of us consider boneless pork roasts to be a welcome modern convenience, like automatic transmissions. Why deal with a clutch and a stick shift—or with bones—if you don't have to? I can't complain about the convenience of a boneless pork roast—little to no butchering on the front end, and fuss-free slicing at the table—but I also know that meat cooked on the bone just tastes better. Plus, for many people, gnawing on the bone is a satisfying way to finish off a meal.

With those reflections in mind, I decided to reacquaint myself with the pleasures of grilling a bone-in roast. I wanted a succulent, flavor-packed roast with a thick, well-browned crust and subtle smokiness. And while I figured out the best way to achieve those results, I also hoped to learn exactly why it is that bones make meat taste juicier and richer.

A Good Ribbing

The obvious starting place was my supermarket butcher case, where I focused on tender, quick-cooking roasts from the loin section of the animal. From this region, I had my choice of three roasts: the blade-end (sometimes called the rib-end) roast, the center-cut rib roast, and the confusingly named center-cut loin roast. From all the taste tests done in our test kitchen over the years, I already knew that the center-cut loin roast offers the least impressive flavor of the three. So I narrowed my choices to the blade-end and center-cut rib roasts, settling on the center-cut roast for its great ease of preparation: Because the meat is a single muscle attached along one side to the bones, there is no need to tie the roast for a tidy presentation. (See "The Best Bone-In Pork Roast" for more information about the roast choices.)

I began by rubbing the meat with a generous handful of kosher salt and letting it rest in the refrigerator for six hours before starting the fire—a technique we

Scoring the fat on the roast helps the rendered drippings baste the meat during grill-roasting.

prefer to soaking the meat in a brine when our goal is a deeply browned, crisp crust. Next I built a modified two-level fire, banking all the coals on one side of the kettle. This leaves a cooler area where the meat can cook through slowly by indirect heat without risk of burning the exterior. Then I threw the roast on the grates, covered the grill, and walked away.

A little more than an hour later, the roast's internal temperature measured 140 degrees (I knew it would rise to the requisite 150 degrees as it rested). I expected to pull the roast over to the grill's hot side for a quick sear before I took it off the grill, but to my delight the meat's exterior had already formed a thick mahogany crust.

Flavor and Fire

Now that I'd picked the best cut and cooking method for the job, I moved on to consider possible tweaks to the flavorings—though, to be honest, I wasn't sure that the roast needed much improvement. The meat was tender and remarkably juicy and had plenty of rich, deep flavor. Even my dead-simple salt rub enhanced the pork's taste without distraction.

But, being a skeptic and a perfectionist, I wanted to rule out all other options. So I set up a side-by-side test for my colleagues, pitting my plain salt-rubbed roast against identical specimens crusted with black pepper and a range of other spices and herbs. I also tested varying strengths of wood smoke. When the votes were tallied, my original intuition was confirmed: Simpler was better. My tasters opted for nothing more than a little sprinkling of black pepper just before cooking and a subtle tinge of smoke flavor. The latter was easy enough: I soaked one wood chunk, placed it on top of the hot coals, positioned the lid vents over the meat, and opened them halfway to draw smoke over the roast.

SHOPPING The Best Bone-In Pork Roast

The three most common pork loin roasts offer markedly different results in terms of flavor and texture.

TOP CHOICE: Center-Cut Rib Roast
A cut from the center of the loin that contains mostly loin muscle (and sometimes a bit of tenderloin) attached to a neat row of curved rib bones.
Pros: Good flavor; easy availability; no tying necessary
Cons: None when cooked bone-in; tendency to dry out when boneless

CLOSE SECOND: Blade-End Roast
Also known as the "rib-end roast," this cut from the shoulder end of the loin is a hodgepodge of small muscles.
Pros: Exceptionally rich flavor
Cons: Spotty availability; must be tied; tricky to slice cleanly

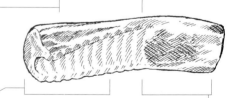

DISTANT THIRD: Center-Cut Loin Roast
A narrow section of loin muscle fused with a larger section of tenderloin, cut from the rear of the loin. The bones are mostly T-shaped vertebrae, not ribs.
Pros: Tender; decent flavor
Cons: Bone structure makes carving difficult; less flavorful than other options

Down to the Bones

My testing was nearly done, but I still wanted to know exactly what makes a bone-in roast so flavorful and juicy. I consulted our science editor as well as a number of unaffiliated meat scientists and experts, and several of them advanced similar theories about the enhanced juiciness and flavor of bone-in meat.

First, there is extra fat and connective tissue around the bones. As the roast cooks, that fat melts and bastes the meat while the connective tissues break down into gelatin, lending the meat perceived juiciness. (We score the fat on the surface of the roast for this reason.) Second, the bones act as insulation. Because they conduct heat poorly, they inhibit evaporation and moisture loss from the meat attached to them, keeping the meat around them juicier. Our science editor also pointed out that many of the flavor compounds in smoke vapor are fat-soluble, and since there is extra fat in the roast—courtesy of the bones—the meat is likely to absorb and retain more flavor from the smoke.

But another, more intriguing theory, and one I had never heard before, credited the bone marrow. Two experts thought some of the flavorful compounds of the marrow might migrate through the porous bone and into the surrounding meat, though they knew of no experiments that proved it. This hypothesis seemed promising, so I asked our science editor to help the test kitchen devise an experiment to test it (see "Flavor from Bones?"). As it turned out, the theory held up.

With all the flavor and tenderness those bones provided, all that this roast needed was a simple orange salsa to provide a counterpoint to its richness. As the man once said, "If it ain't broke, don't fix it."

CHARCOAL-GRILL-ROASTED BONE-IN PORK RIB ROAST
SERVES 6 TO 8

NOTE: If you buy a blade-end roast (sometimes called a "rib-end"), tie it into a uniform shape with kitchen twine at 1-inch intervals; this step is unnecessary with a center-cut roast. For easier carving, ask the butcher to remove the tip of the chine bone and to cut the remainder of the chine bone between the ribs. For instructions on carving the roast, see page 31.

- 1 (4- to 5-pound) center-cut rib or blade-end bone-in pork roast, tip of chine bone removed (see note)
- 4 teaspoons kosher salt
- 1 (3-inch) wood chunk
- 1½ teaspoons ground black pepper
- 1 recipe Orange Salsa with Cuban Flavors, optional (recipe follows)

1. Pat roast dry with paper towels. If necessary, trim thick spots of surface fat layer to about ¼-inch thickness. Using sharp knife, cut slits in surface fat layer, spaced 1 inch apart, in crosshatch pattern, being careful not to cut into meat. Sprinkle roast evenly with salt. Wrap with plastic wrap and refrigerate for at least 6 hours, up to 24 hours.

2. One to 2 hours before grilling, submerge wood chunk in bowl of water to soak.

3. Open bottom grill vents fully. Light large chimney starter filled with charcoal (6 quarts, about 100 briquettes) and allow to burn until coals are fully ignited and partially covered with thin layer of ash, about 20 minutes. Empty coals into grill to cover one-third of grill with coals steeply banked against side of grill. Place wood chunk on top of coals, position cooking grate, cover, and heat until grate is hot and wood is smoking, about 5 minutes. Scrape grate clean with grill brush.

4. Sprinkle roast evenly with pepper. Place roast on grate with meat near, but not over, coals and bones facing away from coals. Open top vents halfway and cover grill, positioning vents over meat. (Initial grill temperature should be about 425 degrees.) Grill roast until instant-read thermometer inserted into thickest part of meat registers 140 degrees, 1¼ to 1½ hours.

5. Transfer roast to carving board, tent loosely with foil, and let rest for 30 minutes (internal temperature should rise to about 150 degrees). Carve into thick slices by cutting between ribs. Serve, passing salsa separately (if using).

GAS-GRILL-ROASTED BONE-IN PORK RIB ROAST

Follow recipe for Charcoal-Grill-Roasted Bone-In Pork Rib Roast through step 2, substituting 2 cups soaked wood chips for wood chunk. Place soaked chips in 9-inch disposable aluminum pie plate and set on primary burner of grill (burner that will stay on during grilling). Position cooking grates over burners. Turn all burners to high and heat grill with lid down until very hot, about 15 minutes. Turn primary burner to medium-high and turn off other burner(s). Scrape grate clean with grill brush. Proceed with recipe from step 4, positioning roast on cooler part of grill, near, but not over, primary burner.

ORANGE SALSA WITH CUBAN FLAVORS
MAKES ABOUT 2½ CUPS

- ½ teaspoon finely grated orange zest, plus 5 oranges, peeled and segmented; each segment quartered crosswise
- ½ red onion, minced (about ½ cup)
- 1 jalapeño, stemmed, seeded if desired, and minced (about 3 tablespoons)
- 2 tablespoons juice from 1 lime
- 2 tablespoons minced fresh parsley leaves
- 2 teaspoons brown sugar
- 1 tablespoon extra-virgin olive oil
- 1½ teaspoons white vinegar
- 1½ teaspoons minced fresh oregano leaves
- 1 medium garlic clove, minced or pressed through garlic press (about 1 teaspoon)
- ½ teaspoon ground cumin
- ½ teaspoon table salt
- ½ teaspoon ground black pepper

Combine all ingredients in small nonreactive bowl.

The Weirdest Roast Ever

We've long known that the fat and connective tissue that surround bones lend moisture and richness to bone-in meats, while the mere presence of bones slows cooking and limits evaporation of juices. But it seemed to us that there must be other reasons why bone-in meat tastes better than the boneless kind. So when two meat experts suggested that some flavor might migrate from the rich marrow at the center of bones through the porous bone itself and right into the meat, our curiosity was piqued. We devised a test to see if this theory made any sense.

EXPERIMENT

To fabricate a neutral-flavored pork substitute, we made a big batch of mashed potatoes and seasoned it with 8 percent butter and 1 percent salt by weight, amounts that mimic the fat and salt found in our pork roast. Then we formed the potatoes into two equal-size, oblong shapes on a baking sheet. Next we scraped three pork rib bones clean of all fat and connective tissue, so that the only flavor would be from the marrow, and placed these bones over the top of one of the "roasts." To create a control, we left the other mashed-potato "roast" alone. Then we cooked both of our imitation roasts in a 425-degree oven for 1½ hours. After a 20-minute rest, we compared the plain sample to the one with bones.

RESULTS

A majority of tasters found that the sample cooked with bones tasted noticeably meaty.

EXPLANATION

As bones are heated, they expel moisture, salt, amino acids, and nucleotides (the last two being responsible for the "meatiness" that tasters detected) from the richly flavored marrow. However, since those water-soluble flavor molecules must penetrate through a thick layer of bone to reach the meat, the diffusion process is slow and the amount of flavor contributed is not enormous. Nevertheless, when coupled with the considerable moisture- and flavor-enhancing benefits of the fat and connective tissue around the bones, the process certainly provides another good reason to opt for bone-in. –Dan Souza

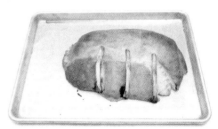

BONE-IN MASHED POTATO "ROAST"
Crazy as it sounds, our imitation roast proved that some flavor from the bone can migrate into the meat.

The Ultimate Pub-Style Burger

Hand-ground beef gave us deep flavor, but getting a crusty exterior plus a juicy interior that was evenly rosy from center to edge required a couple more tricks.

⇒ BY BRYAN ROOF ⇐

Making hamburgers from preground beef sure gets dinner on the table in a hurry. But when my goal is a memorably thick, juicy burger full of big beefy flavor—the kind served in the best high-end pubs—I wouldn't dream of using the preground stuff. The fact is, supermarket ground beef is mediocre. Because it's typically purchased in bulk from beef processing plants, supplemented with meat scraps, and then reground, the flavor and texture vary from package to package. More often than not, I find that the beef has literally been ground to a pulp that cooks up dry and pebbly, no matter how much care I take. And it never has the rich meaty flavor I crave.

So when I received an assignment to create a thick, pub-style burger, I knew that grinding my own beef was a given. What I didn't yet know was which cut of beef I would use, how coarsely or finely I would process the meat, and what cooking method would produce a well-seared, thickly crusted burger that was juicy and evenly medium-rare within.

Cut and Grind

Standing at the butcher case, I was first inclined to reach for a chuck roast. This popular burger cut boasts a robust amount of fat that lubricates and flavors the meat as it cooks. But it also contains a fair amount of sinew—no problem for a dedicated meat grinder, but more work than my food processor (the test kitchen's go-to alternative to a meat grinder) could handle. Instead, I settled on sirloin steak tips. While not quite as rich as chuck, this cut offers supremely beefy flavor without gristly sinew.

As for the grinding process itself, I already had a good lead to follow: our Best Old-Fashioned Burgers recipe (July/August 2008). It calls for cutting the meat into 1-inch chunks, freezing it until just firm, and then pulsing it in the food processor in batches into rough 1/16-inch bits. This relatively coarse grind, coupled with a light touch when packing the meat into disks, is the key to a tender burger. However, when I applied the technique to my heftier, pub-size patties, it didn't translate perfectly. The patties broke apart when I tried to flip them in the skillet. The problem proved easy to solve by cutting the meat into smaller 1/2-inch

Crumbled blue cheese, homemade sauce, and crispy shallots are great enhancements. But the real star is the beef.

chunks before processing, which helped create a more even grind that stuck together better. I also adjusted how I shaped the burgers, first forming the beef into loosely packed meatballs, which I then flattened into patties. Both measures gave the burgers just enough structure to hold their shape when flipped.

Juicing Up

On to the next issue: More than a few tasters hinted that they missed the richness of well-marbled chuck. Supplementing the steak tips with another, fattier cut of beef—a common restaurant trick—would be one way to boost flavor, but I wasn't wild about adding more butchering work to the process. Instead, I experimented with adding straight fat. First I tried olive oil, which was a total flop; it seeped out as soon as the burger started to cook and did little to flavor the meat. But melted butter, which solidified as it hit the cold meat, created pinhead-size particles of fat strewn throughout the patties, which improved the burgers' flavor and juiciness. Even better, the extra fat boosted the browning on its exterior.

But good browning was about the only thing the exterior had going for it. Between their crisp, craggy shells and deep pink centers, the patties were marred by a thick band of gray meat and no amount of extra fat was going to help. Clearly, I needed to rethink my cooking method. Up to now, I had been following a pretty standard approach for pan-fried burgers: preheating a skillet over high heat until it was good and hot, then cooking the patties to medium-rare for about four minutes per side.

But I had an alternative method in mind—one we developed for cooking thick-cut steaks. In that recipe, we used a combination stove-oven technique, in which the intense heat of the burner produced a great crust and the gentler, more ambient heat of the oven prevented the gray band of meat from forming beneath it. I followed suit here, quickly searing the burgers in a skillet and then transferring them

---

KEY STEPS | THICK, JUICY, PERFECTLY COOKED BURGERS

I. FREEZE AND GRIND Chilling the beef chunks until firm and then processing them into 1/16-inch pieces ensures a coarse grind that stays loosely packed.

2. ADD BUTTER Coating the raw ground beef with melted butter not only ensures that the burgers cook up super-juicy, but also encourages flavorful browning.

3. SEAR, THEN BAKE Searing on the stove and then finishing in a low-heat oven trades the usual overcooked exterior for a well-browned crust and juicy center.

(in the pan) to a 350-degree oven. But the results were only marginally better. The problem was that the portion of the burgers in direct contact with the skillet continued to cook faster than the top half. Lowering the oven temperature to 300 degrees helped, but only a little. That's when I decided to transfer the burgers from the skillet after searing to a cool baking sheet for finishing in the oven. That did it. After about 5 minutes, the burgers emerged with perfect interiors—juicy and rosy throughout.

Over the Top

This being a premium pub-style burger, it needed a few premium (yet simple) toppings. I threw together a quick tangy-sweet sauce to smear on each bun and combined it with crispy shallots and blue cheese in one variation and aged cheddar and peppercorn-crusted bacon in another.

Admittedly, this burger required more time and effort than your average patty fashioned from super-market ground beef. But my tasters and I needed only one bite to confirm that the fresh, deeply beefy-tasting, insanely juicy results were well worth the extra trouble.

JUICY PUB-STYLE BURGERS
SERVES 4

NOTE: Sirloin steak tips are also sold as flap meat. When stirring the butter and pepper into the ground meat and shaping the patties, take care not to over-work the meat or the burgers will become dense. The burgers can be topped as desired or with one of the test kitchen's favorite combinations (recipes follow). For our free recipes for Juicy Pub-Style Burgers with Sautéed Onions and Smoked Cheddar and Juicy Pub-Style Burgers with Pan-Roasted Mushrooms and Gruyère, go to www.CooksIllustrated.com/jun11.

- 2 pounds sirloin steak tips, trimmed of excess fat and cut into ½-inch chunks (see note)
- 4 tablespoons unsalted butter, melted and cooled slightly
  Table salt and ground black pepper
- 1 teaspoon vegetable oil
- 4 hamburger buns, toasted and buttered

1. Place beef chunks on baking sheet in single layer. Freeze meat until very firm and starting to harden around edges but still pliable, about 35 minutes.

2. Place one-quarter of meat in food processor and pulse until finely ground into ¹⁄₁₆-inch pieces, about 35 one-second pulses, stopping and redistrib-uting meat around bowl as necessary to ensure beef is evenly ground. Transfer meat to second baking sheet. Repeat grinding with remaining 3 batches of meat. Spread meat over sheet and inspect carefully, discarding any long strands of gristle or large chunks of hard meat or fat.

3. Adjust oven rack to middle position and heat oven to 300 degrees. Drizzle melted butter over ground meat and add 1 teaspoon pepper. Gently

toss with fork to combine. Divide meat into 4 lightly packed balls. Gently flatten into patties ¾ inch thick and about 4½ inches in diameter. Refrigerate pat-ties until ready to cook. (Patties can be refrigerated, covered, for up to 1 day.)

4. Season 1 side of patties liberally with salt and pepper. Using spatula, flip patties and season other side. Heat oil in 12-inch skillet over high heat until just smoking. Using spatula, transfer burgers to skillet and cook without moving for 2 minutes. Using spatula, flip burgers and cook for 2 minutes longer. Transfer patties to rimmed baking sheet and bake until instant-read thermometer inserted into burger registers 125 degrees for medium-rare or 130 degrees for medium, 3 to 6 minutes.

5. Transfer burgers to plate and let rest for 5 min-utes. Transfer to buns, add desired toppings, and serve.

PUB-STYLE BURGER SAUCE
MAKES ABOUT 1 CUP

- ¾ cup mayonnaise
- 2 tablespoons soy sauce
- 1 tablespoon dark brown sugar
- 1 tablespoon Worcestershire sauce
- 1 tablespoon minced fresh chives
- 1 medium garlic clove, minced or pressed through garlic press (about 1 teaspoon)
- ¾ teaspoon ground black pepper

Whisk all ingredients together in bowl.

JUICY PUB-STYLE BURGERS WITH CRISPY SHALLOTS AND BLUE CHEESE

Follow step 1 of recipe for Juicy Pub-Style Burgers. While beef is in freezer, heat ½ cup vegetable oil and 3 thinly sliced shallots in medium saucepan over high heat; cook, stirring frequently, until shallots are golden, about 8 minutes. Using slotted spoon, trans-fer shallots to paper towel–lined plate, season with salt, and set aside. Proceed with recipe, topping each burger with 1 ounce crumbled blue cheese before transferring to oven. Top burgers with Pub-Style Burger Sauce and crispy shallots just before serving.

JUICY PUB-STYLE BURGERS WITH PEPPERED BACON AND AGED CHEDDAR

Follow step 1 of recipe for Juicy Pub-Style Burgers. While beef is in freezer, adjust oven rack to middle position and heat oven to 375 degrees. Arrange 6 slices bacon on rimmed baking sheet and sprinkle with 2 teaspoons coarsely ground black pepper. Place second rimmed baking sheet on top of bacon and bake until bacon is crisp, 15 to 20 minutes. Transfer bacon to paper towel–lined plate and cool. Cut bacon in half crosswise. Reduce oven temperature to 300 degrees. Proceed with recipe, topping each burger with 1 ounce grated aged cheddar cheese before transferring to oven. Top burgers with Pub-Style Burger Sauce and bacon just before serving.

Witness the Burger Creation
Video available FREE for 4 months at
www.CooksIllustrated.com/jun11

Perfecting Grilled Scallops

A blazing-hot live fire can render scallops beautifully crisp on the outside and juicy within—or cement them to the grate like carbonized hockey pucks.

⇒ BY DAVID PAZMIÑO ⇐

Pan-searing is my favorite way to cook scallops indoors: The quick blast of heat deeply browns their exteriors while leaving their centers plump and moist. I've always figured the bivalves would be tailor-made for the grill, too. In theory, the blazing-hot fire would produce even better results than a stove, rendering the scallop crusts extra-crisp, with a hint of smoke. Unfortunately, my outdoor efforts have suggested otherwise. By the time the scallops develop a good sear, they're usually overcooked and rubbery. And then there's the more general problem of trying to flip them: No matter how diligently I coat the scallops with oil before cooking, they inevitably end up sticking to the grates.

Maybe I should be more discouraged by those results, but the seafood lover in me can't shake the idea of savoring scallops at their best: lightly charred on the outside, tender and juicy inside, and tinged with smoke flavor. I set myself up with a charcoal kettle and dozens of scallops, determined to find a way around these pitfalls.

A thin coating of flour, cornstarch, and oil keeps the scallops from sticking to the grate and enhances their crusty exterior.

Adding Fuel to the Fire

The test kitchen's Pan-Seared Scallops recipe (November/December 2009) had already tackled the shopping issues for me. Not only did I want the largest sea specimens I could find—sold as U10s or U20s, which indicates that there are about 10 to 20 per pound—but I would also make sure that I was purchasing "dry," not "wet," scallops. Although pricier and harder to find, dry scallops are worth seeking out because they have not been treated with a preservative solution of water and sodium tripolyphosphate, which gives them a soapy, metallic flavor and causes them to leach out water during cooking, which in turn thwarts browning.

I picked up another trick from the Pan-Seared Scallops recipe to help ensure good browning: blotting the scallops dry between layers of kitchen towels before cooking. From there, I threaded the scallops onto doubled metal skewers, which ensured that all of the scallops could be flipped at the same time and wouldn't spin in the process. Then I brushed them with oil, seasoned them with salt and pepper, and considered my grill setup. To avoid overcooking the scallops but still develop a brown crust, I needed a quick blast of blazing heat. Since most grill grates aren't adjustable, I brainstormed ways to build the biggest fire possible. My first thought was to load the grill with two chimneys full of briquettes, which brought the coals 2 inches from the grate. In four minutes, my scallops were beautifully seared, with succulent interiors. The only problem? Four hours later, the fire was still burning—a ridiculous waste of 200 briquettes.

My next idea was a trick I borrowed from celebrity chef Alton Brown: He grills tuna steaks on a wire rack set directly atop a chimney full of hot coals. Searing food over such a small surface works fine for a piece of fish (if you don't mind the slightly precarious setup), but after grilling my sixth batch of scallops, I realized the idea was absurd for skewers.

Had I dismissed the oversize-fire idea too quickly? Two chimneys were too much, but what if I piled as many coals as possible into a single chimney (7 quarts instead of the usual 6) and made a fire in the center of the grill? I gave it a whirl, and the results were encouraging, though still not ideal. Without anything to contain them, the coals didn't form an even layer, meaning that the skewers set over the center of the fire cooked faster than those sitting over the perimeter. I needed a way to corral the coals and make the fire as level as possible. I rummaged through the test kitchen's grilling equipment and found the simple solution: a disposable aluminum pan. When grilling a roast, we often set one of these deep basins alongside the coals, where it can catch rendered fat, but this time I placed one in the center of the grill, piled in the lit coals from the chimney, and proceeded with my recipe. The result? Scallops with impressive char and juicy centers.

Grill Setup—Trial by Fire

Creating a good sear on scallops without overcooking them requires a quick blast of the hottest heat possible. Here's how we experimented with bringing the food and the fire closer together.

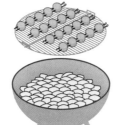

WASTEFUL
Building a huge fire with two chimneys' worth of coals (12 quarts) worked well but was wasteful.

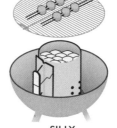

SILLY
Laying the skewers on a rack set directly over the chimney required endless batch work.

RIGHT ON
An aluminum pan filled with 7 quarts of coals created a tall, super-hot, even fire in the center of the grill.

NO-STICK SCALLOPS

Like fish, scallops exude a protein that fuses with the metal grate when they hit the grill bare. To create a barrier between the flesh and the cooking surface, we lightly coat the scallops with a mixture of oil, flour, and cornstarch, along with just a touch of sugar to promote browning.

Sticky Situation

The only problem: I still couldn't get the scallops off the grill in one piece. Then I remembered that I already had a solution at hand. To keep fish fillets from sticking when grilled, the test kitchen uses a two-step approach: We super-heat the grates by briefly covering them with a piece of aluminum foil and then paint them with multiple coats of oil. The latter step creates a super-slick cooking surface that won't instantly burn off, much like the coating on a well-seasoned cast-iron skillet. I applied both techniques here and, sure enough, the scallops released more easily. But if I was going to pay $18 per pound for these scallops, I had to do better.

That's when I decided to try coating the scallops with something more protective than just oil. One suggestion—a spice rub—didn't pan out, since the scallops' delicate flavor was lost and the spices themselves tended to burn. But a trick that another colleague developed to protect lean chicken breasts from drying out during pan-searing sounded at least a little promising: lightly coating the meat with a slurry of melted butter, flour, and cornstarch. This seemed worth trying, although I wondered if such a coating would actually hold up in the much-hotter fire of a grill. To my delight, it worked beautifully—with two

Did You Buy "Wet" Scallops?

We strongly recommend purchasing "dry" scallops (those without chemical additives). To determine if your scallops are "dry" or "wet," place one scallop on a paper towel–lined, microwave-safe plate and microwave on high power for 15 seconds. If the scallop is dry, it will exude very little water. If it is wet, there will be a sizable ring of moisture on the paper towel. In this case, soak the scallops in a solution of 1 quart cold water, ¼ cup lemon juice, and 2 tablespoons table salt for 30 minutes to help disguise any chemical taste before proceeding with step 1, and season only with pepper in step 3.

quick tweaks. To save myself the trouble of melting the butter, I swapped it for vegetable oil, and I added a little sugar to the mixture to expedite browning. When I went to pull this last batch of scallops off the grill, they were crisp-crusted but moist and tender within—and they released without hesitation.

Everyone agreed that these scallops tasted just about perfect with nothing more than a squeeze of lemon. But since scallops aren't everyday fare for most of us, I whipped up a couple of boldly flavored vinaigrettes—one featuring chile and lime, the other basil—for more dressed-up occasions.

CHARCOAL-GRILLED SEA SCALLOPS
SERVES 4

NOTE: Double-skewering the scallops makes flipping easier. To skewer, thread four to six scallops onto one skewer and then place a second skewer through the scallops parallel to and about ¼ inch from the first. You will need a deep (at least 2¾ inches) disposable 13 by 9-inch aluminum roasting pan. For our free recipes for Barbecue Sauce Vinaigrette and Bacon and Brown Butter Vinaigrette, go to www.CooksIllustrated.com/jun11.

1½	pounds large dry sea scallops, 10 to 20 per pound, small side muscles removed (see "Did You Buy 'Wet' Scallops?")
8–12	12-inch metal skewers
	Disposable 13 by 9-inch aluminum roasting pan (see note)
2	tablespoons vegetable oil, plus extra for cooking grate
1	tablespoon unbleached all-purpose flour
1	teaspoon cornstarch
1	teaspoon sugar
	Kosher salt and ground black pepper
	Lemon wedges, for serving
1	recipe vinaigrette, optional (recipes follow)

1. Place scallops on rimmed baking sheet lined with clean kitchen towel. Place second clean kitchen towel on top of scallops and press gently on towel to blot liquid. Let scallops sit at room temperature, covered with towel, for 10 minutes. With scallops on flat work surface, thread onto doubled skewers so that flat sides will directly touch grill grate, 4 to 6 scallops per doubled skewer. Return skewered scallops to towel-lined baking sheet; refrigerate, covered with second towel, while preparing grill.

2. Light large chimney starter mounded with charcoal (7 quarts, about 120 briquettes) and allow to burn until coals are fully ignited and partially covered with thin layer of ash, about 25 minutes. Meanwhile, poke twelve ½-inch holes in bottom of disposable aluminum roasting pan and place in center of grill. Empty coals into pan. Loosely cover cooking grate with large piece of heavy-duty aluminum foil; position grate over coals, cover grill, and heat grate until hot, about 5 minutes. Remove foil with tongs and discard; scrape grate clean with grill brush. Lightly

dip wad of paper towels in oil; holding wad with tongs, wipe grate. Continue to wipe grate with oiled paper towels, redipping towels in oil between applications, until grate is black and glossy, 5 to 10 times.

3. While grill is heating, whisk oil, flour, cornstarch, and sugar together in small bowl. Remove towels from scallops. Brush both sides of skewered scallops with oil mixture and season with salt and pepper. Place skewered scallops directly over hot coals. Cook without moving scallops until lightly browned, 2½ to 4 minutes. Carefully flip skewers and continue to cook until second side is browned, sides of scallops are firm, and centers are opaque, 2 to 4 minutes longer. Serve immediately with lemon wedges and vinaigrette (if using).

GAS-GRILLED SEA SCALLOPS

Follow recipe for Charcoal-Grilled Sea Scallops through step 1. While scallops dry, loosely cover cooking grate with large piece of heavy-duty aluminum foil, leaving 2-inch exposed border on each side of grate. (NOTE: This technique, which works well with metal grill grates, is not advisable for ceramic grill grates, as it has the potential to damage the grates.) Turn all burners to high, cover, and heat grill until very hot, about 15 minutes. Remove foil with tongs and discard. Scrape grate clean and oil grill as directed in step 2. Proceed with recipe from step 3, grilling scallops with lid down over high heat.

CHILE-LIME VINAIGRETTE
MAKES ABOUT 1 CUP

1	teaspoon finely grated zest and 3 tablespoons juice from 1 to 2 limes
1	tablespoon sriracha sauce
2	tablespoons honey
2	teaspoons fish sauce
½	cup vegetable oil

Whisk lime zest, lime juice, sriracha sauce, honey, and fish sauce until combined. Whisking constantly, slowly drizzle in oil until emulsified.

BASIL VINAIGRETTE
MAKES ABOUT 1 CUP

2	tablespoons champagne vinegar
1	cup packed fresh basil leaves
3	tablespoons minced fresh chives
2	medium garlic cloves, minced or pressed through garlic press (about 2 teaspoons)
2	teaspoons sugar
1	teaspoon table salt
½	teaspoon ground black pepper
⅔	cup vegetable oil

Pulse vinegar, basil, chives, garlic, sugar, salt, and pepper in jar of blender until roughly chopped. With blender running, slowly drizzle in oil until emulsified, scraping down sides as necessary.

Fried Rice, Indonesian-Style

Replicating the complex flavors of this Southeast Asian staple took some thoughtful shopping. But the real challenge was producing firm grains of rice without the usual overnight chill.

⇒ BY YVONNE RUPERTI ⇐

Fried rice has always been the frugal chef's template for using up leftovers: Take cold cooked rice, stir-fry it with whatever meat, vegetables, and aromatics are on hand, and toss it in a sauce that lightly coats the mixture and rehydrates the grains. When done well, the result is a satisfying one-dish meal.

And yet after years of eating the typical Chinese takeout versions—in which the rice is chock-full of meat and vegetables cut to the same size, cooked together, and tossed in a garden-variety "brown sauce"—I often crave something a bit more inspired. Indonesia's spin on the approach, *nasi goreng*, provides an answer. In this Southeast Asian rendition, the grains themselves are more thoroughly seasoned with a pungent chili paste called *sambal*, along with fermented shrimp paste and a syrupy-sweet soy sauce known as *kecap manis*. Then, instead of being loaded up with a hodgepodge of meats and vegetables, the rice is garnished with crunchy fried shallots, egg, and crisp fresh vegetables. The final product boasts so much complexity in flavor and texture that it hardly seems like the typical afterthought. But how best to replicate the dish in my own kitchen?

Paste Makers

A quick survey of Indonesian fried rice recipes revealed the source of this dish's heady flavor: chili paste. This coarse mixture is nothing more than a puree of shallots, garlic, and fresh Thai chiles. In most recipes, sautéing the chili paste in oil is the

The spirals of thin, tender omelet that garnish the dish take less than five minutes to create.

first step in the process. This way, the paste develops complexity and heat before the other ingredients hit the pan. (Note: The test kitchen prefers a skillet for stir-frying, since its flat bottom is better suited to a Western-style burner than a wok.)

The chili paste, I discovered, isn't hard to reproduce. I easily found the ingredients at the supermarket, and the paste was a snap to make, requiring just

a few quick pulses in the food processor. As for duplicating the flavors of the shrimp paste, glutamate-rich anchovies packed a rich, salty punch but were a little too fishy. Pungent fish sauce made a better substitute, but didn't single-handedly capture the paste's brininess. For that, I ended up going directly to the source, sautéing 12 ounces of chopped extra-large shrimp with the chili paste.

Bottled versions of kecap manis consist of palm sugar, which has a rich, almost caramelized flavor, and soy sauce. But simply adding brown sugar, which also has caramel notes, to soy sauce didn't quite replicate this condiment's complex flavor and viscosity. I had the best luck sweetening the soy with equal amounts of dark brown sugar and molasses.

In a series of quick motions, I added the shrimp to the pan in which I had been sautéing the paste, followed by the sweet soy mixture (including the fish sauce) and, finally, the rice. Each bite of this fried rice revealed that famously addictive balance of sweetness, heat, and pungency. A scattering of sliced scallions and a squirt of lime juice gave the dish a fresh finish.

Holding Firm

With the flavors of this dish locked down, I moved on to tackle a more fundamental fried rice problem: hastening the crucial rice-chilling step. Unlike freshly cooked rice, which forms soft, mushy clumps when stir-fried too soon, chilled rice undergoes a process called retrogradation, in which the starch molecules form crystalline structures that make the grains firm enough to withstand a second round of cooking. That's why this dish is tailor-made for last night's leftover rice: After hours in the fridge, the grains are cold and firm. But since cold cooked rice is

Re-Creating the Flavors of Indonesia

No need to hunt down esoteric ingredients. The various components that give this dish complex flavors and textures can be found at your local supermarket.

DARK BROWN SUGAR, SOY SAUCE, MOLASSES
Soy sauce sweetened with dark brown sugar and molasses approximates the flavors of the Indonesian condiment *kecap manis*.

GARLIC, SHALLOT, THAI CHILES
We create an Indonesian chili paste by coarsely pureeing these aromatics and sautéing them in oil to develop their flavors.

FISH SAUCE AND FRESH SHRIMP
The combination of fish sauce and fresh shrimp captures the rich, briny essence of hard-to-find Asian shrimp paste.

SIMPLE OMELET
A thin Asian-style omelet that gets rolled into a log and sliced into spirals brings tender texture to the dish.

CRISP SHALLOTS
Sliced thin and fried until golden, a traditional topping of shallot rings adds sweetness and addictive crunch.

Leftover white rice that's been thoroughly chilled—essential to making fried rice—is a staple in Asian households but not something that most of us keep on hand. To condense the overnight chilling process, we came up with a three-pronged approach that produces comparably dry, firm rice in less than an hour.

I. COAT WITH OIL Sautéing the rinsed rice in oil before steaming helps keep the grains from clumping.

2. USE LESS WATER Cooking the rice in slightly less water yields more rigid grains that don't require an overnight chill.

3. REST AND CHILL Resting and then briefly refrigerating the rice ensures that it is dry and firm enough for a second round of cooking.

something that I rarely have on hand, I had to take the extra step of cooking the rice the day before—a process that required more forethought than I wanted to give the dish.

I wondered: Was the 12 to 24 hours in the fridge really necessary? Hoping that I could get away with less chill time, I tried my recipe with rice that had been refrigerated for two, three, and four hours. While the results weren't bad, they hardly compared with the batches made with stiffer, drier grains that had chilled overnight. The freezer was no help: Although the rice felt cold and dry, it cooked up surprisingly mushy. Our science editor offered an explanation: Once the rice freezes, retrogradation comes to a halt, since freezing prevents the starch from crystallizing.

If I couldn't figure out a way to speed up retrogradation, maybe I could produce similarly firm, dry results by cooking the rice in less water. Getting the amount of liquid just right took some fiddling; the standard 3:2 ratio of water to rice was saturating the grains too much, so I drained varying amounts of water from the pot before achieving the ideal texture with just a third of a cup less liquid in the mix. Then I briefly rested the pot on the counter with a dish towel under the lid (to absorb excess moisture), spread the rice on a baking sheet, and popped the tray in the fridge. Twenty minutes later, the rice felt almost as firm as the overnight-chilled batches. The only holdup: The grains were a bit sticky. My two-pronged solution? Rinsing the raw rice and then briefly sautéing it in a splash of oil to form a greasy barrier before adding the water.

Gilding with Garnishes

All that remained was adding the traditional trimmings: a fried egg or omelet, frizzled shallots, and fresh-cut cucumbers and tomatoes. The latter three were no problem, but I had to decide how to prepare the egg, and everyone agreed that avoiding the last-minute work of egg frying would be a plus. With that in mind, I whipped up a quick omelet, which I rolled into a tight log, sliced into spirals, and set aside until I was ready to garnish.

With its sweet-salty flavors, spicy kick, and contrasting textures, this take on fried rice had officially eclipsed the more familiar humdrum versions. And since I didn't even have to wait a day to make it, it was a recipe that I'd turn to again and again.

INDONESIAN-STYLE FRIED RICE (NASI GORENG)
SERVES 4 TO 6

NOTE: If Thai chiles are unavailable, substitute two serranos or two medium jalapeños. Reduce the spiciness of this dish by removing the ribs and seeds from the chiles. This dish progresses very quickly at step 4; it's imperative that your ingredients are in place by then and ready to go. If desired, serve the rice with sliced cucumbers and tomato wedges.

- 5 green or red Thai chiles, stemmed (see note)
- 7 large shallots, peeled
- 4 large garlic cloves, peeled
- 2 tablespoons dark brown sugar
- 2 tablespoons light or mild molasses
- 2 tablespoons soy sauce
- 2 tablespoons fish sauce
  Table salt
- 4 large eggs
- ½ cup vegetable oil
- I recipe Faux Leftover Rice (recipe follows)
- 12 ounces extra-large shrimp (21 to 25 per pound), peeled, deveined, tails removed, and cut crosswise into thirds
- 4 large scallions, sliced thin
- 2 limes, cut into wedges

1. Pulse chiles, 4 shallots, and garlic in food processor until coarse paste is formed, about fifteen 1-second pulses, scraping down sides of bowl as necessary. Transfer mixture to small bowl and set aside. In second small bowl, stir together brown sugar, molasses, soy sauce, fish sauce, and 1¼ teaspoons salt. Whisk eggs and ¼ teaspoon salt together in medium bowl.

2. Thinly slice remaining 3 shallots and place in

12-inch nonstick skillet with oil. Fry over medium heat, stirring constantly, until shallots are golden and crisp, 6 to 10 minutes. Using slotted spoon, transfer shallots to paper towel–lined plate and season with salt to taste. Pour off oil and reserve. Wipe out skillet with paper towels.

3. Heat 1 teaspoon reserved oil in now-empty skillet over medium heat until shimmering. Add half of eggs to skillet, gently tilting pan to evenly coat bottom. Cover and cook until bottom of omelet is spotty golden brown and top is just set, about 1½ minutes. Slide omelet onto cutting board and gently roll up into tight log. Using sharp knife, cut log crosswise into 1-inch segments (leaving segments rolled). Repeat with another teaspoon reserved oil and remaining egg.

4. Remove rice from refrigerator and break up any large clumps with fingers. Heat 3 tablespoons reserved oil in now-empty skillet over medium heat until just shimmering. Add chile mixture and cook until mixture turns golden, 3 to 5 minutes. Add shrimp, increase heat to medium-high, and cook, stirring constantly, until exterior of shrimp is just opaque, about 2 minutes. Push shrimp to sides of skillet to clear center; stir molasses mixture to recombine and pour into center of skillet. When molasses mixture bubbles, add rice and cook, stirring and folding constantly, until shrimp is cooked, rice is heated through, and mixture is evenly coated, about 3 minutes. Stir in scallions, remove from heat, and transfer to serving platter. Garnish with egg segments, fried shallots, and lime wedges; serve immediately.

FAUX LEFTOVER RICE
MAKES 6 CUPS

NOTE: To rinse the rice, place it in a fine-mesh strainer and rinse under cool water until the water runs clear.

- 2 tablespoons vegetable oil
- 2 cups jasmine or long-grain white rice, rinsed (see note)
- 2⅔ cups water

Heat oil in large saucepan over medium heat until shimmering. Add rice and stir to coat grains with oil, about 30 seconds. Add water, increase heat to high, and bring to boil. Reduce heat to low, cover, and simmer until all liquid is absorbed, about 18 minutes. Off heat, remove lid and place clean kitchen towel folded in half over saucepan; replace lid. Let stand until rice is just tender, about 8 minutes. Spread cooked rice onto rimmed baking sheet, set on wire rack, and cool 10 minutes. Transfer to refrigerator and chill for 20 minutes.

Yvonne Demonstrates How to Make It
Video available FREE for 4 months at www.CooksIllustrated.com/jun11

A Guide to Cooking Greens

We've blanched, steamed, stir-fried, and sautéed enough greens over the years to know that some taste best cooked quickly over a high flame, while others benefit from slow, gentle heat. To pair the right leaf with the right cooking method, follow our thoroughly tested guidelines. BY KEITH DRESSER

STORING

If you're buying greens in advance, we recommend storing them in an open plastic produce bag or zipper-lock bag. In tests, we've found that trapped gases and too much constriction encourage rotting.

CLEANING

To ensure that every bit of dirt and grime gets washed off our greens, we trade the smaller confines of a salad spinner for a clean sink full of water, where there is ample room to swish the leaves. Unless you're stir-frying the greens, don't bother patting or spinning them dry; a little water clinging to their leaves helps them cook.

Gently swish greens under water to loosen grit. Give dirt several minutes to settle to bottom before gently lifting greens into colander to drain. Repeat if necessary to remove all dirt.

Pack It Down (Lightly)

Recipes often call for cups of "loosely packed" greens. Here's how to make sure you don't overdo it: Drop greens by the handful into a measuring cup and then gently pat down, using your fingertips rather than the palm of your hand.

PREPPING

KALE AND COLLARD GREENS

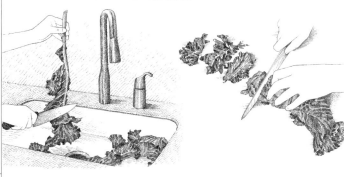

1. Hold each leaf at base of stem and use knife to slash leafy portion from either side of tough stem.

2. Stack several washed leaves, roll into cigar shape, and coarsely chop.

GREEN, RED, AND SAVOY CABBAGE

1. Cut cabbage into quarters and cut away hard piece of core from each quarter.

2. Separate quarters into manageable stacks; press each stack to flatten. Cut stacks crosswise into thin strips.

BOK CHOY AND NAPA CABBAGE

1. Trim bottom inch from head. Wash and pat dry leaves and stalks. Cut away leafy green portion from either side of white stalk.

2. Cut each stalk in half lengthwise, then crosswise into strips.

3. Layer leaves in manageable stacks; cut stacks crosswise into thin strips.

MATURE SPINACH

Curly spinach has thick stems that should be removed before cooking. Grasp each leaf at base of stem and pull stem from leaf.

SWISS CHARD AND BEET, MUSTARD, AND TURNIP GREENS

Fold leaves in half. Cut along edge of rib to remove thickest part of rib and stem.

Which Method Works for Which Green?

GREEN	TEXTURE	COOKING METHOD
Beet Greens	Medium-Tender	S
Bok Choy	Crisp, High Moisture	SF
Collards	Sturdy	SB, PS
Green Cabbage	Crisp, High Moisture	QB
Kale	Sturdy	SB, PS
Mustard Greens	Sturdy	SB, PS
Napa Cabbage	Crisp, High Moisture	SF
Red Cabbage	Crisp, High Moisture	QB
Savoy Cabbage	Crisp, High Moisture	QB, SF
Spinach (mature)	Medium-Tender	S
Swiss Chard	Medium-Tender	S
Turnip Greens	Sturdy	SB, PS

Key: PS=Pan-Steam; QB=Quick-Braise; S=Sauté; SB=Slow-Braise; SF=Stir-Fry

FIVE WAYS TO COOK GREENS

QUICK-BRAISE

Best For: Green, Red, and Savoy Cabbage

Why Use It: Cooking cabbage in a small amount of flavorful liquid preserves its bite. This method also creates a flavor exchange with the cooking liquid and builds complexity. Adding butter to the liquid deepens cabbage flavor and improves texture.

Basic Method: Melt 2 tablespoons butter in Dutch oven; add 1 pound thinly sliced cabbage and ½ cup braising liquid. Simmer, covered, until cabbage is wilted, about 9 minutes.

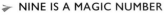

NINE IS A MAGIC NUMBER

Cabbage notoriously gives off an unpleasant odor when it cooks due to the breakdown of the leaves' cell walls, which releases sulfur-bearing flavor compounds. The key to minimizing that smell is all in the timing: We've found that about nine minutes of braising is just long enough to tenderize the sturdy leaves but brief enough to avoid producing an overabundance of sulfurous odor.

STIR-FRY

Best For: Bok Choy and Napa and Savoy Cabbage

Why Use It: Stir-frying over high heat lightly browns the greens, enhancing flavor while preserving some crunch.

Basic Method: Heat oil in nonstick skillet (preferred to wok when cooking on flat-top burner) over high heat. If using bok choy or napa cabbage, add sliced stalks and cook briefly. Add aromatics and cook briefly, then add 1½ pounds thinly sliced leaves and cook until tender, about 1 minute.

GIVE STALKS A HEAD START

Unlike many other greens, bok choy and napa cabbage contain both edible stalks and edible leaves. We add the stiffer stalks to the pan first, cooking them until crisp-tender and just starting to brown before adding the more delicate leaves.

FIVE WAYS TO COOK GREENS, CONTINUED

PAN-STEAM

Best For: Kale, Collards, and Mustard and Turnip Greens

Why Use It: Pan-steaming quickly wilts assertive greens while preserving some of their pungent flavor and hearty texture.

Basic Method: Heat garlic in olive oil in Dutch oven over medium heat. Add 2 pounds damp chopped greens (lots of water should still cling to leaves), cover pan, and cook until wilted, about 7 to 9 minutes for kale and turnip and mustard greens and 9 to 12 minutes for collards.

SLOW-BRAISE

Best For: Kale, Collards, and Mustard and Turnip Greens

Why Use It: This one-pot method slow-cooks assertive greens in a small amount of liquid. The long cooking mellows the bitterness of the greens more than pan-steaming and yields a more tender texture. To ensure that the greens don't taste watery, we increase the heat at the end of cooking to evaporate excess liquid.

Basic Method: Cook onions in oil in Dutch oven until softened. Add 2 pounds damp chopped greens and cook until beginning to wilt. Add 2 cups braising liquid, cover, and cook over medium-low heat until tender, 25 to 35 minutes for kale and turnip and mustard greens and 35 to 45 minutes for collards. Uncover, increase heat to medium-high, and cook until pot is almost dry.

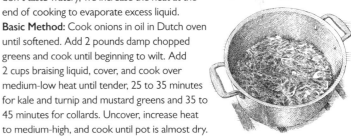

SAUTÉ

Best For: Mature Spinach, Swiss Chard, and Beet Greens

Why Use It: The relatively high heat cooks down medium-tender, high-moisture greens before they have a chance to get soggy.

Basic Method: Heat garlic in oil in Dutch oven over medium-high heat. Add 2 pounds damp greens and cook, tossing with tongs, until wilted, about 2 minutes for spinach and 5 minutes for Swiss chard and beet greens.

QUICK SQUEEZE

While sautéing evaporates most of the greens' moisture, we like to transfer hot greens to a colander in the sink and gently press them against the side to remove any excess water before serving.

Parcook Baby Spinach, Then Sauté

Sautéing baby spinach usually results in a watery mess. Our solution: Wilt this very delicate green in the microwave on high power for three to four minutes with 1 tablespoon of water per 6-ounce bag. Parcooking softens the leaves so moisture can be removed. Press the wilted leaves against the sides of a colander to squeeze out moisture; chop and press again. Then proceed with sautéing.

Spring Vegetable Pasta

When the original primavera method took hours—and produced washed-out vegetables and stodgy sauce—we took inspiration from an entirely different classic.

⇒ BY ANDREW JANJIGIAN ⇐

You'd never know that pasta primavera, a pseudo-Italian dish that appears on virtually every chain restaurant menu, actually has roots in French haute cuisine. The usual reproduction—a random jumble of produce tossed with noodles in a heavy, flavor-deadening cream sauce—tastes nothing like spring. Surprisingly, when I dug up the original recipe from New York's famed Le Cirque restaurant, my colleagues found it wasn't all that inspiring either, despite taking about two hours to prepare and dirtying five pans. First, the vegetables (which had been painstakingly blanched one by one) were bland. Second, the cream-, butter-, and cheese-enriched sauce dulled flavor and didn't really unify the dish. If I wanted a true spring-vegetable pasta—with a few thoughtfully chosen vegetables and a light, but full-bodied sauce that clung well to the noodles and brought the dish together—I'd have to start from the beginning.

Our creamy, glossy sauce clings well to ruffled, bell-shaped campanelle.

Growing Vegetable Flavor

Before I began cooking, I had some produce shopping to do. Freely testing my way through various spring staples, I landed on a pair of classics—asparagus and green peas—plus garlic and leeks for their aromatic depth and sweetness, chives for their fresh bite and onion-y overtones, and mint, a natural match for peas.

I also decided at the outset to do away with the tedious blanching step. I found that by sautéing the vegetables in stages in a large Dutch oven, I was able to ensure that each one maintained its crisp-tender texture while taking on a touch of flavorful browning. First went the leeks, followed by the chopped asparagus, the minced garlic, and finally the frozen baby peas, which needed only a minute over the heat to lend sweetness to the mix.

But as I'd learned from the original recipe, simply tossing sautéed vegetables with the pasta didn't add up to a dish any greater than the sum of its parts. What I needed was a way to tie the dish together and give it depth of flavor—a job that's usually reserved for the sauce. The chicken broth used in the original recipe didn't seem like the best way to enhance the vegetable flavor, so I swapped it for vegetable broth. To give it depth, I simmered the broth with the pile of scraps I'd peeled and trimmed away from the vegetables (the green parts of the leeks and the woody ends of the asparagus), along with some extra garlic and peas. But once I'd strained the broth and added the cream and butter—necessary to give the sauce body—any flavor advantage I had gained was lost. I tried cutting back on the dairy, but the result was so thin that it just slid off the pasta. The bottom line: The vegetables alone weren't enough to give the dish flavor.

The Pot Thickens

I was thinking of calling it quits when a colleague reminded me that Italian cookery has a tradition of parboiling pasta in water and then letting it finish cooking for a minute or two in whatever sauce is being served. The technique has a twofold benefit: As the pasta cooks, it absorbs some of the sauce and takes on its flavors. In exchange, the noodles release some of their starches into the sauce, which helps build body. It wouldn't hurt to try this approach. I prepared another batch, this time boiling the pasta (spaghetti, for now) for a couple of minutes in the water, draining it, and then allowing it to finish cooking in my enhanced vegetable broth. Everyone agreed that while this was a step in the right direction, the results were still too subtle.

Then a thought occurred to me: If I was going to add the pasta to the broth eventually, why not get the full benefit of the broth's flavor and use it to cook the pasta from the start? The concept was nothing new, of course: It's a classic risotto technique, in which the rice and broth work together to produce a glossy, full-bodied "sauce" that thoroughly flavors and coats each grain. When I tried the approach with pasta, the results weren't quite perfect, but they were promising: The noodles, which I had boiled in a modest 5 cups of liquid (4 cups of broth, 1 cup of water) until they were al dente and the Dutch oven was almost dry, emerged more flavorful and lightly coated with the silky, starchy pot liquor. In fact, the sauce was thick enough that I didn't even need to add any cream or butter to give it body.

Now that I was on a roll, I wondered if I couldn't stretch the risotto technique even farther. Traditionally, the raw rice grains "toast" for a few minutes in some hot fat before the liquid is added, taking on a nutty richness. Adapting this technique for my pasta recipe seemed like a natural move, except for the problem of the long spaghetti strands, which I'd need to break up first. It seemed easier to just change the shape of the noodle. After testing half a dozen shorter shapes, I opted for bell-shaped campanelle: They held on to the sauce nicely, without clinging to one another or compressing into a mass. (Bow tie–shaped farfalle and penne quills made fine substitutes.)

Now that I had the right pasta shape, I went back to the cooking technique. After sautéing the vegetables, I wiped out the pot, added a splash of extra-virgin olive oil, and toasted the pasta until it started

Look: A New Way to Cook Pasta

Video available FREE for 4 months at www.CooksIllustrated.com/jun11

to color. Continuing with the classic risotto method, I poured in some dry white wine (its crisp acidity would brighten the sauce), stirring the mixture until most of the liquid had cooked off, and added the hot broth and cranked up the heat to a boil. When I stuck in my fork about 10 minutes later, the results were remarkably improved: tender pasta pieces coated with a light but lustrous and creamy sauce that more than hinted at the sweet, grassy flavors of the vegetables.

Once the sautéed vegetables were incorporated, all the dish needed was a little flavor tweaking here and there. Along with the minced garlic, I added a dash of hot pepper flakes and, just before serving, a handful of grated Parmesan. Finally, I brightened the whole lot with a splash of lemon juice plus a handful of combined fresh chopped mint, chives, and lemon zest.

Nothing against the folks at Le Cirque, mind you, but unlike their original primavera, my recipe—a match-up of grassy, bright-tasting vegetables and nutty pasta in a complex, richly flavored sauce—truly tasted like spring, and came together in a fraction of the time.

SPRING VEGETABLE PASTA
SERVES 4 TO 6

NOTE: For tips on trimming asparagus, see page 30. Campanelle is our pasta of choice in this dish, but farfalle and penne are acceptable substitutes. The test kitchen's preferred brand of vegetable broth is Swanson Vegetable Broth.

- 3 medium leeks, white and light green parts halved lengthwise, washed, and cut into ½-inch-thick slices (about 5 cups); 3 cups roughly chopped dark green parts reserved
- 1 pound asparagus, tough ends snapped off, chopped coarsely, and reserved; spears cut on bias into ½-inch-thick pieces (see note)
- 2 cups frozen baby peas, thawed
- 4 medium garlic cloves, minced or pressed through garlic press (about 4 teaspoons)
- 4 cups vegetable broth (see note)
- 1 cup water
- 2 tablespoons minced fresh mint leaves
- 2 tablespoons minced fresh chives
- ½ teaspoon finely grated zest plus 2 tablespoons juice from 1 lemon
- 6 tablespoons extra-virgin olive oil
  Table salt
- ¼ teaspoon red pepper flakes
- 1 pound campanelle (see note)

- 1 cup dry white wine
- 1 ounce grated Parmesan cheese (about ½ cup), plus extra for serving
  Ground black pepper

1. Place dark green leek trimmings, asparagus trimmings, 1 cup peas, 2 teaspoons garlic, vegetable broth, and water in large saucepan. Bring to simmer over high heat, then lower heat to medium-low and gently simmer 10 minutes. While broth simmers, combine mint, chives, and lemon zest in small bowl; set aside.

2. Strain broth through fine-mesh strainer into 8-cup measuring cup, pressing on solids to extract as much liquid as possible (you should have 5 cups broth; add water as needed to measure 5 cups). Discard solids and return broth to saucepan. Cover and keep warm over low heat.

3. Heat 2 tablespoons oil in Dutch oven over medium heat until shimmering. Add sliced leeks and pinch salt; cook, covered, stirring occasionally, until leeks begin to brown, about 5 minutes. Add asparagus pieces and cook until crisp-tender, 4 to 6 minutes. Add remaining 2 teaspoons garlic and pepper flakes; cook until fragrant, about 30 seconds. Add remaining cup peas and continue to cook 1 minute. Transfer vegetables to plate and set aside. Wipe out pot.

4. Heat remaining 4 tablespoons oil in now-empty Dutch oven over medium heat until shimmering. Add pasta and cook, stirring frequently, until just beginning to brown, about 5 minutes. Add wine and cook, stirring constantly, until absorbed, about 2 minutes.

5. When wine is fully absorbed, add hot broth. Increase heat to medium-high and bring to boil. Cook, stirring frequently, until most of liquid is absorbed and pasta is al dente, 8 to 10 minutes.

6. Remove pot from heat, stir in lemon juice, Parmesan, half of herb mixture, and vegetables. Season with salt and pepper to taste. Serve immediately, passing Parmesan cheese and remaining herb mixture separately.

Spicing Up Sauces for the Grill

Tired of the same ketchup-y barbecue sauces, we looked for more exciting flavors—and made an unconventional stop at the candy-making department.

⋺ BY KEITH DRESSER ⋸

A trip down the condiment aisle of any supermarket is bound to turn up a dizzying array of tomato-based barbecue sauces, most of which are carbon copies of one another—terribly sweet and not the least bit interesting. The only thing they manage to get right? They stick to the food like gangbusters. That tackiness was something I wanted to preserve as I set out to create a handful of homemade grilling sauces to enliven chicken and pork. What I wanted to ditch were those tired, saccharine flavors in favor of something that tasted more balanced and exciting.

To get my bearings, I tried a few recipes. Most were so thin and runny that they slid right off the meat, and those that were sufficiently gooey relied on gobs of flavor-dulling flour or cornstarch.

The ingredient labels of bottled barbecue sauces didn't offer any useful clues either. Manufacturers build viscosity in their products by adding a glut of chemically fabricated emulsifiers—not a route I was about to take. Instead, I brainstormed for alternatives to ketchup or tomato sauce that would lend viscosity, stickiness, and an ability to serve as a foundation for a variety of flavorful add-ins. I came up with an unconventional idea: caramel. Super-adhesive and plenty thick, melted sugar seemed ideal. And it couldn't have been simpler to make: It took all of five minutes to caramelize ⅓ cup of sugar until it turned golden-amber and its one-note sweetness deepened into something richer. At this point, I added a few placeholder sauce ingredients. The sauce thickened up as it cooled, and the caramel produced enough tackiness to keep it glued to the meat during cooking.

Now came the fun part: deciding what other ingredients to add. I wanted each sauce to have a balance of sweet-tangy flavors and maybe a spicy kick. Hoisin and pineapple juice, apple butter and whole-grain mustard, orange marmalade and orange juice, and coconut milk spiced with red curry paste created pairings with a tempered sweetness that worked nicely against the caramel. For brightness, I worked an acidic component into each sauce—clean-tasting cider and white vinegar in some, and a healthy splash of rice vinegar or tart lime juice in the Asian-inspired versions. Finally, I whisked in bold elements: Chipotle chiles,

red pepper flakes, dry mustard, and Chinese five-spice powder added punch, while fish sauce and soy sauce built a salty dimension.

My sauces might take a few minutes longer to make than twisting open a cap, but they're far more complex than anything from a bottle.

APPLE-MUSTARD GRILLING SAUCE
MAKES ABOUT 1 CUP

- ⅔ cup apple cider or apple juice
- ⅓ cup apple butter
- 3 tablespoons whole-grain mustard
- 1 teaspoon dry mustard
- 2 tablespoons cider vinegar
- ½ teaspoon table salt
- ⅛ teaspoon cayenne pepper
- ⅓ cup water
- ⅓ cup sugar

1. Whisk cider, apple butter, whole-grain and dry mustards, vinegar, salt, and cayenne in medium bowl.

2. Place water in heavy-bottomed 2-quart saucepan; pour sugar in center of pan, taking care not to let sugar crystals adhere to sides of pan. Cover and bring mixture to boil over high heat; once boiling, uncover and continue to boil until syrup is thick and straw-colored, 3 to 4 minutes. Reduce heat to medium and continue to cook until syrup is golden amber, 1 to 2 minutes longer. Quickly remove saucepan from heat and whisk in apple-mustard mixture. Return to medium heat and cook, whisking constantly, until caramel has dissolved and sauce has thickened, about 2 minutes. Transfer ½ cup sauce to medium bowl to use for grilling. Set aside remaining sauce for serving.

HOISIN GRILLING SAUCE
MAKES ABOUT 1 CUP

- ½ cup hoisin sauce
- 3 tablespoons rice vinegar
- 3 tablespoons pineapple juice
- 1 tablespoon soy sauce
- 1 tablespoon minced fresh ginger
- ¼ teaspoon red pepper flakes
  Pinch Chinese five-spice powder
- ⅓ cup water
- ⅓ cup sugar

Whisk hoisin, rice vinegar, pineapple juice, soy sauce, ginger, red pepper flakes, and five-spice

powder in medium bowl. Follow recipe for Apple-Mustard Grilling Sauce from step 2.

ORANGE-CHIPOTLE GRILLING SAUCE
MAKES ABOUT 1 CUP

- ½ cup orange marmalade
- ⅓ cup juice plus ½ teaspoon finely grated zest from 1 orange
- ¼ cup white vinegar
- 1 chipotle chile in adobo, minced (about 1 tablespoon)
- ½ teaspoon table salt
- ⅓ cup water
- ⅓ cup sugar

Whisk marmalade, orange juice, zest, vinegar, chipotle, and salt in medium bowl. Follow recipe for Apple-Mustard Grilling Sauce from step 2.

COCONUT–RED CURRY GRILLING SAUCE
MAKES ABOUT 1 CUP

- 1¼ cups coconut milk
- ¼ cup juice and ½ teaspoon finely grated zest from 2 limes
- 1 tablespoon red curry paste
- 1 tablespoon fish sauce
- ⅓ cup water
- ⅓ cup sugar

Whisk coconut milk, lime juice, zest, curry paste, and fish sauce in medium bowl. Follow recipe for Apple-Mustard Grilling Sauce from step 2, increasing final sauce thickening time to 6 to 7 minutes.

How to Use Them

Our grilling sauces work equally well on pork or chicken and yield enough to coat 6 to 8 pieces (3 to 4 pounds) of meat, plus extra for the table. Wait to apply until the last five minutes of grilling (the meat should be about five degrees below the desired final internal temperature). Brush one side of the meat with ¼ cup of sauce reserved for cooking, then flip it and cook until browned, about two minutes. Brush the second side with another ¼ cup of sauce reserved for cooking, then flip it and cook until browned on the second side, two to three minutes. Serve, passing the remaining ½ cup sauce separately.

Best Sweet and Tangy Coleslaw

We wanted a quick, bright alternative to creamy coleslaw, but how do you make a speedy slaw that's not awash in watery dressing?

⇒ BY ANDREA GEARY ⇐

Confronted with heavyweight backyard barbecue offerings like loaded burgers, buttery corn on the cob, and creamy potato salad, I often yearn for something light to go with them—and a mayonnaise-based coleslaw doesn't cut it. An alternative slaw that has its roots in Amish cooking ditches the mayo for a dressing of oil, cider vinegar, and sugar. But I've always found this style—typically featuring just green cabbage and chopped onion—a little too plain. And like many slaws, creamy or tangy, it usually comes drowning in watery dressing. I wanted a sweet, tangy slaw in which all the flavors were in balance, not washed out.

The test kitchen already had a very effective way to deal with the moisture issue: tossing the shredded cabbage leaves with a teaspoon or so of salt and leaving them to drain for several hours while osmosis pulled water to their surface, eliminating moisture that would otherwise dilute the dish. I applied this technique to a basic slaw recipe, allowing a pound of salted shredded cabbage to rest three hours, which released a good half cup of liquid. When I dressed the cabbage, the loss of moisture transformed the slaw, allowing its simple flavors to come to the fore. With a few more tweaks—I replaced the domineering onion with grated carrot and chopped parsley, and added ¼ teaspoon of celery seed for zip—I had a refreshing slaw that would go with almost anything.

But it nagged at me that, for optimal results, such an easy recipe required hours for salting (albeit unattended). In the past we've found that combining the salting step with a quick stint in the microwave speeds moisture loss in other watery foods, including eggplant. Though heating a dish I planned to serve cold seemed counterintuitive, I decided to try it anyway. But after two minutes on high power—I didn't dare go longer for fear of wilting the cabbage—the salted leaves had released only a scant tablespoon.

At a loss for what to try next, I pulled out my science books and learned something new: It turns out that the speed with which water gets pulled to the surface of a salted food is determined by how many dissolved particles are in the solution. In other words, the more salt I used on the cabbage, the faster it should release water. I didn't want to increase the salt for fear of turning the slaw overly salty. But any dissolved molecule will exert osmotic force, and I hadn't considered the other water-soluble ingredient in my recipe: sugar. Though it wouldn't be as effective as salt (sugar remains one particle when dissolved, whereas salt

breaks down into two particles), it should still hasten water loss. I tossed a new batch of shredded slaw with 1 teaspoon of salt and ¼ cup of sugar, and—for good measure—stuck it in the microwave. Remarkably, with both salt and sugar in the mix, in just two minutes the cabbage shed the same ½ cup of liquid it had taken three hours to release at room temperature.

The only remaining issue: I now had warm slaw that required chilling. I had worked so hard to cut back the time, I didn't want to add too much back. The easy solution? I chilled the dressing in the freezer for 15 minutes as I prepped the cabbage. For a final cool-down—and to let the flavors meld—I popped the finished slaw in the fridge for 15 minutes more. By the time I'd finished cleaning up, I had a bright, crisp slaw to go with my grilled burger.

SWEET AND TANGY COLESLAW
SERVES 4

NOTE: If you don't have a salad spinner, use a colander to drain the cabbage and press with a rubber spatula. To adjust the sweetness or tanginess of the coleslaw, prepare as directed and season to taste with up to 2 teaspoons of sugar or up to 2 teaspoons of vinegar, adding 1 teaspoon at a time. For our free recipe for Sweet and Tangy Coleslaw with Fennel and Orange, go to www.CooksIllustrated.com/jun11.

- ¼ cup cider vinegar, plus extra for seasoning
- 2 tablespoons vegetable oil
- ¼ teaspoon celery seed
- ¼ teaspoon ground black pepper
- ½ large green cabbage (about 1 pound), cored and shredded fine (about 6 cups)
- ¼ cup sugar, plus extra for seasoning Table salt
- 1 large carrot, peeled and grated
- 2 tablespoons chopped fresh parsley leaves

1. Combine ¼ cup vinegar, oil, celery seed, and pepper in medium glass or metal bowl. Place bowl in freezer until vinegar mixture is well chilled, at least 15 minutes and up to 30 minutes.

2. While mixture chills, toss cabbage with ¼ cup sugar and 1 teaspoon salt in large microwave-safe bowl. Cover with large plate and microwave on high power for 1 minute. Stir briefly, re-cover, and continue to microwave on high power until cabbage is partially wilted and has reduced in volume by

This crisp slaw starts out with a stint in the microwave.

one-third, 30 to 60 seconds longer.

3. Transfer cabbage to salad spinner and spin cabbage until excess water is removed, 10 to 20 seconds. Remove bowl from freezer, add cabbage, carrot, and parsley to cold vinegar mixture, and toss to combine. If desired, adjust flavor with sugar or vinegar. Season with salt to taste. Refrigerate until chilled, about 15 minutes. Toss again before serving.

SWEET AND TANGY COLESLAW WITH RED BELL PEPPER AND JALAPEÑO

Follow recipe for Sweet and Tangy Coleslaw, substituting 2 tablespoons lime juice for celery seed, ½ thinly sliced red bell pepper and 1 or 2 seeded and minced jalapeños for carrot, and 1 thinly sliced scallion for parsley.

SWEET AND TANGY COLESLAW WITH APPLE AND TARRAGON

Follow recipe for Sweet and Tangy Coleslaw, reducing amount of cider vinegar to 3 tablespoons. Substitute ½ teaspoon Dijon mustard for celery seed, 1 Granny Smith apple cut into matchsticks for carrot, and 2 teaspoons minced tarragon for parsley.

Three Steps to Slaw
Video available FREE for 4 months at
www.CooksIllustrated.com/jun11

Foolproof Crêpes

These thin French pancakes have a reputation for being temperamental divas demanding pampered batter, a specialized pan, and supremely delicate handling. Oh, really?

> BY ANDREA GEARY

In cooking school I was yelled at only once, but I remember it vividly. The instructor was an old-school French chef, and bellowing was an integral part of his teaching style. The subject was crêpes. A crêpe is nothing but a thin pancake cooked quickly on each side and wrapped around a sweet or savory filling, but despite its apparent simplicity, there were a number of conventions to learn, and I was all thumbs that day. The classic steel crêpe pan was too hot or too cool, and I used too much batter or not enough. Unnerved by the chef's rage, I flipped too soon, producing crêpes that were limp and anemic, or I let them linger too long and they stuck and tore. The experience left me with singed fingertips and a firm resolve to avoid crêpe making forever.

Years later, I happened upon the crêpe episode of Julia Child's vintage PBS series *The French Chef*. She made the process look so easy, throwing together the batter in a blender and—using an ordinary nonstick pan—blithely flipping crêpe after crêpe. I was transfixed. Could making great crêpes—thin and delicate yet rich and flavorfully browned in spots—really be so painless, or did Child's expertise just make it look that way?

In the Mix

I was determined to face my bête noire, so I dug deep into the test kitchen's collection of French cookbooks to uncover a range of ingredients and techniques. But surprisingly, the 50-odd recipes I surveyed were remarkably similar: Flour and milk (and sometimes water) were either blended or hand-whisked with eggs, salt, and melted butter to form a creamy batter. Several recipes were spiked with brandy or lightly sweetened with sugar. The cooking instructions were universal: Spread the batter as thin as possible in the skillet, cook until the edges are golden and lacy, and then flip the crêpe to brown

We briefly microwave the stack of cooked crêpes before filling them to ensure they're warm for serving.

spottily on the other side. The only significant difference? About half of the recipes called for resting the batter for one to two hours after mixing, while the others skipped straight to cooking.

I didn't see much need for fiddling with the batter itself. A couple of quick tests determined that a 1½:1 ratio of milk to flour touched with sugar produced the best rich-tasting, lightly sweet thin pancakes. The type of flour in the mix and the mixing method, both of which I thought might affect the texture of the crêpes, didn't seem to matter. When I tested low-protein cake flour against higher-protein all-purpose and bread flours, my tasters deemed the results virtually indistinguishable. And batters simply whisked together by hand turned out crêpes every bit as good as those made from batters whirred by countertop or immersion blenders (for more information, see "Whisk Away"). Even the cooking vessel was nothing to fuss over: After making just a few crêpes, I followed Child's lead and ditched the specialty crêpe pan in favor of a plain old 12-inch nonstick skillet.

The Rest Is History

I was beginning to wonder if all that hullabaloo from my culinary instructor about the fastidiousness of the recipe wasn't just a lot of hot air—but I also hadn't yet tackled the central controversy about whether or not to rest the batter. The traditional justification is twofold: First, resting allows the starch granules in the flour to hydrate more fully, which purportedly produces a more tender crêpe. Second, a rest means that there's time for any air incorporated into the batter during mixing to dissipate, so the crêpe will be as thin as possible.

Curious, I made a batch of crêpe batter and placed it in the fridge. Then, just to take the resting test to the extreme, I waited two hours and made two more batches—one with all-purpose flour and (though I was loath to introduce specialty ingredients) the other with Wondra flour. (Child used this instantly hydrating flour in place of a rest in a later edition of *The French Chef Cookbook*.) Tasters compared crêpes from all three batches. Once again, their votes indicated no clear winner. I repeated the test just to be certain, but it seemed that neither the rest nor the specialty flour intended to mimic the rest made any noticeable difference.

Precision Pointers

Save for a few ingredient tweaks here and there, my recipe hadn't changed much since I began developing it. But these later batches of crêpes were

---

Whisk Away

Most recipes for traditional American pancakes caution against overmixing the batter; doing so activates the formation of gluten and will render the results tough and dense. In theory, the same logic would apply to crêpes, but our mixing tests showed that all that worry was for naught. Why? It all comes down to the liquid-to-flour ratio. The high proportion of liquid in crêpe batter makes it so dilute that gluten development—that is, the network of proteins that give baked goods their chew—is not actually a factor. This also means that you can use anything from low-protein cake flour to high-protein bread flour and get a similarly tender crêpe.

noticeably better—more tender and uniformly brown—than earlier attempts, and I realized that while the batter itself was relatively forgiving, there were some crucial crêpe-cooking tricks that I'd picked up along the way.

First, heat the pan properly. When I made it too hot, the batter set up before it evenly coated the surface, yielding a crêpe marred by thick, spongy patches and holes. When I made it too cool, the crêpe was pale (read: bland) and too flimsy to flip without tearing. To ensure steady, even cooking, I borrowed a technique that we used in our Perfect French Omelet recipe (January/February 2009): I slowly heated the oiled skillet over low heat for at least 10 minutes. I even found a quick test to determine when the pan was ready: Spoon a teaspoon of batter into the center of the preheated, lightly oil-slicked pan. If it turns perfectly golden brown in exactly 20 seconds, your skillet has hit that temperature "sweet spot."

Second, add just enough batter to coat the bottom of the pan. After trial and error, I settled on ¼ cup of batter as the ideal amount. The only glitch: The classic approach taught in culinary school—tilting the pan to swirl the batter around it—wasn't distributing the batter as evenly as I liked. My minor adjustment? Tilting the pan and giving it a gentle shake at the same time.

Finally, pinpoint the precise moment to flip the crêpe. My stopwatch tests showed that if the batter was added to a properly heated pan, it took about 25 seconds for it to go from wet to ready to flip—appearing dry, matte, and lacy around the edges. But to truly overcome all of my crêpe-cooking fears, I needed a way to flip the pancake without

singeing my fingers. Opting for a blunt-edged tool to loosen the crêpe, I nudged it from underneath with a rubber spatula before grasping its edge, then nimbly turned it to the flip side to cook until spotty brown—about another 20 seconds.

Once I had these tactics down, I whipped up a few simple sweet fillings—banana-Nutella, chocolate-orange, honey-almond, and utterly simple lemon-sugar were test kitchen favorites—and mused over how, with some careful testing and a few subtle tweaks, I'd turned my culinary school fall from grace into an opportunity to create the simplest, friendliest of recipes.

CRÊPES WITH SUGAR AND LEMON
SERVES 4

NOTE: Crêpes will give off steam as they cook, but if at any point the skillet begins to smoke, remove it from the heat immediately and turn down the heat. Stacking the crêpes on a wire rack allows excess steam to escape so they won't stick together. To allow for practice, the recipe yields 10 crêpes; only eight are needed for the filling. For our free recipe for Crêpes with Dulce de Leche and Toasted Pecans, go to www.CooksIllustrated.com/jun11.

- ½ teaspoon vegetable oil
- 1 cup (5 ounces) unbleached all-purpose flour
- 1 teaspoon sugar, plus 8 teaspoons sugar for sprinkling
- ¼ teaspoon table salt
- 1½ cups whole milk
- 3 large eggs
- 2 tablespoons unsalted butter, melted and cooled
- 1 lemon, cut into wedges

1. Place oil in 12-inch nonstick skillet and heat over low heat for at least 10 minutes.

2. While skillet is heating, whisk together flour, 1 teaspoon sugar, and salt in medium bowl. In separate bowl, whisk together milk and eggs. Add half of milk mixture to dry ingredients and whisk until

smooth. Add butter and whisk until incorporated. Whisk in remaining milk mixture until smooth.

3. Using paper towel, wipe out skillet, leaving thin film of oil on bottom and sides. Increase heat to medium and let skillet heat for 1 minute. After 1 minute, test heat of skillet by placing 1 teaspoon batter in center and cook for 20 seconds. If mini crêpe is golden brown on bottom, skillet is properly heated; if it is too light or too dark, adjust heat accordingly and retest.

4. Pour ¼ cup batter into far side of pan and tilt and shake gently until batter evenly covers bottom of pan. Cook crêpe without moving it until top surface is dry and crêpe starts to brown at edges, loosening crêpe from side of pan with rubber spatula, about 25 seconds. Gently slide spatula underneath edge of crêpe, grasp edge with fingertips, and flip crêpe. Cook until second side is lightly spotted, about 20 seconds. Transfer cooked crêpe to wire rack, inverting so spotted side is facing up. Return pan to heat and heat for 10 seconds before repeating with remaining batter. As crêpes are done, stack on wire rack.

5. Transfer stack of crêpes to large microwave-safe plate and invert second plate over crêpes. Microwave on high power until crêpes are warm, 30 to 45 seconds (45 to 60 seconds if crêpes have cooled completely). Remove top plate and wipe dry with paper towel. Sprinkle upper half of top crêpe with 1 teaspoon sugar. Fold unsugared bottom half over sugared half, then fold into quarters. Transfer sugared crêpe to second plate. Continue with remaining crêpes. Serve immediately, passing lemon wedges separately.

CRÊPES WITH BANANAS AND NUTELLA

Follow recipe for Crêpes with Sugar and Lemon, omitting 8 teaspoons sprinkling sugar and lemon wedges. Spread 2 teaspoons Nutella over top half of each crêpe followed by eight to ten ¼-inch-thick banana slices. Fold crêpes into quarters. Serve immediately.

CRÊPES WITH HONEY AND TOASTED ALMONDS

Follow recipe for Crêpes with Sugar and Lemon, omitting 8 teaspoons sprinkling sugar and lemon wedges. Drizzle 1 teaspoon honey over top half of each crêpe and sprinkle with 2 teaspoons finely chopped toasted sliced almonds and small pinch salt. Fold crêpes into quarters. Serve immediately.

CRÊPES WITH CHOCOLATE AND ORANGE

Follow recipe for Crêpes with Sugar and Lemon, omitting 8 teaspoons sprinkling sugar and lemon wedges. Using fingertips, rub 1 teaspoon finely grated orange zest into ¼ cup sugar. Stir in 2 ounces finely grated bittersweet chocolate. Sprinkle 1½ tablespoons chocolate-orange mixture over top half of each crêpe. Fold crêpes into quarters. Serve immediately.

Troubleshooting Crêpes

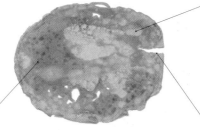

PROBLEM: Batter spreads unevenly
SOLUTION: Tilt and shake
Too much batter creates thick, spongy pockets; too little batter won't fully coat the pan. To guarantee that the batter thinly but completely covers the cooking surface, we add just enough (¼ cup), then tilt and shake the skillet until the batter is evenly distributed.

PROBLEM: Crêpe tears when flipped
SOLUTION: Wait, then try again
If the crêpe begins to tear, the batter hasn't had a chance to fully set and isn't ready to be flipped. Wait a few seconds, until the edge of the crêpe turns light brown, and then gently slide a rubber spatula underneath, grasp it with your fingertips, and flip.

PROBLEM: Splotchy browning
SOLUTION: Preheat pan 10 minutes
Exposing the skillet to too much heat too fast can create hot spots and yield unevenly browned crêpes. To ensure steady, even cooking, we warm the oiled pan over low heat for at least 10 minutes.

Fresh Strawberry Pie

The key to this dessert's bright flavor—plump, uncooked berries—can also be its soupy downfall. But how do you firm up the filling without making it gluey and dull-tasting?

⪢ BY DAWN YANAGIHARA ⪡

Growing up in Southern California, I could hardly wait for the kickoff of strawberry season. In the late spring months, farm stands overflowed with baskets of ripe red berries, which local bakeries would pile whole into fresh strawberry pies. This sweet, juicy dessert traded on nothing more than the fresh-picked berries, a sheer glaze that just barely held the fruit together while making it sparkle, and a flaky, buttery crust. Serving neat slices was downright impossible—the pie inevitably split into shards of pastry and a tumble of berries—but in a dessert so good, looks hardly mattered. Besides, mounds of whipped cream always covered the mess.

Though strawberry pie was a treat my family indulged in on an annual basis, I never learned to make it myself. When I moved back to California a few years ago, I was determined to nail down my own approach. I figured it couldn't be hard, since, with the best ripe berries, the pie would practically make itself. But to my dismay, most of the recipes I tried were flawed, and the fruit's sweet juice was the culprit. Because the uncooked berries shed so much liquid (even when they were left whole), the filling had to be firmed up with some sort of thickener, producing results that ranged from stiff and bouncy to runny and gloppy—hardly the dessert I remembered.

Clearly, re-creating my ideal—fresh berries lightly held together by a sheer, glossy glaze that would make their flavor pop in the buttery pastry shell—hinged on my getting the thickener just right.

Body Builder

Most recipes attacked the excess liquid problem with cornstarch; I also found a few that called for gelatin. The thickener of choice was simmered in a pan with liquid (often a juice like pineapple or grape, even water), sugar, and a dash of salt; mixed with the fresh whole berries; mounded in a prebaked pie shell; and chilled to set. Predictably, the gelatin produced a stiff and springy filling. And the cornstarch was no better, rendering the berry mixture cloudy, gummy, and not at all firm. Adjusting the amount of each type of thickener didn't improve matters. Ramping up the corn-

Using whole strawberries, instead of the usual sliced ones, cuts down on exuded juices and helps keep the filling from turning too soupy.

starch simply led to an increasingly gloppy, dull-tasting filling that never actually firmed up. As for the gelatin, the line between lightly thickened and stiff proved impossible to nail down (⅓ teaspoon, anyone?).

Maybe I was just using the wrong type of thickener. I spent the next few days working through alternatives (flour, arrowroot, potato starch, tapioca), as well as strawberry jam and even a grated apple—a trick from our Blueberry Pie recipe (July/August 2008), in which the apple's natural pectin seamlessly gels up the juicy fruit filling. But nothing panned out, and I was left with pies that were off-flavored, unpredictable, or gluey. The jam offered a reasonably thick texture, but its flavor was dull and cloying, and in this (mostly) fresh-fruit filling, bits of grated apple were hardly a subtle fix.

Frustrated, I decided to try a recipe I'd found that didn't use any added liquid or thickener at all. Instead, half of the uncooked berries were turned into a smooth, thick puree in the food processor, mixed with sugar, simmered briefly in a saucepan to thicken, and then combined with the fresh berries. The puree tasted bright and sweet and added body to the cut-up fruit, but I wasn't surprised when it didn't prove to be sufficient. Even after I assembled and chilled the pie for a couple of hours, the filling oozed from each cut slice.

It Takes Two

The cooked puree was a keeper, but there was no getting around it: Some form of added thickener was a must. I circled back to my earlier tests. Of all the thickeners I'd tried, jam had been the most promising, at least texture-wise. The gelling agent in jam, of course, is pectin. What if I made my own jam by adding pectin to the cooked puree? That way I could control how much of it to add and how long to simmer it with the puree, ideally preserving as much fresh-fruit flavor as possible. Pectin comes in two varieties, regular and low-sugar, the latter engineered to set without a surplus of sugar or acid. Since I didn't want to overload my naturally sweet berries with excess sugar, I mixed some of the low-sugar product into the puree and proceeded with my recipe. But as soon as the knife hit the pie's stiff, springy surface, I knew that I still hadn't found the solution.

RECIPE DIAGNOSIS **Through Thick and Thin**

Most fresh strawberry pies fail because they're overloaded with thickeners that either gum up the filling or never manage to thicken it at all.

TOO STIFF
Thicken strawberry pie filling with gelatin and the result resembles Jell-O.

TOO RUNNY
Thicken strawberry pie filling with cornstarch and the result typically turns out gloppy, dull-tasting, and still not firm enough.

I was tempted to give up on strawberry pie altogether when our science editor suggested something so obvious I couldn't believe I hadn't thought of it before: If I couldn't get the effect I wanted from one thickener, why not try two? After all, combining thickeners to produce a particular effect is exactly what the processed food industry does. Pectin still seemed like my best bet, so I considered what I might use with it. Gelatin was out—it would only exacerbate pectin's springiness. The "alternative" starches I tried had too many issues, and I crossed them off the list as well. That left cornstarch. The more I thought about it, the better the idea seemed. Since cornstarch on its own produced a filling that was too loose and pectin produced a filling that was too firm, a combination of the two might actually do the trick. Excited, I headed back into the test kitchen. After some tinkering, I finally hit upon a formula that worked. With ¾ cup puree, 2 tablespoons cornstarch, and 1½ teaspoons pectin, I managed to produce just the right supple, lightly clingy glaze.

I knew the berry juices would leach out eventually (sugar extracts moisture), but that didn't worry me. A pie this irresistible would never sit around.

FRESH STRAWBERRY PIE
MAKES ONE 9-INCH PIE, SERVING 8 TO 10

NOTE: To account for any imperfect strawberries, the ingredient list calls for several more ounces of berries than will be used in the pie. If possible, seek out ripe, farmers' market–quality berries. Make certain that you use Sure-Jell engineered for low- or no-sugar recipes (packaged in a pink box) and not regular Sure-Jell (in a yellow box); otherwise, the glaze will not set properly. The pie is at its best after two or three hours of chilling; as it continues to chill, the glaze becomes softer and wetter, though the pie will taste just as good.

Filling
- 4 pints (about 3 pounds) fresh strawberries, gently rinsed and dried, hulled (see note)
- ¾ cup (5¼ ounces) sugar
- 2 tablespoons cornstarch
- 1½ teaspoons Sure-Jell for low-sugar recipes (see note)
  Generous pinch table salt
- 1 tablespoon juice from 1 lemon
- 1 Baked Pie Shell (recipe follows)

Whipped cream
- 1 cup cold heavy cream
- 1 tablespoon sugar

1. FOR THE FILLING: Select 6 ounces misshapen, underripe, or otherwise unattractive berries, halving those that are large; you should have about 1½ cups. In food processor, process berries to smooth puree, 20 to 30 seconds, scraping down bowl as needed. You should have about ¾ cup puree.
2. Whisk sugar, cornstarch, Sure-Jell, and salt in

medium saucepan. Stir in berry puree, making sure to scrape corners of pan. Cook over medium-high heat, stirring constantly with heatproof rubber spatula, and bring to full boil. Boil, scraping bottom and sides of pan to prevent scorching, for 2 minutes to ensure that cornstarch is fully cooked (mixture will appear frothy when it first reaches boil, then will darken and thicken with further cooking). Transfer to large bowl and stir in lemon juice. Let cool to room temperature.

3. Meanwhile, pick over remaining berries and measure out 2 pounds of most attractive ones; halve only extra-large berries. Add berries to bowl with glaze and fold gently with rubber spatula until berries are evenly coated. Scoop berries into pie shell, piling into mound. If any cut sides face up on top, turn them face down. If necessary, rearrange berries so that holes are filled and mound looks attractive. Refrigerate pie until chilled, about 2 hours. Serve within 5 hours of chilling.

4. FOR THE WHIPPED CREAM: Just before serving, beat cream and sugar with electric mixer on low speed until small bubbles form, about 30 seconds. Increase speed to medium; continue beating until beaters leave trail, about 30 additional seconds. Increase speed to high; continue beating until cream is smooth, thick, and nearly doubled in volume and forms soft peaks, 30 to 60 seconds.

5. Cut pie into wedges. Serve with whipped cream.

BAKED PIE SHELL
MAKES ONE 9-INCH PIE SHELL

- 1¼ cups (6¼ ounces) unbleached all-purpose flour, plus more for work surface
- ½ teaspoon table salt
- 1 tablespoon sugar
- 6 tablespoons (¾ stick) cold unsalted butter, cut into ¼-inch slices
- ¼ cup (about 1¾ ounces) chilled vegetable shortening, cut into 4 pieces
- 2 tablespoons vodka, cold
- 2 tablespoons cold water

1. Process ¾ cup flour, salt, and sugar together in food processor until combined, about two 1-second pulses. Add butter and shortening and process until homogeneous dough just starts to collect in uneven clumps, about 10 seconds (dough will resemble cottage cheese curds with some very small pieces of butter remaining, but there should be no uncoated flour). Scrape down sides and bottom of bowl with rubber spatula and redistribute dough evenly around processor blade. Add ½ cup flour and pulse until mixture is evenly distributed around bowl and mass

of dough has been broken up, 4 to 6 quick pulses. Empty mixture into medium bowl.

2. Sprinkle vodka and water over mixture. With rubber spatula, use folding motion to mix, pressing down on dough until dough is slightly tacky and sticks together. Flatten dough into 4-inch disk. Wrap in plastic wrap and refrigerate at least 45 minutes or up to 2 days.

3. Adjust oven rack to lowest position, place rimmed baking sheet on oven rack, and heat oven to 425 degrees. Remove dough from refrigerator and roll out on generously floured (up to ¼ cup) work surface to 12-inch circle about ⅛ inch thick. Roll dough loosely around rolling pin and unroll into pie plate, leaving at least 1-inch overhang on each side. Working around circumference, ease dough into plate by gently lifting edge of dough with 1 hand while pressing into plate bottom with other hand. Leave overhanging dough in place; refrigerate until dough is firm, about 30 minutes.

4. Trim overhang to ½ inch beyond lip of pie plate. Fold overhang under itself; folded edge should be flush with edge of pie plate. Flute dough or press tines of fork against dough to flatten against rim of pie plate. Refrigerate dough-lined plate until firm, about 15 minutes.

5. Remove pie plate from refrigerator, line crust with foil, and fill with pie weights or pennies. Bake for 15 minutes. Remove foil and weights, rotate plate, and bake for 5 to 10 additional minutes, until crust is golden brown and crisp. Let cool to room temperature.

SCIENCE Doubling Up to Thicken Juicy Fruit

To create a filling with just enough sticking power to hold the berries together gently, we turned to a thickener more common in jam than pie—low-sugar pectin—and used it in combination with cornstarch. Both products work similarly: When combined with liquid, then heated and cooled, some of their molecules bond together, trapping water and creating a solid, jelly-like structure. But the strength and properties of the two structures differ. Amylose, one of two types of starch molecules in cornstarch, forms a weak structure that easily comes apart under the weight of heavy, juice-filled strawberries. Low-sugar pectin (which, unlike regular pectin, gels without added sugar and acid) contains bigger molecules that form a firmer structure held together more forcefully by calcium ions. Once created, this matrix resists coming apart.

When used independently, neither product resulted in a suitable pie filling, but together they yielded a glaze with just the right texture. –D.Y.

LOW-SUGAR PECTIN   **CORNSTARCH**

Which Cup Measures Up?

A glut of unusual shapes and gimmicky features is getting in the way of the one thing you want from this basic kitchen tool: accuracy.

> BY LISA McMANUS <

What has happened to the simple liquid measuring cup? When I began shopping for this story, I figured I was on easy street. All I wanted was a 2-cup size, with legible markings. Something I could throw in the dishwasher and use in the microwave. No problem, right? Wrong.

A liquid measuring cup doesn't have to be glamorous. It's a basic kitchen tool, meaning that accuracy matters more than looks, and form should follow function. But manufacturers have let their imaginations run wild. I found cup after wacky cup, in silly shapes and candy colors, made of materials that were squishy or flimsy, with markings that ran from overly minimal (no quarter-cup measures? no thirds?) to ridiculously excessive (pints, tablespoons, and cubic centimeters, anyone?).

Disappointment with the winner of our most recent liquid measuring cup testing sent me on this mission. Made by Cuisipro, the cup comes with a red plastic clip that you set to the desired level. Instead of crouching down to check precise measurements at eye level (a necessity with traditional cups), you pour until liquid reaches the level marked off by the clip. However, this cup hasn't held up in the test kitchen—the clip falls off and gets lost, eliminating the very feature that made it our winner.

I was ready to promote our then runner-up, which has survived years of daily use with sturdy grace: the familiar Pyrex glass measuring cup, with its simple red markings. But I found that Pyrex had discontinued this kitchen classic, which requires you to crouch to read it properly, in favor of an updated "read-from-above" design.

Unsure whether any of the new, unusual shapes and features might prove useful, I bought 15 models ranging from $3.99 to $34.99, made variously of glass, silicone, and plastic. After the first few tests, I tossed out seven (for a look at some, see "Losers' Gallery"). How did they fail so quickly? First, some simply weren't accurate. We had two ways of evaluating accuracy: We poured 236.6 ml of water (equivalent to 1 cup) measured in a laboratory graduated cylinder into each cup to see if it reached the marking exactly. We also checked to see if 1 cup of water

measured in each model weighed the correct 236.2 grams. We found a few off by small amounts, but one was short by more than 2 tablespoons—a quantity that could turn your baked goods dry. We also automatically rejected models with no markings for quarters and thirds—a nonstarter in a measuring cup.

Hot and Sticky

Since we often use liquid measuring cups to check our progress while reducing sauces, a good model must be heatproof and sturdy enough not to tip when filled with boiling liquid. To test this, I ladled bubbling hot stock into each cup, then poured it out. Two cups that lacked handles quickly became too hot to hold, particularly one made of silicone. The squishy silicone softened with the heat and narrowed where I held it, raising the level of the steaming liquid so high that it scorched my fingers. It was clear that for a measuring cup to be really useful, handles are a must.

Next, I poured hot pan sauce from a skillet into each cup and then poured it out. When I realized I was worried about letting the searing hot pan touch the plastic measuring cups, I decided to pursue that fear—and rested the hot pan right on the rim of each cup, leaving it there for five seconds. None melted.

Sticky liquids pose special measuring challenges. Here, we found that in a chilly kitchen, a thick glass measuring cup retained more of the cold than plastic cups, so honey didn't flow or level out as well, and it was harder to remove. One plastic model, which displays markings along two angled ramps inside the cup that can be read from above, created more surface and thus extra scraping work. The very best cups were just an inch or two wider than the spatula, with rounded bottoms instead of sharp corners that trap honey.

Measure for Measure

No matter how accurate the cup is technically, its design features determine how well it works for different users. I rounded up a dozen volunteers to use the cups. After they measured 1 cup of water, I poured it onto a scale to weigh it. With each tester, we repeated the process three times.

It was clear that certain cups facilitated accuracy, with crisp, unambiguous markings, while others—with busy designs and small type—were much more difficult to use correctly. To our surprise, the worst offender in this test was the redesigned Pyrex cup. Thick bands of red paint circle the cup at the 1-cup mark and all markings are printed on the inside, to be read from a standing position. But tester after tester complained that the water level was nearly impossible to see against the red paint.

After all our testing, the top-ranked cups—the Good Cook by Bradshaw International 2-Cup Measuring Cup ($3.99) and the Arrow Cool Grip 2.5-Cup Measuring Cup ($11.80)—are recommended because they work just fine. They're not especially durable, though. Our otherwise high-ranking plastic cups began showing faint scratches after fewer than 25 trips through the dishwasher. That comes with being plastic. Will they hold up to years of hard test kitchen use? I am skeptical. Luckily, they come cheap.

This conclusion leaves me as disappointed as ever. After all my searching and testing, I never found the perfect liquid measuring cup. Whether its fatal flaw was a gimmicky design, lack of critical measurement markings, poor material, or—worst of all—inaccuracy, there wasn't a single cup I could highly recommend. My best advice? Before they're all gone from store shelves, buy up a stash of the classic Pyrex liquid measuring cups.

Losers' Gallery

Check out the ratings chart for other big-time losers—including Pyrex.

DECEPTIVE MEASURES
The Anchor Hocking 16-Ounce Glass Measuring Cup ($7.99) has a hidden flaw—the markings are off by nearly 14 percent. No matter how carefully you measure, you'll be wrong.

ALL STYLE, NO SUBSTANCE
With all the zany markings and candy colors on the Zak! Designs Measuring Cup ($12.99), they couldn't find a spot to mark a quarter cup?

NO WEIGH OUT
The Taylor Digital Scale with Measuring Cup ($34.95) has a scale in the handle—but you can't submerge it, use it in the microwave, or put it in the dishwasher.

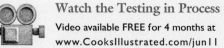

TESTING LIQUID MEASURING CUPS

We tested eight models of 2-cup liquid measuring cups. All were purchased online and are listed below in order of preference. A source for the winner is on page 32. We eliminated the following models in a pretesting: Anchor Hocking 16-Ounce Glass Measuring Cup; Anchor Hocking 16-Ounce Triple Pour Measuring Cup; Zak! Designs Measuring Cup; Leifheit Comfortline 2-Cup Measuring Cup; Rubbermaid Commercial Bouncer 1-Pint Cup; Taylor Digital Scale with Measuring Cup; and Catamount's Bennington Flameware 2-Cup.

DISHWASHER- AND MICROWAVE-SAFE: We downgraded models that weren't microwave-safe; all models were dishwasher-safe.

BPA: Cups were downgraded for containing Bisphenol A as reported by manufacturers. Research has linked this controversial material to health issues.

ACCURACY: Using a laboratory graduated cylinder, we measured 236.6 ml of water (equivalent to 1 cup) and poured it into each measuring cup. We also weighed the water. Because accuracy was crucial, this test was weighted heavily in determining final rankings.

PERFORMANCE: Twelve volunteers measured 1 cup of water and transferred it to a bowl; we then weighed the water to determine accuracy, repeating this three times for each cup. We ladled hot broth and poured hot pan sauce into each cup and tipped the liquid out. We measured honey and scraped it out of the cups. We boiled water in the cups in the microwave, downgrading those that became uncomfortable to handle. The score is composite, reflecting overall performance.

DESIGN: We evaluated the cup's dimensions, shape, gradation markings, and materials.

DURABILITY: We ran all cups through 25 dishwasher cycles (using the Dry Heat mode), dropped them from counter height, and rested a hot skillet on the rims of plastic cups for five seconds to check for melting. Cups lost points for signs of wear.

RECOMMENDED

	CRITERIA		TESTERS' COMMENTS

GOOD COOK by Bradshaw International 2-Cup Measuring Cup
Model: 19864; Price: $3.99
Material: Plastic
Dishwasher: Top rack
Microwave: Yes
BPA: None

Accuracy	★★★
Performance	★★★
Design	★★★
Durability	★★

While we'd prefer a cup that feels more substantial, this lightweight, crisply marked model was accurate and easy to read and provided all the measurements we needed—and no more. Its thin, clear walls and slim gradation lines provided unambiguous readings. Most testers found it "easy and basic." And it's cheap.

ARROW Cool Grip 2.5-Cup Measuring Cup
Model: 473812 (00031); Price: $11.80
Material: Plastic
Dishwasher: Top rack
Microwave: Yes; 15-minute limit
BPA: None

Accuracy	★★★
Performance	★★★
Design	★★★
Durability	★★

We liked this simple plastic cup with its blue, easy-on-the-eyes markings and stay-cool handle. Rounded corners made it easy to scrape out sticky honey. One quibble—the manufacturer got greedy, squeezing in 2½-cup markings right up to the rim, where liquids are likely to spill.

RECOMMENDED WITH RESERVATIONS

OXO Good Grips 2-Cup Angled Measuring Cup
Model: 70981; Price: $9.99
Material: Plastic
Dishwasher: Yes
Microwave: Yes; 4-minute limit; no fats or oils
BPA: Yes

Accuracy	★★★
Performance	★★★
Design	★★
Durability	★★

Comfortable to pour, with an ergonomic handle, oval shape, and sharp, drip-free spout. Angled measurement panels inside the cup, readable from above, were clear to testers, who got accurate results, but these extra ridges were a nuisance when testers scraped out honey.

WILTON 2-Cup Liquid Measure
Model: 2103-334; Price: $10.78
Material: Plastic
Dishwasher: Top rack
Microwave: No
BPA: None

Accuracy	★★★
Performance	★★
Design	★★
Durability	★★

Accurate, comfortable, and lightweight, its oval shape helped control pouring. We liked the "stepped" design, with each step a measurement, but some testers found the yellow markings hard to read. Can't be microwaved.

NOT RECOMMENDED

ISI Basics Flex-It 2-Cup Measuring Cup
Model: B 26400; Price: $8.99
Material: Silicone
Dishwasher: Yes
Microwave: Yes
BPA: None

Accuracy	★★★
Performance	★★
Design	★
Durability	★★★

This simple silicone cylinder was soft and pliable—a fatal flaw when boiling liquid turned it overly squishy and too hot to hold. Still, scraping honey out of the smooth, tubular body was easy, and while testers complained that the milky silicone was hard to see through, they were able to achieve accurate results.

ZYLISS Mix-n-Measure Measuring Cup Set with Lid (1, 2 & 4 Cup)
Model: 13850; Price: $19.99
Material: Plastic
Dishwasher: Yes
Microwave: No
BPA: Yes

Accuracy	★★★
Performance	★★
Design	★
Durability	★★★

We liked the idea of markings readable from the top or side, but these were printed in such small, busy type that the information was lost on several testers; many also disliked the handle's sharp edges. A slanting top rim tricked testers into holding it level under a faucet, throwing off measurements once it was set down.

EMSA Perfect Beaker with Seal by Frieling
Model: 2206990096; Price: $12.46
Material: Plastic
Dishwasher: Yes
Microwave: Yes; 3-minute limit
BPA: None

Accuracy	★
Performance	★★
Design	★★
Durability	★★

The "perfect beaker" it isn't. The 1-cup marking was short by nearly 1 tablespoon. It was easy to pour from, except when full of boiling water, when the lack of a handle was a true disadvantage. The design is busy with six measuring scales; testers turned the cup around and around to figure out which scale they wanted.

PYREX 2-Cup Measuring Cup with Read from Above Graphics
Model: 1085812; Price: $6.49
Material: Glass
Dishwasher: Yes
Microwave: Yes
BPA: None

Accuracy	★
Performance	★★
Design	★
Durability	★★★

This redesigned cup was a disaster. Testers struggled to tell if they'd hit the mark and couldn't double-check from the outside (for one thing, markings appear backward); their uncertainty showed up in poor measuring results. The big, conical shape is hard to pour from and eats up storage space. Accuracy was off by 2 teaspoons.

The Truth About Greek Yogurt

If all Greek yogurt starts with the same basic ingredients—milk and cultures—what makes some brands thick, rich, and creamy while others are watery and sour?

⇒ BY LISA McMANUS ⇐

You wouldn't know from the recent surge in Greek yogurt sales that Americans have never cared much for the tangy plainness of yogurt. In recent months, sales of the Greek variety have jumped 160 percent compared with a mere 3 percent hike for regular yogurt—and for good reason. Like much of the yogurt traditionally made across Europe and the Middle East, Greek yogurt is considerably thicker, richer, and creamier than the American stuff. Even the low-fat and nonfat versions taste remarkably decadent. Greek yogurt is good eaten plain, swirled with honey or jam, or sprinkled with nuts, and in the test kitchen we prefer it to thinner, runnier American yogurt in creamy dips and sauces.

But nowhere is the trend toward Greek yogurt more obvious than in grocery stores. Where once only one or two brands were available, supermarkets now carry nearly a dozen national brands with a variety of fat levels. Even longtime producers of regular yogurt like Dannon and Yoplait have entered the game, launching their own lines of Greek-style yogurt to keep from getting pushed out of the market.

Being fans of the Greek stuff ourselves, we weren't surprised by the impressive sales figures. But we did wonder if all of these new brands measured up to the hype. To find out, we rounded up 10 nonfat plain Greek yogurts (nonfat is the most widely available variety; for the results of our low-fat and full-fat Greek yogurt tastings, go to www.CooksIllustrated.com/jun11). As soon as we pulled back their foil seals, we noticed clear differences. Some yogurts stood up in stiff peaks, while others were loose and glossy, even a little watery. Those discrepancies became even more apparent once we started eating. Flavors ranged from utterly bland to lightly tangy to strongly sour. A few samples boasted a rich, luxurious consistency, while others revealed their nonfat status all too obviously. Our least favorite sample was grainy and curdled and reminded tasters of cottage cheese.

When the scores were tallied, we found three brands that almost nobody liked, six that ranged from barely acceptable to very pleasing, and one that we all loved. Now we just needed to know why.

Clearing the Whey

First, some background information about the yogurt-making process. Like ordinary yogurt, the Greek style is made by adding two active bacterial cultures—*S. thermophilus* (St) and *L. bulgaricus* (Lb)—to milk. During fermentation, these cultures digest the milk's sugar (lactose) and produce the lactic acid that makes yogurt thick and tangy. The major difference between the two types is that true Greek yogurt is strained to remove most of its liquid whey. The result is not only thicker than American-style yogurt, but also considerably higher in protein. In fact, it can take up to four times as much milk to make Greek yogurt using the straining process as it does to make ordinary yogurt. This high-protein product is also lower in carbohydrates and salt and usually less acidic, since much of the lactic acid (along with the carbs and salt) drains out with the whey.

But as we discovered, some manufacturers are getting at this thicker, creamier product in other ways. Rather than draining the whey with an expensive mechanical separator, they skip the straining process altogether and fortify the yogurt with thickeners like milk protein concentrate, pectin, or gelatin. Adding milk protein concentrate boosts the percentage of milk solids, buffering acidity; pectin and gelatin gel the more fluid yogurt so that it mimics the thickness of a strained product. Whichever additive is used, fortification is faster and cheaper—but, not surprisingly, it produces an inferior product. The two yogurts we liked the least, made by Yoplait and The Greek Gods, were fortified and had considerably higher levels of carbohydrates than most other brands—a pretty good indication (although neither company would confirm it) that those manufacturers are not straining out the whey. Tasters found both samples sour to the point of almost tasting spoiled and their textures equally unpleasant. To many, the gelatin-thickened Yoplait resembled pudding. The Greek Gods yogurt, which includes pectin and inulin (a flavorless dietary fiber that absorbs liquid) and contains less than half the protein of other brands, was not only "watery" and "broken," but also "curdled."

A Matter of Culture

Fortification is one factor that likely sank those two brands to the bottom of the rankings. Another equally important variable that determines yogurt flavor and texture is the specific cocktail of bacterial cultures. According to Dr. Mirjana Curic-Bawden, a senior scientist for Chr. Hansen, a leading international supplier of food cultures, all yogurts must contain St and Lb, but exactly which strains of those cultures are added will affect how tangy, rich, or smooth the yogurt will be. The tricky part for manufacturers, Curic-Bawden said, is getting the combination just right. Manufacturers that select a bacteria cocktail prone to heavy acidification might produce a harsh, sour yogurt even if they strain out a good bit of the acidic whey. Similarly, employing a mix of mild cultures (and adding milk proteins) will help compensate for the acidity of unstrained yogurt, although as we seemed to find with Yoplait, it won't necessarily be a perfect solution.

As with any finicky recipe, matching up the right ingredients with the right method (some manufacturers have their own patented approach to straining) makes all the difference. To us, most of the yogurts we sampled didn't hit the mark perfectly. In fact, we found only one that we'd enthusiastically seek out, and it wasn't one of the better-known producers of Greek yogurt like Chobani or Fage (a Greek company whose products have grown so popular in the U.S. that it now produces yogurt here). Our favorite, a strained product made by market newcomer Olympus, boasted just the right combination of thick, unctuous creaminess and mellow tang. Olympus was also the winner and runner-up, respectively, of our full-fat and low-fat tastings, and it happens to be the only brand imported from Greece. In fact, this is one yogurt that we're happy to eat with—or without—a spoonful of honey.

Cooking with Greek Yogurt

After discovering that we have very particular tastes when it comes to eating Greek yogurt plain, we wondered if we'd pick up on those differences when the yogurt was used as a cooking ingredient in tzatziki sauce (a Greek condiment) and our Light New York Cheesecake. It turns out that the other ingredients in the sauce (garlic, mint, and cucumbers) didn't blur the differences among the brands much at all; in fact, the tzatziki scores almost exactly matched the scores we gave these yogurts in the plain tasting: The top-ranked yogurts made thick, creamy, well-balanced sauce, while sauces made with bottom-ranked brands were "runny" and "sour."

But the baked application was more forgiving. Here, the bottom-ranked Greek Gods yogurt was acceptable—even preferred by several tasters, who appreciated the extra moisture and stronger tanginess that it brought to this dense, rich dessert. The bottom line? We'll stick with our favorite, Olympus Greek Yogurt, but in a pinch, we won't worry about the brand if we're baking. –L.M.

TASTING NONFAT GREEK YOGURT

Focusing on the plain, unflavored variety, we chose 10 brands of nonfat Greek yogurt from a list of top-selling national supermarket brands compiled by SymphonyIRI Group, a Chicago-based market research company. Twenty-one staffers from America's Test Kitchen sampled each yogurt in a blind tasting, rating them on flavor, texture, and tanginess, as well as on overall appeal. Note: Because serving sizes were inconsistent from brand to brand, we recalculated protein content for a 6-ounce serving but list original container sizes and prices. The results are listed below according to preference. (For our tasting results for low-fat and full-fat brands, see www.CooksIllustrated.com/jun11.)

HIGHLY RECOMMENDED

OLYMPUS Traditional Greek Nonfat Yogurt Strained, Plain
Price: 6 oz. for $1.99
Protein in 6-ounce serving: 15g
Ingredients: Grade A pasteurized nonfat milk, yogurt culture
Comments: This yogurt—the lone Greek import—won raves for its "smooth, fatty," "seriously creamy" consistency and "pleasantly tangy," well-balanced flavor. In sum: "Hard to believe it's nonfat."

RECOMMENDED

VOSKOS Greek Yogurt Plain Nonfat
Price: 8 oz. for $2.69
Protein in 6-ounce serving: 18g
Ingredients: Grade A pasteurized skim milk, live and active cultures
Comments: Though a bit on the runny side for some tasters, this "creamy" yogurt was "bright, clean, and rich," with the kind of "nice tang" and "complex flavor" that you'd "expect from Greek yogurt."

BROWN COW Greek Yogurt 0% Fat, Plain
Price: 5.3 oz. for $0.99
Protein in 6-ounce serving: 17g
Ingredients: Cultured pasteurized nonfat milk. Contains live active cultures.
Comments: Most tasters found this Greek-style relative of our favorite regular plain yogurt "very thick," "super silky," and "smooth." Many noted that its "good, rich tang" reminded them of sour cream and cream cheese. Others found this sample "a bit too acidic."

DANNON Greek Plain 0% Fat
Price: 5.3 oz. for $1.39
Protein in 6-ounce serving: 17g
Ingredients: Cultured Grade A nonfat milk. Contains active yogurt cultures.
Comments: Most tasters agreed that this yogurt's consistency was "ideal": "thick, smooth, and lush." One happy taster even called it "a guilty pleasure" and compared it to ice cream. Still, others felt that richness wasn't enough to temper its "super-duper sour" flavor and "slightly chalky aftertaste."

OIKOS Organic Greek Yogurt 0% Fat, Plain
Price: 5.3 oz. for $1.99
Protein in 6-ounce serving: 17g
Ingredients: Cultured pasteurized organic nonfat milk. Contains live active cultures.
Comments: This Greek-style offering from the folks at Stonyfield Farm boasted "lots of tang," a quality that some found "distracting." Texture-wise, this product was on the "watery" side, with a "puddle-y" consistency.

FAGE Total 0% Greek Strained Yogurt
Price: 6 oz. for $1.99
Protein in 6-ounce serving: 15g
Ingredients: Grade A pasteurized skimmed milk, live active yogurt cultures
Comments: Unlike other samples, this well-known Greek brand (by the way, it's pronounced "fa-yeh"), which now produces yogurt in the U.S., met no criticism for excessive tanginess. In fact, most tasters found it a tad "muted." Others described it as "nice and creamy, with just enough tang to remind you, 'Yes, this is yogurt.'"

RECOMMENDED WITH RESERVATIONS

CHOBANI Greek Yogurt Plain Nonfat
Price: 6 oz. for $1.25
Protein in 6-ounce serving: 18g
Ingredients: Cultured pasteurized nonfat milk. Contains live active cultures.
Comments: While some tasters found this yogurt's texture "buttery" and like "clotted cream," others deemed it "ricotta-like." Several tasters also inquired about the missing "tang," noting that it "would work to cool down a spicy dish" but wasn't worth eating on its own.

NOT RECOMMENDED

ATHENOS Greek Strained Nonfat Plain Yogurt
Price: 16 oz. for $3.29
Protein in 6-ounce serving: 16g
Ingredients: Cultured pasteurized nonfat milk
Comments: As we like to say in Boston, this sample from Kraft was "wicked sour." The texture was "wrong," too. Tasters described it as "smooth" but "runny," "thin," and "on a par with regular yogurt."

YOPLAIT Greek Fat Free Plain Yogurt
Price: 6 oz. for $1.29
Protein in 6-ounce serving: 14g
Ingredients: Cultured pasteurized Grade A nonfat milk, milk protein concentrate, kosher gelatin, Vitamin A acetate, Vitamin D_3
Comments: The source of this unstrained yogurt's "weird, gelatinous" texture? Gelatin, of course. How did it taste? "Metallic," "sour," and just plain "awful." As of press time, this was the only yogurt in the lineup fortified with protein and gelatin, although a spokesperson noted that the company was in the process of reformulating its product.

THE GREEK GODS Nonfat Plain Greek Yogurt
Price: 6 oz. for $2.19
Protein in 6-ounce serving: 6g
Ingredients: Pasteurized Grade A nonfat milk, inulin, pectin, and active cultures
Comments: "My yogurt is sitting in a pool of liquid!" remarked one dismayed taster. And no wonder: With less than half the protein content of other samples, this unstrained yogurt was not only "soupy" and "way too watery," but also "full of tiny curds." What's more, it was "unpleasantly sour." The general consensus: "Not Greek to me."

Real—or Faking It?

True Greek yogurts have been painstakingly strained of liquid whey to create a thick, creamy product. The faux kind skips the straining and adds thickeners, which results in an inferior, watery yogurt.

CREAMY
Our winning Greek yogurt, from Olympus, has been thoroughly strained, so it stands up in stiff, creamy peaks.

WEEPY
Bottom-ranking Greek Gods yogurt, which has not been strained, is loose and watery.

⇒ BY ANDREW JANJIGIAN & DAN SOUZA ⇐

TEST KITCHEN TIP
Color Taste-Off: White vs. Brown Mushrooms

Despite their differing appearance, white button and cremini mushrooms (and porto-bellos) actually belong to the same mushroom species, *Agaricus bisporus*. Creminis are a brown-hued variety, and portobellos are creminis that have been allowed to grow large. We think of creminis as a recent introduction to the marketplace, but all button mushrooms were actually brown until 1926, when a mushroom farmer in Pennsylvania found a cluster of white buttons growing in his beds, which he cloned and began selling as a new variety. But does the loss of color mean a loss of flavor? To find out, we sautéed white button and cremini mushrooms and tasted them side-by-side in risotto and atop pizza. The flavor of the creminis was noticeably deeper and more complex. This difference in taste was also apparent, though less obvious, when we compared both types of mushroom sprinkled raw over salads. The lesson? If bolder mushroom flavor is what you're after, it's worth shelling out a little extra for creminis.

CREMINI
Brown-hued cremini boast
rich, complex flavor.

WHITE BUTTON
White button mushrooms are
comparatively mild in flavor.

TEST KITCHEN TIP ## We Did the Mash

For the fluffiest mashed potatoes, the goal is to use the gentlest touch possible to avoid bursting the potatoes' swollen starch granules. Once released, the sticky gel inside will turn the mash gluey. We've found that the vigorous action of a food processor guarantees glueyness—and although a potato masher is fine for producing a rustic chunky texture, it yields a mash that's far from fluffy. In tests, we've zeroed in on the ricer as the best tool for producing a fluffy texture. But is a ricer really the top choice if your goal is not only a fluffy mash, but a supremely smooth one as well? We made two identical batches of our Fluffy Mashed Potatoes (March/April 2008), putting one through a ricer and the other through a food mill. While tasters found the riced potatoes a tad fluffier, they were also a bit grainy. The potatoes that passed under the food mill's sweeping blade were almost as fluffy and boasted a far smoother texture. We still stand by the ricer as the most effective tool for fluffy potatoes, but there's no need to rush out and buy one if you have the more versatile food mill in your cabinet.

ULTRA-FLUFFY
A ricer provides the gentlest touch for the
fluffiest mash.

ULTRA-SMOOTH
More aggressive than a ricer, a food mill
will still produce fluffy results—and a
super-smooth texture.

TEST KITCHEN TIP ## Keeping the Freshness in Fresh Chiles

Fresh chiles like jalapeños and serranos have a relatively brief shelf life in the refrigerator. We tried four different refrigerator storage methods to see if any would help these chiles keep their crisp texture and fresh flavor longer. We sealed whole chiles in a plastic bag; left them loose in the crisper drawer; sliced them in half (to allow liquid to penetrate) and stored them in plain white vinegar; and sliced them in half and submerged them in a brine solution (1 tablespoon salt per cup of water). In both the bag and the crisper, the chiles began to soften and turn brown within a week. Storing in vinegar was also not ideal; after about a week, the chiles began tasting more pickled than fresh. The brine-covered chiles, however, retained their crispness, color, and bright heat for several weeks and, after a quick rinse to remove excess brine, were indistinguishable from fresh chiles when we sampled them raw and in salsa. After a month they began to soften, but they remained perfectly usable in cooked applications for several more weeks.

**PRESERVED IN SALT
SOLUTION**
Halved and stored in brine,
fresh chiles will keep their
crisp texture and bright
flavor for up to a month.

RECIPE TESTING ## Successfully Subbing Whole-Wheat Flour for White

The starting point for our Whole-Wheat Sandwich Bread (March/April 2011) was an ordinary white sandwich-loaf recipe, in which we incrementally replaced the white flour with the whole-wheat kind. We found that every time we upped the whole wheat, we also had to increase the water in the recipe or the bread turned out overly dry. This is because the bran and germ in whole-wheat flour absorb more water than the nearly pure starch in white flour. After experimenting, we determined that whole-wheat flour holds about 13 percent more water by weight than white flour. In practical terms, this means that if you want to replace some of the white flour with whole wheat in a given baked goods recipe—whether for bread, muffins, or cookies—you'll need to use either more water or less flour to avoid dryness. The simplest approach is to add liquid. For every cup of whole-wheat flour added to a recipe, add 2 additional tablespoons of liquid. We found that this approach will not affect the texture of the final product (aside from the coarser quality whole wheat lends to baked goods). For the best results, we don't recommend replacing more than 25 percent of the white flour in a recipe with whole wheat.

TECHNIQUE | TRIMMING ASPARAGUS: IT'S A SNAP

Even the most thin, delicate asparagus spears still have tough, woody ends that must be removed. To break off the ends at precisely the right point, all you need is your hands

Grip the stalk about halfway down; with the other hand, hold the stem between the thumb and index finger about an inch or so from the bottom and bend the stalk until it snaps.

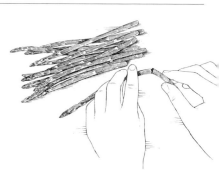

RECIPE TESTING Gauging When Bread Is Done

We commonly advise checking the internal temperature of a loaf of bread before making the decision to pull it from the oven. A properly baked loaf should register a temperature between 195 and 210 degrees on an instant-read thermometer, depending upon the type of bread. But is internal temperature by itself sufficient proof that bread is fully baked?

We placed temperature probes in the center of two loaves of rustic Italian bread and monitored them as they baked. Halfway into the baking time, the internal temperature of the loaves had already passed 200 degrees, and they reached the optimal 210 degrees a full 15 minutes before the end of the recommended baking time. We pulled one loaf from the oven as soon as it neared 210 degrees and left the other in the oven for the recommended baking time. (The temperature of the longer-baked loaf never rose above 210, because the moisture it contains, even when fully baked, prevents it from going past the boiling point of water, or 212 degrees.) The differences between the two loaves were dramatic: The loaf removed early had a pale, soft crust and a gummy interior, while the loaf that baked the full hour had a nicely browned, crisp crust and a perfectly baked crumb.

The takeaway? Internal temperature is less useful than appearance as a sign of a well-baked loaf.

210° BUT HALF BAKED   210° AND FULLY BAKED

We found that bread can reach the optimal temperature for doneness—210 degrees for the rustic Italian bread above—well before the loaf is actually baked through. You can take the temperature of your bread, but stick to the recommended baking time and make sure the crust has achieved the appropriate color before removing the loaf from the oven.

SHOPPING Crabmeat

Crabmeat is almost always sold in cans or containers rather than fresh; it's cooked, cleaned, pasteurized, and then packaged. Though the crabmeat sold in the United States may come from different species of the crustacean, all are closely related with a similar taste and texture. Differences in grade correspond to the part of the crab the meat comes from and the size of the pieces in the package. Below are the most common grades of crabmeat available in U.S. supermarkets.

JUMBO LUMP: Derived from the two large muscles connected to the swimming legs, jumbo lump is the largest and most expensive grade of crabmeat. It boasts a bright white color and delicate flavor. Its size and meaty texture can be best appreciated on cocktail platters or in sautés.

LUMP: Lump crabmeat is composed of smaller or broken pieces of jumbo lump, along with other smaller pieces of body meat. Like jumbo lump, it's white and has a delicate flavor. Because lump is a mixture of large and small pieces, it's a good choice for seafood salads or crab cakes.

BACKFIN: Backfin is a mixture of smaller "flake" pieces of body meat (there's no meat from the legs). Backfin is finer textured than lump meat, but its flavor is similar. It is commonly used in crab cakes.

CLAW MEAT: Claw meat comes from the swimming fins and claws of the crab. Because these are very active muscles—much like dark meat in poultry—the meat is pink or brown, high in fat, and has a much stronger crab flavor. Its texture is similar to backfin, but it's oilier. Claw meat is best in dishes requiring a bold crab taste, such as soups or bisques.

TECHNIQUE

CARVING PORK ROAST, BONE-IN AND BONE-OUT

Our Grill-Roasted Bone-In Pork Rib Roast (page 9) can be served on the bone in thick slabs, or the meat can be removed from the bone and sliced into thinner pieces.

FOR THICK BONE-IN CHOPS
Stand the roast on the carving board with the bones pointing up, and cut between the bones into separate chops.

FOR THIN BONELESS SLICES
1. Holding the tip of the bones with one hand, use a sharp knife to cut along the rib to sever the meat from the bones.

2. Set the meat cut side down on the carving board and slice across the grain into ½-inch-thick slices.

SHOPPING An Eye for an Eye

Some readers have had trouble finding chuck-eye beef roast, a cut we like for its compact, uniform shape, deep flavor, and tenderness in pot roast and stews. So what's a more common but equally good alternative? The chuck eye is a long, narrow group of muscles that runs along the center of the chuck, or shoulder section of the cow, from front to back. It is a continuation of the same muscles that make up the rib eye, one of the most flavorful and tender cuts of beef. This is also the reason why it may be hard to find: Its proximity to the rib eye allows butchers to portion and sell chuck-eye "steak" as a less expensive alternative to boneless rib-eye steaks. If your butcher can't (or won't) fashion you a chuck-eye roast, we've found that other boneless, uniformly shaped cuts from the chuck (such as the top blade roast or bottom chuck roast) will work nearly as well, since they often contain a portion of chuck eye and the meat is similar in texture and flavor.

TEST KITCHEN TIP To Dimple or Not to Dimple

To prevent hamburgers from puffing up during cooking, many sources recommend making a slight depression in the center of the raw patty before placing it on the heat. But we find the need for a dimple depends entirely on how the burger is cooked. Meat inflates upon cooking when its connective tissue, or collagen, shrinks at temperatures higher than 140 degrees. If burgers are cooked on a grill or under a broiler, a dimple is in order. Cooked with these methods, the meat is exposed to direct heat not only from below or above but also on its sides; as a result, the edges of the patty shrink, cinching the hamburger like a belt, compressing its interior up and out. But when the patty is cooked in a skillet, as in our recipe for Juicy Pub-Style Burgers (page 11), only the part of the patty in direct contact with the pan gets hot enough to shrink the collagen. Because the edges of the burger never directly touch the heat, the collagen it contains doesn't shrink much at all, and the burger doesn't puff.

DIMPLED FOR GRILL   NOT DIMPLED
AND BROILER   FOR SKILLET

Don't bother "dimpling" burgers cooked in a skillet. Unlike burgers cooked on a grill or under a broiler, their edges never get hot enough to shrink, pushing the interior up and out and resulting in a puffy patty.

⋟ BY MEREDITH BUTCHER, AMY GRAVES & TAIZETH SIERRA ⋞

EQUIPMENT TESTING Cherry Pitters

Anyone who has ever made a dessert with fresh cherries knows that the most daunting task is the pitting. A cherry pitter saves time, but not without risking mauled fruit and juice-stained countertops. To find out which pitter was both speedy and tidy, we tested four brands, from $15 to a whopping $260, all designed to pit multiple cherries at a time. At the high end, a mammoth machine boasting a 10-cherry hopper certainly pitted a lot of cherries, but given its price, it seemed unnecessary for anyone but a cherry orchard owner. We prefer the simpler (and much cheaper) Progressive International Cherry-It Pitter ($15), which looks like a stapler and pits four cherries at once. Unlike other tools we tried, this pitter is completely mess-free, keeping juice and stones contained in its plastic holder and leaving cherries more neatly pitted and intact than other models, which frequently jammed, sprayed juice, and chewed up the fruit. Best of all, the whole shebang is dishwasher-safe.

PERFECT PITTER
The Progressive International Cherry-It Pitter pits cherries quickly and easily without the mess.

EQUIPMENT TESTING Smoker Boxes

For years, whenever we wanted a smoky flavor in gas-grilled food, we wrapped soaked wood chips in aluminum foil packets and placed them over the burners. Would vented metal smoker boxes filled with soaked wood chips do a better job? To find out, we gathered four smoker boxes ranging from just under $7 to over $80, in stainless steel or cast iron. Using our favorite Weber Spirit E-210 gas grill, we smoked a chicken with each one as well as with our tried-and-true foil packet. Tasted side by side, all but one—the $80 Fire Magic Smoker Box, which bellowed smoke too quickly, yielding acrid results—produced chicken that was at least as good as the chicken smoked with a foil packet. The best-tasting bird was smoked with the GrillPro Cast Iron Smoker Box, a small unit by Onward Manufacturing Company. ($8.50) that will fit in almost any grill. Its thick cast iron was slow to heat, which let the chips smolder a good long while, providing clean smoke flavor without bitterness or soot. It was easy to fill, and at less than $9, it's a worthy, reusable investment that beats fussing with foil.

CAST OUT THE FOIL
When it's time for gas-grill smoking, forget making a foil packet and reach for this cast-iron box.

NEW PRODUCT Compost Buckets

Compost buckets offer a "green" solution to the odor of food scraps mingling with the kitchen trash: A carbon filter on the lid keeps the smells in, cutting down on trips to the compost heap. These small buckets fit in a cabinet beneath the sink, and some are attractive enough to keep on the counter. We had test cooks use three kinds of compost buckets over several weeks. All were easy to empty, all had carbon filters, and each passed daily sniff tests with flying colors. Then one day the lid popped off a bucket that had gotten knocked off the counter, and the stench cleared the kitchen. The virtue of the 2.4-gallon Exaco Trading Co. ECO Kitchen Compost Waste Collector ($19.98) was now evident: Its latching lid won't pop open even when banged about.

OSCAR'S ODOR-FREE FRIEND
The Exaco Trading Co. ECO Kitchen Compost Waste Collector holds 12 recipes' worth of scraps before it must be emptied, and a latch keeps the lid shut in the meantime.

EQUIPMENT TESTING Seltzer Makers

In 2010 we crowned the Penguin, by Sodastream, our favorite seltzer maker, thanks to the crisp bubbles it produced at the press of a lever. But the initial investment (just under $200) and counter-hogging design left some of us flat. Now, a cheaper model has arrived: the iSi Twist 'n Sparkle ($49.95), which, thanks to its contained carbonation system, doesn't require a whole station atop the counter. Instead, it uses a twist-top design to release CO_2 bubbles into a carafe holding 4 cups of water, juice, or any other non-dairy beverage—$1\frac{1}{2}$ cups more than the Penguin. (Sodastream warns against carbonating anything besides water with the Penguin.) We still like the Penguin, but consider the iSi a great space-saving alternative that costs less at the outset. Just take note of which CO_2 chargers you buy; the iSi runs on single-use chargers ($19.95 for twenty-four 4-cup units, or about 20 cents per cup), but equally effective generic chargers produce seltzer costing less than half that price. (Sodastream's chargers produce seltzer at about 10 cents per cup.)

BUBBLY NEWCOMER
The iSi Twist 'n Sparkle seltzer maker saves space while putting CO_2 in your H_2O.

EQUIPMENT UPDATE Goldtouch Loaf Pan

We recently learned that our favorite $8\frac{1}{2}$ by $4\frac{1}{2}$-inch loaf pan, the Williams-Sonoma Goldtouch Nonstick Loaf Pan ($21), has a new manufacturer, though its name remains the same. Curious as to whether this new pan could live up to the original, we made double batches of our Classic Pound Cake and American Loaf Bread and divvied them up to bake in the new and old versions. Good news: The similarity wasn't just a matter of looks (the pans were almost impossible to tell apart). The new pan produced even browning and effortless, perfect release for both pound cake and bread, and remains our favorite brand.

GOOD AS GOLD
The recently relaunched Goldtouch Nonstick Loaf Pan still offers even, golden browning and perfect release.

For complete testing results on each item, go to www.CooksIllustrated.com/jun11.

Sources

The following are mail-order sources for items recommended in this issue. Prices were current at press time and do not include shipping. Contact companies to confirm information or visit www.CooksIllustrated.com for updates.

PAGE 11: MEAT GRINDERS
- Waring Professional Meat Grinder: $199.99, item #MG800, Waring (877-798-7776, www.waringwebstore.com).
- KitchenAid Food Grinder Attachment: $48.74, item #FGA, KitchenAid (800-541-6390, www.shopkitchenaid.com).

PAGE 19: ROTARY GRATER
- Zyliss All Cheese Grater: $19.95, item #11355, Cutlery and More (800-650-9866, www.cutleryandmore.com).

PAGE 27: LIQUID MEASURING CUP
- Good Cook by Bradshaw International 2-Cup Plastic Measuring Cup: $3.99, item #19864, Good Cook (www.goodcook.com).

PAGE 32: CHERRY PITTER
- Progressive International Cherry-It Pitter: $15, item #636852, Sur La Table (800-243-0852, www.surlatable.com).

PAGE 32: SMOKER BOX
- Onward Manufacturing Company Cast Iron Smoker Box: $8.50, item #SPM660942901, Sears (800-697-3277, www.sears.com).

PAGE 32: COMPOST BUCKET
- Exaco Trading Co. ECO Kitchen Compost Waste Collector: $19.98, item #ECO-2000, Home Depot (800-466-3337, www.homedepot.com).

PAGE 32: SELTZER MAKER
- iSi Twist 'n Sparkle: $49.95, item #2963411, Williams-Sonoma (877-812-6235, www.williams-sonoma.com).

PAGE 32: LOAF PAN
- Williams-Sonoma Goldtouch Nonstick Loaf Pan: $21, item #1983915, Williams-Sonoma.

INDEX
May & June 2011

NEW RECIPES ON THE WEB
Available free for four months at
www.CooksIllustrated.com/jun11
Bacon and Brown Butter Vinaigrette
Barbecue Sauce Vinaigrette
Crêpes with Dulche de Leche and Toasted
    Pecans
Juicy Pub-Style Burgers with Pan-Roasted
    Mushrooms and Gruyère
Juicy Pub-Style Burgers with Sautéed Onions
    and Smoked Cheddar
Sweet and Tangy Coleslaw with Fennel and
    Orange

COOK'S LIVE VIDEOS
Available free for four months at
www.CooksIllustrated.com/jun11

BARBECUED CHICKEN KEBABS
Watch: It really works
CRÊPES WITH SUGAR AND LEMON
Watch us tame the diva
FRESH STRAWBERRY PIE
See the pie take shape
GRILL-ROASTED PORK ROAST
See how juicy it is
GRILLED SEA SCALLOPS
Watch our technique in action
GRILLING SAUCES
Caramel for grilling? Just watch
INDONESIAN-STYLE FRIED RICE
See all the tricks
JUICY PUB-STYLE BURGERS
See how to create the burgers
SPRING VEGETABLE PASTA
Look: New way to cook pasta
SWEET AND TANGY COLESLAW
See the three key steps
TESTING: LIQUID MEASURING CUPS
We put them through their paces

AMERICA'S TEST KITCHEN TV
Public television's most popular cooking show

Join the millions of home cooks who watch our show, *America's Test Kitchen*, on public television every week. For more information, including recipes and program times, visit www.AmericasTestKitchenTV.com.

AMERICA'S TEST KITCHEN RADIO
Tune in to our new radio program featuring answers to listener call-in questions, ingredient-taste-test and equipment-review segments, and in-depth reporting on a variety of topics. To listen to episodes, visit www.AmericasTestKitchen.com/Radio.

DOWNLOAD OUR FREE *Cook's Illustrated* iPhone App

Inside you'll find a collection of our top recipes, along with videos that explain how to make them. You can also access many of our most popular taste test results, useful kitchen timers, and an interactive shopping list that helps you plan ahead. Are you a member of CooksIllustrated.com? If so, our app gives you access to every recipe, video, and taste test on the website. Go to CooksIllustrated.com/iPhone.

Follow us on Twitter: twitter.com/TestKitchen
Find us on Facebook: facebook.com/CooksIllustrated

Grill-Roasted Bone-In Pork Rib Roast, 9

Indonesian-Style Fried Rice, 15

Spring Vegetable Pasta, 19

Crêpes with Sugar and Lemon, 23

Fresh Strawberry Pie, 25

Juicy Pub-Style Burger, 11

Apple-Mustard Grilling Sauce, 20

Grilled Sea Scallops, 13

Sweet and Tangy Coleslaw, 21

Grilled Barbecued Chicken Kebabs, 7

Skeena

Sweetheart

Early
Richmond

Bing

Montmorency

Rainier

Van

Balaton

North Star

CHERRIES

NUMBER 111

JULY & AUGUST 2011

COOK'S
ILLUSTRATED

Grill-Smoked Chicken
Getting the Smoke Just Right

Homemade Vanilla Ice Cream
Rich and Dense as Super-Premium

Complete Guide to Grilling Vegetables

Perfect Scrambled Eggs
Unique Two-Heat Method

Summer Peach Cake
Intense Flavor, Lush Texture

Best Canned Tuna
Old Favorite Dethroned

Rating Coolers
Grilled Stuffed Pork Tenderloin
Tuscan Tomato-Bread Salad
Lighter Corn Chowder
Salmon Cakes
Crisp Cucumber Salads

www.CooksIllustrated.com

$5.95 U.S./$6.95 CANADA

0 8>

0 74470 62805 7

CONTENTS

July & August 2011

COOK'S
ILLUSTRATED

Founder and Editor	Christopher Kimball
Editorial Director	Jack Bishop
Executive Editor, Magazines	John Willoughby
Executive Editor	Amanda Agee
Test Kitchen Director	Erin McMurrer
Managing Editor	Rebecca Hays
Senior Editors	Keith Dresser
	Lisa McManus
	Bryan Roof
Associate Features Editor	Elizabeth Bomze
Senior Copy Editor	Catherine Tumber
Copy Editor	Nell Beram
Associate Editors	Andrea Geary
	Amy Graves
	Andrew Janjigian
	Yvonne Ruperti
	Dan Souza
Assistant Editors	Hannah Crowley
	Taizeth Sierra
Executive Assistant	Christine Gordon
Editorial Assistant	Shannon Friedmann Hatch
Assistant Test Kitchen Director	Gina Nistico
Senior Kitchen Assistants	Meryl MacCormack
	Leah Rovner
Kitchen Assistants	Maria Elena Delgado
	Ena Gudiel
Executive Producer	Melissa Baldino
Associate Producer	Stephanie Stender
Contributing Editors	Matthew Card
	Dawn Yanagihara
Consulting Editor	Scott Brueggeman
Science Editor	Guy Crosby, Ph.D.
Managing Editor, Special Issues	Todd Meier
Assistant Editor, Special Issues	Chris Dudley
Assistant Test Cook, Special Issues	Danielle DeSiato-Hallman
Editorial Assistant, Special Issues	Brittany Allen
Online Managing Editor	David Tytell
Online Editor	Kate Mason
Online Assistant Editors	Eric Grzymkowski
	Mari Levine
Video Operations Manager	Peter Tannenbaum
Media Producer	Alexandra Pournaras
Associate Editor/Camera Operator	Nick Dakoulas
Assistant Editor/Camera Operator	Jesse Prent
Design Director	Amy Klee
Art Director, Magazines	Julie Bozzo
Designer	Lindsey Timko
Art Director, Marketing/Web	Christine Vo
Associate Art Directors, Marketing/Web	Erica Lee
	Jody Lee
Designers, Marketing/Web	Elaina Natario
	Mariah Tarvainen
Staff Photographer	Daniel J. van Ackere
Online Photo Editor	Steve Kilse
Vice President, Marketing	David Mack
Circulation Director	Doug Wicinski
Circulation & Fulfillment Manager	Carrie Horan
Partnership Marketing Manager	Pamela Putprush
Marketing Assistant	Lauren Perkins
Database & Direct Mail Director	Adam Perry
Senior Database Analyst	Marina Sakharova
Product Operations Director	Steven Browall
Product Promotions Director	Tom Conway
E-Commerce Marketing Director	Hugh Buchan
E-Commerce Marketing Manager	Laurel Zeidman
E-Commerce Marketing Coordinator	Sandra Greenberg
Marketing Copywriter	David Goldberg
Customer Service Manager	Jacqueline Valerio
Customer Service Representatives	Jillian Nannicelli
Retail Sales & Marketing Manager	Emily Logan
Client Service Manager, Sponsorship	Bailey Snyder
Production Director	Guy Rochford
Senior Project Manager	Alice Carpenter
Production & Traffic Coordinator	Kate Hux
Senior Production Manager	Jessica L. Quirk
Asset & Workflow Manager	Andrew Mannone
Production & Imaging Specialists	Judy Blomquist
	Heather Dube
	Lauren Pettapiece

PRINTED IN THE USA

CRABS

CRABS The turquoise-tinged blue crab is caught in the waters off the Atlantic and Gulf coasts and is highly prized in its soft-shell form (immediately after molting). With a deep purple body, the Dungeness crab offers tender flesh reminiscent of lobster. The claws and legs of the peekytoe crab—also known as Atlantic rock—hold delicate pink meat. Jonah crab claws, available year-round, make a thrifty substitute for black-tipped stone crab claws, which are harvested only from October to May in the warm waters of south Florida. Only the claws of the stone crab are eaten, as laws require that the body be thrown back into the ocean to regenerate for another season. The king crab can reach upward of 20 pounds and span 8 feet in length, although most are half that size. This crustacean is fished in the Bering Sea. The leggy snow crab, with its sweet taste similar to that of the king crab, is fished in the same waters.

COVER (Figs): Robert Papp; **BACK COVER** (Crabs): John Burgoyne

America's TEST KITCHEN

America's Test Kitchen is a very real 2,500-square-foot kitchen located just outside of Boston. It is the home of *Cook's Illustrated* and *Cook's Country* magazines and is the workday destination of more than three dozen test cooks, editors, and cookware specialists. Our mission is to test recipes over and over again until we understand how and why they work and until we arrive at the best version. We also test kitchen equipment and supermarket ingredients in search of brands that offer the best value and performance. You can watch us work by tuning in to *America's Test Kitchen* (www.AmericasTestKitchenTV.com) on public television.

COOK'S
ILLUSTRATED

Technology Director	Rocco Lombardo
Systems Administrator	Marcus Walser
Lead Developer	Scott Thompson
Software Architect	Robert Martinez
Web Developer II	Christopher Candelora
Web Developers	Bach Bui
	James Madden
	Alphonse Shiwala
Software Project Manager	Michelle Rushin
Business Analyst	Wendy Tsang
Quality Assurance Specialist	Micquella Bradford
IT Support Specialist	Geoffrey Clark
Senior Web Production Coordinator	Evan Davis
Web Production Assistant	Debbie Chiang
VP New Media Product Development	Barry Kelly
Lead Developer	Bharat Ruparel
Senior Information Director	Melissa MacQuarrie
Social Media Manager	Steph Yiu
Online Editor	Christine Liu
Graphic Designer	Eggert Ragnarsson
Web Developer	Brian Runk
Instructional Designer	Miriam Manglani
Chief Financial Officer	Sharyn Chabot
Human Resources Director	Adele Shapiro
Controller	Mandy Shito
Financial Director	Wayne Saville
Senior Accountant	Aaron Goranson
Staff Accountant	Connie Forbes
Accounts Payable Specialist	Steven Kasha
Office Manager	Michael Pickett
Receptionist	Henrietta Murray
Publicity	Deborah Broide

FOR LIST RENTAL INFORMATION, CONTACT
Specialists Marketing Services, Inc., 777 Terrace Ave., 4th Floor, Hasbrouck Heights, NJ 07604; 201-865-5800.

EDITORIAL OFFICE 17 Station St., Brookline, MA 02445; 617-232-1000; fax 617-232-1572. Subscription inquiries, visit www.AmericasTestKitchen.com/customerservice or call 800-526-8442.

POSTMASTER Send all new orders, subscription inquiries, and change-of-address notices to *Cook's Illustrated*, P.O. Box 6018, Harlan, IA 51593-1518.

FOR INQUIRIES, ORDERS, OR MORE INFORMATION

www.CooksIllustrated.com
At www.CooksIllustrated.com, you can order books and subscriptions, sign up for our free e-newsletter, or renew your magazine subscription. Join the website and gain access to 18 years of *Cook's Illustrated* recipes, equipment tests, and ingredient tastings, as well as companion videos for every recipe in this issue.

COOKBOOKS
We sell more than 50 cookbooks by the editors of *Cook's Illustrated*. To order, visit our bookstore at www.CooksIllustrated.com.

COOK'S ILLUSTRATED MAGAZINE
Cook's Illustrated magazine (ISSN 1068-2821), number 111, is published bimonthly by Boston Common Press Limited Partnership, 17 Station St., Brookline, MA 02445. Copyright 2011 Boston Common Press Limited Partnership. Periodicals postage paid at Boston, Mass., and additional mailing offices USPS #012487. Publications Mail Agreement No. 40020778. Return undeliverable Canadian addresses to P.O. Box 875, Station A, Windsor, ON N9A 6P2. POSTMASTER: Send address changes to *Cook's Illustrated*, P.O. Box 6018, Harlan, IA 51593-1518. For subscription and gift subscription orders, subscription inquiries, or change-of-address notices, visit us at www.AmericasTestKitchen.com/customerservice or write us at *Cook's Illustrated*, P.O. Box 6018, Harlan, IA 51593-1518.

EDITORIAL

ZERO DEGREES OF SEPARATION

In the early 1960s, I spent my share of afternoons haying with Charlie Bentley, a farmer; Dave Trachte, a local kid my age; and Herbie and Onie, two farmhands who helped out during the summer months. On sleepless nights I still recall the chugging of the baler, the whirring fingers of the tedder, the warm, throaty exhaust of the tractor, the hot vinyl seat of the green Ford pickup, the swallows swooping low to pick exposed bugs off the naked field, and the chaff of timothy as it showered down from the bale launched upwards from outstretched arms toward the towering stack above. Heat radiated in waves up from the field and outward from the hot metal of machinery; the nose was filled with the ripe, corn-mash scent of mown, compressed hay; rivulets of sweat made cool tracks as they ran in stops and starts down my neck; half-blind eyes watered and itched, and the mind was frozen with one crystal-clear image: a cold glass bottle of orange soda pop dispensed from the machine planted outside of Carl Hess's Texaco station. And the afternoon stretched on as the universe expanded, more bales and more rows to come, until Charlie yelled out, "That's the one we've been looking for," the last bale was hoisted high, and our devout procession headed back toward the barn, the top-loaded pickup swaying as if in heavy seas, field hands walking behind like troops in retreat.

Christopher Kimball

Sensory experts tell us that one's sense of taste has much to do with the brain, with matching sensory data with stored memories. One might have perfectly healthy taste receptors as well as a keen sense of smell, yet the way in which the brain stores and retrieves this information is determinate. One experiment asked participants to sniff 10 common household odors and then to identify them; most correctly matched up fewer than half. Perhaps that's because our modern brains have such lousy source material to work with; laundry detergent doesn't make much of an impression.

As a kid in Vermont, however, I collected unforgettable memories: the aching cold of a swimming pond, the sweet smell of fern-dappled wetland, a good snort of wood smoke drifting through the first cold October evening, the wet vanilla-and-caramel steam from a sugarhouse, the scent of a workhorse—all dried sweat, heat, and manure—and afternoon light filtered through spider-webbed, fly-specked windows in the dairy barn. There was nothing between sensation and memory: The senses smashed headlong into the mind, burying deep, leaving immutable patterns of smells, sights, tastes, and sounds.

The modern world, however, filters the pleasure of living through infinite layers. And yet . . . I pull a Macoun apple off a tree in late September. It's marred by a small crescent of rust and the excavation of a hungry borer, but it snaps under my bite and the juice is sweet but sour, complex, even spicy, unlike any shiny Delicious snatched from a wooden bowl in a hotel lobby. It's not just an apple, it's that apple off that tree on that day. I stand in the garden in August and pull a carrot and then a radish by their leafy tops. I rub off the dirt and in the mouth they go, alive and vibrant. Mouthfuls of raspberries in late June, blueberries in July, Sun Gold tomatoes in August, and then the digging of potatoes before Labor Day—bushel baskets strung out along the rows and the warm breath of dirt and roots washing upwards as I dig.

Millions of words have been written about junk and processed foods, about the failings of the USDA, about school lunches, about our diets and our health, to little effect. (McDonald's sales rose 5 percent the year after *Super Size Me* hit theaters.) But few have commented on the loss of experience, about the degrees of separation between our noses and the rich scent of life. Forgive the metaphor, but the smell of Charlie Bentley's dairy barn in July has been stamped on my brain as if hit by a locomotive, and I wouldn't give up that memory sensation for anything. A whiff of manure—shit, if you like—is simply part of life. If you are reading this editorial now and no strong odor memories come flooding back, go out and find a dairy barn this weekend, stick your head in, and take a long, deep whiff. It'll do you good.

Unhappiness steps through the front door when we find our lives removed from the world, from the shock and pleasure of our five senses. That's why we cook, to remind ourselves that we are alive, that we are connected to the food chain (the less fortunate become part of it) and to the ebb and flow of nature.

Breathing filtered, conditioned air, eating processed foods, and experiencing adventure while sitting in an armchair is certainly not what *Homo sapiens* was designed for. I have no idea what life is really about or whether it holds meaning, but happiness is not to be found in a box of cereal, even if it does contain a prize. Living with zero degrees of separation entails risk—yes, that glass of raw milk might contain pathogens—but nothing worth doing is entirely risk-free.

So we can either turn to our kitchens as a lifestyle, or we can do it to remind ourselves that we are alive, because we want to run our fingers across a silky side of salmon or grab hold of a bloody point-cut of brisket. Damn it, don't talk to me about calories, saturated fat, or healthy choices. I just want to experience life as fully as I can before memories of life outside my window fade forever. And that's something that even our kids will understand.

≥ BY ANDREA GEARY & DAN SOUZA ≤

Low–Salt Brining

Is it OK to use a salt substitute in a brine?

JOHN SCHAENMAN
NEWTON, MASS.

➤Salt substitutes fall into two categories: salt-free brands that replace all of the sodium chloride with potassium chloride, and low-salt brands that are a combination of the two minerals. We recently sampled both types in various cooking applications and found some sodium to be necessary to buffer the bitterness of the potassium chloride. To test whether a low-salt brand would be effective in a brine, we cut up two whole chickens and soaked one in a standard saltwater solution and the other in a brine made with our taste-test winner, LoSalt, which is made up of two-thirds potassium chloride and one-third sodium chloride. We pan-roasted the chickens and made a quick sauce with the drippings.

The results surprised us. While we expected to dislike the flavor of the chicken brined in the salt substitute, only a few tasters detected minor bitter notes—and most considered the flavor completely acceptable. Even more surprising was the finding that both samples were equally moist and juicy. When we did some further investigation, we learned that while the positive sodium ions in table salt are responsible for adding flavor, it's the negative chloride ions that bind to the proteins and cause them to swell and absorb moisture. Potassium chloride provides the same negative ions as table salt, and thus has a nearly identical effect when used in a brine.

The bottom line: It's fine to brine with a salt substitute. Just be sure to use a low-salt (not a salt-free) brand.

FINE FOR BRINING
LoSalt works as well as regular table salt for brining.

Corn Syrup Quandary

Is Karo corn syrup the same thing as the high-fructose corn syrup ubiquitous in soft drinks and other processed foods?

SARAH EWING
SPRINGFIELD, MO.

➤In a word, no. Corn syrup (the most popular brand being Karo, introduced in 1902) is made by adding enzymes to a mixture of cornstarch and water to break the long starch strands into glucose molecules. It's valuable in candy making because it discourages crystallization; it also helps baked goods retain moisture. And because it is less sweet than granulated sugar, corn syrup makes an excellent addition to savory glazes, contributing body and sticking power.

High-fructose corn syrup (HFCS) is a newer product, coming on the market in the 1960s. It is made by putting regular corn syrup through an additional enzymatic process that converts a portion of the glucose molecules into fructose, boosting its sweetness to a level even higher than that of cane sugar. Because HFCS is considerably less expensive than cane sugar, it is widely used in processed foods, but it is not sold directly to consumers.

Vintage Beer

I have some lager in my fridge that's about to have an anniversary: It's six months past its "drink by" date. Is it still good?

BRYAN CHU
BRIGHTON, MASS.

➤The simple answer to your question is yes, your beer is still good insofar as it is safe to drink. Since most beer is either pasteurized or filtered to eliminate bacteria, it's extremely resistant to spoiling. How the beer will taste is another matter. For a taste test, we met with Grant Wood, senior brewing manager of the Boston Beer Company, to sample fresh lager next to one that, like yours, had seen its first anniversary. (Typically, the drink-by dates on beers are four to six months out; this is based on how long the brewer thinks the beer can retain fresh flavor.) The difference was dramatic. While the fresh lager presented bright hops flavor and refreshing bitterness, the year-old bottle was distinctly malty, sweet, and, according to most tasters, "flat." The difference was even more pronounced when we repeated the tasting with a bottle that had been forgotten in a basement since 2004.

According to Wood, the explanation is twofold. First, all beer contains a minute amount of oxygen, and as the aroma and flavor compounds found in hops oxidize over time, those compounds dissipate. (Conversely, certain aromatic compounds increase with prolonged exposure to oxygen, resulting in sweet, sherry-like flavors.) Second, the speed of these reactions depends on the alcohol content of the beer and how it's stored. Beers with more alcohol by volume have a longer shelf life, as do those that are refrigerated.

The lesson: To enjoy beer at its finest, buy it cold, store it in the fridge, and drink it before the date on the bottle.

HEED THE DATE
Beer consumed after the "best by" date tastes flatter and more sweet.

Keeping the Kick in Fresh Horseradish

I love the taste of fresh horseradish, but its pungency doesn't seem to last. Grated right away, it tastes stronger than the prepared stuff in a jar, but over time its flavor fades. Is there a way to preserve that complex heat?

PEGGY KAUFFMAN
RUMFORD, MAINE

➤We agree that the flavor of the fresh root is far more vibrant and complex than the jarred stuff. To see if we noticed the flavor fading, we grated the fresh root and tasted it plain and in tomato juice after two hours, four hours, and overnight. Like you, we found that the more time passed, the milder the flavor. We did some research and learned that when horseradish is grated (or otherwise cut), its cells rupture, releasing an enzyme known as myrosinase. This enzyme rapidly reacts with another compound to form allyl isothiocyanate, the chemical that provides horseradish with its characteristic punch. But that sharpness is short-lived: Left unchecked, the enzymatic reaction quickly exhausts itself and the condiment loses pungency. We've found that commercial prepared horseradish, on the other hand, can last for weeks in the refrigerator without losing its punch. It turns out that the key is the vinegar it's steeped in. The acetic acid preserves the root's heat by slowing down the activity of the myrosinase, resulting in a more constant and gradual production of the potent compound allyl isothiocyanate. The upshot: more robust, longer-lasting pungency.

The lesson: To keep the kick in horseradish once you've grated it, add some vinegar. For an 8- to 10-inch-long horseradish root finely grated on a rasp-style grater (peel it first), add 6 tablespoons of water, 3 tablespoons of white vinegar, and ½ teaspoon of salt. Refrigerated in an airtight container, the mixture will hold the heat for up to two weeks.

HORSERADISH HELPER
Once grated, fresh horseradish needs vinegar to hold on to its heat.

SEND US YOUR QUESTIONS We will provide a complimentary one-year subscription for each letter we print. Send your inquiry, name, address, and daytime telephone number to Notes from Readers, *Cook's Illustrated*, P.O. Box 470589, Brookline, MA 02447, or to NotesFromReaders@ AmericasTestKitchen.com.

King Oyster Mushrooms

What do you think of the huge mushrooms called king oysters that are showing up in supermarkets?

TIFFANY SLAYTON
WORCESTER, MASS.

The king oyster mushroom (not the same species as the regular oyster mushroom) is native to the Mediterranean region, Asia, and North Africa but is now cultivated worldwide. Its white stem can measure up to 8 inches long and 2 inches wide, and it's topped by a stout brown cap. We sautéed the sliced stems and quartered caps of this bulky fungus in oil until tender and compared them with regular white mushrooms prepared the same way. The king mushrooms stood out because of their dense, chewy, almost resilient texture, which several tasters likened to that of squid or scallops. The king mushrooms' flavor, while very savory, had little of the characteristic earthiness that even mild white mushrooms boast. Still, we wouldn't hesitate to use these hearty mushrooms in a recipe, especially if the goal is to add meaty texture.

KING OF MUSHROOMS?
King oyster mushrooms boast a meaty flavor and firm, resilient texture.

Taking Multiple Measures

Since I have only one set of measuring cups, I often use a small cup multiple times to measure a larger amount (for instance, I use a ⅓-cup measure three times to get 1 cup of flour). My wife warns me that this method risks inaccuracy. Is she right?

CHRIS RHODES
GAINESVILLE, FLA.

Sticklers for precision, we were also skeptical about your strategy but decided to give it a whirl. We asked 10 volunteers to measure flour using our preferred dip-and-sweep method (dipping the cup into the flour and leveling it off with a straight edge). As they scooped, we recorded the weight of 1 cup of flour measured with a 1-cup dry measure, 1 cup of flour measured by filling a ⅓-cup dry measure three times, and 1 cup of flour measured by filling a ¼-cup dry measure four times. We compared the weight of the flour that the testers measured in the 1-cup dry measure with the weights of their other samples. To our surprise, the discrepancies were not huge. In most cases, the weight difference among the individuals' samples was less than 3 percent.

Our conclusion: Though weighing ingredients will always give you the most accurate results, "doubling up" with a smaller measure is no less accurate than taking one larger measurement as long as you use the dip-and-sweep technique, which we've found is more precise than spooning the dry ingredient into the cup.

WHAT IS IT?

My French grandmother was an avid cook. Several years ago, we inherited her full kitchen arsenal. In it, we found these rather strange-looking tongs. Do you have any idea what they were used for?

AGNES MORAUX
DETROIT, MICH.

TRICKY TONGS
When it comes to escargot, we prefer to use our fingers.

Your tongs are for escargot. While some of us were familiar with this item from our days working in restaurants, it took quite a while to track down its origin. We eventually found the first mention of such a tool in an 1892 publication of *Nouvelles Scientifiques*, a supplement to the French weekly science journal *La Nature*. The inventor, Mr. Munier, found it frustrating to grip slippery, buttery snail shells with his fingers while fishing out the edible morsel inside with a specialized miniature fork. This inspired him to design tongs to firmly grasp the shell (and keep his hands clean). On your model, the pincers open when the handle is squeezed; they clutch the shell as the handle is released. It sounds simple enough, but when we sat down to a plateful of escargot with this relic in hand, many of us found it awkward to use.

Storing Grapes

I've heard that rinsing grapes before storing them causes them to spoil more quickly. Is that true?

AL RISELL
SKIPPACK, PA.

To answer your question, we took bunches of red and white grapes and removed any on-the-verge or obviously rotten ones. Then we rinsed and dried half of each bunch, leaving the other half unrinsed. We also wondered if leaving the fruit on the stem hastens or delays spoilage, so we plucked some of the grapes from their stems and left the remaining clusters intact. Then we refrigerated all the samples in the perforated bags that we bought them in.

All of the rinsed grapes spoiled within just a couple of days. Why? Even though we had dried them as much as possible, moisture exposure encouraged bacterial growth. The unrinsed loose grapes were the next to rot, as the now-exposed stem attachment point became an entryway for bacteria. Unrinsed stem-on grapes fared best, lasting nearly two weeks before starting to decay. In fact, as long as we periodically inspected the bunches and removed any decaying grapes, most of them—both red and white samples—kept for an entire month.

In sum: Don't pull grapes from their stems before refrigeration. Simply discard any that show signs of rotting and hold off on rinsing until just before serving.

FRESHER GRAPES, LONGER
For long-lasting fruit, rinse later.

Milk Substitute

In your March/April 2011 issue, you determined that Carnation evaporated milk is not a good substitute for fresh milk in the 1:1 ratio recommended on the can. How about watering it down?

KERSTIN DOELL
SEATTLE, WASH.

Evaporated milk has been heated to remove half of its water. When we tested a straight 1:1 substitution for fresh milk as recommended on a can of Carnation (the most widely available brand), we found that the concentrated sugars, fats, and proteins in the milk caused recipes to fail: Cakes were denser and puddings were overly thick.

To see if a dilution would work better, we tested three different ratios of evaporated milk and water in vanilla pudding, sponge cake, and béchamel sauce. A mixture of 75 percent evaporated milk to 25 percent water was still too concentrated—pudding was gluey, sponge cake was dense, and béchamel was thick and cloying. Dialing the ratios down to 67 percent evaporated milk and 33 percent water helped only a little. But a 50-50 mix produced results that were close to the all-regular-milk versions in all three cases. It's good to know that we can keep a ready substitute for fresh milk in the cupboard.

Quick Tips

⇛ COMPILED BY SHANNON FRIEDMANN HATCH ⇚

Splash-Proof Mixer

After seeing ingredients splatter out of the bowl one too many times when using her hand mixer, Abigail Sikma of Sussex, Wis., took a plastic gallon-size ice-cream lid, cut it to fit around the beater, and placed it on top of the bowl. No more dirty countertops.

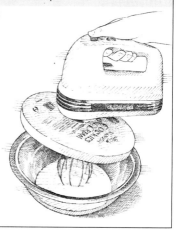

Rinsing Greens for One

When Anna Petranich of San Rafael, Calif., needs to prepare just a handful of greens or herbs, here's how she avoids hauling out the salad spinner.

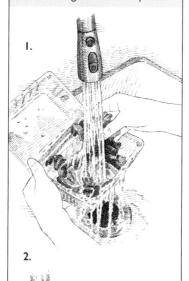

1.

2.

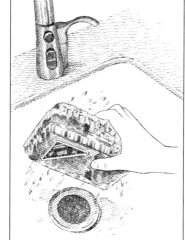

1. Place the greens inside an empty, perforated plastic clamshell container (like those used for strawberries) and give them a quick rinse.
2. Close the container and shake vigorously to drive off water from the leaves.

Neater Crab Cakes

Warren Rheaume of Seattle, Wash., uses his adjustable measuring cup to form tidy, uniform crab cakes.

1.

2.

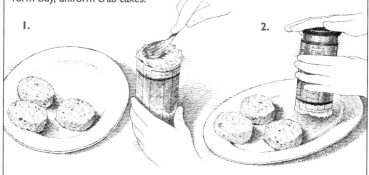

1. Set the cup to the desired cake size, lightly coat the inside with oil, and load it with the filling.
2. Invert the cake onto a plate.

Semipermanent Labeling

It's a good idea to clearly mark what's inside your freezer-bound containers, but many labels leave a sticky residue, and permanent markers offer a one-time solution. Instead, Sandra Robertson of McDonalds Corners, Ontario, uses an inexpensive hardware-store staple: painter's tape. Made for clean removal, it pulls away without leaving a gummy trace.

Corralling Cross-Contamination

When handling raw chicken, Bob McLeod of Vancouver, B.C., avoids cross-contamination of bacteria by placing the plastic-wrapped chicken on a rimmed baking sheet. He cuts open the package with kitchen shears, leaving the empty package, shears, and any other dirty utensils on the sheet, and pats the chicken dry. He then discards the packaging and transfers the baking sheet and tools to the sink to clean.

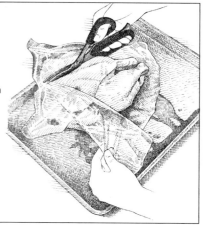

Connect-the-Dots Frosting

When frosting a cake, John Robinson of Athens, Ohio, finds that the act of spreading can dislodge some of the crumbs, which then get incorporated into the frosting, muddying its smoothness. Here's how he minimizes the problem.

1.

2.

1. Place large, evenly spaced dollops of frosting over the top of the cake.
2. Using an offset spatula, spread one dollop to another until the frosting is smooth and equally distributed.

SEND US YOUR TIPS We will provide a complimentary one-year subscription for each tip we print. Send your tip, name, and address to Quick Tips, *Cook's Illustrated*, P.O. Box 470589, Brookline, MA 02447, or to QuickTips@AmericasTestKitchen.com.

ILLUSTRATION: JOHN BURGOYNE

Keeping Appetizers Chilled

Inspired by the ice-ring tip in our March/April 2011 issue, W. F. Schryer of Gansevoort, N.Y., developed a similar method to keep shrimp cocktail chilled while serving. It's a cool trick for crudités and fruit, too.

1.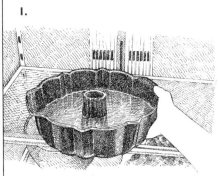

2.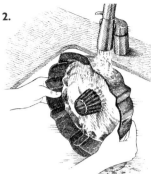

3.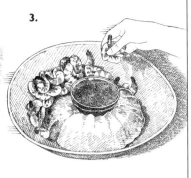

1. Fill a Bundt pan halfway with water; freeze until firm.
2. Just prior to serving, run the bottom of the mold under warm water to loosen the ice ring.
3. Place the ring in a large serving bowl and set a container of cocktail sauce in the center. Top the ice with cooked shrimp.

Mess-Free Pepper Grinding

Mary McKeon of Phoenixville, Pa., has discovered a way to catch her peppermill's loose grinds and make neat work of measuring fresh-ground pepper.

1.

2.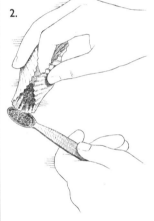

3.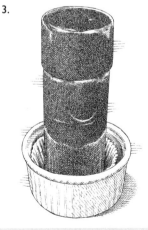

1. Grind the pepper into a cupcake liner.
2. Bend the liner edges to pour the pepper into a measuring spoon.
3. Discard any extra pepper and store the mill and liner inside a ramekin.

Travel-Ready Frozen Dinner

Donny Copeland of Baltimore, Md., preps skirt or flank steak for camping and tailgating with this method.

1.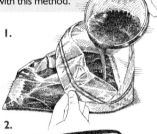

2.

1. At least one day in advance, combine the meat with a low-acid marinade (that won't turn the exterior of the meat mushy) in a zipper-lock bag; place the bag in the freezer.
2. About three hours before you're ready to grill, remove the steak from the freezer and place it in a cooler. The meat should stay cold but defrost in time for cooking.

Tagging with Toothpicks

When grilling for a crowd, Travis Lewis of Birmingham, Ala., has discovered a way to tell well-done burgers from medium-rare at a glance: He assigns each level of doneness a particular number of toothpicks (e.g., one for rare, two for medium, three for well-done) and pegs the proper marker into the patties as they come off the fire.

Chimney-Roasting Bell Peppers

Carol Torrell of Farmville, N.C., takes advantage of a chimney starter full of hot coals when grilling: She uses it to roast a bell pepper. After the charcoal is hot (about 10 minutes), she places a wire rack over the chimney and tops it with a pepper, turning with tongs until all sides have charred. (The hot coals can now be poured into the kettle and used to cook other food.) She allows the pepper to steam in a bowl covered with plastic wrap to loosen its skin, and peels it when cool.

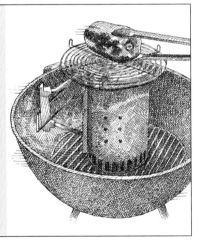

Alternative Citrus Juicer

While handheld juicers work well for smaller citrus, bulky grapefruit hardly fits inside the small chamber. Lacking an electric option, Stephanie Streeter of Brookline, N.H., uses a potato ricer to extract juice from her grapefruit. She quarters the fruit, loads it into the hopper, and squeezes.

Grilled Stuffed Pork Tenderloin

A savory filling boosts flavor and helps this lean cut stay moist on the grill—if you can keep the stuffing from leaking out.

⇒ BY BRYAN ROOF ⇐

When I have plenty of time on my hands, my go-to summer pork roast is a bone-in, well-marbled cut that I can throw on the grill for as long as it takes for the meat to become tender and juicy while picking up plenty of smoke flavor from the fire. But when a laid-back meal isn't possible, a fast-cooking alternative like pork tenderloin can come in handy. This readily available cut has the added advantages of being supremely tender and uniformly shaped for even cooking and slicing. But what it makes up for in convenience, the lean, mild-mannered roast—basically the pork equivalent of boneless, skinless chicken breast—sorely lacks in flavor and juiciness. Throw the unpredictable heat of the grill into the equation, and you're well on your way to producing a dry, bland log.

Most recipes tackle these issues by dressing the cooked roast with relishes or sauces, but those solutions are only skin-deep. For a flavor boost that would literally get at the interior of the tenderloin—arguably the blandest part—I wanted to try stuffing the roast with a rich-tasting filling.

Cut and Paste

I decided to work with two tenderloins, which would make enough to feed four to six people. The average pork tenderloin is only 2 inches in diameter, so I had to think carefully about the most effective way to butterfly it for stuffing. I had two options in mind. One was a simple hinge method, in which the meat is bisected lengthwise about half an inch shy of its back edge, opened up like a book and stuffed, and then closed and secured with twine. The other approach took this method further, pounding the butterflied meat until it was wide and thin, so that once stuffed, it could be rolled up. The first technique seemed less fussy, but I found that it allowed too much stuffing to ooze from the seams. Though

For fillings with maximum flavor and minimal bulk, we use ultra-savory ingredients like olives, porcini, and cheese.

it took a little more effort, pounding and rolling turned out to have two benefits. Pounding the meat created more surface area for the filling, and rolling the pork around the stuffing helped prevent leakage during cooking and carving.

But even with this wider plane to work with, I had to keep the filling's bulk to a minimum. That meant forgoing a traditional bread stuffing. What I needed was some sort of intense-tasting paste, of which a little would go a long way. I perused the test kitchen's pantry for flavor-packed ingredients that wouldn't require extensive prep or precooking. It

didn't take me long to come up with three robustly flavored combinations that required nothing more than a whirl in the food processor. One featured briny kalamata olives, sweet sun-dried tomatoes, and a few flavor-enhancing anchovies. Another balanced spicy roasted piquillo peppers with buttery Manchego cheese and smoked paprika. The third brought together porcini with artichoke hearts and Parmesan. Layering raw baby spinach leaves over the fillings freshened their rich flavors and added bright color.

An Indirect Solution

Now for the grilling method. Lean pork tenderloin needs a forgiving heat source that won't parch the meat's exterior before the interior has a chance to cook through. I opted for a modified two-level fire, where all the coals are spread evenly over one side of the grill, leaving the other side cooler. But when I grilled the roasts across from the coals for 25 minutes, I found that the indirect heat produced mixed results. While the roasts were quite tender with perfectly warmed-through fillings, they looked utterly pale.

Fortunately, this was a problem the test kitchen had tackled before. When we want to boost browning on lean meat, we coat the exterior with a little sugar. Sure enough, when I mixed about 4 teaspoons of sugar with the salt and pepper I was rubbing on the roasts just before grilling, they came off the fire nicely browned with deeper flavor. The effect was even more profound when I traded granulated sugar for dark brown sugar.

When I have the time, I still like to take it slow with a fatty bone-in cut. But my buttery-tender, faintly smoky tenderloins with their robustly flavored fillings were on the table in less than an hour. Who could argue with that?

RECIPE TESTING The Right (and Wrong) Way to Stuff Pork Tenderloin

The trick to keeping the stuffing intact depends on how you butcher and bind the roast.

COMING UNHINGED
Butterflying the roast and simply folding the hinged flaps of meat around the stuffing can lead to oozing filling.

POUNDED AND ROLLED
Pounding the butterflied roast before stuffing allows the meat to be tightly rolled, not folded, around the filling.

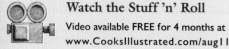

GRILLED STUFFED PORK TENDERLOIN
SERVES 4 TO 6

    4   teaspoons packed dark brown sugar
    2¼   teaspoons kosher salt
    1¼   teaspoons pepper
    2   (1¼- to 1½-pound) pork tenderloins, trimmed
    1   recipe stuffing (recipes follow)
    1   cup baby spinach
    2   tablespoons olive oil

1. Combine sugar, 2 teaspoons salt, and 1 teaspoon pepper in bowl. Cut each tenderloin in half horizontally, stopping ½ inch away from edge so halves remain attached. Open up tenderloins, cover with plastic wrap, and pound to ¼-inch thickness. Trim any ragged edges to create rough rectangle about 10 inches by 6 inches. Sprinkle interior of each tenderloin with ⅛ teaspoon salt and ⅛ teaspoon pepper.

2. With long side of pork facing you, spread half of stuffing mixture over bottom half of one tenderloin followed by ½ cup spinach. Roll away from you into tight cylinder, taking care not to squeeze stuffing out ends. Position tenderloin seam side down, evenly space 5 pieces twine underneath, and tie. Repeat with remaining tenderloin, stuffing, and spinach.

3A. FOR A CHARCOAL GRILL: Light large chimney starter filled with charcoal briquettes (6 quarts). When top coals are partially covered with ash, pour evenly over half of grill. Set cooking grate in place, cover, and heat grill until hot, about 5 minutes.

3B. FOR A GAS GRILL: Turn all burners to high, cover, and heat grill until hot, about 15 minutes. Leave primary burner on high and turn off other burner(s).

4. Clean and oil cooking grate. Coat pork with oil, then rub entire surface with brown sugar mixture. Place pork on cooler side of grill, cover, and cook until center of stuffing registers 140 degrees, 25 to 30 minutes, rotating pork once halfway through cooking.

5. Transfer pork to carving board, tent loosely with foil, and let rest for 5 to 10 minutes. Remove twine, slice pork into ½-inch-thick slices, and serve.

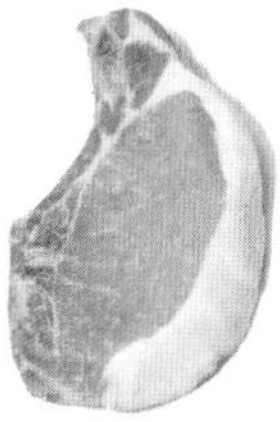

OLIVE AND SUN-DRIED TOMATO STUFFING
MAKES ABOUT 1 CUP, ENOUGH FOR 2 TENDERLOINS

    ½   cup pitted kalamata olives
    ½   cup oil-packed sun-dried tomatoes, rinsed
         and chopped coarse
    4   anchovy fillets
    2   garlic cloves, minced
    1   teaspoon minced fresh thyme
    1   teaspoon finely grated lemon zest
         Salt and pepper

Pulse all ingredients except salt and pepper in food processor until coarsely chopped, 5 to 10 pulses; season with salt and pepper to taste.

PIQUILLO PEPPER AND MANCHEGO STUFFING
MAKES ABOUT 1 CUP, ENOUGH FOR 2 TENDERLOINS

Roasted red peppers may be substituted for the piquillo peppers.

    1   slice hearty white sandwich bread, torn into
         ½-inch pieces
    ¾   cup jarred piquillo peppers, rinsed and
         patted dry
    2   ounces Manchego cheese, shredded (½ cup)
    ¼   cup pine nuts, toasted
    2   garlic cloves, minced
    1   teaspoon minced fresh thyme
    ½   teaspoon smoked paprika
         Salt and pepper

Pulse all ingredients except salt and pepper in food processor until coarsely chopped, 5 to 10 pulses; season with salt and pepper to taste.

PORCINI AND ARTICHOKE STUFFING
MAKES ABOUT 1 CUP, ENOUGH FOR 2 TENDERLOINS

    ½   ounce dried porcini mushrooms, rinsed
    3   ounces frozen artichoke hearts, thawed and
         patted dry (¾ cup)
    1   ounce Parmesan cheese, grated (½ cup)
    ¼   cup oil-packed sun-dried tomatoes, rinsed
         and chopped coarse
    ¼   cup fresh parsley leaves
    2   tablespoons pine nuts, toasted
    2   garlic cloves, minced
    1   teaspoon finely grated lemon zest plus
         2 teaspoons juice
         Salt and pepper

Microwave ½ cup water and porcini in covered bowl until steaming, about 1 minute. Let stand until softened, about 5 minutes. Use fork to remove porcini from liquid and pat dry with paper towels. Discard soaking liquid. Pulse porcini, artichokes, Parmesan, tomatoes, parsley, pine nuts, garlic, lemon zest, and lemon juice in food processor until coarsely chopped, 5 to 10 pulses; season with salt and pepper to taste.

TASTING Premium Pork

Is pedigreed pork such as Berkshire (known as Kurobuta in Japan) and Duroc worth its premium price tag? (Once shipping is factored in, upscale pork can cost at least twice as much as supermarket meat.) Seeking a more flavorful cut than tenderloin, we mail-ordered bone-in chops and a roast we cut into chops from five different specialty producers and compared them with chops from the grocery store. Three of the mail-order chops were 100 percent Berkshire pork; one was pure Duroc; and the last was a Duroc blend. Before we put the chops in the pan, we couldn't help but notice the startling differences in their color. The pure Berkshire meat was a rich crimson; the blends were not quite as dark but had more color than the pale supermarket chops. When we pan-seared all the chops, the 100 percent Berkshire meat won us over with its tender texture and juicy, smoky, intensely pork-y—even bacon-like—taste. The supermarket chops were bland and chewy in comparison, and surprisingly, the heritage-blend samples weren't significantly better.

We wondered if the richer flavor of the pure Berkshire pork was at all related to its deep red tint. As it turns out, there is a connection. According to Kenneth Prusa, professor of food science at Iowa State University, color reflects the meat's pH level. The higher the pH, the darker the meat—and the better its flavor and texture. Berkshire pigs are genetically predisposed to have a slightly higher pH than the norm—and even a few tenths of a point can have a significant impact, says Prusa. Conversely, a low pH translates to paler, softer, and blander meat. (When we measured the pH of the meat in the test kitchen, we found that these claims were borne out: Our two top-rated chops had a significantly higher average pH—6.2—than the supermarket chops, which averaged 5.7.)

Bottom line: Our top-rated samples of Berkshire pork are worth the occasional splurge. In the meantime, we'll be picking out the reddest pork at the supermarket. For complete tasting results, go to www.CooksIllustrated.com/aug11. –Amy Graves

BERKSHIRE
SNAKE RIVER FARMS
Price: $10 per pound, plus shipping
Comments: Tasters raved about the extremely tender texture and "intense pork-y" flavor of these reddish pink chops (cut from a roast).

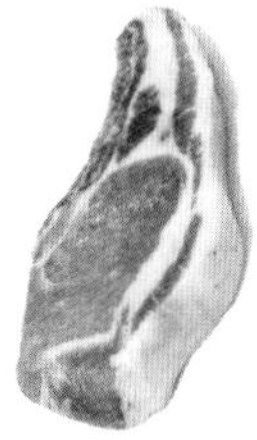

BERKSHIRE
D'ARTAGNAN
Price: $10.99 per pound, plus shipping
Comments: Just as crimson-colored as our winner, these second-place chops were "rich, nutty, tender, and juicy."

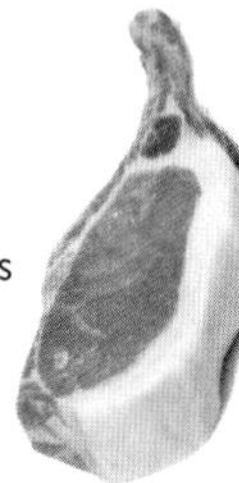

DUROC-YORKSHIRE BLEND
VERMONT QUALITY MEATS
Price: $5.45 per pound, plus shipping
Comments: These faintly pink chops, which rated just above the supermarket chops, were "not amazing—just decent."

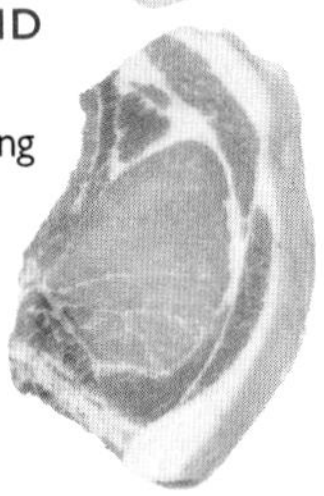

GENERIC
SUPERMARKET
Price: $3.99 per pound
Comments: These last-place chops dulled in comparison with the Berkshire pork. Their off-white meat was "moist enough" but "chalky" and "bland."

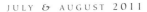

Grill-Smoked Chicken

Surprisingly, the trick to perfecting smoke flavor isn't getting the wood to smolder for as long as possible. It's just the opposite: knowing when to let it burn out.

⇒ BY ANDREW JANJIGIAN ⇐

Though they are cooked under seemingly similar conditions, grill-roasted chickens and smoked chickens are birds of very different feathers. Grill-roasting is a relatively fast, hot cooking method that produces chicken with crisp skin and subtle smoke flavor. Smoking is a gentler process in which a low fire burns slowly to keep pieces of wood smoldering while cooking the chicken more gradually. When done right, the meat is juicy, tender, and imbued throughout with insistent yet balanced smokiness. The skin is just as well rendered as you'd find on a good grilled bird, but instead of being crackly-crisp, it's moist, supple, and stained a deep brown.

Early tests, however, taught me that smoking a chicken is definitely the more challenging proposition. When grill-roasting, it's tricky enough to balance the relationship between the heat level and the cooking time. Add smoke to the equation, and the situation becomes even more complicated. When I built a fire that was too hot, the delicate breast meat overcooked before the smoke had a chance to penetrate beyond the skin. When the fire wasn't hot enough, the heat dwindled too quickly and forced me to refuel the charcoal multiple times. And the smoke flavor was fickle—sometimes barely there, other times harsh and bitter. My task was clear: Nail down a fire setup and a specific window of smoking time that would produce tender, juicy meat with clean, full-bodied smoke flavor.

The Slow Burn

As with all chicken recipes, I had a preliminary decision to make: brine or salt the bird? Both treatments season the meat and help it retain its own juices; the difference is that brining plumps up the bird with additional moisture, which I knew would be a boon in a recipe in which the meat is prone to drying out.

While the chicken soaked, I stepped outside to

Chicken parts not only cook faster than a whole bird, but their increased surface area absorbs smoke flavor more evenly.

figure out the grill setup. It seemed to me that my best bet would be to adopt the method that we devised for our recipe for slow-barbecued, smoky Texas brisket. Rather than bank a full chimney's worth of hot coals to one side of the kettle while leaving the other side empty—a traditional indirect setup known as a modified two-level fire—we mounded a smaller pile of unlit briquettes against one side of the grill and added a batch of lit coals on top. Over time, the heat from the lit briquettes trickles down and lights the cold coals, thereby extending the life of the fire without the need for opening the grill to refuel and allowing precious heat to escape.

The other trick I borrowed from that brisket recipe: stowing a pan of water under the chicken on the cool side of the grill. The humidity provided by the water stabilizes the temperature of the grill and (along with brining) helps prevent the delicate breast meat from drying out. Set up this way (for now, I'd stick with 3 quarts each of lit and unlit coals), the grill jumped to 375 degrees early on and then quickly dropped to the 300 to 325 range, where it held steady.

Parting with the Whole Bird

Now came the harder part: incorporating well-balanced smoke flavor into a whole chicken. I already knew that I'd use wood chunks, since they smolder more steadily and evenly than smaller chips do, and that I'd soak them in water for at least 30 minutes before cooking, since the absorbed moisture keeps the wood from burning too quickly.

Several of the recipes that I found called for keeping up the smolder for the duration of cooking, so I followed their lead, adding two soaked wood chunks to the coals and throwing two more onto the coals when the smoke died out after about 45 minutes. After two hours of indirect cooking, the chicken was up to temperature (160 degrees for the breast and 175 degrees for the leg quarters); I pulled it off the grill, let it rest briefly to ensure that the juices redistributed, and called over my colleagues for a tasting. The results? Unimpressive. The delicate breast meat was parched, and the smoke flavor (not to mention the exterior color of the bird) was uneven. I soon realized that the problem was actually fundamental to all whole chickens grill-roasted in a kettle-style vessel: With an indirect fire, a good bit of the heat travels up and under the lid and then bounces back down onto the meat, so that the top of the chicken cooks faster than the side closest to the grate. Trying to compensate for this effect, I started another bird breast side down and flipped it halfway through cooking, but that got me nowhere. The smoke flavor was still uneven, and now the bird was unattractively branded from the grill grate. Plus, heat escaped when I opened the grill, adding 15 minutes to the cooking time.

There was an easy answer to these problems: Forget the whole bird and start with parts. That way, the white meat could sit as far from the heat as possible, and the smoke could evenly surround the smaller individual pieces. I gave it a whirl and saw immediate progress. Not only were the dark and white components evenly tender and juicy, but I was able to cut down the cooking time from two hours to 90 minutes and the unlit briquettes from 3 quarts to 2 quarts. Best of all, this new setup was far more space-efficient, allowing me to fit another half chicken's worth of pieces on the grill.

Check Out the Grill Setup
Video available FREE for 4 months at www.CooksIllustrated.com/aug11

To produce tender, juicy, smoky chicken, we devised a three-part fire setup in our charcoal kettle. It mimics the slow, steady, indirect heat that pit masters get from a dedicated smoker, plus it avoids sooty flavors.

TWO QUARTS OF UNLIT COALS banked to one side of the grill with 3 quarts of lit coals piled on top kept the fire going without it being necessary to open the lid.

A WATER PAN placed underneath the grill grate opposite the coals created steam, which helped stabilize the temperature and keep the meat moist.

TWO SOAKED WOOD CHUNKS placed on top of the coals smoldered for about 45 minutes—just long enough to infuse the chicken with smoky (not sooty) flavor.

Up in Smoke

Unfortunately, the one problem I still had to contend with—the smoke flavor—had just gone from bad to worse. Whereas smoke only spottily infused the whole chicken, it now so heavily saturated the smaller pieces that tasters likened their flavor to a wet ashtray. I tried adding only one extra wood chunk midway through cooking, but the improvement was negligible. I even tested a slightly hotter fire so that the chicken would get a brief blast of smoke, but this batch was barely tinged with smoke. The problem was that the chicken could absorb only so much smoke flavor at one time, so although the wood was smoldering heavily around the meat, the meat was taking in only a small bit of that smoke and the rest was blowing right out the vent.

At this point I wondered if continuously smoking the meat wasn't the best idea after all, so I tried an altogether different approach: I prepared another batch of chicken, and when the initial pair of chunks burned out, I let the meat finish cooking without refueling the wood. I had my doubts—smoking the meat for only half of the cooking time sounded inadequate—but to my delight, this batch was markedly better. The meat was deeply smoky but not overpoweringly so. In fact, the results were so improved that I mentioned the test to our science editor. He explained that while the smoke flavor that meat develops early on during cooking is fresh and clean-tasting, those pleasant flavors will turn harsh if the meat is exposed to smoke for too long (for more information, see "Don't Oversmoke Your Chicken").

Lesson learned, I had just one holdover issue to resolve: the skin, which had been rendering nicely but was a tad leathery and not quite as glossy as I'd hoped. The obvious fix? A little extra fat. When I brushed the pieces with a coat of vegetable oil just before cooking, the skin emerged supple and tender, with a polished mahogany sheen.

This, finally, was the smoked chicken I'd been working toward: moist and juicy, richly (but not harshly) infused with smoke, and beautifully tanned.

And since most of the cooking time was unattended and there was no fussy carving to worry about, the recipe was dead simple.

SMOKED CHICKEN
SERVES 6 TO 8

Avoid mesquite wood chunks for this recipe; we find that the meat can turn bitter if they smolder too long. When using a charcoal grill, we prefer wood chunks to wood chips whenever possible. If using a gas grill, you will need to use wood chips.

- 1 cup salt
- 1 cup sugar
- 6 pounds bone-in chicken parts (breasts, thighs, and drumsticks), trimmed
- 3 tablespoons vegetable oil
  Pepper
  Large disposable aluminum roasting pan (if using charcoal) or disposable aluminum pie plate (if using gas)
- 2 wood chunks soaked in water for 30 minutes and drained (if using charcoal) or 3 cups wood chips, half of chips soaked in water for 30 minutes and drained (if using gas)

1. Dissolve salt and sugar in 4 quarts cold water in large container. Submerge chicken in brine, cover, and refrigerate for 30 minutes to 1 hour. Remove chicken from brine and pat dry with paper towels. Brush both sides of chicken with oil and season with pepper.

2A. FOR A CHARCOAL GRILL: Open bottom vent halfway. Arrange disposable pan filled with 2 cups water on 1 side of grill and 2 quarts unlit charcoal briquettes against empty side of grill. Light large chimney starter filled halfway with charcoal briquettes (3 quarts). When top coals are partially covered with ash, pour on top of unlit briquettes, keeping coals steeply banked against side of grill. Place wood chunks on top of coals. Set cooking grate in place, cover, and open lid vent halfway. Heat grill until hot

and wood chunks begin to smoke, about 5 minutes.

2B. FOR A GAS GRILL: Use large piece of heavy-duty aluminum foil to wrap soaked chips into foil packet and cut several vent holes in top. Wrap unsoaked chips in second foil packet and cut several vent holes in top. Place wood chip packets directly on primary burner. Place disposable pie plate with 2 cups water on other burner(s). Turn all burners to high, cover, and heat grill until hot and wood chips begin to smoke, about 15 minutes. Turn primary burner to medium-high and turn off other burner(s).

3. Clean and oil cooking grate. Place chicken, skin side up, as far away from fire as possible with thighs closest to fire and breasts furthest away. Cover (positioning lid vent over chicken if using charcoal) and cook until breasts register 160 degrees and thighs/drumsticks register 175 degrees, 1¼ to 1½ hours.

4. Transfer chicken to cutting board, tent loosely with foil, and let rest for 5 to 10 minutes before serving.

SCIENCE EXPERIMENT
Don't Oversmoke Your Chicken

To infuse our chicken pieces with full-bodied smoke flavor, we figured it was necessary to keep the wood chunks smoldering for the entire time that the meat was on the grill. But when the finished product tasted not just smoky, but also harsh and ashy, we wondered: Was there a limit to the amount of smoke that the chicken could take?

EXPERIMENT

We smoked two batches of chicken. For the first, we added two soaked wood chunks to the fire at the beginning of cooking; when those had burned out about 45 minutes later, we added two more soaked chunks to keep the smoldering going for the duration of cooking. For the second batch, we didn't replenish the wood after the initial chunks had burned out.

RESULTS

The chicken exposed to smoke the entire time tasted bitter and sooty, while the pieces that were exposed to smoke for only 45 minutes or so (about half of the overall cooking time) had just enough smoky depth.

EXPLANATION

Smoke contains both water- and fat-soluble compounds. As the chicken cooks, water evaporates and fat drips away, eventually halting meat's capacity to continue absorbing smoke flavor. Once that happens, any additional smoke flavor that's not absorbed by the meat gets deposited on the exterior of the chicken, where the heat of the grill breaks it down into harsher-flavored compounds. –A.J.

ONE ROUND OF WOOD CHUNKS = BALANCED SMOKINESS

Great Salmon Cakes

What's a nice fresh fillet doing mixed up in a fried cake? Three good reasons: a crispy exterior, a moist interior, and a super-simple cooking technique.

> BY ANDREA GEARY

As a small child, I was convinced that all fish were perfectly cylindrical—sort of like dachshunds with fins—because when my family ate fish, it was in the form of puck-shaped cakes. While I have a soft spot for those starch-heavy cod and haddock cakes of my youth, I sometimes crave a more refined version, in which the fish itself isn't camouflaged by gluey binders (usually potatoes) and heavy-handed seasoning. Enter salmon cakes. When done well, these pan-fried patties are tender and moist on the inside, crisp and golden brown on the outside. Any seasoning complements—rather than overpowers—the flavor of the fish, and there is just enough binder to hold the cakes together. Unfortunately, most salmon cakes I've tried stray far from this ideal. Their interior is mushy and their flavor overly fishy. And then there's the fussy breading process.

With a lifetime of fish cake–eating experience, I knew I could do better. My goal: salmon cakes that tasted first and foremost of salmon, with a moist, delicate texture. I'd dump the potatoes in favor of a less stodgy binder and keep it to a minimum. And although I'd make them from scratch, these cakes would be quick and simple to prepare.

To Cook or Not to Cook?

Fish cakes have long been a mainstay of New England cuisine, designed for using up leftover fish and potatoes. But today, most of us buy and cook only as much fish as we plan to eat in one sitting. Which led me to my first question: Should I use cooked or raw fish? I was pretty sure raw would be the way to go if I wanted a moist cake. But to be sure, I tried both approaches.

Keeping things simple for now, I chopped raw salmon fillets by hand into small pieces, then stirred in two typical binders (bread crumbs and mayonnaise), shaped the mixture into cakes, and

Once formed, our cakes need nothing more than a roll in coarse bread crumbs to create a satisfying crunch.

(per standard breading procedure) coated them in all-purpose flour, egg, and bread crumbs. I fried the cakes on both sides in about ¼ inch of vegetable oil until they were crisp and golden brown. Then I repeated this method with cooked salmon, which I prepared three different ways—poached, roasted, and pan-seared—before flaking it and mixing it with the binders.

Just as I'd expected, the cakes made with cooked salmon lacked moisture. Plus, they tasted noticeably "fishier" than the fresh-fish batch. And the two-step cooking process was a pain. But making raw salmon cakes was no joy either. Hand-chopping slippery raw fish into ¼-inch pieces was messy, sticky, and tedious. Larger chunks weren't an option—with bigger salmon bits the cakes fell apart, even with strong binders.

That said, my colleagues deemed the cakes made from raw salmon "pretty darn good." They were tender and moist inside, and boasted pleasantly rich, almost creamy flavor with none of the "fishiness" of the twice-cooked samples. They just needed a bit of flavor enhancement and, for the sake of weeknight cooking, an easier method.

Speeding Up the Process

To this end, I took out my food processor. I cut the fillet into 2-inch pieces, chucked them in, and let the processor whirl. This resulted in big chunks of salmon bound by finely ground fish paste. Processing the salmon in two batches yielded smaller pieces, but the mixture was still too pasty; when I formed the mixture into rounds and fried them, the finished cakes had a ground-meat consistency that was dense rather than delicate.

But that ground meat analogy gave me an idea. When we make burgers, we grind the meat ourselves using an easy three-step process: We cut the meat into 1-inch pieces, briefly freeze them to firm them up, and then batch-grind them into smaller chunks in the food processor. The method ensures small, discrete pieces rather than mush. I didn't have time for the freezer, but smaller pieces and smaller batches were both doable. I cut the salmon into 1-inch chunks and pulsed them in three batches. This approach—pulsing, rather than letting the processor run continuously—allowed for more even chopping. Some of the pieces were still a bit bigger than the ideal ¼-inch morsels and some were smaller, but taken as a whole, they produced a cake very similar to those I'd made with hand-minced fish.

Having succeeded in making the chopping easier, I now could address an issue that had been annoying me from the start: The raw cakes were so wet that dipping them in egg made them as slippery and awkward to handle as mud pies. Adding more bread crumbs made the patties less goopy but masked the delicate sweetness of the fish. I had a radical thought: Was the full-on breading process really necessary? What if I ditched the egg and flour and simply coated the salmon cakes in bread crumbs before frying? This made the patties easier to handle and the bread crumbs clung surprisingly well to the fish on their own, but the results weren't stellar. Without a little bit of flour to act as a buffer from the moisture in the cakes, the fresh bread crumbs came out too pale and soft. But when I traded the fresh crumbs for ultra-crisp Japanese panko, the salmon cakes emerged from the pan crisp and golden brown. For convenience, I decided to use panko for a binder as well.

Curious why the traditional breading procedure proved superfluous in this case—a happy state of affairs that both cut down on mess and resulted in a simpler process—I consulted our science editor. A typical breading process works because the egg contains sticky soluble proteins called ovalbumin that (along with the flour) helps the mixture hold together. But it turns out that salmon also contains tacky soluble proteins, called myosin, that migrate to the surface with the moisture in the fish and help the bread crumbs stick. Salmon has more of these water-soluble proteins than many other kinds of fish, as well as chicken and shrimp, making it the perfect candidate for a nontraditional breading.

Fishy Fish

Spurred on by these successes, I decided to reach for one more: Could I streamline my recipe even further by "oven-frying" the salmon cakes on an oiled sheet pan? I tried a range of temperatures and rack settings, but the results took longer (10 to 12 minutes—double the time) and were consistently disappointing: pale, dry, and not at all crisp. Worst of all, tasters began to murmur again about a "fishy" flavor.

That last problem baffled me. I'd been using beautifully fresh salmon, but tasters had dismissed both the oven-fried cakes and those made with cooked fish as assertively "fishy," while praising the pan-fried cakes made with raw chopped salmon for their mellow yet rich flavor. When I mentioned the results to our science editor, he explained that the highly unsaturated fat in salmon oxidizes both when it is exposed to the air and when it is cooked, resulting in that characteristic salmon aroma and flavor. The more lengthy and thorough the cooking, the stronger the flavor. Not only was pan-frying the quickest method; it also kept fishiness in check.

Now that I had settled on a technique, it was time to jazz up the cakes' somewhat plain taste in a way that would enhance the fish flavor rather than disguise it. I added some finely chopped shallot for depth and both scallion and parsley for freshness. Lemon juice brightened the flavor and cut the richness of the salmon, while a teaspoon of mustard and a pinch of cayenne added punch.

Served with tartar sauce or simply spritzed with lemon, these moist-yet-crisp salmon cakes managed to be both elegant fare and comfort food. What's more, I could whip them up for a weeknight dinner.

EASY SALMON CAKES
SERVES 4

If buying a skin-on salmon fillet, purchase 1⅓ pounds of fish. This will yield 1¼ pounds of fish after skinning. When processing the salmon it is OK to have some pieces that are larger than ¼ inch. It is important to avoid overprocessing the fish. Serve the salmon cakes with lemon wedges and/or tartar sauce.

- 3   tablespoons plus ¾ cup panko bread crumbs
- 2   tablespoons minced fresh parsley
- 2   tablespoons mayonnaise
- 4   teaspoons lemon juice
- 1   scallion, sliced thin
- 1   small shallot, minced
- 1   teaspoon Dijon mustard
- ¾   teaspoon salt
- ¼   teaspoon pepper
-     Pinch cayenne pepper
- 1   (1¼-pound) skinless salmon fillet, cut into 1-inch pieces
- ½   cup vegetable oil

1. Combine 3 tablespoons panko, parsley, mayonnaise, lemon juice, scallion, shallot, mustard, salt, pepper, and cayenne in bowl. Working in 3 batches, pulse salmon in food processor until coarsely chopped into ¼-inch pieces, about 2 pulses, transferring each batch to bowl with panko mixture. Gently mix until uniformly combined.

2. Place remaining ¾ cup panko in pie plate. Using ⅓-cup measure, scoop level amount of salmon mixture and transfer to baking sheet; repeat to make 8 cakes. Carefully coat each cake in bread crumbs, gently patting into disk measuring 2¾ inches in diameter and 1 inch high. Return coated cakes to baking sheet.

3. Heat oil in 12-inch skillet over medium-high heat until shimmering. Place salmon cakes in skillet and cook without moving until golden brown, about 2 minutes. Carefully flip cakes and cook until second side is golden brown, 2 to 3 minutes. Transfer cakes to paper towel–lined plate to drain 1 minute. Serve.

EASY SALMON CAKES WITH SMOKED SALMON, CAPERS, AND DILL

Reduce amount of fresh salmon to 1 pound and salt to ½ teaspoon. Substitute 1 tablespoon chopped dill for parsley. Add 4 ounces finely chopped smoked salmon and 1 tablespoon chopped capers to bowl with salmon mixture.

SCIENCE EXPERIMENT

Something's Fishy

As we developed our recipe for salmon cakes, we experimented with different ways of preparing the fish. During testing, we noticed that sometimes the fish smelled (and tasted) far fishier than other times. Could the way we cooked the fish be the cause?

EXPERIMENT

We made salmon cakes three ways: with flaked precooked fish that we then pan-fried, with chopped raw fish that we baked in the oven, and with chopped raw fish seared until just cooked through.

RESULTS

The twice-cooked cakes had the strongest odor and flavor, with the baked cakes a close second. The pan-seared cakes were the mildest.

EXPLANATION

First, it helps to know that there are two different kinds of "fishy": One is a sign of spoilage; the other is an indication of the presence of healthy fats. The flesh of all fish contains an odorless, nonvolatile chemical called trimethylamine oxide (or TMAO). During storage, bacteria on the surface of the raw fish convert TMAO into a volatile compound called trimethylamine (TMA), which produces the unmistakable smell of rotten fish.

The fishy smell of cooked salmon (and other fatty fish such as mackerel and tuna) comes from a different source. Salmon fat is highly unsaturated, which makes it susceptible to oxidation when cooked. Oxidation causes the breakdown of the fatty acids into strong-smelling aldehydes, which are the source of salmon's characteristic flavor. Cooking the salmon twice resulted in very thoroughly cooked fish and, thus, a high level of aldehydes. Baking the cakes had a similar effect because the ambient heat of the oven cooked the fish more thoroughly than the stove did. The pan-fried cakes were mildest because the least amount of the fat oxidized. In sum: Fish shouldn't smell "fishy" when raw; if it does, don't buy it. And for the mildest flavor, cook salmon and other fatty fish as briefly as possible.

TECHNIQUE | 3 EASY STEPS TO CRISPY SALMON CAKES

1. CHOP INTO PIECES Hand-chop fish into 1-inch pieces before adding them to food processor. Any bigger, and you'll end up with some large chunks and some finely ground paste.

2. PULSE INTO BITS To ensure that pieces grind evenly, pulse chopped fish in 3 batches into ¼-inch bits. (Be careful not to overprocess.) Mix with breadcrumb binder and flavorings.

3. COAT Gently coat shaped cakes in coarse panko bread crumbs. Salmon's high concentration of tacky water-soluble proteins glues crumbs to patties without need for egg or flour.

Thai Grilled-Beef Salad

Our goal was to look no further than the supermarket to replicate this salad's complex range of flavors and textures. Along the way, we learned a neat trick for grilling meat.

⇒ BY ANDREW JANJIGIAN ⇐

In winter when I crave Thai food, it's often a rich, coconut milk–based curry or a wok-charred noodle dish. But in the summer months, I'm more tempted by the country's famous salads, particularly the grilled-beef rendition known as *nam tok*. Served warm or at room temperature, this preparation features slices of deeply charred steak tossed with thinly sliced shallots and handfuls of torn mint and cilantro in a bright, bracing dressing. In the best versions, the cuisine's five signature flavor elements—hot, sour, salty, sweet, and bitter—come into balance, making for a light but satisfying dish that's traditionally served with steamed jasmine rice.

I paged through the test kitchen's stack of Thai cookbooks for some nam tok recipes to try and was pleased to find that both the shopping list and the cooking time—about half an hour from start to finish—were very manageable. The most unusual ingredient was toasted rice powder, which I knew would be easy enough to make at home. Still, the salads that I produced in the test kitchen, while not bad, fell short of the versions that I've eaten in good Thai restaurants. Either the dressing's flavors were unbalanced—too sweet, too salty, too sour—or the beef itself didn't boast enough char to give the salad its hallmark smoky, faintly bitter edge. Clearly, I had some tinkering to do.

High-Steaks Decisions

The obvious place to start my testing was with the beef. Surprisingly, the recipes that I consulted were all over the map. Some specified lean cuts like tenderloin, others more marbled choices like skirt

A scoop of rice turns this steak salad into a meal.

steak or New York strip steak. A few recipes called for marinating the meat before grilling; others suggested simply seasoning it with salt and white pepper (a staple ingredient in Thai cuisine). Most of them didn't even specify a grilling method. As a starting point, I built a standard single-level fire—a full chimney's worth of coals spread in an even layer over the kettle—and seared a variety of beef cuts: New York

strip steak, boneless short ribs, tenderloin, and flank steak, each one sprinkled with salt and white pepper. Once each piece had developed a thick, dark crust, I pulled it off the fire, let it rest briefly (to allow the interior juices to be reabsorbed), cut thin slices, and tossed them in a standard dressing of equal parts fresh lime juice and fish sauce, a little sugar, and a thinly sliced Thai chile.

Just as I had expected, the more marbled pieces of beef fared better than the lean tenderloin, which started out woefully bland and ended up overcooked by the time it developed even the barest crust. Flavorwise, any of these fattier cuts would have been a fine choice, but two came with a caveat. Boneless short ribs vary in quality: Some are evenly marbled and ideally shaped, almost like small strip steaks, while others are misshapen and full of interior fat and connective tissue that requires trimming. Meanwhile, New York strip steaks boast good flavor and pleasantly tender chew but don't come cheap. I settled on flank steak. The uniformly shaped, moderately priced slab was also beefy, juicy, and sliced neatly.

Next decision: whether or not to marinate the meat in a mixture of the dressing ingredients. A quick side-by-side test made my decision easy. Since moisture thwarts browning, the crust on the marinated flank steak was markedly thin and pale compared with that on the nonmarinated sample. Besides, once the slices of grilled steak were tossed with the dressing, they were plenty flavorful.

Five Tastes of Thai Grilled-Beef Salad—and One More

One of the keys to this salad is balancing the signature flavor elements of Thai cuisine. In addition to achieving this, we added one more complementary flavor: the earthiness of toasted cayenne and sweet paprika.

HOT
A fresh Thai bird chile creates bright, fruity heat in the dressing.

SOUR
A generous 3 tablespoons of fresh lime juice adds bracing acidity.

SALTY
Derived from salted, fermented fish, pungent fish sauce acts as a rich flavor enhancer.

SWEET
A half teaspoon of sugar tames the dressing's salty-sour flavors without becoming cloying.

BITTER
Thoroughly charred steak adds both a pleasing textural contrast and a subtle bitter edge.

EARTHY
Though nontraditional, ground cayenne and sweet paprika add earthy flavor without too much heat.

Falling Water

With the cut of meat decided, I could now focus my attention on the grilling method. The single-level fire had produced decently charred results, but for this salad, the contrast of a crisp, smoky, faintly bitter crust and a juicy center was a must, and I knew I could do better. To get a true blaze going, I turned to the test kitchen's favorite high-heat grill method: a modified two-level fire, in which all the coals are concentrated in an even layer over half of the grill. This way, the meat's exterior would caramelize almost on contact and would cook more rapidly, ensuring that the interior would stay medium-rare.

The recipes that I consulted may have been vague about the fire setup, but they did offer one grilling pointer: As the steak cooks, beads of moisture will appear on its surface—an indication that the meat is ready to be flipped. In fact, the dish is named for this visual cue; "nam tok" translates as "water falling." Grateful for the cue, I flipped the meat as soon as beads of moisture showed up, let it sear another five minutes on the second side, and pulled it off the grill. To my delight, this steak was not only perfectly charred on the exterior, but also spot-on medium-rare within. (For more information on the topic, see "Unbeadable Thai Trick: Knowing When to Flip.")

Well Dressed

With perfectly grilled and subtly, satisfyingly bitter meat in hand, I moved back indoors to address the other four flavor elements: hot, sour, salty, and sweet. Everyone agreed that my initial dressing needed some tweaking—a bit more sweetness, a more balanced (and less heady) salty-sour punch, and more complex heat. The first two requests were easy to fix: I quickly landed on a 2:3 ratio of fish sauce to lime juice, plus ½ teaspoon of sugar and 2 tablespoons of water to tone it all down a touch. But the chile situation required a bit more attention. A fresh chile was a given, and I'd been using a Thai bird chile; when sliced thin and tossed with the other vegetable components, it adds a fruity, fiery blaze to each bite. So why did something still seem to be missing? I found the answer in a recipe from Thai cuisine guru David Thompson: His grilled-beef salad calls for not only fresh Thai bird chile, but also a toasted powder made from the dried pods.

Hoping that regular old cayenne powder toasted in a skillet would suffice, I compared its effects on the salad with that of a powder made with ground, toasted chiles following Thompson's instructions. The consensus was unanimous: The powder made from the dried Thai bird chiles added a deeper, earthier complexity than the hotter, more one-dimensional cayenne. Just ½ teaspoon of cayenne, in fact, overpowered the meat's smoky char. I was about to resign myself to the extra step of grinding my own powder when I spied a jar of sweet paprika in the spice cabinet. Could this give me the earthy, fruity red pepper flavor that was missing from the cayenne? As it turned out, a 50-50 mix of cayenne

and paprika did the trick. I added just a dash of the toasted spice mixture to the dressing and put the rest aside as a seasoning for those who wanted to kick up the heat another notch.

The other condiment that I had to address was the *kao kua*, or toasted rice powder. These days most Thai recipes call for the commercially made product, but it can be hard to find. It was simple enough to make my own by toasting rice in a dry skillet and pulverizing it in a spice grinder. Tossing half of the powder with the salad components gave the dressing fuller body, while sprinkling on the rest at the table added faint but satisfying crunch.

As for the vegetable components, it was really a matter of personal taste. Some salads called for incorporating only the requisite sliced shallots and torn mint leaves and cilantro, while others required adding green beans, cabbage, cucumbers, and lettuce. My tasters and I agreed that any accoutrements should complement—not compete with—the grilled beef. We settled on just one extra: a thin-sliced cucumber, which contributed a cool crispness to this nicely balanced, complexly flavored Thai classic.

THAI GRILLED-BEEF SALAD
SERVES 4 TO 6

Serve with steamed jasmine rice, if desired, although any style of white rice can be used. Don't skip the toasted rice; it's integral to the texture and flavor of the dish. If a fresh Thai chile is unavailable, substitute half of a serrano chile.

- 1 teaspoon sweet paprika
- 1 teaspoon cayenne pepper
- 1 tablespoon white rice
- 3 tablespoons lime juice (2 limes)
- 2 tablespoons fish sauce
- 2 tablespoons water
- ½ teaspoon sugar
- 1 (1½-pound) flank steak, trimmed
  Salt and white pepper, coarsely ground
- 4 shallots, sliced thin
- 1½ cups fresh mint leaves, torn
- 1½ cups fresh cilantro leaves
- 1 Thai chile, stemmed and sliced thin into rounds
- 1 seedless English cucumber, sliced ¼ inch thick on bias

1. Heat paprika and cayenne in 8-inch skillet over medium heat; cook, shaking pan, until fragrant, about 1 minute. Transfer to small bowl. Return now-empty skillet to medium-high heat, add rice, and toast, stirring frequently, until deep golden brown, about 5 minutes. Transfer to second small bowl and cool for 5 minutes. Grind rice with spice grinder, mini food processor, or mortar and pestle until it resembles fine meal, 10 to 30 seconds (you should have about 1 tablespoon rice powder).

2. Whisk lime juice, fish sauce, water, sugar, and ¼ teaspoon toasted paprika mixture in large bowl and set aside.

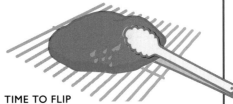
3A. FOR A CHARCOAL GRILL: Open bottom vent completely. Light large chimney starter filled with charcoal briquettes (6 quarts). When top coals are partially covered with ash, pour evenly over half of grill. Set cooking grate in place, cover, and open lid vent completely. Heat grill until hot, about 5 minutes.

3B. FOR A GAS GRILL: Turn all burners to high, cover, and heat grill until hot, about 15 minutes. Leave primary burner on high and turn off other burner(s).

4. Clean and oil cooking grate. Season steak with salt and white pepper. Place steak over hot part of grill and cook until beginning to char and beads of moisture appear on outer edges of meat, 5 to 6 minutes. Flip steak and continue to cook on second side until charred and center registers 125 degrees, about 5 minutes longer. Transfer to plate, tent loosely with aluminum foil, and let rest for 5 to 10 minutes (or allow to cool to room temperature, about 1 hour).

5. Slice meat, against grain, on bias into ¼-inch-thick slices. Transfer sliced steak to bowl with fish sauce mixture. Add shallots, mint, cilantro, chile, and half of rice powder; toss to combine. Transfer to platter lined with cucumber slices. Serve, passing remaining rice powder and toasted paprika mixture separately.

Lighter Corn Chowder

Usually awash in a glut of dairy, sweet corn doesn't stand a chance in this classic summer soup. So we put the squeeze on the traditional approach.

≥ BY DAVID PAZMIÑO ≤

I'm all for the simplicity of eating sweet summer corn straight from the cob, but sometimes I have a bumper crop of ears and need a good corn chowder recipe. I can't say I've ever made a really bad version, but I've never made a great one either. Usually, the results are excessively rich—and while I enjoy cream-based chowders as much as the next New Englander, too much dairy can muddle the bottom line: fresh corn flavor. My ideal version? A simple but substantial soup that lets the kernels' crisp sweetness stand out against a creamy (not stodgy) backdrop seasoned with bits of pork, aromatic vegetables, and fresh herbs.

The most promising recipe I tried was pretty traditional: The cobs were stripped of their kernels and "milked" with the back of a knife to extract all their pulp and juices; chopped onion was sautéed in rendered salt pork fat to build a flavor base, followed by a touch of flour for thickening; liquid—a combination of chicken broth and milk—was added along with cubed red potatoes, herbs, and the corn pulp. Once the potatoes were tender, in went the kernels and a big glug of heavy cream just before serving. My tasters and I decided that, besides the almost undetectable pork, the key flavor elements were generally there, but given the weakness of the corn flavor, the proportions were clearly way off.

The pork problem was easily fixed. Salt pork may have been the go-to for early chowder recipes, but over time it has evolved from a meaty slab often cut from portions other than the belly to the muscle-streaked pieces of fat available today. Instead, I used bacon for its subtle sweet smokiness, adding it to the pot along with the onion and a pat of butter to keep it from browning and overwhelming the other elements.

As for the corn, I looked over the ingredient list and pinpointed the one component I knew was dulling its flavor: the dairy. I started dialing back on both the milk and the heavy cream until I had traded them for water and a mere cup of half-and-half, respectively. The results? Still plenty rich with much clearer corn flavor—but not fresh and sweet enough for a soup made with peak-season produce. Plus, without the cream, the broth lacked body. Adding more flour would have thickened things up a little, but not without undoing my flavor-boosting efforts.

As I thought more about the consistency problem, I realized that adding extra starch wasn't necessary. I already had all the thickening power I needed right in the pot with the potatoes. The trick would be to treat this chowder like other hearty soups and puree a portion of it in a blender. Sure enough, this method worked beautifully; when I poured the pureed portion back into the pot and gave the contents a stir, I had exactly the fluid yet spoon-coating results I was hoping for. But the nutty, sweet corn flavor I was after was still a work in progress.

Looking for other opportunities to highlight the corn, I scanned my recipe again and stopped at the chicken broth. What if I swapped this for a homemade corn broth, as some recipes suggest? I tried—but with little success. Simmering the denuded cobs and husks in water didn't produce anything better than chowder made with plain water. There was only one outlier technique that looked intriguing: "juicing" the corn pulp and adding the flavorful liquid to a water base. I admit, I balked at the idea at first, but I couldn't ignore its potential. So I stripped the kernels and milked the cobs as I had been doing, but instead of adding the pulp (2 cups or so) straight to the pot, I wrapped it in a clean kitchen towel, squeezed out every last bit of liquid into a bowl, and discarded the solids. When I measured the output, I had about ⅔ cup of "*jus*," which I stirred into the chowder just before serving to preserve its fresh sweetness. That did it. When my tasters slurped up this batch and reached for seconds, I knew that shot of pure corn extract was worth the trouble. With one final flourish—a small handful of chopped basil leaves sprinkled over the top—I had a chowder every bit as fresh and sweet as corn straight from the cob.

Strip It Off

To make chowder with fresh, sweet corn flavor, we first needed to remove the kernels from the cob. This can be done by running a sharp chef's knife down the length of the ear, but a good corn stripper can make the job easier and safer. Our favorite model, the OXO Good Grips Corn Stripper ($12.99), resembles a computer mouse and cleanly cuts several rows of kernels at a time as you run its oval body along the cob; even better, it deposits the kernels into an attached cup instead of all over your counter.

OXO GOOD GRIPS CORN STRIPPER

CORN CHOWDER
SERVES 6

Be careful to remove only the part of the corn kernel sticking out of the cob; cutting deeper will pull off fibrous material. Yukon Gold potatoes can be substituted for the red potatoes, minced chives for the basil. Depending on the sweetness of your corn, the finished chowder may need to be seasoned with sugar.

- 8 ears corn, husks and silk removed
- 3 tablespoons unsalted butter
- 1 onion, chopped fine
- 4 slices bacon, halved lengthwise, then cut crosswise into ¼-inch pieces
- 2 teaspoons minced fresh thyme
  Salt and pepper
- ¼ cup all-purpose flour
- 5 cups water
- ¾ pound red potatoes, cut into ½-inch pieces
- 1 cup half-and-half
  Sugar
- 3 tablespoons chopped fresh basil

1. Using chef's knife or corn stripper, cut kernels from corn; transfer to bowl and set aside (you should have 5 to 6 cups kernels). Holding cobs over second bowl, use back of butter knife to firmly scrape any remaining pulp on cobs into bowl (you should have 2 to 2½ cups pulp). Transfer pulp to center of clean kitchen towel set in medium bowl. Wrap towel tightly around pulp and squeeze tightly until dry. Discard pulp in towel and set corn juice aside (you should have about ⅔ cup juice).

2. Melt butter in Dutch oven over medium heat; add onion, bacon, thyme, 2 teaspoons salt, and 1 teaspoon pepper; cook, stirring frequently, until onion is softened and edges are beginning to brown, 8 to 10 minutes. Stir in flour and cook, stirring constantly, for 2 minutes. Whisking constantly, gradually add water and bring to boil. Add corn kernels and potatoes. Return to simmer; reduce heat to medium-low and cook until potatoes have softened, 15 to 18 minutes.

3. Process 2 cups chowder in blender until smooth, 1 to 2 minutes. Return puree to chowder; add half-and-half and return to simmer. Remove pot from heat and stir in reserved corn juice. Season to taste with salt, pepper, and up to 1 tablespoon sugar. Serve, sprinkling with basil.

Crisp Cucumber Salad

A watery salad is usually a given when cucumbers are in the mix. But what if, instead of trying to get rid of the excess liquid, we used it to our advantage?

≥ BY YVONNE RUPERTI ≤

A crisp, cool cucumber salad would be the ideal accompaniment to any hot-off-the-grill entrée if the typical recipe didn't result in soggy disks awash in an insipid dressing. The problem: Cucumbers are full of water. While all that moisture gives cucumber its fresh, clean bite, liquid begins to seep out as soon as the vegetable is cut, diluting the dressing almost as soon as the two come together.

Some recipes address this issue by salting the cucumbers and leaving them to drain before tossing them with dressing. The only dilemma? That process takes at least an hour and leaves the cucumbers slightly wilted. I found that I could get rid of some of the liquid with almost no added time by draining the slices on paper towels while I mixed the dressing, but this didn't entirely solve the problem. Could I do more?

I knew the variety of cucumber I chose would also affect the crispness of the salad. In past tests, we've found that common American cucumbers have more crunch than their seedless English cousins. While all cucumbers contain a "softening" enzyme that's activated when the vegetable is cut, breaking down its cell walls, the cell structure of the English variety is naturally weaker and thus collapses more easily

The cuke choice settled, I moved on to how I might compensate for the dressing's inevitable dilution. I tried doubling and even tripling the amount of dressing to lessen the impact of the cucumber water, but all that soupy liquid at the bottom of the bowl was unappealing. What if instead of trying to mask the excess liquid, I worked with it? For my next batch I tossed the cucumbers with an ultra-potent dressing made with 3 tablespoons of vinegar and just 2 teaspoons of oil. This latest batch was better, if a bit harsh. Could I do better?

I recalled a recipe that concentrated and smoothed out the flavor of the dressing by reducing the vinegar. I did the same: I boiled ½ cup of vinegar until it measured 3 tablespoons; let it cool for about 10 minutes; mixed it with oil, a little salt and sugar, and the cucumbers; and let the salad stand for a few minutes—just long enough for the cucumbers to shed some of their liquid into the dressing. But curiously, instead of tasting more concentrated, the flavor of the dressing had flattened out. It turns out that heating vinegar drives off some of the acetic acid that gives it its tartness, and boiling is the most detrimental way to heat it, driving off many of its other flavors. Our science editor suggested that gently simmering the vinegar might preserve more of its

character while still mellowing its sharp bite. I gave it a whirl, this time reducing the ½ cup of vinegar over medium-low heat for about five minutes and then proceeding with my recipe. The results were remarkably improved. The dressing now had a concentrated depth that could hold up to an influx of water.

But all was still not perfect. I found I actually missed some of the brightness of the uncooked dressing. Adding back even a little raw vinegar would only result in the harshness I was trying to avoid, so I swapped in another, rounder-flavored source of acid: lemon juice. I cut the reduced vinegar to 2 tablespoons (⅓ cup before reducing) and added 1 tablespoon of fresh lemon juice, which punched up the flavors without oversharpening the acidity.

My tasters' only outstanding complaint was that the ¼-inch-thick slices of cucumber were a bit chunky and didn't allow enough dressing to cling to them. I sliced the cucumbers very thin (⅛ inch to 3⁄16 inch) so each piece would be coated in plenty of vinaigrette.

All my salad needed now was some jazzing up. Clean-tasting cucumbers take well to bolder elements, so I added parsley and oregano, kalamata olives, and a handful of chopped almonds to one version and fresh chiles, mint, and basil to another. With salads this good, why even wait for summer?

CUCUMBER SALAD WITH OLIVES, OREGANO, AND ALMONDS
SERVES 4 TO 6

This salad is best served within one hour of being dressed. For our free recipes for Cucumber Salad with Jalapeño, Cilantro, and Pepitas and Cucumber Salad with Ginger, Sesame, and Scallion, go to www.CooksIllustrated.com/aug11.

4	cucumbers, peeled, halved lengthwise, seeded, and sliced very thin
⅓	cup white wine vinegar
1	tablespoon lemon juice
2	teaspoons extra-virgin olive oil
1½	teaspoons sugar
1	teaspoon salt
⅛	teaspoon pepper
½	cup pitted kalamata olives, chopped coarse
1	shallot, sliced very thin
½	cup chopped fresh parsley
1	teaspoon minced fresh oregano
3	tablespoons sliced almonds, toasted and chopped coarse

Thin-slicing the cucumbers allows plenty of flavorful dressing to cling to them.

1. Evenly spread cucumber slices on paper towel–lined baking sheet. Refrigerate while preparing dressing.

2. Bring vinegar to simmer in saucepan over medium-low heat; cook until reduced to 2 tablespoons, 4 to 6 minutes. Transfer vinegar to bowl and set aside to cool to room temperature, about 10 minutes. Whisk in lemon juice, oil, sugar, salt, and pepper.

3. When ready to serve, add cucumbers, olives, shallot, parsley, and oregano to dressing and toss to combine. Let stand for 5 minutes; retoss, sprinkle with almonds, and serve.

CUCUMBER SALAD WITH CHILE, MINT, AND BASIL

Substitute lime juice for lemon juice and vegetable oil for olive oil. Omit pepper and increase sugar to 2 teaspoons. Add 1 tablespoon fish sauce and 2 seeded and minced Thai chiles to dressing in step 2. Substitute ¼ cup chopped mint and ¼ cup chopped basil for parsley and ¼ cup coarsely chopped toasted peanuts for almonds. Omit olives, shallot, and oregano.

Essential Guide to Grilling Vegetables

Why heat up your kitchen to cook vegetables when you can get crisp-tender texture and deep, smoky char from your grill? Here are our proven methods for getting the best results.

BY KEITH DRESSER

14 FAVORITE PICKS THAT DON'T REQUIRE PRECOOKING

ASPARAGUS

Prep: Snap off tough ends by holding asparagus halfway down stalk with one hand, then bend bottom half of stalk with other hand until it breaks.

Cook Time: 5 to 7 minutes, turning once

Test Kitchen Tip: Pencil-thin asparagus will wither in the heat, while bulky specimens will burn before they cook through. If possible, purchase ½-inch-thick spears.

BABY BOK CHOY

Prep: Halve head through stem; rinse but don't dry.

Cook Time: 6 to 7 minutes, turning once

Test Kitchen Tip: Water left clinging to the leaves will turn to steam on the grill, helping the bok choy cook evenly.

CORN

Prep: Remove all but innermost layer of husk; snip off silk.

Cook Time: 8 to 10 minutes, turning every 1½ to 2 minutes

Test Kitchen Tip: By leaving the innermost layer of husk attached, the corn takes on good grilled flavor without charring and becoming tough.

EGGPLANT

Prep: Slice crosswise into ¾-inch rounds.

Cook Time: 8 to 10 minutes, turning once

Test Kitchen Tip: There's no need to salt eggplant destined for the grill. The intense heat will vaporize excess moisture.

ENDIVE

Prep: Halve lengthwise through core.

Cook Time: 5 to 7 minutes, turning once

Test Kitchen Tip: Keeping the core intact helps the leaves stay together for easy turning.

FENNEL

Prep: Trim fronds and cut thin slice from base. Cut bulb vertically through base into ¼-inch-thick slices, leaving core intact.

Cook Time: 7 to 9 minutes, turning once

Test Kitchen Tip: Cover the fennel with an overturned aluminum pan while charcoal grilling to create an oven-like environment that cooks the interiors before the outside burns. (For gas grills, just use the lid.)

GREEN BEANS

Prep: Rinse but don't dry.

Cook Time: 6 minutes, turning once

Test Kitchen Tip: Green beans (choose thick, mature specimens) are the one vegetable for which a grill pan is a must-have.

MUSHROOMS

Prep: For portobellos, wipe caps clean and snap off stems; for button and cremini, skewer through cap and stem so they are less likely to rotate when flipped.

Cook Time: For portobellos, 8 to 10 minutes, turning once; for button and cremini, 8 to 12 minutes, turning every 3 minutes

Test Kitchen Tip: To keep mushrooms from becoming dry and leathery, brush liberally with oil before grilling.

ONIONS

Prep: Cut into ½-inch-thick slices parallel to equator; skewer parallel to work surface.

Cook Time: 10 to 12 minutes, turning once

Test Kitchen Tip: It's awkward to flip a skewer by the rounded "handle." Instead, grasp a centrally located onion slice with tongs and turn.

PEPPERS

Prep: Halve lengthwise; remove core, seeds, and ribs. Cut each half in thirds lengthwise.

Cook Time: 7 to 9 minutes, turning once

Test Kitchen Tip: To grill-roast peppers, cook them whole until charred, transfer them to a bowl, and cover them with plastic wrap to loosen their skins. Then remove their skins, core, and seeds.

RADICCHIO

Prep: Cut head into 4 equal wedges.

Cook Time: 4 to 5 minutes, turning every 1½ minutes

Test Kitchen Tip: For maximum grill flavor, turn each wedge twice so that each side (including the rounded one) spends some time facing the fire.

SCALLIONS

Prep: Trim off root end and discard any loose or wilted outer leaves.

Cook Time: 4 to 5 minutes, turning once

Test Kitchen Tip: To achieve a well-charred exterior and a tender interior, use scallions that are at least ¼ inch in diameter.

TOMATOES

Prep: For round and plum, halve cored tomato along equator. Squeeze gently and shake out seeds. For cherry, thread onto skewers through stem end of fruit.

Cook Time: For round and plum, 4 to 5 minutes, turning once; for cherry, 3 minutes, turning twice

Test Kitchen Tip: Start round and plum tomatoes skin side up to maximize charring.

ZUCCHINI/SUMMER SQUASH

Prep: Slice lengthwise into ½-inch-thick planks.

Cook Time: 8 to 10 minutes, turning once

Test Kitchen Tip: Cutting the squash into planks keeps it from falling through the grates and maximizes moisture evaporation.

TOP 5 VEGETABLE GRILLING PRINCIPLES

1. BUILD A MEDIUM-HOT FIRE: Most vegetables respond better to moderate heat than to a blazing fire. To test the temperature of your grill, hold your hand 5 inches above the grill grate. You should be able to hold it there for three to four seconds.

2. MAKE THE (RIGHT) CUT: Preparing vegetables for the grill is all about maximizing their surface area to increase flavorful browning, and cutting shapes that discourage them from falling apart or slipping through the grill grates.

3. BRUSH WITH OIL: Applying a thin layer of extra-virgin olive oil to vegetables (except corn) before grilling encourages even browning and helps prevent them from sticking to the grill grates. To contain the mess, lay the vegetables on a sheet pan and use a basting brush. Season with salt and pepper before cooking.

4. GO EASY ON THE CHAR: Browning vegetables is one thing; incinerating them is another. For the best results, keep the pieces moving to avoid hot spots and grill until they're just tender and streaked with grill marks.

5. GRILL MEAT FIRST ON A CHARCOAL GRILL: When grilling vegetables to accompany steak, chicken, or pork, we cook the meat first, while the fire is at its hottest. By the time the meat is done, the heat has subsided a bit and the vegetables can cook at more moderate temperatures while the meat rests. (Note: This plan works equally well on a gas grill, and waiting for the fire to die down is not an issue.)

GET IN GEAR

Most grilling equipment you can do without, but these three well-designed tools make the job much easier.

NORPRO 12-Inch Stainless Steel Skewers
($8.99 for 6 skewers)
Unlike wooden skewers, these thin, metal spears are reusable and won't burn. Plus, their flat (not round) surface prevents food from spinning around the blade during turns.

OXO Good Grips 16-Inch Locking Tongs
($14.99)
While keeping our hands far away from the fire, these long-handled tongs can firmly cup an ear of corn or grasp multiple spears of asparagus in one swoop.

WEBER Professional-Grade Grill Pan
($19.99)
Narrow slits, rather than holes, prevent even thin-cut vegetables from slipping into the coals. The pan's raised sides keep food from sliding off and are easy to grip, even with heavy mitts.

Putting It All Together
Smoky char makes this classic dish even better.

GRILLED VEGETABLE RATATOUILLE
SERVES 6 TO 8

Depending on the size of your grill, you may have to cook the vegetables in multiple batches. When grilling more than one vegetable at a time, be prepared to take each off the grill as it is done cooking.

1	red onion
2	pounds eggplant
1½	pounds zucchini or summer squash
2	bell peppers
1	pound tomatoes
	Extra-virgin olive oil
	Salt and pepper
3	tablespoons sherry vinegar
¼	cup chopped fresh basil
1	tablespoon minced fresh thyme
1	garlic clove, peeled and grated to fine paste on rasp-style grater

1. Prepare vegetables according to instructions on page 16. Brush both sides of vegetables with oil and season with salt and pepper. Whisk ¼ cup oil, vinegar, basil, thyme, and garlic together in large bowl.

2. Grill vegetables over medium-hot fire, turning once, until tender and streaked with grill marks, 10 to 12 minutes for onion, 8 to 10 minutes for eggplant and squash, 7 to 9 minutes for peppers, and 4 to 5 minutes for tomatoes. Remove vegetables from grill as they are done and cool slightly.

3. When cool enough to handle, chop vegetables into ½-inch pieces and add to oil mixture; toss to coat. Season with salt and pepper to taste, and serve warm or at room temperature.

Perfect Scrambled Eggs

The classic low-heat approach will never give you tender scrambled eggs with big, pillowy curds. But you've got to do more than just turn up the heat.

> BY DAN SOUZA <

I take pains with just about everything I cook, but not scrambled eggs. Usually my goal is just to get them on the table, fast. My method, such as it is, goes something like this: Whisk eggs, add a splash of milk, pour the mixture into a hot skillet, and stir over medium-high heat until the eggs puff up into large, moist curds. Trouble is, that's not what usually happens. All it takes is the merest distraction for my eggs to go from glossy, fluffy, and wobbly to tough, dry slabs. But even when I take my time and gently stir the eggs over lower heat, I still don't get the results I want. Instead, I end up with spoon food: curds so pebbly and fine that the mixture looks like oatmeal.

It was time to get serious, to stop leaving everything to chance and nail down an approach to foolproof, fluffy, tender scrambled eggs.

Of Eggs and Bondage

I did a little investigation into the science of cooking eggs, and the first thing I discovered was that to produce the ideal voluptuous curds, my slapdash approach over higher heat wasn't far off. Only relatively high heat will produce enough steam (from the dairy and the water in eggs) to puff up the scramble. As the proteins in the eggs continue to heat, they unfold and then bond together to form a latticed gel in a process known as coagulation. The texture of the eggs depends on exactly how much unfolding and bonding occurs. To create moist curds, I needed the egg proteins to bond enough to transform from a liquid into a semisolid, but not so much that they seized up into a tough mass. Fortunately, I could

Extra yolks give these tender, fluffy curds exceptionally rich flavor.

fall back on some lessons learned in the test kitchen over the years to address this problem.

Lesson one: Adding salt to the raw eggs makes for more-tender curds. In the same way that soaking a piece of pork in a brine solution tenderizes its protein network, salt dissolves egg proteins so that they are unable to bond as tightly when cooked.

Lesson two: Don't overbeat the eggs or you'll have a tough scramble. This may seem counterintuitive (since physical agitation usually destroys structure), but the principle is easily illustrated by what happens when you whip egg whites into peaks. Vigorous whisking unfolds proteins in much the same way that heat does; once unfolded, the protein strands readily bond together to form a tighter structure. Since the last thing you want to do is accelerate the unfolding process before the eggs hit the heat, beat them until just combined with the gentler action of a fork rather than a whisk.

The Dairy Godmother

I kept those points in mind as I assumed the role of short-order cook, whipping up batch after batch of scrambled eggs to see how the other major component in the mix—dairy—affected the texture. Some of the recipes I consulted called for milk, others for half-and-half or heavy cream, but all three options contain two important tenderizers: water and fat. What I needed to know was how the water-to-fat ratio in each would affect coagulation; I also needed to know exactly how dairy-rich my tasters liked their eggs.

To feed four people, I beat eight eggs with both salt and pepper and varying proportions of all three dairy options; poured the eggs into a medium-hot, butter-slicked 12-inch skillet; and dragged a heatproof rubber spatula around the pan for about two minutes, until the eggs appeared clumpy but still shiny and wet. My tasters and I mulled over the pros and cons of each dairy ingredient. Milk produced slightly fluffier, cleaner-tasting curds, but they were particularly prone to weeping. Heavy cream, on the other hand, rendered the eggs very stable but dense, and some tasters found their flavor just too rich. One-quarter cup of half-and-half fared best: Though everyone agreed that these curds could stand to be fluffier, they were decently puffed and stable thanks to the tandem effects of the liquid's water and fat.

The benefits of the dairy are threefold: First, the water it contains (80 percent in half-and-half) interrupts the protein network and dilutes the molecules, thereby raising the temperature at which eggs coagulate and providing a greater safety net against overcooking (and disproving the classic French theory that adding the dairy at the end of cooking is best). Second, as the water in the dairy vaporizes, it provides lift (just as in a loaf of baking bread), which causes the eggs to puff up. And third, the fat in the dairy also raises the coagulation temperature by coating and insulating part of each protein molecule so that they cannot stick together as tightly.

Half-and-half wasn't a perfect solution, however: Some tasters still found the dairy flavor too prominent. Less dairy would only make the recipe less foolproof, so I researched ways to boost egg flavor. The best suggestion came from a colleague. She

TECHNIQUE | TURN IT DOWN

When your spatula just leaves a trail through the eggs, that's your cue in our dual-heat method to turn the dial from medium-high to low.

mentioned that when her grandmother makes fresh pasta, she adds an extra yolk or two to the dough to approximate the richer flavor of farm-fresh eggs. I followed suit, and sure enough, the more yolks I added to the mix, the richer the results. There was no need to overdo it, though: Two yolks per eight eggs balanced the flavor nicely. Even better, the high proportion of fat and emulsifiers in the yolks further raised the coagulation temperature, helping to stave off overcooking.

Before I moved on to fine-tune the cooking method, I tried a couple of unconventional stir-ins that promised either fluffier or more tender eggs: vinegar and baking powder. The acidity in the former tenderized the eggs in much the same way that salt did but far more drastically: Just a drop rendered the curds mushy. A dash of baking powder was also too much of a good thing, puffing the eggs like a diner-style omelet as well as imparting a chemical aftertaste.

I also experimented with the advice of old-school French cookbooks to start with room-temperature eggs. While we've proved that egg temperature can influence the structure of some delicate cakes, I found that cold eggs and room-temperature eggs produced virtually identical scrambles.

So much for "secret weapons." It was time to face the fire.

Beating the Heat

The bottom line was that no matter how perfectly I balanced the ratios of protein, fat, and water, the scrambled eggs would still fail if they overcooked. Low heat would curb overcooking, but I needed higher heat to produce nicely puffed curds. Suddenly it hit me like a whack with a cast-iron skillet: What if I used both high and low heat?

I mixed up another batch of eggs, tossed a piece of cold butter into the pan, and turned the heat to medium-high. Once the butter was melted but not brown (a cue that a pan is too hot), I added the eggs, constantly scraping the bottom and sides of the skillet to form large curds and prevent any spots from overcooking. As soon as my spatula could just leave

a trail in the pan with minimal raw egg filling in the gap (about two minutes in), I dropped the heat to low and switched to a gentle folding motion to keep from breaking up the large curds. When the eggs looked cooked through but still glossy (about 45 seconds later), I slid them onto a plate to stop the cooking process. To my delight, the results were almost perfect—fluffy and tender, for sure—and the method was far more fail-safe than my high-heat-only attempts.

My tasters' only holdover request? Larger curds, please. I tried scraping a bit less frequently, but while the curds were certainly bigger, they were also overcooked in spots. Stymied, I looked over all the elements in my recipe and realized that there was one component I hadn't addressed: the size of the pan. In theory, my vessel choice mattered more here than in any other recipe, since a smaller skillet would keep the eggs in a thicker layer, thereby trapping more steam and producing heartier curds. Whisking together one more batch of eggs, I put aside my 12-inch skillet and grabbed a 10-inch pan instead, and then proceeded with my recipe. About three minutes later, I had the best batch of scrambled eggs yet: big billowy curds that were perfect with or without a last-minute sprinkle of fresh herbs.

I was finished with slapdash. A simple, foolproof version of my favorite breakfast was finally served.

PERFECT SCRAMBLED EGGS
SERVES 4

It's important to follow visual cues, as pan thickness will affect cooking times. If using an electric stove, heat one burner on low heat and a second on medium-high heat; move the skillet between burners when it's time to adjust the heat. If you don't have half-and-half, substitute 8 teaspoons of whole milk and 4 teaspoons of heavy cream. To dress up the dish, add 2 tablespoons of chopped parsley, chives, basil, or cilantro or 1 tablespoon of dill or tarragon to the eggs after reducing the heat to low.

- 8 large eggs plus 2 large yolks
- ¼ cup half-and-half
  Salt and pepper
- 1 tablespoon unsalted butter, chilled

1. Beat eggs, yolks, half-and-half, ⅜ teaspoon salt, and ¼ teaspoon pepper with fork until eggs are thoroughly combined and color is pure yellow; do not overbeat.

Unscrambling Perfect Scrambled Eggs

To get big, fluffy, tender, and rich-tasting curds, we experimented with every element of the process until we nailed the right formula.

8 EGGS PLUS 2 YOLKS
Adding yolks not only enriches the egg flavor, but the extra fat and emulsifiers raise the coagulation temperature to stave off overcooking.

HALF-AND-HALF
Half-and-half offers more rich-flavored fat than milk but also contains enough water to generate the steam necessary to make the eggs puff up.

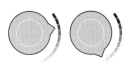

10-INCH SKILLET
Trading the usual 12-inch pan for a smaller 10-inch one keeps the eggs in a thicker layer, thereby trapping more steam and producing heartier curds.

DUAL-HEAT METHOD
Starting the egg mixture over medium-high heat creates puffy curds; turning the heat to low once the eggs coagulate ensures that they won't overcook.

2. Heat butter in 10-inch nonstick skillet over medium-high heat until fully melted (butter should not brown), swirling to coat pan. Add egg mixture and, using rubber spatula, constantly and firmly scrape along bottom and sides of skillet until eggs begin to clump and spatula just leaves trail on bottom of pan, 1½ to 2½ minutes. Reduce heat to low and gently but constantly fold eggs until clumped and just slightly wet, 30 to 60 seconds. Immediately transfer eggs to warmed plates and season with salt to taste. Serve immediately.

PERFECT SCRAMBLED EGGS FOR TWO

Reduce eggs to 4, yolks to 1, half-and-half to 2 tablespoons, and salt and pepper to ⅛ teaspoon each. In step 2, reduce butter to ½ tablespoon. Cook eggs in 8-inch skillet for 45 to 75 seconds over medium-high heat, then for 30 to 60 seconds over low heat.

PERFECT SCRAMBLED EGGS FOR ONE

Reduce eggs to 2, yolks to 1, half-and-half to 1 tablespoon, and salt and pepper to pinch each. In step 2, reduce butter to ¼ tablespoon. Cook eggs in 8-inch skillet for 30 to 60 seconds over medium-high heat, then for 30 to 60 seconds over low heat.

Dual-Heat Method in Action
Video available FREE for 4 months at www.CooksIllustrated.com/aug11

Really Good Panzanella

The biggest challenge in making this classic Italian tomato-bread salad is solving an age-old quandary: What's the best way to deal with the bread?

≥ BY RACHEL TOOMEY KELSEY ≤

Ripe summer tomatoes require nothing more than to be sliced, drizzled with fruity extra-virgin olive oil, and sprinkled with sea salt and fresh pepper. But when I need a side dish that's a little more substantial, I'm often tempted by panzanella, the rustic Italian tomato-bread salad in which the fruit is cut into chunks, tossed with bread pieces, and dressed with olive oil and vinegar. When done well, the tomatoes give up some of their sweet juice, which mixes with the tangy dressing and moistens the dry bread until it's soft and just a little chewy.

In my experience, the line between lightly moistened and unpleasantly soggy is very thin, even when I start with a good-quality bakery loaf. This summer I was determined to aim higher. Besides using ripe, juicy tomatoes (nothing but farmers' market–quality specimens would do), I'd get the bread just right: a thick-crusted loaf cut into chunks and moderately soaked—not drenched—with a bright vinaigrette.

Like many other peasant dishes, panzanella started out as a way to make use of day-old bread. But in the test kitchen, we've stopped cooking with naturally stale bread. Instead, we prefer to cut up a fresh loaf and "quick-stale" the pieces by drying them in a low oven. Here's why: As bread stales naturally, its starch molecules recrystallize in a process called retrogradation, causing the bread to become hard and crumbly but not necessarily dry. Oven-dried bread, on the other hand, loses a fair bit of moisture, thereby enhancing its ability to soak up any added liquid.

I cobbled together a working recipe by cutting a rustic loaf into bite-size (1-inch) pieces, tossing them with a little olive oil and salt, spreading them in an even layer on a baking sheet, and sliding the tray into a 225-degree oven. After about 15 minutes, I took the bread out of the oven, let it cool, and then combined it with the tomato chunks and a 2:1 ratio of olive oil to red wine vinegar. The results? Not bad, but not stellar. The bread was a little dry and unevenly moistened, and the whole thing tasted a smidge flat. Plus, the salad didn't meld together as a whole: The bread and tomatoes seemed like two separate components occupying the same bowl.

Leaving the bread alone for the moment, I switched

Toasted—not stale—bread is a key to this dish.

gears to focus on the tomatoes. Since not enough of the juice from the ripe, sweet fruit was making it into the bread, maybe it would work better if I removed some of the juice first and added it directly to the salad. I tossed the cut-up tomatoes with ½ teaspoon of salt and set them in a colander to drain. Fifteen minutes later, they'd shed a good bit of juice into which I whisked the oil and vinegar. I added the bread and tomatoes and summoned my colleagues for a tasting. Everyone agreed that the bread still hadn't absorbed much of the dressing's flavor.

Reviewing my research, I remembered that the traditional approach to panzanella calls for giving the bread a lengthy soak in water before tossing it with the other ingredients—a frugal step that meant cooks didn't have to rely as much on tomatoes and olive oil to moisten the stale loaf. I wasn't about to dilute the flavor of the bread with water, but what if I gave it a few extra minutes in the dressing before adding the other components? I mixed up the dressing, added the bread, and let it soak for about 10 minutes before stirring in the tomatoes. My tasters said that the bread was now perfectly moistened, but they clamored for just a bit more flavor from the bread itself.

When making bruschetta, I always toast the bread first, since browning brings out fuller flavor. Figuring that the technique would translate here, I cranked up the oven to 400 degrees and baked the bread until it turned light golden brown before proceeding with my recipe. This was the winning batch: The browned bread pieces were nutty-tasting and lightly saturated with the flavorful dressing.

Now for the finishing touches. Thinly sliced cucumber and shallot made the cut for their crunch and fresh bite, as did chopped basil. And because I knew that this salad would become a staple, I whipped up a version with sweet red bell pepper and spicy arugula.

ITALIAN BREAD SALAD (PANZANELLA)
SERVES 4

The success of this recipe depends on ripe, in-season tomatoes and a fruity, high-quality olive oil (the test kitchen prefers Columela Extra-Virgin). For our free recipes for Italian Bread Salad with Garlic and Capers and Italian Bread Salad with Olives and Feta, go to www.CooksIllustrated.com/aug11.

- **6** cups rustic Italian or French bread, cut or torn into 1-inch pieces (½ to 1 pound)
- **½** cup extra-virgin olive oil
  Salt and pepper
- **1½** pounds tomatoes, cored, seeded, and cut into 1-inch pieces
- **3** tablespoons red wine vinegar
- **1** cucumber, peeled, halved lengthwise, seeded, and sliced thin
- **1** shallot, sliced thin
- **¼** cup chopped fresh basil

1. Adjust oven rack to middle position and heat oven to 400 degrees. Toss bread pieces with 2 tablespoons oil and ¼ teaspoon salt; arrange bread in single layer on rimmed baking sheet. Toast bread pieces until just starting to turn light golden, 15 to 20 minutes, stirring halfway through. Set aside to cool to room temperature.

2. Gently toss tomatoes and ½ teaspoon salt in large bowl. Transfer to colander and set over bowl; set aside to drain for 15 minutes, tossing occasionally.

3. Whisk remaining 6 tablespoons oil, vinegar, and ¼ teaspoon pepper into reserved tomato juices. Add bread pieces, toss to coat, and let stand for 10 minutes, tossing occasionally.

4. Add tomatoes, cucumber, shallot, and basil to bowl with bread pieces and toss to coat. Season with salt and pepper to taste, and serve immediately.

ITALIAN BREAD SALAD
WITH RED BELL PEPPER AND ARUGULA

Substitute 1 thinly sliced red bell pepper for cucumber and 1 cup roughly chopped baby arugula for basil.

The Best Vanilla Ice Cream

The main reason more people don't make their own ice cream? It's never as creamy, smooth, or dense as the best stuff from the store. We decided to change that.

⇒ BY DAN SOUZA ⇐

In the five years that I've owned my canister-style ice-cream maker, I'd say that it has produced, optimistically, a mere couple of gallons of ice cream. It's not that I don't love the taste of homemade ice cream—believe me, I do. Rather, it's that the texture of my homemade creations never measures up to the ultra-dense, impossibly smooth "super-premium" ice cream at the grocery store. Instead of thick, dense, and velvety, my results invariably turn out crumbly, fluffy, and icy. And forget about storing homemade ice cream for more than a few hours; an overnight stint in the freezer only amplifies the iciness. Before I decided to sell off my machine at my next yard sale, I wanted to exhaust any lead that might allow me to make ice cream with a texture rivaling the highest quality commercial stuff.

I reviewed what I knew about custard-based ice cream, which typically calls for nothing more than milk, cream, sugar, eggs, and flavorings. Once the custard has frozen, the ice cream is composed of three basic elements: ice crystals of pure water; the proteins, sugars, and fats left behind as the water in the mix is crystallized; and air. The amount of air affects denseness, whereas both the makeup of the custard and how it is frozen contribute to smoothness. I decided to start with a standard custard base and focus first on finding the most effective way to freeze it.

Our super-premium quality ice cream stays dense and creamy for five days.

The Importance of Fast Freezing

Smooth ice cream isn't technically less icy than "icy" ice cream. Instead, its ice crystals are so small that our tongues can't detect them. One way to encourage the creation of small ice crystals is to freeze the ice-cream base as quickly as possible. Fast freezing, along with agitation, causes the formation of thousands of tiny seed crystals, which in turn promote the formation of more tiny crystals. Speed is such an important factor in ice-cream making that commercial producers as well as restaurant kitchens spend tens of thousands of dollars on super-efficient "continuous batch" churners. The best of these can turn a 40-degree custard base (the coldest temperature it can typically achieve in a refrigerated environment) into soft-serve ice cream in 24 seconds, at which point roughly half of the freezable water has crystallized. Even the slowest commercial freezer will get the job done in 10 minutes. To maintain this super-fine ice-crystal structure, the churned ice cream is then transferred to a blast freezer in smaller ice-cream shops or a hardening room in large commercial operations, where the temperature ranges from 20 to 50 degrees below zero. Under these arctic conditions, the remaining freezable water freezes in a matter of minutes.

I took stock of what I was working with: My canister-style machine takes roughly 35 minutes to turn a chilled custard into soft-serve consistency—more than three times as long as the slowest commercial option. Even our favorite self-refrigerating model takes that long. Then, depending on how often the freezer door is opened, the partially frozen custard from either style of machine can take up to eight hours to fully freeze. No wonder my results are always icy.

Since the speed of freezing is critical, I wondered if I could improve my results by starting with a colder base. After letting my hot custard cool for a few minutes, I transferred a cup of it to a small bowl, which I popped into the freezer. I then put the rest of the custard in the fridge to cool overnight, per the usual method. The next day, I scraped the frozen custard into the refrigerated stuff and stirred it until the frozen custard dissolved, at which point the mixture registered

Creating smooth ice cream means cutting back on ice crystals—or preventing them from forming in the first place. We tried a slew of ingredients promising to do just that, most with unfortunate side effects.

NO	NO	NO	YES
Condensed and evaporated milk contribute less water to the mix, leading to fewer ice crystals. But ice cream made from each tasted "cooked."	Cornstarch traps water so it can't form ice crystals, but it produced a "weird," "gummy" texture. Gelatin and pectin bombed, too.	Nonfat dry milk ups the overall milk solids in the custard base, thus blocking ice crystal formation, but it left a "cheesy" flavor.	Some granulated sugar plus corn syrup, which also interferes with crystal formation, made for a super-smooth texture—with no funky side effects.

around 30 degrees. Once in the canister, this base reached soft-serve consistency in just 18 minutes and, tasted straight from the machine, exhibited less iciness than previous batches had. Another bonus of this shortened churning time was that it allowed less air to be beaten into the mix; I needed some air, but too much only diluted the ice cream's flavor and lightened the texture. To my great disappointment, however, after four hours of hardening, this ice cream was almost as icy as before.

With no way to make my freezer colder, it would have seemed that I was out of luck. However, since the rate of cooling is a function of both temperature and surface area, there was still hope. For my next batch, instead of scraping my churned ice cream into a tall container before placing it in the freezer, I spread it into a thin layer in a chilled square metal baking pan (metal conducts heat faster than glass or plastic). In about an hour, my ice cream had firmed up significantly and could be easily scooped and transferred to an airtight container. Its hardening time had been cut significantly, and you could taste the difference—this was my smoothest batch yet.

SCIENCE **Combating Iciness with Corn Syrup**

One key to our ice cream's smoothness was to replace some of the sugar with corn syrup. This sweetener has a twofold effect: First, it is made up of glucose molecules and large tangled chains of starch that interrupt the flow of water molecules in a custard base. Since the water molecules can't move freely, they are less likely to combine and form large crystals as the ice cream freezes. Second, corn syrup creates a higher freezing point in ice cream than granulated sugar does. This makes the ice cream less susceptible to the temperature shifts inevitable in a home freezer. These shifts cause constant thawing and refreezing, which creates crystallization even in the smoothest ice cream. Our ice cream stayed smooth for nearly a week— far longer than most homemade ice creams do.

However, as improved as the ice cream was, it still wasn't as smooth as store-bought. Could the ingredients themselves provide any help?

A Custardy Battle
Playing with the amounts of sugar and fat was out: My tasters felt that the ice cream had optimal sweetness and richness with ¾ cup sugar, 6 egg yolks, and slightly more cream than milk. That left me with trying to manipulate the milk solids and water amounts. Milk solids interfere with the formation of crystals, so the more of them the better (up to a point—too much creates a sandy texture). And since crystals are created from water, the less of it the better (up to a point—too little water leads to gumminess).

A few of the recipes that I came across called for replacing a portion of the milk or cream with condensed or evaporated milk, which contain less water than fresh dairy does. While both products proved effective at reducing iciness, they contributed a "stale" and "cooked" flavor to the ice cream, even in relatively small doses. I also tried stirring in nonfat powdered milk to boost milk solids. Unfortunately, in order to be effective, I needed at least ¼ cup, at which point tasters deemed the ice cream "cheesy" and "funky."

With these options exhausted, I began researching the ingredients in commercial ice cream. Many commercial producers use powerful stabilizer mixes

to immobilize free water in a gel, preventing it from freezing into large ice crystals. I didn't have ready access to these magic powders, but I wondered if I couldn't approximate their effect with something else.

In the test kitchen, we often rely on cornstarch, gelatin, and pectin to provide body to recipes. Though each works slightly differently, I knew that they all thicken by trapping water in a weak gel. To test their effectiveness, I made three custards, adding cornstarch to one, bloomed gelatin to another, and pectin to the third. The ice crystals in all three batches were far less noticeable—in fact, the batch with gelatin was completely smooth. But this easy success came at a price: Each ice cream had an artificial texture and strange melting properties. The sample with gelatin refused to melt, even after 10 minutes at room temperature.

After racking up so many failures, I was tempted to throw in the towel and cede victory to the pros. Instead, I decided to call on a few of them for help.

Expert Advice
I sought advice from two of the Boston area's best-known ice-cream makers: Gus Rancatore of Toscanini's, in nearby Cambridge, and Rick Katz, chef and owner of Pizza and Ice Cream Company, in Boston's South End. Each provided me with a different perspective on ice-cream theory (yes, ice-cream theory is a real thing). But each man circled back to an ingredient that I had all but glossed over in my testing: sugar. I'd stuck with granulated white sugar, without looking further. But ice-cream producers rely on a laundry list of different sweeteners to achieve particular textures and sweetness levels. One highly valued sweetener is invert sugar, a syrup made by cooking sugar water with an acid—a slow, finicky process that converts sucrose into glucose and fructose. With even more molecules than table sugar to interfere with ice formation, invert sugar dramatically lowers the freezing point of the ice-cream mixture so that more of the water remains liquid in

Meet the Makers: Winning Ice-Cream Machines

Our new approach to making ice cream improves the results from each of these winning models.

WHYNTER SNÖ Professional Ice Cream Maker
Price: $219.99
Comments: This self-refrigerating model, our favorite, makes continuous batches of ice cream without the need to freeze a canister. For the smoothest results, we recommend letting the machine run for 5 to 10 minutes to prechill it before adding the custard.

CUISINART Automatic Frozen Yogurt–Ice Cream & Sorbet Maker
Price: $49.95
Comments: For the best results, the canister in this remake of our Best Buy (the old model was discontinued) must be frozen for 24 hours before each use. But given its modest price, you can hardly go wrong.

STEP BY STEP | FOR SUPER–PREMIUM SMOOTHNESS, KEEP IT COLD

Freezing the custard as quickly as possible ensures the formation of small (versus large) ice crystals that are critical to smooth ice cream. Commercial producers use blast freezers or hardening rooms, where the temperature can hover as low as -50 degrees. We resorted to far humbler methods—with surprisingly similar results.

1. REFRIGERATE MOST OF CUSTARD Transfer all but 1 cup cooled custard to large bowl and chill in refrigerator at least 4 hours, until it registers 40 degrees.

2. FREEZE 1 CUP CUSTARD Place remaining 1 cup custard in small bowl and freeze for same amount of time.

3. COMBINE CUSTARDS Scrape frozen custard into chilled custard and stir until fully dissolved; now deeply chilled base registers around 30 degrees.

4. CHURN SUPER-CHILLED BASE Strain custard and churn until ice cream has soft-serve texture and registers about 21 degrees, 15 to 25 minutes.

5. FAST FREEZE Transfer ice cream to chilled metal baking pan, where it will freeze faster than in usual tall container, and freeze until firm around edges, about 1 hour.

6. FULLY FREEZE Transfer ice cream to airtight container, press out air pockets, and freeze until firm, at least 2 hours.

the freezer. While a boon to an ice-cream shop that can hold its product at super-cold temperatures, a depressed freezing point spelled disaster in my home freezer. Even the smoothest ice cream eventually becomes coarse and icy in a home freezer due to inevitable shifts in temperature that cause thawing and refreezing. These temperature shifts have a more dramatic effect on ice creams with a depressed freezing point—they melt much more easily—than they have on ice creams that freeze harder at warmer temperatures. Furthermore, while professionals can buy ready-made invert syrup, I had to make my own—an activity that proved both time-consuming and unreliable. I crossed it off my list, along with two other unobtainable sweeteners: atomized glucose and dextrose powder.

I desperately rummaged through the pantry in search of neutral-tasting alternative sweeteners that I could use. The list was depressingly short: corn syrup. Containing about 25 percent water, corn syrup seemed like the last ingredient that might work in an effort to eliminate large ice crystals. But what did I have to lose?

I mixed up batches of my working recipe, replacing some of the sugar with increasing amounts of corn syrup. Right away, I could tell that something was different. The custard bases were more viscous than my all-sugar recipe straight out of the fridge, and they all churned to a thick, soft-serve consistency in record time. The real revelation, however, came when it was time to taste. The batch with ⅓ cup of corn syrup was the closest thing to super-premium perfection I had ever achieved. Not only was it dense, but, most important, it showed no trace of iciness. Though I was tempted to sit in the kitchen and finish off the rest of the quart, I was too eager to get back to my desk and figure out why this solution had worked so well.

After a few exchanges with our science editor, I had my answer. First, due to its viscosity, corn syrup prevents water molecules from grouping and freezing into large ice crystals. Second, corn syrup doesn't depress the freezing point as much as sugar does. My corn-syrup ice cream froze faster in the canister and remained harder at home-freezer temperatures than did the all-sugar recipe. This stuff was virtually free of large ice crystals, and it stayed that way for nearly a week in my freezer.

After months of churning countless batches of ice cream, I had tasted sweet victory. Another thing I could count on: My ice-cream machine wouldn't be showing up at a yard sale anytime soon.

VANILLA ICE CREAM
MAKES ABOUT 1 QUART

Two teaspoons of vanilla extract can be substituted for the vanilla bean; stir the extract into the cold custard in step 3. An instant-read thermometer is critical for the best results. Using a prechilled metal baking pan and working quickly in step 4 will help prevent melting and refreezing of the ice cream and will speed the hardening process. If using a canister-style ice-cream machine, be sure to freeze the empty canister at least 24 hours and preferably 48 hours before churning. For self-refrigerating ice-cream machines, prechill the canister by running the machine for 5 to 10 minutes before pouring in the custard. For our free recipes for Triple Ginger Ice Cream and Coffee Crunch Ice Cream, go to www.CooksIllustrated.com/aug11.

1	vanilla bean
1¾	cups heavy cream
1¼	cups whole milk
½	cup plus 2 tablespoons sugar
⅓	cup light corn syrup
¼	teaspoon salt
6	large egg yolks

1. Place 8- or 9-inch-square metal baking pan in freezer. Cut vanilla bean in half lengthwise. Using tip of paring knife, scrape out vanilla seeds. Combine vanilla bean, seeds, cream, milk, ¼ cup plus 2 tablespoons sugar, corn syrup, and salt in medium saucepan. Heat over medium-high heat, stirring occasionally, until mixture is steaming steadily and registers 175 degrees, 5 to 10 minutes. Remove saucepan from heat.

2. While cream mixture heats, whisk yolks and remaining ¼ cup sugar in bowl until smooth, about 30 seconds. Slowly whisk 1 cup heated cream mixture into egg yolk mixture. Return mixture to saucepan and cook over medium-low heat, stirring constantly, until mixture thickens and registers 180 degrees, 7 to 14 minutes. Immediately pour custard into large bowl and let cool until no longer steaming, 10 to 20 minutes. Transfer 1 cup custard to small bowl. Cover both bowls with plastic wrap. Place large bowl in refrigerator and small bowl in freezer and cool completely, at least 4 hours and up to 24 hours. (Small bowl of custard will freeze solid.)

3. Remove custards from refrigerator and freezer. Scrape frozen custard from small bowl into large bowl of custard. Stir occasionally until frozen custard has fully dissolved. Strain custard through fine-mesh strainer and transfer to ice-cream machine. Churn until mixture resembles thick soft-serve ice cream and registers about 21 degrees, 15 to 25 minutes. Transfer ice cream to frozen baking pan and press plastic wrap on surface. Return to freezer until firm around edges, about 1 hour.

4. Transfer ice cream to airtight container, pressing firmly to remove any air pockets, and freeze until firm, at least 2 hours. Serve. (Ice cream can be stored for up to 5 days.)

Rescuing Peach Cake

Loading a cake with fresh peaches sounds like a great idea— until the flavor fizzles out and the crumb is drenched in juice.

≥ BY YVONNE RUPERTI ≤

Bakers have been adding fresh peaches to cake for ages, in as many forms as one can dream up. Peach upside-down cake, layer cake stacked with sweet peach filling, and yeasted dough topped with the fruit (known as Baltimore-style peach cake) are a few noteworthy approaches. But the version I like best is the most straightforward, taking its inspiration from the buckle, a classic American pairing of fruit folded into a cake batter or arranged on top of it before baking. The dessert I had in mind would adopt this humble construct and boast plenty of sweet peach flavor.

Little did I know that I'd end up reengineering just about every aspect of the traditional approach to get full fruit flavor without soggy cake.

Juicy Predicament

I ordered a couple of bushels of peaches and got down to business. I mixed together a basic cake batter: White and brown sugar (its caramel taste would pair nicely with peaches), flour, baking powder, and salt went in one bowl; eggs, melted butter, sour cream (for richness), and vanilla extract in another. I stirred the dry ingredients into the wet, folded in two peaches (cut into ½-inch chunks so that they would incorporate easily), scraped the batter into a springform pan for easy serving, and slid it into a 350-degree oven for 60 minutes. My colleagues offered nods of approval as they tucked into the golden-brown, moist, and buttery cake. And yet each bite offered only the mildest suggestion of peach flavor—and I wanted something really fruity.

Accordingly, I whipped up a second cake using four peaches. My dessert was now chock-full of fruit, but it still didn't taste very peachy—and now it was a soggy mess. The peach chunks had settled to the bottom of the pan in a gummy pile, their juices flooding the cake. To achieve the right texture, I would have to remove some peaches.

This cake's fruity flavor comes from fresh peach wedges arranged on top and roasted chunks layered in the batter.

Or would I? In a pie, juicy fruit is kept in check with a thickener, so why not dust the peaches with cornstarch before incorporating them? No go. A cake made with cornstarch-coated fruit still exhibited a horribly sodden crumb. It struck me that instead of trying to thicken the juices, I needed to eliminate them altogether.

Macerating is an effective way to draw juice from fruit, so for my next try I sprinkled the peaches with sugar and let them drain in a colander set over a bowl. After an hour, ¼ cup of juice had dripped out. I poured off the liquid, folded the peaches into the batter, and baked the cake. I took a taste, discovering that while I'd made a small step in the right direction, the cake was still soggy. Would heating the peach-sugar mixture in the microwave expel even more fluid?

I piled the peach chunks into a bowl and zapped them for two minutes. The fruit certainly exuded more juice, but it also turned mushy in spots. Next, I microwaved the chunks in a single layer on a plate, hoping that this would allow for more even cooking. Although this offered some improvement, the peaches still didn't dry out as much as I wanted them to.

Perhaps the oven would be a better option for dehydrating the peaches. I spread the chunks on a baking sheet (lined with aluminum foil spritzed with vegetable oil spray to prevent sticking) and baked them in a 425-degree oven for 20 minutes. When a blast of steam whooshed out as I opened the oven door, I knew I was doing something right. The peaches had softened and shriveled a bit—a clear indication of moisture loss. Once they cooled, I assembled and baked a cake. Finally, the sludgy layer at the base of the dessert had been eliminated. What's more, the sweet flavor of the peaches concentrated during roasting.

There was just one more quandary to deal with: During roasting, the peach chunks became coated in a flavorful but unpleasantly gooey, viscous film. Cornstarch hadn't worked to eliminate watery peach juices, but perhaps a coarser ingredient would sop up this sticky covering. I gently tossed ⅓ cup of crushed

RECIPE DIAGNOSIS Peach Cake Run Amuck

Things aren't all that peachy with most peach cakes.

PROBLEM: Fruit that isn't fruity •
HOW TO SOLVE IT: Macerate peaches Unless you're working with the best farm-stand fruit, peaches are notoriously bland. To boost fruity taste, we macerate the peach wedges we've reserved for shingling on top of the cake in peach schnapps and a little sugar and lemon juice.

PROBLEM: Soggy fruit sinks to bottom •
HOW TO SOLVE IT: Roast peaches Roasting the peach chunks destined for the batter concentrates their flavor and drives off moisture, so there's not as much to weigh them down or to flood the cake.

PROBLEM: Wet, gummy crumb •
HOW TO SOLVE IT: Toss peaches with panko Tossing the roasted peach chunks with bread crumbs helps absorb any remaining sticky juices, ensuring a cake that's moist, not soggy.

panko bread crumbs with the roasted peaches, finding that they clung firmly to the syrup. Fearing that the batter would pull the crumbs off of the peaches if I folded them in, I spooned half of the batter into the pan, arranged the panko-coated peaches on the batter, and then spooned on the remaining batter. Presto. As the cake baked, the panko disappeared into the crumb, taking any trace of sticky, gloppy peach syrup with it.

Just Peachy

The cake was now terrific when made with just-picked peaches, but I wanted to ensure intense peach flavor even when farm-fresh fruit wasn't available. To that end, I considered all of the peach-flavored ingredients I could get my hands on. My first try—swapping peach-flavored yogurt for the sour cream—was ineffectual. I next contemplated adding peach jam, but I'd worked so hard to eliminate gooeyness that introducing a sticky ingredient seemed like a mistake. Chopped dried peaches, although intensely flavored, were too chewy. At last, I hit the jackpot when I spiked the macerating fruit with peach schnapps. The sweet, intense liquor bolstered the flavor of not-so-perfect peaches. Finally, ¼ teaspoon of almond extract (a classic partner with stone fruit) stirred into the batter added a subtle complementary background note.

To make the cake look as good as it tasted, I decked out the top with fanned peach slices and a sprinkling of almond extract–enhanced sugar. As it baked, the sugary fruit caramelized, creating a glazed topping. Now that's one peach of a cake.

SUMMER PEACH CAKE
SERVES 8 TO 10

To crush the panko bread crumbs, place them in a zipper-lock bag and smash them with a rolling pin. If you can't find panko, ¼ cup of plain, unseasoned bread crumbs can be substituted. Orange liqueur can be substituted for the peach schnapps. If using peak-of-season, farm-fresh peaches, omit the peach schnapps.

- 2½ pounds peaches, pitted and cut into ½-inch-thick wedges
- 5 tablespoons peach schnapps
- 4 teaspoons lemon juice
- 6 tablespoons plus ⅓ cup granulated sugar
- 1 cup (5 ounces) all-purpose flour
- 1¼ teaspoons baking powder
- ¾ teaspoon salt
- ½ cup packed (3½ ounces) light brown sugar
- 2 large eggs
- 8 tablespoons unsalted butter, melted and cooled
- ¼ cup sour cream
- 1½ teaspoons vanilla extract
- ¼ teaspoon plus ⅛ teaspoon almond extract
- ⅓ cup panko bread crumbs, crushed fine

1. Adjust oven rack to middle position and heat oven to 425 degrees. Line rimmed baking sheet with aluminum foil and spray with vegetable oil spray. Gently toss 24 peach wedges with 2 tablespoons schnapps, 2 teaspoons lemon juice, and 1 tablespoon granulated sugar in bowl; set aside.

2. Cut remaining peach wedges crosswise into thirds. Gently toss chunks with remaining 3 tablespoons schnapps, remaining 2 teaspoons lemon juice, and 2 tablespoons granulated sugar in bowl. Spread peach chunks in single layer on prepared sheet and bake until exuded juices begin to thicken and caramelize at edges of sheet, 20 to 25 minutes. Transfer sheet to wire rack and let peaches cool to room temperature, about 30 minutes. Reduce oven temperature to 350 degrees.

3. Spray 9-inch springform pan with vegetable oil spray. Whisk flour, baking powder, and salt together in bowl. Whisk brown sugar, ⅓ cup granulated sugar, and eggs together in second bowl until thick and homogeneous, about 45 seconds. Slowly whisk in butter until combined. Add sour cream, vanilla, and ¼ teaspoon almond extract; whisk until combined. Add flour mixture and whisk until just combined.

4. Transfer half of batter to prepared pan; using offset spatula, spread batter evenly to pan edges and smooth surface. Sprinkle crushed bread crumbs evenly over cooled peach chunks and gently toss to coat. Arrange peach chunks on batter in even layer, gently pressing peaches into batter. Gently spread remaining batter over peach chunks and smooth top. Arrange reserved peach wedges, slightly overlapping, in ring over surface of cake, placing smaller wedges in center. Stir together remaining 3 tablespoons granulated sugar and remaining ⅛ teaspoon almond extract in small bowl until sugar is moistened. Sprinkle sugar mixture evenly over top of cake.

5. Bake until center of cake is set and toothpick inserted in center comes out clean, 50 to 60 minutes. Transfer pan to wire rack; cool 5 minutes. Run paring knife around sides of cake to loosen. Remove cake from pan and let cool completely, 2 to 3 hours. Cut into wedges and serve.

EQUIPMENT TESTING Springform Pans

Our favorite springform pan from Frieling ($49.99) features handles and a tempered glass bottom that lets us track browning. But like every other model we've tested, its seal fails to prevent water from trickling in when you place it in a water bath. That drawback has kept us on the lookout for the perfect pan, so we baked cheesecake and Summer Peach Cake in four competitor models ($15 to $48) to see if anything could outclass our old standby.

Unfortunately, not one pan avoided leaking without help (see "Leak-Proofing Springform Pans" on page 30 for our new solution). Hence, our evaluations came down to cake release, evenness of browning, and design.

Nonstick coatings on each model helped the sides release, but the lightest and darkest models produced under- and overbrowned cakes, respectively. We also preferred pans with flat (not rimmed) bases that could double as a serving plate. The Frieling fulfilled all of those requirements and is still our top choice. For complete testing results, go to www.CooksIllustrated.com/aug11. –Amy Graves

TOP PICK

FRIELING Handle-It 9-Inch Glass Bottom Springform Pan

Price: $49.99

Comments: This pricey pan may not be perfect—its seal isn't leakproof—but it boasts plenty of features that make it our two-time favorite: near flawless release; a glass bottom that lets us monitor browning; helper handles; and sturdy, dishwasher-safe parts.

BEST BUY

NORDIC WARE Pro Form 9-Inch Leak-Proof Springform Pan

Price: $15

Comments: Despite its name, this pan allowed water to seep in, just like all the others. While it performed admirably, its nonstick-coated base wasn't as scratch-resistant as the glass-bottomed Frieling, and it didn't release quite as easily as our winner.

PRICEY AND IMPERFECT

KAISER BAKEWARE La Forme Plus Springform Pan, 9 Inch

Price: $48

Comments: For the price, we expected picture-perfect results. Instead, we got a cheesecake with an unsightly seam where the buckle fastened and, thanks to its exceptionally dark coating, a peach cake that overbrowned on the exterior before the middle cooked through.

The Coolest Cooler

The difference between a good cooler and a great one isn't add-ons like cup holders and telescoping handles. The decisive element is much more fundamental: air.

⇒ BY AMY GRAVES ⇐

The first modern cooler, trademarked in 1953 by Richard Laramy of Joliet, Illinois, as a "portable ice chest," was a simple insulated box. Nowadays, coolers are part of just about every American household—but they come in all shapes, sizes, and materials. Bells and whistles range from wheels and telescoping handles to removable dividers and cup holders, and many are made from collapsible fabrics that allow the unit to fold up as small as a gym bag.

Modern innovations aside, we wanted to know how effectively these coolers serve the bottom line: keeping food and drinks cold and securely contained when being hauled to outdoor activities. We surveyed the marketplace and tested five models in varying styles, sizes, and prices, including soft-sided totes, a hard plastic tub, and a $4 Styrofoam box from the supermarket. (In a separate testing, just to see what all the fuss was about, we splurged on two thermoelectric units that cost roughly 35 times the price of the Styrofoam model. See "It's Electric!")

The Big Chill

At the very least, a cooler should keep its contents as cold as they were when they went into the box for several hours on a hot day. But could any of these coolers take it one step further and cool down items that were not perfectly chilled to begin with? We loaded up each model with 45-degree sodas (by most people's standards they weren't yet cool enough to drink) and ice packs (1 pound for every 2 quarts of cooler capacity, per the manufacturers' instructions) and placed them in a stuffy room that we cranked to 95 degrees. We cracked open a can from each cooler every hour for four hours and stuck an instant-read thermometer into the liquid. The first good piece of news was that every model—even the cheap foam box—maintained the temperature of the sodas for the full four hours. Even more impressive, two models exceeded our expectations and actually dropped the sodas to a colder temperature.

We were intrigued: A cooler that can act like a refrigerator wasn't a requirement for us, but it was an appealing feature. Curious why a couple of models had this ability, we looked closer to see how

manufacturers were insulating their products. As it turns out, all coolers in our lineup—whether hard- or soft-sided—are made from the polystyrene foam known as Styrofoam. This plastic is widely used for insulation because it's porous and, therefore, slows the transfer of heat. But with the exception of the $4 Lifoam Styrofoam Cooler, that foam was just one component of insulation. Every other manufacturer used additional materials or design features to improve its product's performance.

The most effective feature we came across was a layer of plastic lining on the interior of the T-Rex from California Cooler Bags ($75), which created an insulating air pocket between the cooler's interior and the foam. Gases like air make very good insulators because they contain relatively few molecules, hence they conduct heat poorly (for more information, see "Full of Cool Air"). That explained why this was the only model to not only keep the sodas cool, but to actually chill them to an optimal 40 degrees. (The other model to drop the sodas' temperature, also from California Cooler Bags, only brought them down to 42 degrees.) What's more, the T-Rex had a small hatch sewn into its zip top that allowed us to grab a soda without opening the entire box, thereby keeping the release of cool air to a minimum.

Material Differences

That last point got us thinking about a cooler's other functions. Besides a beverage chiller, we wanted a container roomy enough to accommodate a weekend's worth of groceries, but not a bear to move when full or a hog that consumed lots of floor space when not in use.

Storage-wise, the T-Rex and the Coleman had the largest capacities, but it was their flexible fabric walls that gave them, as well as the smaller collapsible model from California Cooler Bags, a real advantage. Not only did these coolers fold down like a duffle bag, but their sides were flexible enough for even the smaller California tote to house multiple bags of groceries.

Meanwhile, the rigid Lifoam box was about half as roomy as the largest coolers. When it couldn't accommodate all of the cold-storage goods, we had to perform triage—and only a whole chicken, 1 pound of bacon, and a package of ground beef made the cut.

Most of the soft-sided coolers fared well in the durability test, too. When we tipped them off the tailgate of a station wagon, their zip tops prevented

them from bursting open and hurling their contents onto the pavement as the Lifoam model did, and they didn't suffer any permanent structural damage. The one soft-sided model to fail this test? The Coleman. A peek inside after the tumble revealed a split-open hummus container and a few broken eggs.

The ideal cooler should also clean up odor- and stain-free without a lot of scrubbing. Of the fabric models, the Coleman was the only one to pass the cleanup tests with flying colors, thanks to its smooth sides and antimicrobial material. When we left fresh cod fillets in each cooler for a weekend and then scrubbed them with hot soapy water, baking soda, and cleaning wipes, the fishy aroma stubbornly clung to the other fabric coolers. Meanwhile, spilled milk dyed green with food coloring mopped up easily from the smooth, hard-sided Rubbermaid tub, which also features a handy spout for draining liquid.

By the end of testing, we decided that the California T-Rex was a cooler we'd be happy to take anywhere. Its large fabric-covered frame was lightweight and durable, and its interior plastic lining added an extra layer of insulation. Plus, it rolls on small wheels, pulls along with a telescoping handle, and collapses to the size of a gym bag.

Full of Cool Air

While all of the coolers maintained the sodas' starting temperatures equally well, the California Cooler Bags' T-Rex Large Collapsible Rolling Cooler was particularly effective at chilling, thanks to its unique three-layer insulation: Styrofoam walls, a thick interior plastic lining that zippered shut, and, most important, a pocket of air in between those two layers. Air (like other gases) contains a limited number of molecules that don't transmit energy efficiently, which makes it a poor conductor of heat and therefore a very effective insulator.

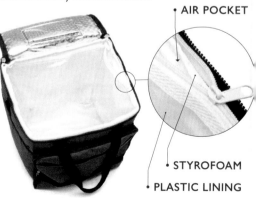

AIR POCKET

STYROFOAM

PLASTIC LINING

Watch the Testing

Video available FREE for 4 months at www.CooksIllustrated.com/aug11

TESTING COOLERS

KEEPING IT COLD We filled each model with partially chilled sodas and ice packs (1 pound per 2 quarts cooler capacity, per manufacturer instructions) and placed them in a 95-degree room. We checked the temperature inside one can from each model every hour for four hours, giving the highest marks to the coolers that maintained—or even dropped (see "Cooling Ability," below)—the sodas' starting temperatures.

PORTABILITY We looked for vessels that were sturdy but not heavy or awkward to move when full. Wheels and handles were plusses.

COOLING ABILITY The sodas we placed in the coolers were less-than-optimally chilled (45 degrees). We gave the highest marks to coolers that were able to drop their temperatures closer to 39 to 40 degrees.

DURABILITY We dropped each cooler from a car tailgate to make sure that it could take a good amount of wear and tear. Models that suffered permanent damage were downgraded.

CLEANUP We dyed milk with green food coloring and spilled a small amount inside each model to test how difficult it was to mop up the mess. We also left fresh cod fillets in the coolers over a weekend and scrubbed the vessels with soap and water, baking soda, and cleaning wipes to test odor retention.

We tested five coolers in a variety of styles, materials, and price points. All models were purchased online. A source for the winner appears on page 32.

RECOMMENDED

	CRITERIA		TESTERS' COMMENTS

CALIFORNIA COOLER BAGS T-Rex Large Collapsible Rolling Cooler
Price: $75
Model: 20109KYC
Interior Dimensions: 15 inches high, 16 inches wide, 14.5 inches deep

Criteria	Rating
Keeping It Cold	★★★
Portability	★★★
Cooling Ability	★★★
Durability	★★★
Cleanup	★★

Thanks to an ultra-insulating layer of plastic lining, this was the only nonelectric model to not only keep the sodas cool, but also chill them to 40 degrees. Wheels, a telescoping handle, a hatch in the lid to limit airflow, and a collapsible frame earned it plenty of convenience points, too. The only downside was cleaning its zip-in lining: Crumbs got caught in the teeth and a very slight fishy odor clung to the fabric.

CALIFORNIA COOLER BAGS Large 48–52 Classic Collapsible Cooler
Price: $36.40
Model: 5-22010KYC
Interior Dimensions: 12 inches high, 16 inches wide, 12 inches deep

Criteria	Rating
Keeping It Cold	★★★
Portability	★★★
Cooling Ability	★★
Durability	★★★
Cleanup	★

This collapsible cooler isn't equipped with its larger sibling's insulating lining, but it still cooled sodas to 42 degrees. It also scored big for portability (a padded shoulder strap), space efficiency (stretchy fabric), and ruggedness. Odors clung to this cooler's interior.

RECOMMENDED WITH RESERVATIONS

RUBBERMAID 5-Day Wheeled Cooler
Price: $48
Model: 802697
Interior Dimensions: 14.5 inches high, 20 inches wide, 10.5 inches deep

Criteria	Rating
Keeping It Cold	★★★
Portability	★★★
Cooling Ability	★
Durability	★
Cleanup	★★★

While this hard plastic tub sports bells and whistles like a split lid and cup holders, and cleanup-friendly features like a spout for emptying liquid, it isn't as durable as it looks. When we dropped it, one of the wheels came loose.

COLEMAN Collapsible Chest Cooler
Price: $39.99
Model: 2000004139
Interior Dimensions: 12 inches high, 22 inches wide, 13 inches deep

Criteria	Rating
Keeping It Cold	★★★
Portability	★
Cooling Ability	★
Durability	★★★
Cleanup	★★★

This cooler's spacious interior may seem like a perk, but once it's loaded up with food and drink, its wheel-free body is almost impossible to move by the short loop handle. That said, it can take a good bit of wear and tear and cleans up nicely, thanks to its smooth sides and antimicrobial fabric.

LIFOAM Styrofoam Cooler
Price: $4
Model: 3542
Interior Dimensions: 12 inches high, 17 inches wide, 10 inches deep

Criteria	Rating
Keeping It Cold	★★★
Portability	★★★
Cooling Ability	★
Durability	★
Cleanup	★½

You can't beat the price—but you don't get much for it. Though this Styrofoam cube kept drinks cool, it was too small to hold more than a few items. And given the crack that developed on the side during cleaning, it clearly wasn't meant for multiple uses.

It's Electric!

Thermoelectric coolers are not refrigerators, but they operate similarly: You plug them into a port (such as your car's cigarette lighter), and they lower the interior temperature of the container by pumping warm air out. When we put two models, the Igloo Cool Chill 40-Quart Cooler and the Koolatron P-95 Travel Saver Cooler, through the same battery of tests as the nonelectric coolers, they predictably outshined the competition by chilling the drinks to an optimal 39 degrees. Their temperatures recovered quickly when their lids were opened; plus, not adding ice packs meant there was more room for food. Of the two, we slightly preferred the Igloo. It featured a pull-out handle that made it easy to cart around, and when we dropped both units, the Igloo's hard-wearing frame and snap-shut lid kept its contents well-contained, while the Koolatron's lid got knocked loose and never fit tightly again.

Cooling efficiency aside, however, these coolers have two major drawbacks that keep us from wholeheartedly recommending them. First, price: They cost roughly twice as much as our favorite nonelectric model, which cooled the sodas almost as well. Second, because they must be plugged in to keep their chill (unplugged, their temperatures rose dramatically after 1 hour), they lack one feature that we consider essential for a cooler: portability.

IGLOO
$139.99

KOOLATRON
$144.61

A Revolution in the Canned Tuna Aisle

Canned tuna has never been high-class fare, but nowadays some manufacturers are promising top-quality fish and processing methods that preserve fresh flavor. Have the tides turned?

≥ BY LISA McMANUS ≤

Canned tuna tastes nothing like fresh fish, but according to American sales figures that's just fine. Reeling in $1.1 billion a year in industry sales, it's the country's most popular seafood after shrimp and has been since the early 20th century, when it gained recognition as a low-cost, pantry-ready source of protein. Apparently, nobody minds that it doesn't taste like fresh tuna. In fact, the appeal of the canned stuff is that, as one well-known brand proclaims on its label, its flavor is as mild as chicken.

With such high demand for inexpensive tuna, the "big three" companies (Chicken of the Sea, StarKist, and Bumble Bee) have tweaked their methods to get the highest rate of "recovery"—the yield of flesh from the fish—at the lowest cost. In some cases, the results bear a smaller resemblance to fish than ever before. At the same time, tuna has gone upscale. In addition to chunk light and solid white, oil- and water-packed, pouch and can, and regular and low-sodium, some brands now offer premium versions with gourmet-sounding names like "select" grade and "prime fillet." A few new companies have even entered the game, claiming to bring not only higher-quality fish but also the advantages of better processing methods (including environmentally friendly fishing practices) to the game.

Wondering if these new products were really any better, we trawled the tuna aisle and returned with eight cans of solid white albacore tuna, most packed in water—our preferred style from a 2006 tasting.

These included two new brands, two "gourmet" lines from the "big three," and four regular samples that we grew up eating. (Just to see if it was worth its staggering price tag and the inconvenience of mail-ordering, we also sampled the crème de la crème of tinned fish—*ventresca* tuna packed in oil—in a separate tasting. See below.) Our questions: Would any of the new versions really taste more like fresh tuna? And given that the most common preparation is to mix it with mayonnaise and pickles for tuna salad, would we even care?

A Double-Edged Sword

As it turned out, the answer was "yes" in both cases. The tuna salad test proved that even after the fish was loaded up with condiments, differences among the samples were still plenty clear—and that what we look for in a can of tuna has come a long way. While several of the lower-ranking sandwich fillings were so wet and spongy that they elicited comparisons to cat food, the two salads we liked best boasted not only heartier, more substantial chunks of fish, but richer, more flavorful meat that—as one taster noted in astonishment—"actually tastes like tuna." But what exactly accounted for the differences? For starters, those alternative processing methods touted by the new-school tuna companies.

First, a little information about how most tuna gets from the ocean into a can. The majority of large-scale manufacturers haul in flash-frozen fish from the boats, thaw it, inspect it, and then cook

it twice—once before canning it and again after sealing it. The first heating maximizes the amount of meat that can be pulled off the fish. Raw fish clings tightly to the skin and bones and must be hand-packed because it clogs machinery. Cooked fish separates more easily from the carcass, allowing manufacturers to not only recover every scrap of meat, but also to machine-pack it quickly and cheaply. The second heating takes place after canning, as a precaution against harmful bacteria. The upshot: a faster process with a higher yield and, in turn, lower prices for the consumer.

The problem is that while the double-cook method cuts down on the cost of the product, it also cheapens the quality. Though all of the samples made acceptable tuna salad, our least favorites (which included the conventional samples from all three of the major brands) had lost so much of their natural flavor, moisture, and meaty bite that some tasters couldn't even tell they were eating fish. Mayonnaise turned the "teeny shreds" in the StarKist can to a "wet paste." One taster likened the "squishy," "loose" Bumble Bee tuna salad to fishy "dip."

The effects of double-cooking became even more apparent when we compared the big-brand tunas to samples from industry newcomers Wild Planet and American Tuna. Both of these smaller companies pack raw fish into the cans by hand and cook the meat only once, and the results had the fresher flavor and firmer, heartier texture to prove it.

Swimming in Liquid

The way the fish was processed accounted for some of the difference between these two brands and the rest of the lineup, but we discovered another likely factor. When we pulled back the lids, we noticed that most cans contained a fair bit of liquid that had to be drained off, while the Wild Planet and American Tuna cans contained almost no liquid. The ingredient labels confirmed our observation: Every manufacturer except those two packed their fish in either water or a combination of water and vegetable broth. Why? Three reasons.

First, producers use the double-cook method to add moisture back to the precooked (and drier) fish. Second, supplementing the water with vegetable broth is a trick used by all three of the bottom-ranking big-brand tuna companies to enhance their products' woefully bland flavor—although in most cases we found that it only made the tuna taste salty. The premium versions of StarKist

---

TASTING SUPERMARKET CANNED TUNA

We tasted eight brands of canned solid white albacore tuna, identified from a list of top-selling national brands compiled by SymphonyIRI Group, a Chicago-based market research firm, as well as through additional editorial research. We sampled them in our recipe for Classic Tuna Salad, rating them on tuna flavor, fishy flavor, saltiness, texture, and overall appeal. Prices were paid in Boston-area supermarkets; per-ounce prices were calculated based on the weight of tuna in the can minus any liquid, which was separated out in our test kitchen. Ingredients appear as listed on labels. Brands appear below in order of preference.

RECOMMENDED

WILD PLANET
Wild Albacore Tuna
Price: $3.39 for 5-ounce can
(85 cents per ounce of meat)
Tuna in Can: 3.99 ounces (80% of total content)
Ingredients: Albacore tuna and sea salt
Sodium: 250 mg per 2-oz serving
Comments: "Rich and flavorful, but not fishy," this hand-packed tuna containing no extra liquid held its own in the mayonnaise-y salad and seemed "substantial" to tasters, who praised its "hearty" yet "tender" bite. In sum: "This one is aces."

AMERICAN TUNA
Pole Caught Wild Albacore
Price: $4.99 for 6-ounce can ($1.00 per ounce of meat)
Tuna in Can: 5 ounces (83% of total content)
Ingredients: Albacore tuna
Sodium: 20 mg per 2-oz serving
Comments: The only other brand not packed in liquid, this product stood out to tasters because it "actually tastes like tuna." The "distinct chunks" boasted fish flavor that was "pronounced" but not overpowering, and a texture that was "meaty," if "a little dry."

RECOMMENDED WITH RESERVATIONS

STARKIST SELECTS
Solid White Albacore Tuna in Water
Price: $1.69 for 4.5-ounce can
(47 cents per ounce of meat)
Tuna in Can: 3.6 ounces (80% of total content)
Ingredients: White meat tuna, water, salt, pyrophosphate
Sodium: 170 mg per 2-oz serving
Comments: Most tasters appreciated that this supposedly higher quality tuna's "solid chunks" were "large enough to stand out" in the salad, but flavor-wise it was a mixed bag: To some the meat had "decent" tuna flavor, while others thought the fish fell flat in the presence of pickles, onions, and mayo. As we went to press, StarKist slightly changed the formulation of this product. Tasters felt the new version was comparable in taste and texture.

BUMBLE BEE Prime Fillet Solid White
Albacore Tuna in Water
Price: $1.99 for 5-ounce can
(54 cents per ounce of meat)
Tuna in Can: 3.7 ounces (74% of total content)
Ingredients: White tuna, water, salt, pyrophosphate added
Sodium: 140 mg per 2-oz serving
Comments: The general consensus about this product whose manufacturer claims comes from a superior grade tuna? Ambivalence. Tasters described the meat's "very fine" texture as "shredded without being squished," and though its flavor was "rather bland" and "mild," it was "moist and pretty tasty" and made a "good, basic tuna sandwich."

RECOMMENDED WITH RESERVATIONS (CONTINUED)

CHICKEN OF THE SEA
Solid White Albacore Tuna in Water
Price: $1.99 for 5-ounce can
(57 cents per ounce of meat)
Tuna in Can: 3.5 ounces (70% of total content)
Ingredients: Solid white tuna, water, vegetable broth (contains soy), salt, pyrophosphate
Sodium: 180 mg per 2-oz serving
Comments: The favorite non-gourmet offering of the "big three" brands, this tuna tasted familiar to many of us. Almost everyone found the meat "decent" but "watery," and some admitted that this met their expectations. Others complained that it reminded them "why I never wanted this in my lunchbox as a kid."

CROWN PRINCE
Natural Solid White Albacore Tuna in Water
Price: $2.99 for 6-ounce can
(70 cents per ounce of meat)
Tuna in Can: 4.3 ounces (72% of total content)
Ingredients: Albacore tuna, spring water, sea salt
Sodium: 105 mg per 2-oz serving
Comments: Though this tuna consistently racked up points for its "distinct," "hearty" texture, tasters' votes were split when it came to flavor. Depending on whom you asked, the fish tasted "meaty" and "pleasant," or was "very, very fishy" and "fermented tasting."

STARKIST
Solid White Albacore Tuna in Water
Price: $1.67 for 5-ounce can
(51 cents per ounce of meat)
Tuna in Can: 3.3 ounces (66% of total content)
Ingredients: White tuna, water, vegetable broth, salt, pyrophosphate; contains soy
Sodium: 190 mg per 2-oz serving
Comments: Without much tuna flavor to speak of, this conventional StarKist sample was more of a "family-friendly protein delivery system" than its premium sibling. That said, a few tasters picked up on a big hit of salt—presumably a result of the meat soaking in vegetable broth, which seemed to affect this brand more than others.

BUMBLE BEE
Solid White Albacore Tuna in Water
Price: $1.69 for 5-ounce can
(46 cents per ounce of meat)
Tuna in Can: 3.7 ounces (74% of total content)
Ingredients: White tuna, water, vegetable broth, salt, pyrophosphate added; contains soy
Sodium: 140 mg per 2-oz serving
Comments: Though the tuna's "mild" flavor didn't offend anyone, it didn't impress either. Where this lesser Bumble Bee sample really lost points was in the texture department, where it elicited censure for tasting "soupy" and "watery" and so "loose" that it seemed "more like a dip than a sandwich filling."

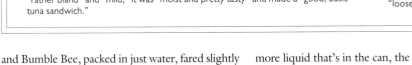

and Bumble Bee, packed in just water, fared slightly better with tasters, but we found that no matter what kind of liquid was in the can, the results weren't as flavorful as those preparations that start with raw tuna and let it cook in its own juices. The third reason is obvious: It's a cost-cutting measure. The more liquid that's in the can, the less room there is for the fish.

That last point prompted us to do one more test: We drained each can and weighed both the fish and the liquid, to see what your money buys. While our top-rated tunas from Wild Planet and American Tuna, respectively, cost more for the same size can than the rest of the lineup, you get more meat per can—up to an additional half-ounce more. But above all, we think the fresher flavor and heartier texture make these brands worth a few extra pennies for our next tuna sandwich.

KITCHEN NOTES

≥ BY ANDREW JANJIGIAN & DAN SOUZA ≤

RECIPE TESTING Almost Pop 'n' Serve Dough

For most of us, fresh-baked bread is a treat rather than an everyday event, since mixing the dough and allowing it to rise (or "proof") typically takes at least four hours (around three hours for the first proof and one hour for the second). But what about freezing the dough ahead of time? We froze dough for a rustic white loaf at three separate junctures: immediately after mixing, after the first proof (just before the dough was divided and shaped into loaves), and after forming the loaves and proofing the final time. Several weeks later, we thawed the dough in the refrigerator overnight and then baked it.

TOO SOON

Freezing the dough just after mixing killed too many of the yeast cells before they had a chance to ferment—a process that creates more complex flavor compounds and releases the carbon dioxide that makes dough rise. In addition, freezing before proofing reduces gluten development, so the loaf doesn't have enough structure to fully expand. The result: a small, squat loaf with bland flavor.

TOO LATE

Dough frozen late in the game—after the second rise—was overproofed: As the already fully risen dough slowly thawed, the random remaining viable yeast cells continued to produce gas in some parts of the dough but not in others, weakening its structure. The result: a misshapen loaf that collapsed during baking.

JUST RIGHT

Freezing the dough between the first and second proofs was the best strategy. The first proof ensured that enough yeast had fermented for the dough to develop complex flavors and some rise. The remaining viable yeast cells then finished the job as the dough thawed and proofed for the second time.

Making Metal Behave Like Glass

We prefer to bake pies in glass or ceramic pie plates because they conduct heat slowly, preventing the crusts from overbrowning before the filling has fully set. (Glass also allows us to easily monitor the browning progress.) But what if metal or disposable aluminum pie plates are all you have? To figure out the best way to prevent overcooking, we lined both types of plates with pie pastry and tried a few tricks. We lowered the oven temperature, and we baked the shells on a single aluminum sheet tray, as well as on a double stack to insulate the bottom of the plate from the oven's direct heat.

Dialing back the temperature was the wrong approach: The crusts baked up not only pale, but also soggy because the temperature wasn't hot enough to cook off the moisture in the dough. Sliding a single sheet tray underneath the pie plate was more effective, and using two was even better. The double layer of insulation ensured that the crusts cooked gradually and evenly. We still prefer glass plates, but it's nice to know how to make metal ones behave more like glass if the need arises.

Leak-Proofing Springform Pans

We'd love to find a springform pan that doesn't let moisture seep in when you place it in a water bath (our preferred method for baking delicate desserts like cheesecake), but so far a less-than-watertight seal seems unavoidable on pans with removable bottoms. Our solution has always been to wrap the pan with a double layer of aluminum foil and tightly crimp it around the pan's edge. But foil is not a perfect fix: Steam from the water bath condenses inside the foil, so that the pan still sits in liquid.

Recently, we came up with a better way to address the problem: placing the springform pan inside a slightly larger metal pan or pot—a 10 by 3-inch cake pan or deep-dish pizza pan is ideal—before lowering it into the bath. The slight gap between the pans isn't wide enough to prevent the water from insulating the springform pan, and there is zero danger of exposing the cheesecake to water, since any moisture that condenses on the sides of the pan rapidly evaporates.

If you bake cheesecakes regularly, this method is more than worth the minimal expense of buying a large metal cake pan.

WATERTIGHT SOLUTION
Setting a springform pan inside a slightly larger vessel guarantees that the cake will stay dry while the water bath does its job.

Oil Before You Knead

Most recipes for hand-kneaded bread call for dusting the countertop with flour to prevent sticking. But depending on the type of bread and how heavily you flour the surface, the dough can absorb the flour and become dry and stiff, or it can take up the flour without absorbing it, leaving pockets of raw flour in the finished loaf.

We prefer a less common approach that replaces the flour with vegetable oil. Rubbing a teaspoon of the neutral-flavored fat onto the countertop works just as well as flour does to minimize sticking, and the dough readily absorbs excess oil without any negative effect on its consistency when either raw or baked. Note: When swapping flour for oil, it's still necessary to reapply the oil if kneading multiple portions of dough.

Fast Track to Soft Cheese

Soft, creamy cheeses like Brie and Camembert firm up in the refrigerator and should be brought to room temperature before serving, but that can take as long as two hours. Looking for a faster route, we placed a wedge of chilled Brie in an airless zipper-lock bag (see "Thrifty Cook's Vacuum Sealer," right) in 4 quarts of 80-degree water and microwaved another wedge on the low-temperature "defrost" function. Microwaving was a bad idea: The tip of the cheese melted after just 25 seconds. But submerging the wedge in a water bath worked well, gently warming the cheese to 72 degrees in less than an hour.

OVERLY OOZY
Even on defrost, a microwave heats too rapidly to properly soften cheese.

EVENLY CREAMY
A warm water bath gently and effectively softens cheese.

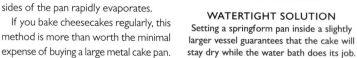

TEST KITCHEN TIP Freezing Brined Beans

In the test kitchen, we have found that soaking dried beans overnight in a saltwater solution will ensure soft, tender skins. During the long soak, sodium ions from the salt displace magnesium and calcium ions in the cell walls of the tough outer shell of the beans. Because sodium ions weaken the pectin in the cell walls more than these other minerals, water has an easier time penetrating the skins, softening their texture as they cook. A bonus: The brine thoroughly seasons the beans.

But brining beans means you've got to wait at least eight hours before you can cook them. We wondered if it would be possible to brine beans and then freeze them prior to cooking. To test this, we brined two batches of dried pinto and black beans, rinsed and drained them, and then froze them in zipper-lock bags for several weeks before cooking. When these beans were compared side by side with beans brined the night before cooking, tasters could not tell them apart. So if you want ready-to-cook beans on hand anytime, just brine and freeze them.

BEANS AT THE READY
For ready-to-cook beans that end up tender and well seasoned, brine and then freeze them.

TECHNIQUE | THRIFTY COOK'S VACUUM SEALER

We think vacuum sealers are a worthwhile investment if you freeze a lot of food. But they're pricey: Our favorite, the Pragotrade Vacuum Sealer Pro, retails for a whopping $469.95, and our Best Buy, the Foodsaver V2240 Vacuum Sealer Kit, costs $100. After much experimentation (including trying to suck air out of an almost-sealed zipper-lock bag), we came up with an approach that costs mere pennies. Sealed according to the method below, chicken breasts stored in the freezer for a month exhibited almost no ice crystals (they are a sure sign of freezer burn).

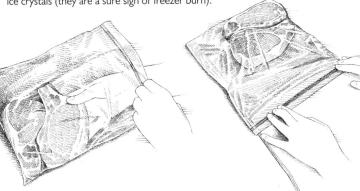

1. Pack food snugly into corner of large zipper-lock bag.

2. Starting from side closest to food, close zipper almost all the way, leaving small opening at end opposite food. Insert straw ½ inch into opening.

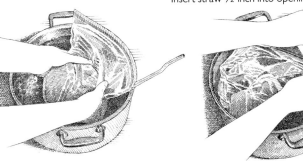

3. Place bag in pot of water. Slowly pull down on bag with one hand while massaging out air through straw with other hand.

4. When all of air is removed from bag and water level almost reaches top, remove straw and seal bag.

Adding Mix-Ins to Homemade Ice Cream

While developing our recipe for Vanilla Ice Cream (page 23), we uncovered a few ground rules for adding mix-ins. These guidelines apply to any homemade ice cream.

FREEZE FIRST To keep mix-ins from raising the ice cream's temperature, freeze them for at least 15 minutes before adding them to the ice-cream maker.
STRAIN TINY BITS Shake chopped ingredients like chocolate and nuts in a mesh strainer to remove small particles that can detract from the ice cream's smooth consistency.
ADD JUST ENOUGH Add no more than ¾ cup of coarsely chopped (¼- to ½-inch) mix-ins per quart of ice cream to provide textural contrast without dominating the ice cream. Scale down to ½ cup when using potent ingredients such as crystallized ginger or crushed peppermint candies.
WAIT UNTIL LAST MINUTE Add mix-ins during the final minute of churning to ensure even distribution without interrupting the freezing process.

Prettier Poached Eggs

Poached egg recipes call for adding vinegar to the cooking water to help the whites firm up, but it's not always a sure fix. Older eggs in particular can form shaggy, uneven edges when they hit the boiling water. This is because as eggs age, the proteins (albumen) in the white break down into a more watery substance that doesn't coagulate as well. Fortunately, this problem is easily avoided by removing the watery part before cooking. Break the egg into a small mesh strainer placed over a bowl and gently run a finger around the edges of the white. The watery portion will drain away, leaving behind only the firm albumen. Given that it's hard to pinpoint the exact age of supermarket eggs, this method will help ensure that they never look shaggy.

SHAGGY
Older egg whites are watery and form ragged edges when poached.

TIDY
Draining the watery part of the whites before poaching ensures a smooth edge.

No More Curdled Milk

If you're prone to accidentally allowing milk to come to a boil when heating it for hot drinks or other purposes, here's a neat trick that will prevent it from curdling: Add a pinch of baking soda before heating. Excessive heat causes the whey proteins in milk to unravel and bind with the casein proteins. The addition of alkaline baking soda raises the milk's pH slightly, creating more negative charges on both types of proteins, which prevents them from binding together as readily and forming curds. A pinch of baking soda added to 2 cups of milk will do the job without creating any soapy off-flavors.

Slow Down Your Mixer

In the past, we've recommended kneading bread dough on high speed (speed 4) on the Kitchen Aid Pro 600 stand mixer to expedite the kneading process. Though we've never experienced problems in the test kitchen, some readers have reported that kneading thick dough on high speed overtaxes the Kitchen Aid's motor to the point that the mixer actually stops. To avoid this problem, Kitchen Aid recommends kneading dough at speed 2 for all of its mixers. Our favorite model, the Cuisinart 5.5 Quart Mixer, also recommends a lower speed: 3. From now on, we'll be using speed 2 for all but the wettest of bread doughs. (The dough for our Pizza Bianca [September/October 2008], with a 90 percent hydration, is too loose for high speed to be a problem.)

BY AMY GRAVES & TAIZETH SIERRA

EQUIPMENT TESTING

Grilling Baskets for Whole Fish

Fish baskets can make the task of wrestling whole fish off the grill a lot less dicey. These oblong, two-piece metal cages keep skin from sticking to the grill and corral your catch for easier flipping. We grilled large whole striped bass and smaller whole red snapper in six heavy-gauge wire baskets costing $11 to $25, most featuring nonstick coatings and two boasting removable handles. Only the two largest baskets easily cradled a 2½-pound striped bass; of these, the Charcoal Companion Ultimate Nonstick Fish-Grilling Basket ($24.99) also allowed successful turning of fish as small as ¾ pound. (The wide-set wires of the other large model, from Steven Raichlen, let the little ones get away.) And because the Charcoal Companion's handle is removable, we could lay the basket flat and, if necessary, close the grill lid. A removable handle was a must for another reason: It allowed the basket to fit easily in the dishwasher.

BEST BASKET
This grilling basket from Charcoal Companion makes flipping whole fish a whole lot easier.

NEW PRODUCT iGrill Remote Thermometer

What could be better than a remote thermometer that talks to your iPhone, transmitting constant readouts of your meat's temperature and even predicting when it will be done? We put steaks on the grill and monitored them with the iGrill ($99.99), a two-part device that communicates via Bluetooth with the iPhone, iPod Touch, or iPad, along with our favorite (and far cheaper) remote thermometer, the Taylor Wireless Thermometer with Remote Pager ($21). The latter beeps when food is within 10 degrees of a target. The good news: The iGrill offers a range comparable to the Taylor, letting us wander 200 feet from the base unit while still receiving readouts. Even when our phone went into "sleep" mode, the iGrill stayed in touch, waking up to report when a target temperature had been reached. What's more, we could even reset the temperature remotely via our phone. The bad news: The iGrill occasionally gave us readouts that were 2 to 3 degrees cooler than measurements taken directly with our gold standard, the Thermapen. It also communicates with just one Bluetooth device at a time, and switching to another one is an involved process. Finally, the digital readout of the

NOT YET A BETA
The iGrill remote thermometer, which reports readouts to your iPhone, has a few flaws to work out.

temperature on the base unit was too faint to be visible in daylight, so using it during the day without a Bluetooth device isn't feasible. With these flaws, and at this price, we can't wholeheartedly recommend the iGrill. We'll be on the lookout for version 2.0.

PRODUCT UPDATE Technivorm Brew-Thru Lid

Our favorite drip coffee maker, the Technivorm Moccamaster Coffeemaker ($299) is pricey but produces great-tasting coffee. But the original didn't come with a brew-through, pour-through lid, requiring you to screw on its airtight lid the instant the brewing stopped—and to unscrew it each time you poured a cup. Now the machine comes with a new, second lid (also sold separately): the Technivorm Brew-Thru Lid ($7.35). We brewed coffee in the machine using the new accessory, then took its temperature at intervals for one hour. Thanks to the lid's small opening that channels into a 5-inch-long tube, the coffee lost just 11 degrees over the course of an hour, dropping from 191 to 180 degrees—well above the 150- to 175-degree serving range recommended by many coffee experts. We're sold.

PUT A LID ON IT
The Technivorm Brew-Thru Lid is more convenient than the original airtight lid.

EQUIPMENT TESTING

Asian/Western Manual Knife Sharpeners

Western knives have a wider cutting angle on the blade than their Asian counterparts, so owning both kinds of knives used to mean owning two different sharpeners—if you expected to get back a razor edge. The pricey Chef'sChoice AngleSelect 1520 Electric Knife Sharpener ($169) solved the problem with two sharpening slots: one for 15-degree Asian knives and one for 20-degree Western knives. But now far more affordable manual sharpeners have come on the market that also accommodate both cutting edges. We compared two of these with the electric device by dulling and then sharpening multiple copies of our favorite Japanese and Western chef's knives and slicing tomatoes. While the Wüsthof Universal Knife Sharpener ($29.95) actually chipped a knife, the diamond abrasives on the manual Chef'sChoice AngleSelect 4623 Knife Sharpener ($29.95) restored the edges almost as effectively as the company's plug-in sharpener. It takes more strokes—but it's a good bargain alternative.

SHARP SAVINGS
The manual Chef'sChoice AngleSelect 4623 Knife Sharpener is an affordable option for honing both Asian and Western blades.

New Product Zoku Quick Pop Maker

When we poured a homemade fruit blend into the Zoku Quick Pop Maker's ($49.95) three 2-ounce slots, in just seven minutes the mixture was rock solid—our cue to insert the special key in each pop handle to release the treat. We could repeat the process for two more rounds of pops (nine pops in total) before the unit needed to be refrozen; pops took six to 10 extra minutes to freeze after the first round. While we love the quick gratification this nifty gadget provides, it doesn't entirely eliminate the need for planning ahead: The console, which contains a proprietary liquid that gets colder than ice, must be placed in the freezer 24 hours before use.

ALMOST INSTANT I
The Zoku Quick Pop Mal produces ice pops in les than 10 minutes.

For complete testing results for each item, go to www.CooksIllustrated.com/aug11.

Sources

The following are sources for items recommended in this issue. Prices were current at press time and do not include shipping. Contact companies to confirm information or visit www.CooksIllustrated.com/aug11 for updates.

PAGE 22: ICE-CREAM MAKERS
- Whynter Snö Professional Ice Cream Maker: $219.99, model #IC-2L, Target (800-591-3869, www.target.com).
- Cuisinart Automatic Frozen Yogurt–Ice Cream & Sorbet Maker: $49.95, item #ICE-21, Cuisinart (800-211-9604, www.cuisinart.com).

PAGE 25: SPRINGFORM PANS
- Frieling Handle-It 9-Inch Glass Bottom Springform Pan: $49.99, item #157723, Cooking.com (800-663-8810, www.cooking.com).
- Nordic Ware Pro Form 9-Inch Leak-Proof Springform Pan: $15, item #55742, Nordic Ware (877-466-7342, www.nordicware.com).

PAGE 27: COOLER
- California Cooler Bags T-Rex Large Collapsible Rolling Cooler: $75, item #20109KYC, Keep Your Cooler (877-838-0500, www.keepyourcooler.com).

PAGE 32: FISH BASKET
- Charcoal Companion Ultimate Nonstick Fish-Grilling Basket: $24.99, item #09-0402, Chef Tools (206-933-0700, www.cheftools.com).

PAGE 32: TECHNIVORM CARAFE LID
- Technivorm Brew-Thru Lid: $7.35, item #SCG80196, Seattle Coffee Gear (866-372-4734, www.seattlecoffeegear.com).

PAGE 32: KNIFE SHARPENER
- Chef'sChoice AngleSelect Professional Knife Sharpener model 4623: $29.95, item #25816, Chef's Catalog (800-338-3232, www.chefscatalog.com).

PAGE 32: POP MAKER
- Zoku Quick Pop Maker: $49.95, item #1742345, Williams-Sonoma (877-812-6425, www.williams-sonoma.com).

INDEX

July & August 2011

NEW RECIPES ON THE WEB
Available free for four months at
www.CooksIllustrated.com/aug11
Coffee Crunch Ice Cream
Cucumber Salad with Ginger, Sesame, and .
    Scallion
Cucumber Salad with Jalapeño, Cilantro,
    and Pepitas
Italian Bread Salad with Garlic and Capers
Italian Bread Salad with Olives and Feta
Triple Ginger Ice Cream

🎥 COOK'S LIVE VIDEOS
Available free for four months at
www.CooksIllustrated.com/aug11
CORN CHOWDER
See every key step
CUCUMBER SALAD
Watch the slice, simmer, and toss
EASY SALMON CAKES
See the right texture
**GRILLED STUFFED PORK
TENDERLOIN**
Watch the stuff 'n' roll
PANZANELLA
Look: Toast, salt, soak
PERFECT SCRAMBLED EGGS
Dual-heat method in action
SMOKED CHICKEN
Check out the grill setup
SUMMER PEACH CAKE
Yvonne makes the cake
TESTING: COOLERS
Watch the testing
THAI GRILLED-BEEF SALAD
Look: The moisture beads
VANILLA ICE CREAM
Watch Dan make it

AMERICA'S TEST KITCHEN TV
Public television's most popular cooking show

Join the millions of home cooks who watch our show, *America's Test Kitchen*, on public television every week. For more information, including recipes and program times, visit www.AmericasTestKitchenTV.com.

AMERICA'S TEST KITCHEN RADIO
Tune in to our new radio program featuring answers to listener call-in questions, ingredient-taste-test and equipment-review segments, and in-depth reporting on a variety of topics. To listen to episodes, visit www.AmericasTestKitchen.com/Radio.

DOWNLOAD OUR FREE *Cook's Illustrated* iPhone App
Inside you'll find a collection of our top recipes, along with videos that explain how to make them. You can also access many of our most popular taste test results, useful kitchen timers, and an interactive shopping list that helps you plan ahead. Are you a member of CooksIllustrated.com? If so, our app gives you access to every recipe, video, and taste test on the website. Go to CooksIllustrated.com/iPhone.

Follow us on Twitter: twitter.com/TestKitchen
Find us on Facebook: facebook.com/CooksIllustrated

Easy Salmon Cakes, 11

Vanilla Ice Cream, 23

Cucumber Salad, 15

Smoked Chicken, 9

Corn Chowder, 14

Thai Grilled-Beef Salad, 13

Italian Bread Salad (Panzanella), 20

Summer Peach Cake, 25

Perfect Scrambled Eggs, 19

Grilled Stuffed Pork Tenderloin, 7

PHOTOGRAPHY: CARL TREMBLAY; STYLING: MARIE PIRAINO, CATRINE KELTY

Blue

Jonah

Stone

Snow

Dungeness

Peekytoe

King

CRABS

NUMBER 112

SEPTEMBER & OCTOBER 2011

COOK'S
ILLUSTRATED

Weeknight Roast Chicken
Great Flavor, No Fuss

Pot-Roasted Pork Loin
Rich, Tender, and Juicy

25 Tips for Improving Flavor
Test Kitchen's Top Tricks

Best Vegetable Lasagna
Full-Flavored, Not Watery

Testing Cutting Boards
Which Material Works Best?

Creamy Chocolate Pudding
Childhood Favorite Gets Better

Tasting "Pizza Cheese"
Foolproof Potato Gnocchi
Cranberry-Nut Muffins
Salt-Baked Potatoes
Butternut Squash Soup

www.CooksIllustrated.com
$5.95 U.S./$6.95 CANADA

CONTENTS

September & October 2011

COOK'S
ILLUSTRATED

Founder and Editor	Christopher Kimball
Editorial Director	Jack Bishop
Executive Editor, Magazines	John Willoughby
Executive Editor	Amanda Agee
Test Kitchen Director	Erin McMurrer
Managing Editor	Rebecca Hays
Senior Editors	Keith Dresser
	Lisa McManus
	Bryan Roof
Associate Features Editor	Elizabeth Bomze
Copy Editor	Nell Beram
Associate Editors	Andrea Geary
	Amy Graves
	Andrew Janjigian
	Yvonne Ruperti
	Dan Souza
Assistant Editors	Hannah Crowley
	Taizeth Sierra
Executive Assistant	Christine Gordon
Editorial Assistant	Shannon Friedmann Hatch
Assistant Test Kitchen Director	Gina Nistico
Senior Kitchen Assistants	Meryl MacCormack
	Leah Rovner
Kitchen Assistants	Maria Elena Delgado
	Ena Gudiel
Executive Producer	Melissa Baldino
Associate Producer	Stephanie Stender
Contributing Editors	Matthew Card
	Dawn Yanagihara
Consulting Editor	Scott Brueggeman
Science Editor	Guy Crosby, Ph.D.
Online Managing Editor	David Tytell
Online Editor	Kate Mason
Online Assistant Editors	Eric Grzymkowski
	Mari Levine
Video Operations Manager	Peter Tannenbaum
Media Producer	Alexandra Pournaras
Associate Editor/Camera Operator	Nick Dakoulas
Assistant Editor/Camera Operator	Jesse Prent
Design Director	Amy Klee
Art Director, Magazines	Julie Bozzo
Designer	Lindsey Timko
Art Director, Marketing/Web	Christine Vo
Associate Art Directors, Marketing/Web	Erica Lee
	Jody Lee
Designers, Marketing/Web	Elaina Natario
	Mariah Tarvainen
Staff Photographer	Daniel J. van Ackere
Online Photo Editor	Steve Kilse
Vice President, Marketing	David Mack
Circulation Director	Doug Wicinski
Circulation & Fulfillment Manager	Carrie Horan
Partnership Marketing Manager	Pamela Putprush
Marketing Assistant	Lauren Perkins
Customer Service Manager	Jacqueline Valerio
Customer Service Representatives	Jessica Amato
	Morgan Ryan
Retail Sales & Marketing Manager	Emily Logan
Client Service Manager, Sponsorship	Bailey Snyder
Production Director	Guy Rochford
Senior Project Manager	Alice Carpenter
Production & Traffic Coordinator	Kate Hux
Asset & Workflow Manager	Andrew Mannone
Production & Imaging Specialists	Judy Blomquist
	Heather Dube
	Lauren Pettapiece
Technology Director	Rocco Lombardo
Systems Administrator	Marcus Walser
Lead Developer	Scott Thompson
Software Architect	Robert Martinez
Software Project Manager	Michelle Rushin
Business Analyst	Wendy Tseng
Senior Web Production Coordinator	Evan Davis
VP New Media Product Development	Barry Kelly
Social Media Manager	Steph Yiu
Chief Financial Officer	Sharyn Chabot
Human Resources Director	Adele Shapiro
Publicity	Deborah Broide

PRINTED IN THE USA

WINTER SQUASHES are harvested after their exteriors toughen into thick topcoats that protect the flesh during prolonged cellar storage. Sugar pumpkins are a classic choice for pies, but the sweet blue hubbard squash and the heirloom-variety sweet meat squash (prized in the Northwest) are worthy stand-ins. Once sautéed or roasted, butternut squash takes on a delicate nuttiness. When cooked and scraped with a fork, the flesh of spaghetti squash separates into long strands. Acorn squash is often roasted and sweetened with brown sugar or maple syrup. With its proportions, carnival squash can be confused with acorn, but its dark green stripes and spots, along with its deep ridges, help set it apart. Earthy turban squash is named for a bulbous swelling at the blossom end. While most winter squash must be peeled, the skin of the oblong delicata is edible; like its Japanese cousin *kabocha*, its flavor is similar to that of sweet potatoes.

COVER (Summer Squash and Zucchini): Robert Papp; BACK COVER (Winter Squash): John Burgoyne

America's Test Kitchen is a very real 2,500-square-foot kitchen located just outside of Boston. It is the home of *Cook's Illustrated* and *Cook's Country* magazines and is the workday destination of more than three dozen test cooks, editors, and cookware specialists. Our mission is to test recipes over and over again until we understand how and why they work and until we arrive at the best version. We also test kitchen equipment and supermarket ingredients in search of brands that offer the best value and performance. You can watch us work by tuning in to *America's Test Kitchen* (www.AmericasTestKitchen.com) on public television.

PLAYING BY THE RULES

Vermont has always been considered the "outlaw" state, in part because the mountains and dark hollows are hard to navigate and easily swallow up bank robbers, revolutionaries, and worse. In fact, Daniel Shays, the Massachusetts farmer who turned against the government due to a fight about property taxes, brought his followers up to a mountaintop a half day's walk from our farm. This ragged group of outlaws spent the better part of 10 years on top of Egg Mountain, enduring killing flu epidemics, ice storms, and rocky soil until they were finally pardoned. Some of their stone walls are still visible today, though I can no longer find the overgrown graveyard and the exact location of the old schoolhouse. A lot has changed since my guided tour by a local hunter back in the 1960s.

This outlaw legacy has given Vermonters the freedom to play by their own rules, at least when it comes to the social order. In our small town, a few still remember the hanging tree down on Lincoln Lane, and there have been rumors for years of bodies buried up in Beartown. At least one neighbor constructed a whiskey still in his basement; plenty of weed has been grown in the middle of cornfields or high up in the mountains; and small, half-rotten hunting camps are occupied in mid-November by long-johns-clad souls looking for a bit of peace and quiet and the first unlucky three-pointer who happens to walk by. Diets are often a bit odd too: Some eat home-pickled cow tongue, Sonny Skidmore held up his parlor ceiling with crates of Pepsi, and others have been known to sneak out at night to secret locations to harvest large clumps of hen of the woods

mushrooms. Some neighbors have made a handsome living off of sidehill gravel pits; others have gotten paid for carting away junk, some hazardous, that was then deposited in their own backyard, while others still cling to the old mountain farm ways: trading cattle and haying fields. Dogs have been shot for straying once too often, deer are often jacked out of season for meat, and I once came across a severed moose head in the woods during rabbit season. (Not quite sure where the other 1,000 pounds went to.)

Vermonters rarely play by the rules (unless we are talking about the golden rule: being neighborly). In fact, their first question is often, "Whose rules are they, anyway?"—a query that too many of us avoid. Who decided that nonfat yogurt was worth eating? Who thought up the idea of a $250 dinner? Who convinced us that hunting for our own food is a sin? Who decided that e-books are better than paper? Who invented yellow-colored egg whites for breakfast? Who introduced revolving credit lines, derivatives, and variable rate mortgages? Who pushed us to visit China rather than our own backyards? What happened to black and white, warm comforters in cold bedrooms, hot wood cookstoves on Thanksgiving, bird dogs stiffening to a full point, and the notion of conversation around the dinner table? Plus we have passed a lot of nonsense about happy, safe childhoods along to our kids. It was quite a while ago, but I seem to remember my mother stepping aside now and then, allowing me to pick

Christopher Kimball

myself up off the ground, nose bloodied, to give it another try.

Vermonters like folks who have a set of rules, but they like them better if they follow them. That way, folks know what to expect; you stand for something. About a year ago, Matthew Waite died suddenly when a tree crushed the cab of his pickup in a windstorm, and hundreds showed up to pay their respects. He stood for something. Charlie Bentley had a terrible tractor accident when his head got trapped between a set of moving disc harrows and the ground. A few months later, he was back farming. He stands for something. Everybody who ever walked into the yellow farmhouse was fed well by Marie Briggs: a thick slice of buttered homemade bread, a couple of biscuits, a molasses cookie or two, or a seat at the table at noon dinner if you showed up on time. She stood for something. In the sixties, Jenny Skidmore invited the hungry, unwashed hippie outcasts over to her Saturday night saunas and gave them a good feed to boot. She stood for something. And anytime somebody needs to find a lost cow, gets locked out in the middle of winter stark naked, or needs a horse put down and buried, they call Tom. He stands for something.

Whenever someone says that we are playing by a new set of rules, that we can indeed get something for nothing, I remember what a bachelor farmer once told me at a corner-house social: "A poor man who stands for something isn't poor." That's not a new rule; it's an old one.

FOR INQUIRIES, ORDERS, OR MORE INFORMATION

www.CooksIllustrated.com
At www.CooksIllustrated.com, you can order books and subscriptions, sign up for our free e-newsletter, or renew your magazine subscription. Join the website and gain access to 18 years of *Cook's Illustrated* recipes, equipment tests, and ingredient tastings, as well as companion videos for every recipe in this issue.

COOKBOOKS
We sell more than 50 cookbooks by the editors of *Cook's Illustrated*. To order, visit our bookstore at www.CooksIllustrated.com.

COOK'S ILLUSTRATED MAGAZINE
Cook's Illustrated magazine (ISSN 1068-2821), number 112, is published bimonthly by Boston Common Press Limited Partnership, 17 Station St., Brookline, MA 02445. Copyright 2011 Boston Common Press Limited Partnership. Periodicals postage paid at Boston, Mass., and additional mailing offices USPS #012487. Publications Mail Agreement No. 40020778. Return undeliverable Canadian addresses to P.O. Box 875, Station A, Windsor, ON N9A 6P2. POSTMASTER: Send address changes to *Cook's Illustrated*, P.O. Box 6018, Harlan, IA 51593-1518. For subscription and gift subscription orders, subscription inquiries, or change-of-address notices, visit us at www.AmericasTestKitchen.com/customerservice or write us at *Cook's Illustrated*, P.O. Box 6018, Harlan, IA 51593-1518.

FOR LIST RENTAL INFORMATION, CONTACT Specialists Marketing Services, Inc., 777 Terrace Ave., 4th Floor, Hasbrouck Heights, NJ 07604; 201-865-5800.
EDITORIAL OFFICE 17 Station St., Brookline, MA 02445; 617-232-1000; fax 617-232-1572. Subscription inquiries, visit www.AmericasTestKitchen.com/customerservice or call 800-526-8442.
POSTMASTER Send all new orders, subscription inquiries, and change-of-address notices to *Cook's Illustrated*, P.O. Box 6018, Harlan, IA 51593-1518.

⇒ BY ANDREA GEARY & DAN SOUZA ⇐

Nutritional Yeast

I recently went to an independent movie theater that offered nutritional yeast as a topping for popcorn. The option sounded odd but intriguing. What is it?

LARRY WEBB
SPOKANE, WASH.

➤Like baker's yeast, nutritional yeast is a member of the fungus kingdom. It's grown on a mixture of beet molasses and sugarcane, and then heated to deactivate its leavening power. There are several brands available—usually in the form of fluffy yellow flakes—at natural foods stores and mail-order sources. Vegans and vegetarians find it especially valuable because it contains the essential nutrient vitamin B_{12}, which is usually obtained from animal products. We'd also heard that it packs big savory flavor, so we popped a batch of popcorn and sprinkled a little on to evaluate.

POPCORN PICK-ME-UP
Ignore the unappealing terminology. Nutritional yeast is a savory seasoning alternative to salt.

Despite its clinical-sounding name, nutritional yeast was a big hit for seasoning popcorn, with tasters describing its effect as "tangy," "nutty," "cheesy," and "addictive." The key is its high level of glutamic acid, the main chemical compound responsible for boosting the *umami* taste in food. Just don't confuse the product with brewer's yeast, which looks similar but tastes bitter.

Poison Beans?

I've heard that dried red kidney beans must be boiled—not just simmered—to make them safe to eat. Is this true? And if so, how long should I boil them?

FRANK DUNN
RICHMOND, IND.

➤Many dried beans contain proteins called lectins that, if ingested raw or partially cooked, can produce symptoms similar to those of food poisoning. Red kidney beans are higher in lectins than other beans, but there's no need to fret: A 1985 research paper published in the *Journal of Food Science* reported that lectins are completely destroyed when beans are boiled for 10 minutes. To keep them from turning mushy, we suggest boiling the beans at the beginning of cooking (when they are at their sturdiest). After that, you can turn down the heat and simmer them until tender.

Cinnamon as a Thickener

I've noticed that when I add ground cinnamon to my hot cocoa or oatmeal, they get thicker. Why does this happen?

JOE WALSTON
DURHAM, N.C.

➤We added 1 teaspoon of ground cinnamon to 1 quart of hot chocolate and experienced the same phenomenon: The spiced version was noticeably thicker than the cinnamon-free sample.

A little investigation revealed that more than half of cinnamon consists of carbohydrates known as polysaccharides, including pectin and cellulose, which can absorb water from liquid and swell. These compounds give cinnamon the power to thicken hot, fluid foods nearly as effectively as cornstarch. But that doesn't mean cinnamon can serve as a spicy-tasting stand-in for starch. Just to see what would happen, we put the thickening power of the spice to the test by preparing two batches of pastry cream: one thickened with 3 tablespoons of cornstarch (per the recipe), the other with an equal amount of ground cinnamon (we'd never want to actually eat this one). While the batches turned out equally viscous, the cinnamon version had an unpleasant stretchy, ropy quality, thanks to the other carbohydrates present in the spice.

Bottom line: A teaspoon or so of ground cinnamon used in baking applications won't noticeably affect texture. But if you want to avoid its thickening effect in warm beverages like hot chocolate or mulled cider, try steeping a cinnamon stick in your drink instead (polysaccharides don't disperse from the whole spice).

Storing Used Frying Oil

I make doughnuts a few times a year and find that my used frying oil—which I store in an airtight container in a dark cupboard—tastes fishy and stale when I reuse it. Is there a better way to store it?

SHIRLEY GOODALE
BROCKTON, MASS.

➤A cool dark cupboard is fine for the short term, since exposure to air and light hastens oil's rate of oxidative rancidification and the creation of off-flavors and odors. But for long-term storage (beyond one month), the cooler the storage temperature the better. We fried chicken in vegetable oil and then divided the oil (strained first) among three containers and stored them in various locations: in a cool, dark cupboard; in the refrigerator; and in the freezer. Two months later, we sautéed chunks of white bread in

each sample and took a taste. Sure enough, the oil from the cupboard had turned fishy and unpleasant and the refrigerated sample only somewhat less so, while the oil kept in the freezer tasted remarkably clean. Why? Though an absence of light is important, very cold temperatures are most effective at slowing oxidation and the production of peroxides, which are the source of rancid oil's unpleasant taste and smell. That's why storing oil in the super-cold, dark freezer is your best bet for keeping it fresh.

A Breath of Fresh Air

I've read that blowing into a bag of salad greens will help them last longer. Does this really work?

LESLIE JOHNSON
DUBUQUE, IOWA

➤The notion seemed pretty wacky to us (not to mention unsanitary), but in the interest of science we divided fresh salad greens into two batches, placing both samples in zipper-lock bags and lightly inflating one of them with a few exhales before sealing. The salad leaves stored in the regular bag started to wilt after five days, while—much to our surprise—those that had received a few puffs lasted almost twice as long.

Here's why: Fresh produce ripens and eventually decomposes by the process of respiration (the conversion of glucose into carbon dioxide and water). However, exposing produce to elevated levels of carbon dioxide can retard the process. Air contains only 0.03 percent carbon dioxide, human breath as much as 4 to 5 percent. A couple of breaths into a zipper-lock bag full of salad greens increased the concentration of carbon dioxide enough to decelerate the respiration process. Despite its effectiveness, we don't recommend this practice since the human breath can contain airborne pathogens.

Manufacturers harness the power of carbon dioxide in a much more sophisticated way, using a method called modified atmosphere packaging to replace some of the oxygen in packages of greens.

POWERFUL PUFF?
Though for sanitary reasons we don't recommend it, breathing into and then sealing a storage bag for salad greens mimics professional methods for prolonging shelf life.

SEND US YOUR QUESTIONS We will provide a complimentary one-year subscription for each letter we print. Send your inquiry, name, address, and daytime telephone number to Notes from Readers, *Cook's Illustrated*, P.O. Box 470589, Brookline, MA 02447, or to NotesFromReaders@ AmericasTestKitchen.com.

Keeping Zested Lemons Juicy

What's the best way to store lemons once their zest has been removed? My zested lemons often become dry, shriveled, and hard before I get a chance to juice them.

NORMA COLEMAN
NORTH SALEM, N.Y.

➤ The flavorful oil that is found in the outer layer, or zest, of lemon skin protects the fruit from drying out. Once you remove that layer, you remove its primary defense against dehydration.

We stripped the zest (but not the white pith) from four lemons and stored them in the fridge in three different ways: wrapped in plastic, enclosed in a zipper-lock bag, and rubbed with a thin layer of vegetable oil. As a control, we refrigerated a fourth zested lemon that we left alone. To measure moisture loss, we weighed the lemons before and after three weeks of refrigeration. The plastic-wrapped and bagged lemons lost only 2.5 percent and 6 percent of their weight, respectively, yielding plenty of juice. By contrast, the oil-coated lemon suffered a 40 percent loss in weight and was almost indistinguishable from the shriveled control sample, in both its firmness and the miserly portion of bitter juice it released. (Without skin or other protection, the juice in a lemon oxidizes, changing its flavor profile.)

The upshot? If you're not going to be juicing a zested lemon for a while, wrap it in plastic before refrigerating it.

When Good Buttermilk Goes Bad

Since buttermilk always smells sour, how do I know when it has gone bad?

SUSAN RUTHERFORD
BURLINGTON, VT.

➤ When we asked this question of the folks at the dairy farm that produces the buttermilk we use in the test kitchen, they told us to consume their product within five to seven days after opening. However, guidelines from agricultural programs at various universities extend that period to two weeks. Then there's our experience, which has shown that refrigerated buttermilk won't turn truly bad (signified by the growth of blue-green mold) until at least three weeks after opening. That it can last this long is not surprising, since buttermilk is high in lactic acid, which is hostile to the growth of harmful bacteria. That said, we wondered if the flavor of buttermilk changes the longer it's stored. To find out, we held a series of tastings, comparing pancakes made with freshly opened buttermilk with those made with buttermilk that had been refrigerated for one week, two weeks, and three weeks. We found that as time went on, the pancakes tasted increasingly bland.

Here's why: The bacteria in buttermilk produce lactic acid and diacetyl, a flavor compound that gives buttermilk its characteristic buttery aroma and taste (diacetyl is also the dominant flavor compound in

butter). As time passes, the buttermilk continues to ferment and becomes more acidic. The abundance of acid kills off virtually all of the bacteria that produce the buttery-tasting diacetyl. So three-week-old buttermilk will retain its tartness (from lactic acid) but lose much of its signature buttery taste, giving it less dimension. The good news is that there is a way to prolong the shelf life and preserve the flavor of buttermilk: Freeze it.

Old-Fashioned Leavener

I have a very old recipe for Hungarian Christmas cookies that calls for baker's ammonia. What is it?

IDA STAVOR
MULLICA HILL, N.J.

➤ Baker's ammonia, also known as ammonium bicarbonate (and often sold as ammonium carbonate), was the primary leavening agent used by bakers before the advent of baking soda and baking powder in the 19th century. In fact, certain recipes for European and Middle Eastern cookies and crackers still call for it today.

When we purchased the powder from a mail-order source (it can also be found at some Greek and Middle Eastern markets), we quickly discovered its biggest drawback: an extremely potent smell. (In fact, it turns out baker's ammonia is the stuff that was passed under Victorian ladies' noses to revive them when they swooned.) Because of its noxious scent,

it is used to leaven only low-moisture baked goods like crisp cookies and crackers that thoroughly dry out during baking, lest the ammonia linger.

When we tried trading baker's ammonia for baking powder in a recipe for crisp sugar cookies, we found that not only can the two products be used interchangeably, but the baker's ammonia produced a lighter, crunchier crumb. This is because when its tiny crystals decompose in the heat of the oven, they leave minuscule air cells in their wake from which moisture easily escapes. Furthermore, this leavener leaves none of the soapy-tasting residue of baking powder or baking soda. It works so well, we'd be tempted to use it for crisp baked goods all the time if it were more readily available.

BAKING POWDER'S PREDECESSOR
Baker's ammonia leavens cookies and crackers at least as well as modern products do.

My father, who was a doctor, was also an avid duck hunter. One of his patients gave him this gift, which she said was a duck press. Can you give me some information about it?

BROOKE OSBORNE BROWN
WESTWOOD, MASS.

PRESS YOUR DUCK
Old-school French chefs use this specialty contraption to press juices out of a duck.

Your sterling silver duck press, which stands 17 inches tall and weighs a hefty 60 pounds, was made by the French manufacturer Christofle. It closely resembles the late-19th-century press used by the famed Parisian restaurant La Tour d'Argent to make its signature dish, Caneton Tour d'Argent—a preparation that exemplifies the extremes of French haute cuisine. First, a Rouen duck specially bred for the restaurant and slaughtered without being bled is par-roasted and its breasts and thighs removed. Its carcass is then inserted into the press's perforated basket (along with a little consommé to help the juices flow), which sits inside a larger cylinder. When the handle is cranked, a silver plate compresses the carcass, directing blood and juices through a spout. The precious jus is combined with cognac and Madeira, reduced until thickened, and served with the breasts. (The thighs are reserved for a subsequent course.)

We couldn't get our hands on an unbled Rouen duck, so we had a little fun experimenting with an eggplant. The press effortlessly crushed the fruit, expelling a considerable amount of juice.

Quick Tips

⇒ COMPILED BY SHANNON FRIEDMANN HATCH ⇐

Refined Trussing

When Wylie Johnson of Bethesda, Md., was out of butcher's twine to truss a chicken, he grabbed a leftover champagne cage instead. He inserted the legs in the cage, twisted the wire to tighten—and the chicken was ready for roasting. (Note: The metal will get hot in the oven, so use caution when removing the cage.)

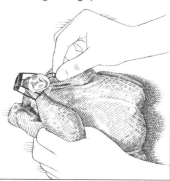

Pasta Water Substitute

Carla Landry of Baton Rouge, La., used to kick herself when she forgot to save pasta water for thinning sauce and instead poured it all down the drain. Now when this happens, she has an easy fix: She mixes ¼ teaspoon of cornstarch with 1 cup of water and microwaves it for 1 to 2 minutes until hot. Just a splash or two of the slightly thickened liquid creates a sauce with just the right consistency.

Swift Scrap Cleanup

Shelly Brandler of Queens, N.Y., saves plastic produce bags from the supermarket and uses them to clean up kitchen scraps. She spreads a bag on the counter next to her cutting board and sweeps scraps such as vegetable peelings and onion skins onto it as she preps. When she's done, she just gathers up the bag and tosses it away.

Clean-Cut Desserts

Cutting brownies or bar cookies with a knife can be a crumby job. Instead, Stella Werman of Cambridge, Mass., finds that her bench scraper makes the cleanest cuts.

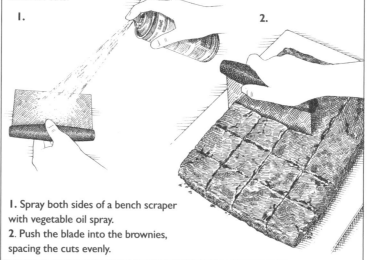

1. Spray both sides of a bench scraper with vegetable oil spray.
2. Push the blade into the brownies, spacing the cuts evenly.

Well-Pressed Spinach

Squeezing cooked spinach dry is a tedious but necessary step before incorporating it into a recipe. Dawna Ellis of Silverdale, Wash., discovered a very effective method for doing so: She places the waterlogged spinach in a colander in the sink and positions a slightly smaller glass bowl on top. She then squeezes the two vessels together, pressing out the unwanted liquid.

Slow-Cooker Clarified Butter

James Erthein of Sandgate, Vt., puts his slow cooker to work to make large batches of clarified butter, which he likes for its higher smoke point and its ability to be used for cooking at higher temperatures.

1. Place 2 to 3 pounds of unsalted butter in the slow-cooker insert. Cover and cook on low until the butter is melted and the milk solids surface, 1 to 1½ hours.
2. Skim the milk solids from the surface until the liquid is clear.
3. Strain the clear liquid through cheesecloth into clean jars. Store clarified butter in the refrigerator for several weeks or freeze it for up to a year.

ILLUSTRATION: JOHN BURGOYNE

Safer Cake Transfer

Eileen Baione of Jensen Beach, Fla., found a new purpose for her cookie sheet: She uses it as a giant spatula to safely separate the thin, delicate layers created after halving cake horizontally—and to put them back together again.

1. 2. 3.

1. Slide the flat end of a cookie sheet between the top and bottom layers of a halved cake until the top half is fully on the sheet. Lift off the top layer and set aside.
2. Frost the bottom layer of the cake.
3. Slide the other round back on top, tilting the cookie sheet and gently shimmying the cake off the flat end.

No Sugar Shaker? No Problem.

When Caitlin Howlett of Waterloo, Ontario, wants to apply a light dusting of powdered sugar to brownies, cakes, or French toast, she turns to her wide-plane rasp grater. A tablespoon of powdered sugar and a few quick taps create the same effect as a sifter or shaker, and the cleanup is a quick rinse under the faucet.

Get a Grip on Slick Bottles

Pouring olive oil from the bottle always leaves a slick drip down the side. Debora Dunsiger of Côte Saint-Luc, Quebec, discovered a fix for this slippery situation: She took the mesh netting used on fruit to keep it from bruising and pulled it over the bottle. The netting creates traction so that she can get a secure grip on the bottle, even with drips.

Taking the Guesswork Out of Measuring

After a few cycles in the dishwasher, the size markings on plastic measuring cups can rub away. Guy Pugh and Steve Yakutis of Jamaica Plain, Mass., turned to their toolbox for help: With an electric drill fit with a very thin bit (⅛ or 1/16 inch), they drilled holes in the cup handles to indicate volume—four holes for the quarter cup, three for the third, and two for the half. (The full cup is hard to misidentify.)

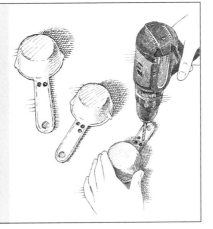

Quick Measure

When he's at the stove, instead of digging around for a tablespoon, David Thornberry of Palm Bay, Fla., measures cooking oil with the lid of the bottle. He's found that the lids on most bottled oils hold about that amount, and cleanup is as easy as wiping the cap.

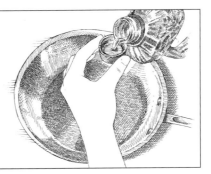

A Corker of an Idea

Very few tools bring order to the kitchen like a utensil holder. However, Catherine Brault of Oroville, Calif., found that her holder knocked against the sides of the drawer every time she opened and closed it. For a better fit, she cut a wine cork to fill the space between the holder and the drawer, creating a wedge that locks the holder in place.

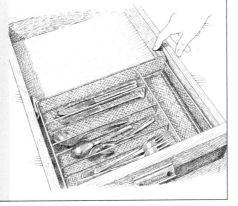

Keeping Tabs on the Coffee Scoop

Ford Fox of San Antonio, Texas, never loses his coffee scoop, thanks to this trick.

1.

2.

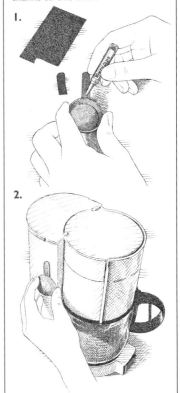

1. Place a coffee scoop facedown on a flat magnet (such as the kind that are often given away free for promotion), trace an outline of the handle, and cut it out. Glue the magnet to the handle's front side.
2. The scoop will now attach to any metal surface on the coffee maker.

French-Style Pot-Roasted Pork

Pot roast almost always starts with a fatty, flavorful cut that turns tender and juicy after hours of cooking. Is it possible to produce the same results from today's lean, bland pork loin?

> BY DAN SOUZA <

French cuisine is well known for its many dishes featuring a lackluster cut of meat turned sumptuous and flavorful by surprisingly simple methods, but the one that impresses me most is *enchaud Périgourdin*. A specialty in the southwest Périgord region of France, it throws the loin—one of the least promising cuts for slow-cooking—into a covered casserole with garlic and a trotter (or pig's foot) to bake for several hours. You'd expect that a roast with so little fat or collagen to protect it would emerge from the pot dried out and tasteless. Instead, the finished meat is astonishingly moist and flavorful, with plenty of rich-tasting, viscous jus to drizzle on top.

Unfortunately, my attempts to make this dish at home have always turned out exactly as I had expected: bland and stringy meat sitting in a flavorless pool of juice. I'm never sure what gets lost in translation, but the promise of a dish that eked out juicy, tender, savory results from this bland (but widely available) roast was motivation enough for me to find an approach of my own. I had just one stipulation: The trotter had to go. Though it imparts body and flavor to the sauce, hunting one down would complicate this genuinely simple dish.

The French Connection

The basic method for preparing enchaud Périgourdin is simple: Season a loin with salt and pepper, tie it with twine so it cooks evenly, and sear it in a Dutch oven. Then remove the roast, sauté garlic (and a little onion) in the rendered fat, add seasonings (and a trotter or two), bake in a covered casserole, and, finally, let it rest briefly before serving to allow the juices to redistribute. I gave a few new recipes a try, and when not one of the roasts—cooked at both high heat and more moderate temperatures—turned out like the juicy, rich-tasting pot-roasted loins I've enjoyed in Périgord, I realized I had a very

Though untraditional, a diced apple sautéed in the pot with the onion and garlic brightens the meaty richness of the jus.

fundamental problem to deal with: the pork itself. While French pigs are bred to have plenty of fat, American pork contains far less marbling, with the center-cut roast that I was using perhaps the leanest cut of all. The blade-end roast, the part of the loin closest to the shoulder, has more fat and flavor, but it's not nearly as readily available.

I was stuck with the center-cut loin and wondered if I could improve the results by dropping the oven temperature (the lowest I'd tried so far was 325 degrees) and pulling out the roast when it hit the medium mark (140 degrees). Sure enough, this test proved that the lower the oven temperature, the more succulent the roast. My tasters clearly favored the pork cooked in the 225-degree oven for about 70 minutes. In this very low oven, the outer layers of the loin absorbed less heat (and consequently squeezed out less moisture) during the time it took the center to climb to 140 degrees. And not only was it far juicier than any of my previous attempts, but a small pool of concentrated jus had accumulated at the bottom of the pot.

There was just one texture-related setback: The bottom of the roast, which was in direct contact with the pot, cooked more quickly than the top. I easily solved this problem by searing just the top and sides of the roast while leaving the bottom raw. But I still had work to do. Engineering juicier meat hadn't improved its bland flavor. Plus, without the trotter, the sauce lacked body.

A Seasoned Approach

Salting and brining are our go-to methods when we want to draw seasoning into large cuts of pork and help the meat retain moisture during cooking. Brining wouldn't be helpful here, because soaking in a salt solution adds extra water to the meat, which would simply leach out and dilute the jus. Salting was the better option. The downside was that it took at least six hours (with superior results after 24 hours) for the salt to penetrate deep into the thick roast. I wondered if I could find a faster way.

It seemed that splitting the loin lengthwise into two smaller pieces and liberally sprinkling each one with salt might hasten the seasoning process, but when I gave it a shot, tasters complained that the interior of each mini loin was still bland. Slicing a pocket into the top of the loin and sprinkling the interior with salt was strike two. Though the center of the roast was well seasoned, it was just as easy to get an unseasoned bite.

After some further experimentation I landed on an effective technique: "double-butterflying." By making two sweeping cuts—the first one-third of the way up the loin and the second into the thicker portion that I created with the first cut—I was able to open up the loin like a tri-fold book and expose a vast amount of surface area. Then I rubbed each side with 1½ teaspoons of kosher salt, folded the loin back up, and secured it with twine. While this method required a bit more knife work, it produced perfectly seasoned meat. Even better, this technique made it possible to add fat and flavor directly to the meat, bringing me closer to the French original.

For "fattening up" the roast, bacon fat, rendered salt-pork fat, and butter all seemed like viable options. Though each produced richly flavorful, supremely juicy roasts, tasters particularly enjoyed the subtly sweet flavor imparted by butter. In fact,

SECRETS TO JUICY, RICH-TASTING POT-ROASTED PORK LOIN

Thanks to their well-marbled pork, the French can get away with pot-roasting the loin, one of the leanest cuts of the pig, without drying it out. Here's how we adapted their approach to super-lean American pork loin.

"DOUBLE-BUTTERFLY" AND SALT Opening up the roast like a tri-fold book creates more surface area for seasoning, ensuring that the salt thoroughly penetrates the meat.

ADD FAT Spreading garlic butter over the surface enriches this lean cut, bringing it closer in flavor and juiciness to well-marbled French pork. We then fold up and tie the roast.

SEAR TIED ROAST ON 3 SIDES Browning only the sides of the roast that are not in contact with the pan during roasting prevents the bottom of the meat from overcooking.

COOK IN LOW OVEN Roasting the pork in a gentle 225-degree oven until medium guarantees that the meat will cook up tender and juicy, not chalky and dry.

ADD GELATIN Adding gelatin to the exuded meat juices replaces the body and richness lost by omitting the pig's trotter used in the French original.

I pushed that sweetness one step further and added 1 teaspoon of sugar to the salt rub. To round out the roast's savory depth, I then sliced a few garlic cloves and caramelized them in the butter before using the mixture to coat the meat. Finally, I sprinkled the rolled roast with *herbes de Provence*, a heady combination that includes dried basil, fennel, lavender, marjoram, rosemary, sage, and thyme.

Enriching the Jus

That left just the flavorful-but-thin jus to attend to. I knew one way to bulk up the jus would be to put bones in the pot. Not only do the bones themselves contain gelatin, but the connective tissue surrounding them also turns into gelatin over the course of long cooking. I wanted to see what would happen if I started with a bone-in loin, removed the bones, and then used them to make a quick stock to add to the pork as it roasted. This worked beautifully. When I opened the pot about an hour later, the jus was as glossy and thickened as the trotter-enhanced liquid. The only problem was that making the stock tacked on 30 minutes to an already lengthy cooking time. I wondered if adding powdered gelatin, which we've used in the past to mimic slow-cooked stocks, would do the trick here, and found that 1 tablespoon bloomed in ¼ cup of chicken broth lent just the right viscosity.

But bones also contribute flavor, and I still had to make up for that loss. Reducing ⅓ cup of white wine (after sautéing the onions) and whisking in 1 tablespoon of butter along with the gelatin rendered the sauce rich and balanced but not remarkable. It was only my final inspiration—a diced apple cooked along with the onions—that really brought the sauce together. Enchaud is traditionally served with pickles as a counterpoint to its rich flavors, and tasters raved that the softened bits of sweet-tart fruit worked in the same way. A variation with port and figs was equally satisfying.

The French method had started me off, but it was kitchen testing that made slow-cooking this super-lean cut something truly great.

FRENCH-STYLE POT-ROASTED PORK LOIN

SERVES 4 TO 6

We strongly prefer the flavor of natural pork in this recipe, but if enhanced pork (injected with a salt solution) is used, reduce the salt to 2 teaspoons (1 teaspoon per side) in step 2. For tips on "double-butterflying," see page 30. For our free recipe for French-Style Pot-Roasted Pork Loin with Marsala and Mushrooms, go to www.CooksIllustrated.com/oct11.

2	tablespoons unsalted butter, cut into 2 pieces
6	garlic cloves, sliced thin
1	(2½-pound) boneless center-cut pork loin roast, trimmed
	Kosher salt and pepper
1	teaspoon sugar
2	teaspoons herbes de Provence
2	tablespoons vegetable oil
1	Granny Smith apple, peeled, cored, and cut into ¼-inch pieces
1	onion, chopped fine
⅓	cup dry white wine
2	sprigs fresh thyme
1	bay leaf
¼–¾	cup low-sodium chicken broth
1	tablespoon unflavored gelatin
1	tablespoon chopped fresh parsley

1. Adjust oven rack to lower-middle position and heat oven to 225 degrees. Melt 1 tablespoon butter in 8-inch skillet over medium-low heat. Add half of garlic and cook, stirring frequently, until golden, 5 to 7 minutes. Transfer mixture to bowl and refrigerate.

2. Position roast fat side up. Insert knife one-third of way up from bottom of roast along 1 long side and cut horizontally, stopping ½ inch before edge. Open up flap. Keeping knife parallel to cutting board, cut through thicker portion of roast about ½ inch from bottom of roast, keeping knife level with first cut and stopping about ½ inch before edge. Open up this flap. If uneven, cover with plastic wrap and use meat

pounder to even out. Sprinkle 1 tablespoon salt over both sides of loin (½ tablespoon per side) and rub into pork until slightly tacky. Sprinkle sugar over inside of loin, then spread with cooled toasted garlic mixture. Starting from short side, fold roast back together like business letter (keeping fat on outside) and tie with twine at 1-inch intervals. Sprinkle tied roast evenly with herbes de Provence and season with pepper.

3. Heat 1 tablespoon oil in Dutch oven over medium heat until just smoking. Add roast, fat side down, and brown on fat side and sides (do not brown bottom of roast), 5 to 8 minutes. Transfer to large plate. Add remaining 1 tablespoon oil, apple, and onion; cook, stirring frequently, until onion is softened and browned, 5 to 7 minutes. Stir in remaining sliced garlic and cook until fragrant, about 30 seconds. Stir in wine, thyme, and bay leaf; cook for 30 seconds. Return roast, fat side up, to pot; place large sheet of aluminum foil over pot and cover tightly with lid. Transfer pot to oven and cook until pork registers 140 degrees, 50 to 90 minutes (short, thick roasts will take longer than long, thin ones).

4. Transfer roast to carving board, tent loosely with foil, and let rest for 20 minutes. While pork rests, sprinkle gelatin over ¼ cup chicken broth and let sit until gelatin softens, about 5 minutes. Remove and discard thyme sprigs and bay leaf from jus. Pour jus into 2-cup measuring cup and, if necessary, add chicken broth to measure 1¼ cups. Return jus to pot and bring to simmer over medium heat. Whisk softened gelatin mixture, remaining 1 tablespoon butter, and parsley into jus and season with salt and pepper to taste; remove from heat and cover to keep warm. Slice pork into ½-inch-thick slices, adding any accumulated juices to sauce. Serve pork, passing sauce separately.

FRENCH-STYLE POT-ROASTED PORK LOIN WITH PORT AND FIGS

Substitute ¾ cup chopped dried figs for apple and port for white wine. Add 1 tablespoon balsamic vinegar to sauce with butter in step 4.

Weeknight Roast Chicken

If you can plan ahead, by all means brine or salt your bird. But when you want dinner on the table in an hour, you need a different way to get juicy, tender chicken.

≥ BY BRYAN ROOF ≤

If there's one thing we've learned from years of experience in the test kitchen, it's that the best way to guarantee a juicy, well-seasoned roast chicken is to brine or salt the bird (at least 30 minutes for brining and up to 24 hours for salting) before it hits the oven. We've found that such pretreatment reliably solves the classic roast-poultry predicament: how to keep the lean, delicate breast meat from overcooking by the time the fattier leg quarters come up to temperature. The salt in both methods buffers the meat against overcooking by restructuring its proteins, enabling it to retain more of its natural juices.

While we stand by these methods, we realize that on a weeknight, many cooks just don't have time to salt or brine. We got to thinking: Wouldn't it be great if we could come up with a foolproof way to roast chicken that didn't call for any preroasting treatment?

Rethinking the Rack

The best approach, it seemed to me, was to modify our standard method for roasting chicken, which calls for submerging the bird in a salt-sugar brine (sugar encourages good browning) for an hour; brushing it with melted butter; and roasting it in a 375-degree oven in a V-rack, starting wing side up. We flip the bird twice (once to expose the other wing and the second time to expose the breast), pulling the chicken from the oven when the breast and thigh meat hit 160 and 175 degrees, respectively. I would take that recipe, skip the brine, and then put every other step under the microscope—from the roasting pan, to the V-rack, to the oven temperature, to whether or not to flip.

I started with the V-rack. This piece of equipment elevates the bird so the oven's heat can circulate evenly around it. The V-rack also prevents the skin from sitting in juices that would keep it from crisping up. I definitely wanted crisp skin, but I

A skillet makes maneuvering the chicken in and out of the oven a lot easier than when it's in a roasting pan.

also knew that I could use the pan's surface to my advantage. If I preheated the pan and then placed the chicken in it breast side up, the thighs would get a jump-start on cooking, much as they would if I seared them first in a skillet. This change would mean the flipping would also go, since that would entail placing the breast directly against the pan's hot surface for part of the cooking time, which would dry it out even faster.

I compared a pan-seared bird against one roasted in the traditional rack setup and found the results surprisingly decent. The skin was poorly browned, but tasters agreed that the breast meat was better now that the thigh meat had a head start in the pan and I could shave a few minutes off the cooking time. The V-rack and flipping were out; preheating the roasting pan was in.

Oven On, Oven Off

Now what about oven temperature? Since the 375-degree oven wasn't really doing the breast meat any favors, I reasoned my next move should

be lowering the heat to cook that delicate meat more gently. I readied a few more birds and experimented with dropping the temperature down to 300 degrees, but the results were disappointing. Though the white meat became marginally juicier, there was an obvious—and unacceptable—trade-off: The skin had gone from patchily browned to pale. Cranking the heat above 375 degrees improved the skin but, not surprisingly, reversed the slight gains I'd made with juicier breast meat.

Without any clear idea of how to proceed, I decided to roast a chicken according to a recipe developed by celebrated French chef Joël Robuchon that is widely regarded as one of the best. He places the bird in a buttered baking dish and rubs it with softened butter—and then does something totally unexpected: He puts it in a cold oven and promptly cranks the heat to 410 degrees. I found that while the hotter temperature did color the skin a deeper shade of bronze, it didn't produce meat any juicier than chickens I'd roasted in preheated ovens. And with this method, I was back to constant flipping.

But could there be something to the idea of a dramatic shift in oven temperature? What if I reversed Robuchon's method by starting the chicken at a relatively hot temperature to brown the skin, but then turned off the oven midway through cooking? I'll admit that I wouldn't be the first cook in the test kitchen to try something like this. A few years back, a colleague shut off the heat partway through cooking a notoriously tough eye-round roast as a way to make the meat tender and keep it juicy.

I decided to give this radical approach a shot but go back to using a preheated roasting pan and no rack. I set the dial to Robuchon's recommended 410 degrees, brushed the chicken with melted butter, seasoned it aggressively with salt and pepper, and lowered it into the hot pan breast side up so that the thighs would start cooking immediately. Then after about 30 minutes, I shut off the heat, let the bird idle in the oven until the breast and thigh meat hit their target temperatures about 30 minutes later, and let it sit on the counter for its requisite 20-minute rest, during which juices would be released and then drawn back into the meat.

HOW TO GET GREAT ROAST CHICKEN IN ONE HOUR. TRULY.

Our unique high-heat/no-heat method ensures crisp skin and super-moist breast meat.

CRANK THE HEAT
Turning the oven up to 450 degrees, instead of roasting at a more typical 350 to 375 degrees, ensures nicely browned, well-rendered skin.

USE A SKILLET
Swapping a roasting pan for a skillet allows the juices to pool deeper in its smaller surface area, so less evaporates and more is left over for pan sauce.

"SEAR" THE THIGHS
Placing the bird breast side up onto the preheated skillet sears the thighs, giving them a head start so that they cook in sync with the delicate breast meat.

TURN OFF THE HEAT
Turning off the oven when the meat is halfway done allows the chicken to finish cooking very gently (it will rise 40 degrees) and not dry out.

I'm not exaggerating when I say that this latest bird was a huge success: Beneath the layer of nicely tanned skin was white meat so tender and moist that even the dark meat loyalists among us were reaching for second helpings. A quick conversation with our science editor helped me understand why the approach was so effective: In meat with a lot of surface area like chicken, most of the moisture loss that occurs during cooking is through surface evaporation. Shutting off the oven will cool the chicken's exterior relatively rapidly, in turn slowing the evaporation of juices. In the meantime, heat that's already inside the chicken will continue to be conducted deeper into the interior, eventually bringing it to the desired safe temperature (the same carryover cooking that occurs when meat is resting). The net result is a juicier chicken with virtually no chance of overcooking.

I was very happy with the progress I'd made with the meat, but I wondered if I could darken the skin on the breast another shade by increasing the oven's heat. I tested temperatures all the way up to 500 degrees and found the ceiling when the hottest ovens filled with smoke midway through cooking as the rendered fat burned in the roasting pan. The finest of the flock emerged from a 450-degree oven: beautifully dark amber skin encasing tender, juicy meat.

Still, all was not well. The higher heat forced more of the juices to evaporate, leaving me with less for a pan sauce. I reasoned that if I replaced the roasting pan with a skillet, the juices would pool in the smaller space and not evaporate as quickly. Plus, its long handle and less cumbersome shape would make shuffling the chicken in and out of the oven easier. When I made the switch, I found the only minor downside was that the skin on the back of the chicken sat in the juices, which turned it soggy. But since this skin is rarely eaten anyway—and the rest of the skin was so gorgeous—I wasn't too bothered.

I made two other small adjustments: I swapped the melted butter for olive oil, which gave me equally good results with even less work. I also broke with our older recipe by trussing the legs. I wasn't worried that tying the legs together would slow down the cooking of the inner thigh (the main reason we avoided this technique in the past); in fact, now that I was relying on carryover cooking, it might even help keep the heat in.

A Jus(t) Ending

The only item left on my checklist? Making good use of the pan drippings. I spooned out and discarded all but 1 tablespoon of the fat, making sure to leave the flavorful browned bits in the pan, and worked up a simple sauce with mustard, tarragon, and lemon juice.

I looked at my watch. I had started cooking only an hour beforehand, but thanks to my new foolproof, dead-simple technique, I was already sitting down to the best roast chicken I'd ever made without brining or salting. This was definitely going to be my standard method for weeknight roast chicken.

WEEKNIGHT ROAST CHICKEN
SERVES 4

We prefer to use a 3½- to 4-pound chicken for this recipe. If roasting a larger bird, increase the time when the oven is on in step 2 to 35 to 40 minutes. Cooking the chicken in a preheated skillet will ensure that the breast and thigh meat finish cooking at the same time. For our free recipe for Thyme and Sherry Vinegar Pan Sauce, go to www.CooksIllustrated.com/oct11.

- 1 tablespoon kosher salt
- ½ teaspoon pepper
- 1 (3½- to 4-pound) whole chicken, giblets discarded
- 1 tablespoon olive oil
- 1 recipe pan sauce (optional)

1. Adjust oven rack to middle position, place 12-inch ovensafe skillet on rack, and heat oven to 450 degrees. Combine salt and pepper in bowl. Pat chicken dry with paper towels. Rub entire surface with oil. Sprinkle evenly all over with salt mixture and rub in mixture with hands to coat evenly. Tie legs together with twine and tuck wing tips behind back.

2. Transfer chicken, breast side up, to preheated skillet in oven. Roast chicken until breasts register 120 degrees and thighs register 135 degrees, 25 to 35 minutes. Turn off oven and leave chicken in oven until breasts register 160 degrees and thighs register 175 degrees, 25 to 35 minutes.

3. Transfer chicken to carving board and let rest, uncovered, for 20 minutes. While chicken rests, prepare pan sauce, if using. Carve chicken and serve.

TARRAGON-LEMON PAN SAUCE
MAKES ABOUT ¾ CUP

- 1 shallot, minced
- 1 cup low-sodium chicken broth
- 2 teaspoons Dijon mustard
- 2 tablespoons unsalted butter
- 2 teaspoons minced fresh tarragon
- 2 teaspoons lemon juice
   Pepper

While chicken rests, remove all but 1 tablespoon of fat from now-empty skillet (handle will be very hot) using large spoon, leaving any fond and jus in skillet. Place skillet over medium-high heat, add shallot, and cook until softened, about 2 minutes. Stir in broth and mustard, scraping skillet bottom with wooden spoon to loosen fond. Simmer until reduced to ¾ cup, about 3 minutes. Off heat, whisk in butter, tarragon, and lemon juice. Season with pepper to taste; cover and keep warm. Serve with chicken.

TECHNIQUE | PROPER TEMPING

Inserting the thermometer too far, not far enough, or at the wrong angle can give you an inaccurate reading. Here's our method:

WHITE MEAT
Insert probe low into thickest part of breast, just above bone (typically the coolest spot, as bone conducts heat poorly). Withdraw probe slowly, checking for lowest registered temperature.

DARK MEAT
Insert probe down into space between tip of breast and thigh. Angle probe outward ever so slightly so it pierces meat in lower part of thigh.

Light-as-Air Potato Gnocchi

What's the secret to transforming two heavyweight ingredients—flour and potatoes—into featherweight dumplings? It comes down to the simplest of strategies: precision.

≥ BY DAN SOUZA ≤

In Italy, gnocchi can mean any number of different styles of dumpling, from ricotta to semolina. In this country, gnocchi usually means the potato-based type. At their best, these thimble-size dumplings boast a pillowy texture and an earthy flavor that needs nothing more than a gloss of browned butter sauce to be fit for the table. Creating them always looks straight-forward enough: Just mash the cooked potatoes, bind them with flour and knead into dough, shape into dumplings, and boil. And yet the surplus of mediocre versions is astonishing. Most of the time, these dumplings turn out dense, gluey, or rubbery—and sometimes all of the above.

The fact is that even in a seemingly simple recipe such as this, there's plenty of room for error. First, the moisture in the potato will affect how much flour the dough absorbs—and, in turn, will impact the density of the gnocchi. Second, mashing the potatoes presents a Catch-22. While obviously necessary, the action of mashing bursts starch cells in the potatoes, and the more they burst, the gluier the gnocchi. Third, developing a modest amount of gluten is what lends these dumplings their pleasantly faint chew, but mix in too much flour or overknead the dough, and you'll end up with leaden sinkers. Add to this the fact that sometimes even the most perfectly textured gnocchi can lack distinct potato flavor and the challenge looms even larger.

Surely there was some way to make this simple recipe foolproof so that light, delicate, and potato-y gnocchi were not a happy accident, but a guarantee.

Baked or Boiled?

I wasn't shocked to find that the majority of gnocchi recipes I surveyed called for russet potatoes, since their low-moisture flesh absorbs less flour than other spuds. The trouble is, they're also comparatively bland. I tried out two other types of potato, but the resulting dumplings were as dense as rubber balls. Clearly russets were the way to go.

A three-minute browned butter sauce is all these gnocchi need.

No need to give up on potato flavor just yet, however. The precooking step was my opportunity to enhance the spuds' earthiness, and I quickly set up a side-by-side test between baked and boiled samples. Not surprisingly, the oven deepened the potatoes' flavor, while the hot water bath washed them out. Even better, the former's dry heat evaporated some of the spuds' moisture, yielding fluffier results. I pulled out an old test kitchen trick to hasten the process. I zapped the potatoes in the microwave for 10 minutes before moving them into a hot 450-degree oven, where they needed just 20 minutes to finish cooking. (Microwaving them the whole time led to unevenly cooked, bland potatoes.) I then pulled the spuds from the oven and grabbed an oven mitt and paring knife to remove the skins. Again, since the drier the potatoes the better, working quickly was essential to ensuring that the spuds would give off as much steam as possible.

Light Starch, Please

It was time to mash, and for the gentlest method possible, I chose a ricer. We've found that this tool ruptures fewer starch cells than hand-mashing, since it only compresses the potatoes once. I then followed the lead of many recipes and spread the riced strands onto a baking sheet, where they continued to release steam.

Once the potatoes had cooled slightly, the flour could be incorporated—but exactly how much was not clear. The existing recipes I'd tried didn't specify an amount of flour but offered a range that varied by as much as 1 cup in some cases. The idea is to form the dough with the lesser amount of flour and boil a few test dumplings to see if it's enough. If the gnocchi fall apart, gradually work more flour into the dough. But therein lies the problem: Because you're starting on the low end of the scale, the dough invariably requires more flour, which means extra kneading—and more gluten development—as you work it in. To limit the dough manipulation, the trick would be to weigh out an exact amount of cooked potato and then determine the precise amount of flour that corresponds to it. Not only would I avoid guesswork during mixing, but the dough would turn out the same way every time.

To determine the minimum amount of flour required to bind 16 ounces of potato together, I made several batches of dough, using a fork to gently stir different amounts into each and kneading them for just a minute. The magic number turned out to be 5 ounces; any less and the gnocchi feathered apart in the water. But although these gnocchi cooked up relatively light and airy, they still weren't the delicate puffs I had envisioned.

Reasoning that I could do no more than I already had with the potatoes and flour, I pulled out what I thought might be a ringer from my pantry: baking powder. This batch definitely puffed up but, unfortunately, also absorbed some cooking water and turned mushy. And the same was true for baking soda. With so little gluten, the dough couldn't hold the gases created by leavening, and it blew apart, allowing water to seep in.

I was running low on ideas when a colleague asked why I hadn't tried incorporating an egg, a relatively common addition. I have to admit that this omission wasn't entirely accidental: I'd deliberately avoided recipes calling for egg because I thought its proteins would coagulate during cooking and bind the dough together too firmly. But at this point, I had nothing to lose.

I whipped up another batch of dough, this time stirring in a beaten egg before adding the 5 ounces of flour. Predictably, the dough was a little wetter than usual. Because I resisted compensating with flour, I was skeptical about the gnocchi holding together when they hit the boiling water. I needn't have feared. These gnocchi not only held their shape but also emerged from the water puffed and tender. The egg turned out to be exactly what the dough needed after all: a more tender building block than gluten-rich flour, with the proteins creating just the right amount of structure.

I wondered if I could press this advantage even further. I made another batch, dropping the flour to a mere 4 ounces. After 90 seconds of simmering, the gnocchi had the impossibly light texture and rich potato flavor I'd been aiming for.

As for shaping, I kept my method traditional: Cut the dough into eight pieces, roll each into a ½-inch-thick rope, and cut ¾-inch lengths. From there, I simply pressed each dumpling against the back of a fork to create an indentation and then rolled them down the tines to create ridges. This classic technique serves two purposes: The ridges trap sauce, while the indentation helps each gnocchi cook more evenly.

These potato-y puffs were good enough to eat straight from the pot, drizzled with a little extra-virgin olive oil, but I also wanted to whip up a simple sauce. The traditional nutty browned butter with shallot and fresh sage fit the bill perfectly—and took just three minutes to make.

In the end, it turns out that you don't need to be Italian or an accomplished cook to make perfect gnocchi. All it takes is a little precision—and an egg.

POTATO GNOCCHI WITH BROWNED BUTTER AND SAGE
SERVES 2 TO 3 AS A MAIN DISH OR 4 TO 6 AS AN APPETIZER

For the most accurate measurements, weigh the potatoes and flour. After processing, you may have slightly more than the 3 cups (16 ounces) of potatoes required for this recipe. Discard any extra or set it aside for another use. Besides the browned butter sauce, try our Gorgonzola Cream Sauce, Parmesan Sauce with Pancetta and Walnuts, and Porcini Mushroom Broth, available free at www.CooksIllustrated.com/oct11.

Gnocchi

- 2 pounds russet potatoes
- 1 large egg, lightly beaten
- ¾ cup plus 1 tablespoon (4 ounces) all-purpose flour, plus extra for counter
- 1 teaspoon plus 1 tablespoon salt

Sauce

- 4 tablespoons unsalted butter, cut into 4 pieces
- 1 small shallot, minced
- 1 teaspoon minced fresh sage
- 1½ teaspoons lemon juice
- ¼ teaspoon salt

1. FOR THE GNOCCHI: Adjust oven rack to middle position and heat oven to 450 degrees. Poke each potato 8 times with paring knife over entire surface. Microwave potatoes until slightly softened

---

KEYS TO AIRY, EARTHY-TASTING POTATO GNOCCHI

BAKE, DON'T BOIL Boiled potatoes taste dull. Instead, jump-start cooking in the microwave and then finish them in the oven.

PEEL 'EM WHILE THEY'RE HOT Peel hot potatoes to release steam. This ensures drier spuds that hold together with less flour.

SPREAD OUT Press the cooked potatoes through a ricer, then allow more steam to escape by spreading the potatoes on a sheet pan.

BE PRECISE Start with an exact amount of cooked potato and flour so you knead only once.

ADD AN EGG Egg helps dough hold its shape with less flour, for lighter results.

KNEAD BRIEFLY Knead dough until it just holds together to avoid overdeveloping gluten.

---

at ends, about 10 minutes, flipping potatoes halfway through cooking. Transfer potatoes directly to oven rack and bake until skewer glides easily through flesh and potatoes yield to gentle pressure, 18 to 20 minutes.

2. Holding each potato with potholder or kitchen towel, peel with paring knife. Process potatoes through ricer or food mill onto rimmed baking sheet. Gently spread potatoes into even layer and let cool for 5 minutes.

3. Transfer 3 cups (16 ounces) warm potatoes to bowl. Using fork, gently stir in egg until just combined. Sprinkle flour and 1 teaspoon salt over potato mixture. Using fork, gently combine until no pockets of dry flour remain. Press mixture into rough ball, transfer to lightly floured counter, and gently knead until smooth but slightly sticky, about 1 minute, lightly dusting counter with flour as needed to prevent sticking.

4. Line 2 rimmed baking sheets with parchment paper and dust liberally with flour. Cut dough into 8 pieces. Lightly dust counter with flour. Gently roll piece of dough into ½-inch-thick rope, dusting with flour to prevent sticking. Cut rope into ¾-inch lengths. Holding fork with tines facing down in 1 hand, press each dough piece cut side down against tines with thumb of other hand to create indentation. Roll dough down tines to form ridges on sides. If dough sticks, dust thumb or fork with flour. Transfer formed gnocchi to sheets and repeat with remaining dough.

5. FOR THE SAUCE: Melt butter in 12-inch skillet over medium-high heat, swirling occasionally,

until butter is browned and releases nutty aroma, about 1½ minutes. Off heat, add shallot and sage, stirring until shallot is fragrant, about 1 minute. Stir in lemon juice and salt; cover to keep warm.

6. Bring 4 quarts water to boil in large pot. Add remaining 1 tablespoon salt. Using parchment paper as sling, gently lower gnocchi from 1 sheet into water and cook until firm and just cooked through, about 90 seconds (gnocchi should float to surface after about 1 minute). Using slotted spoon, transfer cooked gnocchi to skillet with sauce. Repeat with remaining gnocchi. Gently toss gnocchi with sauce and serve.

TECHNIQUE

MAKE THE RIGHT IMPRESSION

Ridges and indentations help gnocchi hold on to sauce. To create them, hold fork with tines facing down. Press each dough piece (cut side down) against tines with thumb to make indentation. Roll dumpling down tines to create ridges on sides.

Better Beef Satay

American restaurants have sapped the magic from this Thai street-food favorite with flavorless meat that's either mushy or overcooked. What would it take to get it back?

> ≥ BY BRYAN ROOF ≤

In Bangkok's outdoor markets, the pungent fragrance of charring meat hovers in the air. It's grilled *satay*—Southeast Asia's most famous street fare, featuring tender swaths of assertively flavored pork, chicken, or beef that have been marinated for hours, threaded onto bamboo skewers, and then cooked over charcoal to achieve a lightly burnished crust.

But something funny happened on satay's journey from Thai food stall to stateside sit-down restaurant: The magic got lost. And the worst offender, hands down, is the beef version. Whether cut too thick and overcooked (making it chewy like leather) or "tenderized" by a long marinade (giving it a mealy exterior), the texture is unappealing—to say nothing of the meat's lackluster flavor, which relies far too much on the chile-spiked peanut sauce served on the side.

How hard could it be to bring beef satay back to its streetwise roots? I headed to the test kitchen to find out.

Right Flank

Figuring out the best cut of beef—and how to slice it—would go far toward improving the situation, so I started there. I ruled out luxury cuts from the outset and narrowed the field to less expensive flank, skirt, top round, and top sirloin, all of which have good flavor and can be tender, too, if treated right.

I cut each of these steaks into pieces small enough to thread onto skewers, taking care to slice the flank and skirt against the grain (a tenderizing trick we use for heavily striated cuts of beef). I soaked the meat for 30 minutes in a simple coconut milk–based marinade before skewering it and throwing it onto the grill.

Top round was the loser, coming out tough with liver-y off-notes. Sirloin had great flavor, but inconsistent texture. Skirt and flank ended up in a dead heat for first place, thanks to plenty of evenly distributed fat. I went with symmetrical flank, which would be far easier to prep than tapered skirt.

Basting the beef just three times is enough to give it great flavor.

Experimenting with butchering methods, I found that halving the flank steak lengthwise first, and then slicing the two long, thin portions on a slight bias, about ¼ inch thick, yielded the optimal size and shape for skewering—and for consuming in a bite or two.

Trough Going

Small pieces of flank steak cook in a matter of minutes, and it's a race to get the exterior adequately crusted before the interior overcooks—a chronic problem in the satay recipes I'd tested. The solution seemed easy enough: Just make the fire hotter. Our usual setup for that—piling the coals on one side of the grill—gave me the firepower I wanted but required seriously nimble work with tongs to keep every morsel on the 12-inch skewers directly over this more contained fire. Add basting—which I did right as I put the meat on the grill, again when I flipped the skewers, and once

more right before I took them off—and the whole process became more trouble than it was worth.

Trolling the Internet for a better idea, I happened upon videos of satay vendors in action and was reminded of the unique style of grill they use for the job. Instead of a kettle with grates, the street vendors cook over a trough-shaped grill, about as wide as the skewers are long, which allows them to suspend the meat mere inches above the coals. Mimicking this setup, I took a 13 by 9-inch disposable aluminum roasting pan—my makeshift "trough"—poked several holes in the bottom of it (to allow for air circulation), positioned it atop the cooking grate of my kettle grill, and filled it with hot coals. I strategically threaded the steak onto only the middle 9 inches of each skewer—so the ends could rest on the edge of the pan—and positioned them just above the coals, Thai-style. I imagined street vendors in Bangkok giving me the thumbs up for my ingenuity—until reality set in. The meat was now so close to the fire that I needed to flip it as constantly and frenetically as they did in the video, and doing so still didn't prevent me from overcooking it.

Maybe what I needed to do was mimic the setup but introduce a little more space between the coals and the meat. This time I positioned the pan inside the kettle, poured the hot coals inside, and replaced the cooking grate. I then lined up the skewers over the pan. This method worked like a charm. When I basted the satay, the coals smoldered just enough to impart a subtle smokiness, yet the heat was sufficiently powerful to yield a lovely burnished exterior—but not so hot that I had to flip the skewers more than once.

Grill Setup for Satay: East Meets West

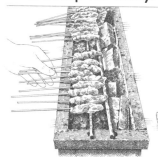

THAI WAY
The trough-shaped grills used by Thai street-food vendors concentrate the firepower but require flipping the skewered meat constantly so it doesn't burn.

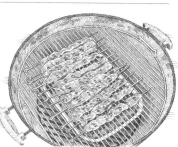

OUR WAY
We corralled the coals in an aluminum pan in the center of the grill to bring them closer to the meat—but not so close that we needed to flip it more than once.

The "Root" of the Problem

Finally, I turned my attention back to the marinade. The test kitchen has spent years determining what works and what doesn't. So, it was with a touch of hubris that I picked off ingredients I knew would be problematic. Acids—gone. We've found they do nothing but weaken the surface of the meat, giving it a mushy texture. Likewise, enzyme-rich juices like pineapple and papaya were sent packing. Though many recipes incorporate them to help "tenderize" tough cuts of meat, our tests have shown that all they do is break down the exterior. Besides, my choice of cut and cooking method yielded ample tenderness; what I needed now was big flavor.

From the ingredients left standing, I assembled the marinade: oil, to facilitate the transfer of oil-soluble flavorings; salty fish sauce, for its brining and flavor-boosting qualities; brown sugar, for complexity and enhanced browning; plus coconut milk, a smattering of dried spices, and a generous amount of minced fresh lemon grass, shallots, and ginger root.

Confidently, I tossed the sliced flank steak with the marinade, letting it chill in the refrigerator for an hour. (We've found there is little benefit to longer marinating times.) I skewered them, grilled them, and dug in. As expected, the flavor was terrific. The problem was the texture: The exterior suffered the mealiness I thought I'd taken every precaution to avoid. Cutting the marinating time in half, I tried again. The flavor was every bit as good (so I kept the marinade brief in the final recipe), but the texture was just as mealy.

Puzzled, I went down the ingredient list, omitting each component of the marinade one by one in subsequent batches. It was only when I eliminated the ginger that I fingered the culprit—without this root, the meat wasn't mealy in the least. Additional research revealed that ginger contains zingibain, an enzyme that aggressively breaks down protein. And my recipe had called for 2 tablespoons of the stuff. I hated to remove such a key flavoring, but what could I do?

Then it occurred to me: What if I kept the marinade very simple—and ramped up the basting sauce with ginger and most of the other flavorings instead? I cooked one more batch, this time marinating the steak in just fish sauce, oil, and sugar. During grilling, I basted the meat heavily with the coconut milk mixture, redolent with ginger, lemon grass, and spices. This was my breakthrough: The texture was flawless and the flavors from the basting sauce really stuck to the meat, so no one missed them in the marinade.

Lastly, I focused on the peanut sauce. Using chunky peanut butter as a base, I spiced things up with Thai red curry paste and garlic. Coconut milk contributed body, and chopped roasted peanuts offered additional texture. A final hit of lime juice, coupled with soy and fish sauce, lent brightness.

Served with the peanut sauce, this beef satay was as good as it gets. And who knows? Maybe one day a Thai street vendor will look to my method for tips.

GRILLED BEEF SATAY
SERVES 4 AS A MAIN DISH OR 6 AS AN APPETIZER

See page 30 for tips on prepping lemon grass. Bamboo skewers soaked in water for 30 minutes can be substituted for metal skewers. The aluminum pan used for charcoal grilling should be at least 2¾ inches deep; you will not need the pan for a gas grill. Note: Unless you have a very high-powered gas grill, these skewers will not be as well seared as they would be with charcoal. Serve with Peanut Sauce (recipe follows). For our free recipe for another garnish, Cucumber Relish, go to www.CooksIllustrated.com/oct11.

Basting Sauce

- ¾ cup regular or light coconut milk
- 3 tablespoons packed dark brown sugar
- 3 tablespoons fish sauce
- 2 tablespoons vegetable oil
- 3 shallots, minced
- 2 stalks lemon grass, trimmed to bottom 6 inches and minced
- 2 tablespoons grated fresh ginger
- 1½ teaspoons ground coriander
- ¾ teaspoon red pepper flakes
- ½ teaspoon ground cumin
- ½ teaspoon salt

Beef

- 2 tablespoons vegetable oil
- 2 tablespoons packed dark brown sugar
- 1 tablespoon fish sauce
- 1 (1½- to 1¾-pound) flank steak, halved lengthwise, then sliced on slight angle against grain into ¼-inch-thick slices
  Disposable aluminum deep roasting pan

1. FOR THE BASTING SAUCE: Whisk all ingredients together in bowl. Reserve one-third of sauce in separate bowl. (Use reserved sauce to apply to raw beef.)

2. FOR THE BEEF: Whisk oil, sugar, and fish sauce together in medium bowl. Toss beef with marinade and let stand at room temperature for 30 minutes. Weave beef onto 12-inch metal skewers, 2 pieces per skewer, leaving 1½ inches at top and bottom of skewer exposed. You should have 10 to 12 skewers.

3A. FOR A CHARCOAL GRILL: Poke twelve ½-inch holes in bottom of roasting pan. Open bottom vent completely and place roasting pan in center of grill. Light large chimney starter mounded with charcoal briquettes (7 quarts). When top coals are partially covered with ash, pour into roasting pan. Set cooking grate over coals with grates parallel to long side of roasting pan, cover, and open lid vent completely. Heat grill until hot, about 5 minutes.

3B. FOR A GAS GRILL: Turn all burners to high, cover, and heat grill until very hot, about 15 minutes. Leave all burners on high.

4. Clean and oil cooking grate. Place beef skewers on grill (directly over coals if using charcoal) perpendicular to grate. Brush meat with one-third

basting sauce (portion reserved for raw meat) and cook (covered if using gas) until browned, about 3 minutes. Flip skewers, brush with half of remaining basting sauce, and cook until browned on second side, about 3 minutes. Brush meat with remaining basting sauce and cook 1 minute longer. Transfer to large platter and serve with peanut sauce.

PEANUT SAUCE
MAKES ABOUT 1½ CUPS

- 1 tablespoon vegetable oil
- 1 tablespoon Thai red curry paste
- 1 tablespoon packed dark brown sugar
- 2 garlic cloves, minced
- 1 cup regular or light coconut milk
- ⅓ cup chunky peanut butter
- ¼ cup roasted unsalted peanuts, chopped
- 1 tablespoon lime juice
- 1 tablespoon fish sauce
- 1 teaspoon soy sauce

Heat oil in small saucepan over medium heat until shimmering. Add curry paste, sugar, and garlic; cook, stirring constantly, until fragrant, about 1 minute. Add coconut milk and bring to simmer. Whisk in peanut butter until smooth. Remove from heat and stir in peanuts, lime juice, fish sauce, and soy sauce. Cool to room temperature.

Introducing Salt-Baked Potatoes

What can 2 pounds of salt do to a potato that an oven can't?

> BY MATTHEW CARD

I had always assumed that salt-baked potatoes were a novelty act akin to dishwasher-steamed salmon or manifold-roasted meatloaf. How could burying a potato beneath a mound of salt possibly improve on basic baking? Well, if you believe the press, all that salt intensifies the potato's flavor and makes its texture particularly moist and fluffy. After hearing yet another paean sung to the method, I decided it was time to separate fact from fiction.

I bought a sack of russets and rounded up some recipes. Most called for simply burying the potatoes in salt and popping them into the oven. Others instructed the cook to set the potatoes on a bed of salt in a baking dish and cover the whole thing with foil. I also found an approach that called for brushing the potatoes with an egg wash and then encrusting them in salt before baking. I tried all three methods—and to my great surprise, I was hooked. While each approach had drawbacks, they all significantly improved on plain baked potato.

Though their skin was as tough and desiccated as an old baseball mitt, the "buried" potatoes were remarkably light and flaky inside. The interiors of the salt-crusted potatoes were also wonderfully fluffy—plus their skins were less leathery—but painting on the egg wash was messy and chiseling off the crust at the table inelegant. And the potatoes cooked in the sealed dish? Really good—without a doubt some of the best baked potatoes I'd ever tasted. Their flesh was fluffy and moist, their flavor deep and well seasoned (though by no means salty). Even the skin was noticeably improved: Though the exposed portion was a tiny bit damp (a minor flaw I'd come back to), it was paper-thin and far more tender than the tough hide on a plain baked spud or the wet casing around one baked in foil.

After giving it some thought, I realized why baking potatoes on a bed of salt in a covered pan worked so much better than either of the conventional ways of baking potatoes: It allows for moisture exchange between the salt and the spud. The moisture that escapes from the potato is contained in the covered

Besides surprisingly tender skins and fluffy interiors, this method yields a head of roasted garlic—ideal for flavored butter.

pan and absorbed by the salt crystals. Some of that moisture is then reabsorbed by the potato, helping to make its skin tender and its flesh light and fluffy.

Now that I had the mechanics behind the method straight, I began refining the details. After some experimentation, I settled on baking the potatoes in a spacious 13 by 9-inch baking dish (where the potatoes wouldn't touch one another) atop a thick 2½-cup layer of either kosher or table salt. Ninety minutes in a 450-degree oven also proved optimal.

But I wondered if I could perfect the skin by making the dampness of the exposed area go away. (I could live with the slight dryness where the skin touched the salt.) Figuring a bit of dry heat might help to burn off some moisture, I baked another batch, but this time removed the foil once the potatoes were almost cooked through—about 75 minutes in. I then let them finish uncovered. This improved matters, but I was able to get rid of the dampness entirely (without causing any ill effects to the interior) by cranking the oven temperature to 500 degrees after I removed the foil. I also found that brushing the potatoes with olive oil after uncovering them boosted the skins' flavor and gave them an appealing glossy look.

The potatoes couldn't get much better, but I wondered if I could put this method to further use. As it

turned out, a few rosemary sprigs laid over the salt scented the potatoes with their fresh, piney aroma. Even better, I threw a head of garlic alongside the spuds as they cooked and used their creamy, sweet flesh to whip up a quick roasted garlic-butter topping.

I'm still not ready to steam fish in my dishwasher or cook meatloaf over my car engine, but in my household, salt-baked potatoes are here to stay.

SALT-BAKED POTATOES WITH ROASTED GARLIC AND ROSEMARY BUTTER
SERVES 4

Kosher or table salt can be used in this recipe. The salt can be strained to remove solid bits and reused for this recipe. The potatoes can be prepared without the roasted garlic butter and topped with other garnishes such as sour cream, chives, crumbled bacon, and/or shredded cheese. For our free recipe for Salt-Baked Potatoes with Roasted Shallot and Thyme Butter, go to www.CooksIllustrated.com/oct11.

- 2½ cups plus ⅛ teaspoon salt
- 4 russet potatoes, scrubbed and dried
- 2 sprigs plus ¼ teaspoon minced fresh rosemary
- 1 whole head garlic, outer papery skin removed and top quarter of head cut off and discarded
- 4 teaspoons olive oil
- 4 tablespoons unsalted butter, softened

1. Adjust oven rack to middle position and heat oven to 450 degrees. Spread 2½ cups salt in even layer in 13 by 9-inch baking dish. Gently nestle potatoes in salt, broad side down, leaving space between potatoes. Add rosemary sprigs and garlic, cut side up, to baking dish. Cover baking dish with foil and crimp edges to tightly seal. Bake 1¼ hours; remove pan from oven. Increase oven temperature to 500 degrees.

2. Carefully remove foil from baking dish. Remove garlic and set aside to cool. Brush exposed portion of each potato with 1 teaspoon oil. Return uncovered baking dish to oven and bake until potatoes are tender when pierced with tip of paring knife and skins are glossy, 15 to 20 minutes.

3. Meanwhile, once garlic is cool enough to handle, squeeze root end until cloves slip out of their skins. Using fork, mash garlic, butter, ⅛ teaspoon kosher salt (or pinch table salt) and minced rosemary to smooth paste. Remove any clumped salt from potatoes (holding with kitchen towel if necessary), split lengthwise, top with portion of butter, and serve immediately.

Look: It Really Works
Video available FREE for 4 months at
www.CooksIllustrated.com/oct11

Great Butternut Squash Soup

Forget cream and spices. The secret to squashier squash soup is concentration.

BY ADAM RIED

It sounds obvious, but butternut squash soup should taste first and foremost of squash. Too often you can barely detect its flavor, either because recipes mask the squash with an overload of cream, stock, and potent herbs or spices, or because, like all vegetables, butternut squash is full of water. Unless some of that moisture is eliminated, the flavor of the soup can't help but be thin.

Many recipes roast the squash to rid it of its excess moisture and concentrate its flavor. But there are times when I simply don't want to turn on the oven, or need to leave it free for something else. Plus, roasting is time-consuming. I wondered if I could get soup with deep, roasted-squash flavor a little faster—and without using the oven.

Because cutting, peeling, and seeding winter squash can be a tedious process, I was curious to find out if using prepeeled, precut squash might work. Unfortunately, tasters vetoed the packaged squash for tasting woody and dried out. After prepping the squash myself, I decided to try browning it on the stovetop before simmering, hoping I'd get caramelization similar to that produced in the oven, along with the super-flavorful brown bits (the fond) that developed on the bottom of the pan. But even in a large Dutch oven with a generous 10-inch cooking surface, I couldn't fit the 2½ pounds of squash I needed for my recipe in a single layer. If I piled it in, it wouldn't brown properly, and working in batches would take as long as roasting.

Then I remembered our recipe for Best French Onion Soup (January/February 2008). Here, virtually an entire pot of sliced onions slowly cooks down to less than half its original volume, all the while creating a rich, dark fond at the bottom of the pan that flavors the soup almost as much as the onions themselves. I loved the idea of creating the thickest, most intensely flavored fond I could. But cooking down waterlogged squash would take all day. What if I jump-started the process? I looked to the quickest, easiest way: using the microwave. I placed the peeled chunks in a bowl, covered them, and microwaved them on high for about 15 minutes. I then drained off the liquid (reserving it for later use) and piled the lot into the Dutch oven, in which I had melted a couple of tablespoons of butter. Since I was mainly after the development of fond, it no longer mattered that the squash didn't fit in a single layer. After about 12 minutes, much of the moisture from the squash had cooked off, and a thick brown fond had developed on the bottom of the pot. I deglazed the pot with a bit of water for now, scraped up the

fond, and added about 6 more cups of water, along with the reserved squash liquid. I then allowed the squash to simmer briefly before pureeing it in a blender. This soup had all the deep flavor of a roasted squash soup, but I had shaved about 15 minutes off the usual preparation time—and the oven was still stone-cold.

Still, my soup was a little on the thin side. I suspected that adding thickeners like potato, rice, white bread, flour, cornstarch, and heavy cream would only serve to dilute the squash flavor—and they did. Instead, I simply reduced the amount of water I was adding to the pot to about 5 cups. This gave my soup the silky smooth texture and medium-bodied consistency I sought, all without masking the taste of squash.

The rest of the testing proceeded quickly. I compared soup made with water with ones made with chicken broth and vegetable broth. Both types of broth added depth, but tasters liked the subtle sweetness of the vegetable broth. I settled on roughly 2 parts vegetable broth to 1 part water. Mild, slightly herbal leeks (favored over onions and shallots) provided an aromatic base. Finally, a simple combination of thyme, bay leaf, and a touch of cayenne beat out carrots, celery, and tomato paste as flavor builders that complemented the squash without overpowering it.

Now, in less time than it takes to roast squash, never mind turn it into soup, I could tuck into a bowl of truly squashy-tasting squash soup.

BUTTERNUT SQUASH SOUP
SERVES 6 TO 8

Do not use prepeeled squash in this recipe. Our favorite vegetable broth is Swanson Vegetable Broth. Low-sodium chicken broth can be substituted for the vegetable broth. If you use a blender to puree the soup, fill the jar two-thirds full—not more—and process in batches. Alternatively, use an immersion blender to puree the soup right in the pot. In addition to sour cream, serve the soup with Fried Leeks (recipe follows), which provide nice textural contrast.

2½ pounds butternut squash, peeled, seeded, and cut into 2-inch chunks (about 7 cups)
2 tablespoons unsalted butter
1 leek, white and light green parts only, quartered lengthwise, sliced thin, and washed thoroughly (about 1½ cups)
  Salt and pepper
4 cups vegetable broth
1–2 cups water
2 sprigs fresh thyme
1 bay leaf
  Pinch cayenne pepper
  Sour cream

1. Place squash in bowl, cover, and microwave until paring knife glides easily through flesh, 14 to 18 minutes, stirring halfway through. Carefully transfer squash to colander set in bowl (squash will be very hot) and drain for 5 minutes; reserve liquid.

2. Melt butter in Dutch oven over medium-high heat. Add squash, leek, and 1 teaspoon salt; cook, stirring occasionally, until squash pieces begin to break down and brown fond forms in bottom of pot, 10 to 13 minutes.

3. Add 2 cups broth and scrape bottom of pot to loosen and dissolve fond. Add remaining 2 cups broth, reserved squash liquid, 1 cup water, thyme sprigs, bay leaf, and cayenne. Increase heat to high and bring to simmer. Reduce heat to medium and simmer until leeks are fully tender, 6 to 7 minutes.

4. Remove and discard bay leaf and thyme sprigs. Working in batches, process soup in blender until smooth, 1 to 2 minutes. Return soup to clean pot and bring to simmer, thinning with up to 1 cup water to desired consistency. Season with salt and pepper to taste; serve with dollop of sour cream. (Soup can be made up to 2 days in advance.)

FRIED LEEKS
MAKES ABOUT ½ CUP

1 leek, white and light green parts only, halved lengthwise, sliced into very thin 2-inch-long strips, washed thoroughly, and dried
2 tablespoons all-purpose flour
  Salt and pepper
½ cup olive oil

Toss leeks, flour, and pinch each salt and pepper in medium bowl. Heat oil in 12-inch skillet until shimmering. Add half of leeks and fry, stirring often, until golden brown, about 6 minutes. Using slotted spoon, transfer leeks to paper towel–lined plate; sprinkle with salt and pepper to taste. Repeat with remaining leeks.

What Is Fond? Watch.
Video available FREE for 4 months at www.CooksIllustrated.com/oct11

25 Tips for Improving Flavor

Reliable recipes and top-quality equipment will get you far, but sometimes it's the small touches that make the biggest difference. From knowing when to pepper meat to saving browned bits at the bottom of a pan, here are the tricks we turn to most often. BY KEITH DRESSER

PREPPING

1 Avoid advance prep for garlic and onions
Chopping garlic and onions causes them to release sharp odors and flavors that intensify over time, so it's best to cut them at the last minute. Soaking sliced or chopped onions in a solution of baking soda and water (1 tablespoon per cup of water) tames their pungency for raw applications; just be sure to rinse them thoroughly before using.

2 Out, damn sprout!
Remove any green shoots from garlic cloves before chopping. They contain bitter-tasting compounds that persist even after cooking.

3 Keep the taste in tomatoes
If excess moisture isn't an issue, ignore any instructions to remove the seeds and "jelly" from tomatoes. The guts are where the flavor is; in fact, they contain three times the amount of flavor-enhancing glutamic acid as the flesh.

4 Score meat before marinating
To help a marinade penetrate as quickly and deeply as possible (especially in thick cuts), prick the surface of the meat with a fork or make shallow scores with a knife.

5 Flip or stir meat while marinating
Place meat in a zipper-lock bag or use a large baking dish covered with plastic wrap. Flip the bag or stir the meat halfway through the soaking time to ensure that all of the meat gets equal exposure to the marinade.

6 Trim beef stew meat thoroughly; leave a little fat on pork
Remove all hard fat and connective tissue from the exterior of beef stew meat before cooking; its intramuscular marbling will keep it plenty moist and tender during cooking. But a thin layer (⅛ inch) of fat left on pork will baste and flavor the leaner meat.

7 Keep fat fresh-tasting
Fat equals flavor. But because the fatty acids in butter, oil, and oil-rich ingredients like nuts are particularly prone to rancidity—and because these ingredients easily absorb off-flavors—it's important to minimize their exposure to oxygen and heat.

FAT/NUT	BEST STORAGE METHOD
Butter	Slip the wrapped sticks into a zipper-lock bag and store them in the back of the fridge—not in the small door compartment—where it's coldest for up to 2½ weeks. For longer storage (up to four months), move the bag to the freezer.
Oil	Keep vegetable oils in a dark pantry or cupboard. Nut and seed oils should be stored in the fridge.
Nuts	The pantry is no place for nuts, unless you plan to use them within a couple of months. Placed in a zipper-lock bag (with the air pressed out) and stored in the freezer, they'll keep for at least a year.

COOKING

8 Strike—but not until the pan is hot
The temperature of the cooking surface will drop the minute food is added, slowing down flavorful browning, so don't rush the preheating step. If shallow- or deep-frying, check the temperature of the oil with an instant-read thermometer.

9 Sprinkle a little sugar on top
Lightly sprinkling lean proteins (and even vegetables) with sugar helps them brown better and faster, enhancing their flavor without the risk of overcooking.

10 Add a rind to soups and stews
Save your Parmesan rinds and do as the Italians do: Toss one into a soup or stew. It's an age-old trick for adding savory depth. Stored in a zipper-lock bag in the freezer, the rinds will keep indefinitely (no need to thaw them before using).

11 Don't forget the fond
The caramelized brown bits that stick to the bottom of the pan after searing meat are packed with savory flavor. To incorporate them into a soup, stew, or pan sauce, deglaze the hot pan with liquid (wine, broth, etc.) and scrape them free with a wooden spoon.

12 Capitalize on meat's juices
As cooked meat rests, it releases flavorful juices that can be added back to the skillet when making a pan sauce. If the juices are plentiful enough to thin the sauce, allow it to simmer an additional minute or two to restore its proper consistency.

13 Make nuts nuttier
Toasting nuts brings out their aromatic oils, contributing to a stronger, more complex flavor and aroma. When using more than 1 cup, oven-toast nuts on a roomy sheet pan. The oven offers not only more space than a skillet but also more even heat than the stove, with less need for stirring.

14 Spice up spices
To intensify the flavor of commercially ground spices—particularly blends such as chili powder and curry powder—cook them for a minute or two in a little butter or oil before adding liquid to the pan. If the recipe calls for sautéing aromatics, add the spices to the pan when the vegetables are nearly cooked.

BAKING

15 Brown your bread

Always bake bread until the crust is well browned—even if that means leaving the loaf in the oven beyond its recommended doneness temperature (most dough contains plenty of moisture and won't dry out). Flavor compounds in a browned crust are volatile and travel inward toward the crumb, enhancing the flavor of the loaf inside as well as out.

16 Go for deep golden pastry

Browning is also important in pastry: A well-browned crust will be more flavorful than a blond one. We bake all pies in glass pie plates so we can track color development. When working with puff pastry or other flaky dough on a baking sheet, we lift up the bottom of individual pieces and look for even browning.

17 Beware of overbaking chocolate desserts

Baking chocolate cakes and brownies past the point of doneness will not only dry them out but also dull the chocolate's flavor. To determine doneness, use a skewer and look for moist crumbs.

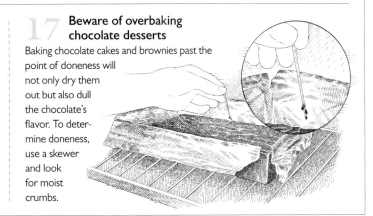

SEASONING

18 Drop (salt for) acid

In addition to grabbing the saltshaker to boost flavor in soups, stews, and sauces, try a drop of lemon juice or vinegar. Like salt, acid competes with bitter flavor compounds, reducing our perception of them as they "brighten" other flavors. Just a dash—⅛ teaspoon—can go a long way.

19 Use coarse salt when seasoning meat

Use kosher salt—rather than table salt—when seasoning meat. Its larger grains distribute more easily and cling well to the meat's surface. When a recipe calls for seasoning meat "to taste," we suggest using about ⅛ teaspoon of kosher salt per portion.

20 Pep up—or tone down—your pepper

When exactly you apply black pepper to meat—before or after searing—will affect the strength of its bite. If you want assertive pepper flavor, season meat after searing; keeping the pepper away from heat will preserve its volatile compounds. Alternatively, seasoning before cooking will tame pepper's punch.

21 Season cold foods aggressively

Chilling foods dulls their flavors and aromas, so it's important to compensate by seasoning generously—but judiciously. To keep from overdoing it, season with a normal amount of salt before chilling and then taste and add more salt as desired just before serving.

22 Incorporate fresh herbs at the right time

Add hearty herbs like thyme, rosemary, oregano, sage, and marjoram to dishes early on in the cooking process; this way, they release maximum flavor while ensuring that their texture will be less intrusive. Save delicate herbs like parsley, cilantro, tarragon, chives, and basil for the last minute, lest they lose their fresh flavor and bright color.

23 Add a little *umami*

Common pantry staples like soy sauce, Worcestershire sauce, and anchovies contain high levels of glutamates that can give a savory umami boost to a dish. Try mixing a teaspoon or two of soy sauce into chili or adding a couple of finely minced anchovies to a chicken braise.

24 Make adjustments when seasonings go awry

If you've added too much salt, sugar, or spice to a dish, the damage is usually done. In mild cases, however, the overpowering ingredient can sometimes be masked by the addition of another from the opposite end of the flavor spectrum. Consult this chart for ideas. And remember to account for the reduction of liquids when seasoning a dish—a perfectly seasoned stew will likely taste too salty after several hours of simmering. Your best bet is to season with a light hand during the cooking process and then adjust the seasoning just before serving.

IF YOUR FOOD IS ...	ADD ...	SUCH AS ...
Too salty	An acid or sweetener	Vinegar; lemon or lime juice; canned, unsalted tomatoes; sugar, honey, or maple syrup
Too sweet	An acid or seasonings	Vinegar or citrus juice; chopped fresh herb; dash of cayenne; or, for sweet dishes, a bit of liqueur or espresso powder
Too spicy or acidic	A fat or sweetener	Butter, cream, sour cream, cheese, or olive oil; sugar, honey, or maple syrup

25 Add a finishing touch

Even the most perfectly cooked soup, stew, or pasta dish can benefit from a last-minute burst of flavor. One of our favorite ways to liven up rich lasagnas or hearty braises is to sprinkle them with the classic Mediterranean garnish known as *gremolata*. This mixture features minced fresh garlic, citrus zest, and fresh herbs such as parsley or basil. Soups, pasta, fish, and just about any cut of meat will benefit from a dollop of herb butter made from blending finely minced herbs, garlic, and often shallot into softened butter. For our free recipes for Gremolata and Herb Butter, go to www.CooksIllustrated.com/oct11.

Really Good Lentil Salads

The key to creamy but firm lentils lies in the relationship between legume and salt.

≥ BY ANDREW JANJIGIAN ≤

Lentils may not get points for glamour, but when properly cooked and dressed up in a salad with bright vinaigrette and herbs, nuts, and cheeses, the legumes' earthy, almost meaty depth and firm-tender bite make a satisfying side dish for almost any meal.

The trouble is, perfectly cooked lentils are never a given. Too often, either their skins burst and their flesh disintegrates into starchy mush, or they don't cook through completely and retain chewy skin and a hard, crunchy core. Before I started adding accoutrements, I had to nail down a reliable way to produce tender, buttery lentils with soft, unbroken skins. And because the tiny, shape-retaining French green lentils we favor can be hard to come by, I was also determined to develop an approach that would yield perfect results with whatever lentil variety my supermarket had to offer.

Fortunately, the test kitchen's previous work with bean cookery gave me a good idea of how to improve the skins. We've discovered that, odd as it may sound, brining beans overnight softens their outer shells and makes them less likely to burst. The explanation is twofold: As the beans soak, the sodium ions from the salt replace some of the calcium and magnesium ions in the skins. By replacing some of the mineral ions, the sodium ions weaken the pectin in the skins, allowing more water to penetrate and leading to a more pliable, forgiving texture. But with beans, brining requires an overnight rest to be most effective. Fortunately, due to the lentils' smaller, flatter shape, I found that just a few hours of brining dramatically cuts down on blowouts. I also had another idea for hastening the process: Since heat speeds up all chemical reactions, I managed to reduce that time to just an hour by using warm water in the salt solution.

Another way to further reduce blowouts would be to cook the lentils as gently as possible. But I could see that even my stovetop's low setting still agitated the lentils too vigorously. I decided to try the oven, hoping that its indirect heat would get the job done more gently—and it did. And while the oven did increase the cooking time from less than 30 minutes to nearly an hour, the results were worth the wait: Virtually all of the lentil skins were tender yet intact.

Despite the lentils' soft, perfect skins, their insides tended to be mushy, not creamy. It occurred to me that I could try another very simple trick with salt: adding it to the cooking water. Many bean recipes (including ours) shy away from adding salt during cooking because it produces firmer interiors that can be gritty. Here's why: While a brine's impact is mainly confined to the skin, heat (from cooking) affects the inside of the bean, causing sodium ions to move to the interior, where they slow the starches' ability to absorb water. But a firmed-up texture was exactly what my mushy lentils needed. Could a problem for beans prove to be the solution for lentils? Sure enough, when I added ½ teaspoon of salt to the cooking water, the lentils went from mushy to firm yet creamy.

I had just two remaining tasks to tackle: enriching the flavor of the lentils and creating a few salad variations. Swapping some of the cooking water for chicken broth solved the first problem, while tossing the lentils with tart vinaigrette and bold mix-ins—feta, olives, and mint in one salad; spinach, walnuts, and Parmesan in another; hazelnuts and goat cheese in another; and carrots and cilantro in a final version—brightened and balanced their rich, earthy flavor.

LENTIL SALAD WITH OLIVES, MINT, AND FETA
SERVES 4 TO 6

French green lentils, or *Lentilles du Puy*, are our preferred choice for this recipe, but it works with any type of lentil except red or yellow. (See page 31 for more information about lentils.) Brining helps keep the lentils intact, but if you don't have time, they'll still taste good without it. The salad can be served warm or at room temperature. For our free recipe for Lentil Salad with Pomegranates and Walnuts, go to www.CooksIllustrated.com/oct11.

1	cup lentils, picked over and rinsed
	Salt and pepper
6	cups water
2	cups low-sodium chicken broth
5	garlic cloves, lightly crushed and peeled
1	bay leaf
5	tablespoons extra-virgin olive oil
3	tablespoons white wine vinegar
½	cup coarsely chopped pitted kalamata olives
½	cup fresh mint leaves, chopped
1	large shallot, minced
1	ounce feta cheese, crumbled (¼ cup)

1. Place lentils and 1 teaspoon salt in bowl. Cover with 4 cups warm water (about 110 degrees) and soak for 1 hour. Drain well. (Drained lentils can be refrigerated for up to 2 days before cooking.)

2. Adjust oven rack to middle position and heat oven to 325 degrees. Place drained lentils, 2 cups water, broth, garlic, bay leaf, and ½ teaspoon salt in medium saucepan. Cover and bake until lentils are tender but remain intact, 40 to 60 minutes. Meanwhile, whisk oil and vinegar together in large bowl.

3. Drain lentils well; remove and discard garlic and bay leaf. Add drained lentils, olives, mint, and shallot to dressing and toss to combine. Season with salt and pepper to taste. Transfer to serving dish, sprinkle with feta, and serve.

LENTIL SALAD WITH SPINACH, WALNUTS, AND PARMESAN CHEESE

Substitute sherry vinegar for white wine vinegar. Place 4 ounces baby spinach and 2 tablespoons water in bowl. Cover and microwave until spinach is wilted and volume is halved, 3 to 4 minutes. Remove bowl from microwave and keep covered for 1 minute. Transfer spinach to colander; gently press to release liquid. Transfer spinach to cutting board and roughly chop. Return to colander and press again. Substitute chopped spinach for olives and mint and 1½ ounces coarsely grated Parmesan cheese for feta. Sprinkle with ⅓ cup coarsely chopped toasted walnuts before serving.

LENTIL SALAD WITH HAZELNUTS AND GOAT CHEESE

Substitute red wine vinegar for white wine vinegar and add 2 teaspoons Dijon mustard to dressing in step 2. Omit olives and substitute ¼ cup chopped parsley for mint. Substitute 2 ounces crumbled goat cheese for feta and sprinkle with ⅓ cup coarsely chopped toasted hazelnuts before serving.

LENTIL SALAD WITH CARROTS AND CILANTRO

Substitute lemon juice for white wine vinegar. Toss 2 carrots, peeled and cut into 2-inch-long matchsticks, with 1 teaspoon ground cumin, ½ teaspoon ground cinnamon, and ⅛ teaspoon cayenne pepper in bowl. Cover and microwave until carrots are tender but still crisp, 2 to 4 minutes. Substitute carrots for olives and ¼ cup chopped cilantro for mint. Omit shallot and feta.

Rescuing Vegetable Lasagna

Ever made a vegetable lasagna that wasn't laden with watery vegetables and dry, grainy patches of cheese? Neither had we.

> BY BRYAN ROOF

There's no reason why a vegetable lasagna made with the classic trio of eggplant, zucchini, and summer squash should be any less satisfying than a meat-based casserole, especially when the produce is in season and locally grown. But I've rarely cooked one that I've been moved to make again. Some versions look tempting enough with a topcoat of bubbly cheese and thick tomato gravy, but cutting out a square of it invariably reveals trouble at the core. Often placed between the pasta sheets raw, the zucchini and squash turn out steamy and limp, flooding the dish with their juices—or, in some instances, undercooked and crunchy. Then there's the eggplant, which is typically not only soggy, but greasy from pre-frying. Add to that the usual patches of dry, grainy ricotta and it's a wonder this dish ever became an Italian-American standard.

So what would it take to make a full-flavored lasagna with vegetables that could stand up to—not wash out—the cheese and sauce? Ridding the produce of some of its moisture and boosting its flavor before adding it to the dish would be steps in the right direction.

Shedding Water

I first focused my efforts on the most unruly element: the eggplant. Besides being full of water, eggplant is extremely porous and readily soaks up any available liquid (or oil). It therefore requires some sort of pretreatment that not only rids the fruit of water but also breaks down its absorbent air pockets. Fortunately, the test kitchen had already devised an effective—and novel—approach to both problems in

Precooking the eggplant, zucchini, summer squash, and spinach not only concentrates their flavor and reduces their juices but also ensures that the lasagna slices cleanly.

another recipe: salting the eggplant and then heating it in the microwave. Salt pulls water out of the fruit through osmosis at the same time the microwave causes it to steam. Microwaving also collapses the eggplant's air pockets, leaving the fruit shrunken, wrinkled, and less prone to absorbing oil or liquid.

Following this method, I cut the eggplant into ½-inch cubes, sprinkled them with 1 teaspoon of salt, and placed the pieces on a double layer of coffee filters. (The filters absorb moisture like a paper towel so that liquid doesn't pool on the plate.) I then microwaved the pieces for 10 minutes. When I sautéed the pretreated eggplant to give it more flavor and color, it hardly picked up any oil at all.

I considered salting the zucchini and yellow squash to remove their excess water, but I was fairly certain that a turn in the skillet would burn off enough fluid and deepen their flavor. I cut the squashes (one pound of each) into ½-inch cubes and, to save myself an extra step, combined them with the microwaved eggplant. I then sautéed the mixture in two batches with minced garlic and healthy dashes of salt and pepper. About seven minutes later, the vegetables had developed good color and picked up some garlicky flavor, but I wondered if I could do better. I minced a few more cloves of garlic, this time letting the bits soak in a tablespoon of olive oil along with some minced fresh thyme. Added to the skillet as each batch of vegetables finished

RECIPE DIAGNOSIS What Ails Vegetable Lasagna

The classic trio of eggplant, zucchini, and summer squash is typically rife with issues.

- Placed in the dish raw, zucchini and squash contribute almost no flavor, plus their moisture washes out the sauce.

- Soggy, greasy eggplant also doesn't do the casserole any favors.

- Ricotta cheese, the traditional choice in lasagna, tends to bake up dry and grainy.

- The red sauce often tastes dull and overcooked.

cooking, this super-garlicky, herbal-infused mixture gave the eggplant and squash so much flavor that they were good enough to eat straight from the pan.

Now it was time to see how the vegetables would fare in the lasagna. I made a placeholder tomato sauce by briefly simmering crushed tomatoes with garlic, olive oil, basil, and a dash of pepper flakes. I then layered a dozen no-boil noodles (our favorite alternative to fresh pasta) with the sauce, the sautéed eggplant and vegetables, and generous helpings of ricotta, mozzarella, and nutty Parmesan cheese. I baked the casserole in a 375-degree oven until golden and bubbly.

The good news was that starting with precooked vegetables allowed me to cut the baking time from the usual hour-plus down to about 35 minutes. But improvements were still needed here and there. Instead of acting as a creamy binder, the ricotta had cooked up into grainy slicks, and some tasters wanted the dairy element to be even richer. Plus, we all agreed that the tomato sauce tasted a bit flat.

On the Sauces

I had one quick idea about the ricotta, thanks to the efforts of another colleague who'd encountered similar graininess when he tried incorporating the tiny, pebbly curds into baked ziti. To solve the problem, he substituted cottage cheese, which boasts a creamier consistency (not to mention slightly tangier flavor), for the ricotta. When I made the switch with my next batch, everyone agreed that things were looking up, but that the cheese was still a bit dry and lean-tasting. In fact, this round of testing convinced me that what we all really wanted was the richness and creaminess of a béchamel sauce, the classic roux-thickened milk mixture found in countless meat and vegetable lasagna recipes. My only hesitation was that it involved extra work. I didn't want to add more fuss to the dish by cooking a third element, so I tried a lazy man's approach and whipped up a no-cook

Shrinking Eggplant Down to Size

Eggplant is full of water that will wash out the flavors of lasagna as it bakes in the oven. It's also riddled with air pockets that act as a magnet for oil. Salting the cubed fruit and then microwaving it solves both problems: Microwaving not only speeds up salt's ability to pull moisture out of the eggplant but also collapses the eggplant's air pockets. (We set the eggplant on a double layer of coffee filters to absorb the excess moisture as it is released.) The result: Low-moisture, meaty-tasting eggplant that doesn't soak up too much oil when sautéed.

RAW　　　**SALTED + MICROWAVED**

KEYS TO HEARTY, FULL–FLAVORED VEGETABLE LASAGNA

In addition to these steps, meaty kalamata olives and lots of chopped fresh basil bring dimension to the dish.

GO FOR CREAMIER CHEESE Cottage cheese boasts not only a creamier consistency than drier, more pebbly ricotta but also tangier flavor.

ADD RICH, NO-COOK CREAM SAUCE Instead of a traditional cooked béchamel, we whisk together a quick version made with heavy cream, Parmesan, the cottage cheese, and garlic, which we add directly to the casserole.

ADD BRIGHT, NO-COOK TOMATO SAUCE Simply stirring together crushed tomatoes, basil, garlic, and olive oil guarantees a sauce with bright flavor—and saves time at the stove, too.

PUT A STOP TO OILY EGGPLANT Salting, then microwaving the cubes of eggplant for 10 minutes eliminates moisture that would flood the lasagna and collapses its air pockets so it soaks up less oil.

"DEHYDRATE" AND BROWN VEGGIES We toss the microwaved eggplant into a hot skillet with the squashes to rid them of water and develop flavorful browning. (Sautéing the spinach also helps rid it of moisture.)

INFUSE VEGGIES WITH FLAVORFUL OIL A shot of garlic-thyme oil stirred in with the sautéed eggplant, summer squash, and zucchini near the end of cooking adds depth.

white sauce by whisking together 1 cup each of milk and cottage cheese with a generous 2 cups of Parmesan and a couple of minced garlic cloves.

I wasn't expecting much from this experiment, but the results were surprisingly good. All that cheese produced a "sauce" that was considerably richer, if still a bit thin and curdled. The first problem I easily fixed by swapping the milk for an equal amount of heavy cream. The second took a bit more experimentation, but a glossy, silky-smooth sauce finally came together after I whisked 1 teaspoon of cornstarch in with the other dairy ingredients. (When the starch granules in cornstarch absorb water and swell, they get in the way of the dairy proteins and prevent them from clumping together in curds.)

As for the tomato sauce, I couldn't help but wonder if a similar no-cook approach might not liven up its dull flavor—and save a few extra minutes at the stove. I prepared another batch, this time simply stirring together the ingredients and adding the sauce to the casserole without simmering it first. The results were better than ever. Even after baking and cooling, the sauce still tasted bright, punching up the filling with just enough acidity.

Final Flourishes

And yet balancing the complexity of the dairy-rich "béchamel" sauce with the fruity tomato sauce didn't quite perk up tasters' interest in the filling. I needed something bolder and fresher to complement the eggplant, zucchini, and squash. Rummaging through the refrigerator for ideas, I spotted a jar of kalamata olives. A handful of these, chopped, added meaty texture and a briny, salty jolt of flavor. For freshness, I added a bag of baby spinach, which took no time to sauté in a touch of olive oil until wilted and then drain before layering into the filling. My final touch was a generous amount of chopped fresh basil leaves sprinkled on the casserole right before serving. Each of these additions was small, but they made a big difference in the flavor of the dish.

At last, this lasagna more than had it all with its rich flavors, creamy cheese, and substantial texture—along with a summery brightness that set it apart from the meat kind. I had to restrain a smile when I saw that even the most dedicated meat lovers among my tasters couldn't help but come back for more.

VEGETABLE LASAGNA
SERVES 8 TO 10

We prefer the lasagna made with our favorite whole-milk, block-style mozzarella from Sorrento, but Kraft part-skim preshredded mozzarella is also fine (for more information on mozzarella, see page 28). Our preferred brands of crushed tomatoes are Tuttorosso and Muir Glen.

No-Cook Tomato Sauce

- 1 (28-ounce) can crushed tomatoes
- ¼ cup chopped fresh basil
- 2 tablespoons extra-virgin olive oil
- 2 garlic cloves, minced
- 1 teaspoon kosher salt
- ¼ teaspoon red pepper flakes

No-Cook Cream Sauce

- 4 ounces Parmesan cheese, grated (2 cups)
- 1 cup whole-milk cottage cheese
- 1 cup heavy cream
- 2 garlic cloves, minced
- 1 teaspoon cornstarch
- ½ teaspoon kosher salt
- ½ teaspoon pepper

Vegetable Filling

- 1½ pounds eggplant, peeled and cut into ½-inch cubes (about 7 cups)
  Kosher salt and pepper
- 1 pound zucchini, cut into ½-inch pieces (about 4 cups)
- 1 pound yellow squash, cut into ½-inch pieces (about 4 cups)
- 5 tablespoons plus 1 teaspoon extra-virgin olive oil
- 4 garlic cloves, minced
- 1 tablespoon minced fresh thyme
- 12 ounces baby spinach (about 12 cups)

- 12 no-boil lasagna noodles
- ½ cup minced pitted kalamata olives
- 12 ounces low-moisture whole-milk mozzarella cheese, shredded (about 3 cups)
- 2 tablespoons chopped fresh basil

1. FOR THE TOMATO SAUCE: Whisk all ingredients together in bowl; set aside.

2. FOR THE CREAM SAUCE: Whisk all ingredients together in bowl; set aside.

3. FOR THE FILLING: Adjust oven rack to middle position and heat oven to 375 degrees. Toss eggplant with 1 teaspoon salt in large bowl. Line surface of large plate with double layer of coffee filters and lightly spray with vegetable oil spray. Spread eggplant in even layer over filters. Wipe out and reserve now-empty bowl. Microwave eggplant, uncovered, until dry to touch and slightly shriveled, about 10 minutes, tossing once halfway through to ensure that eggplant cooks evenly. Let cool slightly. Return eggplant to bowl and toss with zucchini and squash.

4. Combine 1 tablespoon oil, garlic, and thyme in small bowl. Heat 2 tablespoons oil in 12-inch nonstick skillet over medium-high heat until shimmering. Add half eggplant mixture, ¼ teaspoon salt, and ¼ teaspoon pepper; cook, stirring occasionally, until vegetables are lightly browned, about 7 minutes. Push vegetables to sides of skillet; add half of garlic mixture to clearing and cook, mashing with spatula, until fragrant, about 30 seconds. Stir to combine garlic mixture with vegetables and transfer to medium bowl. Repeat with remaining eggplant mixture, 2 tablespoons oil, and remaining garlic mixture.

5. Return skillet to medium-high heat, add remaining teaspoon oil, and heat until shimmering. Add spinach and cook, stirring frequently, until wilted, about 3 minutes. Transfer spinach to paper towel–lined plate and drain 2 minutes. Stir into eggplant mixture.

6. TO ASSEMBLE: Spray 13 by 9-inch baking dish with vegetable oil spray. Spread 1 cup tomato sauce in bottom of baking dish; shingle 4 noodles on top of sauce. Spread half of vegetable mixture over noodles, followed by half of olives, half of cream sauce, and 1 cup of mozzarella. Repeat layering with 4 noodles, 1 cup tomato sauce, remaining vegetables, remaining olives, remaining cream sauce, and 1 cup mozzarella. Place remaining 4 noodles on top layer of cheese. Spread remaining 1 cup tomato sauce over noodles and sprinkle with remaining 1 cup mozzarella. Lightly spray large sheet of aluminum foil with vegetable oil spray and cover lasagna. Bake until bubbling, about 35 minutes. Cool on wire rack 25 minutes. Cut into pieces, sprinkle with basil, and serve.

TASTING Whole Wheat Lasagna Noodles

When last year's whole wheat spaghetti tasting turned up more than one pasta that offered pleasantly nutty flavor and tender-firm chew, we wondered if the trend extended to noodle shapes like lasagna. We sampled four national brands—three made from 100 percent whole wheat flour and one a whole wheat/white flour blend—plain and baked in our Vegetable Lasagna.

We thought the most important factor driving our preferences would be the type of lasagna noodle: Three of the samples were traditional noodles that must be cooked before layering into the casserole, while the fourth was a no-boil product. Our recipes typically call for no-boil noodles (which are precooked and dehydrated before packaging) because we find their thinner, more delicate texture closer to that of fresh pasta. They're also a cinch to work with.

As it turned out, we thought wrong: Tasters' likes and dislikes were mainly grouped around wheat flavor. As they had during the spaghetti tasting, tasters panned noodles that were too gritty and cardboard-y. But pasta that too closely resembled the white kind—including the no-boil lasagna—wasn't their top pick either. Our champ turned out to be none other than our whole wheat spaghetti winner, Bionaturae. Tasters appreciated this brand's complex flavor and substantial chew so much that they were willing to put up with the extra step of boiling the traditional noodles. For complete tasting results, go to www.CooksIllustrated.com/oct11. –Hannah Crowley

WHEATY WINNER
BIONATURAE Organic 100% Whole Wheat Lasagne
Price: $3.99 for 12 oz
Comments: Like their spaghetti sibling, these 100 percent whole wheat lasagna sheets won us over with their "nutty," "rich" wheat flavor and a texture that was pleasantly "chewy" without being gritty.

SECOND BEST (AND NO-BOIL)
DELALLO 100% Organic Whole Wheat Lasagna
Price: $4.48 for 9 oz
Comments: Thin and wafer-like, these no-boil second-place noodles won fans for their delicate texture, which "rivals that of traditional pasta." But flavorwise, tasters were on the fence. Some liked that these sheets could "pass for white flour noodles"; others wished they packed more of a wheaty punch.

THIRD-RATE FLAVOR
RONZONI HEALTHY HARVEST Whole Grain Lasagna
Price: $2.29 for 13.25 oz
Whole Wheat: 54%
Comments: The only blended pasta of the bunch, these third-place noodles had "good structure that holds up well to sauce and cheese." But as they had with the DeLallo lasagna, tasters criticized the noodles for a flavor that wasn't white—but that wasn't whole wheat either.

FOR HEALTH NUTS ONLY
HODGSON MILL Whole Wheat Whole Grain Lasagna
Price: $2 for 8 oz
Whole Wheat: 100%
Comments: Their dark tan color was the first indication that these last-place noodles were seriously wheaty. A few tasters praised their "nutty" flavor, but most found the whole grain flavor overwhelming. As one taster summed it up: "This is like eating burlap."

The Best Creamy Chocolate Pudding

Nostalgia isn't enough to make a dessert worthwhile. To rescue chocolate pudding from obscurity, we'd have to ramp up the flavor while preserving the silky texture.

≥ BY ANDREA GEARY ≤

In the 1980s, a *New Yorker*-style cartoon of a woman and a child examining a dessert menu made its way through food circles. The caption—"Chocolate pudding? Oh, you'll like that. It's like chocolate mousse"—suggests that even 25 years ago, chocolate pudding had fallen into obscurity. It had been pushed off the table by more glamorous, intensely flavored concoctions like truffle tarts and molten chocolate cakes. Today, diners' appetites for increasingly darker, more bitter chocolate have ensured that this trend won't reverse itself. (But instant pudding, mystifyingly, lives on.)

Call me a wimp, but I don't always want my chocolate in lethal doses or in ever-higher cacao percentages. I miss the simplicity—and the restraint—of a good homemade chocolate pudding: that wonderfully smooth, dense yet light marriage of chocolate and dairy thickened with cornstarch and maybe a few egg yolks. I can manage only a few bites of dense, ganache-like *pot de crème*, but I can easily devour a generous serving of chocolate pudding.

Intent on bringing back this homey dessert, I went to the test kitchen library to gather recipes and was happily reminded that making chocolate pudding from scratch couldn't be easier: Simmer dairy and sugar with cornstarch, whisk in chocolate and (sometimes) a few yolks, add vanilla extract, and chill.

That said, when I gave the recipes a closer look, the variety among them was startling for a dish with so few steps and ingredients. Some called for unsweetened chocolate, others bittersweet. Amounts ranged from a modest ounce to more than 10 times that amount. Still others ditched the solid chocolate for cocoa powder. As for the egg yolks, many recipes didn't include them, instead opting for a heftier dose of cornstarch to thicken things up. Then there was the dairy question: Should it be milk, cream, half-and-half—or some combination? And would adding butter be a good thing or overkill?

See How Easy It Is
Video available FREE for 4 months at www.CooksIllustrated.com/oct11

A careful balance of bittersweet chocolate and cocoa powder gives our pudding rich flavor and a remarkably creamy texture.

More Is Less

I decided to start conservatively, preparing a pudding from the 1975 edition of *The Joy of Cooking* that called for 1 ounce of unsweetened chocolate, milk, cornstarch, and no eggs. No surprise: Tasters panned this pudding for its wan flavor and loose consistency. Fast-forwarding to 1990, I tried the version in Craig Claiborne's *The New York Times Cookbook*, which kicked everything up a notch, increasing the unsweetened chocolate to 3 ounces, swapping in some half-and-half for the milk, and adding a few tablespoons of butter. But still no fans.

Putting the old tomes aside, I went for a more drastic change and tried a blog-hyped bittersweet chocolate pudding recipe from the Scharffen Berger website. This formula—4 ounces of bittersweet chocolate, milk, and no eggs—produced a markedly richer, more complex chocolate pudding, and I can't say we were all that surprised.

Though 4 ounces of bittersweet chocolate is the rough equivalent of 3 ounces of unsweetened, we usually find the quality of good bittersweet far superior. (Unsweetened chocolate, we think, is best reserved for recipes such as brownies, where nuance isn't as important and where we want strict control over the amount of sugar.) But I hadn't hit the mark yet. Sure, this pudding's chocolate flavor had more oomph and dimension, but according to my tasters, I had yet to reach the chocolate ceiling.

I'd done a pretty thorough sweep of traditional recipes so far; perhaps it was time to consider a more scientific approach. The book I had in mind was a recently released food science volume called *Ideas in Food* by Aki Kamozawa and H. Alexander Talbot. Their recipe boasted a whopping 12 ounces of bittersweet chocolate and sounded like it was developed with only die-hard chocoholics in mind. But it did embolden me to increase the chocolate in my placeholder pudding base (made with milk, cornstarch, and no eggs) to 8 ounces. As I poured this latest batch into a bowl to chill, I sneaked a taste. The rich, dark, glossy pudding had a robust flavor that had been missing in the previous versions. But when the pudding set, my hopes were dashed; the once-smooth pudding was now marred by a distinctly grainy texture. I could only guess that the high proportion of chocolate solids was to blame.

I began dialing back the chocolate to see how much I could incorporate while still keeping a velvety texture. To my disappointment, I found that the 4 ounces I'd used in the Scharffen Berger recipe was as high as I could go before the pudding turned gritty.

My only recourse was to highlight the modest chocolate flavor I had by cutting back on flavor-dulling

The Gritty Truth about Cocoa Butter

As we developed our pudding recipe, we found that there was a limit to how much bittersweet chocolate we could add before the texture turned gritty—but that we could continue to add chocolate in the form of cocoa powder without affecting smoothness. Why should this be the case? The culprit in causing grittiness, it turns out, is cocoa butter—and solid chocolate has far more of it than cocoa powder. Chocolate is manufactured so that its fat remains solid at room temperature but literally melts in the mouth. But when melted chocolate is allowed to re-solidify, the crystalline structure of its cocoa butter is reorganized. It becomes more stable and melts at higher-than-body temperature. If present in high enough amounts, this more-stable form of cocoa butter can create the grainy mouthfeel we detected in the pudding.

ingredients like cornstarch and dairy. Replacing some of the cornstarch with low-sugar pectin—a combination that we used to thicken our Fresh Strawberry Pie (May/June 2011)—produced pudding that was marginally more chocolaty but also considerably wetter. Trading some of the cornstarch for gelatin worked no better, turning out pudding that was slick and springy. And when I swapped out 1 cup of milk for equal portions of water, coffee, or stout, these tests were also a bust. As a last-ditch effort, I tried a vegan chocolate pudding recipe from *New York Times* columnist Mark Bittman that replaces both the thickener and the dairy with silken tofu. Foiled again. What this pudding gained in rich chocolate punch, it lost in creaminess.

Chocolate Flavor, Hold the Chalk

With no other leads, I circled back to a recipe that I'd skipped because it sounded, well, uninspiring. The pudding, from the "Big Red" *Betty Crocker's Cookbook* (1986 edition), calls for ⅓ cup of cocoa powder and no bar chocolate at all. My hesitation was twofold: First, gritty cocoa particles, in my mind, would equal gritty pudding; second, without richer-tasting solid chocolate, I didn't have high hopes for the chocolate flavor. Sure enough, my colleagues deemed this pudding's flavor simply "OK." But to my surprise, they raved about its silky texture—by far the smoothest pudding I'd turned out to date.

Why would cocoa powder—which typically consists of 80 to 90 percent cocoa solids and 10 to 20 percent fat, while a typical bar of 60 percent cacao bittersweet chocolate averages about 25 percent cocoa solids and 35 percent cocoa butter—make for a smoother pudding? Could it actually be that cocoa butter, not cocoa solids, caused grittiness in pudding when used in overly high amounts?

As a test, I took my working recipe with 4 ounces of solid chocolate and began adding cocoa powder to it, stopping when I got to 3 tablespoons. This pudding boasted not only deep chocolate flavor but also perfect smoothness. It seemed certain that cocoa butter—not cocoa solids—was the culprit.

Our science editor explained this curious phenomenon: Solid chocolate is manufactured so that its cocoa butter remains solid at room temperature but melts precisely at human body temperature. But when the same chocolate is melted, the crystalline structure of the cocoa butter is reorganized; it becomes more stable and melts at higher temperatures. If present in high enough amounts, this more-stable form of cocoa butter creates a grainy mouthfeel. The upshot: For a pudding with both potent chocolate flavor and a supremely smooth texture, a combo of bittersweet chocolate and cocoa powder is the way to go.

With that mystery solved and the chocolate flavor exactly where I wanted it, I had just a few more tweaks to make. Thus far, I hadn't used egg yolks in my recipe, but the pudding was lacking a certain richness and body that yolks would surely provide. After a few tests, I determined that three yolks did the trick. Tasters also liked the added creaminess brought

Pudding Through the Ages

Whether it's because our tastes have grown increasingly sophisticated or we just desire more taste sensation, the amount of chocolate in chocolate pudding recipes has inched steadily upward over the years. Here is the amount of chocolate per 3 cups of dairy in classic American recipes since the 1970s—along with our test kitchen's assessment of each pudding's flavor and our modern fix.

ERA		SOURCE	CHOCOLATE	RESULTS
1970s		*The Joy of Cooking*	1½ oz unsweetened	No surprise: A minuscule amount of chocolate corresponded to minimal chocolate flavor.
1980s		The "Big Red" *Betty Crocker's Cookbook*	½ cup cocoa powder	All cocoa powder made for an extremely smooth texture but one-dimensional taste.
1990s		Craig Claiborne's *The New York Times Cookbook*	3 oz unsweetened	A big increase in unsweetened chocolate wasn't enough. This pudding still lacked oomph.
2011		*Cook's Illustrated*	4 oz bittersweet + 3 tbs cocoa powder	At last, the winning formula for a super smooth pudding chock-full of chocolaty flavor.

about by swapping ½ cup of the milk with heavy cream. Even better, with these adjustments, I was able to drop the cornstarch from 3 tablespoons to 2.

And yet something was still missing—some depth and roundness to the chocolate flavor. I thought back to my testing of nondairy liquids. While 8 ounces of coffee had competed with the chocolate, a smaller amount might perfectly enhance its roast-y undertones. I added just ½ teaspoon of espresso powder, and my pudding was finally complete.

With the help of two kinds of chocolate in a goodly—but not lethal—amount, I daresay I had engineered a new classic.

CREAMY CHOCOLATE PUDDING
SERVES 6

We recommend using one of our favorite dark chocolates—Callebaut Intense Dark Chocolate, L-60-40NV, or Ghirardelli Bittersweet Chocolate Baking Bar. If you like, garnish the pudding with whipped cream and chocolate shavings. For our free recipes for Creamy Mexican Chocolate Pudding and Creamy Mocha Pudding, go to www.CooksIllustrated.com/oct11.

- 2 teaspoons vanilla extract
- ½ teaspoon espresso powder
- ½ cup (3½ ounces) sugar
- 3 tablespoons Dutch-processed cocoa
- 2 tablespoons cornstarch
- ¼ teaspoon salt
- 3 large egg yolks
- ½ cup heavy cream
- 2½ cups whole milk
- 5 tablespoons unsalted butter, cut into 8 pieces
- 4 ounces bittersweet chocolate, chopped fine

1. Stir together vanilla and espresso powder in bowl; set aside. Whisk sugar, cocoa, cornstarch, and salt together in large saucepan. Whisk in yolks and

cream until fully incorporated, making sure to scrape corners of saucepan. Whisk in milk until incorporated.

2. Place saucepan over medium heat; cook, whisking constantly, until mixture is thickened and bubbling over entire surface, 5 to 8 minutes. Cook 30 seconds longer, remove from heat, add butter and chocolate, and whisk until melted and fully incorporated. Whisk in vanilla mixture.

3. Pour pudding through fine-mesh strainer into bowl. Press lightly greased parchment paper against surface of pudding, and place in refrigerator to cool, at least 4 hours. Whisk pudding briefly and serve.

Great Cranberry-Nut Muffins

Most cranberry-nut-muffin recipes call for loading sour berries and chopped nuts into any old batter. Could that be why they always seem out of whack?

⇒ BY YVONNE RUPERTI ⇐

Most recipes for cranberry-nut muffins follow the same course as those for any fruit-studded muffin: Just toss a few handfuls of fresh berries and coarsely chopped nuts into the batter and bake. It's an approach that works well enough when using ripe, sweet blueberries or raspberries, but the method is never as successful with cranberries. I find that cranberries' ultra-sour burst can completely overwhelm the delicate flavor of the muffin. As for the nuts, after steaming in the moist batter, their rich, toasty flavor washes away. And then there's the usual problem of unevenly distributed mix-ins. Depending on where you bite, you might get a mouthful of sour berries, a cluster of nuts, or plain old cake.

Hankering for a not-so-sweet breakfast pastry, I decided to reinvent the concept. My muffin would feature a moist crumb with plenty of its own flavor, punctuated by zingy but not harsh cranberries and rich-tasting, crunchy nuts.

A pecan-streusel topping makes these muffins even nuttier.

Going Nutty

First things first: creating a muffin that could stand up to the heft of two mix-ins. As with all cake recipes, I could choose either the creaming method or the hand-mixed "quick-bread" method. In this case, only the latter's coarser, sturdier crumb would do. I whisked sugar, eggs, melted butter, and milk in one bowl and flour, baking powder, and salt in another. Then I gently combined the two components with a generous 2 cups of whole cranberries and 1¼ cups of toasted chopped pecans (my preference over more-common walnuts for their richer, sweeter, more buttery flavor), before filling and loading the pan into a 425-degree oven. About 18 minutes later, I had a good-looking batch of muffins—nicely domed and sturdy enough to accommodate the fruit and nuts. But that's all this batch had going for it, as the nuts offered nothing but a little crunch and the cake's ho-hum flavor was no match for the sour berries.

Brainstorming for ways to enliven the muffin base, I gave my spice pantry a quick glance—and then thought better of it. Hits of cinnamon, cloves, or allspice would not add the kind of complexity I had in mind. My other idea was to trade some of the all-purpose flour for a heartier grain like cornmeal, oat flour, or whole wheat flour, but those batches baked up respectively gritty, gummy, and dense.

However, cutting the all-purpose flour with a heftier, more flavorful flour wasn't a bad idea. It then dawned on me that just the right kind of ingredient had been sitting under my nose the whole time: nuts. In fact, not long ago in my Chocolate-Raspberry Torte recipe (November/December 2010), I swapped out some of the all-purpose flour for almond flour that I ground myself from whole nuts in the food processor. Taking the same approach with the pecans in this recipe, it seemed, might remedy both the blandness of the

muffin and the washed-out flavor of the steamed chopped nuts. I knew the trade would mean losing some of the wheat's gluten-forming proteins and, in turn, some of the muffins' tall, sturdy structure, but I decided to worry about that later. I processed the toasted pecans into a coarse, sand-like meal, which I then substituted for the regular flour in varying amounts—from just ¼ cup all the way up to 1¼ cups.

The results bore out my suspicion: These batches of muffin batter looked looser and runnier than those made with regular flour and, rather than baking up tall and self-contained, they spread out—particularly those with more nut flour. But once my tasters took a bite I knew the trade-off hadn't been for naught. Despite their now-disappointing structure, these nut-based muffins boasted a richer-tasting, heartier crumb that helped counter the cranberries' acidity. As for how much nut flour to put in the batter, tasters were definitive: the more, the better.

Stopping the Spread

To compensate for the nut flour's inability to form gluten, I committed baker's treason: I overmixed the batter. Though doing so is a surefire way to overdevelop the gluten strands and toughen up the final product, I thought it might be exactly what this batter needed. I even went for a second count by mixing up another batch and trading the remaining all-purpose flour for bread flour, hoping that the latter's protein boost would build up some structure. But instead of the domed tops that I wanted, I got squat, chewy muffins with stunted peaks—two classic

TESTING Muffin-Top Pans

Muffin-top pans allow you to bake just the part of the muffin that many people like most: the browned, crispy top. We tested five pans priced from $11.95 to $16.50, each boasting wide, shallow cups ½ inch deep. All the pans held almost a full batch of our Cranberry-Pecan Muffins batter and produced similarly crispy muffin tops, but some looked a whole lot better than others. Three models had flared sides that allowed the batter to rise up and spread across the pan, leading to flattened, lopsided tops. Our winner, the Cuisinart Chef's Classic 6-Cup Nonstick Muffin-Top Pan ($15.95), featured cups with curving sides that contained the batter and guided it upward to create even, elegantly domed muffin tops. For full testing results, go to www.CooksIllustrated. com/oct11. –Hannah Crowley

IT'S TOPS
This pan by Cuisinart makes crispy, perfectly shaped muffin tops.

RAMPING UP NUTTINESS, TONING DOWN TANG

MAKE NUT FLOUR Instead of chopped nuts, we incorporate homemade toasted pecan "flour" into the batter, which lends the muffins richer, heartier flavor.

CHOP CRANBERRIES WITH SUGAR—AND SALT Processing the berries with confectioners' sugar sweetens them; a dash of salt masks their bitter edge.

TOP WITH STREUSEL A classic nut streusel sprinkled over the top of the muffins adds rich buttery crunch and just a hint of sweetness.

---

signs of overworking. Apparently, I'd been wrong: More gluten was not the answer.

But if a lack of gluten wasn't the problem, what was? I was pondering this question while throwing together another batch of batter when I was called across the kitchen to a colleague's tasting. When I returned 30 minutes later, a curious thing had happened: The batter had thickened up considerably. Intrigued, I baked the muffins and was rewarded with the best batch yet. The batter hadn't spread across the pan and the muffins were symmetrical, with gently rounded tops. When I described the outcome to our science editor, he explained that, while the rest undoubtedly allowed a little more gluten to form, its main effect was to hydrate the batter. Because this batter contained relatively little flour, there were very few starch granules to absorb the liquid and thicken the batter. Letting the batter rest allowed what starch granules that were available to more fully absorb the free water, which, in turn, resulted in batter with more body. (For more information, see "Thickening Thin Batter.")

A Not-So-Bitter Ending

The mystery of the spreading batter solved, it was time to temper the berries' sour punch. Sugar was the obvious go-to, but further sweetening the batter wouldn't help once the whole berries burst and released their sharp juice. The more effective solution was chopping the berries to expose some of their inner flesh—a fix that also helped distribute the fruit more evenly throughout the batter—and tossing them with sugar. I saved myself some knife-work and pulsed the berries in the food processor with a spoonful of confectioners' sugar (which dissolves more quickly than granulated sugar). Sugar took the edge off, but tasters complained that the rough-chopped berries were still too tart—even bitter. That latter description triggered an idea: In the past, we've used salt to tame bitterness in eggplant and coffee. Sure enough, adding ¼ teaspoon to the processor bowl along with the berries and sugar did the trick.

These muffins were in good shape, but my tasters requested still more nut flavor. They also wanted

to get back the crunchy element that had been eliminated when I switched from chopped to ground pecans. To meet the first request, instead of grinding the nuts by themselves, I processed them with the granulated sugar. The sugar's abrasiveness helped the nuts break down further, releasing more of their flavorful oils and preventing clumping. Recovering some of the crunchy texture was as simple as creating a topping. A sweet streusel mixture of flour, sugar, butter, and chopped pecans worked perfectly. The nuts browned nicely during baking and lent a toasty, buttery touch along with satisfying crunch.

With its crunchy topping and the pop of tart berries against the nutty-tasting crumb, here, finally, was a cranberry muffin I could go nuts for.

CRANBERRY-PECAN MUFFINS
MAKES 12 MUFFINS

If fresh cranberries aren't available, substitute frozen: Microwave them in a bowl until they're partially but not fully thawed, 30 to 45 seconds.

Streusel Topping

3	tablespoons all-purpose flour
4	teaspoons granulated sugar
1	tablespoon packed light brown sugar
2	tablespoons unsalted butter, cut into ½-inch pieces, softened
	Pinch salt
½	cup pecan halves

Muffins

1⅓	cups (6⅔ ounces) all-purpose flour
1½	teaspoons baking powder
1	teaspoon salt
1¼	cups pecan halves, toasted and cooled
1	cup plus 1 tablespoon (7½ ounces) granulated sugar
2	large eggs
6	tablespoons unsalted butter, melted and cooled slightly
½	cup whole milk
2	cups fresh cranberries
1	tablespoon confectioners' sugar

SCIENCE **Thickening Thin Batter**

We thought a lack of gluten was causing our nut flour–based muffin batter to be thin and runny, leading to muffins that baked up flat. But when we accidentally let the batter rest briefly—a fluke occurrence when we walked away for 30 minutes—the batter thickened and the muffins baked up nice and tall. Could the rest be what improved the muffins' structure? We prepared another batch, this time deliberately letting the batter rest for 30 minutes before baking, and compared the results with muffins we baked right away. Once again, the rested batter thickened considerably and produced muffins with nicely domed tops, while the unrested batter was thin and created predictably flat muffins that spread across the tin.

After a chat with our science editor, we understood why: As batter rests, a small amount of gluten develops, providing structure. But the main effect is that water more fully hydrates the starches, causing them to swell. This swelling thickens the batter and helps prevent it from spreading during baking.

JUST MIXED **AFTER 30 MINUTES— SHAZAM!**

1. FOR THE STREUSEL: Adjust oven rack to upper-middle position and heat oven to 425 degrees. Process flour, granulated sugar, brown sugar, butter, and salt in food processor until mixture resembles coarse sand, 4 to 5 pulses. Add pecans and process until pecans are coarsely chopped, about 4 pulses. Transfer to small bowl; set aside.

2. FOR THE MUFFINS: Spray 12-cup muffin tin with baking spray with flour. Whisk flour, baking powder, ¾ teaspoon salt together in bowl; set aside.

3. Process toasted pecans and granulated sugar until mixture resembles coarse sand, 10 to 15 seconds. Transfer to large bowl and whisk in eggs, butter, and milk until combined. Whisk flour mixture into egg mixture until just moistened and no streaks of flour remain. Set batter aside 30 minutes to thicken.

4. Pulse cranberries, remaining ¼ teaspoon salt, and confectioners' sugar in food processor until very coarsely chopped, 4 to 5 pulses. Using rubber spatula, fold cranberries into batter. Use ice cream scoop or large spoon to divide batter equally among prepared muffin cups, slightly mounding in middle. Evenly sprinkle streusel topping over muffins, gently pressing into batter to adhere. Bake until muffin tops are golden and just firm, 17 to 18 minutes, rotating muffin tin from front to back halfway through baking time. Cool muffins in muffin tin on wire rack, 10 minutes. Remove muffins from tin and cool for at least 10 minutes before serving.

The Last Cutting Board You'll Ever Need

We thought we'd picked a winner—until our favorite board warped after just a few years.
This time we upped the ante: three months of test kitchen boot camp.

> BY AMY GRAVES

Choosing a cutting board can feel like a roll of the dice. You think you're buying a solid, hard-wearing piece of equipment that will last for decades, only to find that it eventually suffers deep gouges, dulls the edge of your knife, or even warps or splits. That's what happened to our once-favorite board, the Totally Bamboo Congo. While it initially passed every test with flying colors, several copies of this model became distorted after a few years of hard-core use in the test kitchen, some even cracking at the seams. Hardly the lifelong purchase we had in mind.

Back at square one, we restarted the search process with nine new boards—wood, bamboo, plastic, and composite models priced from $22 to nearly $200—and a firm list of criteria. First and foremost, we wanted space, and lots of it: at least 15 by 20 inches. Any smaller and we feel cramped when butchering chickens and end up chasing carrot coins that roll off the board's edge. We also wanted some heft to keep the boards from slipping and sliding around the counter while we're working. Finally, durability was crucial. We expected shallow scratches, since a blade should stick to the surface just a little; it makes for safer, steadier knife work. Deep gashes, however, would be a deal breaker, as they trap food, odors, and bacteria and can lead to splintering. To get the toughest board we could find, we distributed copies of each model to our test cooks, who put them through three solid months of daily use—the equivalent of years of use in the average home kitchen.

Get a Grip

Our first consideration was how well each of the boards accommodated the knife. More specifically, we observed how the blade responded to the board's surface, and how securely the board stayed anchored to the counter. We wanted a surface smooth enough to allow the knife's edge to glide and make nimble cuts, but nothing so slippery that either the blade or the food slides out of control while in use. This is where most of the wood and bamboo boards excelled: Their soft, subtly textured surfaces offered just enough give and "grip" for the knife to stick

lightly with each stroke as we diced onions and chiles. Conversely, the blade practically slid across the slick surface of one of the plastic boards. And the hard facade of one composite model actually wore down the blade after just 350 strokes. (Knives used on every other board retained edges sharp enough to slice through a piece of paper well beyond 750 strokes.)

As for countertop stability, many cooks slip a nonskid pad or damp paper towel under their boards, but we wanted one that stayed put on its own. That ability depended on one of two factors: the weight of the board and whether it had built-in traction. Thanks to grippy rubber strips affixed to the two lightest boards (both weighing less than 4 pounds), these featherweights stayed anchored to the counter, even as we hacked at chicken with a cleaver. Other models used sheer heft—though the disadvantages of too much bulk became clear when we had to haul the 19-pound composite block to the sink for cleaning.

Wear and Tear

We also evaluated how well the boards survived testing. Each model endured repeated blows from cleavers and chef's knives, and some of them—the plastic boards in particular—had the scars to prove it. With the exception of one model that cleaned up easily despite incurring deep scores, the cleaver gouges acted like mini trenches that trapped food and made them a pain to clean. But the surprise failure was the priciest slab of them all (at nearly $200). Despite its seemingly indestructible paper-resin composite construction (resin is also used to make skateboard ramps), the board splintered from the cleaver's whack, forcing us to pluck stray bits of it from the chicken.

The durability of the wood and bamboo models mostly depended on how the boards were constructed: end-grain or edge-grain. The former is made by gluing together blocks of wood or bamboo with the grain running perpendicular to the surface of the board, the latter by gluing together longer strips with the grain running parallel to the surface. End-grain models showed fewer scars than the edge-grain boards because their wood fibers faced the surface, and as a result, the knife marks actually closed up within minutes.

Unfortunately, those exposed wood fibers also soaked up liquid and stains like a sponge, making them prone to warping. The end-grain models in our lineup began to warp—and eventually split—after just a few rinses in the sink. The edge-grain boards, on the other hand, showed no evidence of warping.

A Cut Above

Finally, we considered how much nurture the boards required to stay in good shape. The wood and bamboo models need to be oiled regularly lest they dry out and shrink, absorb too much water, split, or crack. But the fact is, most people don't oil their cutting boards with any regularity. That's why we were intrigued when, even after four weeks of use, the Proteak Edge Grain Teak Cutting Board never appeared "thirsty." Even more impressive, after months of slicing, chopping, hacking, and washing, it retained its satiny, flat surface. With a little research, we discovered that teak, a tropical wood, contains *tectoquinones*, components of oily resins that are resistant to moisture, allowing this particular board to survive far better than the other wood and bamboo models. (Sailboats and expensive outdoor furniture are often made of teak because it can withstand the elements.) At $85, it's not cheap, but it's far from the most expensive board we tested and offers all the features we want: plenty of space, a knife-friendly surface, and longevity with minimal fuss. We think that makes it worth the price—and the trouble of oiling it every now and then. But if a carefree, dishwasher-safe board is a must, the reversible plastic OXO Good Grips Carving & Cutting Board ($21.99) makes a good, considerably cheaper alternative.

Soaking Up Water at Warp Speed

The alignment of the grain in the wood and bamboo boards in our lineup proved key to their durability.

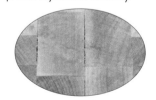 

END-GRAIN = MORE WARPING
In this model from Catskill, blocks of wood are glued together with the exposed grain facing up, which allowed the board to easily soak up liquid and warp.

EDGE-GRAIN = LESS WARPING
This winning model from Proteak is made from planks in which the grain runs parallel to the surface. The planks absorb less moisture and are less prone to warping.

TESTING CUTTING BOARDS

We tested nine cutting boards by evaluating their user-friendliness, wear on a chef's knife, ease of cleanup, and durability. All boards were purchased online and appear in order of preference. Sources for the top-rated boards are on page 32.

CUTTING We diced onions, chopped chipotle chiles, minced herbs, and hacked up chicken thighs. Boards with a slight "grip" that kept the blade (and food) from sliding around got higher marks. Those that dulled a knife were downgraded.

DURABILITY We gave copies of each board to test cooks for three months of hard-core use. We ran the dishwasher-safe boards through the test kitchen's high-heat commercial dishwasher 40 to 75 times; we also ran duplicate copies in the top rack of a home dishwasher. After testing was complete, we shoved each board off the countertop. Our ideal: no warping, splitting, cracking, or splintering, and only minimal gouging or scuffing.

USER-FRIENDLINESS Roominess and countertop stability were key, but a good board also was a snap to maneuver (handles were a plus), came clean easily, and didn't require frequent oiling or special care.

HIGHLY RECOMMENDED

PROTEAK Edge Grain Teak Cutting Board
Model: 107 Price: $84.99
Material: Mexican teak
Dimensions: 18 by 24 in
Weight: 15.05 lb

CRITERIA		TESTERS' COMMENTS
Cutting	★★★	Roomy, knife-friendly, and exceptionally durable, this teak slab was worth every penny. It resisted warping and cracking, showed only minor scratches, never seemed "thirsty," and—despite its heft—was easy to lift and clean, thanks to handholds on each end.
Durability	★★★	
User-friendliness	★★★	
Dishwasher-safe	No	

RECOMMENDED

OXO Good Grips Carving & Cutting Board
Model: 1063789 Price: $21.99
Material: Polypropylene (plastic)
Dimensions: 14.5 by 21 in
Weight: 3.85 lb

BEST BUY

Cutting	★★★	Our favorite bargain board sports rubber strips on both sides that keep its lightweight frame anchored to the counter—and make it reversible. It did suffer deep scratches and gouges but never split or warped, and it cleaned up stain-free in the dishwasher.
Durability	★★	
User-friendliness	★★★	
Dishwasher-safe	Yes	

JOHN BOOS Chop-N-Slice Reversible
Model: 214 Price: $44.95
Material: Maple
Dimensions: 15 by 20 in
Weight: 9.4 lb

Cutting	★★★	A classic wood model, this reversible, edge-grain board's slightly rough surface offered twofold control: It securely held the counter and gently gripped the knives. Though it absorbed stains and developed hairline cracks after a few months, it never warped.
Durability	★★	
User-friendliness	★★★	
Dishwasher-safe	No	

NOT RECOMMENDED

SAGE Non-Skid Chop Board
Model: SNS-141619S Price: $46.95
Material: Wood-laminate composite
Dimensions: 16 by 19 in
Weight: 3.15 lb

Cutting	★	This model had its perks: It was thin and lightweight, dishwasher-safe, and stayed put thanks to its nonskid feet. Unfortunately, it warped after several commercial dishwasher runs and was the only model to commit the ultimate cutting board no-no: It dulled a knife.
Durability	★★	
User-friendliness	★★★	
Dishwasher-safe	Yes	

THE CUTTING BOARD FACTORY Industrial Grade Polymer Cutting Board
Model: CG-18024 Price: $27.93
Material: Polyethylene (plastic)
Dimensions: 18 by 25.25 in
Weight: 7.7 lb

Cutting	★★	The good news: This plastic board is reversible and can be custom-cut to any size. It never warped, even in the commercial dishwasher. The bad news: Chef's knives couldn't grip its slick surface, and the cleaver left cuts so deep that it pulled up strips of plastic.
Durability	★	
User-friendliness	★★	
Dishwasher-safe	Yes	

CATSKILL CRAFTSMEN End Grain Chopping Block
Model: 1822 Price: $79
Material: Yellow birch
Dimensions: 17 by 20.75 in
Weight: 17.6 lb

Cutting	★★½	What this hefty end-grain block offered in knife-friendliness (a cushiony, grippy surface for controlled cutting) it lacked in durability. Despite a starter coat of oil, both copies cracked after a few rinses and eventually warped, developing bent corners.
Durability	★	
User-friendliness	★	
Dishwasher-safe	No	

TOTALLY BAMBOO CONGO Large Prep Board
Model: 20-3476 Price: $140
Material: Butcher block-style bamboo
Dimensions: 16.5 by 21.75 in
Weight: 13.75 lb

Cutting	★★	Both copies of this end-grain board arrived slightly distorted, and the warping worsened somewhat over time. Though its feet kept it steady, the rubber pads peeled off. The knife gripped the surface well enough but made a harsh, grating, scissor-like sound as it cut.
Durability	★	
User-friendliness	★	
Dishwasher-safe	No	

THINK BAMBOO Heavy Duty Cutting Board
Model: TB002 Price: $89.87
Material: Edge-grain bamboo encased by end-grain bamboo
Dimensions: 17.5 by 23.5 in
Weight: 14.85 lb

Cutting	★	Small cracks visible upon arrival in this hybrid-grain board widened after the first wash. Eventually, it warped so badly that it looked shingled. Scratches marred the surface and the cleaver left deep scores. Lacking handles, its 15-pound body was a beast to maneuver.
Durability	★	
User-friendliness	★	
Dishwasher-safe	No	

EPICUREAN Big Block Series Thick Cutting Board with Cascade Effect
Model: 014-241802015 Price: $199
Material: Richlite (paper and resin composite)
Dimensions: 18 by 24 in
Weight: 19 lb

Cutting	★	We figured this model—the heaviest and priciest in the lineup—was in it for the long haul. We were wrong. Cleaver whacks left gouges and raised splinters. Its two best features, roominess and dishwasher-safety, clashed with each other, as this large version (it's available smaller) doesn't fit in most dishwashers.
Durability	★	
User-friendliness	★	
Dishwasher-safe	Yes	

The Truth about "Pizza Cheese"

What's the difference between one supermarket mozzarella and another? The difference between deliciously creamy and dry and grainy.

BY AMY GRAVES

For such a mild-mannered cheese, mozzarella sure is popular. In 2006, it passed cheddar to become the leading cheese in the United States in per-capita consumption, with most supermarkets stocking two main varieties: fresh (usually packed in brine) and low-moisture (available either as a block or preshredded). Both kinds are made by stretching and pulling the curds by hand or machine, which aligns the proteins into long chains and gives the cheese its trademark elasticity. However, the final products differ considerably, particularly when it comes to water weight. According to federal standards, fresh mozzarella must have a moisture content between 52 percent and 60 percent by weight, which makes it highly perishable. Drier, firmer low-moisture mozzarella hovers between 45 and 52 percent and is remarkably shelf-stable—it can last in the fridge for weeks.

We prefer the sweet richness and tender bite of the fresh stuff for snacking, sandwiches, and caprese salad but tend not to use it in cooked applications, since heat can destroy its delicate flavor and texture. For most baked dishes, we turn to the low-moisture kind: It offers mellow flavor that blends seamlessly with bolder ingredients and melts nicely in everything from lasagna to pizza. It's a staple in the test kitchen and in many of our home refrigerators. But given mozzarella's unassuming reputation, does it really matter which brand you buy?

We sampled nine nationally available brands of low-moisture supermarket mozzarella, both block-style and preshredded, made with whole or part-skim

Got (Fresh) Milk?

The form of milk that manufacturers use to make their mozzarella affects not only flavor but also texture.

CREAMY
Our winning mozzarella from Sorrento, made with fresh milk, won raves for its clean dairy flavor and creamy, gooey elasticity.

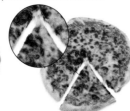

LEATHERY
Condensed milk gave the losing cheese from Sargento an oddly sweet taste and rubbery texture. It also overbrowned.

milk. Because we knew that the subtle (some would say "bland") flavor of this cheese would be most easily assessed uncooked and unadorned, we first sampled the brands plain. But since low-moisture mozzarella's biggest claim to fame is as "pizza cheese," we also melted the products on pizza. The perfect specimen's profile: creamy and clean-tasting with a bit of soft (not rubbery) chew, plenty of gooey stretch, and just a touch of flavorful browning.

Block Party

Straight out of the package, the mozzarellas were surprisingly distinct (we'd carefully shredded the blocks beforehand to match the preshredded samples). Some boasted tender, supple chew and flavor so "fresh" that it reminded tasters of drinking milk. Others were rubbery and virtually tasteless. The worst samples were downright unpleasant—overly sharp or weirdly sweet as well as chalky. This tasting confirmed that when we ate block-style cheeses plain, we preferred those made from whole milk. In contrast, the three part-skim blocks in the lineup, all passable, hovered in the middle of the rankings, while three out of four preshredded part-skim cheeses lost points for an unpleasant powdery coating and flavor that was either weak or off-kilter.

Those results more or less held up on pizza, too. Even though the powder on the preshredded brands dispersed in the fat when the cheese melted, and tasters praised how the oven's heat rendered them "gooey" and "bubbly," these cheeses were criticized for being "bland" or "flat" and "sweet." The lowest-ranked cheese in the plain tasting also failed on pizza; both times tasters noted the preshredded cheese's objectionably sweet aftertaste. This sample was also pockmarked with overly dark, leathery patches. Most of the block samples, on the other hand, boasted richer flavor (including more oil on the surface), softer texture, more stretch, and just a little appealing browning.

So what, exactly, accounted for these differences?

Cheese by Design

One obvious factor was that dusty coating. Manufacturers toss the preshredded cheese with powdered cellulose (and sometimes potato starch) to absorb moisture, which prevents clumping and slows spoilage. The powder itself is flavorless, but it can dull the flavor of already-mild cheese. The fat content in the cheeses also played a role in flavor. All of our top-ranked cheeses boasted more fat—between 6 and 7 grams per serving—than the low-

ranked cheeses, which contained roughly 5 grams. As a result, these leaner samples were drier and less capable of melting cohesively. They were also unusually bland—or, worse, sour and sharp.

But beyond that, there were very few clues as to why some brands did better than others, as the ingredient and nutrition labels didn't offer much insight. In fact, aside from variations in their dairy-fat content, the ingredient lists were virtually the same. Digging deeper, we learned that it was the manufacturing process that tweaks a cheese's taste and alters its ability to shred, melt, stretch, brown, and bubble to an exact set of specifications.

That information is not easy to come by. While the U.S. Food and Drug Administration sets standards for the amount of moisture and fat in mozzarella, manufacturers aren't required to reveal their processing methods or to spell out the exact form an ingredient may take in their product. For example, we learned from Dean Sommer, a cheese and food technologist at the Wisconsin Center for Dairy Research, that the "milk" listed on a mozzarella label can mean the fresh stuff—or it can mean a cheaper alternative like condensed skim milk or nonfat dry milk. Because condensed milk and nonfat dry milk have more sugars, Sommer said, they can lead to blistering and overbrowning in melted cheese—and oddly sweet, off-flavors. Conversely, the relatively small amount of sugar in fresh milk produces minimal spotting and, as a result, just a pleasant hint of sweetness.

It seemed obvious to us that some of the cheeses in our lineup weren't made entirely from fresh milk. When we asked, only one manufacturer, Sargento, would confirm that it allows processed milk products to be used in its mozzarella. Sure enough, that brand turned out to be the very same one that had placed in the bottom of the rankings for a sweet "cooked," "flat" flavor. At the same time, a few companies—including the maker of our favorite mozzarella, Sorrento—stated outright that they use only fresh milk. Checking the labels, we found that Sargento listed 2 grams of carbohydrates per 28-gram serving; all the other cheeses in our lineup contained less than 1 gram. More carbs in the Sargento cheese means that its sweet taste likely derives from condensed or nonfat dry milk.

It turned out that some of the other flavors we noticed—sourness, tang, and even Parmesan- and cheddar-like sharpness—are products of aging. According to Sommer, while low-moisture mozzarella can be sold for up to 150 days after manufacture,

COOK'S ILLUSTRATED

28

TASTING MOZZARELLA CHEESE

We sampled nine top-selling supermarket low-moisture mozzarella cheese products, compiled from data gathered by Chicago-based market research firm SymphonyIRI Group. The lineup included shredded and block-style, whole milk and part-skim cheeses, which we sampled in two blind tastings, first plain and then melted on our Thin-Crust Pizza. We rated them on flavor, milkiness, rubberiness, and overall appeal. Scores were averaged and the cheese products appear below in order of preference.

RECOMMENDED

SORRENTO Whole Milk Mozzarella (sold as Precious on the West Coast)
Style: Block
Price: $5.29 for 16 oz (33 cents per oz)
Fat: 6.5 grams per 28g serving
Comments: Tasters raved that our favorite mozzarella's flavor was so "clean," "mellow," and "buttery" that it was "practically like drinking milk." Even better, its "smooth" texture boasted just a hint of "nice chew" that was great both eaten out of hand and melted on pizza.

KRAFT Low-Moisture Part-Skim Mozzarella
Style: Block
Price: $3.68 for 8 oz (46 cents per oz)
Fat: 6 grams per 28g serving
Comments: The "creamy," "milky," "fresh-tasting" flavors that tasters praised when sampling this cheese plain turned up again when the cheese had been melted on pizza. There, it earned bonus points for its "stretchy," "gooey" texture.

BOAR'S HEAD Whole Milk Low Moisture Mozzarella
Style: Block
Price: $7.49 for 16 oz (47 cents per oz)
Fat: 7 grams per 28g serving
Comments: Though a few of us found this cheese's texture a bit too "chewy" on pizza, its flavor more than made up for it. Tasters noted that its balance of "creamy" and "milky" overtones, with "a touch of tang," made it ideal as a pizza topper—and as a snack.

RECOMMENDED WITH RESERVATIONS

KRAFT Low-Moisture Part-Skim Mozzarella
Style: Shredded
Price: $4.29 for 8 oz (54 cents per oz)
Fat: 6 grams per 28g serving
Comments: Our favorite among the shredded cheeses, this sample's "creamy," "milky" flavor came through particularly well on pizza, where the dusty coating dissolved and gave way to a "smooth," "not too stringy" texture with "nice chewiness" and "good brown spots."

ORGANIC VALLEY Low-Moisture Part Skim Organic Mozzarella
Style: Block
Price: $6.99 for 8 oz (87 cents per oz)
Fat: 6 grams per 28g serving
Comments: Most tasters thought that this sample's "sharp," "sour," "cheddar"-like flavors, which stood out distractingly in the plain tasting, mellowed to become "nice" and "milky" once it was melted on pizza. Texture, however, was a mixed bag: Several tasters found it unpleasantly "rubbery"; others applauded its "moderate chew."

RECOMMENDED WITH RESERVATIONS (CONTINUED)

SORRENTO Part-Skim Mozzarella
Style: Block
Price: $5.29 for 16 oz (33 cents per oz)
Fat: 5.6 grams per 28g serving
Comments: Almost everyone noted that this cheese was comparatively "damp," "wet," and "a bit spongy," but that meant different things to different tasters. Many happily compared it to "fresh mozzarella"; others panned it as "limp," particularly when it was melted on pizza.

HORIZON Organic Low-Moisture Part-Skim Mozzarella
Style: Shredded
Price: $3.99 for 6 oz (67 cents per oz)
Fat: 5 grams per 28g serving
Comments: One of the two leanest cheeses of the bunch, this sample—our least favorite in the plain tasting—was nothing you'd want to snack on. Many found it "dry" and "bland." Some picked up on sharp "pungent" flavors. On pizza, however, those harsh notes faded to a "creamy," "milky tang."

ORGANIC VALLEY Low-Moisture Part-Skim Mozzarella
Style: Shredded
Price: $4.29 for 6 oz (72 cents per oz)
Fat: 6 grams per 28g serving
Comments: "Looks like cheap grated Parm—and kinda tastes like it, too," said one taster about these wispy shreds. Others agreed, citing "sharper, tangier" flavor than you'd expect from mozzarella. Its pizza performance redeemed it—but only slightly: Its higher fat content rendered it "stretchier" and "creamier" than other low-ranking samples.

NOT RECOMMENDED

SARGENTO Classic Mozzarella
Style: Shredded
Price: $3.49 for 8 oz (44 cents per oz)
Fat: 5 grams per 28g serving
Comments: Though "void of flavor" to some, most found this cheese "overly sweet." The anti-caking residue made it "super-dry," "like there's a packet of mac and cheese powder dumped over it." On pizza, it was "dry and leathery," even "crunchy," with an odd "sweet" flavor.

---

the fresh milky taste begins to fade after two to four weeks. This is because the enzymes and starter cultures that turn the milk into cheese continue to break down its proteins into peptides, developing sour, tangy, or even bitter notes. One brand in our lineup, Organic Valley, said it deliberately targeted a later sale date—90 to 120 days after production—to create this more intensely flavored profile. But in the main, our tasters didn't appreciate the age-related tang. Some sharpness on pizza was OK, but too much was distracting. And eaten out of hand, these samples got a near-unanimous thumbs-down.

The Cheese Stands Alone

As we looked at the averaged scores from the two tastings, two cheeses stood apart. One was our winner, block-style Sorrento Whole Milk Mozzarella. Its gooey creaminess and clean dairy flavor were exactly what we wanted on pizza. Like all low-moisture supermarket mozzarellas, it doesn't rival the just-churned taste of the fragile fresh kind, but it comes as close as this style of cheese can get. It was so good that we even found ourselves snacking on it straight out of the package.

The other standout was something of an anomaly:

Kraft's Low-Moisture Part-Skim shredded mozzarella. This was the lone shredded sample to make it into the upper half of the rankings. (We also liked the brand's part-skim block mozzarella enough to rank it number two in the lineup.) The company wouldn't disclose any manufacturing information, but this sample did have a little more fat than most of the preshredded cheeses. Although it didn't dazzle us with its flavor, our tasters found it a reliable pizza topping—smooth and melty—and gave it convenience points for those times when we want shredded cheese at the ready.

KITCHEN NOTES

⇒ BY ANDREW JANJIGIAN & DAN SOUZA ⇐

TECHNIQUE | "DOUBLE-BUTTERFLYING" A ROAST

When butterflying a narrow roast like pork tenderloin, a single bisecting cut will usually suffice. But to open up wider roasts like the center-cut pork loin used in our French-Style Pot-Roasted Pork Loin (page 7), we make two parallel cuts. This technique exposes more of the meat's surface area to flavorful seasoning.

1. Holding chef's knife parallel to cutting board, insert knife one-third of way up from bottom of roast and cut horizontally, stopping ½ inch before edge. Open up flap.

2. Make another horizontal cut into thicker portion of roast about ½ inch from bottom, stopping about ½ inch before edge. Open up this flap, smoothing out rectangle of meat.

Drying Fresh Herbs in a Flash

The traditional method of hanging fresh herbs to dry can take days, if not weeks. Since the microwave targets and heats water molecules, we wondered if we could use it to drive off moisture from herbs more quickly.

We experimented with a variety of hearty herbs, including sage, rosemary, thyme, oregano, mint, and marjoram, placing them in a single layer between two paper towels on the microwave turntable and microwaving on high power. We found that it took just one to three minutes for the leaves to turn brittle and fall easily from the stems—a sure sign of dryness. (We didn't try the technique on delicate herbs such as parsley and cilantro, which are best eaten fresh.) With a method this quick, we'll never go back to hanging fresh herbs out to dry.

ZAPPED DRY
Drying fresh herbs takes just minutes in the microwave.

Another Reason to Pat Steaks Dry

With regard to searing meat, we have long recommended patting the exterior dry with paper towels before adding it to the hot pan; this ensures rapid, flawless browning. We recently retested this assumption, cooking two sets of steaks in a hot skillet side by side: one set patted dry, the other left untouched. The dry steaks achieved a crisp, dark, even sear and left behind flavorful golden bits (or fond) on the skillet—the perfect base for a pan sauce. After initially steaming, the moist steaks achieved a reasonably dark sear, but it was much softer than that on the dried steaks, showing clearly that the excess moisture did not cook off but remained trapped between the meat and the surface of the hot pan. In addition, excess moisture allowed soluble proteins to migrate out from under the steaks (where it's cooler) to exposed areas of the pan, producing a fond that quickly burned and turned bitter by the time the meat had cooked, making it unusable for pan sauce. This is yet one more reason to pat meat dry before searing.

PATTED DRY
Dry meat leaves behind a golden fond that's the perfect base for pan sauce.

LEFT WET
Wet meat produces fond too quickly: It burns before the meat finishes cooking.

Save Energy: Soak Your Noodles

If you're planning to parboil pasta for a baked dish like ziti or lasagna, but the burners on your stove are in high demand, here's an energy-saving way to get the noodles to the proper texture: Soak 'em. We experimented with different types of pasta, including ziti, rigatoni, and elbow noodles, and found that soaking them in cold water (4 quarts per pound of pasta, along with 1 teaspoon of salt for proper seasoning) for 90 minutes hydrated their starches just enough: When baked the rest of the way in sauce, the pasta had the desired texture. When we asked tasters to compare ziti baked with soaked noodles with ziti baked with parboiled noodles, they couldn't tell them apart.

TECHNIQUE | HOW TO PREP LEMON GRASS

The tender heart of the lemon grass stalk is used to flavor many Southeast Asian dishes, including our Grilled Beef Satay (page 13). While lemon grass is often steeped in soups and stews and removed before serving, it can also be minced and left in the dish. When buying lemon grass, look for green (not brown) stalks that are firm and fragrant.

1. Trim dry leafy top (this part is usually green) and tough bottom of each stalk.

2. Peel and discard dry outer layer until moist, tender inner stalk is exposed.

3. Smash peeled stalk with bottom of heavy saucepan to release maximum flavor from fibrous stalk.

4. Cut smashed stalk into long, thin strips; cut crosswise to mince.

All About Lentils

Lentils come in numerous varieties, each of which has a distinct appearance, flavor, and texture. We prepared different types using the slow-cooking method developed for our lentil salad recipes (page 18) and asked our tasters to evaluate them.

TYPE	APPEARANCE	FLAVOR	TEXTURE	APPLICATION
French green	Small, dark green	Earthy, slightly starchy taste	Firm, resilient texture that won't fall apart even when long-cooked	Salads and side dishes
Black or "beluga"	Tiny, jet black	Robust, meaty taste	Firm, creamy texture that holds shape well	Salads and side dishes
Green, brown	Medium, pale green or brown	Vegetal, mineral taste	Relatively firm texture when cooked	Salads, soups, and side dishes
Red	Small, orange	Delicate taste with floral hints	Disintegrates completely when cooked	Soups, Indian dal
Yellow	Medium, pale golden	Bland, starchy taste	Disintegrates completely when cooked	Soups, Indian dal

SCIENCE EXPERIMENT

Cutting Out Curdling in Cultured Dairy

Dishes like beef stroganoff, chicken paprikash, and many of the Moroccan stews known as *tagines* wouldn't be complete without a little sour cream or yogurt stirred in at the end. However, these cultured dairy products are sensitive to heat and can easily curdle if the stew is too hot or reheated. We wondered if another dairy product would provide a more stable tang.

EXPERIMENT

We stirred dollops of whole-milk yogurt, full-fat sour cream, and crème fraîche (which boasts much more fat) into water that we brought to just a simmer (185 degrees). After letting the samples sit for 10 seconds, we examined the liquid for signs of curdling.

RESULTS

Both the yogurt and the sour cream mixtures quickly curdled, while the crème fraîche mixture remained perfectly creamy.

EXPLANATION

Curdling occurs when excessive heat causes the whey proteins in dairy to denature (unfold) and bind with casein proteins, forming clumps of larger proteins. The greater amount of butterfat in crème fraîche (30 to 40 percent, versus 18 to 20 percent and roughly 4 percent in sour cream and yogurt, respectively) protects against this process by more thoroughly coating the proteins and preventing them from binding together. Plus, with more fat, crème fraîche has far fewer proteins to bind together in the first place. It's now our go-to dairy product for hot dishes; in fact, we found that crème fraîche is so resistant to curdling that it can withstand reheating.

SOUR CREAM
Curdled

YOGURT
Curdled

CRÈME FRAÎCHE
Creamy

TECHNIQUE | TURN YOUR OVEN INTO A SAUNA

Professional bread ovens boast pressurized valves for injecting steam into the oven at the beginning of baking for three important reasons. For starters, a moist environment transfers heat more rapidly than dry heat does, allowing the gases inside the loaf to rapidly expand in the first few minutes of baking, ensuring maximum volume. At the same time, steam prevents the bread's exterior from drying out too quickly, which would create a rigid structure that limits rise. Finally, moisture converts the exterior starches into a thin coating of gel that eventually results in the glossy, crackly crust that is a hallmark of a great artisanal loaf.

Our usual approach to creating steam in a home oven is to pour boiling water into a preheated loaf pan placed on the oven's bottom rack, but the water doesn't continue to boil for very long. Inspired by the superheated stones used to generate steam in Swedish saunas, we've come up with a more effective approach: using lava rocks. These irregularly shaped rocks (available at many hardware stores for use in gas grills) have a lot of surface area for absorbing and retaining heat, maximizing the amount of steam produced when boiling water is introduced.

1. Place a wide pan filled with lava rocks on the bottom oven rack beneath the baking stone (which we use to heat the bread's interior as quickly as possible) and preheat. If you bake bread regularly, consider designating a pan for this purpose, since it will eventually get scratched.

2. Pour about ¼ cup of boiling water onto the preheated rocks. Keep the oven door closed for one minute to create steam. Place the bread on the stone, pour another ¼ cup of water over the rocks, and bake the bread as usual.

Taking the Temperature of Scallops

We typically recommend cooking scallops until their sides are firm and their centers are slightly translucent. Since determining whether the scallop's interior is done requires cutting into it, we decided that it would be useful to have a more precise (and less destructive) way of assessing doneness. After searing a few batches, we determined that scallops are perfectly cooked when their centers reach 115 degrees. Because scallops are so small and are usually cooked over high heat, carryover cooking will add another 10 to 15 degrees, for an ideal final temperature of 125 to 130 degrees.

Why Charcoal Browns Best

We love the convenience of gas grills, but only the most powerful models can produce the same dark, crusty exterior on food as charcoal. Here's why: Grilled foods brown quickly through intense radiant heat produced by the frenetic motion of charged particles in the air around the food. Charcoal, once it has burned down to glowing coals and ash, emits almost all radiant heat. Gas, on the other hand, though it burns about 75 percent hotter than charcoal, gives off very little radiant heat. To compensate, manufacturers insert ceramic rods, metal bars, or lava rocks above the flames of gas grills to capture the energy from the burning fuel and convert it into radiant heat. But as the hot gases travel from the flames to these radiant surfaces, some are simply carried away by air currents. This makes it difficult to raise the temperature of the radiant emitters as high as that of glowing coals, putting most gas grills at a disadvantage. Case in point: Three minutes over charcoal created a thick, dark sear on our Grilled Beef Satay (page 13), while the sear produced by three minutes on a gas grill literally paled in comparison.

⇒ BY LISA McMANUS, DAVID PAZMIÑO & SARAH SEITZ ⇐

EQUIPMENT TESTING

Weber Gourmet BBQ System

The new Weber Gourmet BBQ System offers three cast-iron accessories that expand the functions of our longtime favorite charcoal grill. Replacing the cooking grate on the Weber 22½-Inch One-Touch or Performer Grill with a stainless steel grate featuring a removable inner 12-inch circle ($29) allows you to insert a crosshatched sear grate, a griddle, or a wok. Though these components sounded fun to play with, all proved to have limitations. The sear grate ($29) left a beautiful diamond pattern on meat—but only on large cuts. While delicate proteins such as scallops and salmon developed a great crust and released easily from the griddle ($29), a solid pan bottom doesn't allow much smoke flavor to penetrate. The wok ($49.99) seared meat nicely for a beef and vegetable stir-fry, but it was heavy (10 pounds!) and cumbersome as well as very slow to heat, adding prep time and, again, imparting little grill flavor. The bottom line: We might consider buying the sear grate and griddle for the fun of it, but the wok is definitely not worth the expense. (Note: The sear grate and griddle are sold in sets with the grate for $54.99. The wok is only sold separately.)

FUN BUT FRIVOLOUS
Weber's Gourmet BBQ System adds novel—but impractical—accessories to your charcoal kettle grill.

NEW PRODUCT Toss and Chop Salad Scissors

The Toss and Chop Salad Scissors ($24), an odd-looking pair of large kitchen shears, sports dual spring-loaded curved blades and a plastic scoop beneath the blades to capture items for slicing. The idea is that you can use them directly in a bowl, scooping and snipping lettuce, tomatoes, and more to create chopped salads. When we tried them on an assortment of vegetables, our first problem was that the scissors don't open wide enough to get around anything thicker than a carrot or stalk of celery. A whole tomato or onion, say, or a head of romaine or iceberg is out of the question—so you still have to precut such items with a knife and cutting board before the scissors can go to work. (At that point, why not just finish the job with the knife?) As for the mashed, oozing, irregular-size chunks that the scissors made, even someone with lousy knife skills could do better.

DIDN'T MAKE THE CUT
The Toss and Chop Salad Scissors were designed to simplify chopped salads. They don't.

NEW PRODUCT Silicone Ice Cube Trays

Hip lounges and artisan bartenders tout the virtues of superior ice. Now, silicone trays producing cubes ranging from tiny to glass-hogging are available to home mixologists. Do they make a better drink? To find out, we bought four: Tovolo's King Cube ($7.95) and Perfect Cube Trays ($10.75 for two) and Casabella's Big Ice Cube Trays ($12.21 for two) and Mini Cube Ice Trays ($11.99 for two).

Filled with water, the squishy silicone of the Casabella Big Ice Cube Trays sagged, resulting in bulged ice. The sturdier silicone of the Tovolo "King" and Casabella "Mini" trays produced samples with clean, impressively crisp edges. The ½-inch Mini cubes melted the fastest but did a great job of cooling juice: Even after 30 minutes, the juice was a noticeable 4 degrees more chilled than the sample cooled by the 2-inch King cubes, which melted the slowest. For thirst quenchers that will be rapidly consumed, we recommend the Mini cubes. For slowly sipped drinks like Scotch, the Jumbo cubes not only look sharp but also keep dilution to a minimum.

SO COOL
Tovolo's King Cube Ice Tray eliminates watered-down drinks.

NEW PRODUCT Pancake Batter Dispensers

Pancake batter dispensers are the secret behind restaurants' quick-to-the-plate, perfectly shaped disks. Seeking similarly professional results at home, we tested five batter dispensers priced from about $10 to $30, comparing each with our usual method of scooping up batter with a quarter-cup measure. Although dispensers eliminate the messy batter trail left by that method, the narrow mouths on three of the models made them nearly impossible to fill cleanly, and their small capacities forced us to refill (and spill) repeatedly. The bulky design on one model made it hard to see the batter as it hit the pan—as well as gauge how much to release. Two others trapped up to a ½ cup of batter in their mechanisms. We fared better with a French press look-alike with settings for different pancake sizes and a plunger that smoothly pushed out batter. But our favorite, the Tovolo Pancake Pen ($9.95), was beautifully simple. Just a squeeze of this tall plastic cylinder with a heat-resistant silicone nozzle allowed us to draw letters and shapes in addition to creating perfect pancakes.

PLAYING WITH PANCAKES
The Tovolo Pancake Pen dispenses batter into round cakes and more creative shapes without mess or fuss.

EQUIPMENT UPDATE Universal Knife Blocks

Unlike traditional knife blocks with slots for specific blades, universal models are "slotless" frames filled with a nest of spaghetti-like plastic rods that accommodate any arsenal of cutlery. The Kapoosh 650 Universal Knife Block ($37.35) has been our favorite—with one caveat: Blades longer than 8 inches stick out.

Recently, we discovered two new models—a bi-level block from Kapoosh ($56.26) and a newcomer from Bodum ($44.95). The Kapoosh held just as many blades as its predecessor, but it wobbled and its shorter lower level shielded only 5 inches of blade. The Bodum, however, represented an upgrade: Not only did its narrow frame hold nine knives in a more compact footprint, but it completely sheathed all but a 12-inch slicer once the knives were inserted diagonally.

COMPACT COVERA...
The Bodum Bistro Univer...
Knife Block holds any
assortment of knives an...
tools—and sheathes blad...
up to 10 inches long—in...
trim 8 by 2-inch containe...

For complete testing results, go to www.CooksIllustrated.com/oct11.

Sources

Prices were current at press time and do not include shipping. Contact companies to confirm information or visit www.CooksIllustrated.com for updates.

PAGE 24: MUFFIN-TOP PAN
- Cuisinart Chef's Classic 6-Cup Nonstick Muffin-Top Pan: $15.95, item #AMB-6MTP, Cuisinart Webstore (800-211-9604, **www.cuisinartwebstore.com**).

PAGE 27: CUTTING BOARDS
- Proteak Edge Grain Teak Cutting Board: $84.99, item #PC-KCB3006, Kitchensource.com (800-667-8721, **www.kitchensource.com**).
- OXO Good Grips Carving & Cutting Board: $21.99, item #1063789, OXO (800-545-4411, **www.oxo.com**).

PAGE 32: WEBER GRILL ATTACHMENTS
- Weber Gourmet BBQ System Sear Grate Set: $54.99, item #001602409, Walmart.com (800-925-6278, **www.walmart.com**).
- Weber Gourmet BBQ System Griddle: $29, item #7421, AJ Madison (800-570-3355, **www.ajmadison.com**).

PAGE 32: ICE CUBE TRAYS
- Tovolo King Cube Silicone Ice Cube Tray: $7.95, item #06-2375, ChefTools.com (206-933-0700, **www.cheftools.com**).
- Casabella Silicone Mini Cube Ice Trays, set of 2: $11.99, item #028484533104, Organize-It (800-210-7712, **www.organizeit.com**).

PAGE 32: BATTER DISPENSER
- Tovolo Pancake Pen: $9.95, item #298919, Cooking.com (800-663-8810, **www.cooking.com**).

PAGE 32: KNIFE BLOCK
- Bodum Bistro Universal Knife Block: $44.95, item #11089, Bodum (800-232-6386, **www.bodumusa.com**).

INDEX
September & October 2011

NEW RECIPES ON THE WEB
Available free for 4 months at
www.CooksIllustrated.com/oct11

Creamy Mexican Chocolate Pudding
Creamy Mocha Pudding
Cucumber Relish
French-Style Pot-Roasted Pork Loin with
  Marsala and Mushrooms
Gorgonzola Cream Sauce
Gremolata
Herb Butter
Lentil Salad with Pomegranates and Walnuts
Parmesan Sauce with Pancetta and Walnuts
Porcini Mushroom Broth
Salt-Baked Potatoes with Roasted Shallot
  and Thyme Butter
Thyme and Sherry Vinegar Pan Sauce

 COOK'S LIVE VIDEOS
Available free for 4 months at
www.CooksIllustrated.com/oct11

Butternut Squash Soup
Cranberry-Pecan Muffins
Creamy Chocolate Pudding
French-Style Pot-Roasted Pork Loin
Grilled Beef Satay
Lentil Salads
Potato Gnocchi
Salt-Baked Potatoes
Testing Cutting Boards
Vegetable Lasagna
Weeknight Roast Chicken

AMERICA'S TEST KITCHEN TV
Public television's most popular cooking show
Join the millions of home cooks who watch our show,
America's Test Kitchen, on public television every week.
For more information, including recipes and program
times, visit www.AmericasTestKitchenTV.com.

AMERICA'S TEST KITCHEN RADIO
Tune in to our new radio program featuring answers to listener call-in questions, ingredient
taste test and equipment-review segments, and in-depth reporting on a variety of topics.
To listen to episodes, visit www.AmericasTestKitchen.com/Radio.

DOWNLOAD OUR FREE *Cook's Illustrated* iPhone App
Inside you'll find a collection of our top recipes, along with videos that
explain how to make them. You can also access many of our most popular
taste test results, useful kitchen timers, and an interactive shopping list
that helps you plan ahead. Are you a member of CooksIllustrated.com?
If so, our app gives you access to every recipe, video, and taste test on the
website. Go to CooksIllustrated.com/iPhone.

 Follow us on Twitter: twitter.com/TestKitchen
Find us on Facebook: facebook.com/CooksIllustrated

Salt-Baked Potatoes, 14

French-Style Pot-Roasted Pork Loin, 7

Cranberry-Pecan Muffins, 25

Lentil Salad with Olives, Mint, and Feta, 18

Vegetable Lasagna, 21

Butternut Squash Soup, 15

Potato Gnocchi, 11

Creamy Chocolate Pudding, 23

Grilled Beef Satay, 13

Weeknight Roast Chicken, 9

PHOTOGRAPHY: CARL TREMBLAY; STYLING: MARIE PIRAINO

Acorn

Sweet
Meat

Delicata

Carnival

Sugar
Pumpkin

Turban

Kabocha

Blue
Hubbard

Spaghetti

Butternut

WINTER SQUASHES

NUMBER 113

NOVEMBER & DECEMBER 2011

COOK'S
ILLUSTRATED

Easy Braised Turkey
Perfect Light & Dark Meat
Bonus: Great Gravy

Guide to Perfect Holiday Cookies

Best-Ever Prime Rib
The Secret? A 200-Degree Oven

Ultimate Pasta alla Bolognese
Throw Out the Dairy

Testing Knife Sets
What Do You Get for $700?

Farmhouse Vegetable Soup
Deep Flavor Without Meat

Christmas Eve Showstopper
Tasting High-End Butters
Roasted Brussels Sprouts
Gingersnaps with Real Snap

www.CooksIllustrated.com
$5.95 U.S./$6.95 CANADA

CONTENTS
November & December 2011

COOK'S
ILLUSTRATED

Founder and Editor	Christopher Kimball
Editorial Director	Jack Bishop
Executive Editor, Magazines	John Willoughby
Executive Editor	Amanda Agee
Test Kitchen Director	Erin McMurrer
Managing Editor	Rebecca Hays
Senior Editors	Keith Dresser
	Lisa McManus
	Bryan Roof
Associate Features Editors	Elizabeth Bomze
	Danette St. Onge
Copy Editor	Nell Beram
Associate Editors	Andrea Geary
	Amy Graves
	Andrew Janjigian
	Yvonne Ruperti
	Dan Souza
Assistant Editors	Hannah Crowley
	Shannon Friedmann Hatch
	Taizeth Sierra
Executive Assistant	Christine Gordon
Assistant Test Kitchen Director	Gina Nistico
Senior Kitchen Assistants	Meryl MacCormack
	Leah Rovner
Kitchen Assistants	Maria Elena Delgado
	Ena Gudiel
	Andrew Straaberg Finfrock
Executive Producer	Melissa Baldino
Associate Producer	Stephanie Stender
Contributing Editors	Matthew Card
	Dawn Yanagihara
Consulting Editor	Scott Brueggeman
Science Editor	Guy Crosby, Ph.D.
Online Managing Editor	David Tytell
Online Editor	Kate Mason
Online Assistant Editors	Eric Grzymkowski
	Mari Levine
Video Operations Manager	Peter Tannenbaum
Media Producer	Alexandra Pournaras
Associate Editor/Camera Operator	Nick Dakoulas
Assistant Editor/Camera Operator	Jesse Prent
Design Director	Amy Klee
Art Director, Magazines	Julie Bozzo
Designer	Lindsey Timko
Art Director, Marketing/Web	Christine Vo
Associate Art Directors, Marketing/Web	Erica Lee
	Jody Lee
Designers, Marketing/Web	Elaina Natario
	Mariah Tarvainen
Staff Photographer	Daniel J. van Ackere
Online Photo Editor	Steve Klise
Vice President, Marketing	David Mack
Circulation Director	Doug Wicinski
Circulation & Fulfillment Manager	Carrie Horan
Partnership Marketing Manager	Pamela Putprush
Marketing Assistant	Lauren Perkins
Customer Service Manager	Jacqueline Valerio
Customer Service Representatives	Jessica Amato
	Morgan Ryan
Retail Sales & Marketing Manager	Emily Logan
Client Service Manager, Sponsorship	Bailey Snyder
Production Director	Guy Rochford
Senior Project Manager	Alice Carpenter
Production & Traffic Coordinator	Kate Hux
Asset & Workflow Manager	Andrew Mannone
Production & Imaging Specialists	Judy Blomquist
	Heather Dube
	Lauren Pettapiece
Technology Director	Rocco Lombardo
Systems Administrator	Marcus Walser
Lead Developer	Scott Thompson
Software Architect	Robert Martinez
Software Project Manager	Michelle Rushin
Business Analyst	Wendy Tseng
Senior Web Production Coordinator	Evan Davis
VP New Media Product Development	Barry Kelly
Social Media Manager	Steph Yiu
Chief Financial Officer	Sharyn Chabot
Human Resources Director	Adele Shapiro
Publicity	Deborah Broide

PRINTED IN THE USA

FRENCH PASTRIES To create *palmiers*, puff pastry is folded, rolled, cut into double spirals, and sprinkled with sugar. *Mille-feuille* includes puff pastry stacked with pastry cream and glazed. Cold butter incorporated into yeasted dough creates the flaky texture of the *croissant*. *Pain au chocolat* is a variation on the croissant that calls for tucking chocolate into the dough. The flaky crust of *chaussons aux pommes* ("apple slippers") is achieved by *fraisage*, a kneading method in which dough and butter are smeared with the heel of the hand. Oblong *éclairs* are made with *pâte à choux*, a paste-like dough of flour, boiling water, butter, and eggs. The hollow pastries are filled with pastry cream and topped with ganache. *Tarte au citron* contains a tangy lemon-curd filling, while *tarte aux fruits* holds fresh fruits tossed with melted jelly and arranged atop pastry cream. The chocolate ganache exterior of *dôme au chocolat* hides layers of chocolate mousse and liqueur-soaked génoise cake. **COVER** *(Apples)*: Robert Papp; **BACK COVER** *(French Pastries)*: John Burgoyne

RECIPES THAT WORK

America's Test Kitchen is a very real 2,500-square-foot kitchen located just outside of Boston. It is the home of *Cook's Illustrated* and *Cook's Country* magazines and is the workday destination of more than three dozen test cooks, editors, and cookware specialists. Our mission is to test recipes over and over again until we understand how and why they work and until we arrive at the best version. We also test kitchen equipment and supermarket ingredients in search of brands that offer the best value and performance. You can watch us work by tuning in to *America's Test Kitchen* (www.AmericasTestKitchen.com) on public television.

THE SAME OLD THING

Two years ago, Tom and Nate seeded down a small field near the brook, just past the pig lot and right across from the upper field where we keep the Randall Linebacks. It was two weeks before deer season and Tom mentioned that at exactly 4:17 every day, a large doe, followed a minute later by a very cautious buck, made her way out of the woods and down into the field. The next day I sat with my back against a sugar maple and timed it, and sure enough, at exactly 4:17, there came the doe and the buck. Evening after evening, it was the same old thing.

Every August, on the first day that offers the promise of autumn—a whisker of wet leaves and humus, a chance patch of hoary frost—Tom jumps up and talks about where we will put our tree stands this year and the first buck sightings, racks covered with felt. Summer gives up all of a sudden, the evenings fade sooner, and the night is darker and more pressing—no zephyr kisses on a warm breeze. The sugar-dusted fried dough of Old Home Day is behind us and we march through potato and honey harvest, pumpkins on the porch, thorn bushes and beagles pounding after rabbits, snowshoes and dim snowfalls, days and nights in sugarhouses, trucks stuck in mud, the planting of potatoes, beans, and corn, and then tacking up the horses for the July 4 parade.

Some might say that life has few surprises if you live long enough: accidents, marriages, births, deaths, luck, no luck, bad coffee, dry spells, frozen pipes, a cold LaBatts on a hot day, and Parker House Rolls on Thanksgiving. But then your neighbor drops off a half cord of dried, split oak. A turkey shows up drunk on fermented apples at the country store. A seven-point buck appears on the first Sunday of hunting season, just a hundred yards uphill. A neighbor tells you about his secret fishing hole in the Green River. They're unexpected moments but part and parcel of everyday living.

Watching our town's annual Old Home Day parade, I am on the lookout for the familiar. The bearded drummer with the Abe Lincoln face. The bagpipe band from Cambridge. Young kids and dogs, faces peering down from the high cabs of firetrucks. The muscle cars. The float with someone sitting on a toilet (a popular theme in our town).

Christopher Kimball

The veterans. The bright red 1949 Farmall. The couple on horseback. The cheese float. And whatever crazy entry Jed has thought up. He was the Cat in the Hat this year driving a bright red Seuss car.

A few years ago, I took three of my kids up SE Corners Road, where I grew up. If you know just where to look for it, there sits the prettiest small waterfall in Vermont, hidden in a stand of pines. At the bottom is a small pool, lit by shifting circles of sun, overshadowed by the rushing sound of the falls. It was a perfect match in memory but mirrored how much I had changed.

A few months back a neighbor took me aside and offered a few words of kindness. Her manner was a tad different than usual: more personal, more focused. She had thought hard about what she was about to say and wanted her words to make a difference. They did. It was a familiar face with an unfamiliar message. Words of kindness at the right time can be something truly new, not the same old thing.

DID YOU KNOW? All products reviewed by America's Test Kitchen, home of *Cook's Illustrated* and *Cook's Country* magazines, are independently chosen, researched, and reviewed by our editors. We buy products for testing at retail locations and do not accept unsolicited samples for testing. We do not accept or receive payment or consideration from product manufacturers or retailers. Manufacturers and retailers are not told in advance of publication which products we have recommended. We list suggested sources for recommended products as a convenience to our readers but do not endorse specific retailers.

FOR INQUIRIES, ORDERS, OR MORE INFORMATION

www.CooksIllustrated.com
At www.CooksIllustrated.com, you can order books and subscriptions, sign up for our free e-newsletter, or renew your magazine subscription. Join the website and gain access to 18 years of *Cook's Illustrated* recipes, equipment tests, and ingredient tastings, as well as companion videos for every recipe in this issue.

COOKBOOKS
We sell more than 50 cookbooks by the editors of *Cook's Illustrated*. To order, visit our bookstore at www.CooksIllustrated.com.

COOK'S ILLUSTRATED MAGAZINE

Cook's Illustrated magazine (ISSN 1068-2821), number 113, is published bimonthly by Boston Common Press Limited Partnership, 17 Station St., Brookline, MA 02445. Copyright 2011 Boston Common Press Limited Partnership. Periodicals postage paid at Boston, Mass., and additional mailing offices USPS #012487. Publications Mail Agreement No. 40020778. Return undeliverable Canadian addresses to P.O. Box 875, Station A, Windsor, ON N9A 6P2. POSTMASTER: Send address changes to *Cook's Illustrated*, P.O. Box 6018, Harlan, IA 51593-1518. For subscription and gift subscription orders, subscription inquiries, or change-of-address notices, visit us at www.AmericasTestKitchen.com/customerservice or write us at *Cook's Illustrated*, P.O. Box 6018, Harlan, IA 51593-1518.

FOR LIST RENTAL INFORMATION, CONTACT Specialists Marketing Services, Inc., 777 Terrace Ave., 4th Floor, Hasbrouck Heights, NJ 07604; 201-865-5800.
EDITORIAL OFFICE 17 Station St., Brookline, MA 02445; 617-232-1000; fax 617-232-1572. Subscription inquiries, visit www.AmericasTestKitchen.com/customerservice or call 800-526-8442.
POSTMASTER Send all new orders, subscription inquiries, and change-of-address notices to *Cook's Illustrated*, P.O. Box 6018, Harlan, IA 51593-1518.

⇒ BY ANDREA GEARY & DAN SOUZA ⇐

Taking the Bite out of Radicchio

I love the deep red color of radicchio in a salad, but my family complains that it's too bitter. Is there any way to tame it?

MABEL HOWARD
GARDEN CITY, N.Y.

➤ Radicchio owes its characteristically bitter edge to naturally occurring chemical compounds released when the vegetable is cut or chewed. However, because these bitter compounds are water soluble, you can tone down the bitterness by soaking the cut leaves in water. After testing at various time intervals, we found that a soak of at least 30 minutes was necessary to tame the vegetable's bite. To tone it down even more, we cut the radicchio into fine shreds before soaking, as the greater amount of exposed surface area allows more of the bitter compounds to leach out.

That said, we like the sharpness of this lettuce and will stick to giving it just a quick rinse to preserve its bite before incorporating it into recipes. We find that radicchio's bitterness helps balance flavors, particularly in salads that contain rich ingredients, such as cheese or nuts, or sweet components like fruit.

ASSERTIVE   **EASIER-GOING**
Finely cutting radicchio and then soaking
it in water tames some of its bite.

Goat Butter

I love goat cheese, so I was intrigued when I recently spotted goat butter at my local cheese shop. Can it be used in the same way as butter made from cow's milk?

RACHAEL ROBERTSON
ALBUQUERQUE, N.M.

➤ The first thing we noticed when we unwrapped our goat butter was its translucent white color—quite different from the yellow of cow's-milk butter. The difference is due to the fact that goats transform the beta-carotene in their diets into colorless vitamin A, while cows do not.

Goat butter and cow butter have very similar fat content, but goat butter's different fatty acid structure gives it a lower melting point and makes it softer at room temperature. As for taste, we found that goat butter has a much milder flavor than goat cheese but still retains enough tang and grassiness to set it apart from cow butter when spread on bread. Most tasters loved this "barnyard" quality—though some couldn't get past the butter's resemblance to shortening. The subtle flavor differences between goat butter and cow butter were lost, however, when we used them to sauté carrots.

There was one surprising area in which goat butter really shone: butter cookies. The butter's low melting temperature gave cookies an extra-tender, sandy texture. This is because the melted fat is able to more effectively coat the proteins in the flour, resulting in less hydration and less gluten development—and a cookie that's more delicate and "short." Plus, tasters loved how the slight tanginess of the goat butter served as a counterpoint to the cookie's sweetness.

Still, with the Liberté Goat Milk Butter we tasted selling for about $10.99 per 250-gram package (the equivalent of marginally more than two 8-tablespoon sticks), we'll save it for special occasions.

Resting Clabbered Milk

Directions for making a buttermilk substitute by adding lemon juice to milk always call for letting the mixture sit for a while. Can I skip this rest if I'm short on time, or is it important?

MOLLIE SULLIVAN
DURHAM, N.C.

➤ "Clabbered" milk is widely recommended as a substitute for buttermilk in baked goods. The usual approach is to stir lemon juice into milk (1 tablespoon per cup) and let the mixture sit for 10 minutes to "clabber" (or thicken) before proceeding with the recipe. But after following this method and closely observing what transpired, we discovered that clabbering milk doesn't give it the smooth, thick consistency of buttermilk. Small curds formed almost instantly, but after a 10-minute rest, most of the milk had not thickened at all. And more waiting still didn't give clabbered milk the consistency of buttermilk.

It turns out that when lemon juice is added to milk, the citric acid changes the electrical charge on the dairy's casein proteins, causing them to coagulate tightly into clumps. On the other hand, the *Lactobacillus* bacteria added to milk to produce commercial buttermilk remove some of the sugar molecules bonded to the proteins, allowing them to form a gel that gradually becomes thicker over time.

So, does waiting after treating milk with lemon juice impact its baking properties? To find out, we made multiple batches of biscuits and buttermilk pancakes: one set with clabbered milk that had rested for 10 minutes and one set in which we mixed the milk into the batter immediately after adding the lemon juice. All of the biscuits and pancakes were virtually identical in appearance, flavor, and texture.

Our conclusion: Adding lemon juice to milk simply acidifies it, allowing the leavening in the batter to do its job—the same role played by buttermilk. Since this change happens immediately, you can safely skip the resting time.

Swapping Nut Butters

Peanut allergies have become so commonplace. Can I substitute other nut butters for peanut butter in cookie recipes?

HOWARD CHOW, MD
SAN CARLOS, CALIF.

➤ To find the answer to your question, we substituted almond butter and cashew butter, the two most commonly available "alternative" nut butters, for peanut butter in chewy peanut butter cookies. Since we could only find them unsalted, we bumped up the salt in our recipe to compensate.

The cashew butter cookies were very similar in texture and appearance to those made with peanut butter, but the cashew flavor was so subtle that it was easy to miss, making this nut a poor stand-in for peanuts. The almond butter cookies fared worse: The almond skins made the cookies taste noticeably bitter, and the cookies also spread more than their peanut and cashew counterparts, looking comparatively flat and unattractive. It turns out that almonds contain not only slightly more fat than peanuts and cashews (which share a similar fat percentage) but also a much higher proportion of unsaturated fat. Because unsaturated fat has a lower melting point than the saturated kind, cookies made with almond butter are more fluid, allowing the batter to spread before their structure is set.

In a nutshell: If you're concerned about peanut allergies, look for cookie recipes specifically designed for other nut butters. A direct substitution with cashew or almond butter won't produce the same results.

**CASHEW BUTTER =
BLANDER**

**ALMOND BUTTER =
FLATTER**
Neither cashew nor almond
butter works well as a
direct substitute for peanut
butter in a cookie recipe.

Artichokes on Acid

I've always been taught that to keep artichokes from darkening, they must be stored in lemon water as soon as they are cut and then also cooked in lemon water. Are both steps really essential? And will vinegar work just as well?

JANE HINCKLEY
BREWER, MAINE

➤When the cell walls of artichokes (as well as avocados, apples, and potatoes) are cut or crushed, enzymes in their tissues are exposed to the air and react with polyphenols, producing black- or brown-colored pigments that mar their appearance. Contact with an acid will slow the rate of this browning. We found that vinegar (which is high in acetic acid) and parsley (which is high in ascorbic acid) each minimized darkening when added to cooking water. However, lemon juice proved more effective than either of these substances. This is because lemon juice contains both citric and ascorbic acids, which together not only slow the enzymatic reaction but also limit its activity in the first place.

As for whether soaking cut artichokes in lemon juice before cooking is also necessary to prevent them from browning, the answer is no. Since browning occurs only on surfaces where the tissues are ruptured, the acid's impact is limited to cut areas during a precooking soak. Adding lemon juice to the cooking water is far more important, as many more cells of the artichoke will burst in the boiling water, potentially creating browning throughout the vegetable.

WITH LEMON   **WITHOUT LEMON**
Lemon juice in the cooking water inhibits the enzymatic reaction that causes browning in cut artichokes.

Plastic Wrap Safety

Is it safe to place plastic wrap directly on the surface of still-warm, fatty foods such as puddings or pastry creams?

JUNE REDFORD
MONROE, CONN.

➤For an answer, we consulted Daniel Schmidt, an associate professor in the Department of Plastics Engineering at the University of Massachusetts Lowell. He explained that in the past, plastic wraps were made with one of two types of plastic—polyvinyl chloride (PVC) or polyvinylidene chloride (PVDC)—along with compounds known as "plasticizers" that enhanced their clinginess and stretchiness. However, health concerns associated with these plastics as well as many plasticizers have led most manufacturers to switch to polyethylene, which requires no plasticizers, at the expense of some

clinginess. That said, if plasticizers or additives were present in a plastic wrap, they would indeed be more likely to migrate into warm, fatty foods. Not only are many plastic additives more soluble in fats and oils than in water, but small molecules in general migrate at much higher rates at elevated temperatures.

The bottom line: While there is no evidence to suggest that the newer, reformulated plastic wraps leach harmful compounds into food, keeping the wrap at least 1 inch from food surfaces will eliminate any potential risk. Another solution is to use parchment paper for direct surface contact, as we do in the test kitchen for puddings and custards.

Gentle Giant

I've started seeing enormous bulbs of "elephant garlic" at my supermarket. Can I use it just like regular garlic?

GARY GARCIA
CHARLESTON, S.C.

➤Despite the name, elephant garlic is not actually garlic. Though both aromatics are part of the allium genus, they belong to different species. Elephant garlic belongs to *ampeloprasum*, the same species as leeks; garlic is from the species *sativum*. And while at first glance elephant garlic might look like garlic on steroids (it's two to three times larger), closer examination reveals some differences. Conventional garlic heads can boast as many as 20 cloves, but elephant garlic never has more than about six, and its cloves have a yellowish cast.

To see how their tastes compared, we made *aïoli*

and garlic-potato soup, using regular garlic in one batch and the same amount of elephant garlic in another. Raw in aïoli, the elephant garlic had a mild, garlicky onion flavor. This weak flavor virtually disappeared when it was simmered in soup. Tasters much preferred the sharper, more pungent taste of regular garlic in both recipes. It turns out that elephant garlic produces the same flavor compounds as regular garlic when it's crushed—as well as those produced by onions and leeks—just less of each type. The upshot is that elephant garlic doesn't taste as potent as its allium cousins.

In short: Elephant garlic is not a substitute for true garlic. If you want milder garlic flavor, use less of the real stuff.

ELEPHANT   **CONVENTIONAL**
Elephant garlic is big in stature but small in flavor. We'll stick with the regular kind.

SEND US YOUR QUESTIONS We will provide a complimentary one-year subscription for each letter we print. Send your inquiry, name, address, and daytime telephone number to Notes from Readers, *Cook's Illustrated*, P.O. Box 470589, Brookline, MA 02447, or to NotesFromReaders@ AmericasTestKitchen.com.

WHAT IS IT?

I picked up this peculiar-looking contraption at a garage sale for a few bucks. The seller thought it was a kitchen tool. Can you tell me how it might have been used?

MARTHA BOSS
HARRISBURG, PA.

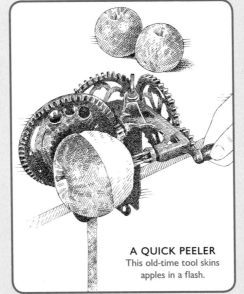

A QUICK PEELER
This old-time tool skins apples in a flash.

Your item is an antique fruit peeler, invented by Elmer H. Lupton of Baltimore, Maryland, in 1950. The mishmash of cast-iron gears directs a rotating blade around fruits positioned on a stationary trident. Much of the mechanism was originally encased to hide the working parts, but those panels, likely made of wood, are long gone. A C-clamp secures the peeler to a countertop or shelf.

As the patent states, the object of the invention was "to provide a new and improved vegetable or fruit peeler or parer that will be compact, easy to keep clean and sanitary and capable of being manufactured economically." The patent also describes portability as a goal. By today's standards, we're not sure that "compact" and "portable" are accurate descriptors. But when we tried it out, this machine did work extremely well in spite of its age. It skinned apples and peaches as fast as we could line them up.

Quick Tips

⇒ COMPILED BY SHANNON FRIEDMANN HATCH ⇐

No More Dried-Out Cookies

It's a different kind of holiday rush—trying to eat an entire tin of soft, chewy cookies before they grow stale and harden. Dissatisfied with the two common techniques for keeping cookies moist—storing them with apple pieces (which can impart off-flavors) or bread slices (which are bulky)—Lum Pennington of Salida, Colo., came up with a new way. She slips layers of flour tortillas and parchment between the layers of cookies. The tortillas fit tidily into the tin, where their moisture keeps cookies soft for days.

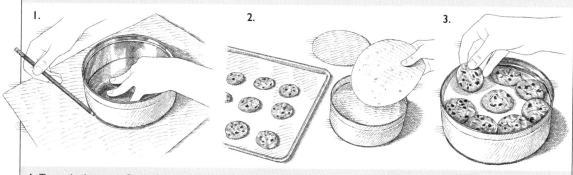

1. Trace the bottom of a cookie tin on a sheet of parchment paper. Cut out the circle and repeat as needed.
2. Layer parchment, a tortilla, parchment, and then a layer of completely cooled cookies.
3. Repeat until the tin is full, ending with a layer of cookies.

Have Cupcakes or Pie, Will Travel

Rather than buying a carrier dedicated to transporting baked goods, Sue Redman of San Diego, Calif., totes hers in a bamboo steamer basket. Cupcakes and pie fit snugly inside, the lid protects it, and a ribbon (tied from bottom to top) secures it en route.

Smart Cookie Shaping

Elizabeth Sudbey of South Grafton, Mass., doesn't let the lack of a cookie scoop stand in the way of swiftly portioning cookie dough. She fills a quarter-cup measure (equal to 4 tablespoons) with dough and then divides it according to the desired size (e.g., halved for 2 tablespoons).

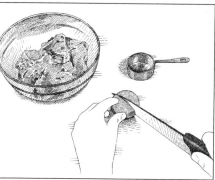

A Nonstick Solution for Chopping Candied Ginger

The sticky interior of candied ginger makes chopping it a chore: What doesn't cling to the knife clumps together on the cutting board. Angela Elliott of Quincy, Calif., stores her candied ginger in a zipper-lock bag in the freezer. When she needs a bit for cooking, she pulls out the brittle frozen ginger and breaks it into pieces with her meat tenderizer.

Evenly Sliced Bread

Slicing a boule of bread straight across like a sandwich loaf delivers smaller slices at the ends and bigger slices toward the middle. To create more even-size pieces, Alex Tonnisson of San Francisco, Calif., cuts circular loaves in a unique pattern.

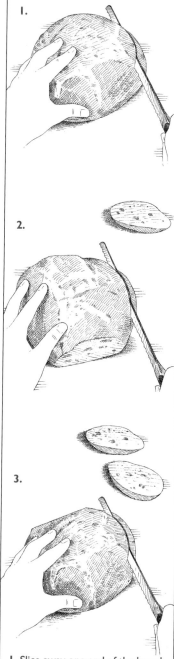

1. Slice away one end of the bread.
2. Rotate the bread one-quarter turn to the right and cut a slice.
3. Rotate the bread one-quarter turn to the left and slice again. Continue to rotate the bread after each cut.

ILLUSTRATION: JOHN BURGOYNE

Clean Shave for Burnt Spatulas

A plastic spatula is a must with a nonstick pan to prevent a scratched surface. Over time, however, the tool's edge can melt into an uneven, rough lip. Anne Awh of Eugene, Ore., has a simple solution: She uses a vegetable peeler to shave off the singed plastic and restore an even edge.

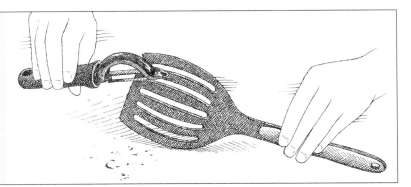

A New Bacon Wrap

Freezing is a great way to preserve bacon, but if it's frozen into a solid slab, it's impossible to remove just a few slices when needed. Instead of rolling slices into cylinders before freezing them, Jonathan May of Los Angeles, Calif., uses this wrapping method, which keeps the strips flat.

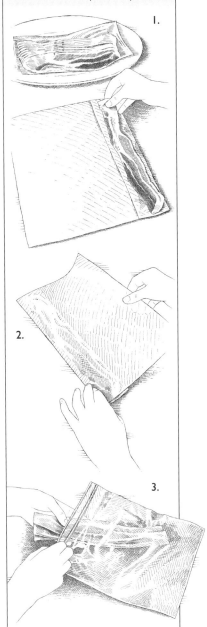

1.

2.

3.

1. Place a single slice of bacon on one end of a 12 by 16-inch piece of waxed paper. Fold the paper over the bacon, then top with another slice.
2. Continue folding and stacking in an accordion fashion.
3. Place wrapped slices in a zipper-lock bag and freeze until ready to use.

Getting a Grip on Cooking Spray

Because grabbing a can of cooking spray with floured or greasy hands can be a slippery task, Murni Gondokusumo of Oklahoma City, Okla., decided to add some traction. She placed a rubber band around the can. Now she has a no-slip grip on the nonstick spray.

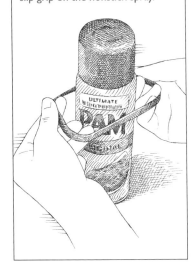

Control Your Tempering

Tempering—the process of gradually increasing the temperature of a heat-sensitive ingredient (such as eggs or dairy) with hot liquid to avoid breaking or curdling—usually requires a measuring cup and a steady hand. Michael Goodwin of Wayland, Mass., uses a turkey baster. After sucking up hot liquid into the baster, he can control the speed at which it is mixed into the cool ingredient with a gentle squeeze. A baster is also easier to grasp than a full measuring cup while simultaneously whisking with the opposite hand.

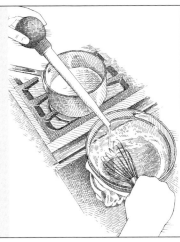

Ensuring Maximum Extraction

Whether she's making meringues or decorating a cake, Andrea King of Quincy, Mass., has devised a method to extract all of the contents of her pastry bag. She lays the bag flat on her countertop and gently presses a rolling pin toward the tip, pushing the contents to the bottom of the bag where they can be easily piped.

Short-Order Bouquet Garni

When making soup recently, Charles Christiansen of Melrose, Mass., discovered that he had no cheesecloth to bundle the herbs for a bouquet garni. Instead, he decided to try an old-fashioned method that's fallen out of favor: wrapping the herbs in leek greens. He found that this worked so well he may never go back to cheesecloth.

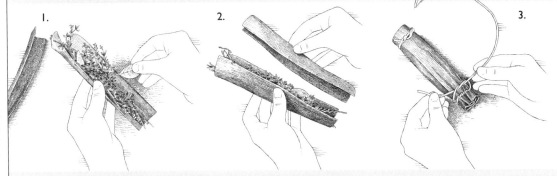

1. Trim two leek greens to 6 inches long and rinse thoroughly. Lay one green flat and place the desired herbs inside.
2. Cover them with the remaining green.
3. Tie each end closed with butcher's twine, leaving the twine long on one end. The twine can be tied to the handle of the pot to facilitate easy removal of the bundle.

Oven-Braised Turkey

Roast turkey is the norm today, but early American cookbooks often recommended another cooking method. We wondered if maybe they knew something worth learning.

⇒ BY ANDREW JANJIGIAN ⇐

Roast turkey has become synonymous with Thanksgiving, but many early American cookbook authors actually advocated a very different method: cooking the whole bird (or its parts) in liquid in a covered pot set over an open fire. Braising, after all, would have been uniquely suited to the tough wild fowl put on the table in those days, as hours of simmering would have broken down the dark meat's chewy connective tissue and turned it meltingly tender. But it's also a terrific way to cook today's mass-produced domestic turkey. Since the temperature in the pot can never rise above the boiling point of water (212 degrees), the method is inherently gentle, minimizing the risk of drying out the breast. On top of that, simmering the pieces in broth creates a flavor exchange between the meat and the liquid, giving the turkey a flavor boost and producing a rich, ready-made gravy. (The only trade-off I could think of might be less-than-crisp skin, but it was a compromise I was willing to make for supremely tender, juicy meat.) Braising parts instead of a whole bird makes the situation even more advantageous, providing extra insurance that the white and dark meat cook at a more even rate.

But I knew that a successful recipe would require more than just sticking some parts in broth, covering them up, and placing the whole thing in the oven. Contrary to what you might expect, simmering meat in liquid is no guarantee of juiciness. In fact, if cooked too long or at the wrong temperature, braised meat can dry out just as readily as roasted meat. The trick would be to find the optimal cooking time and oven temperature and just the right ingredients to add deeper complexity to the meat.

Braising the Stakes

Turkey parts are readily available at the supermarket, so I wouldn't have to bother with any butchering myself. I assembled enough bone-in, skin-on breasts, drumsticks, and thighs to total around 10 pounds per batch—enough to feed a crowd of 10 to 12.

Before I figured out the nitty-gritty of what would go in the braising liquid, I wanted to get the basics

The flavorful braising liquid for the turkey is thickened to make a rich gravy.

of the cooking method down. First, I arranged the parts skin side up in a roasting pan. (The traditional vessel for braising—a covered casserole or Dutch oven—was out, as all the parts would never fit in one layer.) I added about 5 cups of chicken broth—just enough to come about three-quarters of the way up the sides of the thighs. Then I covered the pan tightly with aluminum foil.

The oven temperature was a more complicated matter. The curious thing about braising is that despite the fact that the meat is sitting in liquid, it never actually absorbs moisture. On the contrary, once its muscle fibers reach around 140 degrees, they begin to contract and wring out juices. But when the meat in the pot has a lot of collagen, this shriveling reaction is mitigated by a second reaction: Between 160 and 180 degrees, the collagen rapidly dissolves into gelatin, which then holds on to some of the juices squeezed from the muscle fibers. If enough collagen dissolves, it lends something akin to juiciness to the meat. The challenge in braising turkey, however, is that the dark meat has a good bit of collagen while the breast meat has almost none. In other words, I had a timing issue on my

hands: I'd need to keep the thighs above the minimum temperature for dissolving collagen long enough for most of it to turn into gelatin—but not so long that the breast dried out.

Playing it safe, I dialed the oven temperature to a very gentle 275 degrees and put the turkey parts in. Without the insulating effect of the backbone and the breast, the thighs and drumsticks came up to their ideal temperature of 175 degrees at the same time that the breast reached its ideal 160 degrees: about four hours later. Both types of meat were very tender and juicy. Even the outermost layers of the breast were moist and succulent—an almost impossible feat when roasting. Still, as good as the turkey tasted, monopolizing the oven for four hours during the holidays was something I wanted to avoid.

Wondering what would happen if I took the opposite tack and cranked the heat a lot higher, I prepped a new batch of turkey parts and braised them in a 400-degree oven. That got things moving for sure—it took barely more than an hour for the meat to come up to temperature—but the results were markedly inferior. Though the center of the breast was still juicy, the outer layers were dried out and the thighs, while moist, were tough. The higher heat was obviously to blame. Because the liquid was going at a rapid boil, the cooking time sped up and, as a result, the collagen in the thighs didn't have a chance to sufficiently break down. And despite the fact that the temperature inside the covered roasting pan was limited to 212 degrees, it was still hot enough to dry out the exterior of the breast. When I checked, I found that the meat just below the surface of the breast had climbed a good 20 degrees higher than its center.

The compromise solution was 325 degrees. At this temperature, braising took a reasonable two hours, during which time the collagen in the thighs still had a chance to break down into gelatin, while the breast meat remained relatively moist. Still, I couldn't get the super-juiciness of the low-and-slow-cooked batch out of my head—and I knew that meant introducing brining into the equation. I'd been avoiding the extra step until now but was well aware of its benefits: Salt in a brine solution denatures the meat's proteins, making them better

COOK'S ILLUSTRATED

6

Contrary to what you might expect, it's possible for braised meat to turn out dry. To guarantee moist, juicy meat, we brine the turkey and cook it in a low oven.

1. BRINE Brining the turkey parts in water, salt, and sugar not only ensures that the outer layers of the breast don't dry out during cooking but also seasons the meat thoroughly.

2. BROWN To boost complexity and lend roasted flavor to the mix, briefly brown the turkey parts in a 500-degree oven along with the aromatics and flavorings.

3. ADD LIQUID To ensure a concentrated braising liquid, pour 1 cup of wine and 4 cups of broth into the pan—just enough to partially submerge the meat.

4. BRAISE Cover the pan with parchment and foil and then braise gently in a 325-degree oven until the white and dark meat are cooked through, about two hours.

5. MAKE GRAVY Making gravy from the rich-flavored braising liquid is easy: Strain the liquid, use some of its fat to make a roux, add back the liquid, and simmer until thickened.

---

able to hold on to their moisture. It also thoroughly seasons meat. Per our usual approach, I also amped up the flavor of the solution by stirring in some sugar. Finally, both the breast and the dark meat were super juicy and tender.

Taking Stock

Now that the meat was perfect, it was time to address the turkey's sallow skin. I had no expectations, of course, that truly crisp skin was in the cards, but some browning was a must. Not only would it improve the look of the skin, but it would also add flavor that would make its way into the braising liquid. Searing the pieces in the oven before adding the liquid would be the most efficient method, so I cranked the heat to 500 degrees, brushed another batch of turkey parts with melted butter, and roasted them until they were lightly tanned. That took about 20 minutes, after which I poured the chicken broth into the pan and returned the meat to a 325-degree oven. Some of the color washed away during the long braise, but the rich, roasted flavor that it added to the broth made for a worthy compromise.

I wasn't finished yet: The braising liquid still needed some tweaking. I started by swapping out 1 cup of the chicken broth for white wine—a classic trick for adding bright sweetness to a pan sauce. To further round out the flavor, I tossed chopped onions, celery, carrots, and garlic with melted butter and arranged them in the pan before placing the parts on top, browning the whole lot in a hot oven for about 20 minutes. The flavor was much improved—but I did even better by adding pepper, bay leaves, thyme, parsley, and a handful of ultra-savory dried porcini mushrooms to the aromatics before browning them. Best of all, as the flavors of the braising liquid improved, so did the flavor of the turkey itself.

All that remained was to turn this rich braising liquid into gravy. Once the turkey was cooked, I let the parts rest while I skimmed the liquid and used some of the flavorful fat to produce a golden roux. Then I whisked in a few cups of the liquid and let the

mixture simmer until it thickened into glossy gravy.

With its juicy, rich meat and sumptuous gravy, braised turkey is worth celebrating. An approach so good—and so tailor-made for turkey—should be as much the stuff of legend as the roasted bird.

BRAISED TURKEY WITH GRAVY
SERVES 10 TO 12

Instead of drumsticks and thighs, you may use 2 whole leg quarters, 1½ to 2 pounds each. The recipe will also work with turkey breast alone; in step 1, reduce the salt and sugar to ½ cup each and the water to 4 quarts. If you are braising kosher or self-basting turkey parts, skip the brining step and instead season the turkey parts with 1½ teaspoons of salt.

Turkey
Salt and pepper
1 cup sugar
1 (5- to 7-pound) whole bone-in turkey breast, trimmed
4 pounds turkey drumsticks and thighs, trimmed
3 onions, chopped
3 celery ribs, chopped
2 carrots, peeled and chopped
6 garlic cloves, peeled and crushed
2 bay leaves
6 sprigs fresh thyme
6 sprigs fresh parsley
½ ounce dried porcini mushrooms, rinsed
4 tablespoons unsalted butter, melted
4 cups low-sodium chicken broth
1 cup dry white wine

Gravy
3 tablespoons all-purpose flour
Salt and pepper

1. FOR THE TURKEY: Dissolve 1 cup salt and sugar in 2 gallons cold water in large container. Submerge turkey pieces in brine, cover, and refrigerate for 3 to 6 hours.

2. Adjust oven rack to lower-middle position and heat oven to 500 degrees. Remove turkey from brine and pat dry with paper towels. Toss onions, celery, carrots, garlic, bay leaves, thyme, parsley, porcini, and 2 tablespoons butter in large roasting pan; arrange in even layer. Brush turkey pieces with remaining 2 tablespoons butter and season with pepper. Place turkey pieces, skin side up, over vegetables, leaving at least ¼ inch between pieces. Roast until skin is lightly browned, about 20 minutes.

3. Remove pan from oven and reduce temperature to 325 degrees. Pour broth and wine around turkey pieces (it should come about three-quarters of way up legs and thighs). Place 12 by 16-inch piece of parchment paper over turkey pieces. Cover roasting pan tightly with aluminum foil. Return covered roasting pan to oven and cook until breasts register 160 degrees and thighs register 175 degrees, 1¾ to 2¼ hours. Transfer turkey to carving board, tent loosely with foil, and let rest for 20 minutes.

4. FOR THE GRAVY: Strain vegetables and liquid from roasting pan through fine-mesh strainer set in large bowl. Press solids with back of spatula to extract as much liquid as possible. Discard vegetables. Transfer liquid to fat separator; allow to settle, 5 minutes. Reserve 3 tablespoons fat and measure out 3 cups braising liquid (reserve any remaining broth for another use).

5. Heat reserved fat in medium saucepan over medium-high heat. Add flour and cook, stirring constantly, until flour is dark golden brown and fragrant, about 5 minutes. Whisk in 3 cups braising liquid and bring to boil. Reduce heat to medium-low and simmer, stirring occasionally, until gravy is thick and reduced to 2 cups, 15 to 20 minutes. Remove gravy from heat and season with salt and pepper to taste.

6. Carve turkey and serve, passing gravy separately.

Watch Andrew Braise It
Video available FREE for 4 months at
www.CooksIllustrated.com/dec11

The Best Prime Rib

Top chefs say that 18 hours in a 120-degree oven is the route to prime rib perfection. So what's a home cook to do?

> BY DAN SOUZA

A chef friend of mine recently served me a slice of prime rib as close to beef perfection as anything I've ever tasted. It featured a crisp, salty crust encasing a large eye of juicy, rose-hued meat interspersed with soft pockets of richly flavored fat. The meat had the buttery texture of tenderloin but the beefiness of a chuck roast—and the usual gray band of overcooked meat under the surface of the crust was practically nonexistent. I found myself reassessing my expectations for this primo cut and asked my friend for his recipe. While he wouldn't divulge all the details, he did direct me to the formula on which he based his own: famed British chef Heston Blumenthal's recipe for "Steak" (translation: a two-rib roast from which he cuts steaks), published in his book *In Search of Perfection*.

To say that Blumenthal goes to extremes for his prime rib would be an understatement. The recipe breaks down as follows: Sear the exterior of the roast with a blowtorch; place the meat in a preheated 120-degree oven until the internal temperature hits 120 degrees—and then hold it there for 18 hours. (You read that right: 18 hours.) Finally, pull the meat out of the oven, let it rest, slice it into steaks, and pan-sear the slabs until crisp.

This exact approach was out of the question. For one thing, even if a cook was willing to keep the meat in the oven all night and most of a day, no home oven can reliably go below 200 degrees. But it did give me some ideas—and an ideal to strive for.

Primal Sear

I had one major decision made—the meat selection—before I even got started. In the test kitchen, our preferences for the exact grade and cut of beef are definitive: a prime first-cut roast for its supreme marbling and large rib-eye muscle. (For more information on prime rib shopping, see "Cattle Roundup," page 31.) As I would with any other

Scoring the fat cap before cooking the roast helps the salt to penetrate the meat and encourages rendering.

roast, I patted the meat dry and seasoned it with a handful of coarse salt. Then came the first hurdle: how best to replicate the effects of a blowtorch. Blumenthal blast-sears meat with this instrument because its intense heat output (over 3,000 degrees) immediately starts to render fat and brown the exterior while leaving the meat beneath the surface virtually untouched (hence the remarkably thin gray band). My options were a hot oven or a skillet—and neither was ideal. Oven-searing at 500 degrees was easy but far too slow; by the time the roast got some decent color, a good half inch of meat below the surface had turned ashen. Unacceptable. Meanwhile, a blazing-hot skillet seared the meat faster, but evenly browning a three-bone roast in a 12-inch pan was cumbersome, to say the least.

I had a quick fix to the unwieldiness problem: I cut the bones off the roast before searing to make it easier to maneuver the meat in the skillet and then tied them back on before roasting so the meat wouldn't lose the insulation they provide, which helps the roast cook more evenly. I even discovered two side benefits to the method: The exposed meat

on the bone side could now be thoroughly seasoned, and carving the finished roast required nothing more than snipping the twine before slicing—no predinner butchery required. But getting a deep sear on the roast (even when I skipped browning the bone side) still took 10 minutes—not because the pan wasn't hot (it clocked 450 degrees) but because even after I had carefully blotted it dry, the meat straight out of the package was still damp. That meant that the surface directly underneath my roast couldn't rise above 212 degrees (the boiling point of water) until the moisture had evaporated. I didn't need a hotter pan. I needed drier meat.

Fortunately, this was familiar territory. We routinely air-dry poultry to allow its moisture to evaporate, making the skin extra-crisp. When I took the same tack here, prepping and seasoning another roast before moving it into the fridge for a 24-hour rest before searing, the exterior did indeed brown better (and faster) than it had in my previous attempts. But that wasn't the only perk. The meat below the surface was beefier and much more tender, and I had the combination of salt and time to thank for it. Given a chance to penetrate deep into the meat, salt enhanced the beefy flavor while dissolving some of the proteins, yielding a buttery-tender roast. In fact, I found that the longer I let the roast sit—up to 96 hours in advance—the beefier, juicier, and more tender the results. (If I let it sit any longer than 96 hours, however, I risked desiccating the exterior.) I also scored the larger swaths of fat on the exterior, which gave the salt a head start on the meat and encouraged rendering.

Rapid Aging

Things were progressing nicely—but I still had a home oven to reckon with. There was good reason for Blumenthal's incredibly long cooking time and incredibly low temperature. By gently raising the temperature of the meat and then holding it at 120 degrees for all those hours, he was cleverly manipulating two active enzymes in the meat: calpains and cathepsins. When the meat is held around the 120-degree mark, these enzymes work at a rapid pace to break down connective tissues and tenderize the meat. (This tenderizing effect is equivalent to aging the beef for almost a month.) Since it was impossible to use the same method with my conventional home oven, I focused my efforts on finding another way to keep my beef close to 120 degrees for as long as I could.

Steakhouse Prime Rib at Home

High-end-restaurant chefs like Heston Blumenthal turn out prime rib that's crisp on the outside and gorgeously rosy from center to edge. For similar results, we used nothing more than a hot skillet, a regular home oven—and a few tricks.

SUPER-CHEF APPROACH	OUR WAY
BLOWTORCH THE MEAT Blasting the roast with the intense heat of a blowtorch jump-starts its exterior without subjecting the interior to any heat. 	**SALT AND SEAR** Salting the roast and then refrigerating it uncovered for at least a day (and up to four) not only seasons the meat thoroughly but also dries out its exterior for better browning. Searing the super-dry roast in a blazing-hot skillet develops a nice thick crust. 
ROAST AT 120° Using a specialized ultra-low-temperature oven—and leaving the roast in it for 18 hours—produces rosy-pink, ultra-tender results.	**ROAST AT 200°** Roasting the meat as low as a conventional oven can go and then shutting off the heat and letting it finish in a turned-off oven produces incredibly tender and evenly cooked meat in about 4 to 5 hours.

The lowest my oven would go was 200 degrees, so I set the dial there and popped in another salted, seared roast. When the meat hit 125 degrees (medium-rare) almost four hours later, the crust was decent and the interior well seasoned and rosy from center to edge. But the texture wasn't ideal: more like run-of-the-mill strip steak than like prime-grade rib eye. I wasn't sure what to do next. Then it occurred to me that I actually did have a way to lower the temperature of my oven: I could turn it off. I ran a series of tests, shutting off the oven when the roasts hit various degrees of doneness. The magic number turned out to be 110 degrees, my trusty probe thermometer indicating exactly when the roast had hit the target temperature. This was a breakthrough technique. In the shut-off oven, the beef stayed in the enzyme sweet spot far longer, about an hour more to reach 120 for rare. I then took it out of the oven to let it rest and to allow the exuded juices to be drawn back into the meat. Thanks to the roast's hefty size, the meat stayed at an ideal serving temperature for more than an hour, giving me plenty of time to cook or reheat side dishes.

A Searing Question

Only one imperfection remained: The crust had lost some of its crispness as it rested under a tent of foil. A quick stint under the broiler before serving was all it took to restore it—well, almost all of it. To ensure that the fatty portion at the top of the ribs got enough exposure to the heat, I rolled up the piece of foil I'd used to tent the roast into a ball and sandwiched it under the ribs to elevate the fat.

All that was left was to snip the twine, lift the meat from the bones, and slice it into hefty ¾-inch-thick slabs. This prime rib was truly the king of all roasts—a deep-colored, substantial crust encasing a rosy-pink center. And making it took nothing more than a humble skillet and regular old oven.

BEST PRIME RIB
SERVES 6 TO 8

Look for a roast with an untrimmed fat cap (ideally ½ inch thick). We prefer the flavor and texture of prime-grade beef, but choice grade will work as well. (See page 31 for more information on prime rib shopping.) To remove the bones from the roast, use a sharp knife and run it down the length of the bones, following the contours as closely as possible until the meat is separated. Monitoring the roast with a meat-probe thermometer is best. If you use an instant-read thermometer, open the oven door as little as possible and remove the roast from the oven while taking its temperature. If the roast has not reached the correct temperature in the time range specified in step 3, heat the oven to 200 degrees, wait for 5 minutes, then shut it off, and continue to cook the roast until it reaches the desired temperature. For our free recipe for Mustard-Cream Sauce, go to www.CooksIllustrated.com/dec11.

1 (7-pound) first-cut beef standing rib roast (3 bones), meat removed from bones, bones reserved
   Kosher salt and pepper
2 teaspoons vegetable oil

1. Using sharp knife, cut slits in surface layer of fat, spaced 1 inch apart, in crosshatch pattern, being careful to cut down to, but not into, meat. Rub 2 tablespoons salt over entire roast and into slits. Place meat back on bones (to save space in refrigerator), transfer to large plate, and refrigerate, uncovered, at least 24 hours and up to 96 hours.

2. Adjust oven rack to middle position and heat oven to 200 degrees. Heat oil in 12-inch skillet over high heat until just smoking. Sear sides and top of roast (reserving bone) until browned, 6 to 8

minutes total (do not sear side where roast was cut from bone). Place meat back on ribs, so bones fit where they were cut, and let cool for 10 minutes; tie meat to bones with 2 lengths of twine between ribs. Transfer roast, fat side up, to wire rack set in rimmed baking sheet and season with pepper. Roast until meat registers 110 degrees, 3 to 4 hours.

3. Turn off oven; leave roast in oven, opening door as little as possible, until meat registers about 120 degrees for rare or about 125 degrees for medium-rare, 30 to 75 minutes longer.

4. Remove roast from oven (leave roast on baking sheet), tent loosely with aluminum foil, and let rest for at least 30 minutes and up to 75 minutes.

5. Adjust oven rack about 8 inches from broiler element and heat broiler. Remove foil from roast, form into 3-inch ball, and place under ribs to elevate fat cap. Broil until top of roast is well browned and crisp, 2 to 8 minutes.

6. Transfer roast to carving board; cut twine and remove roast from ribs. Slice meat into ¾-inch-thick slices. Season with coarse salt to taste, and serve.

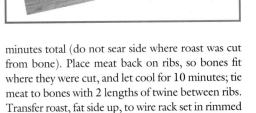

Really Good Roasted Brussels Sprouts

What would it take to create tender, nutty-tasting Brussels sprouts in just one pan?

⇒ BY ANDREA GEARY ⇐

Brussels sprouts are in dire need of a new publicist. The first order of business should be to get the word out that this vegetable doesn't have to taste overly bitter or sulfurous. Like other members of the crucifer family (which also includes broccoli, cabbage, and mustard greens), Brussels sprouts are rich in flavor precursors that react with the vegetable's enzymes to produce pungent new compounds when the sprouts are cut, cooked, and even eaten. But when the sprouts are handled just right, this pungency takes on a nutty sweetness.

The problem is, achieving perfect results is usually a two-part process. To ensure that the interiors of this dense vegetable get sufficiently tender, the sprouts are first blanched or steamed, followed by roasting or pan-searing. The latter process lightly crisps the outer leaves and creates the nice browning that mellows the sprouts' bitter kick. But when Brussels sprouts are part of a holiday feast, this two-step approach is a little too fussy. Could I get the results I wanted using just one step?

I decided to skip the pan-searing, since one batch in a 12-inch skillet barely makes enough for four people, and I wanted my sprouts to feed a crowd. Roasting seemed like a better technique to play with.

I rounded up a little over 2 pounds of sprouts—enough for six to eight people—looking for same-size specimens about 1½ inches long. With parcooking ruled out, the obvious first step was to halve the sprouts, which would help ensure that they cooked through and would create a flat surface for browning. I then tossed them in a bowl with a bit of olive oil, salt, and pepper.

To maximize browning and to jump-start cooking, we often preheat the baking sheet before roasting vegetables. I did precisely this, placing the sprouts cut side down on the hot sheet, which I then put back in a 500-degree oven. But when I pulled the vegetables out 20 minutes later, they were dry, chewy, and even burnt in spots on the outside, while practically crunchy on the inside. Starting with a cool baking sheet didn't help matters, and turning down the heat merely meant that it took a little longer for the sprouts to reach the same unsatisfactory state.

To prevent the outer leaves from drying out too much before the center achieved the ideal tender-firm texture, it seemed clear that I needed to introduce moisture into the equation. I wondered if just covering the sprouts with aluminum foil as they roasted would trap enough steam to do the trick. Once again, I arranged the sprouts cut side down on the baking sheet, but this time I covered the pan tightly with foil before placing it in the oven. After 10 minutes, I removed the foil so that the slightly softened sprouts could brown and get just a little crisp. After 10 minutes more, the Brussels sprouts were perfectly browned on the outside. And undercooked on the inside. And a bit dry and chewy all around.

I reluctantly considered lowering the oven temperature—but that would almost certainly increase the cooking time, and I wanted a side dish that would be done when my turkey finished resting. The solution was as simple as tossing the sprouts with a tablespoon of water along with the oil and seasonings before I put them in the oven. Covered in foil, each halved sprout acted like its own little steam chamber, holding on to a tiny bit of water to finish cooking its interior even as its outside began to brown. The results were perfect: tender, sweet insides and caramelized exteriors.

Now that I'd made perfectly cooked Brussels sprouts in one easy step, I devised some quick variations. They could show off their image makeover not just during the holidays, but all year long.

We found a way to turn each sprout into its own little steam chamber.

ROASTED BRUSSELS SPROUTS
SERVES 6 TO 8

If you are buying loose Brussels sprouts, select those that are about 1½ inches long. Quarter Brussels sprouts longer than 2½ inches; don't cut sprouts shorter than 1 inch.

- 2¼   pounds Brussels sprouts, trimmed and halved
- 3   tablespoons olive oil
- I   tablespoon water
-    Salt and pepper

1. Adjust oven rack to upper-middle position and heat oven to 500 degrees. Toss Brussels sprouts, oil, water, ¾ teaspoon salt, and ¼ teaspoon pepper in large bowl until sprouts are coated. Transfer sprouts to rimmed baking sheet and arrange so cut sides are facing down.

2. Cover sheet tightly with aluminum foil and roast for 10 minutes. Remove foil and continue to cook until Brussels sprouts are well browned and tender, 10 to 12 minutes longer. Transfer to serving platter, season with salt and pepper to taste, and serve.

ROASTED BRUSSELS SPROUTS WITH GARLIC, RED PEPPER FLAKES, AND PARMESAN

While Brussels sprouts roast, heat 3 tablespoons olive oil in 8-inch skillet over medium heat until shimmering. Add 2 minced garlic cloves and ½ teaspoon red pepper flakes; cook until garlic is golden and fragrant, about 1 minute. Remove from heat. After transferring sprouts to platter, toss with garlic oil and season with salt and pepper to taste. Sprinkle with ¼ cup grated Parmesan cheese before serving.

ROASTED BRUSSELS SPROUTS WITH BACON AND PECANS

While Brussels sprouts roast, cook 4 slices bacon in 10-inch skillet over medium heat until crisp, 7 to 10 minutes. Using slotted spoon, transfer bacon to paper towel–lined plate and reserve 1 tablespoon bacon fat. Finely chop bacon. After transferring sprouts to platter, toss with 2 tablespoons olive oil, reserved bacon fat, chopped bacon, and ½ cup finely chopped toasted pecans. Season with salt and pepper to taste, and serve.

ROASTED BRUSSELS SPROUTS WITH WALNUTS AND LEMON

Transfer roasted Brussels sprouts to platter and toss with 3 tablespoons melted unsalted butter, 1 tablespoon lemon juice, and ⅓ cup finely chopped toasted walnuts. Season with salt and pepper to taste, and serve.

Easy Chicken Thighs

Chicken thighs plus the blast of a broiler equals undercooked meat and charred skin. To ensure that both elements cooked evenly, we rethought the equation.

> BY ANDREW JANJIGIAN

When I need chicken dinner on the fly, chicken thighs are what I turn to most. They're more flavorful than lean breasts, meatier than drumsticks, and, thanks to their uniform size and thickness, less prone to overcooking, which eliminates any need for brining or salting. The only catch? The fat underneath the skin that helps keep the meat moist during cooking often leads to flabby skin. I wanted to come up with a quick recipe for thighs sheathed in crackling skin—without sacrificing the succulent, tender meat.

Following the lead of most recipes, I went straight to the broiler, arranging the thighs skin side up on a baking sheet and sliding them into the oven. It didn't take more than a few minutes for the skin to start browning—which unfortunately meant that by the time the meat was fully cooked, the skin was charred on top, with a flabby underbelly.

We've had luck getting poultry skin to render more quickly by poking it with a skewer before cooking, so I punctured about a dozen holes in the skin of each thigh and tried again. Improvement? Yes—but not enough, as the chicken still emerged blackened.

I had two problems: On one hand, I needed a way to more slowly render the skin; on the other, I needed to crisp the skin—but not until the meat had come up to the right temperature. High-temperature roasting, instead of broiling, seemed like the most logical way to more thoroughly render the skin's fat without sacrificing browning. So I dialed the oven temperature down to 500 degrees. This produced skin that was nicely brown but still not rendered enough. Lowering the temperature to 450 degrees helped with rendering, but the skin was now spottily browned. There was no getting around it: These two problems required two separate solutions.

Then I had an idea so logical I was surprised I hadn't thought of it sooner. Why not roast the thighs skin side down on a preheated baking sheet? That way, the sheet would concentrate heat onto the skin and help it brown. I gave it a shot, spritzing the thighs with vegetable oil spray and roasting them skin side down on the rack closest to the oven floor (and the heating element). While this succeeded in producing juicy meat and nicely rendered skin, I had a new problem: Because the skin was now sitting in rendered fat and juices, it wasn't crisp enough. I knew I could do better—and I had a hunch that the broiler might be my trump card.

About 20 minutes into the roasting time, I pulled the baking sheet out of the oven, preheated the broiler, flipped the thighs skin side up, and then slid them back onto the middle rack, where they'd crisp up a little more gently than they would on a higher rack. That did the trick: The meat emerged succulent and juicy under a layer of crackly, deeply browned skin. Best of all, the process took only about 30 minutes.

To take further advantage of my oven technique, I placed a packet of garlic on the middle rack while the chicken roasted and used it to whip up Roasted Garlic Salsa Verde as the meat rested.

Starting the thighs skin side down helps their fat render before they are flipped and crisped under the broiler.

OVEN-ROASTED CHICKEN THIGHS
SERVES 4

For best results, trim all visible fat from the thighs. Use a heavy-duty baking sheet and fully preheat the oven and baking sheet before adding the chicken. The chicken can be served plain or with Roasted Garlic Salsa Verde. For our free recipes for Roasted Shallot and Mint Chutney and Roasted Poblano-Cilantro Salsa, go to www.CooksIllustrated.com/dec11.

- 8 (6- to 8-ounce) bone-in chicken thighs, trimmed
- 1¼ teaspoons salt
- Pepper
- Vegetable oil spray
- 1 recipe sauce, optional (recipe follows)

1. Adjust oven racks to middle and lowest positions, place rimmed baking sheet on lower rack, and heat oven to 450 degrees.

2. Using metal skewer, poke skin side of chicken thighs 10 to 12 times. Season both sides of thighs with salt and pepper; spray skin lightly with vegetable oil spray. Place thighs skin side down on preheated baking sheet. Return baking sheet to bottom rack. If preparing sauce, place foil packet on middle rack.

3. Roast chicken until skin side is beginning to brown and meat registers 160 degrees, 20 to 25 minutes, rotating pan and, if preparing sauce, removing foil packet after 10 minutes. Remove chicken from oven and heat broiler.

4. While broiler heats, flip chicken skin side up. Broil chicken on middle rack until skin is crisp and well browned and meat registers 175 degrees, about 5 minutes, rotating pan as needed for even browning. Transfer chicken to platter and let rest for 5 minutes.

5. While chicken is resting, finish sauce, if using. Serve chicken, passing sauce separately.

ROASTED GARLIC SALSA VERDE
MAKES ABOUT ½ CUP

- 1 head garlic, cloves separated, unpeeled
- 1 tablespoon plus ¼ cup olive oil
- 2 tablespoons lemon juice
- 1 cup fresh parsley leaves
- 2 anchovy fillets, rinsed and patted dry
- 2 tablespoons capers, rinsed
- ¼ teaspoon salt
- ¼ teaspoon red pepper flakes

1. While oven preheats, toss garlic cloves and 1 tablespoon oil in bowl. Cover bowl and microwave until garlic is softened, 2 to 5 minutes, stirring once halfway through. Place garlic in center of 12-inch square of aluminum foil. Cover with second 12-inch square of foil; fold edges together to create packet about 7 inches square. Roast packet as directed in Oven-Roasted Chicken Thighs recipe.

2. Squeeze garlic cloves out of skins. Process garlic, lemon juice, parsley, anchovies, capers, and salt in food processor until coarsely chopped, about 5 seconds. Add remaining ¼ cup oil and pepper flakes; pulse until combined, scraping bowl as necessary.

Farmhouse Vegetable Soup

Richly flavored vegetable soup is no problem when you've fussed over homemade stock. For a weeknight version, we needed to get creative with pantry staples.

≥ BY LAN LAM ≤

Wintertime is soup time, and also the time of year when our crisper drawers are overflowing with cold-weather vegetables like carrots, potatoes, leeks, cabbage, and turnips. That combination of produce would seem to have all the makings of a satisfying vegetable soup, but my attempts often turn out lackluster. The problem is time: The best soups—vegetable or otherwise—start with a rich, full-bodied broth that serves not only as the soup's chief component but also as its flavor foundation, and I usually need the weekend to make a good one. Some recipes call for adding a little meat to the broth to beef up flavor, but it's hardly a shortcut. Many of the most flavorful cuts are also some of the toughest, and they take hours to turn tender. Cured meats such as bacon or pancetta aren't the answer either, since they impart smoky or distinctive tastes that I sometimes don't want in a vegetable soup.

Rather than sideline rustic vegetable soup as a lazy Sunday-afternoon project, I wanted to pack all the earthy-rich flavor and depth of a long-simmered stock into a recipe that only took about an hour's toil. That narrowed my focus to a soup based on prefab broth.

It Takes Two

Curious to see how much mileage I could get out of simply doctoring commercial broth and tossing in vegetables, I threw together a test batch in which I sweated leeks, carrots, and celery in a few pats of butter; added staple aromatics like crushed garlic, a few sprigs of fresh thyme, and a bay leaf; and poured in 10 cups of vegetable broth. I simmered this base for 20 minutes, strained out the solids, then stirred in small chunks of potato and turnip as well as chopped green cabbage, and let everything cook until the vegetables were just tender. My tasters had no complaints about the vegetables

Shortcut techniques help build rich, complex flavor in a hurry.

themselves: Their flavors worked well together, and the crinkly cabbage leaves offered crisp-tender crunch. Nor could I gripe about the time or labor involved, both of which were minimal. But there was no denying that the soup felt thin, in terms of both flavor and body.

The good news was that we'd been here before. A few years back the test kitchen developed a recipe for quick beef and vegetable soup and learned that the most effective way to get big flavor in a hurry is to bolster the prefab broth with ingredients rich in flavor-enhancing *umami*, the fifth taste in Asian cuisine that describes savory, almost "meaty" flavor. Among the ingredients at the top of the list were soy sauce and mushrooms, so I started my testing there, "seasoning" one pot with a few dashes of the salty Asian condiment and another with 2 large pieces of dried porcini, the latter known for their ability to lend intense, earthy depth. The improvement to each batch was obvious but also insufficient. While both flavor boosters provided subtle depth, the commercial-broth taste still prevailed. I hesitantly added a little more of each ingredient to the pot in subsequent batches. But just as I'd feared, the soy and mushrooms began to reveal themselves, pulling the broths squarely into the Asian and mushroom soup camps, respectively.

Clearly soy sauce and mushrooms were imperfect solutions on their own, but I had yet to try them together. I worked up another batch of soup, this time limiting myself to 2 teaspoons of soy sauce and just a few of the dried mushroom slabs, which I fished out of the broth just before serving. To my delight, the impact of using both ingredients was far better than I ever would have imagined. The soup suddenly took on a savory depth and complexity that had previously been missing. The only problem was that I couldn't reliably repeat the results. Sometimes the soup turned out a little less flavorful; other times it tasted a bit too mushroom-y.

SCIENCE **Building Savory Flavor On the Double**

To ramp up savory flavor in our Farmhouse Vegetable and Barley Soup, we tried adding umami boosters like soy sauce and porcini mushrooms and made an interesting discovery. We found that using less of both ingredients—versus more of just one or the other—had a powerful impact on flavor. Here's why: Soy sauce contains high levels of naturally occurring, flavor-enhancing compounds called glutamates, while mushrooms are rich in flavor-amplifying compounds known as nucleotides. Used together, the two compounds can boost savory, umami-like flavors exponentially. Their effect is even more pronounced when the ratio of glutamates to nucleotides is very high. (Studies suggest that an effective ratio is 95:5.)

Of course, we couldn't measure exactly how much of each compound was making it into the pot, so we tinkered with the amount of soy and porcini we were adding until we hit it just right.

GLUTAMATES   +   NUCLEOTIDES = BIG SAVORY FLAVOR
Due to the synergistic effect of their different flavor-enhancing compounds, small amounts of both soy sauce and porcini mushrooms add up to a more profound impact on flavor than a greater amount of just one of these ingredients.

It occurred to me that the issue was the dried-mushroom pieces, which can vary a lot in size. I wondered if it would work better to grind the dried porcini to a powder and then measure out a set amount to add to the pot, instead of rehydrating whole slices in the soup. This turned out to be a great solution: After experimenting with amounts, I found that 2 teaspoons of the porcini powder, along with the 2 teaspoons of soy sauce I'd already been adding, perfectly enhanced savory flavor. (For more information on the tandem effect of these flavor enhancers, see "Building Savory Flavor On the Double," page 12.)

The broth was now so good, I even found that I could substitute water for a good bit of the store-bought broth to eliminate any vestige of heavily cooked commercial flavor. The acidity of a little white wine (added along with the first batch of vegetables) further improved the pot, as did the last-minute introduction of frozen peas, a splash of fresh lemon juice, and a fistful of chopped parsley.

Body Builders

Flavorwise, I was in pretty good shape. The bigger hurdle was the soup's lack of body. The vegetables themselves were substantial, and rough-chopping (rather than fine-dicing) them amped up their heartiness, but even the starchy potatoes didn't do much to thicken the broth. I thought about adding dairy but realized that the fat would dull the flavor of the broth that I'd just worked so hard to build. I started flipping through some Irish cookbooks, recalling that a colleague had mentioned eating some stellar vegetable soups while in Ireland, and I stumbled on an interesting idea: adding oatmeal to the soup. I found this frugal trick for bulking up the broth charming in theory, but it didn't play out as I'd hoped. Tasters complained that even though the dish took on a certain nuttiness, the chewy oats turned it into a vegetable-heavy gruel.

Nonetheless, I liked the idea of bulking up the soup with a grain and immediately turned my attention to a more obvious choice: barley. I added ½ cup of the pearl variety to the pot just as I poured in the liquids. The beads were partially plumped by the time I was ready to add in the potatoes, turnip, and cabbage, and they were perfectly al dente about 20 minutes later, when the soup was ready to be served.

This was exactly the heft and substance that the soup needed—well, almost. A few of my tasters weren't keen on letting me wrap up testing before getting another dimension of flavor and richness into the pot. I had a holdout idea that I'd come across in one of the Irish cookbooks: finishing the soup with flavored butter. It would be an unusual addition for sure. Still, I held out hope that stirring in a dollop at the table would contribute not only a burst of fresh flavor (lemon and fresh thyme seemed like good, soup-brightening mix-ins) but also the plush body that only dairy can give without the cloying, flavor-dampening effect of milk or cream. When I caught my tasters sneaking an extra dollop into their bowls, I knew that I'd hit it right.

At last, a rustic, full-bodied vegetable soup thrown together in under an hour that didn't even need a speck of meat to taste hearty and satisfying.

FARMHOUSE VEGETABLE AND BARLEY SOUP
SERVES 6 TO 8

We prefer an acidic, un-oaked white wine such as sauvignon blanc for this recipe. We love the richness added by the Lemon-Thyme Butter, but the soup can also be garnished with crisp bacon, crumbled cheddar cheese, or croutons. For our free recipe for Herbed Croutons, go to www.CooksIllustrated.com/dec11.

- ⅛ ounce dried porcini mushrooms
- 8 sprigs fresh parsley plus 3 tablespoons chopped
- 4 sprigs fresh thyme
- 1 bay leaf
- 2 tablespoons unsalted butter
- 1½ pounds leeks, white and light green parts sliced ½ inch thick and washed thoroughly
- 2 carrots, peeled and cut into ½-inch pieces
- 2 celery ribs, cut into ¼-inch pieces
- ⅓ cup dry white wine
- 2 teaspoons soy sauce
  Salt and pepper
- 6 cups water
- 4 cups low-sodium chicken broth or vegetable broth
- ½ cup pearl barley
- 1 garlic clove, peeled and smashed
- 1½ pounds Yukon Gold potatoes, peeled and cut into ½-inch pieces
- 1 turnip, peeled and cut into ¾-inch pieces
- 1½ cups chopped green cabbage
- 1 cup frozen peas
- 1 teaspoon lemon juice

1. Grind porcini with spice grinder until they resemble fine meal, 10 to 30 seconds. Measure out 2 teaspoons porcini powder; reserve remainder for other use. Using kitchen twine, tie together parsley sprigs, thyme, and bay leaf.

2. Melt butter in large Dutch oven over medium heat. Add leeks, carrots, celery, wine, soy sauce, and 2 teaspoons salt. Cook, stirring occasionally, until liquid has evaporated and celery is softened, about 10 minutes.

3. Add water, broth, barley, porcini powder, herb bundle, and garlic; increase heat to high and bring to boil. Reduce heat to medium-low and simmer, partially covered, for 25 minutes.

4. Add potatoes, turnip, and cabbage; return to simmer and cook until barley, potatoes, turnip, and cabbage are tender, 18 to 20 minutes.

5. Remove pot from heat and remove herb bundle. Stir in peas, lemon juice, and chopped parsley; season with salt and pepper to taste. Serve, passing Lemon-Thyme Butter separately.

LEMON-THYME BUTTER
MAKES 6 TABLESPOONS

- 6 tablespoons unsalted butter, softened
- 1 tablespoon minced fresh thyme
- ¾ teaspoon finely grated lemon zest plus ¼ teaspoon juice
  Pinch salt

Combine all ingredients in bowl.

Ultimate Ragu alla Bolognese

Our goal was the richest, most savory interpretation of this famous meat sauce.
But how many meats did that require—and would the dairy have to go?

⋛ BY BRYAN ROOF ⋚

Ragu alla Bolognese, the hearty meat sauce native to the northern Italian city for which it is named, has always been a simple concept—but with a lot of complications to hamper its simplicity. Despite its undisputed Bolognese pedigree, there are countless "authentic" interpretations on record. While ground beef is the common starting point, many versions add ground pork and often veal as well. Others supplement the ground meat with finely chopped *salumi*, usually pancetta or prosciutto. Some recipes call for brightening the ragu with crushed tomatoes; others lean toward the drier, more concentrated depth of tomato paste. One version may call for white wine, another for red—some may call for no wine at all. Cooking times range from 90 minutes to 3 hours.

But the most controversial point of all? Dairy. Depending on which source you consult, milk and/or cream is either an essential component, lending further richness and supposedly tenderizing the long-cooked meat, or it has no place in the sauce whatsoever. In other words, what constitutes "real" ragu Bolognese is largely a matter of interpretation.

The only thing that all Italian cooks seem to agree on is this: The end product should be hearty and rich but not cloying, with a velvety texture that lightly clings to the noodles, and tomatoes should be a bit player in this show. The true star is the meat.

I'd never felt strongly about the dairy issue myself, until recently, when I sampled a Bolognese sauce made by Dante de Magistris, an Italian chef in Boston with a big following. His version was by far the meatiest, most complex version I'd ever had. I was so taken with it that I asked him for a breakdown of the recipe. Two points stood out. First, he used a whopping six meats: ground beef, pork, and veal; pancetta; mortadella (bologna-like Italian deli meat); and, to my surprise, chicken livers. Second, de Magistris stood squarely in the no-dairy camp, claiming that when he

How to Add Six Meats

Video available FREE for 4 months at
www.CooksIllustrated.com/dec11

A little gelatin gives this sauce a silky, glossy texture despite the lack of long-simmered, collagen-rich *brodo*.

learned to make the dish in Bologna, milk and cream were definitely not included.

Those clues—plus the test kitchen's library of Italian cookbooks—were enough to get me started on my own dairy-free Bolognese. I was determined to make my version home cook–friendly and yet satisfying to even the most discriminating Italian palate.

The Meat of the Matter

I started with a test batch that I cobbled based on de Magistris's version, loading up the pot with the components of the flavor base, or *soffritto* (chopped carrot, celery, and onion), followed by five different meats. (I wasn't sure I really needed the chicken livers, so I left them out for the time being.) I then stirred in crushed tomatoes.

I let it all simmer, covered, for a couple of hours. The result was acceptably rich and flavorful, but I still had a good bit of tweaking to do, to both the ingredient list and the technique.

I made several more batches, adding a fistful of minced sage to the meat—considered an essential component by some sources—and trying various proportions of all five meats until I landed on an easy 1:1 ratio of the ground beef, pork, and veal and 4 ounces each of pancetta and mortadella. Some of the other classic Bolognese recipes I'd consulted specified that the ground meat should be cooked only until it loses its pink color, lest the browning lead to toughness. But I found the textural compromise to be far subtler than the flavor benefit of a good sear. I also decided to ignore tradition and add the meat to the pot before the soffritto. Without the interference of moisture from the vegetables, I could get a much better sear on the meat, plus sautéing the veggies in the meats' rendered fat built up even richer flavor.

What gave me pause was a more minor complaint: finely chopping the pancetta and mortadella. It was tedious work, so I called on my food processor to take over. The job was literally done with the push of a button. In fact, the appliance worked so efficiently that I also pulsed the soffritto components before sautéing them in the meats' rendered fat.

I moved on to the next major decision: the best kind of tomato product to use. The recipes I'd read didn't help narrow things down—I'd seen everything from the crushed tomatoes I had been using up until now, to sauce, to paste. One source I consulted even suggested that tomatoes were not originally part of the sauce. That idea reminded me that I liked the unobtrusive texture of tomato paste in de Magistris's version, so I added a healthy dollop to the pot, and then let the mixture go. Once the fond had taken on a deep rust tone, I poured in a few

The Mother of All Meat Sauces

For the meatiest-ever ragu alla Bolognese, we didn't stop at ground beef—or even at pork and veal. To bolster the sauce's complex, savory flavor, we packed in pancetta, mortadella, and chicken livers, too.

Ground Pork · Pancetta · Mortadella · Ground Veal · Ground Beef · Chicken Livers

PHOTOGRAPHY: CARL TREMBLAY

big glugs of red wine, deglazed the pan by scraping up the browned bits with a wooden spoon, and let the sauce simmer gently for the better part of two hours. When the sauce was nearly done, I boiled some pasta and tossed the noodles with the ragu.

Flavorwise, the sauce was in good shape: rich and complex and, thanks to the wine and tomato paste, balanced with just enough acidity. But as my tasters noted, this ragu had a textural flaw: Its consistency was pebbly, dry, and not particularly saucelike.

Velvet Underground

There was one element of de Magistris's recipe that I had overlooked in my earlier attempts: Just before the long simmering step, he ladled some homemade *brodo* (or broth) into the ragu, repeating the step twice more during cooking to moisten the reduced sauce. I suspected that the brodo—and the technique of adding the brodo in stages—had an important effect on the texture of Bolognese. Besides boosting the meaty flavor, the bones used to make the broth give up lots of gelatin as they simmer, which renders the liquid glossy and viscous. The more the broth reduced in the Bolognese, the more savory and satiny it became. But homemade broth was out of the question for me. Simmering bones for hours on top of making the ragu was just too much fuss; I'd have to make do with commercial broth.

No surprise here: The ragus I made with store-bought broth didn't measure up to the Bolognese made with homemade broth—especially in regard to texture. I started brainstorming other ways to mimic the velvetiness contributed by the gelatin in real brodo—and realized that the answer was right in front of me: powdered gelatin. It's a trick we've used to lend suppleness to all-beef meatloaf and viscosity to beef stew—two qualities that I was looking for in my ragu. I prepped multiple batches of the sauce, blooming varying amounts of gelatin—from 1 teaspoon all the way up to a whopping 8—in a combination of canned beef and chicken broth (1 cup each) before proceeding with the recipe. Every batch was an improvement over the gelatin-free ragus, but the powder's effect was relatively subtle until I got up into the higher amounts, which rendered the sauce ultra-silky. That settled it: Eight teaspoons it was.

I had one more thought about the canned broth: Since the flavor and body of the canned stuff hardly equaled that of a real brodo, I wondered if the reduction step was really doing that much for the sauce. One side-by-side test gave me my answer: The batch into which I'd added all the broth at once boasted just as much meatiness and body as the one with the staggered additions. It also finished cooking in about 90 minutes.

STEP BY STEP | BUILDING A MEATY, SATINY-TEXTURED BOLOGNESE

1. COOK the ground meats; add depth by sautéing the chopped mortadella, pancetta, and sage in the rendered fat.

2. ADD the soffritto and sweat it until softened and then add concentrated tomato flavor in the form of tomato paste.

3. DEGLAZE the pot with wine; stir in the broth plus the bloomed gelatin to develop luxurious silky texture.

4. STIR in the pureed chicken livers for subtle but rich taste.

And yet while canned broth plus gelatin nicely solved the texture problem, the sauce still lacked a certain depth and roundness of flavor. Fortunately, I still had one card left to play: chicken livers. They'd seemed superfluous to me at first, but I wondered if finely chopping them and tossing them in at the end might get at the complexity I was after. That they did—but according to my tasters, their effect was a bit too strong. Pureeing them in the food processor worked much better; this way, their rich, gamy flavor incorporated seamlessly into the sauce.

Though my sauce could hardly get any more perfect, I just couldn't push away the thought that kept sneaking into my head: What would happen if the sauce included a little dairy? I made one last batch, adding 1 cup of milk along with the broth. But when my tasters sampled this latest version, the consensus was unanimous: Dairy muted its meaty flavor, and they liked it better without.

Without dairy, I knew that some Italian cooks out there would not consider my recipe authentic. But no matter: The sauce was undeniably complex, rich-tasting, and lusciously silky. And besides, how could any version be Bolognese without a little controversy?

RAGU ALLA BOLOGNESE
MAKES ABOUT 6 CUPS

This recipe makes enough sauce to coat 2 pounds of pasta. Leftover sauce may be refrigerated for up to three days or frozen for up to one month. Eight teaspoons of gelatin is equivalent to one (1-ounce) box of gelatin. If you can't find ground veal, use an additional ¾ pound of ground beef.

- 1 cup low-sodium chicken broth
- 1 cup beef broth
- 8 teaspoons unflavored gelatin
- 1 onion, chopped coarse
- 1 large carrot, peeled and chopped coarse
- 1 celery rib, chopped coarse
- 4 ounces pancetta, chopped fine
- 4 ounces mortadella, chopped
- 6 ounces chicken livers, trimmed
- 3 tablespoons extra-virgin olive oil
- ¾ pound 85 percent lean ground beef
- ¾ pound ground veal
- ¾ pound ground pork
- 3 tablespoons minced fresh sage
- 1 (6-ounce) can tomato paste
- 2 cups dry red wine
- Salt and pepper
- 1 pound pappardelle or tagliatelle pasta
- Parmesan cheese, grated, for serving

1. Combine chicken broth and beef broth in bowl; sprinkle gelatin over top and set aside. Pulse onion, carrot, and celery in food processor until finely chopped, about 10 pulses, scraping down bowl as needed; transfer to separate bowl. Pulse pancetta and mortadella in now-empty food processor until finely chopped, about 25 pulses, scraping down bowl as needed; transfer to second bowl. Process chicken livers in now-empty food processor until pureed, about 5 seconds; transfer to third bowl.

2. Heat oil in large Dutch oven over medium-high heat until shimmering. Add beef, veal, and pork; cook, breaking up pieces with spoon, until all liquid has evaporated and meat begins to sizzle, 10 to 15 minutes. Add chopped pancetta mixture and sage; cook, stirring frequently, until pancetta is translucent, 5 to 7 minutes, adjusting heat to keep fond from burning. Add chopped vegetables and cook, stirring frequently, until softened, 5 to 7 minutes. Add tomato paste and cook, stirring constantly, until rust-colored and fragrant, about 3 minutes.

3. Stir in wine, scraping pan with wooden spoon to loosen fond. Simmer until sauce has thickened, about 5 minutes. Stir in broth mixture and return to simmer. Reduce heat to low and cook at bare simmer until thickened (wooden spoon should leave trail when dragged through sauce), about 1½ hours.

4. Stir in pureed chicken livers, bring to boil, and remove from heat. Season with salt and pepper to taste; cover and keep warm.

5. Bring 4 quarts water to boil in large pot. Add pasta and 1 tablespoon salt and cook, stirring occasionally, until al dente. Reserve ¾ cup cooking water, then drain pasta and return it to pot. Add half of sauce and cooking water to pasta and toss to combine. Transfer to serving bowl and serve, passing cheese separately.

Holiday Cookies Made Simple

Basic butter cookies are the perfect template for decorating—provided you start with a dough that's tailor-made for rolling, cutting, and embellishing. Follow these guidelines for cookies that look their holiday best. BY KEITH DRESSER

START WITH THE RIGHT DOUGH

Rolling out the dough is usually sticky business, and the typical solution—adding more flour—makes for tough cookies.

WHY THIS DOUGH IS FOOLPROOF:

➤ We use just enough butter for tenderness and rich flavor.
➤ Superfine sugar makes for a tight, compact crumb.
➤ Cream cheese adds subtle tang, and since it is softer than butter when chilled, it makes the dough easier to roll out.
➤ A "reverse" creaming method—in which the butter is beaten into the flour and sugar rather than creamed with the sugar—makes for flatter cookies that are easier to decorate.

FOOLPROOF HOLIDAY COOKIES

MAKES 3 DOZEN COOKIES

The wrapped disks of dough can be refrigerated for up to three days or frozen for up to one month. If frozen, let the disks thaw in the refrigerator for 24 hours before using.

- 2½ cups (12½ ounces) all-purpose flour
- ¾ cup (5½ ounces) superfine sugar
- ¼ teaspoon salt
- 16 tablespoons unsalted butter, cut into sixteen ½-inch pieces and softened
- 2 teaspoons vanilla extract
- 2 tablespoons cream cheese, softened

1. In bowl of stand mixer fitted with paddle attachment, mix flour, sugar, and salt on low speed until combined, about 5 seconds. With mixer running on low, add butter 1 piece at a time; continue to mix until mixture looks crumbly and slightly wet, about 1 minute longer. Add vanilla and cream cheese and mix on low until dough just begins to form large clumps, about 30 seconds.

2. Remove bowl from mixer; knead dough by hand in bowl for 2 to 3 turns to form large cohesive mass. Turn out dough onto countertop. Divide in half, pat into two 4-inch disks, wrap each in plastic wrap, and refrigerate until dough is firm but malleable, about 30 minutes.

3. Adjust oven rack to middle position; heat oven to 375 degrees. Roll out 1 dough disk to even ⅛-inch thickness. Place rolled dough on baking sheet and refrigerate until firm, about 10 minutes. Meanwhile, repeat with second disk.

4. Working with first portion of rolled dough, cut into desired shapes using cookie cutter(s) and place shapes on parchment paper–lined baking sheet, spacing them about 1½ inches apart. Bake until light golden brown, about 10 minutes, rotating baking sheet halfway through baking time. Repeat with second portion of rolled dough. Cool cookies on wire rack to room temperature.

ROLL WITH THE RIGHT TECHNIQUES

DO roll dough between sheets of parchment paper
Handling the dough causes it to warm up and become tacky. To prevent it from sticking to the counter—and to the rolling pin—roll it between two large pieces of parchment paper.

DON'T skip the chill after rolling
Cold, stiff dough will cut more cleanly than dough that's soft. Slide the bottom piece of parchment with the rolled dough onto a baking sheet to keep it flat, and refrigerate until firm, 10 minutes.

DO minimize scraps
Cut shapes close together, starting from the outside and working your way to the middle. When making large and small cookies, we alternate cutters as we stamp to use as much dough as possible.

DO peel away dough scraps—not the cookie
Use a small spatula to strip away the dough scraps from around the cookies. With excess dough out of the way, it is easier to cleanly lift the cookies and transfer them to a baking sheet.

DON'T reroll more than once
Dough scraps may be packed into a ball and rerolled one time; working the dough any more will develop too much gluten and produce tough cookies. Make sure to chill the dough again before rolling and again before cutting.

USE THE RIGHT TOOLS

1 ATECO Plain Round Cutters (11-Piece Set), $15
No matter the shape, a good cookie cutter should be made of metal, with a thin, sharp cutting edge and a rounded top that won't cut into your hand as you press.

2 VOLLRATH Cookie Sheet, $24.95
Our favorite is roomy, with handles on the short sides, which makes it easy to slide cookies off.

3 ATECO Medium-Sized Offset Spatula (7.75-Inch), $8 Use a medium-sized offset spatula for transferring cookies to and from the cookie sheet.

4 WILTON Angled Spatula (4.5-Inch), $4.79 Smaller versions offer better control for spreading icing on a cookie.

5 FANTE'S French Rolling Pin with Tapered Ends, $6.99
The tapered shape of this model provides plenty of flat rolling surface at the center of the pin, with narrower edges for easy handling.

DECORATE SIMPLY, BUT ELEGANTLY

With the right techniques, decorating cookies with colored glazes in different patterns is an easy way to create professional-looking results.

ALL-PURPOSE WHITE GLAZE
MAKES 1 CUP

To color, stir drops of food coloring into the glaze until it reaches the desired tint. For a citrus-flavored glaze, substitute orange, lemon, or lime juice for the milk. The glaze can also be flavored with ½ teaspoon of your favorite extract.

- 2 cups (8 ounces) confectioners' sugar
- 3 tablespoons milk
- 2 tablespoons cream cheese, softened

Whisk all ingredients together until smooth. Spread glaze onto completely cooled cookies. Let glaze dry completely, about 30 minutes, before serving.

Three Ways to Glaze

➤ **Spread** For a simple, smooth coat, drizzle a little glaze in the center of the cookie and then spread it out in an even layer using the back of a spoon or a small offset spatula.

➤ **Pipe** To apply more intricate detail work, such as dots or lines, pipe the glaze directly onto the cookie. Fill a homemade parchment piping bag or a small pastry bag fitted with a small 1/16-inch round tip with glaze.

➤ **Paint** Use a small paint-brush to apply different colored glazes to a cookie without overlapping or to fill in an outline.

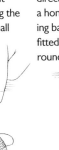

Gussying Up Glazed Cookies

➤ **Dragging** By applying dots of a contrasting colored glaze on top of another glaze and dragging a toothpick or thin skewer carefully through the center, you can create a variety of patterns and designs.

➤ **Embellishing** Place decorations in the glaze while it is still soft; once the glaze dries, it will act like glue. In addition to the usual decorating options, consider cinnamon candies, jelly beans, crushed peppermint candies, gum drops, and chocolate morsels.

➤ **Sugaring** Once a glaze has been applied to a cookie, sprinkle it with colored sugar. For the most even distribution, hold your hand about 12 inches above the work surface. Excess sugar can be brushed or gently shaken off when the glaze is dry.

Make a Parchment Piping Bag

We find that the stiff opening of a homemade parchment bag works just as well as a small piping bag at drawing thin lines (and better than the usual alternative to a pastry bag, a zipper-lock bag, which is best reserved for less delicate piping). You can also make several to hold different colored glazes—with no need for washing out between uses.

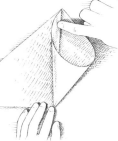

1. Fold 12-inch square of parchment paper in half on diagonal. Using knife, cut it in half on fold into 2 triangles.

2. With long side of triangle facing you, fold bottom right-hand point up and under, giving it half twist until it meets triangle's top point.

3. Holding those points together, wrap left-hand point around outside of cone until all 3 points are perfectly aligned. Tape or staple points together.

4. Use scissors to snip very small hole in point of cone.

Color Your Sugar

Colored sugar is easy to make at home and offers many more color options than the grocery store does.

1. Place ½ cup of granulated sugar in a bowl. Add about five drops of food coloring and mix thoroughly.

2. To ensure even color, push the sugar through a fine-mesh strainer. Spread the sugar in a pie plate and let it dry completely.

DECORATORS' TIPS

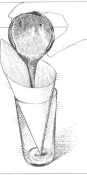

➤ **Mess-Free Filling** To simplify the multi-handed job of filling a piping bag, place the bag upright in a tall drinking glass before filling. The glass also makes a good resting place for the bag while you are decorating.

➤ **Glitter Sticking Points** Unglazed cookies require a little surface preparation to ensure that embellishments will stick. We recommend lightly misting or brushing the surface of the dough with water before applying decorations.

➤ **Tackle Box for Trimmings** Decorating cookies usually means juggling a collection of tiny trimmings. To keep the items close at hand and neatly organized, we corral each one in the individual cups of a muffin pan.

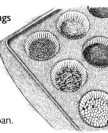

Pasta with Broccoli Rabe and Sausage

To fine-tune this classic combination, we first needed to tame broccoli rabe's bitter edge.

⋝ BY RAQUEL PELZEL ⋜

If each region in Italy can be said to have a signature dish, then orecchiette with broccoli rabe is the one most often associated with the southeastern region of Puglia. Italian-American versions frequently add sausage to create a satisfying study in contrasts: the richness of the meat taming the peppery rabe. Pulled together with a generous helping of garlic, a dash of hot pepper flakes, a gloss of sauce, plus a shower of grated Pecorino, it's one of those quick, satisfying, one-pot meals that are invaluable as part of a winter weeknight repertoire.

That's not to say that the dish is infallible. As in any marriage of dissimilar personalities, the relationship takes finesse to work properly—and it's the broccoli rabe that requires the most attention. Most recipes agree that rabe requires pretreatment to tame its bitter edge, but they differ in their solution: Sautéing, blanching, and boiling are all common.

I gave each method a go, finishing the rough-chopped stalks in the skillet with the rendered sausage fat and aromatics before mixing them with the meat and tossing the two components with the lightly sauced pasta. The rabe pretreatments produced remarkably different results, with tasters overwhelmingly preferring the tender-firm bite of the greens that had been simply sautéed. Their intensely bitter flavor, however, needed some work.

I started by doing some rabe research to understand why the water-based treatments had softened the vegetable's sharp edge. As it turns out, broccoli rabe is rich in flavor precursors that release pungent, bitter compounds called isothiocyanates when the vegetable is cut. Exposing the rabe to boiling water inactivates these acrid compounds. I wondered, though: Since we preferred the firmer texture of the sautéed rabe, was a full pot of boiling water necessary, or could I cut that step and get by with adding just a splash of water to the skillet?

I had my answer after one test, as the boiled and lightly pan-steamed greens tasted virtually identical. Good news: I'd not only eliminated the wait time for the broccoli water to boil but also saved myself the trouble of washing another pot. In fact, I didn't need to introduce any additional liquid to the skillet; the water left clinging to the rabe after washing was enough to render it crisp-tender.

As I turned to fine-tuning the dish itself, I considered one of my taster's milder criticisms: that the large (1- to 3-inch) rabe pieces were clumping together in the pasta. No problem: I simply chopped the stalks into small (¼-inch) pieces. But while this remedied the clumping, it reintroduced the rabe's bitterness. I shouldn't have been surprised: The more the vegetable was broken down, the more of its bitter compounds were released.

Taking a step back, I tried balancing the rabe's bitterness by tweaking the other ingredients. The obvious test—ramping up the sausage, garlic, and pepper flakes—didn't so much round out the flavors as add heft and heat. I had more luck with the sauce: Just as I had been doing, I added a ladle full of the pasta cooking water to the pan (the starchy liquid lends body to the sauce and helps it cling to the pasta), but this time I poured in 1 cup of chicken broth along with it and reduced the liquid to about 1 cup. This gave the sauce more depth. I further enriched it with a pat of butter and some grated Pecorino. Definitely better—but still not quite there.

Then I remembered that in my research I'd seen many recipes for broccoli rabe sautéed with a mashed anchovy paste, a step intended to lend subtle depth. I followed suit, mashing a couple of fillets with some olive oil and a drop of fresh lemon juice and whisking the mixture into the reduced sauce before tossing it with the reserved pasta, sausage, rabe, and cheese (with salty anchovies in the mix, I swapped the super-salty Pecorino for milder Parmesan). That did it: Each bite was bold but balanced, with an addictively bitter—but not fishy—edge. Best of all, after testing more than 40 pounds of rabe, I'd taken one of my standard weeknight pasta recipes and made it even easier to prepare.

PASTA WITH BROCCOLI RABE AND SAUSAGE
SERVES 4 TO 6

It's important that some water still clings to the rabe after washing to help it steam during cooking. Our preference is to make this dish with orecchiette pasta, but fusilli and campanelle also work well. For our free recipe for Pasta with Broccoli Rabe, Raisins, and Pine Nuts, go to www.CooksIllustrated.com/dec11.

- 2 anchovy fillets, rinsed
- 4 tablespoons extra-virgin olive oil
- 1 tablespoon lemon juice
- 4 garlic cloves, minced
- 1 pound orecchiette pasta
   Salt
- 8 ounces hot Italian sausage, casings removed, cut into ¼-inch pieces
- ½ teaspoon red pepper flakes
- 1 pound broccoli rabe, trimmed and cut into ¼-inch pieces
- 1 cup low-sodium chicken broth
- 1½ tablespoons unsalted butter
- 1 ounce Parmesan cheese, grated (½ cup), plus extra for serving

1. Using fork, smear anchovies on cutting board into uniform paste (you should have about 1 teaspoon). Combine anchovy paste, 1 tablespoon oil, lemon juice, and 1 teaspoon garlic in bowl; set aside.

2. Bring 4 quarts water to boil in large pot. Add pasta and 1 tablespoon salt and cook, stirring often, until al dente. Reserve 1 cup cooking water, then drain pasta and return it to pot.

3. While pasta cooks, heat 1 tablespoon oil in 12-inch nonstick skillet over medium-high heat, until shimmering. Add sausage and cook, stirring often, until browned and cooked through, 2 to 4 minutes. Using slotted spoon, transfer sausage to paper towel–lined plate. Leave rendered fat in skillet.

4. Return skillet to medium heat, add remaining 2 tablespoons oil, remaining garlic, and pepper flakes; cook, stirring often, until fragrant, 1 to 2 minutes. Increase heat to high and add half of broccoli rabe; cook, stirring often, until just wilted, about 1 minute. Add remaining broccoli rabe and ½ teaspoon salt; cook, stirring often, until crisp-tender, 2 to 3 minutes. Transfer broccoli rabe to colander set in bowl. Do not wash skillet.

5. Bring broth and ¾ cup pasta water to boil in now-empty skillet over high heat. Reduce heat to medium and simmer until reduced to about 1 cup, 4 to 6 minutes. Remove skillet from heat and whisk in reserved anchovy mixture and butter. Add sauce, reserved broccoli rabe, sausage, and ½ cup Parmesan to pasta and toss to combine. Add remaining cooking water as needed to adjust consistency. Serve immediately, passing remaining Parmesan separately.

TECHNIQUE
PREPPING BROCCOLI RABE

To trim broccoli rabe, cut off the tough bottom ½ inch of the stalks.

Paris-Brest

We knew this showstopper French dessert was both elegant and delicious.
Now that we've perfected its various components, we can say it's reliable as well.

≥ BY ANDREW JANJIGIAN ≤

Paris-Brest is a showstopper dessert with a rather curious history. To make it, a large ring of pâte à choux—the same pastry used to make éclairs and cream puffs—is filled with hazelnut praline pastry cream and then sprinkled with chopped almonds and powdered sugar. Its quirky name dates back to 1910, when an enterprising baker whose shop was located along the route of the Paris-Brest-Paris bicycle race—a 1,200-kilometer journey from Paris to the city of Brest, in Brittany, and back again—invented the dessert to honor the cyclists. His creation was in the shape of a bicycle tire, complete with a pastry "inner tube"—a recent invention at the time. Despite the irony of associating a calorie-laden, decadent confection with grueling feats of athleticism, Paris-Brest cake was an instant hit in France.

In this country, the dessert has achieved a certain cult status as a Christmas Eve specialty. It makes sense, because if you're looking for a holiday dessert, it's hard to beat tender pastry filled with praline-flavored cream. What's more, although it looks as though it would take a professional pastry chef to create it, the dessert is actually assembled from relatively easy-to-prepare elements, each of which can be made hours or days in advance.

That said, I knew that coming up with a foolproof recipe was going to require a bit of athleticism of my own. The recipes I rounded up in my research—from such culinary luminaries as Julia Child, Alain Ducasse, and Pierre Hermé—yielded "wheels" of all shapes and sizes, some considerably more wobbly than others. With several, the pastry ring was crusty and tough; other rings were so tender that they either collapsed upon cooling or were simply unable to contain the filling. Many recipes dispensed with the inner-tube pastry ring, but it seemed necessary to give the dessert both structure and stature. The praline cream presented challenges as well: I didn't want it to be overly rich, yet I needed it to be sturdy enough to stay put in the pastry when it came time to slice. The praline paste—a puree of toasted hazelnuts and caramelized sugar—was straightforward enough, but I knew I'd need to make sure that even the most caramel-phobic cook would be able to prepare it confidently.

Looking for the ultimate Christmas Eve dessert? Look no further.

Down Pâte

Since it was both the backbone of and the container for the Paris-Brest, the pastry dough was where I started my testing. Creating pâte à choux is a particularly rewarding process because it's so easy and the results are so dramatic. To make it, milk, water, granulated sugar, and butter are brought to a simmer, all-purpose flour is stirred in to make a paste, and then it is cooked briefly before eggs are finally whipped into the hot mixture. The dough is piped out through a pastry bag and then baked. Leavened by steam alone, the dough puffs up, creating a crisp, hollow shell surrounding a tender, ethereal lining of soft dough. I was aware from my testing that for pastry this large, it would take some work to achieve just the right balance between a too-crisp shell and one so tender that it would slump once removed from the oven.

Since all choux pastry recipes use the same six ingredients—milk, water, butter, sugar, eggs, and salt—I worked up a spreadsheet to compare the relative ratios of each component in the various recipes I'd tested. The differences were clear. The

recipes that yielded the crispest, most rigid pastries called for the addition of extra egg whites and only small amounts of milk. Egg whites give the pastry structure, while milk and egg yolks both contain tenderizing fat and proteins. After testing several ratios of my own, I eventually landed on a dough made with ⅔ cup of whole eggs (even standard large eggs sometimes vary in size, and exact proportions were essential, so I couldn't just call for three large eggs) and half that amount of both water and milk. These measurements yielded the balance of tenderness and strength that I was looking for. To add crunch to the tender pastry, I sprinkled it with chopped hazelnuts before baking it.

With a reliable dough in hand, I began to sort out the best way to bake my tire and inner tube. Choux pastry is typically baked in three stages. Starting the dough in a high-temperature oven quickly generates steam that inflates the pastry. The oven temperature is then lowered and the pastry is cooked until the exterior is well browned and fully set. Finally, it is removed from the oven, sliced open in spots to help release moisture trapped in its interior, and then returned to a turned-off but still-warm oven with its door propped open—an essential step that prevents the pastry from collapsing by drying it out.

If I'd been making a single tray of small, same-size éclairs or cream puffs, this method would have worked fine. But when baking two sets of rings, one thick and one narrow, it was unworkable: The larger tire never completely set, while the narrow

A Race That Takes the Cake

The cream-filled pastry known as Paris-Brest was created to honor the Paris-Brest-Paris bicycle race—a 1,200-kilometer race from Paris to Brest, in Brittany, and back again. Over the years, culinary luminaries from Julia Child to Alain Ducasse to Pierre Hermé have paid homage to the event (first organized in 1891) with their own versions of this rich yet ethereal dessert.

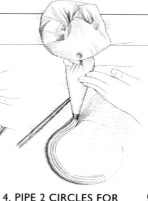

1. ADD NUTS TO CARAMEL As soon as caramel turns golden brown, stir in toasted hazelnuts and pour mixture onto parchment paper–lined baking sheet to set.

2. MAKE PRALINE PASTE Process broken caramel pieces in food processor until finely ground, about 30 seconds. Add salt and vegetable oil and process again until uniform paste forms, 2 to 3 minutes longer.

3. PIPE INNER RING Using bag fitted with ⅜-inch round tip, pipe narrow circle of pastry dough directly on top of guide ring traced on parchment. Set aside.

4. PIPE 2 CIRCLES FOR LARGE OUTER RING Use ½-inch star tip to pipe circle of dough around inside of remaining guide ring. Then pipe second circle around first so they overlap slightly.

5. PIPE THIRD CIRCLE FOR OUTER RING Finish outer ring by piping third circle on top of other 2 circles, directly over seam. Sprinkle with nuts and bake.

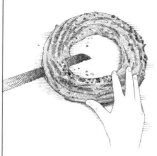

6. HALVE BAKED OUTER RING After cooling outer ring, halve horizontally using serrated knife.

7. PIPE PRALINE CREAM Using pastry bag fitted with ½-inch star tip, pipe narrow zigzag of praline cream onto bottom half of outer ring.

8. TOP WITH INNER RING Place inner ring on top of praline cream and press down gently.

9. PIPE PRALINE CREAM Pipe remaining praline cream over inner ring in zigzag pattern to cover.

10. TOP AND DUST Gently place top half of outer ring over filling and dust with confectioners' sugar.

---

inner tube tended to burn by the end of the baking time. I first tried opening the oven door to remove the narrow ring as soon as it was crisp, but that let so much heat escape that the larger ring collapsed. (I considered baking the rings individually but decided that this recipe didn't need yet another step.) After a long series of tests in which I baked the rings at different temperatures for varying times, I came up with a two-part solution.

First, I discovered that when the narrow ring was placed on the lower rack, it was partially shielded from the oven's heat by the tray above, which helped prevent burning. Second, I lowered the temperature of the initial bake from the standard 450 to 400 degrees and held it there for 25 minutes or so—more than double the duration that most recipes call for. This longer, gentler early cooking period ensured that by the time the narrow ring was browned, the thick ring would be fully set—the upshot being that I could open the oven door, remove the narrow ring, lower the oven temperature to 350, and finish cooking the larger ring. (Because the narrow ring was so thin, it did not need to dry out in the turned-off oven and could simply be cooled on a rack.) Finally, I was pleased to find that the baked pastry ring stored well, turning this dessert into an ideal make-ahead candidate.

The Perils of Praline Cream

Next, I got down to the business of creating that light yet sturdy cream. Praline cream is made by combining pastry cream with praline paste—a pulverized mixture of hardened caramel and nuts—along with one of a variety of components designed to lighten it up.

The praline paste was the sticking point, since caramel-making can be tricky business for many cooks. But when I got to the stove, I was pleasantly surprised to find the paste considerably less finicky than standard caramel. The key is that praline calls for adding nuts to the sugar syrup as soon as it turns golden. Standard caramel requires careful monitoring of the temperature of the sugar syrup to avoid scorching. Adding nuts, however, immediately arrests the cooking and, in turn, makes praline practically foolproof. I was also able to improve on the basic recipe by adding a touch of lemon juice to the sugar and water mixture. The acidity of the juice speeds up the breakdown of the sugars and catalyzes browning. Once the nuts are in, the mixture is transferred to a baking sheet to harden.

To turn praline into a smooth paste, I broke it into small pieces and ground it fine in a food processor along with salt and a little oil. I found that the praline could be held for a week in the refrigerator—another make-ahead boon.

Fortunately, it wasn't necessary to invent a pastry cream recipe, since the one we created for our Boston Cream Pie (March/April 2011) was easy, reliable, and delicious. That recipe's secret: thickening the dairy with flour rather than the usual cornstarch, as the latter is less stable and can break down if overheated or overwhisked.

As for lightening up the pastry cream, there were a number of widely hailed options to try, including whipped butter, softened butter, Italian meringue (boiled sugar syrup whipped into beaten egg whites), and whipped cream. Not surprisingly, butter—even when whipped—added too much richness, while the meringue produced nicely lighter-weight results but fussily required the use of a candy thermometer. In the end, my tasters were happiest with the texture and flavor of whipped cream, since it added little to the filling besides much-needed air.

Ensuring that the filling had enough structure was more complicated. More flour thickened it up somewhat; it also added an unpleasant pastiness. A few teaspoons of gelatin (added after the pastry cream had finished cooking) worked far better, providing the necessary amount of body without rendering the filling firm or bouncy. To fully set, the cream needed to sit in the refrigerator for three to 24 hours, well in advance of dinner.

It All Comes Together

With each component in place, all that remained was the assembly. After halving the larger cooled ring horizontally with a serrated knife, I used a ½-inch star tip to pipe a ribbon of praline cream onto the bottom half of the ring in a zigzag pattern. (Since some home cooks don't own a pastry bag, I also came up with a not quite as elegant but still perfectly effective piping method utilizing a zipper-lock bag; see page 30.) Working my way up, I pressed the narrow inner tube into the bed of cream to secure it in place, piped the remaining praline cream over the inner tube in a wider zigzag pattern, and then gently placed the top half of the large ring on top of it. With a last-minute dusting of confectioners' sugar, this dazzling cake was ready for its grand debut on my holiday table.

PARIS-BREST
SERVES 8 TO 10

An equal amount of slivered almonds can be substituted for hazelnuts. To skin the hazelnuts, simply place them in a clean kitchen towel after toasting, while they are still warm, and rub gently. Use a serrated knife to cut the dessert. See page 30 for instructions on how to pipe the dough and filling using a zipper-lock bag.

Praline
½	cup (3½ ounces) sugar
¼	cup water
1	teaspoon lemon juice
1	cup hazelnuts, toasted and skinned
½	teaspoon salt
1	tablespoon vegetable oil

Pastry Dough
3	large eggs
6	tablespoons unsalted butter, cut into 12 pieces
⅓	cup whole milk
⅓	cup water
2	teaspoons sugar
½	teaspoon salt
¾	cup (3¾ ounces) all-purpose flour
2	tablespoons toasted, skinned, and chopped hazelnuts

Cream Filling
2	teaspoons unflavored gelatin
¼	cup water
1½	cups half-and-half
5	large egg yolks
⅓	cup (2⅓ ounces) sugar
3	tablespoons all-purpose flour
3	tablespoons unsalted butter, cut into 3 pieces and chilled
1½	teaspoons vanilla extract
1	cup heavy cream, chilled
	Confectioners' sugar

1. FOR THE PRALINE: Line rimmed baking sheet with parchment paper; spray parchment with vegetable oil spray and set aside. Bring sugar, water, and lemon juice to boil in medium saucepan over medium heat, stirring once or twice to dissolve sugar. Cook without stirring until syrup is golden brown, 10 to 15 minutes. Remove saucepan from heat, stir in nuts, and immediately pour mixture onto prepared baking sheet. Place baking sheet on wire rack and allow caramel to harden, about 30 minutes.

2. Break hardened caramel into 1- to 2-inch pieces; process pieces in food processor until finely ground, about 30 seconds. Add salt and vegetable oil and continue to process until uniform paste is formed, 1 to 2 minutes. Transfer mixture to bowl, cover with plastic wrap, and set aside.

3. FOR THE PASTRY DOUGH: Adjust oven racks to upper-middle and lower-middle positions and heat oven to 400 degrees. Draw or trace 8-inch circle in center of two 12 by 18-inch sheets of parchment paper; flip parchment over. Spray 2 baking sheets with vegetable oil spray and line with parchment (keeping guide rings on underside).

4. Beat eggs in measuring cup or small bowl; you should have ⅔ cup (discard excess). Heat butter, milk, water, sugar, and salt in medium saucepan over medium heat, stirring occasionally. When mixture reaches full boil (butter should be fully melted), immediately remove saucepan from heat and stir in flour with heatproof spatula or wooden spoon until combined and no mixture remains on sides of pan. Return saucepan to low heat and cook, stirring constantly, using smearing motion, until mixture is slightly shiny and tiny beads of fat appear on bottom of saucepan, about 3 minutes.

5. Immediately transfer mixture to food processor and process with feed tube open for 30 seconds to cool slightly. With machine running, gradually add eggs in steady stream. When all eggs have been added, scrape down sides of bowl, then process for 30 seconds until smooth, thick, sticky paste forms.

6. Transfer ¾ cup dough to pastry bag fitted with ⅜-inch round tip. To make narrow inner ring, pipe single ½-inch-wide circle of dough directly on traced guide ring on 1 baking sheet. For large outer ring, squeeze out any excess dough in pastry bag and change pastry bag tip to ½-inch star tip. Put all remaining dough into pastry bag. Pipe ½-inch-wide circle of dough around inside of traced guide ring on remaining baking sheet. Pipe second ½-inch circle of dough around first so they overlap slightly. Pipe third ½-inch circle on top of other 2 circles directly over seam. Sprinkle chopped nuts evenly over surface of ring.

7. Place sheet with larger outer ring on upper rack and sheet with narrow inner ring on lower rack and bake until narrow ring is golden brown and firm, 22 to 26 minutes. Remove narrow ring and transfer to wire rack. Reduce oven temperature to 350 degrees and continue to bake larger ring for another 10 minutes. Remove baking sheet from oven and turn oven off. Using paring knife, cut 4 equally spaced ¾-inch-wide slits around edges of larger ring to release steam.

Return larger ring to oven and prop oven door open with handle of wooden spoon. Let ring stand in oven until exterior is crisp, about 45 minutes. Transfer ring to wire rack to cool, about 15 minutes.

8. FOR THE CREAM FILLING: Sprinkle gelatin over water in small bowl and let sit until gelatin softens, about 5 minutes. Heat half-and-half in medium saucepan over medium heat until just simmering. Meanwhile, whisk yolks and sugar in medium bowl until smooth. Add flour to yolk mixture and whisk until incorporated. Remove half-and-half from heat and, whisking constantly, slowly add ½ cup to yolk mixture to temper. Whisking constantly, add tempered yolk mixture to half-and-half in saucepan.

9. Return saucepan to medium heat and cook, whisking constantly, until mixture thickens slightly, 1 to 2 minutes. Reduce heat to medium-low and continue to cook, whisking constantly, 8 minutes.

10. Increase heat to medium and cook, whisking vigorously, until bubbles burst on surface, 1 to 2 minutes. Remove saucepan from heat; whisk in butter, vanilla, and softened gelatin until butter is melted and incorporated. Strain pastry cream through fine-mesh strainer set over large bowl. Press lightly greased parchment paper directly on surface and refrigerate until chilled but not set, about 45 minutes.

11. Using stand mixer fitted with whisk, whip cream on medium-low speed until foamy, about 1 minute. Increase speed to high and whip until soft peaks form, 1 to 3 minutes. Whisk praline paste and half of whipped cream into pastry cream until combined. Gently fold in remaining whipped cream until incorporated. Cover and refrigerate until set, at least 3 hours and up to 24 hours.

12. TO ASSEMBLE: Using serrated knife, slice larger outer ring in half horizontally; place bottom on large serving plate. Fill pastry bag fitted with ½-inch star tip with cream filling. Pipe ½-inch-wide strip of cream filling in narrow zigzag pattern around center of bottom half of ring. Press narrow inner ring gently into cream filling. Pipe cream filling over narrow ring in zigzag pattern to cover. Place top half of larger ring over cream filling, dust with confectioners' sugar, and serve.

TO MAKE AHEAD: Cooled pastry rings can be wrapped tightly and stored at room temperature for up to 24 hours or frozen for up to 1 month. Before using, recrisp rings in 300-degree oven for 5 to 10 minutes. Praline can be made up to 1 week in advance and refrigerated. Bring praline to room temperature before using. Pastry dough can be transferred to bowl, with surface covered with sheet of lightly greased parchment, and stored at room temperature for up to 2 hours. Dessert can be assembled and refrigerated up to 3 hours in advance.

Creating Crisp Gingersnaps

What's the secret to gingersnaps that combine bold spice flavor and real snap? To begin with, there's getting rid of all that moisture.

≥ BY ANDREW JANJIGIAN ≤

Sweetened dough spiced with ginger has been around since medieval times, but the term "gingersnap" wasn't coined until the 19th century. To my mind, this nomenclature should have settled once and for all the question of whether a ginger cookie should be crisp or chewy. I've never doubted that "snap" speaks to a cookie that breaks cleanly in half and crunches with every bite. "Snap" also sums up assertive ginger flavor and heat.

But most gingersnap recipes that I've tried don't live up to the name. Once you get past their brittle edges, the cookies turn soft and chewy. In fact, the only gingersnaps I've had that actually snap come from a box. But these cookies always fall short on flavor, lacking sufficiently bold notes of ginger and spice. I wanted freshly baked gingersnaps with a crackly top and a texture to rival the store-bought kind, but with all-natural ginger flavor and lingering heat.

Snap Judgments

I started with the best of all of the flawed recipes I'd tried—one that at least yielded a cookie that boasted crisp edges. Like most gingersnap recipes, it called for creaming butter and brown sugar (preferred to white sugar for its caramel-like undertone) in a stand mixer and then whipping in eggs, molasses, and vanilla and incorporating the dry ingredients (flour, baking soda, salt, and ground ginger). You then chill the dough until firm, form it into balls, and bake.

I wondered if transforming this cookie from mainly chewy to crunchy could be as straightforward as cutting down on moisture. I opted not to tinker with the molasses since the cookies wouldn't be true gingersnaps without its pleasantly bitter, smoky edge. And with just a single egg and a yolk in the recipe, the idea of adjusting the egg amount didn't seem promising either. That left me with just two potential moisture sources to work with: the brown sugar and the butter.

These cookies keep their crunch for up to two weeks when stored in an airtight container.

I turned to the sugar first. I knew that brown sugar was a double-edged sword. It contributes rich, molasses-y flavor—but also creates chewiness in cookies. This is because brown sugar is even more hygroscopic than granulated sugar, attracting moisture during baking. Switching to granulated sugar did produce a crispier, less chewy cookie, but the loss of flavor wasn't worth it. My only choice was to cut back on the sweetener. I found that slashing the brown sugar almost in half—from 2 to 1¼ cups—resulted in cookies noticeably drier and crunchier (albeit not yet worthy of their eponymous "snap"). Reducing the sugar also allowed the ginger flavor to move to the fore.

On to the butter, which is about 16 percent water. Using less butter (I went from 12 tablespoons to 10 tablespoons) dehydrated the cookies a bit, but new problems emerged. Without ample fat, the leaner, stiffer dough refused to spread as it baked. More important, these cookies didn't taste as good. It occurred to me that if I browned the butter, I'd eliminate some of its water while keeping its fat (and creating richer, nutty flavor). Of course, this meant that I could no longer cream the butter with the sugar, so I tried simply whisking the browned

butter with the sugar. I was pleased to find that this lower-moisture dough yielded considerably firmer cookies, and the subtle nutty taste of the browned butter turned out to be an ideal backdrop for the ginger. Eliminating creaming seemed to have helped matters, too: Since I was no longer whipping air into the dough, the cookie crumb was more densely packed and firmly textured. But all was not perfect: The center of the cookie was still a little too moist and didn't have the crackly top I wanted.

Previous experiments in the test kitchen gave me an idea for creating crackles: increase the leavening. In the next series of tests, I gradually upped the baking soda. The intentional overdose caused the cookies to rise dramatically but then collapse, leaving attractive fissures on their surfaces. After experimenting with varying amounts of baking soda, I settled on a full 2 teaspoons, which created nice deep cracks without imparting any soapy flavor. (See "Loading Up on Leavening" for more information.) I found that the overdose had several other positive effects: better browning (and therefore an even richer taste) and cookies that were crispier, since the cracks in the dough were allowing more moisture to escape.

Though these cookies were getting close, they still didn't have quite the clean, definitive snap of the box kind, so I moved on to consider the other major variable: the oven. By reducing the temperature from 350 to 300 degrees, I nearly doubled the overall baking time, which allowed the gingersnaps to gradually (and fully) dry out without burning. I also transferred the cookies to a wire rack immediately after baking, which allowed air to circulate and steam to escape from their undersides. At last, my cookies turned out dry and crackly crisp to the core.

SCIENCE

Loading Up on Leavening

Using a full 2 teaspoons of baking soda in our cookie dough instead of the more typical ½ to 1 teaspoon not only helped create desirable fissures in the final cookie but also helped it dry out. Baking soda is an alkaline substance that weakens the gluten (the network of proteins that gives most baked goods their structure) in a dough or batter. Weaker gluten means a more porous structure from which air bubbles and moisture can burn off. It also means that the dough will collapse after its initial rise in the oven, leading to cracks that also allow more moisture to escape.

PUTTING THE SNAP IN GINGERSNAPS

The hallmark of gingersnap cookie texture—big crunch—came down to one key factor: drying out the dough.

BROWN THE BUTTER
Butter is 16 percent water. Browning it before whisking it with the sugar, eggs, and flour eliminates moisture.

CUT BACK ON SUGAR
The brown sugar in our recipe holds on to water, even after baking. Our solution? Use just 1¼ cups.

TURN DOWN THE OVEN Baking the cookies in a low (300-degree) oven gives the dough ample time to gradually—but thoroughly—dry out.

STAGGER THE BAKING
Baking each tray on the top rack before moving it to the cooler bottom rack creates fissures that allow moisture to escape.

Crack Down

There was just one glitch. When I baked two sheets at once, only the cookies on the upper rack developed a uniformly crackled top, while those on the lower rack sported smoother facades (plus less crispness), despite the amped-up leavening. Rotating the sheets halfway through baking so that each one got time on the top rack didn't improve the situation, suggesting that the cracks were produced right at the beginning of baking, when the heat radiating down from the top of the oven caused the cookies to rise and fall rapidly. The sheet on the lower rack was partially shielded from the oven's heat by the sheet above, causing its cookies to expand more gradually, which resulted in smoother tops. I could just bake the sheets one at a time on the top rack—but that would take forever, given that my recipe was geared toward an extra-large batch (I wanted to have plenty of cookies on hand for the holidays). The solution proved as simple as staggering the baking: I popped one tray onto the upper rack for 15 minutes until fissures formed, moved it to the lower rack to finish baking, and then placed the second sheet of cookies on the upper rack.

The Spice Is Right

With the texture and appearance of my gingersnaps right where I wanted them, all that remained was to punch up their rather mild flavor. Doubling the amount of dried ginger was an obvious starting point, as was incorporating freshly grated ginger. Warm spices seemed appropriate here, and I followed the lead of many other recipes by incorporating cinnamon and cloves. But I wanted yet another layer of heat. I perused the spice cabinet once more, landing on cayenne and black pepper. The combination lent the cookies a judicious but lingering heat. Finally, to make the spices really sing, I bloomed them in the browned butter, the hot fat helping to fully release the spices' pungent aromatic compounds.

As a finishing touch, I rolled the balls of dough in granulated sugar before baking to provide a sweet exterior foil to the spicy interiors. At last, I'd found the gingersnap that I'd been craving: snappy-textured, snappy-flavored, and a snap to make.

GINGERSNAPS

MAKES 80 1½-INCH COOKIES

For the best results, use fresh spices. For efficiency, form the second batch of cookies while the first batch bakes. And no, the 2 teaspoons of baking soda is not a mistake; it's essential to getting the right texture.

2½	cups (12½ ounces) all-purpose flour
2	teaspoons baking soda
½	teaspoon salt
12	tablespoons unsalted butter
2	tablespoons ground ginger
1	teaspoon ground cinnamon
¼	teaspoon ground cloves
¼	teaspoon pepper
	Pinch cayenne
1¼	cups packed (8¾ ounces) dark brown sugar
¼	cup molasses
2	tablespoons finely grated fresh ginger
1	large egg plus 1 large yolk
½	cup (3½ ounces) granulated sugar

1. Whisk flour, baking soda, and salt together in bowl. Heat butter in 10-inch skillet over medium heat until melted. Lower heat to medium-low and continue to cook, swirling pan frequently, until foaming subsides and butter is just beginning to brown, 2 to 4 minutes. Transfer butter to large bowl and whisk in ground ginger, cinnamon, cloves, pepper, and cayenne. Cool slightly, about 2 minutes. Add brown sugar, molasses, and fresh ginger to butter mixture and whisk to combine. Add egg and yolk and whisk to combine. Add flour mixture and stir until just combined. Cover dough tightly with plastic wrap and refrigerate until firm, about 1 hour.

2. Adjust oven racks to upper-middle and lower-middle positions and heat oven to 300 degrees. Line 2 baking sheets with parchment paper. Place granulated sugar in shallow baking dish or pie plate. Divide dough into heaping teaspoon portions; roll dough into 1-inch balls. Working in batches of 10, roll balls in sugar to coat. Evenly space dough balls on prepared baking sheets, 20 dough balls per sheet.

3. Place 1 sheet on upper rack and bake for 15 minutes. After 15 minutes, transfer partially baked top sheet to lower rack, rotating 180 degrees, and place second sheet of dough balls on upper rack. Continue to bake until cookies on lower tray just begin to darken around edges, 10 to 12 minutes longer. Remove lower sheet of cookies and shift upper sheet to lower rack and continue to bake until cookies begin to darken around edges, 15 to 17 minutes. Slide baked cookies, still on parchment, to wire rack and cool completely before serving. Cool baking sheets slightly and repeat step 3 with remaining dough balls.

TO MAKE AHEAD: Dough can be refrigerated for up to 2 days or frozen for up to 1 month. Let dough stand at room temperature for 30 minutes before shaping. Let frozen dough thaw overnight before proceeding with recipe. Cooled cookies can be stored at room temperature for up to 2 weeks in airtight container.

TASTING **Molasses**

Molasses is made by boiling the juice of sugarcane or sugar beets and then extracting sugar crystals through centrifuge. More stages of boiling (and extraction) may follow to produce an increasingly intense flavor. A first boil typically corresponds to mild or "Barbados" molasses; a second boil produces a style sometimes called "full"; and a third creates blackstrap, the most assertive and bitter molasses. We ruled out blackstrap for its overpowering flavor (based on previous tastings) and sampled five national brands in other styles, plain and in our Gingersnaps recipe. (We tasted only unsulfured versions.)

The first thing we discovered is that descriptive names on labels—including "mild," "original," "full," and "robust"—are not a reliable indicator of how the molasses tastes. A brand labeled "mild" rated among the strongest for flavor. But we also found that when it comes to baking, it doesn't matter what molasses you buy (as long as it's not blackstrap). When sampled straight, some brands tasted "burnt" or "like coffee grounds," but baking mellowed out their differences; all five brands were equally acceptable in cookies. Tasted plain, Brer Rabbit All Natural Unsulphured Molasses Mild Flavor was our favorite for its "caramelized," "spicy" taste. For complete tasting results, go to www.CooksIllustrated.com/dec11.
–Hannah Crowley

A BITTER BALANCE
Brer Rabbit All Natural Unsulphured Molasses Mild Flavor has a rich, caramelized taste that struck the right note between bitter and sweet.

Holiday Cranberry Chutney

For a standout sauce, we needed to do more than just fine-tune the sweet-tart classic.

> BY KEITH DRESSER <

There will always be a place at my Thanksgiving table for sauce made with just cranberries, water, and granulated sugar according to the instructions on the back of the cranberry bag. With its sweet-tart flavor and soft jelled texture, this no-fuss condiment is a fine way to cut the richness of the roast turkey, mashed potatoes, and gravy. But when I want a sauce with more dimension and sharpness—whether as an accompaniment for turkey or for more robustly flavored, fattier cuts of pork, lamb, or game—I find the options for a dressed-up sauce disappointing. Usually these sauces incorporate just one more flavor note, and typically it's sweet. Not what I had in mind.

As I cast about for ideas, I realized that I was looking for something with the complexity of an Indian chutney, which, in addition to featuring slow-cooked fruits, boasts vinegar, aromatics, and spices that give the jammy relish kick and savor. I began by thinking of an aromatic element that would add that subtle savory quality to the sauce. Garlic and red onion, both common additions in Indian chutneys, seemed too potent. I settled on milder shallot instead. For an assertive fruit to pair with cranberries, I chopped up tart Granny Smith apples. Fresh ginger was the perfect choice for incorporating spiciness. I mixed all of these ingredients in a pot with the cranberries, sugar, and a little salt. Because I didn't want an overly potent mixture, it seemed unwise to introduce the vinegar typically added to chutney to the two tart fruits. I opted instead for water as the only liquid, simmering the mixture until the cranberries and apples had completely broken down, about 20 minutes. The resulting chutney wasn't terrible, but overall, it lacked complexity. Also, the shallot and ginger were a little too prominent.

I wanted to keep my recipe relatively short, so developing depth via a bunch of additional ingredients was out. But what about my decision to omit vinegar? Indian cooks must have a good reason for its inclusion in chutney. Hoping that fruity cider vinegar would enliven the cranberry-apple mixture, I experimented with using it to replace some of the water, finally settling on swapping ⅓ cup of water for ¼ cup of cider vinegar. To my surprise, rather than making the sauce overly sour, the cider vinegar lent

both brightness and depth, helping to pull the flavors back into balance. After consulting our science editor, I learned that the acetic acid in vinegar reacts with pectin in the cranberries during cooking, reducing the vinegar's potency while preserving its lively taste.

For even more depth, I traded the granulated sugar for molasses-y brown sugar. Finally, I softened the shallot and ginger in oil along with some salt before adding the other ingredients, which drew out more of their flavor nuances while simultaneously toning down their harsh edges.

Now I was close to the chunky sauce that I had imagined, but I had inadvertently created a problem. While tasters appreciated the concentrated flavors of the sauce, many missed the fresh pop of the back-of-the-bag version, which cooks for just 10 minutes. I solved the problem by simmering half of the cranberries with the other ingredients for the full 20 minutes and reserving the other half until the last five minutes of cooking. This created a jamlike base dotted with soft but still intact berries that retained their zing. The textural contrast gave me the idea for one last tweak: I mixed ⅓ cup of minced crystallized ginger into the chutney along with the cranberries at the end of cooking, adding a slight, pleasing chewiness.

I used this concept to create four more versions. In addition to sweet-tart flavors, they all had a bit of punch, a bit of slow-cooked savor, a bit of fresh zing—and a whole lot of complexity.

CRANBERRY CHUTNEY WITH APPLE AND CRYSTALLIZED GINGER
MAKES ABOUT 3 CUPS

If using frozen cranberries, thaw them before cooking.

- 1 teaspoon vegetable oil
- 1 shallot, minced
- 2 teaspoons finely grated fresh ginger
- ½ teaspoon salt
- ⅔ cup water
- ¼ cup cider vinegar
- 1 cup packed brown sugar
- 12 ounces (3 cups) fresh or frozen cranberries
- 2 Granny Smith apples, peeled, cored, and cut into ¼-inch pieces
- ⅓ cup minced crystallized ginger

1. Heat oil in medium saucepan over medium heat until just shimmering. Add shallot, fresh ginger, and salt; cook, stirring occasionally, until shallot has softened, 1 to 2 minutes.

2. Add water, vinegar, and sugar. Increase heat

to high and bring to simmer, stirring to dissolve sugar. Add 1½ cups cranberries and apples; return to simmer. Reduce heat to medium-low and simmer, stirring occasionally, until cranberries have almost completely broken down and mixture has thickened, about 15 minutes.

3. Add remaining 1½ cups cranberries and crystallized ginger; continue to simmer, stirring occasionally, until just beginning to burst, 5 to 7 minutes. Transfer to serving bowl and cool for at least 1 hour before serving. (Sauce can be refrigerated for up to 3 days.)

SPICY CRANBERRY CHUTNEY

Increase oil to 2 teaspoons and substitute 1 stemmed and seeded red bell pepper cut into ¼-inch pieces and 2 seeded and minced jalapeños for fresh ginger in step 1. Increase cooking time in step 1 to 5 minutes. Increase water to ¾ cup and omit apples and crystallized ginger.

CRANBERRY CHUTNEY WITH FENNEL AND GOLDEN RAISINS

Increase oil to 2 teaspoons and substitute 1 cored fennel bulb cut into ¼-inch pieces and ½ teaspoon fennel seed for fresh ginger in step 1. Increase cooking time in step 1 to 5 minutes. Increase water to 1 cup, omit apples, and substitute ⅓ cup golden raisins for crystallized ginger.

CRANBERRY-ORANGE CHUTNEY

Starting with 2 oranges, remove four 2-inch-wide strips zest from 1 orange, then peel both oranges and remove segments. Set aside zest and segments. Increase fresh ginger to 4 teaspoons and add 1 teaspoon yellow mustard seeds to oil together with fresh ginger in step 1. Increase water to ¾ cup and add orange zest and segments to pot with cranberries in step 2. Omit apples and crystallized ginger.

CRANBERRY CHUTNEY WITH PEAR, LEMON, AND ROSEMARY

Remove two 2-inch-wide strips zest from 1 lemon, then peel and remove segments. Set aside zest and segments. Substitute 2 teaspoons chopped fresh rosemary for fresh ginger. Substitute 2 peeled Bosc pears cut into ¼-inch pieces for apples and omit crystallized ginger. Add lemon zest and segments to pot with cranberries in step 2.

The Problem with Knife Sets

Nine pieces of matching cutlery, plus a block for easy storage?
It could be a bargain—or a rip-off.

> BY LISA McMANUS <

We can't help but be skeptical about knife block sets. As with cookware sets, their biggest selling point has always been the number of pieces the manufacturer can cram into the package, not the usefulness or quality of the blades themselves. Most collections are loaded not only with superfluous pieces but also with ones that are impractical or even useless. In the test kitchen, we've always maintained that there are just three truly essential knives: a chef's knife, a paring knife, and a serrated bread knife. Beyond that, a boning knife, a slicing knife (for carving meat), and a good pair of kitchen shears can make certain tasks easier. But anything other than these six pieces is filler.

At the same time, we know that there are occasions (particularly during gift-giving season or when you're outfitting a kitchen from scratch) when an attractive, all-in-one set of cutlery—complete with a block that keeps everything neatly housed and within easy reach—could be a nice convenience. Hoping to find that we'd been a bit hasty in our cynicism, we went shopping and returned to the test kitchen with eight knife block sets that contained anywhere from six to nine pieces and spanned a broad price spectrum: $97 all the way up to nearly $700. We would evaluate these sets against one another as well as against an à la carte selection of our test kitchen favorites. Our criteria would be as follows: how comfortable the pieces were to use and how well each performed; how many pieces in the collection were essential and how many extraneous; and of the extraneous stock, how much of it was actually useful. If the right package was out there, we'd gladly give it our stamp of approval.

The Big Three

The only way to assess the efficacy of a set was to put each piece through the paces. First, we singled out the core blades from each set—the chef's, bread, and paring knives—and went about our everyday tasks. We diced onions, minced herbs, and broke down a whole chicken with each of the chef's knives. We sliced large, crusty loaves and then diced soft Wonder bread with the serrated bread knives (the latter test would reveal the knives' ability to make clean, precise cuts without squishing the food). We peeled, quartered, and cored apples with the paring knives. Later, we'd examine the other pieces to see if they offered any additional value to the set or if they simply took up space.

The good news was that all but one of the chef's knives in the sets boasted our preferred length of 8 inches, and five out of the eight scored well. They were easy to handle and slipped effortlessly through food as we worked. The poorly performing specimens had a common flaw: Their blades were a little thicker than was ideal, and they tended to crush—rather than cleanly slice—onions and to bruise parsley as we minced.

The quality of the paring knives, however, was less impressive. Half of the blades were too wide or ungainly, which made the meticulous task of apple paring feel dicey. When we'd singled out the two we liked best, they turned out to be none other than our reigning favorite and our Best Buy, respectively. Two similar blades also fit our criteria, with slim, pointed, slightly flexible blades that measured 4 inches or less, providing added precision and control.

Meanwhile, blade length turned out to be the single most important—and detrimental—factor for the serrated bread knives. All were too short (8 or 9 inches) to saw a 10-inch-wide bread loaf into even slices. We wondered if manufacturers were including models shorter than the standard 10-inch size because a longer blade would stick out of the wooden block's slots, but we were wrong: When we slid our favorite 10-inch model from Wüsthof into the hole vacated by the 8-inch version included in the brand's set, it fit completely. We figured—and more than one knife company executive admitted—that there was another reason for including shorter models: price. Smaller knives cost less to produce. Block sets are not compiled strictly according to their usefulness to consumers, they told us, but to meet price ceilings set by retailers, who want the maximum number of "pieces" in a block at an attractive price. (And by the way, the block itself always counts as one of the "pieces.")

The Best (and Worst) of the Rest

Then came the other half of the equation: sorting through the extra pieces, the most common of which was a "utility" knife. "Utility" is a seemingly generic industry term for any blade bigger than a paring knife and smaller than a chef's knife (usually measuring between 4½ and 6½ inches). We also found "sandwich," "tomato," and "citrus" knives and other single-task blades, all about the same size as the utility models. Some were serrated and some weren't, but all were too short to cut across larger pieces of fruit without sawing. What's more, those with saw-toothed edges ripped delicate tomato skin

Trimmed Size, Trimmed Cost

Knife manufacturers routinely shrink down knives in block sets to lower production costs. Wüsthof includes an 8-inch version of our favorite 10-inch bread knife in its set; the shorter blade was overwhelmed when cutting a big, crusty loaf of bread.

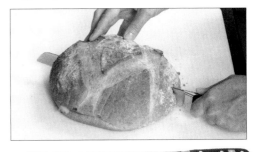

FULL-LENGTH BREAD KNIFE

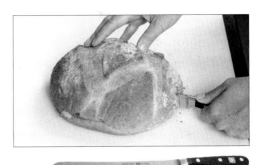

SHORTCHANGED BREAD KNIFE

and tore lemon skin so that fragrant oil spritzed out in the process. Clearly, these models were expendable, but just to confirm that they really were useless, we repeated the tomato- and lemon-slicing tests with each set's corresponding chef's knife. No surprises: In every case, the all-purpose chef's knife outperformed the specialty tool.

In fact, we found very few extra knives in any of the sets that weren't rendered redundant by one of

See the Knives in Action
Video available FREE for 4 months at
www.CooksIllustrated.com/dec11

these core knives. Though the pointed-tipped carving knives included in two of the sets were perfectly functional, neither one did a better job cutting up roast beef or roast chicken than the chef's knife already in these sets. It was the same story with the 5½- to 7-inch santoku or nakiri blades that came in many of the sets. These Asian-inspired knives were nice to have around for vegetable prep—especially the Global nakiri, which effortlessly cleaved through onions, lemons, and tomatoes—but did they do anything the chef's knife couldn't? Not really.

Most of the sets included honing or so-called sharpening steels. Though these metal rods don't actually sharpen at all—they simply realign a bent cutting edge to make it straight again and more effective at cutting—they are useful tune-up devices. The only problem? With the exception of professional chefs, most people don't know how to properly use the rods. (We didn't deduct points for including steels, however.)

The only examples of truly useful extras in the sets were slicing knives, kitchen shears, and boning knives. In all but one set, the boning knives made removing small bones from raw meat and peeling away strips of tough silverskin easy. But most of the collections included flawed models of slicing knives and shears. The Victorinox set came with a slightly too-short (10-inch) version of our favorite (12-inch) round-tipped slicing blade that peels off thinner, more uniform slices than a bulkier chef's blade—and all the other models were way too short at 9 inches or less. One model was also disadvantageously sharp-tipped. (Pointed tips wedge into the meat, forcing you to saw back and forth to finish the task.) Four of the eight sets came with shears, but only one pair (our favorite, from Shun) sported the long, super-sharp blades and comfortable handles that made cutting the backbone from a chicken feel effortless.

Not a Great Deal

In the end, our testing confirmed our suspicion that you are much better off shopping for knives à la carte; that way, you get only what you really need. If you must have a set, those by Wüsthof ($379.99) and Victorinox ($189.95) contained well-constructed knives and more of the types that we found most useful. Because they also contain some knives that we didn't find to be the best length or style, or that we found nonessential, we recommend them with reservations.

"Utility" Knife: Useful or Useless?

Many knife sets come with assorted "utility" knives, a catchall term for any blade too big to be a paring knife and too small to be a chef's knife. Despite their name, these knives are mostly useless filler included only to bulk out a set.

PARING
Perfect for jobs requiring precision and control.

UTILITY
Not good for much.

CHEF'S
Multitasker that can mince, slice, and chop.

HIGHLY RECOMMENDED Test Kitchen à la Carte Knife Set

This "all-star" set of test kitchen favorites (all best-in-class winners in past tests) fits neatly into our favorite universal knife block by Bodum, designed to hold any variety of blades securely in its nest of plastic sticks. Best of all, at $334.65, this ideal collection costs less than many prepackaged knife block sets. (For an even less expensive option, a seven-piece collection that includes Best Buys can be had for just $189.95. To see a list of those inexpensive knives, go to www.CooksIllustrated.com/dec11.)

❶ 3½-INCH PARING KNIFE
WÜSTHOF Classic, Model 4066, $39.95
An essential knife for hand-held tasks such as peeling and trimming fruit and vegetables. The short (less than 4 inches, for better agility), straight blade; slim shape; and pointed tip offer precision, and the handle is comfortable.

❷ 8-INCH CHEF'S KNIFE
VICTORINOX Fibrox, Model 40520, $29.95
This basic, inexpensive blade has consistently bested many competitors over the years—even those costing up to eight times as much. Its sharp, slim blade curves gently at the tip for good rocking motion during chopping, and its comfortable nonslip handle and excellent overall balance make it a kitchen workhorse.

❸ 10-INCH BREAD KNIFE
WÜSTHOF Classic Bread Knife, Model 4151, $109.95
This well-balanced knife with deeply tapered serrations handles with exceptional ease and control, even for lefties. Its 10-inch blade saws through the biggest, crustiest loaves just as easily as it delicately slices soft breads, tall sandwiches, and fine-crumbed cakes.

❹ 12-INCH SLICING KNIFE
VICTORINOX Fibrox Granton Edge Slicing/Carving Knife, Model 47645, $49.95
This moderately heavy knife has enough heft and rigidity to make straight cuts, with just enough flexibility to offer control. The thin, tapered, razor-sharp blade is long and wide, allowing it to draw through a large roast in one stroke.

❺ 6-INCH BONING KNIFE
VICTORINOX Fibrox 6-Inch Straight Boning Knife: Flexible, Model 40513, $19.95
With a nonslip grip and a narrow, straight blade, this knife removes the smallest bones (or bits of silverskin) with precision and complete comfort. Perfectly balanced, with enough flexibility to maneuver around tight joints.

❻ KITCHEN SHEARS
SHUN Classic Kitchen Shears, Model 1120M, $39.95
Thanks to 9-inch, razor-sharp blades (one with fine microserrations, the other with deep grooves), these shears make breaking down a chicken feel effortless. The large, rubbery handles are comfy, and the blades are symmetrical for both right- and left-handed use. Blades come apart for easy cleanup.

❼ KNIFE BLOCK
BODUM Bistro Universal Knife Block, Model 11089, $44.95
Unlike traditional knife blocks with slots for specific blades, universal models are "slotless" frames. This compact box is filled with a nest of spaghetti-like plastic rods that accommodate any arsenal of cutlery. The rods are attached at the base and come out for easy cleaning in the dishwasher.

TOTAL COST: $334.65

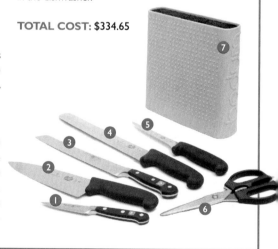

▶ **Tune Up Your Knife Skills** Check out our new online cooking school and take a FREE KNIFE TUTORIAL at www.TestKitchenSchool.com.

TESTING KNIFE BLOCK SETS

We tested eight knife block sets, assessing their performance, ease of use, and usefulness against one another as well as against our à la carte collection of test kitchen favorite knives. Sets appear below in order of preference. All were purchased online, and sources for recommended knives are on page 32.

KEY
GOOD: ★★★
FAIR: ★★
POOR: ★

PERFORMANCE
We compared each component (or the closest equivalents) with its counterparts in other sets on a variety of tasks consistent with its intended purpose. We diced onions, minced parsley, and cut up whole chickens with chef's knives; sliced large, crusty loaves and cubed a stack of Wonder bread slices with bread knives; and peeled, quartered, and cored apples with paring knives. When they were included, we used kitchen shears to cut the backbone from a whole chicken; boned a whole chicken and removed silverskin from short ribs with boning knives; sliced lemons and tomatoes with "utility," citrus, or tomato knives; and carved and sliced roast chicken and roast beef with carving and slicing knives.

EASE OF USE Block design and knife shape, size, weight, and balance were assessed on how comfortable they felt and how easy they were to use.

USEFULNESS Ratings of good, fair, or poor were assigned based on how useful we found each included item. If another knife could be used instead and/or performed the task better, points were deducted. Sets that included several nonessential blades were downgraded.

WEAK LINKS We tallied the number of poor-quality versions of essential pieces as well as redundant or unnecessary pieces.

CRITERIA | **TESTERS' COMMENTS**

HIGHLY RECOMMENDED

TEST KITCHEN à la Carte Knife Set (7 pieces)
Total Price: $334.65

Performance ★★★
Ease of Use ★★★
Usefulness ★★★

See page 26.

RECOMMENDED WITH RESERVATIONS

WÜSTHOF Classic 8-Piece Deluxe Knife Set
Model 8420, $379.99
- 3½-inch paring
- 5-inch boning
- 8-inch chef's
- 8-inch bread
- 8-inch carving
- Sharpening steel
- Shears
- 17-slot wood block

Performance ★★½
Ease of Use ★★
Usefulness ★★
Weak Links 3 of 8

We were eager to try this set featuring our favorite paring knife and a shorter version of our favorite 10-inch bread knife. The results were mixed: The paring and boning blades fared admirably, but the 8-inch bread knife couldn't slice through a large loaf, the shears were wimpy, and the carving knife extraneous.

VICTORINOX 7-Piece Rosewood Knife Set
Model 46054, $189.95
- 3¼-inch paring
- 6-inch boning
- 8-inch chef's
- 8-inch bread
- 10-inch slicing
- Sharpening steel
- 6-slot wood block

Performance ★★½
Ease of Use ★★
Usefulness ★★
Weak Links 2 of 7

While the knives in this set performed well and very few were filler, there was something that seemed cheap about it. The slots chipped as we slid the knives in and out, making the set look worn right away. The bread and slicing knives were sharp but a bit short.

SHUN Classic 9-Piece Knife Set
Model DMS0910, $699.95
- 2½-inch bird's beak
- 3½-inch paring
- 6-inch utility
- 8-inch chef's
- 9-inch bread
- 9-inch slicing
- Sharpening steel
- Shears
- 11-slot bamboo block

Performance ★★½
Ease of Use ★★
Usefulness ★★
Weak Links 5 of 9

These solidly constructed, razor-edged knives generally performed well. That said, even at 9 inches the bread knife couldn't handle large loaves. The stiff parer was like a mini chef's knife, which made it hard to peel an apple. The "utility" knife was useless. At this price, every component should be essential.

NOT RECOMMENDED

MESSERMEISTER Meridian Elite 9-Piece Knife Block Set
Model E/3000-9S, $351.94
- 3½-inch paring
- 5-inch scalloped utility
- 6-inch utility
- 7-inch santoku
- 8-inch chef's
- 9-inch bread
- Sharpening steel
- Shears
- 16-slot wood block

Performance ★★
Ease of Use ★
Usefulness ★
Weak Links 5 of 9

While some blades (particularly the nimble paring knife) shone in tests, this set's two utility knives and santoku were easily outperformed by the chef's blade on identical tasks. The bread knife was too short, and the block's finish chipped a little around the slots with repeated use.

GLOBAL 9-Piece Knife Set
Model G88/91ST, $661.95
- 3-inch paring
- 4-inch paring
- 5¼-inch utility
- 5½-inch nakiri/vegetable
- 6-inch serrated utility
- 7-inch Asian chef's
- 8¼-inch carving
- 8¾-inch bread
- 11-slot steel block

Performance ★★
Ease of Use ★
Usefulness ★
Weak Links 6 of 9

Most of these sleek Japanese blades were agile, but many were also unnecessary: two utility knives, an extra paring knife, a carving knife, and a 5½-inch nakiri blade for vegetable prep. The bread knife lacked at least an inch of necessary length—a feature that we also missed on the curiously short chef's knife.

ZWILLING J.A. HENCKELS Twin Four Star II Elite Knife Block Set, 9 Piece
Model 33404-100, $399.99
- 2¾-inch paring/boning
- 4-inch paring
- 5-inch serrated utility
- 5-inch hollow-edge santoku
- 8-inch chef's
- 8-inch bread
- Sharpening steel
- Shears
- 15-slot wood block

Performance ★★
Ease of Use ★
Usefulness ★
Weak Links 6 of 9

Many pieces in this set were underwhelming. The thicker-bladed chef's knife was just adequate, requiring extra pressure to chop; the bread knife not only was stumpy but also squished soft bread when slicing. The paring/boning knife was tiny, and the utility knife ripped—rather than sliced—tomato skin. One bright spot: the excellent 4-inch paring knife.

RACHAEL RAY Essentials 6-Piece Knife Block Set from Furi
Model 145903, $139.95
- 3½-inch paring
- 5-inch santoku
- 6-inch serrated utility
- 8-inch chef's
- 8-inch bread
- 5-slot bamboo block

Performance ★
Ease of Use ★
Usefulness ★
Weak Links 5 of 6

This set is a dud. The handles were uncomfortable and the blades uniformly clunky. The too-short bread knife struggled through big loaves, the paring knife was too heavy for precision tasks, and the utility blade was utterly dispensable. The only decent blade: the santoku.

PURE KOMACHI II 9-Piece Knife Set in Clear Block
Model ABS0900, $97
- 3½-inch paring
- 4-inch tomato/cheese
- 4-inch citrus
- 5¾-inch sandwich
- 6-inch utility
- 6½-inch santoku
- 8-inch chef's
- 8-inch bread
- 8-slot acrylic block

Performance ★
Ease of Use ★
Usefulness ★
Weak Links 8 of 9

These candy-colored steel blades came suspended in a clear acrylic holder. While the edges were relatively sharp, minced food clung to the supposedly nonstick blades, and the smooth handles were slippery. We found the chef's knife awkward, the bread knife short, and the paring knife stiff and dull. The other five knives in the set were expendable.

The Best Butter

When it comes to butter, whether or not a brand is a fancy, high-fat European style may not matter as much as how it's wrapped.

> BY AMY GRAVES

Since the rise of factory-produced butter in the early 20th century, the vast majority of butter sold in this country has been the sweet-cream kind. This style is quickly and cheaply mass-produced by churning cream that has undergone little or no storage. At the same time, old-fashioned cultured butter—made more slowly, with cream that's allowed to ripen for a few days to develop flavor and then inoculated with bacterial cultures before churning—has typically been an imported, hard-to-find luxury. But these days, the tables seem to be turning: Not only is cultured (also known as European-style) butter increasingly available, but many supermarket shelves now hold more brands of this pricier condiment than brands of the sweet-cream stuff. Fans of cultured butter rave about its fuller, more complex taste.

Given that we go through upwards of 25 pounds of butter per week in the test kitchen, we wondered if we should stick with our longtime favorite supermarket butter, Land O'Lakes—or fork out as much as $12 per pound for a premium butter? With that question in mind, we bought out the butter aisle and returned to the test kitchen with 10 unsalted butters: seven cultured and three sweet cream. Our main criterion was simple: We wanted the best-tasting butter we could find for eating straight up on things like toast, pancakes, and corn on the cob. But since many of the cultured butters also contain more fat than the sweet-cream varieties do, we wanted to see how that extra richness affected flavor and texture in baking; for that test, we baked French butter cookies. The results, we decided, would have to be pretty spectacular for us to shell out nearly double or triple what we pay for regular butter.

Culture Clash

We let the samples soften and then spread them on plain crackers—a blank canvas that could expose their nuanced flavors. When we tallied up the results of this plain tasting, we found that there was something to all the cultured-butter hype: These European-style products took three of the four top spots. Several of the cultured samples inspired high praise for dairy flavor that was "deep," "rich," and even "grassy" and "mineral-y," with a "long and complex finish" that stood apart from the cleaner, more straightforward flavor of the sweet-cream butters. We also found that the higher fat of cultured butters (about 83 to 86 percent butterfat compared with around 81 to 82 percent in the sweet-cream style) lent them a luscious, mouth-coating richness.

That said, the cultured butters weren't preferred across the board in the plain tasting. Though none were unacceptable, a few did suffer distinct off-flavors that made them less pleasant as spreads. These flavors ranged from strong hints of fake-butter popcorn to suggestions of cheap Chardonnay. But that was only part of the story. Coming in second to one of the richest, most assertively cultured butters was Land O'Lakes, which outshone the other two sweet-cream butters—and several of the cultured samples—by a considerable margin. (The two other sweet-cream butters landed at or near the bottom of the heap.) So why doesn't culturing always result in better flavor?

For an answer, we contacted Robert Bradley, a professor emeritus of food science and an expert on butter flavor and texture analysis at the University of Wisconsin. He suggested that the artificial movie-popcorn flavor we detected in some cultured brands was most likely linked to the type and amount of starter cultures added to the cream—in particular, a naturally occurring volatile compound called diacetyl that's responsible for buttery, slightly tangy flavor and yellow color. (Diacetyl is used in margarine to imitate the flavor of butter, and a few California Chardonnays, known as "butter bombs," actually encourage its growth in fermentation.) Ideally, Bradley explained, manufacturers will hit on just the right mix of cultures to develop some acidity, some diacetyl flavor, and a good, well-rounded background. The manufacturer of our

favorite butter nailed the formula, nicely balancing sweet, fresh-cream flavor with complex tang. Other brands proved that getting the bacteria cocktail just right is tricky—and imperfections can be glaringly clear, particularly when you're eating butter straight up on crackers or bread.

And then there were the cookies. While we found that most of the cultured butters' artificial, margarine-like flavors burned off in the oven, so did some of their appealing nuances. Furthermore, some of the cookies made with the highest-fat cultured butter failed to spread as much as they should, baking up firm and dense. We did a little research and discovered that butters with more fat soften at higher temperatures than those with less fat. In cookie dough, this can mean that the starch and protein set before the butter has time to fully soften and spread, so the cookies bake up higher and more dense.

That said, a few of the cultured butters, including the imported brand Plugrá, distinguished themselves in cookies that were both supercrisp and wonderfully buttery. But here again, most couldn't top Land O'Lakes, which produced cookies that boasted "fresh-cream," "clean dairy flavor" and nice sandy texture. So what was it about this supermarket butter that allowed it to repeatedly perform so well?

It's a Wrap

According to Bradley, the answer may be as simple as the brand's wrapping. Butter's high proportion of fat makes its flavor fragile and highly susceptible to picking up odors from anything that's stored near it. And the longer it's exposed to other odors, the more its own flavor will be affected. (The U.S. Department of Agriculture maintains strict sanitation and cream-quality standards for butter production, but no such standards exist for how long and under what conditions butter may be kept in frozen storage or at the market.)

Bradley explained that the waxed parchment that some manufacturers use to cover their product does nothing to block out foreign flavors. Sure enough, in our tasting, three out of the four parchment-wrapped samples elicited complaints about off- or stale-tasting refrigerator flavors. Only the fourth, Land O'Lakes, did not. Bradley was not surprised. Land O'Lakes, he explained, treats its parchment wrapper with a patented coating called FlavorProtect that helps lock in the butter's clean flavor and keep intruding odors out. In fact, its wrapper was just as effective as the foil wrappers that

TASTING SWEET-CREAM AND CULTURED BUTTERS

Twenty-one *Cook's Illustrated* staff members sampled 10 nationally available butters at room temperature, spread on crackers, rating the butters on flavor and texture. Brands were selected from among top-selling supermarket butters, as compiled by SymphonyIRI Group, a market research firm based in Chicago, Illinois. Butters were selected after we contacted each manufacturer to identify its top-selling variety. An independent laboratory determined percentages for butterfat. Brands appear in the order in which they're preferred.

HIGHLY RECOMMENDED

PLUGRÁ European-Style Unsalted Butter

Price (per lb): $9.98
Style: cultured cream
Butterfat: 83%
Comments: The cream of the crop, this "thick and luscious" cultured butter was "complex" and "just a bit tangy" and "grassy." Some deemed its flavor the most "robust" of all the samples.

RECOMMENDED

LAND O'LAKES Unsalted Sweet Butter

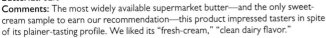
Price (per lb): $4.79
Style: sweet cream
Butterfat: 82%
Comments: The most widely available supermarket butter—and the only sweet-cream sample to earn our recommendation—this product impressed tasters in spite of its plainer-tasting profile. We liked its "fresh-cream," "clean dairy flavor."

VERMONT CREAMERY European-Style Cultured Butter, Unsalted
Price (per lb): $11.98
Style: cultured cream
Butterfat: 86%
Comments: This high-priced, high-fat cultured butter balanced "fresh-sweet dairy richness" with flavor that tasters described as "rich," "refreshing," and "barnyard-y" but also "mineral-y."

PRÉSIDENT Unsalted Butter

Price (per lb): $7.52
Style: cultured cream
Butterfat: 82%
Comments: Though leaner than other cultured butters, this French import came across as "firm" and "silky," with "beautifully sweet and creamy" flavor that was also "buttermilk-y" and "slightly grassy."

ORGANIC VALLEY European-Style Cultured Butter, Unsalted

Price (per lb): $7.58
Style: cultured cream
Butterfat: 86%
Comments: This sample was on the mellow side for a cultured butter, with some tasters deeming it "a bit timid." Others praised its "simple buttery flavor" and "floral undertones."

RECOMMENDED, (CONTINUED)

ORGANIC VALLEY Cultured Butter, Unsalted
Price (per lb): $5.99
Style: cultured cream
Butterfat: 83%
Comments: Though some tasters picked up on nothing but this butter's "rich" flavor and "welcome tartness," several detected an apparent storage problem. Seeping through this sample's waxed parchment wrapper were flavors that tasted "like the inside of a fridge."

LURPAK Imported Butter, Unsalted
Price (per lb): $11.98
Style: cultured cream
Butterfat: 83%
Comments: Though enough tasters praised this butter for its "richness" and "complexity," it barely skated into the "Recommended" category, as others found it so "fake"-tasting that it drew comparisons to margarine.

RECOMMENDED WITH RESERVATIONS

CABOT Natural Creamery Unsalted Butter
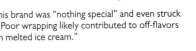
Price (per lb): $5.29
Style: sweet cream
Butterfat: 81%
Comments: At best, this butter was "mild"; but it was a little "boring," too. It was also another victim of poor wrapping: More than a few tasters detected "odd" flavors that reminded them of "the fridge."

KERRYGOLD Pure Irish Butter, Unsalted
Price (per lb): $5.98
Style: cultured cream
Butterfat: 83%
Comments: It wasn't this Irish butter's texture that tasters objected to; in fact, several deemed it "luxurious" and "velvety." It was the "artificial," "movie-theater-popcorn flavor" that put many tasters off.

HORIZON Organic Unsalted Butter
Price (per lb): $5.49
Style: sweet cream
Butterfat: 81%
Comments: Like the Cabot butter, this brand was "nothing special" and even struck some tasters as "watery" and "thin." Poor wrapping likely contributed to off-flavors that reminded one taster of "refrozen melted ice cream."

covered six other butters we tasted—and more protective than the Lurpak block's foil wrapper, which, to the detriment of that butter's flavor, arrived slightly gapped in a few spots. (We sealed all of our samples in zipper-lock bags as soon as they arrived, but that couldn't reverse the damage done to any butter whose flavor was already spoiled.)

Cream of the Crop
When we circled back to our original question—whether or not the cultured stuff measured up to the hype—we realized that we had two answers. Our

top choice, a cultured product from Plugrá, offered everything we look for in good butter: flavor that's at once sweet and creamy and overlaid with a complex, slightly sour tang, plus enough butterfat (almost 83 percent) to make it decadent and glossy but not so rich that it renders baked goods dense and greasy. The only part of Plugrá that's hard to swallow is the price tag. At $10 per pound, it's a splurge and a condiment-only purchase for most of us—especially considering the fact that good old Land O'Lakes was a second-place finisher for less than half the price ($4.79 per pound).

Keeping Flavor Under Wraps
Land O'Lakes's ability to beat out so many of the richer, more complex-tasting cultured butters in our ranking may have something to do with its packaging. The company treats its parchment-paper wrapper with a patented coating called FlavorProtect that blocks out the refrigerator odors that can ruin butter's taste.

ODOR BLOCKER
Land O'Lakes boasts a specially patented wrapper that preserves clean, fresh flavor.

⇒ BY ANDREW JANJIGIAN & DAN SOUZA ⇐

Quick-Chilling Wine

To chill a bottle of wine, you can just pop it into the freezer, but it will take a while to cool down (in our tests, it took about an hour to bring a bottle of room-temperature wine to 50 degrees, the ideal drinking temperature). We've also recommended submerging the bottle in a salt/ice-water solution, which will chill it in about half that time. (When salt is added to ice water, its freezing point and temperature decrease to well below 32 degrees.)

Now we've discovered an equally effective (and less messy) technique for quick chilling: Simply wrap the bottle in a wet kitchen towel before placing it in the freezer. Since cooling occurs when heat is transferred away from an item, the water in the towel—a much more efficient conductor of heat than air—will quickly freeze, dropping the temperature of the wine to 50 degrees in only 30 minutes. (Note: Once the wine is fully chilled, the towel will be frozen solid. To release it from the bottle, just place it briefly under warm running water.)

Flip for the Best Possible Crust

Conventional wisdom dictates that hamburgers or steaks should be flipped just once halfway through the cooking period. Some experts, however, suggest that multiple turns yield a better crust.

To test this notion, we pan-seared two batches of steaks and burgers, flipping one batch of each only once during cooking and the other batch every minute. In both cases, the repeatedly flipped sample boasted a crispier crust and more evenly cooked meat than its single-flipped counterpart. Recurrent turns mean that the developing crust alternates between direct contact with the pan and exposure to air, maximizing evaporation and allowing a drier, crispier coating to form. And because the meat is heated from both sides at the same time—residual heat continues cooking on the top surface—it also cooks more evenly, resulting in a narrower "gray band" of overdone meat on the exterior.

As fond as we are of this method, we don't recommend it for hamburgers, since repeated manipulation causes the patties to crumble in the pan by the time they are fully cooked. But if your primary goal for steaks is the ultimate golden brown, crisp crust, then start flipping.

FAUX PASTRY BAG

If you want to make Paris-Brest (page 21)—or another recipe requiring simple piping—but you don't own a pastry bag and tips, a zipper-lock bag can be fashioned into a substitute. For Paris-Brest, you'll need two bags, one with a ¾-inch-wide opening (to approximate the star tip) and another with a ½-inch-wide opening (to approximate the round tip).

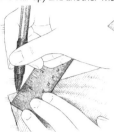

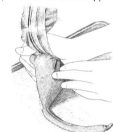

1. Measure desired width diagonally across 1 bottom corner of zipper-lock bag. Use pen to mark bag at both ends of line.

2. Cut from 1 mark to other in slight arc shape to create circular opening. Fill bag with contents to be piped.

3. While squeezing bag with 1 hand, use other hand to guide contents onto baking sheet.

Preserving a Salty Crunch

Since the crunchy texture of a finishing salt is just as important as the seasoning it provides, we were disappointed when the flaky sea salt we sprinkled on fish fillets, steaks, and chicken breasts dissolved almost instantly in the food's juices. In search of a way to maintain the crunch, we tried tossing Maldon Sea Salt Flakes (our favorite finishing salt) in a spoonful of oil to create a moisture barrier. While the oil-coated crystals indeed stayed intact on food (after 10 minutes they were unchanged), the oil caused the salt to clump, making even sprinkling virtually impossible. Next, we turned to vegetable oil spray, which produced a gossamer coating that precluded clumping—and dissolving. Simply discharge a ⅓-second spray into a small bowl (say "one," and you're done), add 1½ teaspoons of flaky sea salt, and stir to coat. (Be sure to spritz first and then add the salt, lest the flakes fly everywhere.)

TECHNIQUE | THE BEST WAY TO SHUCK AN OYSTER

We've come across a number of recommendations for the best way to open an oyster easily and safely. One source suggested that freezing the bivalves for a couple of minutes would relax the muscle that holds the two shells closed. While this did make the shells a little easier to pry apart, we found it hard to get the timing just right: If you overdo it just a little, the oyster meat begins to freeze, ruining its texture. Other sources advised a variety of implements—a flathead screwdriver, a church key, even a butter knife—but each of these proved more dangerous than effective, since none slid readily into the extremely narrow crevice between the shells. In the end, the best tool for the job turned out to be a classic oyster knife. Its pointed tip and sturdy blade are designed to easily shimmy into the oyster's recalcitrant hinge without slipping or breaking.

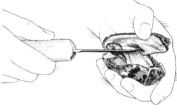

1. Fold kitchen towel several times into thin, tight roll. Grip towel in fist of hand that will be holding oyster, wrapping 1 end over thumb and tucking it between thumb and forefinger.

2. Using towel-protected thumb, hold oyster in place with hinge facing away from thumb. Insert tip of oyster knife into hinge of oyster.

3. Slowly work tip of knife into hinge, using twisting motion. When shells begin to separate, rotate knife to either side to "pop" hinge open.

4. Run knife along inside of top shell to sever muscle, then gently scrape underside of oyster meat to release it from bottom shell.

SCIENCE Carryover Cooking

When you're cooking an expensive roast such as Best Prime Rib (page 9), getting it to the table cooked just the way you like it is critical. To do that, you must hit the meat's target temperature spot-on; 5 or 10 degrees off can make a huge difference. But judging precisely when meat is done is tricky, because what you're actually gauging is not whether the food is ready to eat right now—but whether it will be ready to eat once it has rested. Meat will continue to cook even after it has been removed from the heat source, a phenomenon known as "carryover cooking." This happens for two reasons: First, the exterior of a large roast gets hot much more quickly than the interior. Second, because heat always moves from a hotter to a cooler area, as long as there is a difference in temperature between the two regions, heat will keep moving from the surface to the center even after you remove the meat from the heat source. This transfer will slow, and eventually stop, as internal and external temperatures approach each other and even out. But the process can result in a significant increase in temperature at the center of a large roast, bringing it from a perfect pink to a disappointing gray.

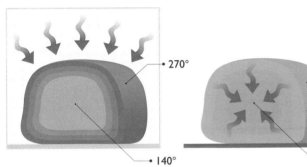

IN THE OVEN
The exterior of meat heats up far more quickly than the interior, resulting in a huge temperature differential between the outside and the center of a roast. The internal temperature is what matters. When the center of a roast comes within 10 degrees of the target, it's time to take it off the heat.

OFF HEAT
As long as there is a difference between the outside and inside temperatures of a cut of meat, heat will continue to travel inward. Off heat, the temperature of this roast continued to rise—a phenomenon known as "carryover cooking." After 15 minutes, it reached its target of 150 degrees.

So when, exactly, should you remove meat from the heat source? Both the size of the roast and the heat level during cooking will impact the answer. A large roast will absorb more heat than a thin steak, which means there will be more heat in the meat and therefore a greater amount of carryover cooking. Similarly, meat cooked in a 400-degree oven absorbs more heat than meat cooked in a 200-degree oven, so carryover cooking is greater in a roast cooked in a hot oven.

Use our guidelines to determine exactly when to take meat off the heat so when you serve it, it's at the desired temperature. (Note: While carryover cooking can occur in poultry, for food safety reasons we usually don't recommend removing it from the heat until it's done.)

	FOR FINAL SERVING TEMPERATURE	STOP COOKING WHEN TEMPERATURE REACHES	
		For large roasts/ high heat	Thin cuts/ moderate heat
BEEF AND LAMB			
Rare	125°F	115°F	120°F
Medium-Rare	130°F	120°F	125°F
Medium	140°F	130°F	135°F
Well Done	160°F	150°F	155°F
PORK			
Medium	150°F	140°F	145°F
Well Done	160°F	150°F	155°F

The Truth About Braising

It's a common misconception that braising—cooking food half-submerged in liquid in a covered pot at low heat—results in moister meat than dry cooking methods do. The reality is that despite the wet conditions, braising does not add moisture to meat. To see the dynamic at work for ourselves, we set up a test designed to simulate braising. We placed samples of beef chuck, along with measured amounts of broth, in individual vacuum-sealed bags to eliminate the possibility of evaporation. We then submerged the bags in water held at 190 degrees (the temperature of a typical braise) for 90 minutes. We found that the weight of the meat decreased an average of 12.5 percent during cooking while the volume of liquid increased, demonstrating that moisture had been pulled from the meat into the surrounding liquid, not the other way around.

So why, then, does braised meat seem so moist? Gentle cooking helps break down the meat's connective tissue and collagen, which lubricate and tenderize its fibers. The resulting soft, tender texture is (mistakenly) perceived as moist.

TECHNIQUE | A PAINLESS WAY TO SEED CHILES

It can be tricky to remove the sticky ribs and seeds from chiles. Here's a simple method that allows you to do so effortlessly. (The same technique can be used to seed sweet peppers.)

 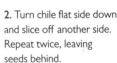 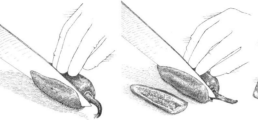

1. Slice lengthwise along 1 side of chile, keeping stem and seedpod intact.

2. Turn chile flat side down and slice off another side. Repeat twice, leaving seeds behind.

3. Discard stem, seeds, and ribs (or add minced ribs and seeds judiciously to your recipe).

Cattle Roundup

While testing our Best Prime Rib recipe (page 9), we discovered that choosing the right roast was almost as important as deciding how to cook it. Butchers tend to cut a whole rib roast (which contains seven ribs) into two 3-rib roasts, known most commonly as first-cut and second-cut roasts. Our recipe calls for a 3-bone first-cut roast, which sits closer to the loin end of the cow and consists of ribs 10 through 12. First-cut roasts feature more of the flavorful, tender rib-eye muscle than do second-cut roasts (ribs 6 through 8 or 9), which are comprised of a mix of smaller muscles and more pockets of fat.

We also found prime-grade prime rib, the darling of steakhouses, to be consistently more tender and flavorful than choice-grade prime rib because of its higher level of intramuscular fat (or "marbling"). It's true that these upgrades add to the sticker price (prime costs roughly 25 percent more than choice), but we think they're well worth the extra money.

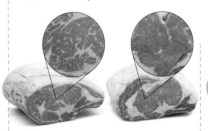 

PRIME VS. CHOICE
With more marbling, prime-grade beef is more tender and flavorful. Choice-grade beef is a bit less expensive than prime, but it also has less marbling; it is our second choice.

FIRST CUT VS. SECOND CUT
A first-cut roast features more of the prized rib-eye muscle. A second-cut roast trades some of the rib eye for a mosaic of different muscles and more pockets of fat.

≥ BY HANNAH CROWLEY, AMY GRAVES, LISA McMANUS & DAVID PAZMIÑO ≤

EQUIPMENT TESTING Cast-Iron Pizza Pan

Since it absorbs and maintains heat so well, cast iron would seem like the ideal material for creating good pizza crust, which requires searingly hot temperatures. That's why we were keen to test the Lodge Pro Logic Cast-Iron 14-Inch Pizza Pan ($28). After preheating the pan to 500 degrees, we used it to bake multiple batches of pizza, looking for crisp, golden crusts on par with those made with our winning Baker's Catalogue Pizza Baking Stone by Old Stone Oven ($54.95). The first surprise: While the stone takes an hour to reach 500 degrees, this pan was ready after a mere 30 minutes. And though it weighs nearly 10 pounds (just a few ounces less than the stone), it was easy to move thanks to a pair of looped handles. Worries that the raised edges of the pan might make it difficult to remove the pizza proved unfounded. Best of all, the pan produced perfect crust. The 14-inch circle does limit the size and shape of your pizza, providing slightly less usable space than the 14½ by 16½-inch rectangular stone (especially if you're baking something other than pizza), but this pan offers identical results in less time.

PIZZA PERFECT
The Lodge Pro Logic Cast-Iron 14-Inch Pizza Pan delivered evenly browned, crisp crust on pizza.

NEW PRODUCT Pomegranate Tool

Picking the juicy seeds (called arils) from a pomegranate can be a messy, painstaking job. Enter the ART—Arils Removal Tool ($14.99) by Shoham. You place half a pomegranate cut side down in its removable plastic sieve, which sits in a steep-sided plastic bowl. Then you cover the fruit with a soft silicone dome and give it a good whack with any heavy, large tool. The arils pass through the sieve and land intact in the bottom of the bowl. The dome and bowl corral any spraying juice, and a small spout lets you drain the juice away, while the sieve catches most of the white membrane and pith. All in all, it's a good tool. It squashes fewer arils than the old-fashioned method of simply holding the fruit over a bowl and thumping it with a spoon—and without any messy red splatter.

SEEDS IN A JIFFY
The ART—Arils Removal Tool quickly extracts pomegranate seeds, with less mess.

EQUIPMENT UPDATE Nutcrackers

Nutcrackers can give your hands a workout—and test your patience as you pick shells out of crushed nutmeats. We tested our favorite from five years ago—the Reed's Rocket ($25.99), an innovative model that uses a lever to crack and remove shells easily without pulverizing the contents—against four new models priced from $14.99 to $35.99. One was another lever-style cracker, two were variations on the traditional V-shaped style, and one resembled a jar with a crushing post in the lid. We used them to crack everything from rock-hard hazelnuts and Brazil nuts to softer pecans, walnuts, and almonds. V-style crackers required force and tended to crush nuts; the jar-style cracker was slow to twist, though it kept messy shells contained. The two lever-style crackers were quickest and excelled at leaving nutmeats intact. Our new favorite is the Get Crackin' Heavy Duty Steel Lever Nutcracker ($35.99). Its extra-long handle cracked the hardest nuts effortlessly, leaving the meat intact. And unlike our old winner, it required no adjustment when we changed the type of nut, and it didn't scatter shells everywhere. Best of all, it cracked a pound of walnuts in nine minutes—record time.

NUTS ABOUT THIS
The Get Crackin' Heavy Duty Steel Lever Nutcracker uses leverage instead of hand strength to crack all types of nuts, and it works fast.

EQUIPMENT TESTING Mini Bundt Pans

Reflecting a recent miniaturizing trend in bakeware, manufacturers have shrunk the Bundt. Miniature Bundt pans come in two styles: single-cup molds and trays of six. We baked cakes in two singletons and in two tray models ranging in price from $3.75 to $40. Since all were nonstick and released cakes effortlessly, picking a winner came down to ease of handling and the visual appeal of the cakes. Both tray-style pans featured handles that made flipping out the cakes easier than flipping from the singleton pans. As the little cakes sat cooling on racks, we focused on looks. Only the cakes from the tray-style models had well-defined ridges. Since the main purpose of a Bundt pan is to produce cakes with a distinctive scalloped surface, we had no problem choosing a favorite: the Nordic Ware Platinum Anniversary Bundtlette Pan ($40), a mini version of our winning full-size Bundt pan.

BEST BABY BUNDTS
Nordic Ware Platinum Anniversary Bundtlette Pan produced six crisply shaped mini Bundt cakes.

EQUIPMENT TESTING Hearth Grill

Cooking over a fire is possible indoors with a Tuscan Hearth Grill. This cast-iron set has a solid frame that fits into your fireplace. Just slide the grill grate into one of three slots, depending on how far above the flames you want to grill. The large version ($199), with a generously proportioned grate (23½ by 30 inches), gave us enough real estate to grill and turn six strip steaks. Wood handles made the grate safe for barehanded adjustment, which proved useful when we moved the food closer to the coals as the flames subsided. Two minor objections: Adding logs to the fire was difficult once the grate was in place, so we had to make sure the fire was just right before we began cooking. Also, the set does not include a drip pan, so we used a disposable aluminum pan to keep the bottom of the fireplace grease-free.

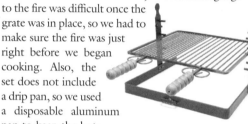

FIRESIDE COOKOUT
The Tuscan Hearth Grill turns your fireplace into an indoor cooking pit.

For complete testing results for each item, go to www.CooksIllustrated.com/dec11.

Sources

Prices were current at press time and do not include shipping. Contact companies to confirm information or visit www.CooksIllustrated.com for updates.

PAGE 9: KNIFE STRIP
• Messermeister Bamboo Knife Magnet: $50, item #BKM-16, Messermeister Inc. (800-426-5134, **www.messermeister.com**).

PAGE 13: ASIAN VEGETABLE CLEAVER
• MAC Japanese Series 6½-Inch Japanese Vegetable Cleaver: $95, item #JU-65, MAC Knife Inc. (888-622-5643, **www.macknife.com**).

PAGE 27: KNIFE SET
• Test Kitchen à la Carte Knife Set: $334.65, all knives available à la carte at **Amazon.com**.

PAGE 32: CAST-IRON PIZZA PAN
• Lodge Pro Logic Cast-Iron 14-Inch Pizza Pan: $28, item #P14P3, KaTom Restaurant Supply, Inc. (800-541-8683, **www.katom.com**).

PAGE 32: POMEGRANATE TOOL
• ART—Arils Removal Tool: $14.99, item #97599, Fante's Kitchen Wares Shop (800-443-2683, **www.fantes.com**).

PAGE 32: NUTCRACKER
• Get Crackin' Heavy Duty Steel Lever Nutcracker: $35.99, item #6126, Fante's Kitchen Wares Shop.

PAGE 32: MINI BUNDT PAN
• Nordic Ware Platinum Anniversary Bundtlette Pan: $40, item #86237, Nordic Ware (877-466-7420, **www.nordicware.com**).

PAGE 32: HEARTH GRILL
• Tuscan Hearth Grill: $199, item #70126, NapaStyle (866-776-6272, **www.napastyle.com**).

INDEX
November & December 2011

NEW RECIPES ON THE WEB
Available free for 4 months at
www.CooksIllustrated.com/dec11

Herbed Croutons
Mustard-Cream Sauce
Pasta with Broccoli Rabe, Raisins, and
  Pine Nuts
Roasted Poblano-Cilantro Salsa
Roasted Shallot and Mint Chutney

🎥 COOK'S LIVE VIDEOS
Available free for 4 months at
www.CooksIllustrated.com/dec11

Best Prime Rib
Braised Turkey with Gravy
Cranberry Chutney with Apple and
  Crystallized Ginger
Farmhouse Vegetable and Barley Soup
Gingersnaps
Oven-Roasted Chicken Thighs
Paris-Brest
Pasta with Broccoli Rabe and Sausage
Ragu alla Bolognese
Roasted Brussels Sprouts
Testing Knife Sets

Roasted Brussels Sprouts, 10

Ragu alla Bolognese, 15

Pasta with Broccoli Rabe and Sausage, 18

Gingersnaps, 23

Braised Turkey with Gravy, 7

Cranberry Chutney, 24

Paris-Brest, 21

Best Prime Rib, 9

Farmhouse Vegetable and Barley Soup, 13

Oven-Roasted Chicken Thighs, 11

AMERICA'S TEST KITCHEN TV
Public television's most popular cooking show
Join the millions of home cooks who watch our show,
America's Test Kitchen, on public television every week.
For more information, including recipes and program
times, visit www.AmericasTestKitchenTV.com.

NEW! **AMERICA'S TEST KITCHEN COOKING SCHOOL**
Learn how to think—and cook—like a pro from the test kitchen experts you know from our
TV shows. Our new online cooking school combines personalized instruction with leading-edge
technology to offer a rich and unparalleled learning experience. To learn more, visit
www.TestKitchenSchool.com.

DOWNLOAD OUR FREE *Cook's Illustrated* **iPhone App**
Inside you'll find a collection of our top recipes, along with videos that
explain how to make them. You can also access many of our most popular
taste test results, useful kitchen timers, and an interactive shopping list
that helps you plan ahead. Are you a member of CooksIllustrated.com?
If so, our app gives you access to every recipe, video, and taste test on the
website. Go to CooksIllustrated.com/iPhone.

Follow us on Twitter: twitter.com/TestKitchen
Find us on Facebook: facebook.com/CooksIllustrated

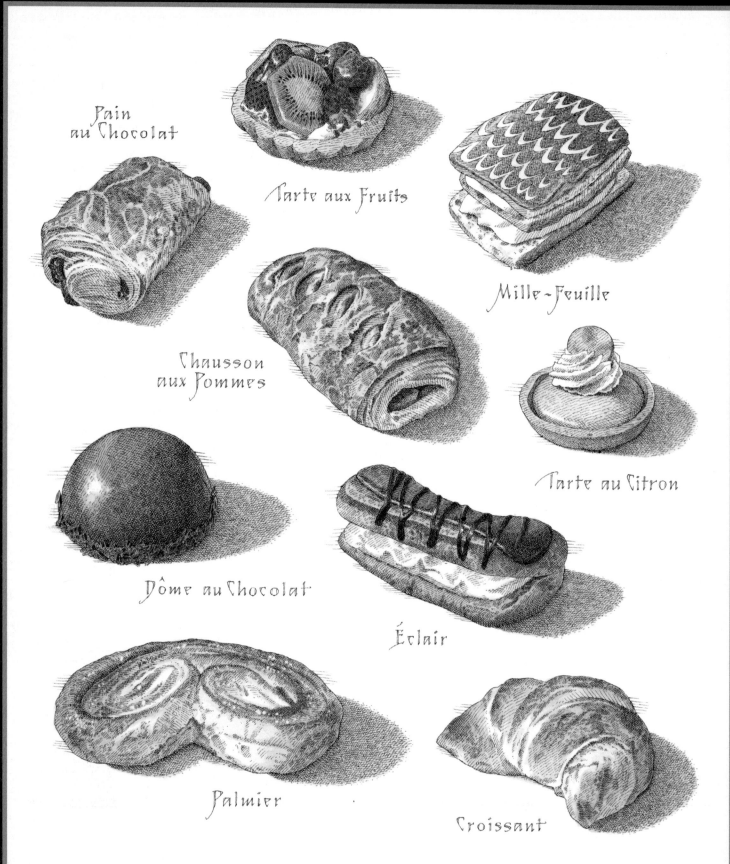

Pain
au Chocolat

Tarte aux Fruits

Mille-Feuille

Chausson
aux Pommes

Tarte au Citron

Dôme au Chocolat

Éclair

Palmier

Croissant

FRENCH PASTRIES